PRIDE AND PREJUDICE

AN AUTHORITATIVE TEXT
BACKGROUNDS
REVIEWS AND ESSAYS IN CRITICISM

NORTON CRITICAL EDITIONS

➤➤ A NORTON CRITICAL EDITION ⫷⫷

JANE AUSTEN

PRIDE AND PREJUDICE

AN AUTHORITATIVE TEXT
BACKGROUNDS
REVIEWS AND ESSAYS IN CRITICISM

➤➤⫷⫷

Edited by

DONALD J. GRAY

INDIANA UNIVERSITY

W·W· NORTON & COMPANY · INC · *New York*

W. W. NORTON & COMPANY, INC.
also publishes

THE NORTON ANTHOLOGY OF ENGLISH LITERATURE
edited by M. H. Abrams et al.

THE NORTON ANTHOLOGY OF POETRY
edited by Arthur M. Eastman et al.

WORLD MASTERPIECES
edited by Maynard Mack et al.

THE NORTON READER
edited by Arthur M. Eastman et al.

THE NORTON FACSIMILE OF
THE FIRST FOLIO OF SHAKESPEARE
prepared by Charlton Hinman
and the NORTON CRITICAL EDITIONS

ISBN 0 393 04274 X (Paper Edition)
ISBN 0 393 09668 8 (Cloth Edition)
PRINTED IN THE UNITED STATES OF AMERICA

6 7 8 9 0

Contents

Preface

In 1796, the year in which she turned twenty-one, Jane Austen began writing a novel she named *First Impressions*. When the novel was completed in 1797, it immediately became the favorite among the many stories and burlesques which for the past six or seven years she had been turning out for the amusement of her family and friends. Her father thought well enough of the novel to offer it, unsuccessfully, to a publisher. Two years later the novel was still being reread by members of her family. Jane wrote to her sister Cassandra in 1799, "I do not wonder at your wanting to read 'First Impressions' again, so seldom as you have gone through it, and that so long ago"; and later the same year, with the same casual sarcasm, "I would not let Martha read 'First Impressions' again upon any account. * * * She is very cunning, but I saw through her design; she means to publish it from memory, and one more perusal must enable her to do it." During these two years she had continued to write, and rewrite. By 1800 she had completed a new novel, entitled *Susan*, and had thoroughly revised another originally called *Elinor and Marianne*, which had been written before *First Impressions* and was now changed from a novel in letters to a third-person narrative entitled *Sense and Sensibility*. She may have touched up *First Impressions* less radically when in 1802 or 1803 she prepared *Susan* for publication (the novel was sold to a publisher in 1803 but not published until 1817, when it appeared as *Northanger Abbey*). She may have revised *First Impressions* again in 1809, when after a five-year recess her interest in writing revived and she began a final revision of *Sense and Sensibility*. Certainly she began working hard on *First Impressions* even before the appearance in November 1811, of *Sense and Sensibility*, the first of her novels to be published. When the book was finally published in January 1813, its title had been changed to *Pride and Prejudice*. It was so different from the story her sister had repeatedly read fifteen years earlier that Jane was "exceedingly pleased" when Cassandra, who had apparently not read the final version through before its publication, wrote to say that she liked it.

The circumstances of the composition of *Pride and Prejudice* describe its place in the development of Jane Austen's fiction. Because the manuscript of *First Impressions* no longer exists, its differences from *Pride and Prejudice* can only be guessed. It has been plausibly suggested [1] that, like *Elinor and Marianne, First Impressions* was a novel in letters which was converted to a third-person narrative. It is certain that *Pride and Prejudice* is shorter than the "manuscript novel * * * about the length of Miss Burney's *Evelina*" which Jane Austen's father offered to a publisher in 1797. Whatever *First Impressions* was like, in short, this apprentice work of a girl of twenty-one was radically changed and cut by the mature writer of thirty-six who took it up again in 1811. At the same time, this mature writer was attracted enough by an early work to revise it, perhaps not for the first time. As a result the novel clearly draws its strengths and interest from both Jane Austen's youth and maturity. In several respects *Pride and Prejudice* retains the impress of the reading and writing Jane Austen did in the last years of the eighteenth century: in the frequent and sometimes (in Darcy's letter in the center of the book, for example) crucial dependence on letters to move the plot; and in the derivative foundations of such characters as the rake Wickham and the toadying clergyman Mr. Collins. In other and more important ways the novel jumps with the authority and excitement of a really good writer moving out from her beginnings as she discovers and extends the range of her powers— as she neglects static simplicities like Mary Bennet to follow the complexities Elizabeth and Darcy go on making for themselves; and advances from the outrages people like Mr. Collins and Lady Catherine practice on others to begin to consider the indignities people like Mr. Bennet and Wickham practice on themselves. After *Pride and Prejudice* Jane Austen was never to draw again so heavily on a work of her apprenticeship. It is the particular interest of the novel, therefore, that it stands at the entrance to its author's mature practice, preserving some of the lessons and traditions from which she learned while demonstrating the uses to which she put them to make for the first time a fiction unmistakably her own.

I have included in the supplementary material in the second part of this edition three examples of Jane Austen's juvenile writing, as well as some remarks in her letters about *Pride and Prejudice*, the writing of fiction, and the delicate tangles of love and courtship, those central topics in her fiction. The juvenile writings show both how much she owed to the books she read and how from the beginning she was working to put the lessons of her reading to uses of her own. The progress from the broad burlesque of "Jack and Alice" to the mobile narrative, solid characterization and setting, and experimentation with first- and third-person points of view in "Catharine" and "Letter the Third," and from there to a

1. By, for example, Q. D. Leavis, B. C. Southam, and Robert Liddell, in works cited in the Bibliography (pp. 448–450). Each of these three critics has different reasons for supposing that *First Impressions* was an epistolary novel.

scene like that between Elizabeth and Lady Catherine at the end of *Pride and Prejudice*, is not accidental. It was directed by the conscious craftsman who later urges on her novel-writing niece her own fidelity to the observed and probable, and who worries about the difficult necessity of modulating tones and making characters serve the turns of the plot without violating the key and consistency of the kind of novel to which she restricted her talent. I have also included an essay by R. W. Chapman which demonstrates how thoroughly this deliberate writer revised *First Impressions* and planned *Pride and Prejudice*, and an essay by Q. D. Leavis which speculates about how much of the original novel remains in the revision.

Jane Austen's nineteenth-century critics were not usually much interested in how she grew from novel to novel. Except to paraphrase plots or choose a favorite, they did not often discuss her novels individually at all. Their usual tactic was rather to regard her six novels as a single achievement and to set about discussing its qualities. For that reason, it would have been misleading to restrict the selection from this commentary to remarks specifically concerning *Pride and Prejudice*. I have tried rather to select passages from essays which represent what nineteenth-century readers and critics thought about Jane Austen's fiction no matter which of her novels they were discussing—from the first reviewers of *Pride and Prejudice*, who like almost everybody else were struck by the economy of craft with which she makes commonplace people and events interesting, to Richard Simpson, one of the few nineteenth-century critics to look closely at her irony in order to see what the aloof, skeptical, didactic presence who tells her stories wants us to think of the people and events in the stories she tells.

Jane Austen's twentieth-century critics are interested in the same characteristics of craft and attitude, particularly in her irony. They are, however, much more given than their predecessors were to studying where those characteristics came from, how they developed, and especially how they work in individual novels. They are also not usually worried by the superficially trivial content of her fiction, which often persuaded earlier admirers to grant her only the kind of second-rank excellence awarded to miniaturists and painters of the Dutch school. Sometimes, as in the essays of Mrs. Leavis, A. C. Bradley, Samuel Kliger, and A. Walton Litz, they seek to relieve the novels from the suspicion of being parochial by connecting their practices and attitudes to those of late eighteenth-century life, letters, and opinion. Sometimes, as in the studies of Reginald Farrer, Mary Lascelles, Andrew Wright, and E. M. Halliday, they assume that the high technical competence with which Jane Austen manipulates plot, character, and style to play out the significance she finds in small actions and unheroic emotions is its own warrant of consequence. Increasingly, in studies like those of Dorothy Van Ghent, Reuben Brower, Marvin Mudrick, and Howard Babb, they study the development of characters and themes, the structure of episodes and sentences, even her very choice of words, in order to explain how novels about three or four families in a country village are also novels about the important business of making a fruitful life in a society and of a character which do not always encourage the best of even the few possibilities they permit. *Pride and Prejudice,* because of its place in Jane Austen's career, has invited and rewarded each of these interests. I have tried, from the many fine studies of the novel by twentieth-century critics, to make a selection which illustrates how a common critical habit of attending very closely to the text of the novel has been variously used to elucidate it, to place it in its historical moment, to specify the ways of its author's craft, and to enlarge—not the novel, which is what it was—but our idea of the character and weight of the matters it addresses.

The text of *Pride and Prejudice* reprinted in this edition is that established by R. W. Chapman and published in Volume II of the third edition of *The Novels of Jane Austen* (New York and London, 1932). To arrive at the text Chapman collated three early editions of the novel, two published in 1813 and the third in 1817. His text is almost entirely that of the first edition of 1813, even to preserving such customary (but not consistent) spellings as "neice" and such now unused spellings as "ancle," "stile" (for "style"), and "staid" (for "stayed"). Variant readings and the few minor corrections Chapman made to the text of the first edition of 1813 are listed in the "Notes" to the Oxford edition; two more important emendations to the first edition offered or accepted by Chapman are noted in the footnotes to this edition. Unless otherwise indicated, the occasional glosses and notes to the texts of the novel and of the letters and juvenilia are not Mr. Chapman's but mine. The text of the novel is reprinted by permission of the Oxford University Press, which has also kindly granted permission to reprint the extracts from Jane Austen's juvenilia and letters.

I am particularly grateful to the authors of the more recent essays for permitting me to reprint them. When I have deleted from their writing passages not immediately relevant to *Pride and Prejudice* or to the matters they and other critics have judged of central importance in the study of the novel, I have tried to preserve the shape and force of their arguments. If I have failed, it is not because their arguments are loose or weak. Except for some of the remarks of early nineteenth-century critics, which I have included largely because it is instructive to see where and how criticism of

Jane Austen's fiction began, I have chosen to reprint only essays I admire and which I think singularly useful in the teaching and study of *Pride and Prejudice*.

DONALD J. GRAY

The Text of
Pride and Prejudice

Pride and Prejudice

Volume I

Chapter I

It is a truth universally acknowledged, that a single man in possession of a good fortune, must be in want of a wife.

However little known the feelings or views of such a man may be on his first entering a neighbourhood, this truth is so well fixed in the minds of the surrounding families, that he is considered as the rightful property of some one or other of their daughters.

"My dear Mr. Bennet," said his lady to him one day, "have you heard that Netherfield Park is let at last?"

Mr. Bennet replied that he had not.

"But it is," returned she; "for Mrs. Long has just been here, and she told me all about it."

Mr. Bennet made no answer.

"Do not you want to know who has taken it?" cried his wife impatiently.

"You want to tell me, and I have no objection to hearing it."

This was invitation enough.

"Why, my dear, you must know, Mrs. Long says that Netherfield is taken by a young man of large fortune from the north of England; that he came down on Monday in a chaise and four to see the place, and was so much delighted with it that he agreed with Mr. Morris immediately; that he is to take possession before Michaelmas,[1] and some of his servants are to be in the house by the end of next week."

"What is his name?"

"Bingley."

"Is he married or single?"

"Oh! single, my dear, to be sure! A single man of large fortune; four or five thousand a year. What a fine thing for our girls!"

"How so? how can it affect them?"

"My dear Mr. Bennet," replied his wife, "how can you be so tiresome! You must know that I am thinking of his marrying one of them."

"Is that his design in settling here?"

1. September 29; or, more generally, autumn.

1

"Design! nonsense, how can you talk so! But it is very likely that he *may* fall in love with one of them, and therefore you must visit him as soon as he comes."

"I see no occasion for that. You and the girls may go, or you may send them by themselves, which perhaps will be still better, for as you are as handsome as any of them, Mr. Bingley might like you the best of the party."

"My dear, you flatter me. I certainly *have* had my share of beauty, but I do not pretend to be any thing extraordinary now. When a woman has five grown up daughters, she ought to give over thinking of her own beauty."

"In such cases, a woman has not often much beauty to think of."

"But, my dear, you must indeed go and see Mr. Bingley when he comes into the neighbourhood."

"It is more than I engage for, I assure you."

"But consider your daughters. Only think what an establishment it would be for one of them. Sir William and Lady Lucas are determined to go, merely on that account, for in general you know they visit no new comers. Indeed you must go, for it will be impossible for *us* to visit him, if you do not."

"You are over scrupulous surely. I dare say Mr. Bingley will be very glad to see you; and I will send a few lines by you to assure him of my hearty consent to his marrying which ever he chuses of the girls; though I must throw in a good word for my little Lizzy."

"I desire you will do no such thing. Lizzy is not a bit better than the others; and I am sure she is not half so handsome as Jane, nor half so good humoured as Lydia. But you are always giving *her* the preference."

"They have none of them much to recommend them," replied he; "they are all silly and ignorant like other girls; but Lizzy has something more of quickness than her sisters."

"Mr. Bennet, how can you abuse your own children in such a way? You take delight in vexing me. You have no compassion on my poor nerves."

"You mistake me, my dear. I have a high respect for your nerves. They are my old friends. I have heard you mention them with consideration these twenty years at least."

"Ah! you do not know what I suffer."

"But I hope you will get over it, and live to see many young men of four thousand a year come into the neighbourhood."

"It will be no use to us, if twenty such should come since you will not visit them."

"Depend upon it, my dear, that when there are twenty, I will visit them all."

Mr. Bennet was so odd a mixture of quick parts, sarcastic humour, reserve, and caprice, that the experience of three and twenty years had been insufficient to make his wife understand his character. *Her* mind was less difficult to develop. She was a woman of mean understanding, little information, and uncertain temper. When she was discontented she fancied herself nervous. The business of her life was to get her daughters married; its solace was visiting and news.

Chapter II

Mr. Bennet was among the earliest of those who waited on Mr. Bingley. He had always intended to visit him, though to the last always assuring his wife that he should not go; and till the evening after the visit was paid, she had no knowledge of it. It was then disclosed in the following manner. Observing his second daughter employed in trimming a hat, he suddenly addressed her with,

"I hope Mr. Bingley will like it Lizzy."

"We are not in a way to know *what* Mr. Bingley likes," said her mother resentfully, "since we are not to visit."

"But you forget, mama," said Elizabeth, "that we shall meet him at the assemblies, and that Mrs. Long has promised to introduce him."

"I do not believe Mrs. Long will do any such thing. She has two neices of her own. She is a selfish, hypocritical woman, and I have no opinion of her."

"No more have I," said Mr. Bennet; "and I am glad to find that you do not depend on her serving you."

Mrs. Bennet deigned not to make any reply; but unable to contain herself, began scolding one of her daughters.

"Don't keep coughing so, Kitty, for heaven's sake! Have a little compassion on my nerves. You tear them to pieces."

"Kitty has no discretion in her coughs," said her father; "she times them ill."

"I do not cough for my own amusement," replied Kitty fretfully.

"When is your next ball to be, Lizzy?" [2]

"To-morrow fortnight."

"Aye, so it is," cried her mother, "and Mrs. Long does not come back till the day before; so, it will be impossible for her to introduce him, for she will not know him herself."

"Then, my dear, you may have the advantage of your friend,

---

2. R. W. Chapman has emended this passage to give this line to Mr. Bennet, for reasons Mr. Chapman advances most persuasively. " '*When is your next ball to be, Lizzy?*' is given to Kitty by all editions. But why should Kitty ask what she must have known? And why should she call it 'your ball'? The speech is of course Mr. Bennet's. In A [the first edition of 1813] it begins a line, and the printer merely failed to indent the first word." *The Novels of Jane Austen*, Oxford edition, II, 391.

and introduce Mr. Bingley to *her*."

"Impossible, Mr. Bennet, impossible, when I am not acquainted with him myself; how can you be so teazing?"

"I honour your circumspection. A fortnight's acquaintance is certainly very little. One cannot know what a man really is by the end of a fortnight. But if *we* do not venture, somebody else will; and after all, Mrs. Long and her neices must stand their chance; and therefore, as she will think it an act of kindness, if you decline the office, I will take it on myself."

The girls stared at their father. Mrs. Bennet said only, "Nonsense, nonsense!"

"What can be the meaning of that emphatic exclamation?" cried he. "Do you consider the forms of introduction, and the stress that is laid on them, as nonsense? I cannot quite agree with you *there*. What say you, Mary? for you are a young lady of deep reflection I know, and read great books, and make extracts."

Mary wished to say something very sensible, but knew not how.

"While Mary is adjusting her ideas," he continued, "let us return to Mr. Bingley."

"I am sick of Mr. Bingley," cried his wife.

"I am sorry to hear *that*; but why did not you tell me so before? If I had known as much this morning, I certainly would not have called on him. It is very unlucky; but as I have actually paid the visit, we cannot escape the acquaintance now."

The astonishment of the ladies was just what he wished; that of Mrs. Bennet perhaps surpassing the rest; though when the first tumult of joy was over, she began to declare that it was what she had expected all the while.

"How good it was in you, my dear Mr. Bennet! But I knew I should persuade you at last. I was sure you loved your girls too well to neglect such an acquaintance. Well, how pleased I am! and it is such a good joke, too, that you should have gone this morning, and never said a word about it till now."

"Now, Kitty, you may cough as much as you chuse," said Mr. Bennet; and, as he spoke, he left the room, fatigued with the raptures of his wife.

"What an excellent father you have, girls," said she, when the door was shut. "I do not know how you will ever make him amends for his kindness; or me either, for that matter. At our time of life, it is not so pleasant I can tell you, to be making new acquaintance every day; but for your sakes, we would do any thing. Lydia, my love, though you *are* the youngest, I dare say Mr. Bingley will dance with you at the next ball."

"Oh!" said Lydia stoutly, "I am not afraid; for though I *am* the youngest, I'm the tallest."

The rest of the evening was spent in conjecturing how soon he would return Mr. Bennet's visit, and determining when they should ask him to dinner.

Chapter III

Not all that Mrs. Bennet, however, with the assistance of her five daughters, could ask on the subject was sufficient to draw from her husband any satisfactory description of Mr. Bingley. They attacked him in various ways; with barefaced questions, ingenious suppositions, and distant surmises; but he eluded the skill of them all; and they were at last obliged to accept the second-hand intelligence of their neighbour Lady Lucas. Her report was highly favourable. Sir William had been delighted with him. He was quite young, wonderfully handsome, extremely agreeable, and to crown the whole, he meant to be at the next assembly with a large party. Nothing could be more delightful! To be fond of dancing was a certain step towards falling in love; and very lively hopes of Mr. Bingley's heart were entertained.

"If I can but see one of my daughters happily settled at Netherfield," said Mrs. Bennet to her husband, "and all the others equally well married, I shall have nothing to wish for."

In a few days Mr. Bingley returned Mr. Bennet's visit, and sat about ten minutes with him in his library. He had entertained hopes of being admitted to a sight of the young ladies, of whose beauty he had heard much; but he saw only the father. The ladies were somewhat more fortunate, for they had the advantage of ascertaining from an upper window, that he wore a blue coat and rode a black horse.

An invitation to dinner was soon afterwards dispatched; and already had Mrs. Bennet planned the courses that were to do credit to her housekeeping, when an answer arrived which deferred it all. Mr. Bingley was obliged to be in town the following day, and consequently unable to accept the honour of their invitation, &c. Mrs. Bennet was quite disconcerted. She could not imagine what business he could have in town so soon after his arrival in Hertfordshire; and she began to fear that he might be always flying about from one place to another, and never settled at Netherfield as he ought to be. Lady Lucas quieted her fears a little by starting the idea of his being gone to London only to get a large party for the ball; and a report soon followed that Mr. Bingley was to bring twelve ladies and seven gentlemen with him to the assembly. The girls grieved over such a number of ladies; but were comforted the day before the ball by hearing, that instead of twelve, he had brought only six with him from London, his five sisters and a cousin. And when the party entered the assembly room, it consisted of only five altogether; Mr. Bingley, his two sisters, the husband of the eldest, and another young man.

Mr. Bingley was good looking and gentlemanlike; he had a pleasant countenance, and easy, unaffected manners. His sisters were fine women, with an air of decided fashion. His brother-in-law, Mr. Hurst, merely looked the gentleman; but his friend Mr. Darcy soon drew the attention of the room by his fine, tall person, handsome features, noble mien; and the report which was in general circulation within five minutes after his entrance, of his having ten thousand a year. The gentlemen pronounced him to be a fine figure of a man, the ladies declared he was much handsomer than Mr. Bingley, and he was looked at with great admiration for about half the evening, till his manners gave a disgust which turned the tide of his popularity; for he was discovered to be proud, to be above his company, and above being pleased; and not all his large estate in Derbyshire could then save him from having a most forbidding, disagreeable countenance, and being unworthy to be compared with his friend.

Mr. Bingley had soon made himself acquainted with all the principal people in the room; he was lively and unreserved, danced every dance, was angry that the ball closed so early, and talked of giving one himself at Netherfield. Such amiable qualities must speak for themselves. What a contrast between him and his friend! Mr. Darcy danced only once with Mrs. Hurst and once with Miss Bingley, declined being introduced to any other lady, and spent the rest of the evening in walking about the room, speaking occasionally to one of his own party. His character was decided. He was the proudest, most disagreeable man in the world, and every body hoped that he would never come there again. Amongst the most violent against him was Mrs. Bennet, whose dislike of his general behaviour, was sharpened into particular resentment, by his having slighted one of her daughters.

Elizabeth Bennet had been obliged, by the scarcity of gentlemen, to sit down for two dances; and during part of that time, Mr. Darcy had been standing near enough for her to overhear a conversation between him and Mr. Bingley, who came from the dance for a few minutes, to press his friend to join it.

"Come, Darcy," said he, "I must have you dance. I hate to see you standing about by yourself in this stupid manner. You had much better dance."

"I certainly shall not. You know how I detest it, unless I am particularly acquainted with my partner. At such an assembly as this, it would be insupportable. Your sisters are engaged, and there is not another woman in the room, whom it would not be a punishment to me to stand up with."

"I would not be so fastidious as you are," cried Bingley, "for a kingdom! Upon my honour, I never met with so many pleasant girls in my life, as I have this evening; and there are several of them you see uncommonly pretty."

"*You* are dancing with the only handsome girl in the room," said Mr. Darcy, looking at the eldest Miss Bennet.

"Oh! she is the most beautiful creature I ever beheld! But there is one of her sisters sitting down just behind you, who is very pretty, and I dare say, very agreeable. Do let me ask my partner to introduce you."

"Which do you mean?" and turning round, he looked for a moment at Elizabeth, till catching her eye, he withdrew his own and coldly said, "She is tolerable; but not handsome enough to tempt *me*; and I am in no humour at present to give consequence to young ladies who are slighted by other men. You had better return to your partner and enjoy her smiles, for you are wasting your time with me."

Mr. Bingley followed his advice. Mr. Darcy walked off; and Elizabeth remained with no very cordial feelings towards him. She told the story however with great spirit among her friends; for she had a lively, playful disposition, which delighted in any thing ridiculous.

The evening altogether passed off pleasantly to the whole family. Mrs. Bennet had seen her eldest daughter much admired by the Netherfield party. Mr. Bingley had danced with her twice, and she had been distinguished by his sisters. Jane was as much gratified by this, as her mother could be, though in a quieter way. Elizabeth felt Jane's pleasure. Mary had heard herself mentioned to Miss Bingley as the most accomplished girl in the neighbourhood; and Catherine and Lydia had been fortunate enough to be never without partners, which was all that they had yet learnt to care for at a ball. They returned therefore in good spirits to Longbourn, the village where they lived, and of which they were the principal inhabitants. They found Mr. Bennet still up. With a book he was regardless of time; and on the present occasion he had a good deal of curiosity as to the event of an evening which had raised such splendid expectations. He had rather hoped that all his wife's views on the stranger would be disappointed; but he soon found that he had a very different story to hear.

"Oh! my dear Mr. Bennet," as she entered the room, "we have had a most delightful evening, a most excellent ball. I wish you had been there. Jane was so admired, nothing could be like it. Every body said how well she looked; and Mr. Bingley thought her quite beautiful, and danced with her twice. Only think of *that* my dear; he actually danced with her twice; and she was the only creature in the room that he asked a second time. First of all, he asked Miss Lucas. I was so vexed to see him stand up with her; but, however, he did not admire her at all: indeed, nobody can, you know; and he seemed quite struck with Jane as she was going down the dance. So, he enquired who she was, and got introduced, and asked her for the two next. Then, the two third he danced with Miss King, and the two fourth with Maria Lucas, and the two fifth with Jane again, and the two sixth with Lizzy, and the Boulanger ———" [3]

"If he had had any compassion for *me*," cried her husband impatiently, "he would not have danced half so much! For God's sake, say no more of his partners. Oh! that he had sprained his ancle in the first dance!"

"Oh! my dear," continued Mrs. Bennet, "I am quite delighted with him. He is so excessively handsome! and his sisters are charming women. I never in my life saw any thing more elegant than their dresses. I dare say the lace upon Mrs. Hurst's gown ———"

Here she was interrupted again. Mr. Bennet protested against any description of finery. She was therefore obliged to seek another branch of the subject, and related, with much bitterness of spirit and some exaggeration, the shocking rudeness of Mr. Darcy.

"But I can assure you," she added, "that Lizzy does not lose much by not suiting *his* fancy; for he is a most disagreeable, horrid man, not at all worth pleasing. So high and so conceited that there was no enduring him! He walked here, and he walked there, fancying himself so very great! Not handsome enough to dance with! I wish you had been there, my dear, to have given him one of your set downs. I quite detest the man."

Chapter IV

When Jane and Elizabeth were alone, the former, who had been cautious in her praise of Mr. Bingley before, expressed to her sister how very much she admired him.

"He is just what a young man ought to be," said she, "sensible, good humoured, lively; and I never saw such happy manners!—so much ease, with such perfect good breeding!"

"He is also handsome," replied Elizabeth, "which a young man ought likewise to be, if he possibly can. His character is thereby complete."

"I was very much flattered by his asking me to dance a second time. I did not expect such a compliment."

"Did not you? *I* did for you. But that is one great difference

3. A round dance.

between us. Compliments always take *you* by surprise, and *me* never. What could be more natural than his asking you again? He could not help seeing that you were about five times as pretty as every other woman in the room. No thanks to his gallantry for that. Well, he certainly is very agreeable, and I give you leave to like him. You have liked many a stupider person."

"Dear Lizzy!"

"Oh! you are a great deal too apt you know, to like people in general. You never see a fault in any body. All the world are good and agreeable in your eyes. I never heard you speak ill of a human being in my life."

"I would wish not to be hasty in censuring any one; but I always speak what I think."

"I know you do; and it is *that* which makes the wonder. With *your* good sense, to be so honestly blind to the follies and non-sense of others! Affectation of candour is common enough;—one meets it every where. But to be candid without ostentation or de-sign—to take the good of every body's character and make it still better, and say nothing of the bad—belongs to you alone. And so, you like this man's sisters too, do you? Their manners are not equal to his."

"Certainly not; at first. But they are very pleasing women when you converse with them. Miss Bingley is to live with her brother and keep his house; and I am much mistaken if we shall not find a very charming neighbour in her."

Elizabeth listened in silence, but was not convinced; their be-haviour at the assembly had not been calculated to please in gen-eral; and with more quickness of observation and less pliancy of temper than her sister, and with a judgment too unassailed by any attention to herself, she was very little disposed to approve them. They were in fact very fine ladies; not deficient in good humour when they were pleased, nor in the power of being agree-able where they chose it; but proud and conceited. They were rather handsome, had been educated in one of the first private seminaries in town, had a fortune of twenty thousand pounds, were in the habit of spending more than they ought, and of associating with people of rank; and were therefore in every re-spect entitled to think well of themselves, and meanly of others. They were of a respectable family in the north of England; a circumstance more deeply impressed on their memories than that their brother's fortune and their own had been acquired by trade.

Mr. Bingley inherited property to the amount of nearly an hundred thousand pounds from his father, who had intended to purchase an estate, but did not live to do it.—Mr. Bingley in-tended it likewise, and sometimes made choice of his county; but as he was now provided with a good house and the liberty of a manor,[4] it was doubtful to many of those who best knew the easiness of his temper, whether he might not spend the remainder of his days at Netherfield, and leave the next generation to purchase.

His sisters were very anxious for his having an estate of his own; but though he was now established only as a tenant, Miss Bingley was by no means unwilling to preside at his table, nor was Mrs. Hurst, who had married a man of more fashion than fortune, less disposed to consider his house as her home when it suited her. Mr. Bingley had not been of age two years, when he was tempted by an accidental recommendation to look at Netherfield House. He did look at it and into it for half an hour, was pleased with the situation and the principal rooms, satisfied with what the owner said in its praise, and took it immediately.

Between him and Darcy there was a very steady friendship, in spite of a great opposition of character.—Bingley was endeared to Darcy by the easiness, openness, ductility of his temper, though no disposition could offer a greater contrast to his own, and though with his own he never appeared dissatisfied. On the strength of Darcy's regard Bingley had the firmest reliance, and of his judgment the highest opinion. In understanding Darcy was the superior. Bingley was by no means deficient, but Darcy was clever. He was at the same time haughty, reserved, and fastidious, and his manners, though well bred, were not inviting. In that respect his friend had greatly the advantage. Bingley was sure of being liked wherever he appeared, Darcy was continually giving offence.

The manner in which they spoke of the Meryton assembly was sufficiently characteristic. Bingley had never met with pleasanter people or prettier girls in his life; every body had been most kind and attentive to him, there had been no formality, no stiffness, he had soon felt acquainted with all the room; and as to Miss Bennet, he could not conceive an angel more beautiful. Darcy, on the contrary, had seen a collection of people in whom there was little beauty and no fashion, for none of whom he had felt the smallest interest, and from none received either attention or pleasure. Miss Bennet he acknowledged to be pretty, but she smiled too much.

Mrs. Hurst and her sister allowed it to be so—but still they admired her and liked her, and pronounced her to be a sweet girl, and one whom they should not object to know more of. Miss Bennet was therefore established as a sweet girl, and their brother felt authorised by such commendation to think of her as he chose.

4. **Right to hunt on its fields.**

Chapter V

Within a short walk of Longbourn lived a family with whom the Bennets were particularly intimate. Sir William Lucas had been formerly in trade in Meryton, where he had made a tolerable fortune and risen to the honour of knighthood by an address to the King, during his mayoralty.[5] The distinction had perhaps been felt too strongly. It had given him a disgust to his business and to his residence in a small market town; and quitting them both, he had removed with his family to a house about a mile from Meryton, denominated from that period Lucas Lodge, where he could think with pleasure of his own importance, and unshackled by business, occupy himself solely in being civil to all the world. For though elated by his rank, it did not render him supercilious; on the contrary, he was all attention to every body. By nature inoffensive, friendly and obliging, his presentation at St. James's had made him courteous.

Lady Lucas was a very good kind of woman, not too clever to be a valuable neighbour to Mrs. Bennet.—They had several children. The eldest of them, a sensible, intelligent young woman, about twenty-seven, was Elizabeth's intimate friend.

That the Miss Lucases and the Miss Bennets should meet to talk over a ball was absolutely necessary; and the morning after the assembly brought the former to Longbourn to hear and to communicate.

"*You* began the evening well, Charlotte," said Mrs. Bennet with civil self-command to Miss Lucas. "*You* were Mr. Bingley's first choice."

"Yes;—but he seemed to like his second better."

"Oh!—you mean Jane, I suppose—because he danced with her twice. To be sure that *did* seem as if he admired her—indeed I rather believe he *did*—I heard something about it—but I hardly know what—something about Mr. Robinson."

"Perhaps you mean what I overheard between him and Mr. Robinson; did not I mention it to you? Mr. Robinson's asking him how he liked our Meryton assemblies, and whether he did not think there were a great many pretty women in the room, and

5. Knighthoods were sometimes conferred on the occasion of a civic dignitary presenting to the sovereign an address setting out the opinions or good wishes of the citizens of his locality. (In 1786, for example, a London alderman was knighted "on presentation of an address from the lord mayor, aldermen, etc. of congratulation on the late escape of the king from an attack endangering his life"—cited in William A. Shaw, *The Knights of England* [London, 1906], II, 209.) When he was knighted, Sir William was presented to the king at the palace of St. James, one of the official residences of the sovereigns of England.

which he thought the prettiest? and his answering immediately to the last question—Oh! the eldest Miss Bennet beyond a doubt, there cannot be two opinions on that point."

"Upon my word!—Well, that was very decided indeed—that does seem as if——but however, it may all come to nothing you know."

"*My* overhearings were more to the purpose than *yours*, Eliza," said Charlotte. "Mr. Darcy is not so well worth listening to as his friend, is he?—Poor Eliza!—to be only just *tolerable*."

"I beg you would not put it into Lizzy's head to be vexed by his ill-treatment; for he is such a disagreeable man that it would be quite a misfortune to be liked by him. Mrs. Long told me last night that he sat close to her for half an hour without once opening his lips."

"Are you quite sure, Ma'am?—is not there a little mistake?" said Jane.—"I certainly saw Mr. Darcy speaking to her."

"Aye—because she asked him at last how he liked Netherfield, and he could not help answering her;—but she said he seemed very angry at being spoke to."

"Miss Bingley told me," said Jane, "that he never speaks much unless among his intimate acquaintance. With *them* he is remarkably agreeable."

"I do not believe a word of it, my dear. If he had been so very agreeable he would have talked to Mrs. Long. But I can guess how it was; every body says that he is ate up with pride, and I dare say he had heard somehow that Mrs. Long does not keep a carriage, and had come to the ball in a hack chaise."[6]

"I do not mind his not talking to Mrs. Long," said Miss Lucas, "but I wish he had danced with Eliza."

"Another time, Lizzy," said her mother, "I would not dance with *him*, if I were you."

"I believe, Ma'am, I may safely promise you *never* to dance with him."

"His pride," said Miss Lucas, "does not offend *me* so much as pride often does, because there is an excuse for it. One cannot wonder that so very fine a young man, with family, fortune, every thing in his favour, should think highly of himself. If I may so express it, he has a *right* to be proud."

"That is very true," replied Elizabeth, "and I could easily forgive *his* pride, if he had not mortified *mine*."

"Pride," observed Mary, who piqued herself upon the solidity of her reflections, "is a very common failing I believe. By all that I have ever read, I am convinced that it is very common indeed,

---

6. A rented carriage. See R. W. Chapman's appendix, "On Carriages and Travel," in Volume III of the Oxford edition of the novels, 560–84.

that human nature is particularly prone to it, and that there are very few of us who do not cherish a feeling of self-complacency on the score of some quality or other, real or imaginary. Vanity and pride are different things, though the words are often used synonimously. A person may be proud without being vain. Pride relates more to our opinion of ourselves, vanity to what we would have others think of us."

"If I were as rich as Mr. Darcy," cried a young Lucas who came with his sisters, "I should not care how proud I was. I would keep a pack of foxhounds, and drink a bottle of wine every day."

"Then you would drink a great deal more than you ought," said Mrs. Bennet; "and if I were to see you at it I should take away your bottle directly."

The boy protested that she should not; she continued to declare that she would, and the argument ended only with the visit.

Chapter VI

The ladies of Longbourn soon waited on those of Netherfield. The visit was returned in due form. Miss Bennet's pleasing manners grew on the good will of Mrs. Hurst and Miss Bingley; and though the mother was found to be intolerable and the younger sisters not worth speaking to, a wish of being better acquainted with *them*, was expressed towards the two eldest. By Jane this attention was received with the greatest pleasure; but Elizabeth still saw superciliousness in their treatment of every body, hardly excepting even her sister, and could not like them; though their kindness to Jane, such as it was, had a value as arising in all probability from the influence of their brother's admiration. It was generally evident whenever they met, that he *did* admire her; and to *her* it was equally evident that Jane was yielding to the preference which she had begun to entertain for him from the first, and was in a way to be very much in love; but she considered with pleasure that it was not likely to be discovered by the world in general, since Jane united with great strength of feeling, a composure of temper and a uniform cheerfulness of manner, which would guard her from the suspicions of the impertinent. She mentioned this to her friend Miss Lucas.

"It may perhaps be pleasant," replied Charlotte, "to be able to impose on the public in such a case; but it is sometimes a disadvantage to be so very guarded. If a woman conceals her affection with the same skill from the object of it, she may lose the opportunity of fixing him; and it will then be but poor consolation to believe the world equally in the dark. There is so much of gratitude or vanity in almost every attachment, that it is not safe to leave any to itself. We can all *begin* freely—a slight preference is natural enough; but there are very few of us who have heart enough to be really in love without encouragement. In nine cases out of ten, a woman had better shew *more* affection than she feels. Bingley likes your sister undoubtedly; but he may never do more than like her, if she does not help him on."

"But she does help him on, as much as her nature will allow. If I can perceive her regard for him, he must be a simpleton indeed not to discover it too."

"Remember, Eliza, that he does not know Jane's disposition as you do."

"But if a woman is partial to a man, and does not endeavour to conceal it, he must find it out."

"Perhaps he must, if he sees enough of her. But though Bingley and Jane meet tolerably often, it is never for many hours together; and as they always see each other in large mixed parties, it is impossible that every moment should be employed in conversing together. Jane should therefore make the most of every half hour in which she can command his attention. When she is secure of him, there will be leisure for falling in love as much as she chuses."

"Your plan is a good one," replied Elizabeth, "where nothing is in question but the desire of being well married; and if I were determined to get a rich husband, or any husband, I dare say I should adopt it. But these are not Jane's feelings; she is not acting by design. As yet, she cannot even be certain of the degree of her own regard, nor of its reasonableness. She has known him only a fortnight. She danced four dances with him at Meryton; she saw him one morning at his own house, and has since dined in company with him four times. This is not quite enough to make her understand his character."

"Not as you represent it. Had she merely *dined* with him, she might only have discovered whether he had a good appetite; but you must remember that four evenings have been also spent together—and four evenings may do a great deal."

"Yes; these four evenings have enabled them to ascertain that they both like Vingt-un better than Commerce;[7] but with respect to any other leading characteristic, I do not imagine that much has been unfolded."

"Well," said Charlotte, "I wish Jane success with all my heart; and if she were married to him to-morrow, I should think she had

7. Vingt-un is a form of the game commonly called blackjack in America. Commerce is a somewhat more complicated game in which players buy individual cards from the dealer or barter for them with other players. In some places in England at the end of the eighteenth century, Commerce was a very fashionable game, sometimes played for high stakes.

as good a chance of happiness, as if she were to be studying his character for a twelve-month. Happiness in marriage is entirely a matter of chance. If the dispositions of the parties are ever so well known to each other, or ever so similar before-hand, it does not advance their felicity in the least. They always continue to grow sufficiently unlike afterwards to have their share of vexation; and it is better to know as little as possible of the defects of the person with whom you are to pass your life."

"You make me laugh, Charlotte; but it is not sound. You know it is not sound, and that you would never act in this way yourself."

Occupied in observing Mr. Bingley's attentions to her sister, Elizabeth was far from suspecting that she was herself becoming an object of some interest in the eyes of his friend. Mr. Darcy had at first scarcely allowed her to be pretty; he had looked at her without admiration at the ball; and when they next met, he looked at her only to criticise. But no sooner had he made it clear to himself and his friends that she had hardly a good feature in her face, than he began to find it was rendered uncommonly intelligent by the beautiful expression of her dark eyes. To this discovery succeeded some others equally mortifying. Though he had detected with a critical eye more than one failure of perfect symmetry in her form, he was forced to acknowledge her figure to be light and pleasing; and in spite of his asserting that her manners were not those of the fashionable world, he was caught by their easy playfulness. Of this she was perfectly unaware;—to her he was only the man who made himself agreeable no where, and who had not thought her handsome enough to dance with.

He began to wish to know more of her, and as a step towards conversing with her himself, attended to her conversation with others. His doing so drew her notice. It was at Sir William Lucas's, where a large party were assembled.

"What does Mr. Darcy mean," said she to Charlotte, "by listening to my conversation with Colonel Forster?"

"That is a question which Mr. Darcy only can answer."

"But if he does it any more I shall certainly let him know that I see what he is about. He has a very satirical eye, and if I do not begin by being impertinent myself, I shall soon grow afraid of him."

On his approaching them soon afterwards, though without seeming to have any intention of speaking, Miss Lucas defied her friend to mention such a subject to him, which immediately provoking Elizabeth to do it, she turned to him and said,

"Did not you think, Mr. Darcy, that I expressed myself uncommonly well just now, when I was teazing Colonel Forster to give us a ball at Meryton?"

"With great energy;—but it is a subject which always makes a lady energetic."

"You are severe on us."

"It will be *her* turn soon to be teazed," said Miss Lucas. "I am going to open the instrument, Eliza, and you know what follows."

"You are a very strange creature by way of a friend!—always wanting me to play and sing before any body and every body!— If my vanity had taken a musical turn, you would have been invaluable, but as it is, I would really rather not sit down before those who must be in the habit of hearing the very best performers." On Miss Lucas's persevering, however, she added, "Very well; if it must be so, it must." And gravely glancing at Mr. Darcy, "There is a fine old saying, which every body here is of course familiar with—'Keep your breath to cool your porridge,'—and I shall keep mine to swell my song."

Her performance was pleasing, though by no means capital. After a song or two, and before she could reply to the entreaties of several that she would sing again, she was eagerly succeeded at the instrument by her sister Mary, who having, in consequence of being the only plain one in the family, worked hard for knowledge and accomplishments, was always impatient for display.

Mary had neither genius nor taste; and though vanity had given her application, it had given her likewise a pedantic air and conceited manner, which would have injured a higher degree of excellence than she had reached. Elizabeth, easy and unaffected, had been listened to with much more pleasure, though not playing half so well; and Mary, at the end of a long concerto, was glad to purchase praise and gratitude by Scotch and Irish airs, at the request of her younger sisters, who with some of the Lucases and two or three officers joined eagerly in dancing at one end of the room.

Mr. Darcy stood near them in silent indignation at such a mode of passing the evening, to the exclusion of all conversation, and was too much engrossed by his own thoughts to perceive that Sir William Lucas was his neighbour, till Sir William thus began.

"What a charming amusement for young people this is, Mr. Darcy!—There is nothing like dancing after all.—I consider it as one of the first refinements of polished societies."

"Certainly, Sir;—and it has the advantage also of being in vogue amongst the less polished societies of the world.—Every savage can dance."

Sir William only smiled. "Your friend performs delightfully;" he continued after a pause, on seeing Bingley join the group;— "and I doubt not that you are an adept in the science yourself, Mr. Darcy."

"You saw me dance at Meryton, I believe, Sir."

"Yes, indeed, and received no inconsiderable pleasure from the sight. Do you often dance at St. James's?"

"Never, sir."

"Do you not think it would be a proper compliment to the place?"

"It is a compliment which I never pay to any place if I can avoid it."

"You have a house in town, I conclude?"

Mr. Darcy bowed.

"I had once some thoughts of fixing in town myself—for I am fond of superior society; but I did not feel quite certain that the air of London would agree with Lady Lucas."

He paused in hopes of an answer; but his companion was not disposed to make any; and Elizabeth at that instant moving towards them, he was struck with the notion of doing a very gallant thing, and called out to her,

"My dear Miss Eliza, why are not you dancing?—Mr. Darcy, you must allow me to present this young lady to you as a very desirable partner.—You cannot refuse to dance, I am sure, when so much beauty is before you." And taking her hand, he would have given it to Mr. Darcy, who, though extremely surprised, was not unwilling to receive it, when she instantly drew back, and said with some discomposure to Sir William,

"Indeed, Sir, I have not the least intention of dancing.—I entreat you not to suppose that I moved this way in order to beg for a partner."

Mr. Darcy with grave propriety requested to be allowed the honour of her hand; but in vain. Elizabeth was determined; nor did Sir William at all shake her purpose by his attempt at persuasion.

"You excel so much in the dance, Miss Eliza, that it is cruel to deny me the happiness of seeing you; and though this gentleman dislikes the amusement in general, he can have no objection, I am sure, to oblige us for one half hour."

"Mr. Darcy is all politeness," said Elizabeth, smiling.

"He is indeed—but considering the inducement, my dear Miss Eliza, we cannot wonder at his complaisance; for who would object to such a partner?"

Elizabeth looked archly, and turned away. Her resistance had not injured her with the gentleman, and he was thinking of her with some complacency, when thus accosted by Miss Bingley,

"I can guess the subject of your reverie."

"I should imagine not."

"You are considering how insupportable it would be to pass many evenings in this manner—in such society; and indeed I am quite of your opinion. I was never more annoyed! The insipidity and yet the noise; the nothingness and yet the self-importance of all these people!—What would I give to hear your strictures on them!"

"Your conjecture is totally wrong, I assure you. My mind was more agreeably engaged. I have been meditating on the very great pleasure which a pair of fine eyes in the face of a pretty woman can bestow."

Miss Bingley immediately fixed her eyes on his face, and desired he would tell her what lady had the credit of inspiring such reflections. Mr. Darcy replied with great intrepidity,

"Miss Elizabeth Bennet."

"Miss Elizabeth Bennet!" repeated Miss Bingley. "I am all astonishment. How long has she been such a favourite?—and pray when am I to wish you joy?"

"That is exactly the question which I expected you to ask. A lady's imagination is very rapid; it jumps from admiration to love, from love to matrimony in a moment. I knew you would be wishing me joy."

"Nay, if you are so serious about it, I shall consider the matter as absolutely settled. You will have a charming mother-in-law, indeed, and of course she will be always at Pemberley with you."

He listened to her with perfect indifference, while she chose to entertain herself in this manner, and as his composure convinced her that all was safe, her wit flowed long.

Chapter VII

Mr. Bennet's property consisted almost entirely in an estate of two thousand a year, which, unfortunately for his daughters, was entailed [8] in default of heirs male, on a distant relation; and their mother's fortune, though ample for her situation in life, could but ill supply the deficiency of his. Her father had been an attorney in Meryton, and had left her four thousand pounds.

She had a sister married to a Mr. Phillips, who had been a clerk to their father, and succeeded him in the business, and a brother settled in London in a respectable line of trade.

The village of Longbourn was only one mile from Meryton; a most convenient distance for the young ladies, who were usually tempted thither three or four times a week, to pay their duty to their aunt and to a milliner's shop just over the way. The two youngest of the family, Catherine and Lydia, were particularly frequent in these attentions; their minds were more vacant than

8. A restriction on an inheritance; in this case, a stipulation that Mr. Bennet's property will pass to another branch of his family if he has no son to continue his line.

their sisters', and when nothing better offered, a walk to Meryton was necessary to amuse their morning hours and furnish conversation for the evening; and however bare of news the country in general might be, they always contrived to learn some from their aunt. At present, indeed, they were well supplied both with news and happiness by the recent arrival of a militia regiment in the neighbourhood; it was to remain the whole winter, and Meryton was the head quarters.

Their visits to Mrs. Philips were now productive of the most interesting intelligence. Every day added something to their knowledge of the officers' names and connections. Their lodgings were not long a secret, and at length they began to know the officers themselves. Mr. Philips visited them all, and this opened to his nieces a source of felicity unknown before. They could talk of nothing but officers; and Mr. Bingley's large fortune, the mention of which gave animation to their mother, was worthless in their eyes when opposed to the regimentals of an ensign.

After listening one morning to their effusions on this subject, Mr. Bennet coolly observed,

"From all that I can collect by your manner of talking, you must be two of the silliest girls in the country. I have suspected it some time, but I am now convinced."

Catherine was disconcerted, and made no answer; but Lydia, with perfect indifference, continued to express her admiration of Captain Carter, and her hope of seeing him in the course of the day, as he was going the next morning to London.

"I am astonished, my dear," said Mrs. Bennet, "that you should be so ready to think your own children silly. If I wished to think slightingly of any body's children, it should not be of my own however."

"If my children are silly I must hope to be always sensible of it."

"Yes—but as it happens, they are all of them very clever."

"This is the only point, I flatter myself, on which we do not agree. I had hoped that our sentiments coincided in every particular, but I must so far differ from you as to think our two youngest daughters uncommonly foolish."

"My dear Mr. Bennet, you must not expect such girls to have the sense of their father and mother.—When they get to our age I dare say they will not think about officers any more than we do. I remember the time when I liked a red coat myself very well— and indeed so I do still at my heart; and if a smart young colonel, with five or six thousand a year, should want one of my girls, I shall not say nay to him; and I thought Colonel Forster looked very becoming the other night at Sir William's in his regimentals."

"Mama," cried Lydia, "my aunt says that Colonel Forster and Captain Carter do not go so often to Miss Watson's as they did when they first came; she sees them now very often standing in Clarke's library."

Mrs. Bennet was prevented replying by the entrance of the footman with a note for Miss Bennet; it came from Netherfield, and the servant waited for an answer. Mrs. Bennet's eyes sparkled with pleasure, and she was eagerly calling out, while her daughter read,

"Well, Jane, who is it from? what is it about? what does he say? Well, Jane, make haste and tell us; make haste, my love."

"It is from Miss Bingley," said Jane, and then read it aloud.

"My dear Friend,

"If you are not so compassionate as to dine to-day with Louisa and me, we shall be in danger of hating each other for the rest of our lives, for a whole day's tête-à-tête between two women can never end without a quarrel. Come as soon as you can on the receipt of this. My brother and the gentlemen are to dine with the officers. Yours ever,

"CAROLINE BINGLEY."

"With the officers!" cried Lydia. "I wonder my aunt did not tell us of *that*."

"Dining out," said Mrs. Bennet, "that is very unlucky."

"Can I have the carriage?" said Jane.

"No, my dear, you had better go on horseback, because it seems likely to rain; and then you must stay all night."

"That would be a good scheme," said Elizabeth, "if you were sure that they would not offer to send her home."

"Oh! but the gentlemen will have Mr. Bingley's chaise to go to Meryton; and the Hursts have no horses to theirs."

"I had much rather go in the coach."

"But, my dear, your father cannot spare the horses, I am sure. They are wanted in the farm, Mr. Bennet, are not they?"

"They are wanted in the farm much oftener than I can get them."

"But if you have got them to day," said Elizabeth, "my mother's purpose will be answered."

She did at last extort from her father an acknowledgment that the horses were engaged. Jane was therefore obliged to go on horseback, and her mother attended her to the door with many cheerful prognostics of a bad day. Her hopes were answered; Jane had not been gone long before it rained hard. Her sisters were uneasy for her, but her mother was delighted. The rain continued the whole evening without intermission; Jane certainly could not come back.

"This was a lucky idea of mine, indeed!" said Mrs. Bennet, more than once, as if the credit of making it rain were all her own. Till the next morning, however, she was not aware of all the felicity of her contrivance. Breakfast was scarcely over when a servant from Netherfield brought the following note for Elizabeth:

"My dearest Lizzy,

"I find myself very unwell this morning, which, I suppose, is to be imputed to my getting wet through yesterday. My kind friends will not hear of my returning home till I am better. They insist also on my seeing Mr. Jones—therefore do not be alarmed if you should hear of his having been to me—and excepting a sore-throat and head-ache there is not much the matter with me.

"Yours, &c."

"Well, my dear," said Mr. Bennet, when Elizabeth had read the note aloud, "if your daughter should have a dangerous fit of illness, if she should die, it would be a comfort to know that it was all in pursuit of Mr. Bingley, and under your orders."

"Oh! I am not at all afraid of her dying. People do not die of little trifling colds. She will be taken good care of. As long as she stays there, it is all very well. I would go and see her, if I could have the carriage."

Elizabeth, feeling really anxious, was determined to go to her, though the carriage was not to be had; and as she was no horse-woman, walking was her only alternative. She declared her resolution.

"How can you be so silly," cried her mother, "as to think of such a thing, in all this dirt! You will not be fit to be seen when you get there."

"I shall be very fit to see Jane—which is all I want."

"Is this a hint to me, Lizzy," said her father, "to send for the horses?"

"No, indeed. I do not wish to avoid the walk. The distance is nothing, when one has a motive; only three miles. I shall be back by dinner."

"I admire the activity of your benevolence," observed Mary, "but every impulse of feeling should be guided by reason; and, in my opinion, exertion should always be in proportion to what is required."

"We will go as far as Meryton with you," said Catherine and Lydia.—Elizabeth accepted their company, and the three young ladies set off together.

"If we make haste," said Lydia, as they walked along, "perhaps we may see something of Captain Carter before he goes."

In Meryton they parted; the two youngest repaired to the

lodgings of one of the officers' wives, and Elizabeth continued her walk alone, crossing field after field at a quick pace, jumping over stiles and springing over puddles with impatient activity, and finding herself at last within view of the house, with weary ancles, dirty stockings, and a face glowing with the warmth of exercise.

She was shewn into the breakfast-parlour, where all but Jane were assembled, and where her appearance created a great deal of surprise.—That she should have walked three miles so early in the day, in such dirty weather, and by herself, was almost incredible to Mrs. Hurst and Miss Bingley; and Elizabeth was convinced they they held her in contempt for it. She was received, however, very politely by them; and in their brother's manners there was something better than politeness; there was good humour and kindness.—Mr. Darcy said very little, and Mr. Hurst nothing at all. The former was divided between admiration of the brilliancy which exercise had given to her complexion, and doubt as to the occasion's justifying her coming so far alone. The latter was thinking only of his breakfast.

Her enquiries after her sister were not very favourably answered. Miss Bennet had slept ill, and though up, was very feverish and not well enough to leave her room. Elizabeth was glad to be taken to her immediately; and Jane, who had only been withheld by the fear of giving alarm or inconvenience, from expressing in her note how much she longed for such a visit, was delighted at her entrance. She was not equal, however, to much conversation, and when Miss Bingley left them together, could attempt little beside expressions of gratitude for the extraordinary kindness she was treated with. Elizabeth silently attended her.

When breakfast was over, they were joined by the sisters; and Elizabeth began to like them herself, when she saw how much affection and solicitude they shewed for Jane. The apothecary came, and having examined his patient, said, as might be supposed, that she had caught a violent cold, and that they must endeavour to get the better of it; advised her to return to bed, and promised her some draughts.[9] The advice was followed readily, for the feverish symptoms increased, and her head ached acutely. Elizabeth did not quit her room for a moment, nor were the other ladies often absent; the gentlemen being out, they had in fact nothing to do elsewhere.

When the clock struck three, Elizabeth felt that she must go; and very unwillingly said so. Miss Bingley offered her the carriage, and she only wanted a little pressing to accept it, when Jane testified such concern in parting with her, that Miss Bingley was obliged to convert the offer of the chaise into an invitation to remain at

9. Medicine.

Netherfield for the present. Elizabeth most thankfully consented, and a servant was dispatched to Longbourn to acquaint the family with her stay, and bring back a supply of clothes.

Chapter VIII

At five o'clock the two ladies retired to dress, and at half past six Elizabeth was summoned to dinner. To the civil enquiries which then poured in, and amongst which she had the pleasure of distinguishing the much superior solicitude of Mr. Bingley's, she could not make a very favourable answer. Jane was by no means better. The sisters, on hearing this, repeated three or four times how much they were grieved, how shocking it was to have a bad cold, and how excessively they disliked being ill themselves; and then thought no more of the matter: and their indifference towards Jane when not immediately before them, restored Elizabeth to the enjoyment of all her original dislike.

Their brother, indeed, was the only one of the party whom she could regard with any complacency. His anxiety for Jane was evident, and his attentions to herself most pleasing, and they prevented her feeling herself so much an intruder as she believed she was considered by the others. She had very little notice from any but him. Miss Bingley was engrossed by Mr. Darcy, her sister scarcely less so; and as for Mr. Hurst, by whom Elizabeth sat, he was an indolent man, who lived only to eat, drink, and play at cards, who when he found her prefer a plain dish to a ragout, had nothing to say to her.

When dinner was over, she returned directly to Jane, and Miss Bingley began abusing her as soon as she was out of the room. Her manners were pronounced to be very bad indeed, a mixture of pride and impertinence; she had no conversation, no stile, no taste, no beauty. Mrs. Hurst thought the same, and added,

"She has nothing, in short, to recommend her, but being an excellent walker. I shall never forget her appearance this morning. She really looked almost wild."

"She did indeed, Louisa. I could hardly keep my countenance. Very nonsensical to come at all! Why must *she* be scampering about the country, because her sister had a cold? Her hair so untidy, so blowsy!"

"Yes, and her petticoat; I hope you saw her petticoat, six inches deep in mud, I am absolutely certain; and the gown which had been let down to hide it, not doing its office."

"Your picture may be very exact, Louisa," said Bingley; "but this was all lost upon me. I thought Miss Elizabeth Bennet looked remarkably well, when she came into the room this morning.

Her dirty petticoat quite escaped my notice."

"*You* observed it, Mr. Darcy, I am sure," said Miss Bingley; "and I am inclined to think that you would not wish to see *your sister* make such an exhibition."

"Certainly not."

"To walk three miles, or four miles, or five miles, or whatever it is, above her ancles in dirt, and alone, quite alone! what could she mean by it? It seems to me to shew an abominable sort of conceited independence, a most country town indifference to decorum."

"It shews an affection for her sister that is very pleasing," said Bingley.

"I am afraid, Mr. Darcy," observed Miss Bingley, in a half whisper, "that this adventure has rather affected your admiration of her fine eyes."

"Not at all," he replied; "they were brightened by the exercise." —A short pause followed this speech, and Mrs. Hurst began again.

"I have an excessive regard for Jane Bennet, she is really a very sweet girl, and I wish with all my heart she were well settled. But with such a father and mother, and such low connections, I am afraid there is no chance of it."

"I think I have heard you say, that their uncle is an attorney in Meryton."

"Yes; and they have another, who lives somewhere near Cheapside." [1]

"That is capital," added her sister, and they both laughed heartily.

"If they had uncles enough to fill *all* Cheapside," cried Bingley, "it would not make them one jot less agreeable."

"But it must very materially lessen their chance of marrying men of any consideration in the world," replied Darcy.

To this speech Bingley made no answer; but his sisters gave it their hearty assent, and indulged their mirth for some time at the expense of their dear friend's vulgar relations.

With a renewal of tenderness, however, they repaired to her room on leaving the dining-parlour, and sat with her till summoned to coffee. She was still very poorly, and Elizabeth would not quit her at all, till late in the evening, when she had the comfort of seeing her asleep, and when it appeared to her rather right than pleasant that she should go down stairs herself. On entering

1. Cheapside is a neighborhood in London's commercial district. To be in business rather than to live, as Bingley and Darcy do, from the income of capital or land is to be judged socially inferior by people like Miss Bingley and Mrs. Hurst, even though their own fortune was earned in trade. To live near one's place of business rather than in more fashionable precincts is to confirm their judgment.

the drawing-room she found the whole party at loo,[2] and was immediately invited to join them; but suspecting them to be playing high she declined it, and making her sister the excuse, said she would amuse herself for the short time she could stay below with a book. Mr. Hurst looked at her with astonishment.

"Do you prefer reading to cards?" said he; "that is rather singular."

"Miss Eliza Bennet," said Miss Bingley, "despises cards. She is a great reader and has no pleasure in anything else."

"I deserve neither such praise nor such censure," cried Elizabeth; "I am *not* a great reader, and I have pleasure in many things."

"In nursing your sister I am sure you have pleasure," said Bingley; "and I hope it will soon be increased by seeing her quite well."

Elizabeth thanked him from her heart, and then walked towards a table where a few books were lying. He immediately offered to fetch her others; all that his library afforded.

"And I wish my collection were larger for your benefit and my own credit; but I am an idle fellow, and though I have not many, I have more than I ever look into."

Elizabeth assured him that she could suit herself perfectly with those in the room.

"I am astonished," said Miss Bingley, "that my father should have left so small a collection of books.—What a delightful library you have at Pemberley, Mr. Darcy!"

"It ought to be good," he replied, "it has been the work of many generations."

"And then you have added so much to it yourself, you are always buying books."

"I cannot comprehend the neglect of a family library in such days as these."

"Neglect! I am sure you neglect nothing that can add to the beauties of that noble place. Charles, when you build *your* house, I wish it may be half as delightful as Pemberley."

"I wish it may."

"But I would really advise you to make your purchase in that neighbourhood, and take Pemberley for a kind of model. There is not a finer county in England than Derbyshire."

"With all my heart; I will buy Pemberley itself if Darcy will sell it."

"I am talking of possibilities, Charles."

"Upon my word, Caroline, I should think it more possible to get Pemberley by purchase than by imitation."

Elizabeth was so much caught by what passed, as to leave her very little attention for her book; and soon laying it wholly aside,

2. A card game similar to whist.

she drew near the card-table, and stationed herself between Mr. Bingley and his eldest sister, to observe the game.

"Is Miss Darcy much grown since the spring?" said Miss Bingley; "will she be as tall as I am?"

"I think she will. She is now about Miss Elizabeth Bennet's height, or rather taller."

"How I long to see her again! I never met with anybody who delighted me so much. Such a countenance, such manners! and so extremely accomplished for her age! Her performance on the piano-forte is exquisite."

"It is amazing to me," said Bingley, "how young ladies can have patience to be so very accomplished, as they all are."

"All young ladies accomplished! My dear Charles, what do you mean?"

"Yes, all of them, I think. They all paint tables, cover skreens and net purses. I scarcely know any one who cannot do all this, and I am sure I never heard a young lady spoken of for the first time, without being informed that she was very accomplished."

"Your list of the common extent of accomplishments," said Darcy, "has too much truth. The word is applied to many a woman who deserves it no otherwise than by netting a purse, or covering a skreen. But I am very far from agreeing with you in your estimation of ladies in general. I cannot boast of knowing more than half a dozen, in the whole range of my acquaintance, that are really accomplished."

"Nor I, I am sure," said Miss Bingley.

"Then," observed Elizabeth, "you must comprehend a great deal in your idea of an accomplished woman."

"Yes; I do comprehend a great deal in it."

"Oh! certainly," cried his faithful assistant, "no one can be really esteemed accomplished, who does not greatly surpass what is usually met with. A woman must have a thorough knowledge of music, singing, drawing, dancing, and the modern languages, to deserve the word; and besides all this, she must possess a certain something in her air and manner of walking, the tone of her voice, her address and expressions, or the word will be but half deserved."

"All this she must possess," added Darcy, "and to all this she must yet add something more substantial, in the improvement of her mind by extensive reading."

"I am no longer surprised at your knowing *only* six accomplished women. I rather wonder now at your knowing *any*."

"Are you so severe upon your own sex, as to doubt the possibility of all this?"

"I never saw such a woman. I never saw such capacity, and taste, and application, and elegance, as you describe, united."

Mrs. Hurst and Miss Bingley both cried out against the injustice of her implied doubt, and were both protesting that they knew many women who answered this description, when Mr. Hurst called them to order, with bitter complaints of their inattention to what was going forward. As all conversation was thereby at an end, Elizabeth soon afterwards left the room.

"Eliza Bennet," said Miss Bingley, when the door was closed on her, "is one of those young ladies who seek to recommend themselves to the other sex, by undervaluing their own; and with many men, I dare say, it succeeds. But, in my opinion, it is a paltry device, a very mean art."

"Undoubtedly," replied Darcy, to whom this remark was chiefly addressed, "there is meanness in *all* the arts which ladies sometimes condescend to employ for captivation. Whatever bears affinity to cunning is despicable."

Miss Bingley was not so entirely satisfied with this reply as to continue the subject.

Elizabeth joined them again only to say that her sister was worse, and that she could not leave her. Bingley urged Mr. Jones's being sent for immediately; while his sisters, convinced that no country advice could be of any service, recommended an express to town for one of the most eminent physicians. This, she would not hear of; but she was not so unwilling to comply with their brother's proposal; and it was settled that Mr. Jones should be sent for early in the morning, if Miss Bennet were not decidedly better. Bingley was quite uncomfortable; his sisters declared that they were miserable. They solaced their wretchedness, however, by duets after supper, while he could find no better relief to his feelings than by giving his housekeeper directions that every possible attention might be paid to the sick lady and her sister.

Chapter IX

Elizabeth passed the chief of the night in her sister's room, and in the morning had the pleasure of being able to send a tolerable answer to the enquiries which she very early received from Mr. Bingley by a housemaid, and some time afterwards from the two elegant ladies who waited on his sisters. In spite of this amendment, however, she requested to have a note sent to Longbourn, desiring her mother to visit Jane, and form her own judgment of her situation. The note was immediately dispatched, and its contents as quickly complied with. Mrs. Bennet, accompanied by her two youngest girls, reached Netherfield soon after the family breakfast.

Had she found Jane in any apparent danger, Mrs. Bennet

would have been very miserable; but being satisfied on seeing her that her illness was not alarming, she had no wish of her recovering immediately, as her restoration to health would probably remove her from Netherfield. She would not listen therefore to her daughter's proposal of being carried home; neither did the apothecary, who arrived about the same time, think it at all advisable. After sitting a little while with Jane, on Miss Bingley's appearance and invitation, the mother and three daughters all attended her into the breakfast parlour. Bingley met them with hopes that Mrs. Bennet had not found Miss Bennet worse than she expected.

"Indeed I have, Sir," was her answer. "She is a great deal too ill to be moved. Mr. Jones says we must not think of moving her. We must trespass a little longer on your kindness."

"Removed!" cried Bingley. "It must not be thought of. My sister, I am sure, will not hear of her removal."

"You may depend upon it, Madam," said Miss Bingley, with cold civility, "that Miss Bennet shall receive every possible attention while she remains with us."

Mrs. Bennet was profuse in her acknowledgments.

"I am sure," she added, "if it was not for such good friends I do not know what would become of her, for she is very ill indeed, and suffers a vast deal, though with the greatest patience in the world, which is always the way with her, for she has, without exception, the sweetest temper I ever met with. I often tell my other girls they are nothing to *her*. You have a sweet room here, Mr. Bingley, and a charming prospect over that gravel walk. I do not know a place in the country that is equal to Netherfield. You will not think of quitting it in a hurry I hope, though you have but a short lease."

"Whatever I do is done in a hurry," replied he; "and therefore if I should resolve to quit Netherfield, I should probably be off in five minutes. At present, however, I consider myself as quite fixed here."

"That is exactly what I should have supposed of you," said Elizabeth.

"You begin to comprehend me, do you?" cried he, turning towards her.

"Oh! yes—I understand you perfectly."

"I wish I might take this for a compliment; but to be so easily seen through I am afraid is pitiful."

"That is as it happens. It does not necessarily follow that a deep, intricate character is more or less estimable than such a one as yours."

"Lizzy," cried her mother, "remember where you are, and do

not run on in the wild manner that you are suffered to do at home."

"I did not know before," continued Bingley immediately, "that you were a studier of character. It must be an amusing study."

"Yes; but intricate characters are the *most* amusing. They have at least that advantage."

"The country," said Darcy, "can in general supply but few subjects for such a study. In a country neighbourhood you move in a very confined and unvarying society."

"But people themselves alter so much, that there is something new to be observed in them for ever."

"Yes, indeed," cried Mrs. Bennet, offended by his manner of mentioning a country neighbourhood. "I assure you there is quite as much of *that* going on in the country as in town."

Every body was surprised; and Darcy, after looking at her for a moment, turned silently away. Mrs. Bennet, who fancied she had gained a complete victory over him, continued her triumph.

"I cannot see that London has any great advantage over the country for my part, except the shops and public places. The country is a vast deal pleasanter, is not it, Mr. Bingley?"

"When I am in the country," he replied, "I never wish to leave it; and when I am in town it is pretty much the same. They have each their advantages, and I can be equally happy in either."

"Aye—that is because you have the right disposition. But that gentleman," looking at Darcy, "seemed to think the country was nothing at all."

"Indeed, Mama, you are mistaken," said Elizabeth, blushing for her mother. "You quite mistook Mr. Darcy. He only meant that there were not such a variety of people to be met with in the country as in town, which you must acknowledge to be true."

"Certainly, my dear, nobody said there were; but as to not meeting with many people in this neighbourhood, I believe there are few neighbourhoods larger. I know we dine with four and twenty families."

Nothing but concern for Elizabeth could enable Bingley to keep his countenance. His sister was less delicate, and directed her eye towards Mr. Darcy with a very expressive smile. Elizabeth, for the sake of saying something that might turn her mother's thoughts, now asked her if Charlotte Lucas had been at Longbourn since *her* coming away.

"Yes, she called yesterday with her father. What an agreeable man Sir William is, Mr. Bingley—is not he? so much the man of fashion! so genteel and so easy!—He has always something to say to every body.—*That* is my idea of good breeding; and those persons who fancy themselves very important and never open their mouths, quite mistake the matter."

"Did Charlotte dine with you?"

"No, she would go home. I fancy she was wanted about the mince pies. For my part, Mr. Bingley, I always keep servants that can do their own work; *my* daughters are brought up differently. But every body is to judge for themselves, and the Lucases are very good sort of girls, I assure you. It is a pity they are not handsome! Not that I think Charlotte so *very* plain—but then she is our particular friend."

"She seems a very pleasant young woman," said Bingley.

"Oh! dear, yes;—but you must own she is very plain. Lady Lucas herself has often said so, and envied me Jane's beauty. I do not like to boast of my own child, but to be sure, Jane—one does not often see any body better looking. It is what every body says. I do not trust my own partiality. When she was only fifteen, there was a gentleman at my brother Gardiner's in town, so much in love with her, that my sister-in-law was sure he would make her an offer before we came away. But however he did not. Perhaps he thought her too young. However, he wrote some verses on her, and very pretty they were."

"And so ended his affection," said Elizabeth impatiently. "There has been many a one, I fancy, overcome in the same way. I wonder who first discovered the efficacy of poetry in driving away love!"

"I have been used to consider poetry as the *food* of love," said Darcy.

"Of a fine, stout, healthy love it may. Every thing nourishes what is strong already. But if it be only a slight, thin sort of inclination, I am convinced that one good sonnet will starve it entirely away."

Darcy only smiled; and the general pause which ensued made Elizabeth tremble lest her mother should be exposing herself again. She longed to speak, but could think of nothing to say; and after a short silence Mrs. Bennet began repeating her thanks to Mr. Bingley for his kindness to Jane, with an apology for troubling him also with Lizzy. Mr. Bingley was unaffectedly civil in his answer, and forced his younger sister to be civil also, and say what the occasion required. She performed her part indeed without much graciousness, but Mrs. Bennet was satisfied, and soon afterwards ordered her carriage. Upon this signal, the youngest of her daughters put herself forward. The two girls had been whispering to each other during the whole visit, and the result of it was, that the youngest should tax Mr. Bingley with having promised on his first coming into the country to give a ball at Netherfield.

Lydia was a stout, well-grown girl of fifteen, with a fine complexion and good-humoured countenance; a favorite with her mother, whose affection had brought her into public at an early age. She had high animal spirits, and a sort of natural self-consequence, which the attentions of the officers, to whom her uncle's good dinners and her own easy manners recommended her, had increased into assurance. She was very equal therefore to address Mr. Bingley on the subject of the ball, and abruptly reminded him of his promise; adding, that it would be the most shameful thing in the world if he did not keep it. His answer to this sudden attack was delightful to their mother's ear.

"I am perfectly ready, I assure you, to keep my engagement; and when your sister is recovered, you shall if you please name the very day of the ball. But you would not wish to be dancing while she is ill."

Lydia declared herself satisfied. "Oh! yes—it would be much better to wait till Jane was well, and by that time most likely Captain Carter would be at Meryton again. And when you have given *your* ball," she added, "I shall insist on their giving one also. I shall tell Colonel Forster it will be quite a shame if he does not."

Mrs. Bennet and her daughters then departed, and Elizabeth returned instantly to Jane, leaving her own and her relations' behaviour to the remarks of the two ladies and Mr. Darcy; the latter of whom, however, could not be prevailed on to join in their censure of *her*, in spite of all Miss Bingley's witticisms on *fine eyes*.

Chapter X

The day passed much as the day before had done. Mrs. Hurst and Miss Bingley had spent some hours of the morning with the invalid, who continued, though slowly, to mend; and in the evening Elizabeth joined their party in the drawing-room. The loo table, however, did not appear. Mr. Darcy was writing, and Miss Bingley, seated near him, was watching the progress of his letter, and repeatedly calling off his attention by messages to his sister. Mr. Hurst and Mr. Bingley were at piquet,[3] and Mrs. Hurst was observing their game.

Elizabeth took up some needlework, and was sufficiently amused in attending to what passed between Darcy and his companion. The perpetual commendations of the lady either on his handwriting, or on the evenness of his lines, or on the length of his

3. A card game, commonly played by two players; similar to the draw-and-discard games called rummy.

letter, with the perfect unconcern with which her praises were received, formed a curious dialogue, and was exactly in unison with her opinion of each.

"How delighted Miss Darcy will be to receive such a letter!"

He made no answer.

"You write uncommonly fast."

"You are mistaken. I write rather slowly."

"How many letters you must have occasion to write in the course of the year! Letters of business too! How odious I should think them!"

"It is fortunate, then, that they fall to my lot instead of to yours."

"Pray tell your sister that I long to see her."

"I have already told her so once, by your desire."

"I am afraid you do not like your pen. Let me mend it for you. I mend pens remarkably well."

"Thank you—but I always mend my own."

"How can you contrive to write so even?"

He was silent.

"Tell your sister I am delighted to hear of her improvement on the harp, and pray let her know that I am quite in raptures with her beautiful little design for a table, and I think it infinitely superior to Miss Grantley's."

"Will you give me leave to defer your raptures till I write again? —At present I have not room to do them justice."

"Oh! it is of no consequence. I shall see her in January. But do you always write such charming long letters to her, Mr. Darcy?"

"They are generally long; but whether always charming, it is not for me to determine."

"It is a rule with me, that a person who can write a long letter, with ease, cannot write ill."

"That will not do for a compliment to Darcy, Caroline," cried her brother—"because he does *not* write with ease. He studies too much for words of four syllables.—Do not you, Darcy?"

"My stile of writing is very different from yours."

"Oh!" cried Miss Bingley, "Charles writes in the most careless way imaginable. He leaves out half his words, and blots the rest."

"My ideas flow so rapidly that I have not time to express them— by which means my letters sometimes convey no ideas at all to my correspondents."

"Your humility, Mr. Bingley," said Elizabeth, "must disarm reproof."

"Nothing is more deceitful," said Darcy, "than the appearance of humility. It is often only carelessness of opinion, and sometimes an indirect boast."

"And which of the two do you call *my* little recent piece of modesty?"

"The indirect boast;—for you are really proud of your defects in writing, because you consider them as proceeding from a rapidity of thought and carelessness of execution, which if not estimable, you think at least highly interesting. The power of doing any thing with quickness is always much prized by the possessor, and often without any attention to the imperfection of the performance. When you told Mrs. Bennet this morning that if you ever resolved on quitting Netherfield you should be gone in five minutes, you meant it to be a sort of panegyric, of compliment to yourself—and yet what is there so very laudable in a precipitance which must leave very necessary business undone, and can be of no real advantage to yourself or any one else?"

"Nay," cried Bingley, "this is too much, to remember at night all the foolish things that were said in the morning. And yet, upon my honour, I believed what I said of myself to be true, and I believe it at this moment. At least, therefore, I did not assume the character of needless precipitance merely to shew off before the ladies."

"I dare say you believed it; but I am by no means convinced that you would be gone with such celerity. Your conduct would be quite as dependant on chance as that of any man I know; and if, as you were mounting your horse, a friend were to say, 'Bingley, you had better stay till next week,' you would probably do it, you would probably not go—and, at another word, might stay a month."

"You have only proved by this," cried Elizabeth, "that Mr. Bingley did not do justice to his own disposition. You have shewn him off now much more than he did himself."

"I am exceedingly gratified," said Bingley, "by your converting what my friend says into a compliment on the sweetness of my temper. But I am afraid you are giving it a turn which that gentleman did by no means intend; for he would certainly think the better of me, if under such a circumstance I were to give a flat denial, and ride off as fast as I could."

"Would Mr. Darcy then consider the rashness of your original intention as atoned for by your obstinacy in adhering to it?"

"Upon my word I cannot exactly explain the matter, Darcy must speak for himself."

"You expect me to account for opinions which you chuse to call mine, but which I have never acknowledged. Allowing the case, however, to stand according to your representation, you must remember, Miss Bennet, that the friend who is supposed to desire his return to the house, and the delay of his plan, has merely desired it, asked it without offering one argument in favour of its propriety."

"To yield readily—easily—to the *persuasion* of a friend is no merit with you."

"To yield without conviction is no compliment to the understanding of either."

"You appear to me, Mr. Darcy, to allow nothing for the influence of friendship and affection. A regard for the requester would often make one readily yield to a request, without waiting for arguments to reason one into it. I am not particularly speaking of such a case as you have supposed about Mr. Bingley. We may as well wait, perhaps, till the circumstance occurs, before we discuss the discretion of his behaviour thereupon. But in general and ordinary cases between friend and friend, where one of them is desired by the other to change a resolution of no very great moment, should you think ill of that person for complying with the desire, without waiting to be argued into it?"

"Will it not be advisable, before we proceed on this subject, to arrange with rather more precision the degree of importance which is to appertain to this request, as well as the degree of intimacy subsisting between the parties?"

"By all means," cried Bingley; "let us hear all the particulars, not forgetting their comparative height and size; for that will have more weight in the argument, Miss Bennet, than you may be aware of. I assure you that if Darcy were not such a great tall fellow, in comparison with myself, I should not pay him half so much deference. I declare I do not know a more aweful object than Darcy, on particular occasions, and in particular places; at his own house especially, and of a Sunday evening when he has nothing to do."

Mr. Darcy smiled; but Elizabeth thought she could perceive that he was rather offended; and therefore checked her laugh. Miss Bingley warmly resented the indignity he had received, in an expostulation with her brother for talking such nonsense.

"I see your design, Bingley," said his friend.—"You dislike an argument, and want to silence this."

"Perhaps I do. Arguments are too much like disputes. If you and Miss Bennet will defer yours till I am out of the room, I shall be very thankful; and then you may say whatever you like of me."

"What you ask," said Elizabeth, "is no sacrifice on my side; and Mr. Darcy had much better finish his letter."

Mr. Darcy took her advice, and did finish his letter.

When that business was over, he applied to Miss Bingley and Elizabeth for the indulgence of some music. Miss Bingley moved with alacrity to the piano-forte, and after a polite request that Elizabeth would lead the way, which the other as politely and more earnestly negatived, she seated herself.

Mrs. Hurst sang with her sister, and while they were thus employed Elizabeth could not help observing as she turned over some music books that lay on the instrument, how frequently Mr. Darcy's eyes were fixed on her. She hardly knew how to suppose that she could be an object of admiration to so great a man; and yet that he should look at her because he disliked her, was still more strange. She could only imagine however at last, that she drew his notice because there was a something about her more wrong and reprehensible, according to his ideas of right, than in any other person present. The supposition did not pain her. She liked him too little to care for his approbation.

After playing some Italian songs, Miss Bingley varied the charm by a lively Scotch air; and soon afterwards Mr. Darcy, drawing near Elizabeth, said to her—

"Do not you feel a great inclination, Miss Bennet, to seize such an opportunity of dancing a reel?"

She smiled, but made no answer. He repeated the question, with some surprise at her silence.

"Oh!" said she, "I heard you before; but I could not immediately determine what to say in reply. You wanted me, I know, to say 'Yes,' that you might have the pleasure of despising my taste; but I always delight in overthrowing those kind of schemes, and cheating a person of their premeditated contempt. I have therefore made up my mind to tell you, that I do not want to dance a reel at all—and now despise me if you dare."

"Indeed I do not dare."

Elizabeth, having rather expected to affront him, was amazed at his gallantry; but there was a mixture of sweetness and archness in her manner which made it difficult for her to affront anybody; and Darcy had never been so bewitched by any woman as he was by her. He really believed, that were it not for the inferiority of her connections, he should be in some danger.

Miss Bingley saw, or suspected enough to be jealous; and her great anxiety for the recovery of her dear friend Jane, received some assistance from her desire of getting rid of Elizabeth.

She often tried to provoke Darcy into disliking her guest, by talking of their supposed marriage, and planning his happiness in such an alliance.

"I hope," said she, as they were walking together in the shrubbery the next day, "you will give your mother-in-law a few hints, when this desirable event takes place, as to the advantage of holding her tongue; and if you can compass it, do cure the younger girls of running after the officers.—And, if I may mention so delicate a subject, endeavour to check that little something, bordering on conceit and impertinence, which your lady possesses."

"Have you any thing else to propose for my domestic felicity?"

"Oh! yes.—Do let the portraits of your uncle and aunt Philips be placed in the gallery at Pemberley. Put them next to your great uncle the judge. They are in the same profession, you know; only in different lines. As for your Elizabeth's picture, you must not attempt to have it taken, for what painter could do justice to those beautiful eyes?"

"It would not be easy, indeed, to catch their expression, but their colour and shape, and the eye-lashes, so remarkably fine, might be copied."

At that moment they were met from another walk, by Mrs. Hurst and Elizabeth herself.

"I did not know that you intended to walk," said Miss Bingley, in some confusion, lest they had been overheard.

"You used us abominably ill," answered Mrs. Hurst, "in running away without telling us that you were coming out."

Then taking the disengaged arm of Mr. Darcy, she left Elizabeth to walk by herself. The path just admitted three. Mr. Darcy felt their rudeness and immediately said,—

"This walk is not wide enough for our party. We had better go into the avenue."

But Elizabeth, who had not the least inclination to remain with them, laughingly answered,

"No, no; stay where you are.—You are charmingly group'd, and appear to uncommon advantage. The picturesque would be spoilt by admitting a fourth. Good bye."

She then ran gaily off, rejoicing as she rambled about, in the hope of being at home again in a day or two. Jane was already so much recovered as to intend leaving her room for a couple of hours that evening.

Chapter XI

When the ladies removed after dinner,[4] Elizabeth ran up to her sister, and seeing her well guarded from cold, attended her into the drawing-room; where she was welcomed by her two friends with many professions of pleasure; and Elizabeth had never seen them so agreeable as they were during the hour which passed before the gentlemen appeared. Their powers of conversation were considerable. They could describe an entertainment with

4. It was customary for the ladies to leave the dinner-table before the gentle- men, who delayed an interval, usually over wine.

accuracy, relate an anecdote with humour, and laugh at their acquaintance with spirit.

But when the gentlemen entered, Jane was no longer the first object. Miss Bingley's eyes were instantly turned towards Darcy, and she had something to say to him before he had advanced many steps. He addressed himself directly to Miss Bennet, with a polite congratulation; Mr. Hurst also made her a slight bow, and said he was "very glad;" but diffuseness and warmth remained for Bingley's salutation. He was full of joy and attention. The first half hour was spent in piling up the fire, lest she should suffer from the change of room; and she removed at his desire to the other side of the fire-place, that she might be farther from the door. He then sat down by her, and talked scarcely to any one else. Elizabeth, at work in the opposite corner, saw it all with great delight.

When tea was over, Mr. Hurst reminded his sister-in-law of the card-table—but in vain. She had obtained private intelligence that Mr. Darcy did not wish for cards; and Mr. Hurst soon found even his open petition rejected. She assured him that no one intended to play, and the silence of the whole party on the subject, seemed to justify her. Mr. Hurst had therefore nothing to do, but to stretch himself on one of the sophas and go to sleep. Darcy took up a book; Miss Bingley did the same; and Mrs. Hurst, principally occupied in playing with her bracelets and rings, joined now and then in her brother's conversation with Miss Bennet.

Miss Bingley's attention was quite as much engaged in watching Mr. Darcy's progress through *his* book, as in reading her own; and she was perpetually either making some inquiry, or looking at his page. She could not win him, however, to any conversation; he merely answered her question, and read on. At length, quite exhausted by the attempt to be amused with her own book, which she had only chosen because it was the second volume of his, she gave a great yawn and said, "How pleasant it is to spend an evening in this way! I declare after all there is no enjoyment like reading! How much sooner one tires of any thing than of a book!—When I have a house of my own, I shall be miserable if I have not an excellent library."

No one made any reply. She then yawned again, threw aside her book, and cast her eyes round the room in quest of some amusement; when hearing her brother mentioning a ball to Miss Bennet, she turned suddenly towards him and said,

"By the bye, Charles, are you really serious in meditating a dance at Netherfield?—I would advise you, before you determine on it, to consult the wishes of the present party; I am much mistaken if there are not some among us to whom a ball would be rather a punishment than a pleasure."

"If you mean Darcy," cried her brother, "he may go to bed, if he chuses, before it begins—but as for the ball, it is quite a settled thing; and as soon as Nicholls has made white soup enough I shall send round my cards." [5]

"I should like balls infinitely better," she replied, "if they were carried on in a different manner; but there is something insufferably tedious in the usual process of such a meeting. It would surely be much more rational if conversation instead of dancing made the order of the day."

"Much more rational, my dear Caroline, I dare say but it would not be near so much like a ball."

Miss Bingley made no answer; and soon afterwards got up and walked about the room. Her figure was elegant, and she walked well;—but Darcy, at whom it was all aimed, was still inflexibly studious. In the desperation of her feelings she resolved on one effort more; and, turning to Elizabeth, said,

"Miss Eliza Bennet, let me persuade you to follow my example, and take a turn about the room.—I assure you it is very refreshing after sitting so long in one attitude."

Elizabeth was surprised, but agreed to it immediately. Miss Bingley succeeded no less in the real object of her civility; Mr. Darcy looked up. He was as much awake to the novelty of attention in that quarter as Elizabeth herself could be, and unconsciously closed his book. He was directly invited to join their party, but he declined it, observing, that he could imagine but two motives for their chusing to walk up and down the room together, with either of which motives his joining them would interfere. "What could he mean? she was dying to know what could be his meaning"—and asked Elizabeth whether she could at all understand him?

"Not at all," was her answer; "but depend upon it, he means to be severe on us, and our surest way of disappointing him, will be to ask nothing about it."

Miss Bingley, however, was incapable of disappointing Mr. Darcy in any thing, and persevered therefore in requiring an explanation of his two motives.

"I have not the smallest objection to explaining them," said he, as soon as she allowed him to speak. "You either chuse this method of passing the evening because you are in each other's confidence and have secret affairs to discuss, or because you are conscious that your figures appear to the greatest advantage in walking;—if the first, I should be completely in your way;—and

5. Invitations.

if the second, I can admire you much better as I sit by the fire."

"Oh! shocking!" cried Miss Bingley. "I never heard any thing so abominable. How shall we punish him for such a speech?"

"Nothing so easy, if you have but the inclination," said Elizabeth. "We can all plague and punish one another. Teaze him—laugh at him.—Intimate as you are, you must know how it is to be done."

"But upon my honour I do *not*. I do assure you that my intimacy has not yet taught me *that*. Teaze calmness of temper and presence of mind! No, no—I feel he may defy us there. And as to laughter, we will not expose ourselves, if you please, by attempting to laugh without a subject. Mr. Darcy may hug himself."

"Mr. Darcy is not to be laughed at!" cried Elizabeth. "That is an uncommon advantage, and uncommon I hope it will continue, for it would be a great loss to *me* to have many such acquaintance. I dearly love a laugh."

"Miss Bingley," said he, "has given me credit for more than can be. The wisest and the best of men, nay, the wisest and best of their actions, may be rendered ridiculous by a person whose first object in life is a joke."

"Certainly," replied Elizabeth—"there are such people, but I hope I am not one of *them*. I hope I never ridicule what is wise or good. Follies and nonsense, whims and inconsistencies *do* divert me, I own, and I laugh at them whenever I can.—But these, I suppose, are precisely what you are without."

"Perhaps that is not possible for any one. But it has been the study of my life to avoid those weaknesses which often expose a strong understanding to ridicule."

"Such as vanity and pride."

"Yes, vanity is a weakness indeed. But pride—where there is a real superiority of mind, pride will be always under good regulation."

Elizabeth turned away to hide a smile.

"Your examination of Mr. Darcy is over, I presume," said Miss Bingley;—"and pray what is the result?"

"I am perfectly convinced by it that Mr. Darcy has no defect. He owns it himself without disguise."

"No"—said Darcy, "I have made no such pretension. I have faults enough, but they are not, I hope, of understanding. My temper I dare not vouch for.—It is I believe too little yielding—certainly too little for the convenience of the world. I cannot forget the follies and vices of others so soon as I ought, nor their offences against myself. My feelings are not puffed about with every attempt to move them. My temper would perhaps be called resentful.—My good opinion once lost is lost for ever."

"*That* is a failing indeed!"—cried Elizabeth. "Implacable resentment *is* a shade in a character. But you have chosen your fault well.—I really cannot *laugh* at it. You are safe from me."

"There is, I believe, in every disposition a tendency to some particular evil, a natural defect, which not even the best education can overcome."

"And *your* defect is a propensity to hate every body."

"And yours," he replied with a smile, "is wilfully to misunderstand them."

"Do let us have a little music,"—cried Miss Bingley, tired of a conversation in which she had no share.—"Louisa, you will not mind my waking Mr. Hurst."

Her sister made not the smallest objection, and the piano forte was opened, and Darcy, after a few moments recollection, was not sorry for it. He began to feel the danger of paying Elizabeth too much attention.

Chapter XII

In consequence of an agreement between the sisters, Elizabeth wrote the next morning to her mother, to beg that the carriage might be sent for them in the course of the day. But Mrs. Bennet, who had calculated on her daughters remaining at Netherfield till the following Tuesday, which would exactly finish Jane's week, could not bring herself to receive them with pleasure before. Her answer, therefore, was not propitious, at least not to Elizabeth's wishes, for she was impatient to get home. Mrs. Bennet sent them word that they could not possibly have the carriage before Tuesday; and in her postscript it was added, that if Mr. Bingley and his sister pressed them to stay longer, she could spare them very well.—Against staying longer, however, Elizabeth was positively resolved—nor did she much expect it would be asked; and fearful, on the contrary, as being considered as intruding themselves needlessly long, she urged Jane to borrow Mr. Bingley's carriage immediately, and at length it was settled that their original design of leaving Netherfield that morning should be mentioned, and the request made.

The communication excited many professions of concern; and enough was said of wishing them to stay at least till the following day to work on Jane; and till the morrow, their going was deferred. Miss Bingley was then sorry that she had proposed the delay, for her jealousy and dislike of one sister much exceeded her affection for the other.

The master of the house heard with real sorrow that they

were to go so soon, and repeatedly tried to persuade Miss Bennet that it would not be safe for her—that she was not enough recovered; but Jane was firm where she felt herself to be right.

To Mr. Darcy it was welcome intelligence—Elizabeth had been at Netherfield long enough. She attracted him more than he liked—and Miss Bingley was uncivil to *her*, and more teazing than usual to himself. He wisely resolved to be particularly careful that no sign of admiration should *now* escape him, nothing that could elevate her with the hope of influencing his felicity; sensible that if such an idea had been suggested, his behaviour during the last day must have material weight in confirming or crushing it. Steady to his purpose, he scarcely spoke ten words to her through the whole of Saturday, and though they were at one time left by themselves for half an hour, he adhered most conscientiously to his book, and would not even look at her.

On Sunday, after morning service, the separation, so agreeable to almost all, took place. Miss Bingley's civility to Elizabeth increased at last very rapidly, as well as her affection for Jane; and when they parted, after assuring the latter of the pleasure it would always give her to see her either at Longbourn or Netherfield, and embracing her most tenderly, she even shook hands with the former.—Elizabeth took leave of the whole party in the liveliest spirits.

They were not welcomed home very cordially by their mother. Mrs. Bennet wondered at their coming, and thought them very wrong to give so much trouble, and was sure Jane would have caught cold again.—But their father, though very laconic in his expressions of pleasure, was really glad to see them; he had felt their importance in the family circle. The evening conversation, when they were all assembled, had lost much of its animation, and almost all its sense, by the absence of Jane and Elizabeth.

They found Mary, as usual, deep in the study of thorough bass and human nature; and had some new extracts to admire, and some new observations of thread-bare morality to listen to. Catherine and Lydia had information for them of a different sort. Much had been done, and much had been said in the regiment since the preceding Wednesday; several of the officers had dined lately with their uncle, a private had been flogged, and it had actually been hinted that Colonel Forster was going to be married.

Chapter XIII

"I hope, my dear," said Mr. Bennet to his wife, as they were at breakfast the next morning, "that you have ordered a good dinner to-day, because I have reason to expect an addition to our family party."

"Who do you mean, my dear? I know of nobody that is coming I am sure, unless Charlotte Lucas should happen to call in, and I hope *my* dinners are good enough for her. I do not believe she often sees such at home."

"The person of whom I speak, is a gentleman and a stranger." Mrs. Bennet's eyes sparkled.—"A gentleman and a stranger! It is Mr. Bingley I am sure. Why Jane—you never dropt a word of this; you sly thing! Well, I am sure I shall be extremely glad to see Mr. Bingley.—But—good lord! how unlucky! there is not a bit of fish to be got to-day. Lydia, my love, ring the bell. I must speak to Hill, this moment."

"It is *not* Mr. Bingley," said her husband; "it is a person whom I never saw in the whole course of my life."

This roused a general astonishment; and he had the pleasure of being eagerly questioned by his wife and five daughters at once.

After amusing himself some time with their curiosity, he thus explained. "About a month ago I received this letter, and about a fortnight ago I answered it, for I thought it a case of some delicacy, and requiring early attention. It is from my cousin, Mr. Collins, who, when I am dead, may turn you all out of this house as soon as he pleases."

"Oh! my dear," cried his wife, "I cannot bear to hear that mentioned. Pray do not talk of that odious man. I do think it is the hardest thing in the world, that your estate should be entailed away from your own children; and I am sure if I had been you, I should have tried long ago to do something or other about it."

Jane and Elizabeth attempted to explain to her the nature of an entail. They had often attempted it before, but it was a subject on which Mrs. Bennet was beyond the reach of reason; and she continued to rail bitterly against the cruelty of settling an estate away from a family of five daughters, in favour of a man whom nobody cared anything about.

"It certainly is a most iniquitous affair," said Mr. Bennet, "and nothing can clear Mr. Collins from the guilt of inheriting Longbourn. But if you will listen to his letter, you may perhaps be a little softened by his manner of expressing himself."

"No, that I am sure I shall not; and I think it was very impertinent of him to write to you at all, and very hypocritical. I hate such false friends. Why could not he keep on quarrelling with you, as his father did before him?"

"Why, indeed, he does seem to have had some filial scruples on that head, as you will hear."

> *Hunsford, near Westerham, Kent,*
> *15th October.*

DEAR SIR,

The disagreement subsisting between yourself and my late honoured father, always gave me much uneasiness, and since I have had the misfortune to lose him, I have frequently wished to heal the breach; but for some time I was kept back by my own doubts, fearing lest it might seem disrespectful to his memory for me to be on good terms with any one, with whom it had always pleased him to be at variance.—"There, Mrs. Bennet."—My mind however is now made up on the subject, for having received ordination at Easter, I have been so fortunate as to be distinguished by the patronage of the Right Honourable Lady Catherine de Bourgh, widow of Sir Lewis de Bourgh, whose bounty and beneficence has preferred me to the valuable rectory of this parish,[6] where it shall be my earnest endeavour to demean myself with grateful respect towards her Ladyship, and be ever ready to perform those rites and ceremonies which are instituted by the Church of England. As a clergyman, moreover, I feel it my duty to promote and establish the blessing of peace in all families within the reach of my influence; and on these grounds I flatter myself that my present overtures of good-will are highly commendable, and that the circumstance of my being next in the entail of Longbourn estate, will be kindly overlooked on your side, and not lead you to reject the offered olive branch. I cannot be otherwise than concerned at being the means of injuring your amiable daughters, and beg leave to apologise for it, as well as to assure you of my readiness to make them every possible amends,—but of this hereafter. If you should have no objection to receive me into your house, I propose myself the satisfaction of waiting on you and your family, Monday, November 18th, by four o'clock, and shall probably trespass on your hospitality till the Saturday se'night[7] following, which I can do without any inconvenience, as Lady Catherine is far from objecting to my occasional absence on a Sunday, provided that some other clergyman is engaged to do

6. **Originally those landowners who built churches or set aside land for the support of the Church were granted advowsons, the right to recommend to bishops candidates for livings or benefices, often the post of rector of a parish. In time the advowsons, which were a useful and often valuable means of patronage, came to be regarded as part of the personal estate of those who held them, and it was literally** through the "bounty and beneficence" of people like Lady Catherine that many ambitious clergymen were given their first and subsequent livings. Once preferred to a living, the clergyman held it for life, unless he resigned or was judged grossly incompetent. See Wickham's remarks on the living he was promised (p. 55), and Darcy's (pp. 138-139).

7. A week.

the duty of the day. I remain, dear sir, with respectful compliments to your lady and daughters, your well-wisher and friend,

WILLIAM COLLINS."

"At four o'clock, therefore, we may expect this peacemaking gentleman," said Mr. Bennet, as he folded up the letter. "He seems to be a most conscientious and polite young man, upon my word; and I doubt not will prove a valuable acquaintance, especially if Lady Catherine should be so indulgent as to let him come to us again."

"There is some sense in what he says about the girls however; and if he is disposed to make them any amends, I shall not be the person to discourage him."

"Though it is difficult," said Jane, "to guess in what way he can mean to make us the atonement he thinks our due, the wish is certainly to his credit."

Elizabeth was chiefly struck with his extraordinary deference for Lady Catherine, and his kind intention of christening, marrying, and burying his parishioners whenever it were required.

"He must be an oddity, I think," said she. "I cannot make him out.—There is something very pompous in his stile.—And what can he mean by apologizing for being next in the entail?— We cannot suppose he would help it, if he could.—Can he be a sensible man, sir?"

"No, my dear; I think not. I have great hopes of finding him quite the reverse. There is a mixture of servility and self-importance in his letter, which promises well. I am impatient to see him."

"In point of composition," said Mary, "his letter does not seem defective. The idea of the olive branch perhaps is not wholly new, yet I think it is well expressed."

To Catherine and Lydia, neither the letter nor its writer were in any degree interesting. It was next to impossible that their cousin should come in a scarlet coat, and it was now some weeks since they had received pleasure from the society of a man in any other colour. As for their mother, Mr. Collins's letter had done away much of her ill-will, and she was preparing to see him with a degree of composure, which astonished her husband and daughters.

Mr. Collins was punctual to his time, and was received with great politeness by the whole family. Mr. Bennet indeed said little; but the ladies were ready enough to talk, and Mr. Collins seemed neither in need of encouragement, nor inclined to be silent himself. He was a tall, heavy looking young man of five and twenty. His air was grave and stately. and his manners were very formal. He had not been long seated before he complimented

Mrs. Bennet on having so fine a family of daughters, said he had heard much of their beauty, but that, in this instance, fame had fallen short of the truth; and added, that he did not doubt her seeing them all in due time well disposed of in marriage. This gallantry was not much to the taste of some of his hearers, but Mrs. Bennet, who quarrelled with no compliments, answered most readily,

"You are very kind, sir, I am sure; and I wish with all my heart it may prove so; for else they will be destitute enough. Things are settled so oddly."

"You allude perhaps to the entail of this estate."

"Ah! sir, I do indeed. It is a grievous affair to my poor girls, you must confess. Not that I mean to find fault with *you*, for such things I know are all chance in this world. There is no knowing how estates will go when once they come to be entailed."

"I am very sensible, madam, of the hardship to my fair cousins, —and could say much on the subject, but that I am cautious of appearing forward and precipitate. But I can assure the young ladies that I come prepared to admire them. At present I will not say more, but perhaps when we are better acquainted——"

He was interrupted by a summons to dinner; and the girls smiled on each other. They were not the only objects of Mr. Collins's admiration. The hall, the dining-room, and all its furniture were examined and praised; and his commendation of every thing would have touched Mrs. Bennet's heart, but for the mortifying supposition of his viewing it all as his own future property. The dinner too in its turn was highly admired; and he begged to know to which of his fair cousins, the excellence of its cookery was owing. But here he was set right by Mrs. Bennet, who assured him with some asperity that they were very well able to keep a good cook, and that her daughters had nothing to do in the kitchen. He begged pardon for having displeased her. In a softened tone she declared herself not at all offended; but he continued to apologise for about a quarter of an hour.

Chapter XIV

During dinner, Mr. Bennet scarcely spoke at all; but when the servants were withdrawn, he thought it time to have some conversation with his guest, and therefore started a subject in which he expected him to shine, by observing that he seemed very fortunate in his patroness. Lady Catherine de Bourgh's attention to his wishes, and consideration for his comfort, appeared very remarkable. Mr. Bennet could not have chosen better. Mr. Collins was eloquent in her praise. The subject elevated him to more than usual solemnity of manner, and with a most important aspect he protested that [8] he had never in his life witnessed such behaviour in a person of rank—such affability and condescension, as he had himself experienced from Lady Catherine. She had been graciously pleased to approve of both the discourses, which he had already had the honour of preaching before her. She had also asked him twice to dine at Rosings, and had sent for him only the Saturday before, to make up her pool of quadrille [9] in the evening. Lady Catherine was reckoned proud by many people he knew, but *he* had never seen any thing but affability in her. She had always spoken to him as she would to any other gentleman; she made not the smallest objection to his joining in the society of the neighbourhood, nor to his leaving his parish occasionally for a week or two, to visit his relations. She had even condescended to advise him to marry as soon as he could, provided he chose with discretion; and had once paid him a visit in his humble parsonage; where she had perfectly approved all the alterations he had been making, and had even vouchsafed to suggest some herself,—some shelves in the closets up stairs."

"That is all very proper and civil, I am sure," said Mrs. Bennet, "and I dare say she is a very agreeable woman. It is a pity that great ladies in general are not more like her. Does she live near you, sir?"

"The garden in which stands my humble abode, is separated only by a lane from Rosings Park, her ladyship's residence."

"I think you said she was a widow, sir? has she any family?"

"She has one only daughter, the heiress of Rosings, and of very extensive property."

"Ah!" cried Mrs. Bennet, shaking her head, "then she is better off than many girls. And what sort of young lady is she? is she handsome?"

"She is a most charming young lady indeed. Lady Catherine herself says that in point of true beauty, Miss De Bourgh is far superior to the handsomest of her sex; because there is that in her features which marks the young woman of distinguished birth. She is unfortunately of a sickly constitution, which has prevented her making that progress in many accomplishments, which she could not otherwise have failed of; as I am informed by the lady who superintended her education, and who still

8. Most editions—including the first American edition, which was based on the second English edition—mark the beginning of Mr. Collins' speech with a quotation mark at this point. The speech is not so punctuated in the first edition, however: there it is closed but not opened by a quotation mark.
9. Quadrille is a four-handed card game which by the end of the eighteenth century had become an old-fashioned pleasure, having been displaced by the popularity of whist.

resides with them. But she is perfectly amiable, and often condescends to drive by my humble abode in her little phaeton and ponies."

"Has she been presented? I do not remember her name among the ladies at court."

"Her indifferent state of health unhappily prevents her being in town; and by that means, as I told Lady Catherine myself one day, has deprived the British court of its brightest ornament. Her ladyship seemed pleased with the idea, and you may imagine that I am happy on every occasion to offer those little delicate compliments which are always acceptable to ladies. I have more than once observed to Lady Catherine, that her charming daughter seemed born to be a duchess, and that the most elevated rank, instead of giving her consequence, would be adorned by her.— These are the kind of little things which please her ladyship, and it is a sort of attention which I conceive myself peculiarly bound to pay."

"You judge very properly," said Mr. Bennet, "and it is happy for you that you possess the talent of flattering with delicacy. May I ask whether these pleasing attentions proceed from the impulse of the moment, or are the result of previous study?"

"They arise chiefly from what is passing at the time, and though I sometimes amuse myself with suggesting and arranging such little elegant compliments as may be adapted to ordinary occasions, I always wish to give them as unstudied an air as possible."

Mr. Bennet's expectations were fully answered. His cousin was as absurd as he had hoped, and he listened to him with the keenest enjoyment, maintaining at the same time the most resolute composure of countenance, and except in an occasional glance at Elizabeth, requiring no partner in his pleasure.

By tea-time however the dose had been enough, and Mr. Bennet was glad to take his guest into the drawing-room again, and when tea was over, glad to invite him to read aloud to the ladies. Mr. Collins readily assented, and a book was produced; but on beholding it, (for every thing announced it to be from a circulating library,) he started back, and begging pardon, protested that he never read novels.—Kitty stared at him, and Lydia exclaimed.—Other books were produced, and after some deliberation he chose Fordyce's Sermons.[1] Lydia gaped as he opened the volume, and before he had, with very monotonous solemnity, read three pages, she interrupted him with,

"Do you know, mama, that my uncle Philips talks of turning away Richard, and if he does, Colonel Forster will hire him.

1. James Fordyce's *Sermons to Young Women* (1766).

My aunt told me so herself on Saturday. I shall walk to Meryton to-morrow to hear more about it, and to ask when Mr. Denny comes back from town."

Lydia was bid by her two eldest sisters to hold her tongue; but Mr. Collins, much offended, laid aside his book, and said,

"I have often observed how little young ladies are interested by books of a serious stamp, though written solely for their benefit. It amazes me, I confess;—for certainly, there can be nothing so advantageous to them as instruction. But I will no longer importune my young cousin."

Then turning to Mr. Bennet, he offered himself as his antagonist at backgammon. Mr. Bennet accepted the challenge, observing that he acted very wisely in leaving the girls to their own trifling amusements. Mrs. Bennet and her daughters apologised most civilly for Lydia's interruption, and promised that it should not occur again, if he would resume his book; but Mr. Collins, after assuring them that he bore his young cousin no ill will, and should never resent her behaviour as any affront, seated himself at another table with Mr. Bennet, and prepared for backgammon.

Chapter XV

Mr. Collins was not a sensible man, and the deficiency of nature had been but little assisted by education or society; the greatest part of his life having been spent under the guidance of an illiterate and miserly father; and though he belonged to one of the universities, he had merely kept the necessary terms, without forming at it any useful acquaintance. The subjection in which his father had brought him up, had given him originally great humility of manner, but it was now a good deal counteracted by the self-conceit of a weak head, living in retirement, and the consequential feelings of early and unexpected prosperity. A fortunate chance had recommended him to Lady Catherine de Bourgh when the living of Hunsford was vacant; and the respect which he felt for her high rank, and his veneration for her as his patroness, mingling with a very good opinion of himself, of his authority as a clergyman, and his rights as a rector, made him altogether a mixture of pride and obsequiousness, self-importance and humility.

Having now a good house and very sufficient income, he intended to marry; and in seeking a reconciliation with the Longbourn family he had a wife in view, as he meant to chuse one of the daughters, if he found them as handsome and amiable as they were represented by common report. This was his plan of amends—of atonement—for inheriting their father's estate; and he thought it an excellent one, full of eligibility and suitableness, and excessively generous and disinterested on his own part.

His plan did not vary on seeing them.—Miss Bennet's lovely face confirmed his views, and established all his strictest notions of what was due to seniority; and for the first evening *she* was his settled choice. The next morning, however, made an alteration; for in a quarter of an hour's tête-à-tête with Mrs. Bennet before breakfast, a conversation beginning with his parsonage-house, and leading naturally to the avowal of his hopes, that a mistress for it might be found at Longbourn, produced from her, amid very complaisant smiles and general encouragement, a caution against the very Jane he had fixed on.—"As to her *younger* daughters she could not take upon her to say—she could not positively answer—but she did not *know* of any prepossession;—her *eldest* daughter, she must just mention—she felt it incumbent on her to hint, was likely to be very soon engaged."

Mr. Collins had only to change from Jane to Elizabeth—and it was soon done—done while Mrs. Bennet was stirring the fire. Elizabeth, equally next to Jane in birth and beauty, succeeded her of course.

Mrs. Bennet treasured up the hint, and trusted that she might soon have two daughters married; and the man whom she could not bear to speak of the day before, was now high in her good graces.

Lydia's intention of walking to Meryton was not forgotten; every sister except Mary agreed to go with her; and Mr. Collins was to attend them, at the request of Mr. Bennet, who was most anxious to get rid of him, and have his library to himself; for thither Mr. Collins had followed him after breakfast, and there he would continue, nominally engaged with one of the largest folios in the collection, but really talking to Mr. Bennet, with little cessation, of his house and garden at Hunsford. Such doings discomposed Mr. Bennet exceedingly. In his library he had been always sure of leisure and tranquillity; and though prepared, as he told Elizabeth, to meet with folly and conceit in every other room in the house, he was used to be free from them there; his civility, therefore, was most prompt in inviting Mr. Collins to join his daughters in their walk; and Mr. Collins, being in fact much better fitted for a walker than a reader, was extremely well pleased to close his large book, and go.

In pompous nothings on his side, and civil assents on that of his cousins, their time passed till they entered Meryton. The attention of the younger ones was then no longer to be gained by *him*. Their eyes were immediately wandering up in the street in quest of the officers, and nothing less than a very smart bonnet indeed, or a really new muslin in a shop window, could recal them.

But the attention of every lady was soon caught by a young man, whom they had never seen before, of most gentlemanlike appearance, walking with an officer on the other side of the way. The officer was the very Mr. Denny, concerning whose return from London Lydia came to inquire, and he bowed as they passed. All were struck with the stranger's air, all wondered who he could be, and Kitty and Lydia, determined if possible to find out, led the way across the street, under pretence of wanting something in an opposite shop, and fortunately had just gained the pavement when the two gentlemen turning back had reached the same spot. Mr. Denny addressed them directly, and entreated permission to introduce his friend, Mr. Wickham, who had returned with him the day before from town, and he was happy to say had accepted a commission in their corps. This was exactly as it should be; for the young man wanted only regimentals to make him completely charming. His appearance was greatly in his favour; he had all the best part of beauty, a fine countenance, a good figure, and very pleasing address. The introduction was followed up on his side by a happy readiness of conversation—a readiness at the same time perfectly correct and unassuming; and the whole party were still standing and talking together very agreeably, when the sound of horses drew their notice, and Darcy and Bingley were seen riding down the street. On distinguishing the ladies of the group, the two gentlemen came directly towards them, and began the usual civilities. Bingley was the principal spokesman, and Miss Bennet the principal object. He was then, he said, on his way to Longbourn on purpose to inquire after her. Mr. Darcy corroborated it with a bow, and was beginning to determine not to fix his eyes on Elizabeth, when they were suddenly arrested by the sight of the stranger, and Elizabeth happening to see the countenance of both as they looked at each other, was all astonishment at the effect of the meeting. Both changed colour, one looked white, the other red. Mr. Wickham, after a few moments, touched his hat—a salutation which Mr. Darcy just deigned to return. What could be the meaning of it?—It was impossible to imagine; it was impossible not to long to know.

In another minute Mr. Bingley, but without seeming to have noticed what passed, took leave and rode on with his friend.

Mr. Denny and Mr. Wickham walked with the young ladies to the door of Mr. Philips's house, and then made their bows, in spite of Miss Lydia's pressing entreaties that they would come in, and even in spite of Mrs. Philips' throwing up the parlour window, and loudly seconding the invitation.

Mrs. Philips was always glad to see her nieces, and the two eldest, from their recent absence, were particularly welcome, and she was eagerly expressing her surprise at their sudden return home, which, as their own carriage had not fetched them, she should have known nothing about, if she had not happened to see Mr. Jones's shop boy in the street, who had told her that they were not to send any more draughts to Netherfield because the Miss Bennets were come away, when her civility was claimed towards Mr. Collins by Jane's introduction of him. She received him with her very best politeness, which he returned with as much more, apologising for his intrusion, without any previous acquaintance with her, which he could not help flattering himself however might be justified by his relationship to the young ladies who introduced him to her notice. Mrs. Philips was quite awed by such an excess of good breeding; but her contemplation of one stranger was soon put an end to by exclamations and inquiries about the other, of whom, however, she could only tell her nieces what they already knew, that Mr. Denny had brought him from London, and that he was to have a lieutenant's commission in the ———shire. She had been watching him the last hour, she said, as he walked up and down the street, and had Mr. Wickham appeared Kitty and Lydia would certainly have continued the occupation, but unluckily no one passed the windows now except a few of the officers, who in comparison with the stranger, were become "stupid, disagreeable fellows." Some of them were to dine with the Philipses the next day, and their aunt promised to make her husband call on Mr. Wickham, and give him an invitation also, if the family from Longbourn would come in the evening. This was agreed to, and Mrs. Philips protested that they would have a nice comfortable noisy game of lottery tickets,[2] and a little bit of hot supper afterwards. The prospect of such delights was very cheering, and they parted in mutual good spirits. Mr. Collins repeated his apologies in quitting the room, and was assured with unwearying civility that they were perfectly needless.

As they walked home, Elizabeth related to Jane what she had seen pass between the two gentlemen; but though Jane would have defended either or both, had they appeared to be wrong, she could no more explain such behaviour than her sister.

Mr. Collins on his return highly gratified Mrs. Bennet by admiring Mrs. Philips's manners and politeness. He protested that except Lady Catherine and her daughter, he had never seen a

---

2. A very simple card game which can be played with many players, who simply bet that a card dealt face down to one player will be found to match that of another player.

more elegant woman; for she had not only received him with the utmost civility, but had even pointedly included him in her invitation for the next evening, although utterly unknown to her before. Something he supposed might be attributed to his connection with them, but yet he had never met with so much attention in the whole course of his life.

Chapter XVI

As no objection was made to the young people's engagement with their aunt, and all Mr. Collins's scruples of leaving Mr. and Mrs. Bennet for a single evening during his visit were most steadily resisted, the coach conveyed him and his five cousins at a suitable hour to Meryton; and the girls had the pleasure of hearing, as they entered the drawing-room, that Mr. Wickham had accepted their uncle's invitation, and was then in the house.

When this information was given, and they had all taken their seats, Mr. Collins was at leisure to look around him and admire, and he was so much struck with the size and furniture of the apartment, that he declared he might almost have supposed himself in the small summer breakfast parlour at Rosings; a comparison that did not at first convey much gratification; but when Mrs. Philips understood from him what Rosings was, and who was its proprietor, when she had listened to the description of only one of Lady Catherine's drawing-rooms, and found that the chimney-piece alone had cost eight hundred pounds, she felt all the force of the compliment, and would hardly have resented a comparison with the housekeeper's room.

In describing to her all the grandeur of Lady Catherine and her mansion, with occasional digressions in praise of his own humble abode, and the improvements it was receiving, he was happily employed until the gentlemen joined them; and he found in Mrs. Philips a very attentive listener, whose opinion of his consequence increased with what she heard, and who was resolving to retail it all among her neighbours as soon as she could. To the girls, who could not listen to their cousin, and who had nothing to do but to wish for an instrument, and examine their own indifferent imitations of china on the mantlepiece, the interval of waiting appeared very long. It was over at last however. The gentlemen did approach; and when Mr. Wickham walked into the room, Elizabeth felt that she had neither been seeing him before, nor thinking of him since, with the smallest degree of unreasonable admiration. The officers of the ——shire were in general a very creditable, gentlemanlike set, and the best of them were of the present party; but Mr. Wickham was as far beyond them all in person, countenance, air, and walk, as *they* were superior to the broad-faced stuffy uncle Philips, breathing port wine, who followed them into the room.

Mr. Wickham was the happy man towards whom almost every female eye was turned, and Elizabeth was the happy woman by whom he finally seated himself; and the agreeable manner in which he immediately fell into conversation, though it was only on its being a wet night, and on the probability of a rainy season, made her feel that the commonest, dullest, most threadbare topic might be rendered interesting by the skill of the speaker.

With such rivals for the notice of the fair, as Mr. Wickham and the officers, Mr. Collins seemed likely to sink into insignificance; to the young ladies he certainly was nothing; but he had still at intervals a kind listener in Mrs. Philips, and was, by her watchfulness, most abundantly supplied with coffee and muffin.

When the card tables were placed, he had an opportunity of obliging her in return, by sitting down to whist.

"I know little of the game, at present," said he, "but I shall be glad to improve myself, for in my situation of life——" Mrs. Philips was very thankful for his compliance, but could not wait for his reason.

Mr. Wickham did not play at whist, and with ready delight was he received at the other table between Elizabeth and Lydia. At first there seemed danger of Lydia's engrossing him entirely, for she was a most determined talker; but being likewise extremely fond of lottery tickets, she soon grew too much interested in the game, too eager in making bets and exclaiming after prizes, to have attention for any one in particular. Allowing for the common demands of the game, Mr. Wickham was therefore at leisure to talk to Elizabeth, and she was very willing to hear him, though what she chiefly wished to hear she could not hope to be told, the history of his acquaintance with Mr. Darcy. She dared not even mention that gentleman. Her curiosity however was unexpectedly relieved. Mr. Wickham began the subject himself. He inquired how far Netherfield was from Meryton; and, after receiving her answer, asked in an hesitating manner how long Mr. Darcy had been staying there.

"About a month," said Elizabeth; and then, unwilling to let the subject drop, added, "He is a man of very large property in Derbyshire, I understand."

"Yes," replied Wickham;—"his estate there is a noble one. A clear ten thousand per annum. You could not have met with a person more capable of giving you certain information on that head than myself—for I have been connected with his family in a particular manner from my infancy."

Elizabeth could not but look surprised.

"You may well be surprised, Miss Bennet, at such an assertion, after seeing, as you probably might, the very cold manner of our meeting yesterday.—Are you much acquainted with Mr. Darcy?"

"As much as I ever wish to be," cried Elizabeth warmly,—"I have spent four days in the same house with him, and I think him very disagreeable."

"I have no right to give *my* opinion," said Wickham, "as to his being agreeable or otherwise. I am not qualified to form one. I have known him too long and too well to be a fair judge. It is impossible for *me* to be impartial. But I believe your opinion of him would in general astonish—and perhaps you would not express it quite so strongly anywhere else.—Here you are in your own family."

"Upon my word I say no more *here* than I might say in any house in the neighbourhood, except Netherfield. He is not at all liked in Hertfordshire. Every body is disgusted with his pride. You will not find him more favourably spoken of by any one."

"I cannot pretend to be sorry," said Wickham, after a short interruption, "that he or that any man should not be estimated beyond their deserts; but with *him* I believe it does not often happen. The world is blinded by his fortune and consequence, or frightened by his high and imposing manners, and sees him only as he chuses to be seen."

"I should take him, even on *my* slight acquaintance, to be an ill-tempered man." Wickham only shook his head.

"I wonder," said he, at the next opportunity of speaking, "whether he is likely to be in this country much longer."

"I do not at all know; but I *heard* nothing of his going away when I was at Netherfield. I hope your plans in favour of the ——shire will not be affected by his being in the neighbourhood."

"Oh! no—it is not for *me* to be driven away by Mr. Darcy. If *he* wishes to avoid seeing *me*, he must go. We are not on friendly terms, and it always gives me pain to meet him, but I have no reason for avoiding *him* but what I might proclaim to all the world; a sense of very great ill usage, and most painful regrets at his being what he is. His father, Miss Bennet, the late Mr. Darcy, was one of the best men that ever breathed, and the truest friend I ever had; and I can never be in company with this Mr. Darcy without being grieved to the soul by a thousand tender recollections. His behaviour to myself has been scandalous; but I verily believe I could forgive him any thing and every thing, rather than his disappointing the hopes and disgracing the memory of his father."

Elizabeth found the interest of the subject increase, and listened with all her heart; but the delicacy of it prevented farther inquiry.

Mr. Wickham began to speak on more general topics, Meryton, the neighbourhood, the society, appearing highly pleased with all that he had yet seen, and speaking of the latter especially, with gentle but very intelligible gallantry.

"It was the prospect of constant society, and good society," he added, "which was my chief inducement to enter the ——shire. I knew it to be a most respectable, agreeable corps, and my friend Denny tempted me farther by his account of their present quarters, and the very great attentions and excellent acquaintance Meryton had procured them. Society, I own, is necessary to me. I have been a disappointed man, and my spirits will not bear solitude. I *must* have employment and society. A military life is not what I was intended for, but circumstances have now made it eligible. The church *ought* to have been my profession—I was brought up for the church, and I should at this time have been in possession of a most valuable living, had it pleased the gentleman we were speaking of just now."

"Indeed!"

"Yes—the late Mr. Darcy bequeathed me the next presentation of the best living in his gift. He was my godfather, and excessively attached to me. I cannot do justice to his kindness. He meant to provide for me amply, and thought he had done it; but when the living fell, it was given elsewhere."

"Good heavens!" cried Elizabeth; "but how could *that* be?—How could his will be disregarded?—Why did not you seek legal redress?"

"There was just such an informality in the terms of the bequest as to give me no hope from law. A man of honour could not have doubted the intention, but Mr. Darcy chose to doubt it—or to treat it as a merely conditional recommendation, and to assert that I had forfeited all claim to it by extravagance, imprudence, in short any thing or nothing. Certain it is, that the living became vacant two years ago, exactly as I was of an age to hold it, and that it was given to another man; and no less certain is it, that I cannot accuse myself of having really done any thing to deserve to lose it. I have a warm, unguarded temper, and I may perhaps have sometimes spoken my opinion *of* him, and *to* him, too freely. I can recal nothing worse. But the fact is, that we are very different sort of men, and that he hates me."

"This is quite shocking!—He deserves to be publicly disgraced."

"Some time or other he *will* be—but it shall not be by *me*. Till I can forget his father, I can never defy or expose *him*."

Elizabeth honoured him for such feelings, and thought him

handsomer than ever as he expressed them.

"But what," said she, after a pause, "can have been his motive?—what can have induced him to behave so cruelly?"

"A thorough, determined dislike of me—a dislike which I cannot but attribute in some measure to jealousy. Had the late Mr. Darcy liked me less, his son might have borne with me better; but his father's uncommon attachment to me, irritated him I believe very early in life. He had not a temper to bear the sort of competition in which we stood—the sort of preference which was often given me."

"I had not thought Mr. Darcy so bad as this—though I have never liked him, I had not thought so very ill of him—I had supposed him to be despising his fellow-creatures in general, but did not suspect him of descending to such malicious revenge, such injustice, such inhumanity as this!"

After a few minutes reflection, however, she continued, "I *do* remember his boasting one day, at Netherfield, of the implacability of his resentments, of his having an unforgiving temper. His disposition must be dreadful."

"I will not trust myself on the subject," replied Wickham, "*I* can hardly be just to him."

Elizabeth was again deep in thought, and after a time exclaimed, "To treat in such a manner, the godson, the friend, the favourite of his father!"—She could have added, "A young man too, like *you*, whose very countenance may vouch for your being amiable"—but she contented herself with "And one, too, who had probably been his own companion from childhood, connected together, as I think you said, in the closest manner!"

"We were born in the same parish, within the same park, the greatest part of our youth was passed together; inmates of the same house, sharing the same amusements, objects of the same parental care. *My* father began life in the profession which your uncle, Mr. Philips, appears to do so much credit to—but he gave up every thing to be of use to the late Mr. Darcy, and devoted all his time to the care of the Pemberley property. He was most highly esteemed by Mr. Darcy, a most intimate, confidential friend. Mr. Darcy often acknowledged himself to be under the greatest obligations to my father's active superintendance, and when immediately before my father's death, Mr. Darcy gave him a voluntary promise of providing for me, I am convinced that he felt it to be as much a debt of gratitude to *him*, as of affection to myself."

"How strange!" cried Elizabeth. "How abominable!—I wonder that the very pride of this Mr. Darcy has not made him just to you!—If from no better motive, that he should not have been too proud to be dishonest,—for dishonesty I must call it."

"It *is* wonderful,"—replied Wickham,—"for almost all his actions may be traced to pride;—and pride has often been his best friend. It has connected him nearer with virtue than any other feeling. But we are none of us consistent; and in his behaviour to me, there were stronger impulses even than pride."

"Can such abominable pride as his, have ever done him good?"

"Yes. It has often led him to be liberal and generous,—to give his money freely, to display hospitality, to assist his tenants, and relieve the poor. Family pride, and *filial* pride, for he is very proud of what his father was, have done this. Not to appear to disgrace his family, to degenerate from the popular qualities, or lose the influence of the Pemberley House, is a powerful motive. He has also *brotherly* pride, which with *some* brotherly affection, makes him a very kind and careful guardian of his sister; and you will hear him generally cried up as the most attentive and best of brothers."

"What sort of a girl is Miss Darcy?"

He shook his head.—"I wish I could call her amiable. It gives me pain to speak ill of a Darcy. But she is too much like her brother,—very, very proud.—As a child, she was affectionate and pleasing, and extremely fond of me; and I have devoted hours and hours to her amusement. But she is nothing to me now. She is a handsome girl, about fifteen or sixteen, and I understand highly accomplished. Since her father's death, her home has been London, where a lady lives with her, and superintends her education."

After many pauses and many trials of other subjects, Elizabeth could not help reverting once more to the first, and saying,

"I am astonished at his intimacy with Mr. Bingley! How can Mr. Bingley, who seems good humour itself, and is, I really believe, truly amiable, be in friendship with such a man? How can they suit each other?—Do you know Mr. Bingley?"

"Not at all."

"He is a sweet tempered, amiable, charming man. He cannot know what Mr. Darcy is."

"Probably not;—but Mr. Darcy can please where he chuses. He does not want abilities. He can be a conversible companion if he thinks it worth his while. Among those who are at all his equals in consequence, he is a very different man from what he is to the less prosperous. His pride never deserts him; but with the rich, he is liberal-minded, just, sincere, rational, honourable, and perhaps agreeable,—allowing something for fortune and figure."

The whist party soon afterward breaking up, the players gathered round the other table, and Mr. Collins took his station between his cousin Elizabeth and Mrs. Philips.—The usual inquiries as to his success were made by the latter. It had not been very great; he had lost every point; but when Mrs. Philips began to express her concern thereupon, he assured her with much earnest gravity that it was not of the least importance, that he considered the money as a mere trifle, and begged she would not make herself uneasy.

"I know very well, madam," said he, "that when persons sit down to a card table, they must take their chance of these things, —and happily I am not in such circumstances as to make five shillings any object. There are undoubtedly many who could not say the same, but thanks to Lady Catherine de Bourgh, I am removed far beyond the necessity of regarding little matters."

Mr. Wickham's attention was caught; and after observing Mr. Collins for a few moments, he asked Elizabeth in a low voice whether her relation were very intimately acquainted with the family of de Bourgh.

"Lady Catherine de Bourgh," she replied, "has very lately given him a living. I hardly know how Mr. Collins was first introduced to her notice, but he certainly has not known her long."

"You know of course that Lady Catherine de Bourgh and Lady Anne Darcy were sisters; consequently that she is aunt to the present Mr. Darcy."

"No, indeed, I did not.—I knew nothing at all of Lady Catherine's connections. I never heard of her existence till the day before yesterday."

"Her daughter, Miss de Bourgh, will have a very large fortune, and it is believed that she and her cousin will unite the two estates."

This information made Elizabeth smile, as she thought of poor Miss Bingley. Vain indeed must be all her attentions, vain and useless her affection for his sister and her praise of himself, if he were already self-destined to another.

"Mr. Collins," said she, "speaks highly both of Lady Catherine and her daughter; but from some particulars that he has related of her ladyship, I suspect his gratitude misleads him, and that in spite of her being his patroness, she is an arrogant, conceited woman."

"I believe her to be both in a great degree," replied Wickham; "I have not seen her for many years, but I very well remember that I never liked her, and that her manners were dictatorial and insolent. She has the reputation of being remarkably sensible and clever; but I rather believe she derives part of her abilities from her rank and fortune, part from her authoritative manner, and the rest from the pride of her nephew, who chuses that every one connected with him should have an understanding of the first class."

Elizabeth allowed that he had given a very rational account of it, and they continued talking together with mutual satisfaction till supper put an end to cards; and gave the rest of the ladies their share of Mr. Wickham's attentions. There could be no conversation in the noise of Mrs. Philips's supper party, but his manners recommended him to every body. Whatever he said, was said well; and whatever he did, done gracefully. Elizabeth went away with her head full of him. She could think of nothing but of Mr. Wickham, and of what he had told her, all the way home; but there was not time for her even to mention his name as they went, for neither Lydia nor Mr. Collins were once silent. Lydia talked incessantly of lottery tickets, of the fish she had lost and the fish [3] she had won, and Mr. Collins, in describing the civility of Mr. and Mrs. Philips, protesting that he did not in the least regard his losses at whist, enumerating all the dishes at supper, and repeatedly fearing that he crouded his cousins, had more to say than he could well manage before the carriage stopped at Longbourn House.

Chapter XVII

Elizabeth related to Jane the next day, what had passed between Mr. Wickham and herself. Jane listened with astonishment and concern;—she knew not how to believe that Mr. Darcy could be so unworthy of Mr. Bingley's regard; and yet, it was not in her nature to question the veracity of a young man of such amiable appearance as Wickham.—The possibility of his having really endured such unkindness, was enough to interest all her tender feelings; and nothing therefore remained to be done, but to think well of them both, to defend the conduct of each, and throw into the account of accident or mistake, whatever could not be otherwise explained.

"They have both," said she, "been deceived, I dare say, in some way or other, of which we can form no idea. Interested people have perhaps misrepresented each to the other. It is, in short, impossible for us to conjecture the causes or circumstances which may have alienated them, without actual blame on either side."

"Very true, indeed;—and now, my dear Jane, what have you got to say in behalf of the interested people who have probably been concerned in the business?—Do clear *them* too, or we shall be obliged to think ill of somebody."

3. Counters of bone or ivory used as stakes in games.

"Laugh as much as you chuse, but you will not laugh me out of my opinion. My dearest Lizzy, do but consider in what a disgraceful light it places Mr. Darcy, to be treating his father's favourite in such a manner,—one, whom his father had promised to provide for.—It is impossible. No man of common humanity, no man who had any value for his character, could be capable of it. Can his most intimate friends be so excessively deceived in him? oh! no."

"I can much more easily believe Mr. Bingley's being imposed on, than that Mr. Wickham should invent such a history of himself as he gave me last night; names, facts, every thing mentioned without ceremony.—If it be not so, let Mr. Darcy contradict it. Besides, there was truth in his looks."

"It is difficult indeed—it is distressing.—One does not know what to think."

"I beg your pardon;—one knows exactly what to think."

But Jane could think with certainty on only one point,—that Mr. Bingley, if he *had been* imposed on, would have much to suffer when the affair became public.

The two young ladies were summoned from the shrubbery where this conversation passed, by the arrival of some of the very persons of whom they had been speaking; Mr. Bingley and his sisters came to give their personal invitation for the long expected ball at Netherfield, which was fixed for the following Tuesday. The two ladies were delighted to see their dear friend again, called it an age since they had met, and repeatedly asked what she had been doing with herself since their separation. To the rest of the family they paid little attention; avoiding Mrs. Bennet as much as possible, saying not much to Elizabeth, and nothing at all to the others. They were soon gone again, rising from their seats with an activity which took their brother by surprise, and hurrying off as if eager to escape from Mrs. Bennet's civilities.

The prospect of the Netherfield ball was extremely agreeable to every female of the family. Mrs. Bennet chose to consider it as given in compliment to her eldest daughter, and was particularly flattered by receiving the invitation from Mr. Bingley himself, instead of a ceremonious card. Jane pictured to herself a happy evening in the society of her two friends, and the attentions of their brother; and Elizabeth thought with pleasure of dancing a great deal with Mr. Wickham, and of seeing a confirmation of every thing in Mr. Darcy's looks and behaviour. The happiness anticipated by Catherine and Lydia, depended less on any single event, or any particular person, for though they each, like Elizabeth, meant to dance half the evening with Mr. Wickham, he was by no means the only partner who could satisfy them, and a ball was at any rate, a ball. And even Mary could assure her family that she had no disinclination for it.

"While I can have my mornings to myself," said she, "it is enough.—I think it no sacrifice to join occasionally in evening engagements. Society has claims on us all; and I profess myself one of those who consider intervals of recreation and amusement as desirable for every body."

Elizabeth's spirits were so high on the occasion, that though she did not often speak unnecessarily to Mr. Collins, she could not help asking him whether he intended to accept Mr. Bingley's invitation, and if he did, whether he would think it proper to join in the evening's amusement; and she was rather surprised to find that he entertained no scruple whatever on that head, and was very far from dreading a rebuke either from the Archbishop, or Lady Catherine de Bourgh, by venturing to dance.

"I am by no means of opinion, I assure you," said he, "that a ball of this kind, given by a young man of character, to respectable people, can have any evil tendency; and I am so far from objecting to dancing myself that I shall hope to be honoured with the hands of all my fair cousins in the course of the evening, and I take this opportunity of soliciting yours, Miss Elizabeth, for the two first dances especially,—a preference which I trust my cousin Jane will attribute to the right cause, and not to any disrespect for her."

Elizabeth felt herself completely taken in. She had fully proposed being engaged by Wickham for those very dances:—and to have Mr. Collins instead! her liveliness had been never worse timed. There was no help for it however. Mr. Wickham's happiness and her own was per force delayed a little longer, and Mr. Collins's proposal accepted with as good a grace as she could. She was not the better pleased with his gallantry, from the idea it suggested of something more.—It now first struck her, that *she* was selected from among her sisters as worthy of being the mistress of Hunsford Parsonage, and of assisting to form a quadrille table at Rosings, in the absence of more eligible visitors. The idea soon reached to conviction, as she observed his increasing civilities toward herself, and heard his frequent attempt at a compliment on her wit and vivacity; and though more astonished than gratified herself, by this effect of her charms, it was not long before her mother gave her to understand that the probability of their marriage was exceedingly agreeable to *her*. Elizabeth however did not chuse to take the hint, being well aware that a serious dispute must be the consequence of any reply. Mr. Collins might never make the offer, and till he did, it was useless to quarrel about him.

If there had not been a Netherfield ball to prepare for and

talk of, the younger Miss Bennets would have been in a pitiable state at this time, for from the day of the invitation, to the day of the ball, there was such a succession of rain as prevented their walking to Meryton once. No aunt, no officers, no news could be sought after;—the very shoe-roses [4] for Netherfield were got by proxy. Even Elizabeth might have found some trial of her patience in weather, which totally suspended the improvement of her acquaintance with Mr. Wickham; and nothing less than a dance on Tuesday, could have made such a Friday, Saturday, Sunday and Monday, endurable to Kitty and Lydia.

Chapter XVIII

Till Elizabeth entered the drawing-room at Netherfield and looked in vain for Mr. Wickham among the cluster of red coats there assembled, a doubt of his being present had never occurred to her. The certainty of meeting him had not been checked by any of those recollections that might not unreasonably have alarmed her. She had dressed with more than usual care, and prepared in the highest spirits for the conquest of all that remained unsubdued of his heart, trusting that it was not more than might be won in the course of the evening. But in an instant arose the dreadful suspicion of his being purposely omitted for Mr. Darcy's pleasure in the Bingley's invitation to the officers; and though this was not exactly the case, the absolute fact of his absence was pronounced by his friend Mr. Denny, to whom Lydia eagerly applied, and who told them that Wickham had been obliged to go to town on business the day before, and was not yet returned; adding, with a significant smile,

"I do not imagine his business would have called him away just now, if he had not wished to avoid a certain gentleman here."

This part of his intelligence, though unheard by Lydia, was caught by Elizabeth, and as it assured her that Darcy was not less answerable for Wickham's absence than if her first surmise had been just, every feeling of displeasure against the former was so sharpened by immediate disappointment, that she could hardly reply with tolerable civility to the polite inquiries which he directly afterwards approached to make.—Attention, forbearance, patience with Darcy, was injury to Wickham. She was resolved against any sort of conversation with him, and turned away with a degree of ill humour, which she could not wholly surmount even in speaking to Mr. Bingley, whose blind partiality provoked her.

But Elizabeth was not formed for ill-humour; and though every prospect of her own was destroyed for the evening, it could not

4. Shoe-ties with ribbons bunched in the form of a rose.

dwell long on her spirits; and having told all her griefs to Charlotte Lucas, whom she had not seen for a week, she was soon able to make a voluntary transition to the oddities of her cousin, and to point him out to her particular notice. The two first dances, however, brought a return of distress; they were dances of mortification. Mr. Collins, awkward and solemn, apologising instead of attending, and often moving wrong without being aware of it, gave her all the shame and misery which a disagreeable partner for a couple of dances can give. The moment of her release from him was exstacy.

She danced next with an officer, and had the refreshment of talking of Wickham, and of hearing that he was universally liked. When those dances were over she returned to Charlotte Lucas, and was in conversation with her, when she found herself suddenly addressed by Mr. Darcy, who took her so much by surprise in his application for her hand, that, without knowing what she did, she accepted him. He walked away again immediately, and she was left to fret over her own want of presence of mind; Charlotte tried to console her.

"I dare say you will find him very agreeable."

"Heaven forbid!—*That* would be the greatest misfortune of all!—To find a man agreeable whom one is determined to hate!—Do not wish me such an evil."

When the dancing recommenced, however, and Darcy approached to claim her hand, Charlotte could not help cautioning her in a whisper not to be a simpleton and allow her fancy for Wickham to make her appear unpleasant in the eyes of a man of ten times his consequence. Elizabeth made no answer, and took her place in the set, amazed at the dignity to which she was arrived in being allowed to stand opposite to Mr. Darcy, and reading in her neighbours' looks their equal amazement in beholding it. They stood for some time without speaking a word; and she began to imagine that their silence was to last through the two dances, and at first was resolved not to break it; till suddenly fancying that it would be the greater punishment to her partner to oblige him to talk, she made some slight observation on the dance. He replied, and was again silent. After a pause of some minutes she addressed him a second time with

"It is *your* turn to say something now, Mr. Darcy.—*I* talked about the dance, and *you* ought to make some kind of remark on the size of the room, or the number of couples."

He smiled, and assured her that whatever she wished him to say should be said.

"Very well.—That reply will do for the present.—Perhaps by and bye I may observe that private balls are much pleasanter than public ones.—But *now* we may be silent."

"Do you talk by rule then, while you are dancing?"

"Sometimes. One must speak a little, you know. It would look odd to be entirely silent for half an hour together, and yet for the advantage of *some*, conversation ought to be so arranged as that they may have the trouble of saying as little as possible."

"Are you consulting your own feelings in the present case, or do you imagine that you are gratifying mine?"

"Both," replied Elizabeth archly; "for I have always seen a great similarity in the turn of our minds.—We are each of an unsocial, taciturn disposition, unwilling to speak, unless we expect to say something that will amaze the whole room, and be handed down to posterity with all the eclat of a proverb."

"This is no very striking resemblance of your own character, I am sure," said he. "How near it may be to *mine*, I cannot pretend to say.—*You* think it a faithful portrait undoubtedly."

"I must not decide on my own performance."

He made no answer, and they were again silent till they had gone down the dance, when he asked her if she and her sisters did not very often walk to Meryton. She answered in the affirmative, and, unable to resist the temptation, added, "When you met us there the other day, we had just been forming a new acquaintance."

The effect was immediate. A deeper shade of hauteur overspread his features, but he said not a word, and Elizabeth, though blaming herself for her own weakness, could not go on. At length Darcy spoke, and in a constrained manner said,

"Mr. Wickham is blessed with such happy manners as may ensure his *making* friends—whether he may be equally capable of *retaining* them, is less certain."

"He has been so unlucky as to lose *your* friendship," replied Elizabeth with emphasis, "and in a manner which he is likely to suffer from all his life."

Darcy made no answer, and seemed desirous of changing the subject. At that moment Sir William Lucas appeared close to them, meaning to pass through the set to the other side of the room; but on perceiving Mr. Darcy he stopt with a bow of superior courtesy to compliment him on his dancing and his partner.

"I have been most highly gratified indeed, my dear Sir. Such very superior dancing is not often seen. It is evident that you belong to the first circles. Allow me to say, however, that your fair partner does not disgrace you, and that I must hope to have this pleasure often repeated, especially when a certain desirable event, my dear Miss Eliza, (glancing at her sister and Bingley,) shall take place. What congratulations will then flow in! I appeal to Mr. Darcy:—but let me not interrupt you, Sir.—You will not thank me for detaining you from the bewitching converse of that young lady, whose bright eyes are also upbraiding me."

The latter part of this address was scarcely heard by Darcy; but Sir William's allusion to his friend seemed to strike him forcibly, and his eyes were directed with a very serious expression towards Bingley and Jane, who were dancing together. Recovering himself, however, shortly, he turned to his partner, and said,

"Sir William's interruption has made me forget what we were talking of."

"I do not think we were speaking at all. Sir William could not have interrupted any two people in the room who had less to say for themselves.—We have tried two or three subjects already without success, and what we are to talk of next I cannot imagine."

"What think you of books?" said he, smiling.

"Books—Oh! no.—I am sure we never read the same, or not with the same feelings."

"I am sorry you think so; but if that be the case, there can at least be no want of subject.—We may compare our different opinions."

"No—I cannot talk of books in a ball-room; my head is always full of something else."

"The *present* always occupies you in such scenes—does it?" said he, with a look of doubt.

"Yes, always," she replied, without knowing what she said, for her thoughts had wandered far from the subject, as soon afterwards appeared by her suddenly exclaiming, "I remember hearing you once say, Mr. Darcy, that you hardly ever forgave, that your resentment once created was unappeasable. You are very cautious, I suppose, as to its *being created*."

"I am," said he, with a firm voice.

"And never allow yourself to be blinded by prejudice?"

"I hope not."

"It is particularly incumbent on those who never change their opinion, to be secure of judging properly at first."

"May I ask to what these questions tend?"

"Merely to the illustration of *your* character," said she, endeavouring to shake off her gravity. "I am trying to make it out."

"And what is your success?"

She shook her head. "I do not get on at all. I hear such different accounts of you as puzzle me exceedingly."

"I can readily believe," answered he gravely, "that report may vary greatly with respect to me; and I could wish, Miss Bennet, that you were not to sketch my character at the present moment, as there is reason to fear that the performance would reflect no credit on either."

"But if I do not take your likeness now, I may never have another opportunity."

"I would by no means suspend any pleasure of yours," he coldly replied. She said no more, and they went down the other dance and parted in silence; on each side dissatisfied, though not to an equal degree, for in Darcy's breast there was a tolerable powerful feeling towards her, which soon procured her pardon, and directed all his anger against another.

They had not long separated when Miss Bingley came towards her, and with an expression of civil disdain thus accosted her,

"So, Miss Eliza, I hear you are quite delighted with George Wickham!—Your sister has been talking to me about him, and asking me a thousand questions; and I find that the young man forgot to tell you, among his other communications, that he was the son of old Wickham, the late Mr. Darcy's steward. Let me recommend you, however, as a friend, not to give implicit confidence to all his assertions; for as to Mr. Darcy's using him ill, it is perfectly false; for, on the contrary, he has been always remarkably kind to him, though George Wickham has treated Mr. Darcy in a most infamous manner. I do not know the particulars, but I know very well that Mr. Darcy is not in the least to blame, that he cannot bear to hear George Wickham mentioned, and that though my brother thought he could not well avoid including him in his invitation to the officers, he was excessively glad to find that he had taken himself out of the way. His coming into the country at all, is a most insolent thing indeed, and I wonder how he could presume to do it. I pity you, Miss Eliza, for the discovery of your favourite's guilt; but really considering his descent, one could not expect much better."

"His guilt and his descent appear by your account to be the same," said Elizabeth angrily; "for I have heard you accuse him of nothing worse than of being the son of Mr. Darcy's steward, and of *that*, I can assure you, he informed me himself."

"I beg your pardon," replied Miss Bingley, turning away with a sneer. "Excuse my interference.—It was kindly meant."

"Insolent girl!" said Elizabeth to herself.—"You are much mistaken if you expect to influence me by such a paltry attack as this. I see nothing in it but your own wilful ignorance and the malice of Mr. Darcy." She then sought her eldest sister, who had undertaken to make inquiries on the same subject of Bingley. Jane met her with a smile of such sweet complacency, a glow of such happy expression, as sufficiently marked how well she was satisfied with the occurrences of the evening.—Elizabeth instantly read her feelings, and at that moment solicitude for Wickham, resentment against his enemies, and every thing else gave way before the hope of Jane's being in the fairest way for happiness.

"I want to know," said she, with a countenance no less smiling than her sister's, "what you have learnt about Mr. Wickham. But perhaps you have been too pleasantly engaged to think of any third person; in which case you may be sure of my pardon."

"No," replied Jane, "I have not forgotten him; but I have nothing satisfactory to tell you. Mr. Bingley does not know the whole of his history, and is quite ignorant of the circumstances which have principally offended Mr. Darcy; but he will vouch for the good conduct, the probity and honour of his friend, and is perfectly convinced that Mr. Wickham has deserved much less attention from Mr. Darcy than he has received; and I am sorry to say that by his account as well as his sister's, Mr. Wickham is by no means a respectable young man. I am afraid he has been very imprudent, and has deserved to lose Mr. Darcy's regard."

"Mr. Bingley does not know Mr. Wickham himself?"

"No; he never saw him till the other morning at Meryton."

"This account then is what he has received from Mr. Darcy. I am perfectly satisfied. But what does he say of the living?"

"He does not exactly recollect the circumstances, though he has heard them from Mr. Darcy more than once, but he believes that it was left to him *conditionally* only."

"I have not a doubt of Mr. Bingley's sincerity," said Elizabeth warmly; "but you must excuse my not being convinced by assurances only. Mr. Bingley's defence of his friend was a very able one I dare say, but since he is unacquainted with several parts of the story, and has learnt the rest from that friend himself, I shall venture still to think of both gentlemen as I did before."

She then changed the discourse to one more gratifying to each, and on which there could be no difference of sentiment. Elizabeth listened with delight to the happy, though modest hopes which Jane entertained of Bingley's regard, and said all in her power to heighten her confidence in it. On their being joined by Mr. Bingley himself, Elizabeth withdrew to Miss Lucas; to whose inquiry after the pleasantness of her last partner she had scarcely replied, before Mr. Collins came up to them and told her with great exultation that he had just been so fortunate as to make a most important discovery.

"I have found out," said he, "by a singular accident, that there is now in the room a near relation of my patroness. I happened to overhear the gentleman himself mentioning to the young lady who does the honours of this house the names of his cousin Miss de Bourgh, and of her mother Lady Catherine. How wonderfully these sort of things occur! Who would have thought of my meeting with—perhaps—a nephew of Lady Catherine de Bourgh in this assembly!—I am most thankful that the discovery is made in time for me to pay my respects to him, which I am now going to do, and trust he will excuse my not having done it before. My total ignorance of the connection must plead my apology."

"You are not going to introduce yourself to Mr. Darcy?"

"Indeed I am. I shall intreat his pardon for not having done it earlier. I believe him to be Lady Catherine's *nephew*. It will be in my power to assure him that her ladyship was quite well yesterday se'nnight."

Elizabeth tried hard to dissuade him from such a scheme; assuring him that Mr. Darcy would consider his addressing him without introduction as an impertinent freedom, rather than a compliment to his aunt; that it was not in the least necessary there should be any notice on either side, and that if it were, it must belong to Mr. Darcy, the superior in consequence, to begin the acquaintance.—Mr. Collins listened to her with the determined air of following his own inclination, and when she ceased speaking, replied thus,

"My dear Miss Elizabeth, I have the highest opinion in the world of your excellent judgment in all matters within the scope of your understanding, but permit me to say that there must be a wide difference between the established forms of ceremony amongst the laity, and those which regulate the clergy; for give me leave to observe that I consider the clerical office as equal in point of dignity with the highest rank in the kingdom—provided that a proper humility of behaviour is at the same time maintained. You must therefore allow me to follow the dictates of my conscience on this occasion, which leads me to perform what I look on as a point of duty. Pardon me for neglecting to profit by your advice, which on every other subject shall be my constant guide, though in the case before us I consider myself more fitted by education and habitual study to decide on what is right than a young lady like yourself." And with a low bow he left her to attack Mr. Darcy, whose reception of his advances she eagerly watched, and whose astonishment at being so addressed was very evident. Her cousin prefaced his speech with a solemn bow, and though she could not hear a word of it, she felt as if hearing it all, and saw in the motion of his lips the words "apology," "Hunsford," and "Lady Catherine de Bourgh."—It vexed her to see him expose himself to such a man. Mr. Darcy was eyeing him with unrestrained wonder, and when at last Mr. Collins allowed him time to speak, replied with an air of distant civility. Mr. Collins, however, was not discouraged from speaking again, and Mr. Darcy's comtempt seemed abundantly increasing with the length of his second speech, and at the end of it he only made him a slight bow, and moved another way. Mr. Collins then returned to Elizabeth.

"I have no reason, I assure you," said he, "to be dissatisfied with my reception. Mr. Darcy seemed much pleased with the attention. He answered me with the utmost civility, and even paid me the compliment of saying, that he was so well convinced of Lady Catherine's discernment as to be certain she could never bestow a favour unworthily. It was really a very handsome thought. Upon the whole, I am much pleased with him."

As Elizabeth had no longer any interest of her own to pursue, she turned her attention almost entirely on her sister and Mr. Bingley, and the train of agreeable reflections which her observations gave birth to, made her perhaps almost as happy as Jane. She saw her in idea settled in that very house in all the felicity which a marriage of true affection could bestow; and she felt capable under such circumstances, of endeavouring even to like Bingley's two sisters. Her mother's thoughts she plainly saw were bent the same way, and she determined not to venture near her, lest she might hear too much. When they sat down to supper, therefore, she considered it a most unlucky perverseness which placed them within one of each other; and deeply was she vexed to find that her mother was talking to that one person (Lady Lucas) freely, openly, and of nothing else but of her expectation that Jane would be soon married to Mr. Bingley.—It was an animating subject, and Mrs. Bennet seemed incapable of fatigue while enumerating the advantages of the match. His being such a charming young man, and so rich, and living but three miles from them, were the first points of self-gratulation; and then it was such a comfort to think how fond the two sisters were of Jane, and to be certain that they must desire the connection as much as she could do. It was, moreover, such a promising thing for her younger daughters, as Jane's marrying so greatly must throw them in the way of other rich men; and lastly, it was so pleasant at her time of life to be able to consign her single daughters to the care of their sister, that she might not be obliged to go into company more than she liked. It was necessary to make this circumstance a matter of pleasure, because on such occasions it is the etiquette; but no one was less likely than Mrs. Bennet to find comfort in staying at home at any period of her life. She concluded with many good wishes that Lady Lucas might soon be equally fortunate, though evidently and triumphantly believing there was no chance of it.

In vain did Elizabeth endeavour to check the rapidity of her mother's words, or persuade her to describe her felicity in a less audible whisper; for to her inexpressible vexation, she could perceive that the chief of it was overheard by Mr. Darcy, who sat opposite to them. Her mother only scolded her for being nonsensical.

"What is Mr. Darcy to me, pray, that I should be afraid of him? I am sure we owe him no such particular civility as to be obliged to say nothing *he* may not like to hear."

"For heaven's sake, madam, speak lower.—What advantage can it be to you to offend Mr. Darcy?—You will never recommend yourself to his friend by so doing."

Nothing that she could say, however, had any influence. Her mother would talk of her views in the same intelligible tone. Elizabeth blushed and blushed again with shame and vexation. She could not help frequently glancing her eye at Mr. Darcy, though every glance convinced her of what she dreaded; for though he was not always looking at her mother, she was convinced that his attention was invariably fixed by her. The expression of his face changed gradually from indignant contempt to a composed and steady gravity.

At length however Mrs. Bennet had no more to say; and Lady Lucas, who had been long yawning at the repetition of delights which she saw no likelihood of sharing, was left to the comforts of cold ham and chicken. Elizabeth now began to revive. But not long was the interval of tranquillity; for when supper was over, singing was talked of, and she had the mortification of seeing Mary, after very little entreaty, preparing to oblige the company. By many significant looks and silent entreaties, did she endeavour to prevent such a proof of complaisance,—but in vain; Mary would not understand them; such an opportunity of exhibiting was delightful to her, and she began her song. Elizabeth's eyes were fixed on her with most painful sensations; and she watched her progress through the several stanzas with an impatience which was very ill rewarded at their close; for Mary, on receiving amongst the thanks of the table, the hint of a hope that she might be prevailed on to favour them again, after the pause of half a minute began another. Mary's powers were by no means fitted for such a display; her voice was weak, and her manner affected.— Elizabeth was in agonies. She looked at Jane, to see how she bore it; but Jane was very composedly talking to Bingley. She looked at his two sisters, and saw them making signs of derision at each other, and at Darcy, who continued however impenetrably grave. She looked at her father to entreat his interference, lest Mary should be singing all night. He took the hint, and when Mary had finished her second song, said aloud,

"That will do extremely well, child. You have delighted us long enough. Let the other young ladies have time to exhibit."

Mary, though pretending not to hear, was somewhat disconcerted; and Elizabeth sorry for her, and sorry for her father's speech, was afraid her anxiety had done no good.—Others of the party were now applied to.

"If I," said Mr. Collins, "were so fortunate as to be able to sing, I should have great pleasure, I am sure, in obliging the company with an air; for I consider music as a very innocent diversion, and perfectly compatible with the profession of a clergyman.—I do not mean however to assert that we can be justified in devoting too much of our time to music, for there are certainly other things to be attended to. The rector of a parish has much to do.—In the first place, he must make such an agreement for tythes as may be beneficial to himself and not offensive to his patron. He must write his own sermons; and the time that remains will not be too much for his parish duties, and the care and improvement of his dwelling, which he cannot be excused from making as comfortable as possible. And I do not think it of light importance that he should have attentive and conciliatory manners towards every body, especially towards those to whom he owes his preferment. I cannot acquit him of that duty; nor could I think well of the man who should omit an occasion of testifying his respect towards any body connected with the family." And with a bow to Mr. Darcy, he concluded his speech, which had been spoken so loud as to be heard by half the room.—Many stared.—Many smiled; but no one looked more amused than Mr. Bennet himself, while his wife seriously commended Mr. Collins for having spoken so sensibly, and observed in a half-whisper to Lady Lucas, that he was a remarkably clever, good kind of young man.

To Elizabeth it appeared, that had her family made an agreement to expose themselves as much as they could during the evening, it would have been impossible for them to play their parts with more spirit, or finer success; and happy did she think it for Bingley and her sister that some of the exhibition had escaped his notice, and that his feelings were not of a sort to be much distressed by the folly which he must have witnessed. That his two sisters and Mr. Darcy, however, should have such an opportunity of ridiculing her relations was bad enough, and she could not determine whether the silent contempt of the gentleman, or the insolent smiles of the ladies, were more intolerable.

The rest of the evening brought her little amusement. She was teazed by Mr. Collins, who continued most perserveringly by her side, and though he could not prevail with her to dance with him again, put it out of her power to dance with others.

In vain did she entreat him to stand up with somebody else, and offer to introduce him to any young lady in the room. He assured her that as to dancing, he was perfectly indifferent to it; that his chief object was by delicate attentions to recommend himself to her, and that he should therefore make a point of remaining close to her the whole evening. There was no arguing upon such a project. She owed her greatest relief to her friend Miss Lucas, who often joined them, and good-naturedly engaged Mr. Collins's conversation to herself.

She was at least free from the offence of Mr. Darcy's farther notice; though often standing within a very short distance of her, quite disengaged, he never came near enough to speak. She felt it to be the probable consequence of her allusions to Mr. Wickham, and rejoiced in it.

The Longbourn party were the last of all the company to depart; and by a manœuvre of Mrs. Bennet had to wait for their carriages a quarter of an hour after every body else was gone, which gave them time to see how heartily they were wished away by some of the family. Mrs. Hurst and her sister scarcely opened their mouths except to complain of fatigue, and were evidently impatient to have the house to themselves. They repulsed every attempt of Mrs. Bennet at conversation, and by so doing, threw a languor over the whole party, which was very little relieved by the long speeches of Mr. Collins, who was complimenting Mr. Bingley and his sisters on the elegance of their entertainment, and the hospitality and politeness which had marked their behaviour to their guests. Darcy said nothing at all. Mr. Bennet, in equal silence, was enjoying the scene. Mr. Bingley and Jane were standing together, a little detached from the rest, and talked only to each other. Elizabeth preserved as steady a silence as either Mrs. Hurst or Miss Bingley; and even Lydia was too much fatigued to utter more than the occasional exclamation of "Lord, how tired I am!" accompanied by a violent yawn.

When at length they arose to take leave, Mrs. Bennet was most pressingly civil in her hope of seeing the whole family soon at Longbourn; and addressed herself particularly to Mr. Bingley, to assure him how happy he would make them, by eating a family dinner with them at any time, without the ceremony of a formal invitation. Bingley was all grateful pleasure, and he readily engaged for taking the earliest opportunity of waiting on her, after his return from London, whither he was obliged to go the next day for a short time.

Mrs. Bennet was perfectly satisfied; and quitted the house under the delightful persuasion that, allowing for the necessary preparations of settlements, new carriages and wedding clothes, she should undoubtedly see her daughter settled at Netherfield, in the course of three or four months. Of having another daughter married to Mr. Collins, she thought with equal certainty, and with considerable, though not equal, pleasure. Elizabeth was the least dear to her of all her children; and though the man and the match were quite good enough for *her*, the worth of each was eclipsed by Mr. Bingley and Netherfield.

Chapter XIX

The next day opened a new scene at Longbourn. Mr. Collins made his declaration in form. Having resolved to do it without loss of time, as his leave of absence extended only to the following Saturday, and having no feelings of diffidence to make it distressing to himself even at the moment, he set about it in a very orderly manner, with all the observances which he supposed a regular part of the business. On finding Mrs. Bennet, Elizabeth, and one of the younger girls together, soon after breakfast, he addressed the mother in these words,

"May I hope, Madam, for your interest with your fair daughter Elizabeth, when I solicit for the honour of a private audience with her in the course of this morning?"

Before Elizabeth had time for any thing but a blush of surprise, Mrs. Bennet instantly answered,

"Oh dear!—Yes—certainly.—I am sure Lizzy will be very happy—I am sure she can have no objection.—Come, Kitty, I want you up stairs." And gathering her work together, she was hastening away, when Elizabeth called out,

"Dear Ma'am, do not go.—I beg you will not go.—Mr. Collins must excuse me.—He can have nothing to say to me that any body need not hear. I am going away myself."

"No, no, nonsense, Lizzy.—I desire you will stay where you are."—And upon Elizabeth's seeming really, with vexed and embarrassed looks, about to escape, she added, "Lizzy, I *insist* upon your staying and hearing Mr. Collins."

Elizabeth would not oppose such an injunction—and a moment's consideration making her also sensible that it would be wisest to get it over as soon and as quietly as possible, she sat down again, and tried to conceal by incessant employment the feelings which were divided between distress and diversion. Mrs. Bennet and Kitty walked off, and as soon as they were gone Mr. Collins began.

"Believe me, my dear Miss Elizabeth, that your modesty, so far from doing you any disservice, rather adds to your other perfections. You would have been less amiable in my eyes had there *not* been this little unwillingness; but allow me to assure you that I have your respected mother's permission for this address. You can hardly doubt the purport of my discourse, however your natural delicacy may lead you to dissemble; my attentions have been too marked to be mistaken. Almost as soon as I entered the house I singled you out as the companion of my future life. But before I am run away with by my feelings on this subject, perhaps it will be advisable for me to state my reasons for marrying —and moreover for coming into Hertfordshire with the design of selecting a wife, as I certainly did."

The idea of Mr. Collins, with all his solemn composure, being run away with by his feelings, made Elizabeth so near laughing that she could not use the short pause he allowed in any attempt to stop him farther, and he continued:

"My reasons for marrying are, first, that I think it a right thing for every clergyman in easy circumstances (like myself) to set the example of matrimony in his parish. Secondly, that I am convinced it will add very greatly to my happiness; and thirdly —which perhaps I ought to have mentioned earlier, that it is the particular advice and recommendation of the very noble lady whom I have the honour of calling patroness. Twice has she condescended to give me her opinion (unasked too!) on this subject; and it was but the very Saturday night before I left Hunsford— between our pools at quadrille, while Mrs. Jenkinson was arranging Miss de Bourgh's foot-stool, that she said, 'Mr. Collins, you must marry. A clergyman like you must marry.—Chuse properly, chuse a gentlewoman for *my* sake; and for your *own*, let her be an active, useful sort of person, not brought up high, but able to make a small income go a good way. This is my advice. Find such a woman as soon as you can, bring her to Hunsford, and I will visit her.' Allow me, by the way, to observe, my fair cousin, that I do not reckon the notice and kindness of Lady Catherine de Bourgh as among the least of the advantages in my power to offer. You will find her manners beyond any thing I can describe; and your wit and vivacity I think must be acceptable to her, especially when tempered with the silence and respect which her rank will inevitably excite. Thus much for my general intention in favour of matrimony; it remains to be told why my views were directed to Longbourn instead of my own neighbourhood, where I assure you there are many amiable young women. But the fact is, that being, as I am, to inherit this estate after the death of your honoured father, (who, however, may live many years longer,) I could not satisfy myself without resolving to chuse a wife from among his daughters, that the loss to them might be as little as possible, when the melancholy event takes place— which, however, as I have already said, may not be for several years. This has been my motive, my fair cousin, and I flatter myself it will not sink me in your esteem. And now nothing remains for me but to assure you in the most animated language of the violence of my affection. To fortune I am perfectly indifferent, and shall make no demand of that nature on your father, since I am well aware that it could not be complied with; and that one thousand pounds in the 4 per cents.[5] which will not be yours till after your mother's decease, is all that you may ever be entitled to. On that head, therefore, I shall be uniformly silent; and you may assure yourself that no ungenerous reproach shall ever pass my lips when we are married."

It was absolutely necessary to interrupt him now.

"You are too hasty, Sir," she cried. "You forget that I have made no answer. Let me do it without farther loss of time. Accept my thanks for the compliment you are paying me. I am very sensible of the honour of your proposals, but it is impossible for me to do otherwise than decline them."

"I an not now to learn," replied Mr. Collins, with a formal wave of the hand, "that it is usual with young ladies to reject the addresses of the man whom they secretly mean to accept, when he first applies for their favour; and that sometimes the refusal is repeated a second or even a third time. I am therefore by no means discouraged by what you have just said, and shall hope to lead you to the altar ere long."

"Upon my word, Sir," cried Elizabeth, "your hope is rather an extraordinary one after my declaration. I do assure you that I am not one of those young ladies (if such young ladies there are) who are so daring as to risk their happiness on the chance of being asked a second time. I am perfectly serious in my refusal. —You could not make *me* happy, and I am convinced that I am the last woman in the world who would make *you* so.—Nay, were your friend Lady Catherine to know me, I am persuaded she would find me in every respect ill qualified for the situation."

"Were it certain that Lady Catherine would think so," said Mr. Collins very gravely—"but I cannot imagine that her ladyship would at all disapprove of you. And you may be certain that when I have the honour of seeing her again I shall speak in the highest terms of your modesty, economy, and other amiable qualifications."

"Indeed, Mr. Collins, all praise of me will be unnecessary. You must give me leave to judge for myself, and pay me the compliment of believing what I say. I wish you very happy and very rich, and by refusing your hand, do all in my power to prevent your being otherwise. In making me the offer, you must have satisfied the delicacy of your feelings with regard to my family, and may

5. Quite secure stock sold by the government to finance its operations.

take possession of Longbourn estate whenever it falls, without any self-reproach. This matter may be considered, therefore, as finally settled." And rising as she thus spoke, she would have quitted the room, had not Mr. Collins thus addressed her,

"When I do myself the honour of speaking to you next on this subject I shall hope to receive a more favourable answer than you have now given me; though I am far from accusing you of cruelty at present, because I know it to be the established custom of your sex to reject a man on the first application, and perhaps you have even now said as much to encourage my suit as would be consistent with the true delicacy of the female character."

"Really, Mr. Collins," cried Elizabeth with some warmth, "you puzzle me exceedingly. If what I have hitherto said can appear to you in the form of encouragement, I know not how to express my refusal in such a way as may convince you of its being one."

"You must give me leave to flatter myself, my dear cousin, that your refusal of my addresses is merely words of course. My reasons for believing it are briefly these:—It does not appear to me that my hand is unworthy your acceptance, or that the establishment I can offer would be any other than highly desirable. My situation in life, my connections with the family of De Bourgh, and my relationship to your own, are circumstances highly in my favour; and you should take it into farther consideration that in spite of your manifold attractions, it is by no means certain that another offer of marriage may ever be made you. Your portion is unhappily so small that it will in all likelihood undo the effects of your loveliness and amiable qualifications. As I must therefore conclude that you are not serious in your rejection of me, I shall chuse to attribute it to your wish of increasing my love by suspense, according to the usual practice of elegant females."

"I do assure you, Sir, that I have no pretension whatever to that kind of elegance which consists in tormenting a respectable man. I would rather be paid the compliment of being believed sincere. I thank you again and again for the honour you have done me in your proposals, but to accept them is absolutely impossible. My feelings in every respect forbid it. Can I speak plainer? Do not consider me now as an elegant female intending to plague you, but as a rational creature speaking the truth from her heart."

"You are uniformly charming!" cried he, with an air of awkward gallantry; "and I am persuaded that when sanctioned by the express authority of both your excellent parents, my proposals will not fail of being acceptable."

To such perseverance in wilful self-deception Elizabeth would make no reply, and immediately and in silence withdrew; determined, if he persisted in considering her repeated refusals as flattering encouragement, to apply to her father, whose negative might be uttered in such a manner as must be decisive, and whose behaviour at least could not be mistaken for the affectation and coquetry of an elegant female.

Chapter XX

Mr. Collins was not left long to the silent contemplation of his successful love; for Mrs. Bennet, having dawdled about in the vestibule to watch for the end of the conference, no sooner saw Elizabeth open the door and with quick step pass her towards the staircase, than she entered the breakfast-room, and congratulated both him and herself in warm terms on the happy prospect of their nearer connection. Mr. Collins received and returned these felicitations with equal pleasure, and then proceeded to relate the particulars of their interview, with the result of which he trusted he had every reason to be satisfied, since the refusal which his cousin had stedfastly given him would naturally flow from her bashful modesty and the genuine delicacy of her character.

This information, however, startled Mrs. Bennet;—she would have been glad to be equally satisfied that her daughter had meant to encourage him by protesting against his proposals, but she dared not to believe it, and could not help saying so.

"But depend upon it, Mr. Collins," she added, "that Lizzy shall be brought to reason. I will speak to her about it myself directly. She is a very headstrong foolish girl, and does not know her own interest; but I will *make* her know it."

"Pardon me for interrupting you, Madam," cried Mr. Collins; "but if she is really headstrong and foolish, I know not whether she would altogether be a very desirable wife to a man in my situation, who naturally looks for happiness in the marriage state. If therefore she actually persists in rejecting my suit, perhaps it were better not to force her into accepting me, because if liable to such defects of temper, she could not contribute much to my felicity."

"Sir, you quite misunderstand me," said Mrs. Bennet, alarmed. "Lizzy is only headstrong in such matters as these. In every thing else she is as good natured a girl as ever lived. I will go directly to Mr. Bennet, and we shall very soon settle it with her, I am sure."

She would not give him time to reply, but hurrying instantly to her husband, called out as she entered the library,

"Oh! Mr. Bennet, you are wanted immediately; we are all in an uproar. You must come and make Lizzy marry Mr. Collins, for she vows she will not have him, and if you do not make haste he will change his mind and not have *her*."

Mr. Bennet raised his eyes from his book as she entered, and fixed them on her face with a calm unconcern which was not in the least altered by her communication.

"I have not the pleasure of understanding you," said he, when she had finished her speech. "Of what are you talking?"

"Of Mr. Collins and Lizzy. Lizzy declares she will not have Mr. Collins, and Mr. Collins begins to say that he will not have Lizzy."

"And what am I to do on the occasion?—It seems an hopeless business."

"Speak to Lizzy about it yourself. Tell her that you insist upon her marrying him."

"Let her be called down. She shall hear my opinion."

Mrs. Bennet rang the bell, and Miss Elizabeth was summoned to the library.

"Come here, child," cried her father as she appeared. "I have sent for you on an affair of importance. I understand that Mr. Collins has made you an offer of marriage. Is it true?" Elizabeth replied that it was. "Very well—and this offer of marriage you have refused?"

"I have, Sir."

"Very well. We now come to the point. Your mother insists upon your accepting it. Is not it so, Mrs. Bennet?"

"Yes, or I will never see her again."

"An unhappy alternative is before you, Elizabeth. From this day you must be a stranger to one of your parents.—Your mother will never see you again if you do *not* marry Mr. Collins, and I will never see you again if you *do*."

Elizabeth could not but smile at such a conclusion of such a beginning; but Mrs. Bennet, who had persuaded herself that her husband regarded the affair as she wished, was excessively disappointed.

"What do you mean, Mr. Bennet, by talking in this way? You promised me to *insist* upon her marrying him."

"My dear," replied her husband, "I have two small favours to request. First, that you will allow me the free use of my understanding on the present occasion; and secondly, of my room. I shall be glad to have the library to myself as soon as may be."

Not yet, however, in spite of her disappointment in her husband, did Mrs. Bennet give up the point. She talked to Elizabeth again and again; coaxed and threatened her by turns. She endeavoured to secure Jane in her interest, but Jane with all possible mildness declined interfering;—and Elizabeth sometimes with real earnestness and sometimes with playful gaiety replied to her attacks.

Though her manner varied however, her determination never did.

Mr. Collins, meanwhile, was meditating in solitude on what had passed. He thought too well of himself to comprehend on what motive his cousin could refuse him; and though his pride was hurt, he suffered in no other way. His regard for her was quite imaginary; and the possibility of her deserving her mother's reproach prevented his feeling any regret.

While the family were in this confusion, Charlotte Lucas came to spend the day with them. She was met in the vestibule by Lydia, who, flying to her, cried in a half whisper, "I am glad you are come, for there is such fun here!—What do you think has happened this morning?—Mr. Collins has made an offer to Lizzy, and she will not have him."

Charlotte had hardly time to answer, before they were joined by Kitty, who came to tell the same news, and no sooner had they entered the breakfast-room, where Mrs. Bennet was alone, than she likewise began on the subject, calling on Miss Lucas for her compassion, and entreating her to persuade her friend Lizzy to comply with the wishes of all her family. "Pray do, my dear Miss Lucas," she added in a melancholy tone, "for nobody is on my side, nobody takes part with me, I am cruelly used, nobody feels for my poor nerves."

Charlotte's reply was spared by the entrance of Jane and Elizabeth.

"Aye, there she comes," continued Mrs. Bennet, "looking as unconcerned as may be, and caring no more for us than if we were at York, provided she can have her own way.—But I tell you what, Miss Lizzy, if you take it into your head to go on refusing every offer of marriage in this way, you will never get a husband at all—and I am sure I do not know who is to maintain you when your father is dead.—I shall not be able to keep you—and so I warn you.—I have done with you from this very day.—I told you in the library, you know, that I should never speak to you again, and you will find me as good as my word. I have no pleasure in talking to undutiful children.—Not that I have much pleasure indeed in talking to any body. People who suffer as I do from nervous complaints can have no great inclination for talking. Nobody can tell what I suffer!—But it is always so. Those who do not complain are never pitied."

Her daughters listened in silence to this effusion, sensible that any attempt to reason with or sooth her would only increase the irritation. She talked on, therefore, without interruption from any of them till they were joined by Mr. Collins, who entered with an air more stately than usual, and on perceiving whom, she said to the girls,

"Now, I do insist upon it, that you, all of you, hold your tongues, and let Mr. Collins and me have a little conversation together."

Elizabeth passed quietly out of the room, Jane and Kitty followed, but Lydia stood her ground, determined to hear all she could; and Charlotte, detained first by the civility of Mr. Collins, whose inquiries after herself and all her family were very minute, and then by a little curiosity, satisfied herself with walking to the window and pretending not to hear. In a doleful voice Mrs. Bennet thus began the projected conversation.—"Oh! Mr. Collins!"

"My dear Madam," replied he, "let us be for ever silent on this point. Far be it from me," he presently continued in a voice that marked his displeasure, "to resent the behaviour of your daughter. Resignation to inevitable evils is the duty of us all; the peculiar duty of a young man who has been so fortunate as I have been in early preferment; and I trust I am resigned. Perhaps not the less so from feeling a doubt of my positive happiness had my fair cousin honoured me with her hand; for I have often observed that resignation is never so perfect as when the blessing denied begins to lose somewhat of its value in our estimation. You will not, I hope, consider me as shewing any disrespect to your family, my dear Madam, by thus withdrawing my pretensions to your daughter's favour, without having paid yourself and Mr. Bennet the compliment of requesting you to interpose your authority in my behalf. My conduct may I fear be objectionable in having accepted my dismission from your daughter's lips instead of your own. But we are all liable to error. I have certainly meant well through the whole affair. My object has been to secure an amiable companion for myself, with due consideration for the advantage of all your family, and if my *manner* has been at all reprehensible, I here beg leave to apologise."

Chapter XXI

The discussion of Mr. Collins's offer was now nearly at an end, and Elizabeth had only to suffer from the uncomfortable feelings necessarily attending it, and occasionally from some peevish allusion of her mother. As for the gentleman himself, *his* feelings were chiefly expressed, not by embarrassment or dejection, or by trying to avoid her, but by stiffness of manner and resentful silence. He scarcely ever spoke to her, and the assiduous attentions which he had been so sensible of himself, were transferred for the rest of the day to Miss Lucas, whose civility in listening to him, was a seasonable relief to them all, and especially to her friend.

The morrow produced no abatement of Mrs. Bennet's ill humour or ill health. Mr. Collins was also in the same state of angry pride. Elizabeth had hoped that his resentment might shorten his visit, but his plan did not appear in the least affected by it. He was always to have gone on Saturday, and to Saturday he still meant to stay.

After breakfast, the girls walked to Meryton to inquire if Mr. Wickham were returned, and to lament over his absence from the Netherfield ball. He joined them on their entering the town and attended them to their aunt's, where his regret and vexation, and the concern of every body was well talked over.—To Elizabeth, however, he voluntarily acknowledged that the necessity of his absence *had* been self imposed.

"I found," said he, "as the time drew near, that I had better not meet Mr. Darcy;—that to be in the same room, the same party with him for so many hours together, might be more than I could bear, and that scenes might arise unpleasant to more than myself."

She highly approved his forbearance, and they had leisure for a full discussion of it, and for all the commendation which they civilly bestowed on each other, as Wickham and another officer walked back with them to Longbourn, and during the walk, he particularly attended to her. His accompanying them was a double advantage; she felt all the compliment it offered to herself, and it was most acceptable as an occasion of introducing him to her father and mother.

Soon after their return, a letter was delivered to Miss Bennet; it came from Netherfield, and was opened immediately. The envelope contained a sheet of elegant, little, hot pressed paper, well covered with a lady's fair, flowing hand; and Elizabeth saw her sister's countenance change as she read it, and saw her dwelling intently on some particular passages. Jane recollected herself soon, and putting the letter away, tried to join with her usual cheerfulness in the general conversation; but Elizabeth felt an anxiety on the subject which drew off her attention even from Wickham; and no sooner had he and his companion taken leave, than a glance from Jane invited her to follow her up stairs. When they had gained their own room, Jane taking out the letter, said,

"This is from Caroline Bingley; what is contains, has surprised me a good deal. The whole party have left Netherfield by this time, and are on their way to town; and without any intention of coming back again. You shall hear what she says."

She then read the first sentence aloud, which comprised the information of their having just resolved to follow their brother to town directly, and of their meaning to dine that day in Grosvenor street, where Mr. Hurst had a house. The next was in these words. "I do not pretend to regret any thing I shall leave in Hertfordshire, except your society, my dearest friend; but we will hope at some future period, to enjoy many returns of the delightful intercourse we have known, and in the mean while may lessen the pain of separation by a very frequent and most unreserved correspondence. I depend on you for that." To these high flown expressions, Elizabeth listened with all the insensibility of distrust; and though the suddenness of their removal surprised her, she saw nothing in it really to lament; it was not to be supposed that their absence from Netherfield would prevent Mr. Bingley's being there; and as to the loss of their society, she was persuaded that Jane must soon cease to regard it, in the enjoyment of his.

"It is unlucky," said she, after a short pause, "that you should not be able to see your friends before they leave the country. But may we not hope that the period of future happiness to which Miss Bingley looks forward, may arrive earlier than she is aware, and that the delightful intercourse you have known as friends, will be renewed with yet greater satisfaction as sisters?—Mr. Bingley will not be detained in London by them."

"Caroline decidedly says that none of the party will return into Hertfordshire this winter. I will read it to you—

"When my brother left us yesterday, he imagined that the business which took him to London, might be concluded in three or four days, but as we are certain it cannot be so, and at the same time convinced that when Charles gets to town, he will be in no hurry to leave it again, we have determined on following him thither, that he may not be obliged to spend his vacant hours in a comfortless hotel. Many of my acquaintance are already there for the winter; I wish I could hear that you, my dearest friend, had any intention of making one in the croud, but of that I despair. I sincerely hope your Christmas in Hertfordshire may abound in the gaieties which that season generally brings, and that your beaux will be so numerous as to prevent your feeling the loss of the three, of whom we shall deprive you."

"It is evident by this," added Jane, "that he comes back no more this winter."

"It is only evident that Miss Bingley does not mean he *should*."

"Why will you think so? It must be his own doing.—He is his own master. But you do not know *all*. I *will* read you the passage which particularly hurts me. I will have no reserves from *you*." "Mr. Darcy is impatient to see his sister, and to confess the truth, *we* are scarcely less eager to meet her again. I really do not think Georgiana Darcy has her equal for beauty, elegance, and accomplishments; and the affection she inspires in Louisa and myself, is heightened into something still more interesting, from the hope we dare to entertain of her being hereafter our sister. I do not know whether I ever before mentioned to you my feelings on this subject, but I will not leave the country without confiding them, and I trust you will not esteem them unreasonable. My brother admires her greatly already, he will have frequent opportunity now of seeing her on the most intimate footing, her relations all wish the connection as much as his own, and a sister's partiality is not misleading me, I think, when I call Charles most capable of engaging any woman's heart. With all these circumstances to favour an attachment and nothing to prevent it, am I wrong, my dearest Jane, in indulging the hope of an event which will secure the happiness of so many?"

"What think you of *this* sentence, my dear Lizzy?"—said Jane as she finished it. "Is it not clear enough?—Does it not expressly declare that Caroline neither expects nor wishes me to be her sister; that she is perfectly convinced of her brother's indifference, and that if she suspects the nature of my feelings for him, she means (most kindly!) to put me on my guard? Can there be any other opinion on the subject?"

"Yes, there can; for mine is totally different.—Will you hear it?"

"Most willingly."

"You shall have it in few words. Miss Bingley sees that her brother is in love with you, and wants him to marry Miss Darcy. She follows him to town in the hope of keeping him there, and tries to persuade you that he does not care about you."

Jane shook her head.

"Indeed, Jane, you ought to believe me.—No one who has ever seen you together, can doubt his affection. Miss Bingley I am sure cannot. She is not such a simpleton. Could she have seen half as much love in Mr. Darcy for herself, she would have ordered her wedding clothes. But the case is this. We are not rich enough, or grand enough for them; and she is the more anxious to get Miss Darcy for her brother, from the notion that when there has been *one* intermarriage, she may have less trouble in achieving a second; in which there is certainly some ingenuity, and I dare say it would succeed, if Miss de Bourgh were out of the way. But, my dearest Jane, you cannot seriously imagine that because Miss Bingley tells you her brother greatly admires Miss Darcy, he is in the smallest degree less sensible of *your* merit than when he took leave of you on Tuesday, or that it will be in her power to persuade him that instead of being in love with you, he is very much in love with her friend."

"If we thought alike of Miss Bingley," replied Jane, "your representation of all this, might make me quite easy. But I know the foundation is unjust. Caroline is incapable of wilfully deceiving any one; and all that I can hope in this case is, that she is deceived herself."

"That is right.—You could not have started a more happy idea, since you will not take comfort in mine. Believe her to be deceived by all means. You have now done your duty by her, and must fret no longer."

"But, my dear sister, can I be happy, even supposing the best, in accepting a man whose sisters and friends are all wishing him to marry elsewhere?"

"You must decide for yourself," said Elizabeth, "and if upon mature deliberation, you find that the misery of disobliging his two sisters is more than equivalent to the happiness of being his wife, I advise you by all means to refuse him."

"How can you talk so?"—said Jane faintly smiling,—"You must know that though I should be exceedingly grieved at their disapprobation, I could not hesitate."

"I did not think you would;—and that being the case, I cannot consider your situation with much compassion."

"But if he returns no more this winter, my choice will never be required. A thousand things may arise in six months!"

The idea of his returning no more Elizabeth treated with the utmost contempt. It appeared to her merely the suggestion of Caroline's interested wishes, and she could not for a moment suppose that those wishes, however openly or artfully spoken, could influence a young man so totally independent of every one.

She represented to her sister as forcibly as possible what she felt on the subject, and had soon the pleasure of seeing its happy effect. Jane's temper was not desponding, and she was gradually led to hope, though the diffidence of affection sometimes overcame the hope, that Bingley would return to Netherfield and answer every wish of her heart.

They agreed that Mrs. Bennet should only hear of the departure of the family, without being alarmed on the score of the gentleman's conduct; but even this partial communication gave her a great deal of concern, and she bewailed it as exceedingly unlucky that the ladies should happen to go away, just as they were all getting so intimate together. After lamenting it however at some length, she had the consolation of thinking that Mr. Bingley would be soon down again and soon dining at Longbourn, and the conclusion of all was the comfortable declaration that, though he had been invited only to a family dinner, she would take care to have two full courses.

Chapter XXII

The Bennets were engaged to dine with the Lucases, and again during the chief of the day, was Miss Lucas so kind as to listen to Mr. Collins. Elizabeth took an opportunity of thanking her. "It keeps him in good humour," said she, "and I am more obliged to you than I can express." Charlotte assured her friend of her satisfaction in being useful, and that it amply repaid her for the little sacrifice of her time. This was very amiable, but Charlotte's kindness extended farther than Elizabeth had any conception of;—its object was nothing less, than to secure her from any return of Mr. Collins's addresses, by engaging them towards herself. Such was Miss Lucas's scheme; and appearances were so favourable that when they parted at night, she would have felt almost sure of success if he had not been to leave Hertfordshire so very soon. But here, she did injustice to the fire and independence of his character, for it led him to escape out of Longbourn House the next morning with admirable slyness, and hasten to Lucas Lodge to throw himself at her feet. He was anxious to avoid the notice of his cousins, from a conviction that if they saw him depart, they could not fail to conjecture his design, and he was not willing to have the attempt known till its success could be known likewise; for though feeling almost secure, and with reason, for Charlotte had been tolerably encouraging, he was comparatively diffident since the adventure of Wednesday. His reception however was of the most flattering kind. Miss Lucas perceived him from an upper window as he walked towards the house, and instantly set out to meet him accidentally in the lane. But little had she dared to hope that so much love and eloquence awaited her there.

In as short a time as Mr. Collins's long speeches would allow, every thing was settled between them to the satisfaction of both; and as they entered the house, he earnestly entreated her to name the day that was to make him the happiest of men; and though such a solicitation must be waved for the present, the lady felt no inclination to trifle with his happiness. The stupidity with which he was favoured by nature, must guard his courtship from any charm that could make a woman wish for its continuance; and Miss Lucas, who accepted him solely from the pure and disinterested desire of an establishment, cared not how soon that establishment were gained.

Sir William and Lady Lucas were speedily applied to for their consent; and it was bestowed with a most joyful alacrity. Mr. Collins's present circumstances made it a most eligible match for their daughter, to whom they could give little fortune; and his prospects of future wealth were exceedingly fair. Lady Lucas began directly to calculate with more interest than the matter had ever excited before, how many years longer Mr. Bennet was likely to live; and Sir William gave it as his decided opinion, that whenever Mr. Collins should be in possession of the Longbourn estate, it would be highly expedient that both he and his wife should make their appearance at St. James's. The whole family in short were properly overjoyed on the occasion. The younger girls formed hopes of *coming out* a year or two sooner than they might otherwise have done; and the boys were relieved from their apprehension of Charlotte's dying an old maid. Charlotte herself was tolerably composed. She had gained her point, and had time to consider of it. Her reflections were in general satisfactory. Mr. Collins to be sure was neither sensible nor agreeable; his society was irksome, and his attachment to her must be imaginary. But still he would be her husband.—Without thinking highly either of men or of matrimony, marriage had always been her object; it was the only honourable provision for well-educated young women of small fortune, and however uncertain of giving happiness, must be their pleasantest preservative from want. This preservative she had now obtained; and at the age of twenty-seven, without having ever been handsome, she felt all the good luck of it. The least agreeable circumstance in the business, was the surprise it must occasion to Elizabeth Bennet, whose friendship she valued beyond that of any other person. Elizabeth would wonder, and probably would blame her; and though her resolution was not to be shaken, her feelings must be hurt by such disapprobation. She resolved to give her the information herself, and therefore charged Mr. Collins when he returned to Longbourn to dinner, to drop no hint of what had passed before any of the family. A promise of secrecy was of course very dutifully given, but it could not be kept without difficulty; for the curiosity excited by his long absence, burst forth in such very direct questions on his return, as required some ingenuity to evade, and he was at the same time exercising great self-denial, for he was longing to publish his prosperous love.

As he was to begin his journey too early on the morrow to see any of the family, the ceremony of leave-taking was performed when the ladies moved for the night; and Mrs. Bennet with great politeness and cordiality said how happy they should be to see him at Longbourn again, whenever his other engagements might allow him to visit them.

"My dear Madam," he replied, "this invitation is particularly gratifying, because it is what I have been hoping to receive; and you may be very certain that I shall avail myself of it as soon as possible."

They were all astonished; and Mr. Bennet, who could by no means wish for so speedy a return, immediately said,

"But is there not danger of Lady Catherine's disapprobation here, my good sir?—You had better neglect your relations, than run the risk of offending your patroness."

"My dear sir," replied Mr. Collins, "I am particularly obliged to you for this friendly caution, and you may depend upon my not taking so material a step without her ladyship's concurrence."

"You cannot be too much on your guard. Risk any thing rather than her displeasure; and if you find it likely to be raised by your coming to us again, which I should think exceedingly probable, stay quietly at home, and be satisfied that *we* shall take no offence."

"Believe me, my dear sir, my gratitude is warmly excited by such affectionate attention; and depend upon it, you will speedily receive from me a letter of thanks for this, as well as for every other mark of your regard during my stay in Hertfordshire. As for my fair cousins, though my absence may not be long enough to render it necessary, I shall now take the liberty of wishing them health and happiness, not excepting my cousin Elizabeth."

With proper civilities the ladies then withdrew; all of them equally surprised to find that he meditated a quick return. Mrs. Bennet wished to understand by it that he thought of paying his addresses to one of her younger girls, and Mary might have been prevailed on to accept him. She rated his abilities much higher than any of the others; there was a solidity in his reflections which often struck her, and though by no means so clever as herself, she thought that if encouraged to read and improve himself by such an example as her's, he might become a very agreeable companion. But on the following morning, every hope of this kind was done away. Miss Lucas called soon after breakfast, and in a private conference with Elizabeth related the event of the day before.

The possibility of Mr. Collins's fancying himself in love with her friend had once occurred to Elizabeth within the last day or two; but that Charlotte could encourage him, seemed almost as far from possibility as that she could encourage him herself, and her astonishment was consequently so great as to overcome at first the bounds of decorum, and she could not help crying out,

"Engaged to Mr. Collins! my dear Charlotte,—impossible!"

The steady countenance which Miss Lucas had commanded in telling her story, gave way to a momentary confusion here on receiving so direct a reproach; though, as it was no more than she expected, she soon regained her composure, and calmly replied,

"Why should you be surprised, my dear Eliza?—Do you think it incredible that Mr. Collins should be able to procure any woman's good opinion, because he was not so happy as to succeed with you?"

But Elizabeth had now recollected herself, and making a strong effort for it, was able to assure her with tolerable firmness that the prospect of their relationship was highly grateful to her, and that she wished her all imaginable happiness.

"I see what you are feeling," replied Charlotte,—"you must be surprised, very much surprised,—so lately as Mr. Collins was wishing to marry you. But when you have had time to think it all over, I hope you will be satisfied with what I have done. I am not romantic you know. I never was. I ask only a comfortable home; and considering Mr. Collins's character, connections, and situation in life, I am convinced that my chance of happiness with him is as fair, as most people can boast on entering the marriage state."

Elizabeth quietly answered "Undoubtedly;"—and after an awkward pause, they returned to the rest of the family. Charlotte did not stay much longer, and Elizabeth was then left to reflect on what she had heard. It was a long time before she became at all reconciled to the idea of so unsuitable a match. The strangeness of Mr. Collins's making two offers of marriage within three days, was nothing in comparison of his being now accepted. She had always felt that Charlotte's opinion of matrimony was not exactly like her own, but she could not have supposed it possible that when called into action, she would have sacrificed every better feeling to worldly advantage. Charlotte the wife of Mr. Collins, was a most humiliating picture!—And to the pang of a friend disgracing herself and sunk in her esteem, was added the distressing conviction that it was impossible for that friend to be tolerably happy in the lot she had chosen.

Chapter XXIII

Elizabeth was sitting with her mother and sisters, reflecting on what she had heard, and doubting whether she were authorised to mention it, when Sir William Lucas himself appeared, sent by his daughter to announce her engagement to the family. With many compliments to them, and much self-gratulation on the prospect of a connection between the houses, he unfolded the matter,—to an audience not merely wondering, but incredulous; for Mrs. Bennet, with more perseverance than politeness, protested he must be entirely mistaken, and Lydia, always unguarded and often uncivil, boisterously exclaimed,

"Good Lord! Sir William, how can you tell such a story?—Do not you know that Mr. Collins wants to marry Lizzy?"

Nothing less than the complaisance of a courtier could have borne without anger such treatment; but Sir William's good breeding carried him through it all; and though he begged leave to be positive as to the truth of his information, he listened to all their impertinence with the most forbearing courtesy.

Elizabeth, feeling it incumbent on her to relieve him from so unpleasant a situation, now put herself forward to confirm his account, by mentioning her prior knowledge of it from Charlotte herself; and endeavoured to put a stop to the exclamations of her mother and sisters, by the earnestness of her congratulations to Sir William, in which she was readily joined by Jane, and by making a variety of remarks on the happiness that might be expected from the match, the excellent character of Mr. Collins, and the convenient distance of Hunsford from London.

Mrs. Bennet was in fact too much overpowered to say a great deal while Sir William remained; but no sooner had he left them than her feelings found a rapid vent. In the first place, she persisted in disbelieving the whole of the matter; secondly, she was very sure that Mr. Collins had been taken in; thirdly, she trusted that they would never be happy together; and fourthly, that the match might be broken off. Two inferences, however, were plainly deduced from the whole; one, that Elizabeth was the real cause of all the mischief; and the other, that she herself had been barbarously used by them all; and on these two points she principally dwelt during the rest of the day. Nothing could console and nothing appease her.—Nor did that day wear out her resentment. A week elasped before she could see Elizabeth without scolding her, a month passed away before she could speak to Sir William or Lady Lucas without being rude, and many months were gone before she could at all forgive their daughter.

Mr. Bennet's emotions were much more tranquil on the occasion, and such as he did experience he pronounced to be of a most agreeable sort; for it gratified him, he said, to discover that Charlotte Lucas, whom he had been used to think tolerably sensible, was as foolish as his wife, and more foolish than his daughter!

Jane confessed herself a little surprised at the match; but she said less of her astonishemnt than of her earnest desire for their happiness; nor could Elizabeth persuade her to consider it as improbable. Kitty and Lydia were far from envying Miss Lucas, for Mr. Collins was only a clergyman; and it affected them in no other way than as a piece of news to spread at Meryton.

Lady Lucas could not be insensible of triumph on being able to retort on Mrs. Bennet the comfort of having a daughter well married; and she called at Longbourn rather oftener than usual to say how happy she was, though Mrs. Bennet's sour looks and ill-natured remarks might have been enough to drive happiness away.

Between Elizabeth and Charlotte there was a restraint which kept them mutually silent on the subject; and Elizabeth felt persuaded that no real confidence could ever subsist between them again. Her disappointment in Charlotte made her turn with fonder regard to her sister, of whose rectitude and delicacy she was sure her opinion could never be shaken, and for whose happiness she grew daily more anxious, as Bingley had now been gone a week, and nothing was heard of his return.

Jane had sent Caroline an early answer to her letter, and was counting the days till she might reasonably hope to hear again. The promised letter of thanks from Mr. Collins arrived on Tuesday, addressed to their father, and written with all the solemnity of gratitude which a twelvemonth's abode in the family might have prompted. After discharging his conscience on that head, he proceeded to inform them, with many rapturous expressions, of his happiness in having obtained the affection of their amiable neighbour, Miss Lucas, and then explained that it was merely with the view of enjoying her society that he had been so ready to close with their kind wish of seeing him again at Longbourn, whither he hoped to be able to return on Monday fortnight; for Lady Catherine, he added, so heartily approved his marriage, that she wished it to take place as soon as possible, which he trusted would be an unanswerable argument with his amiable Charlotte to name an early day for making him the happiest of men.

Mr. Collins's return into Hertfordshire was no longer a matter of pleasure to Mrs. Bennet. On the contrary she was as much disposed to complain of it as her husband.—It was very strange that he should come to Longbourn instead of to Lucas Lodge; it was also very inconvenient and exceedingly troublesome.—She hated having visitors in the house while her health was so indifferent, and lovers were of all people the most disagreeable. Such were the gentle murmurs of Mrs. Bennet, and they gave way only to the greater distress of Mr. Bingley's continued absence.

Neither Jane nor Elizabeth were comfortable on this subject. Day after day passed away without bringing any other tidings of him than the report which shortly prevailed in Meryton of his coming no more to Netherfield the whole winter; a report which highly incensed Mrs. Bennet, and which she never failed to contradict as a most scandalous falsehood.

Even Elizabeth began to fear—not that Bingley was indifferent—but that his sisters would be successful in keeping him away. Unwilling as she was to admit an idea so destructive of Jane's happiness, and so dishonourable to the stability of her lover, she could not prevent its frequently recurring. The united efforts of his two unfeeling sisters and of his overpowering friend, assisted by the attractions of Miss Darcy and the amusements of London, might be too much, she feared, for the strength of his attachment.

As for Jane, *her* anxiety under this suspence was, of course, more painful than Elizabeth's; but whatever she felt she was desirous of concealing, and between herself and Elizabeth, therefore, the subject was never alluded to. But as no such delicacy restrained her mother, an hour seldom passed in which she did not talk of Bingley, express her impatience for his arrival, or even require Jane to confess that if he did not come back, she should think herself very ill used. It needed all Jane's steady mildness to bear these attacks with tolerable tranquillity.

Mr. Collins returned most punctually on the Monday fortnight, but his reception at Longbourn was not quite so gracious as it had been on his first introduction. He was too happy, however, to need much attention; and luckily for the others, the business of love-making relieved them from a great deal of his company. The chief of every day was spent by him at Lucas Lodge, and he sometimes returned to Longbourn only in time to make an apology for his absence before the family went to bed.

Mrs. Bennet was really in a most pitiable state. The very mention of any thing concerning the match threw her into an agony of ill humour, and wherever she went she was sure of hearing it talked of. The sight of Miss Lucas was odious to her. As her successor in that house, she regarded her with jealous abhorrence. Whenever Charlotte came to see them she concluded her to be anticipating the hour of possession; and whenever she spoke in a low voice to Mr. Collins, was convinced that they were talking of the Longbourn estate, and resolving to turn herself and her daughters out of the house, as soon as Mr. Bennet were dead. She complained bitterly of all this to her husband.

"Indeed, Mr. Bennet," said she, "it is very hard to think that Charlotte Lucas should ever be mistress of this house, that *I* should be forced to make way for *her*, and live to see her take my place in it!"

"My dear, do not give way to such gloomy thoughts. Let us hope for better things. Let us flatter ourselves that *I* may be the survivor."

This was not very consoling to Mrs. Bennet, and, therefore,

instead of making any answer, she went on as before,

"I cannot bear to think that they should have all this estate. If it was not for the entail I should not mind it."

"What should not you mind?"

"I should not mind any thing at all."

"Let us be thankful that you are preserved from a state of such insensibility."

"I never can be thankful, Mr. Bennet, for any thing about the entail. How any one could have the conscience to entail away an estate from one's own daughters I cannot understand; and all for the sake of Mr. Collins too!—Why should *he* have it more than anybody else?"

"I leave it to yourself to determine," said Mr. Bennet.

Volume II

Chapter I

Miss Bingley's letter arrived, and put an end to doubt. The very first sentence conveyed the assurance of their being all settled in London for the winter, and concluded with her brother's regret at not having had time to pay his respects to his friends in Hertfordshire before he left the country.

Hope was over, entirely over; and when Jane could attend to the rest of the letter, she found little, except the professed affection of the writer, that could give her any comfort. Miss Darcy's praise occupied the chief of it. Her many attractions were again dwelt on, and Caroline boasted joyfully of their increasing intimacy, and ventured to predict the accomplishment of the wishes which had been unfolded in her former letter. She wrote also with great pleasure of her brother's being an inmate of Mr. Darcy's house, and mentioned with raptures, some plans of the latter with regard to new furniture.

Elizabeth, to whom Jane very soon communicated the chief of all this, heard it in silent indignation. Her heart was divided between concern for her sister, and resentment against all the others. To Caroline's assertion of her brother's being partial to Miss Darcy she paid no credit. That he was really fond of Jane, she doubted no more than she had ever done; and much as she had always been disposed to like him, she could not think without anger, hardly without contempt, on that easiness of temper, that want of proper resolution which now made him the slave of his designing friends, and led him to sacrifice his own happiness to the caprice of their inclinations. Had his own happiness, however, been the only sacrifice, he might have been allowed to sport with it in what ever manner he thought best; but her sister's was involved in it, as she thought he must be sensible himself. It was a subject, in short, on which reflection would be long indulged, and must be unavailing. She could think of nothing else, and yet whether Bingley's regard had really died away, or were suppressed by his friends' interference; whether he had been aware of Jane's attachment, or whether it had escaped his observation; whichever were the case, though her opinion of him must be materially affected by the difference, her sister's situation remained the same, her peace equally wounded.

A day or two passed before Jane had courage to speak of her feelings to Elizabeth; but at last on Mrs. Bennet's leaving them together, after a longer irritation than usual about Netherfield and its master, she could not help saying,

"Oh! that my dear mother had more command over herself; she can have no idea of the pain she gives me by her continual reflections on him. But I will not repine. It cannot last long. He will be forgot, and we shall all be as we were before."

Elizabeth looked at her sister with incredulous solicitude, but said nothing.

"You doubt me," cried Jane, slightly colouring; "indeed you have no reason. He may live in my memory as the most amiable man of my acquaintance, but that is all. I have nothing either to hope or fear, and nothing to reproach him with. Thank God! I have not *that* pain. A little time therefore.—I shall certainly try to get the better."

With a stronger voice she soon added, "I have this comfort immediately, that it has not been more than an error of fancy on my side, and that it has done no harm to any one but myself."

"My dear Jane!" exclaimed Elizabeth, "you are too good. Your sweetness and disinterestedness are really angelic; I do not know what to say to you. I feel as if I had never done you justice, or loved you as you deserve."

Miss Bennet eagerly disclaimed all extraordinary merit, and threw back the praise on her sister's warm affection.

"Nay," said Elizabeth, "this is not fair. *You* wish to think all the world respectable, and are hurt if I speak ill of any body. I only want to think *you* perfect, and you set yourself against it. Do not be afraid of my running into any excess, of my encroaching on your privilege of universal good will. You need not. There are few people whom I really love, and still fewer of whom I think well. The more I see of the world, the more am I dissatisfied with it; and every day confirms my belief of the inconsistency of all human characters, and of the little dependence that can be placed on the appearance of either merit or sense. I have met with two instances lately; one I will not mention; the other is Charlotte's marriage. It is unaccountable! in every view it is unaccountable!"

"My dear Lizzy, do not give way to such feelings as these. They will ruin your happiness. You do not make allowance enough for difference of situation and temper. Consider Mr. Collins's respectability, and Charlotte's prudent, steady character. Remember that she is one of a large family; that as to fortune, it is a most eligible match; and be ready to believe, for every body's sake, that she may feel something like regard and esteem for our cousin."

"To oblige you, I would try to believe almost any thing, but no one else could be benefited by such a belief as this; for were I persuaded that Charlotte had any regard for him, I should only think worse of her understanding, than I now do of her heart. My dear Jane, Mr. Collins is a conceited, pompous, narrow-minded, silly man; you know he is, as well as I do; and you must feel, as well as I do, that the woman who marries him, cannot have a proper way of thinking. You shall not defend her, though it is Charlotte Lucas. You shall not, for the sake of one individual, change the meaning of principle and integrity, nor endeavour to persuade yourself or me, that selfishness is prudence, and insensibility of danger, security for happiness."

"I must think your language too strong in speaking of both," replied Jane, "and I hope you will be convinced of it, by seeing them happy together. But enough of this. You alluded to something else. You mentioned *two* instances. I cannot misunderstand you, but I intreat you, dear Lizzy, not to pain me by thinking *that person* to blame, and saying your opinion of him is sunk. We must not be so ready to fancy ourselves intentionally injured. We must not expect a lively young man to be always so guarded and circumspect. It is very often nothing but our own vanity that deceives us. Women fancy admiration means more than it does."

"And men take care that they should."

"If it is designedly done, they cannot be justified; but I have no idea of there being so much design in the world as some persons imagine."

"I am far from attributing any part of Mr. Bingley's conduct to design," said Elizabeth; "but without scheming to do wrong, or to make others unhappy, there may be error, and there may be misery. Thoughtlessness, want of attention to other people's feelings, and want of resolution, will do the business."

"And do you impute it to either of those?"

"Yes; to the last. But if I go on, I shall displease you by saying what I think of persons you esteem. Stop me whilst you can."

"You persist, then, in supposing his sisters influence him."

"Yes, in conjuction with his friend."

"I cannot believe it. Why should they try to influence him? They can only wish his happiness, and if he is attached to me, no other woman can secure it."

"Your first position is false. They may wish many things besides his happiness; they may wish his increase of wealth and consequence; they may wish him to marry a girl who has all the importance of money, great connections, and pride."

"Beyond a doubt, they *do* wish him to chuse Miss Darcy," replied Jane; "but this may be from better feelings than you are supposing. They have known her much longer than they have known me; no wonder if they love her better. But, whatever may be their own wishes, it is very unlikely they should have opposed their brother's. What sister would think herself at liberty to do it, unless there were something very objectionable? If they believed him attached to me, they would not try to part us; if he were so, they could not succeed. By supposing such an affection, you make every body acting unnaturally and wrong, and me most unhappy. Do not distress me by the idea. I am not ashamed of having been mistaken—or, at least, it is slight, it is nothing in comparison of what I should feel in thinking ill of him or his sisters. Let me take it in the best light, in the light in which it may be understood."

Elizabeth could not oppose such a wish; and from this time Mr. Bingley's name was scarcely ever mentioned between them.

Mrs. Bennet still continued to wonder and repine at his returning no more, and though a day seldom passed in which Elizabeth did not account for it clearly, there seemed little chance of her ever considering it with less perplexity. Her daughter endeavoured to convince her of what she did not believe herself, that his attentions to Jane had been merely the effect of a common and transient liking, which ceased when he saw her no more; but though the probability of the statement was admitted at the time, she had the same story to repeat every day. Mrs. Bennet's best comfort was, that Mr. Bingley must be down again in the summer.

Mr. Bennet treated the matter differently. "So, Lizzy," said he one day, "your sister is crossed in love I find. I congratulate her. Next to being married, a girl likes to be crossed in love a little now and then. It is something to think of, and gives her a sort of distinction among her companions. When is your turn to come? You will hardly bear to be long outdone by Jane. Now is your time. Here are officers enough at Meryton to disappoint all the young ladies in the country. Let Wickham be *your* man. He is a pleasant fellow, and would jilt you creditably."

"Thank you, Sir, but a less agreeable man would satisfy me. We must not all expect Jane's good fortune."

"True," said Mr. Bennet, "but it is a comfort to think that, whatever of that kind may befal you, you have an affectionate mother who will always make the most of it."

Mr. Wickham's society was of material service in dispelling the gloom, which the late perverse occurrences had thrown on many of the Longbourn family. They saw him often, and to his other recommendations was now added that of general unreserve. The whole of what Elizabeth had already heard, his claims on Mr. Darcy, and all that he had suffered from him, was now openly acknowledged and publicly canvassed; and every body was pleased to think how much they had always disliked Mr. Darcy before they had known any thing of the matter.

Miss Bennet was the only creature who could suppose there might be any extenuating circumstances in the case, unknown to the society of Hertfordshire; her mild and steady candour always pleaded for allowances, and urged the possibility of mistakes—but by everybody else Mr. Darcy was condemned as the worst of men.

Chapter II

After a week spent in professions of love and schemes of felicity, Mr. Collins was called from his amiable Charlotte by the arrival of Saturday. The pain of separation, however, might be alleviated on his side, by preparations for the reception of his bride, as he had reason to hope, that shortly after his next return into Hertfordshire, the day would be fixed that was to make him the happiest of men. He took leave of his relations at Longbourn with as much solemnity as before; wished his fair cousins health and happiness again, and promised their father another letter of thanks.

On the following Monday, Mrs. Bennet had the pleasure of receiving her brother and his wife, who came as usual to spend the Christmas at Longbourn. Mr. Gardiner was a sensible, gentlemanlike man, greatly superior to his sister as well by nature as education. The Netherfield ladies would have had difficulty in believing that a man who lived by trade, and within view of his own warehouses, could have been so well bred and agreeable. Mrs. Gardiner, who was several years younger than Mrs. Bennet and Mrs. Philips, was an amiable, intelligent, elegant woman, and a great favourite with all her Longbourn nieces. Between the two eldest and herself especially, there subsisted a very particular regard. They had frequently been staying with her in town.

The first part of Mrs. Gardiner's business on her arrival, was to distribute her presents and describe the newest fashions. When this was done, she had a less active part to play. It became her turn to listen. Mrs. Bennet had many grievances to relate, and much to complain of. They had all been very ill-used since she last saw her sister. Two of her girls had been on the point of marriage, and after all there was nothing in it.

"I do not blame Jane," she continued, "for Jane would have got Mr. Bingley, if she could. But, Lizzy! Oh, sister! it is very hard to think that she might have been Mr. Collins's wife by this time, had not it been for her own perverseness. He made her an offer in this very room, and she refused him. The consequence of it is, that Lady Lucas will have a daughter married before I have, and that Longbourn estate is just as much entailed as ever. The Lucases are very artful people indeed, sister. They are all for what they can get. I am sorry to say it of them, but so it is. It makes me very nervous and poorly, to be thwarted so in my own family, and to have neighbours who think of themselves before anybody else. However, your coming just at this time is the greatest of comforts, and I am very glad to hear what you tell us, of long sleeves."

Mrs. Gardiner, to whom the chief of this news had been given before, in the course of Jane and Elizabeth's correspondence with her, made her sister [6] a slight answer, and in compassion to her nieces turned the conversation.

When alone with Elizabeth afterwards, she spoke more on the subject. "It seems likely to have been a desirable match for Jane," said she. "I am sorry it went off. But these things happen so often! A young man, such as you describe Mr. Bingley, so easily falls in love with a pretty girl for a few weeks, and when accident separates them, so easily forgets her, that these sort of inconstancies are very frequent."

"An excellent consolation in its way," said Elizabeth, "but it will not do for *us*. We do not suffer by *accident*. It does not often happen that the interference of friends will persuade a young man of independent fortune to think no more of a girl, whom he was violently in love with only a few days before."

"But the expression of 'violently in love' is so hackneyed, so doubtful, so indefinite, that it gives me very little idea. It is as

6. Sister-in-law. See also p. 207, where Mr. Gardiner addresses Mr. Bennet as "My Dear Brother."

often applied to feelings which arise from an half-hour's acquaintance, as to a real, strong attachment. Pray, how *violent was* Mr. Bingley's love?"

"I never saw a more promising inclination. He was growing quite inattentive to other people, and wholly engrossed by her. Every time they met, it was more decided and remarkable. At his own ball he offended two or three young ladies, by not asking them to dance, and I spoke to him twice myself, without receiving an answer. Could there be finer symptoms? Is not general incivility the very essence of love?"

"Oh, yes!—of that kind of love which I suppose him to have felt. Poor Jane! I am sorry for her, because, with her disposition, she may not get over it immediately. It had better have happened to *you*, Lizzy; you would have laughed yourself out of it sooner. But do you think she would be prevailed on to go back with us? Change of scene might be of service—and perhaps a little relief from home, may be as useful as anything."

Elizabeth was exceedingly pleased with this proposal, and felt persuaded of her sister's ready acquiescence.

"I hope," added Mrs. Gardiner, "that no consideration with regard to this young man will influence her. We live in so different a part of town, all our connections are so different, and, as you well know, we go out so little, that it is very improbable they should meet at all, unless he really comes to see her."

"And *that* is quite impossible; for he is now in the custody of his friend, and Mr. Darcy would no more suffer him to call on Jane in such a part of London! My dear aunt, how could you think of it? Mr. Darcy may perhaps have *heard* of such a place as Gracechurch Street, but he would hardly think a month's ablution enough to cleanse him from its impurities, were he once to enter it; and depend upon it, Mr. Bingley never stirs without him."

"So much the better. I hope they will not meet at all. But does not Jane correspond with the sister? *She* will not be able to help calling."

"She will drop the acquaintance entirely."

But in spite of the certainty in which Elizabeth affected to place this point, as well as the still more interesting one of Bingley's being withheld from seeing Jane, she felt a solicitude on the subject which convinced her, on examination, that she did not consider it entirely hopeless. It was possible, and sometimes she thought it probable, that his affection might be re-animated, and the influence of his friends successfully combated by the more natural influence of Jane's attractions.

Miss Bennet accepted her aunt's invitation with pleasure;

and the Bingleys were no otherwise in her thoughts at the time, than as she hoped that, by Caroline's not living in the same house with her brother, she might occasionally spend a morning with her, without any danger of seeing him.

The Gardiners staid a week at Longbourn; and what with the Philipses, the Lucases, and the officers, there was not a day without its engagement. Mrs. Bennet had so carefully provided for the entertainment of her brother and sister, that they did not once sit down to a family dinner. When the engagement was for home, some of the officers always made part of it, of which officers Mr. Wickham was sure to be one; and on these occasions, Mrs. Gardiner, rendered suspicious by Elizabeth's warm commendation of him, narrowly observed them both. Without supposing them, from what she saw, to be very seriously in love, their preference of each other was plain enough to make her a little uneasy; and she resolved to speak to Elizabeth on the subject before she left Herfordshire, and represent to her the imprudence of encouraging such an attachment.

To Mrs. Gardiner, Wickham had one means of affording pleasure, unconnected with his general powers. About ten or a dozen years ago, before her marriage, she had spent a considerable time in that very part of Derbyshire, to which he belonged. They had, therefore, many acquaintance in common; and, though Wickham had been little there since the death of Darcy's father, five years before, it was yet in his power to give her fresher intelligence of her former friends, than she had been in the way of procuring.

Mrs. Gardiner had seen Pemberley, and known the late Mr. Darcy by character perfectly well. Here consequently was an inexhaustible subject of discourse. In comparing her recollection of Pemberley, with the minute description which Wickham could give, and in bestowing her tribute of praise on the character of its late possessor, she was delighting both him and herself. On being made acquainted with the present Mr. Darcy's treatment of him, she tried to remember something of that gentleman's reputed disposition when quite a lad, which might agree with it, and was confident at last, that she recollected having heard Mr. Fitzwilliam Darcy formerly spoken of as a very proud, ill-natured boy.

Chapter III

Mrs. Gardiner's caution to Elizabeth was punctually and kindly given on the first favourable opportunity of speaking to her alone; after honestly telling her what she thought, she thus went on:

"You are too sensible a girl, Lizzy, to fall in love merely because you are warned against it; and, therefore, I am not afraid of speaking openly. Seriously, I would have you be on your guard. Do not involve yourself, or endeavour to involve him in an affection which the want of fortune would make so very imprudent. I have nothing to say against *him;* he is a most interesting young man; and if he had the fortune he ought to have, I should think you could not do better. But as it is—you must not let your fancy run away with you. You have sense, and we all expect you to use it. Your father would depend on *your* resolution and good conduct, I am sure. You must not disappoint your father."

"My dear aunt, this is being serious indeed."

"Yes, and I hope to engage you to be serious likewise."

"Well, then, you need not be under any alarm. I will take care of myself, and of Mr. Wickham too. He shall not be in love with me, if I can prevent it."

"Elizabeth, you are not serious now."

"I beg your pardon. I will try again. At present I am not in love with Mr. Wickham; no, I certainly am not. But he is, beyond all comparison, the most agreeable man I ever saw—and if he becomes really attached to me—I believe it will be better that he should not. I see the imprudence of it.—Oh! *that* abominable Mr. Darcy!—My father's opinion of me does me the greatest honor; and I should be miserable to forfeit it. My father, however, is partial to Mr. Wickham. In short, my dear aunt, I should be very sorry to be the means of making any of you unhappy; but since we see every day that where there is affection, young people are seldom withheld by immediate want of fortune, from entering into engagements with each other, how can I promise to be wiser than so many of my fellow creatures if I am tempted, or how am I even to know that it would be wisdom to resist? All that I can promise you, therefore, is not to be in a hurry. I will not be in a hurry to believe myself his first object. When I am in company with him, I will not be wishing. In short, I will do my best."

"Perhaps it will be as well, if you discourage his coming here so very often. At least, you should not *remind* your Mother of inviting him."

"As I did the other day," said Elizabeth, with a conscious smile; "very true, it will be wise in me to refrain from *that*. But do not imagine that he is always here so often. It is on your account that he has been so frequently invited this week. You know my mother's ideas as to the necessity of constant company for her friends. But really, and upon my honour, I will try to do what I think to be wisest; and now, I hope you are satisfied."

Her aunt assured her that she was; and Elizabeth having thanked her for the kindness of her hints, they parted; a wonderful instance of advice being given on such a point, without being resented.

Mr. Collins returned into Hertfordshire soon after it had been quitted by the Gardiners and Jane; but as he took up his abode with the Lucases, his arrival was no great inconvenience to Mrs. Bennet. His marriage was now fast approaching, and she was at length so far resigned as to think it inevitable, and even repeatedly to say in an ill-natured tone that she *"wished* they might be happy." Thursday was to be the wedding day, and on Wednesday Miss Lucas paid her farewell visit; and when she rose to take leave, Elizabeth, ashamed of her mother's ungracious and reluctant good wishes, and sincerely affected herself, accompanied her out of the room. As they went down stairs together, Charlotte said,

"I shall depend on hearing from you very often, Eliza."

"*That* you certainly shall."

"And I have another favour to ask. Will you come and see me?"

"We shall often meet, I hope, in Hertfordshire."

"I am not likely to leave Kent for some time. Promise me, therefore, to come to Hunsford."

Elizabeth could not refuse, though she foresaw little pleasure in the visit.

"My father and Maria are to come to me in March," added Charlotte, "and I hope you will consent to be of the party. Indeed, Eliza, you will be as welcome to me as either of them."

The wedding took place; the bride and bridegroom set off for Kent from the church door, and every body had as much to say or to hear on the subject as usual. Elizabeth soon heard from her friend; and their correspondence was as regular and frequent as it had ever been; that it should be equally unreserved was impossible. Elizabeth could never address her without feeling that all the comfort of intimacy was over, and, though determined not to slacken as a correspondent, it was for the sake of what had been, rather than what was. Charlotte's first letters were received with a good deal of eagerness; there could not but be curiosity to know how she would speak of her new home, how she would like Lady Catherine, and how happy she would dare pronounce herself to be; though, when the letters were read, Elizabeth felt that Charlotte expressed herself on every point exactly as she might have foreseen. She wrote cheerfully, seemed surrounded with comforts, and mentioned nothing which she could not praise. The house, furniture, neighbourhood, and roads, were all to her taste, and Lady Catherine's behaviour was most friendly and obliging. It was Mr. Collins's picture of Hunsford and Rosings rationally softened; and Elizabeth perceived that she must wait for her own visit there, to know the rest.

Jane had already written a few lines to her sister to announce their safe arrival in London; and when she wrote again, Elizabeth hoped it would be in her power to say something of the Bingleys.

Her impatience for this second letter was as well rewarded as impatience generally is. Jane had been a week in town, without either seeing or hearing from Caroline. She accounted for it, however, by supposing that her last letter to her friend from Longbourn, had by some accident been lost.

"My aunt," she continued, "is going to-morrow into that part of the town, and I shall take the opportunity of calling in Grosvenor-street."

She wrote again when the visit was paid, and she had seen Miss Bingley. "I did not think Caroline in spirits," were her words, "but she was very glad to see me, and reproached me for giving her no notice of my coming to London. I was right, therefore; my last letter had never reached her. I enquired after their brother, of course. He was well, but so much engaged with Mr. Darcy, that they scarcely ever saw him. I found that Miss Darcy was expected to dinner. I wish I could see her. My visit was not long, as Caroline and Mrs. Hurst were going out. I dare say I shall soon see them here."

Elizabeth shook her head over this letter. It convinced her, that accident only could discover to Mr. Bingley her sister's being in town.

Four weeks passed away, and Jane saw nothing of him. She endeavoured to persuade herself that she did not regret it; but she could no longer be blind to Miss Bingley's inattention. After waiting at home every morning for a fortnight, and inventing every evening a fresh excuse for her, the visitor did at last appear; but the shortness of her stay, and yet more, the alteration of her manner, would allow Jane to deceive herself no longer. The letter which she wrote on this occasion to her sister, will prove what she felt.

"My dearest Lizzy will, I am sure, be incapable of triumphing in her better judgment, at my expence, when I confess myself to have been entirely decived in Miss Bingley's regard for me. But, my dear sister, though the event has proved you right, do not think me obstinate if I still assert, that, considering what her behaviour was, my confidence was as natural as your suspicion. I do not at all comprehend her reason for wishing to be intimate with me, but if the same circumstances were to happen again,

I am sure I should be deceived again. Caroline did not return my visit till yesterday; and not a note, not a line, did I receive in the mean time. When she did come, it was very evident that she had no pleasure in it; she made a slight, formal, apology, for not calling before, said not a word of wishing to see me again, and was in every respect so altered a creature, that when she went away, I was perfectly resolved to continue the acquaintance no longer. I pity, though I cannot help blaming her. She was very wrong in singling me out as she did; I can safely say, that every advance to intimacy began on her side. But I pity her, because she must feel that she has been acting wrong, and because I am very sure that anxiety for her brother is the cause of it. I need not explain myself farther; and though *we* know this anxiety to be quite needless, yet if she feels it, it will easily account for her behaviour to me; and so deservedly dear as he is to his sister, whatever anxiety she may feel on his behalf, is natural and amiable. I cannot but wonder, however, at her having any such fears now, because, if he had at all cared about me, we must have met long, long ago. He knows of my being in town, I am certain, from something she said herself; and yet it should seem by her manner of talking, as if she wanted to persuade herself that he is really partial to Miss Darcy. I cannot understand it. If I were not afraid of judging harshly, I should be almost tempted to say, that there is a strong appearance of duplicity in all this. But I will endeavour to banish every painful thought, and think only of what will make me happy, your affection, and the invariable kindness of my dear uncle and aunt. Let me hear from you very soon. Miss Bingley said something of his never returning to Netherfield again, of giving up the house, but not with any certainty. We had better not mention it. I am extremely glad that you have such pleasant accounts from our friends at Hunsford. Pray go to see them, with Sir William and Maria. I am sure you will be very comfortable there.

"Your's, &c."

This letter gave Elizabeth some pain; but her spirits returned as she considered that Jane would no longer be duped, by the sister at least. All expectation from the brother was now absolutely over. She would not even wish for any renewal of his attentions. His character sunk on every review of it; and as a punishment for him, as well as a possible advantage to Jane, she seriously hoped he might really soon marry Mr. Darcy's sister, as, by Wickham's account, she would make him abundantly regret what he had thrown away.

Mrs. Gardiner about this time reminded Elizabeth of her

promise concerning that gentleman, and required information; and Elizabeth had such to send as might rather give contentment to her aunt than to herself. His apparent partiality had subsided, his attentions were over, he was the admirer of some one else. Elizabeth was watchful enough to see it all, but she could see it and write of it without material pain. Her heart had been but slightly touched, and her vanity was satisfied with believing that *she* would have been his only choice, had fortune permitted it. The sudden acquisition of ten thousand pounds was the most remarkable charm of the young lady, to whom he was now rendering himself agreeable; but Elizabeth, less clear-sighted perhaps in his case than in Charlotte's, did not quarrel with him for his wish of independence. Nothing, on the contrary, could be more natural; and while able to suppose that it cost him a few struggles to relinquish her, she was ready to allow it a wise and desirable measure for both, and could very sincerely wish him happy.

All this was acknowledged to Mrs. Gardiner; and after relating the circumstances, she thus went on:—"I am now convinced, my dear aunt, that I have never been much in love; for had I really experienced that pure and elevating passion, I should at present detest his very name, and wish him all manner of evil. But my feelings are not only cordial towards *him*; they are even impartial towards Miss King. I cannot find out that I hate her at all, or that I am in the least unwilling to think her a very good sort of girl. There can be no love in all this. My watchfulness has been effectual; and though I should certainly be a more interesting object to all my acquaintance, were I distractedly in love with him, I cannot say that I regret my comparative insignificance. Importance may sometimes be purchased too dearly. Kitty and Lydia take his defection much more to heart than I do. They are young in the ways of the world, and not yet open to the mortifying conviction that handsome young men must have something to live on, as well as the plain."

Chapter IV

With no greater events than these in the Longbourn family, and otherwise diversified by little beyond the walks to Meryton, sometimes dirty and sometimes cold, did January and February pass away. March was to take Elizabeth to Hunsford. She had not at first thought very seriously of going thither; but Charlotte, she soon found, was depending on the plan, and she gradually learned to consider it herself with greater pleasure as well as greater certainty. Absence had increased her desire of seeing Charlotte again, and weakened her disgust of Mr. Collins. There was novelty in the scheme, and as, with such a mother and such uncompanionable sisters, home could not be faultless, a little change was not unwelcome for its own sake. The journey would moreover give her a peep at Jane; and, in short, as the time drew near, she would have been very sorry for any delay. Every thing, however, went on smoothly, and was finally settled according to Charlotte's first sketch. She was to accompany Sir William and his second daughter. The improvement of spending a night in London was added in time, and the plan became perfect as plan could be.

The only pain was in leaving her father, who would certainly miss her, and who, when it came to the point, so little liked her going, that he told her to write to him, and almost promised to answer her letter.

The farewell between herself and Mr. Wickham was perfectly friendly; on his side even more. His present pursuit could not make him forget that Elizabeth had been the first to excite and to deserve his attention, the first to listen and to pity, the first to be admired; and in his manner of bidding her adieu, wishing her every enjoyment, reminding her of what she was to expect in Lady Catherine de Bourgh, and trusting their opinion of her— their opinion of every body—would always coincide, there was a solicitude, an interest which she felt must ever attach her to him with a most sincere regard; and she parted from him convinced, that whether married or single, he must always be her model of the amiable and pleasing.

Her fellow-travellers the next day, were not of a kind to make her think him less agreeable. Sir William Lucas, and his daughter Maria, a good humoured girl, but as empty-headed as himself, had nothing to say that could be worth hearing, and were listened to with about as much delight as the rattle of the chaise. Elizabeth loved absurdities, but she had known Sir William's too long. He could tell her nothing new of the wonders of his presentation and knighthood; and his civilities were worn out like his information.

It was a journey of only twenty-four miles, and they began it so early as to be in Gracechurch-street by noon. As they drove to Mr. Gardiner's door, Jane was at a drawing-room window watching their arrival; when they entered the passage she was there to welcome them, and Elizabeth, looking earnestly in her face, was pleased to see it healthful and lovely as ever. On the stairs were a troop of little boys and girls, whose eagerness for their cousin's appearance would not allow them to wait in the drawing-room, and whose shyness, as they had not seen her for a twelve-month, prevented their coming lower. All was joy and kindness.

The day passed most pleasantly away; the morning [7] in bustle and shopping, and the evening at one of the theatres.

Elizabeth then contrived to sit by her aunt. Their first subject was her sister; and she was more grieved than astonished to hear, in reply to her minute enquiries, that though Jane always struggled to support her spirits, there were periods of dejection. It was reasonable, however, to hope, that they would not continue long. Mrs. Gardiner gave her the particulars also of Miss Bingley's visit in Gracechurch-street, and repeated conversations occurring at different times between Jane and herself, which proved that the former had, from her heart, given up the acquaintance.

Mrs. Gardiner then rallied her niece on Wickham's desertion, and complimented her on bearing it so well.

"But, my dear Elizabeth," she added, "what sort of girl is Miss King? I should be sorry to think our friend mercenary."

"Pray, my dear aunt, what is the difference in matrimonial affairs, between the mercenary and the prudent motive? Where does discretion end, and avarice begin? Last Christmas you were afraid of his marrying me, because it would be imprudent; and now, because he is trying to get a girl with only ten thousand pounds, you want to find out that he is mercenary."

"If you will only tell me what sort of girl Miss King is, I shall know what to think."

"She is a very good kind of girl, I believe. I know no harm of her."

"But he paid her not the smallest attention, till her grandfather's death made her mistress of this fortune."

"No—why should he? If it was not allowable for him to gain *my* affections, because I had no money, what occasion could there be for making love to a girl whom he did not care about, and who was equally poor?"

"But there seems indelicacy in directing his attentions towards her, so soon after this event."

"A man in distressed circumstances has not time for all those elegant decorums which other people may observe. If *she* does not object to it, why should *we*?"

"*Her* not objecting, does not justify *him*. It only shews her being deficient in something herself—sense or feeling."

"Well," cried Elizabeth, "have it as you choose. He shall be mercenary, and *she* shall be foolish."

"No, Lizzy, that is what I do *not* choose. I should be sorry, you know, to think ill of a young man who has lived so long in

---

7. The interval between breakfast (customarily served around 10:00 A.M.) and dinner (served around 4:00 or 5:00 P.M.) was referred to as the morning. See R. W. Chapman's appendix, "Manners of the Age," in volume IV of the Oxford edition of the novels, 497–516.

Derbyshire." ·

"Oh! if that is all, I have a very poor opinion of young men who live in Derbyshire; and their intimate friends who live in Hertfordshire are not much better. I am sick of them all. Thank Heaven! I am going to-morrow where I shall find a man who has not one agreeable quality, who has neither manner nor sense to recommend him. Stupid men are the only ones worth knowing, after all."

"Take care, Lizzy; that speech savours strongly of disappointment."

Before they were separated by the conclusion of the play, she had the unexpected happiness of an invitation to accompany her uncle and aunt in a tour of pleasure which they proposed taking in the summer.

"We have not quite determined how far it shall carry us," said Mrs. Gardiner, "but perhaps to the Lakes." [8]

No scheme could have been more agreeable to Elizabeth, and her acceptance of the invitation was most ready and grateful. "My dear, dear aunt," she rapturously cried, "what delight! what felicity! You give me fresh life and vigour. Adieu to disappointment and spleen. What are men to rocks and mountains? Oh! what hours of transport we shall spend! And when we *do* return, it shall not be like other travellers, without being able to give one accurate idea of any thing. We *will* know where we have gone—we *will* recollect what we have seen. Lakes, mountains, and rivers, shall not be jumbled together in our imaginations; nor, when we attempt to describe any particular scene, will we begin quarrelling about its relative situation. Let *our* first effusions be less insupportable than those of the generality of travellers."

Chapter V

Every object in the next day's journey was new and interesting to Elizabeth; and her spirits were in a state for enjoyment; for she had seen her sister looking so well as to banish all fear for her health, and the prospect of her northern tour was a constant source of delight.

When they left the high road for the lane to Hunsford, every eye was in search of the Parsonage, and every turning expected to bring it in view. The paling of Rosings Park was their boundary on one side. Elizabeth smiled at the recollection of all that she had heard of its inhabitants.

At length the Parsonage was discernible. The garden sloping to the road, the house standing in it, the green pales and the

8. The Lake District in the north of England, above Derbyshire.

laurel hedge, every thing declared they were arriving. Mr. Collins and Charlotte appeared at the door, and the carriage stopped at the small gate, which led by a short gravel walk to the house, amidst the nods and smiles of the whole party. In a moment they were all out of the chaise, rejoicing at the sight of each other. Mrs. Collins welcomed her friend with the liveliest pleasure, and Elizabeth was more and more satisfied with coming, when she found herself so affectionately received. She saw instantly that her cousin's manners were not altered by his marriage; his formal civility was just what it had been, and he detained her some minutes at the gate to hear and satisfy his enquiries after all her family. They were then, with no other delay than his pointing out the neatness of the entrance, taken into the house; and as soon as they were in the parlour, he welcomed them a second time with ostentatious formality to his humble abode, and punctually repeated all his wife's offers of refreshment.

Elizabeth was prepared to see him in his glory; and she could not help fancying that in displaying the good proportion of the room, its aspect and its furniture, he addressed himself particularly to her, as if wishing to make her feel what she had lost in refusing him. But though every thing seemed neat and comfortable, she was not able to gratify him by any sigh of repentance; and rather looked with wonder at her friend that she could have so cheerful an air, with such a companion. When Mr. Collins said any thing of which his wife might reasonably be ashamed, which certainly was not unseldom, she involuntarily turned her eye on Charlotte. Once or twice she could discern a faint blush; but in general Charlotte wisely did not hear. After sitting long enough to admire every article of furniture in the room, from the sideboard to the fender, to give an account of their journey and of all that had happened in London, Mr. Collins invited them to take a stroll in the garden, which was large and well laid out, and to the cultivation of which he attended himself. To work in his garden was one of his most respectable pleasures; and Elizabeth admired the command of countenance with which Charlotte talked of the healthfulness of the exercise, and owned she encouraged it as much as possible. Here, leading the way through every walk and cross walk, and scarcely allowing them an interval to utter the praises he asked for, every view was pointed out with a minuteness which left beauty entirely behind. He could number the fields in every direction, and could tell how many trees there were in the most distant clump. But of all the views which his garden, or which the country, or the kingdom could boast, none were to be compared with the prospect of Rosings, afforded by an opening in the trees that bordered the park nearly opposite the front of his house. It was a handsome modern building, well situated on rising ground.

From his garden, Mr. Collins would have led them round his two meadows, but the ladies not having shoes to encounter the remains of a white frost, turned back; and while Sir William accompanied him, Charlotte took her sister and friend over the house, extremely well pleased, probably, to have the opportunity of shewing it without her husband's help. It was rather small, but well built and convenient; and every thing was fitted up and arranged with a neatness and consistency of which Elizabeth gave Charlotte all the credit. When Mr. Collins could be forgotten, there was really a great air of comfort throughout, and by Charlotte's evident enjoyment of it, Elizabeth supposed he must be often forgotten.

She had already learnt that Lady Catherine was still in the country. It was spoken of again while they were at dinner, when Mr. Collins joining in, observed,

"Yes, Miss Elizabeth, you will have the honour of seeing Lady Catherine de Bourgh on the ensuing Sunday at church, and I need not say you will be delighted with her. She is all affability and condescension, and I doubt not but you will be honoured with some portion of her notice when service is over. I have scarcely any hesitation in saying that she will include you and my sister Maria in every invitation with which she honours us during your stay here. Her behaviour to my dear Charlotte is charming. We dine at Rosings twice every week, and are never allowed to walk home. Her ladyship's carriage is regularly ordered for us. I *should* say, one of her ladyship's carriages, for she has several."

"Lady Catherine is a very respectable, sensible woman indeed," added Charlotte, "and a most attentive neighbour."

"Very true, my dear, that is exactly what I say. She is the sort of woman whom one cannot regard with too much deference."

The evening was spent chiefly in talking over Hertfordshire news, and telling again what had been already written; and when it closed, Elizabeth in the solitude of her chamber had to meditate upon Charlotte's degree of contentment, to understand her address in guiding, and composure in bearing with her husband, and to acknowledge that it was all done very well. She had also to anticipate how her visit would pass, the quiet tenor of their usual employments, the vexatious interruptions of Mr. Collins, and the gaieties of their intercourse with Rosings. A lively imagination soon settled it all.

About the middle of the next day, as she was in her room getting ready for a walk, a sudden noise below seemed to speak the whole house in confusion; and after listening a moment, she heard somebody running up stairs in a violent hurry, and calling loudly after her. She opened the door, and met Maria in the landing place, who, breathless with agitation, cried out,

"Oh, my dear Eliza! pray make haste and come into the dining-room, for there is such a sight to be seen! I will not tell you what it is. Make haste, and come down this moment."

Elizabeth asked questions in vain; Maria would tell her nothing more, and down they ran into the dining-room, which fronted the lane, in quest of this wonder; it was two ladies stopping in a low phaeton at the garden gate.

"And is this all?" cried Elizabeth. "I expected at least that the pigs were got into the garden, and here is nothing but Lady Catherine and her daughter!"

"La! my dear," said Maria quite shocked at the mistake, "it is not Lady Catherine. The old lady is Mrs. Jenkinson, who lives with them. The other is Miss De Bourgh. Only look at her. She is quite a little creature. Who would have thought she could be so thin and small!"

"She is abominably rude to keep Charlotte out of doors in all this wind. Why does she not come in?"

"Oh! Charlotte says, she hardly ever does. It is the greatest of favours when Miss De Bourgh comes in."

"I like her appearance," said Elizabeth, struck with other ideas. "She looks sickly and cross.—Yes, she will do for him very well. She will make him a very proper wife."

Mr. Collins and Charlotte were both standing at the gate in conversation with the ladies; and Sir William, to Elizabeth's high diversion, was stationed in the doorway, in earnest contemplation of the greatness before him, and constantly bowing whenever Miss De Bourgh looked that way.

At length there was nothing more to be said; the ladies drove on, and the others returned into the house. Mr. Collins no sooner saw the two girls than he began to congratulate them on their good fortune, which Charlotte explained by letting them know that the whole party was asked to dine at Rosings the next day.

Chapter VI

Mr. Collins's triumph in consequence of this invitation was complete. The power of displaying the grandeur of his patroness to his wondering visitors, and of letting them see her civility towards himself and his wife, was exactly what he had wished for; and that an opportunity of doing it should be given so soon, was such an instance of Lady Catherine's condescension as he knew not how to admire enough.

"I confess," said he, "that I should not have been at all surprised by her Ladyship's asking us on Sunday to drink tea and spend the evening at Rosings. I rather expected, from my knowledge of her affability, that it would happen. But who could have foreseen such an attention as this? Who could have imagined that we should receive an invitation to dine there (an invitation moreover including the whole party) so immediately after your arrival!"

"I am the less surprised at what has happened," replied Sir William, "from that knowledge of what the manners of the great really are, which my situation in life has allowed me to acquire. About the Court, such instances of elegant breeding are not uncommon."

Scarcely any thing was talked of the whole day or next morning, but their visit to Rosings. Mr. Collins was carefully instructing them in what they were to expect, that the sight of such rooms, so many servants, and so splendid a dinner might not wholly overpower them.

When the ladies were separating for the toilette, he said to Elizabeth,

"Do not make yourself uneasy, my dear cousin, about your apparel. Lady Catherine is far from requiring that elegance of dress in us, which becomes herself and daughter. I would advise you merely to put on whatever of your clothes is superior to the rest, there is no occasion for any thing more. Lady Catherine will not think the worse of you for being simply dressed. She likes to have the distinction of rank preserved."

While they were dressing, he came two or three times to their different doors, to recommend their being quick, as Lady Catherine very much objected to be kept waiting for her dinner.—Such formidable accounts of her Ladyship, and her manner of living, quite frightened Maria Lucas, who had been little used to company, and she looked forward to her introduction at Rosings, with as much apprehension, as her father had done to his presentation at St. James's.

As the weather was fine, they had a pleasant walk of about half a mile across the park.—Every park has its beauty and its prospects; and Elizabeth saw much to be pleased with, though she could not be in such raptures as Mr. Collins expected the scene to inspire, and was but slightly affected by his enumeration of the windows in front of the house, and his relation of what the glazing altogether had originally cost Sir Lewis De Bourgh.

When they ascended the steps to the hall, Maria's alarm was every moment increasing, and even Sir William did not look perfectly calm.—Elizabeth's courage did not fail her. She had heard nothing of Lady Catherine that spoke her awful from any extraordinary talents or miraculous virtue, and the mere stateliness of money and rank, she thought she could witness without trepidation.

From the entrance hall, of which Mr. Collins pointed out, with a rapturous air, the fine proportion and finished ornaments, they followed the servants through an antichamber, to the room where Lady Catherine, her daughter, and Mrs. Jenkinson were sitting.—Her Ladyship, with great condescension, arose to receive them; and as Mrs. Collins had settled it with her husband that the office of introduction should be her's, it was performed in a proper manner, without any of those apologies and thanks which he would have thought necessary.

In spite of having been as St. James's, Sir William was so completely awed, by the grandeur surrounding him, that he had but just courage enough to make a very low bow, and take his seat without saying a word; and his daughter, frightened almost out of her senses, sat on the edge of her chair, not knowing which way to look. Elizabeth found herself quite equal to the scene, and could observe the three ladies before her composedly.—Lady Catherine was a tall, large woman, with strongly-marked features, which might once have been handsome. Her air was not conciliating, nor was her manner of receiving them, such as to make her visitors forget their inferior rank. She was not rendered formidable by silence; but whatever she said, was spoken in so authoritative a tone, as marked her self-importance, and brought Mr. Wickham immediately to Elizabeth's mind; and from the observation of the day altogether, she believed Lady Catherine to be exactly what he had represented.

When, after examining the mother, in whose countenance and deportment she soon found some resemblance of Mr. Darcy, she turned her eyes on the daughter, she could almost have joined in Maria's astonishment, at her being so thin, and so small. There was neither in figure nor face, any likeness between the ladies. Miss De Bourgh was pale and sickly; her features, though not plain, were insignificant; and she spoke very little, except in a low voice, to Mrs. Jenkinson, in whose appearance there was nothing remarkable, and who was entirely engaged in listening to what she said, and placing a screen in the proper direction before her eyes.

After sitting a few minutes, they were all sent to one of the windows, to admire the view, Mr. Collins attending them to point out its beauties, and Lady Catherine kindly informing them that it was much better worth looking at in the summer.

The dinner was exceedingly handsome, and there were all the servants, and all the articles of plate which Mr. Collins had promised; and, as he had likewise foretold, he took his seat at the bottom of the table, by her ladyship's desire, and looked as if he felt that life could furnish nothing greater.—He carved, and ate, and praised with delighted alacrity; and every dish was commended, first by him, and then by Sir William, who was now enough recovered to echo whatever his son in law said, in a manner which Elizabeth wondered Lady Catherine could bear. But Lady Catherine seemed gratified by their excessive admiration, and gave most gracious smiles, especially when any dish on the table proved a novelty to them. The party did not supply much conversation. Elizabeth was ready to speak whenever there was an opening, but she was seated between Charlotte and Miss De Bourgh—the former of whom was engaged in listening to Lady Catherine, and the latter said not a word to her all dinner time. Mrs. Jenkinson was chiefly employed in watching how little Miss De Bourgh ate, pressing her to try some other dish, and fearing she were indisposed. Maria thought speaking out of the question, and the gentlemen did nothing but eat and admire.

When the ladies returned to the drawing room, there was little to be done but to hear Lady Catherine talk, which she did without any intermission till coffee came in, delivering her opinion on every subject in so decisive a manner as proved that she was not used to have her judgment controverted. She enquired into Charlotte's domestic concerns familiarly and minutely, and gave her a great deal of advice, as to the management of them all; told her how every thing ought to be regulated in so small a family as her's, and instructed her as to the care of her cows and her poultry. Elizabeth found that nothing was beneath this great Lady's attention, which could furnish her with an occasion of dictating to others. In the intervals of her discourse with Mrs. Collins, she addressed a variety of questions to Maria and Elizabeth, but especially to the latter, of whose connections she knew the least, and who she observed to Mrs. Collins, was a very genteel, pretty kind of girl. She asked her at different times, how many sisters she had, whether they were older or younger than herself, whether any of them were likely to be married, whether they were handsome, where they had been educated, what carriage her father kept, and what had been her mother's maiden name?— Elizabeth felt all the impertinence of her questions, but answered them very composedly.—Lady Catherine then observed,

"Your father's estate is entailed on Mr. Collins, I think. For your sake," turning to Charlotte, "I am glad of it; but otherwise I see no occasion for entailing estates from the female line.—It was not thought necessary in Sir Lewis de Bourgh's family.—Do you play and sing, Miss Bennet?"

"A little."

"Oh! then—some time or other we shall be happy to hear you. Our instrument is a capital one, probably superior to——You shall try it some day.—Do your sisters play and sing?"

"One of them does."

"Why did not you all learn?—You ought all to have learned. The Miss Webbs all play, and their father has not so good an income as your's.—Do you draw?"

"No, not at all."

"What, none of you?"

"Not one."

"That is very strange. But I suppose you had no opportunity. Your mother should have taken you to town every spring for the benefit of masters."

"My mother would have had no objection, but my father hates London."

"Has your governess left you?"

"We never had any governess."

"No governess! How was that possible? Five daughters brought up at home without a governess!—I never heard of such a thing. Your mother must have been quite a slave to your education."

Elizabeth could hardly help smiling, as she assured her that had not been the case.

"Then, who taught you? who attended to you? Without a governess you must have been neglected."

"Compared with some families, I believe we were; but such of us as wished to learn, never wanted the means. We were always encouraged to read, and had all the masters that were necessary. Those who chose to be idle, certainly might."

"Aye, no doubt; but that is what a governess will prevent, and if I had known your mother, I should have advised her most strenuously to engage one. I always say that nothing is to be done in education without steady and regular instruction, and nobody but a governess can give it. It is wonderful how many families I have been the means of supplying in that way. I am always glad to get a young person well placed out. Four nieces of Mrs. Jenkinson are most delightfully situated through my means; and it was but the other day, that I recommended another young person, who was merely accidentally mentioned to me, and the family are quite delighted with her. Mrs. Collins, did I tell you of Lady Metcalfe's calling yesterday to thank me? She finds Miss Pope a treasure. 'Lady Catherine,' said she, 'you have given me a treasure.' Are any of your younger sisters out,[9] Miss Bennet?"

"Yes, Ma'am, all."

9. Formally entered into adult society.

"All!—What, all five out at once? Very odd!—And you only the second.—The younger ones out before the elder are married! —Your younger sisters must be very young?"

"Yes, my youngest is not sixteen. Perhaps *she* is full young to be much in company. But really, Ma'am, I think it would be very hard upon younger sisters, that they should not have their share of society and amusement because the elder may not have the means or inclination to marry early.—The last born has as good a right to the pleasures of youth, as the first. And to be kept back on *such* a motive!—I think it would not be very likely to promote sisterly affection or delicacy of mind."

"Upon my word," said her Ladyship, "you give your opinion very decidedly for so young a person.—Pray, what is your age?"

"With three younger sisters grown up," replied Elizabeth smiling, "your Ladyship can hardly expect me to own it."

Lady Catherine seemed quite astonished at not receiving a direct answer; and Elizabeth suspected herself to be the first creature who had ever dared to trifle with so much dignified impertinence.

"You cannot be more than twenty, I am sure,—therefore you need not conceal your age."

"I am not one and twenty."

When the gentlemen had joined them, and tea was over, the card tables were placed. Lady Catherine, Sir William, and Mr. and Mrs. Collins sat down to quadrille; and as Miss De Bourgh chose to play at cassino, the two girls had the honour of assisting Mrs. Jenkinson to make up her party. Their table was superlatively stupid. Scarcely a syllable was uttered that did not relate to the game, except when Mrs. Jenkinson expressed her fears Miss De Bourgh's being too hot or too cold, or having too much or too little light. A great deal more passed at the other table. Lady Catherine was generally speaking—stating the mistakes of the three others, or relating some anecdote of herself. Mr. Collins was employed in agreeing to every thing her Ladyship said, thanking her for every fish he won, and apologising if he thought he won too many. Sir William did not say much. He was storing his memory with anecdotes and noble names.

When Lady Catherine and her daughter had played as long as they chose, the tables were broke up, the carriage was offered to Mrs. Collins, gratefully accepted, and immediately ordered. The party then gathered round the fire to hear Lady Catherine determine what weather they were to have on the morrow. From these instructions they were summoned by the arrival of the coach, and with many speeches of thankfulness on Mr. Collins's side, and as many bows on Sir William's, they departed. As soon as they had driven from the door, Elizabeth was called on by her cousin, to give her opinion of all that she had seen at Rosings, which, for Charlotte's sake, she made more favourable than it really was. But her commendation, though costing her some trouble, could by no means satisfy Mr. Collins, and he was very soon obliged to take her Ladyship's praise into his own hands.

Chapter VII

Sir William staid only a week at Hunsford; but his visit was long enough to convince him of his daughter's being most comfortably settled, and of her possessing such a husband and such a neighbour as were not often met with. While Sir William was with them, Mr. Collins devoted his mornings to driving him out in his gig, and shewing him the country; but when he went away, the whole family returned to their usual employments, and Elizabeth was thankful to find that they did not see more of her cousin by the alteration, for the chief of the time between breakfast and dinner was now passed by him either at work in the garden, or in reading and writing, and looking out of window in his own book room, which fronted the road. The room in which the ladies sat was backwards.[1] Elizabeth at first had rather wondered that Charlotte should not prefer the dining parlour for common use; it was a better sized room, and had a pleasanter aspect; but she soon saw that her friend had an excellent reason for what she did, for Mr. Collins would undoubtedly have been much less in his own apartment, had they sat in one equally lively; and she gave Charlotte credit for the arrangement.

From the drawing room they could distinguish nothing in the lane, and were indebted to Mr. Collins for the knowledge of what carriages went along, and how often especially Miss De Bourgh drove by in her phaeton, which he never failed coming to inform them of, though it happened almost every day. She not unfrequently stopped at the Parsonage, and had a few minutes' conversation with Charlotte, but was scarcely ever prevailed on to get out.

Very few days passed in which Mr. Collins did not walk to Rosings, and not many in which his wife did not think it necessary to go likewise; and till Elizabeth recollected that there might be other family livings to be disposed of, she could not understand the sacrifice of so many hours. Now and then, they were honoured

1. I.e., at the back rather at the front of the house, looking out on the lane.

with a call from her Ladyship, and nothing escaped her observation that was passing in the room during these visits. She examined into their employments, looked at their work, and advised them to do it differently; found fault with the arrangement of the furniture, or detected the housemaid in negligence; and if she accepted any refreshment, seemed to do it only for the sake of finding out that Mrs. Collins's joints of meat were too large for her family.

Elizabeth soon perceived that though this great lady was not in the commission of the peace [2] for the county, she was a most active magistrate in her own parish, the minutest concerns of which were carried to her by Mr. Collins; and whenever any of the cottagers were disposed to be quarrelsome, discontented or too poor, she sallied forth into the village to settle their differences, silence their complaints, and scold them into harmony and plenty.

The entertainment of dining at Rosings was repeated about twice a week; and, allowing for the loss of Sir William, and there being only one card table in the evening, every such entertainment was the counterpart of the first. Their other engagements were few; as the style of living of the neighbourhood in general, was beyond the Collinses' reach. This however was no evil to Elizabeth, and upon the whole she spent her time comfortably enough; there were half hours of pleasant conversation with Charlotte, and the weather was so fine for the time of year, that she had often great enjoyment out of doors. Her favourite walk, and where she frequently went while the others were calling on Lady Catherine, was along the open grove which edged that side of the park, where there was a nice sheltered path, which no one seemed to value but herself, and where she felt beyond the reach of Lady Catherine's curiosity.

In this quiet way, the first fortnight of her visit soon passed away. Easter was approaching, and the week preceding it, was to bring an addition to the family at Rosings, which in so small a circle must be important. Elizabeth had heard soon after her arrival, that Mr. Darcy was expected there in the course of a few weeks, and though there were not many of her acquaintance whom she did not prefer, his coming would furnish one comparatively new to look at in their Rosings parties, and she might be amused in seeing how hopeless Miss Bingley's designs on him were, by his behaviour to his cousin, for whom he was evidently destined by Lady Catherine; who talked of his coming with

2. Commissioned as justice of the peace, with the authority to judge and punish minor offenders.

the greatest satisfaction, spoke of him in terms of the highest admiration, and seemed almost angry to find that he had already been frequently seen by Miss Lucas and herself.

His arrival was soon known at the Parsonage, for Mr. Collins was walking the whole morning within view of the lodges opening into Hunsford Lane, in order to have the earliest assurance of it; and after making his bow as the carriage turned into the Park, hurried home with the great intelligence. On the following morning he hastened to Rosings to pay his respects. There were two nephews of Lady Catherine to require them, for Mr. Darcy had brought with him a Colonel Fitzwilliam, the younger son of his uncle, Lord ——— and to the great surprise of all the party, when Mr. Collins returned the gentlemen accompanied him. Charlotte had seen them from her husband's room, crossing the road, and immediately running into the other, told the girls what an honour they might expect, adding,

"I may thank you, Eliza, for this piece of civility. Mr. Darcy would never have come so soon to wait upon me."

Elizabeth had scarcely time to disclaim all right to the compliment, before their approach was announced by the door-bell, and shortly afterwards the three gentlemen entered the room. Colonel Fitzwilliam, who led the way, was about thirty, not handsome, but in person and address most truly the gentleman. Mr. Darcy looked just as he had been used to look in Hertfordshire, paid his compliments, with his usual reserve, to Mrs. Collins; and whatever might be his feelings towards her friend, met her with every appearance of composure. Elizabeth merely curtseyed to him, without saying a word.

Colonel Fitzwilliam entered into conversation directly with the readiness and ease of a well-bred man, and talked very pleasantly; but his cousin, after having addressed a slight observation on the house and garden to Mrs. Collins, sat for some time without speaking to any body. At length, however, his civility was so far awakened as to enquire of Elizabeth after the health of her family. She answered him in the usual way, and after a moment's pause, added,

"My eldest sister has been in town these three months. Have you never happened to see her there?"

She was perfectly sensible that he never had; but she wished to see whether he would betray any consciousness of what had passed between the Bingleys and Jane; and she thought he looked a little confused as he answered that he had never been so fortunate as to meet Miss Bennet. The subject was pursued no farther, and the gentlemen soon afterwards went away.

Chapter VIII

Colonel Fitzwilliam's manners were very much admired at the parsonage, and the ladies all felt that he must add considerably to the pleasure of their engagements at Rosings. It was some days, however, before they received any invitation thither, for while there were visitors in the house, they could not be necessary; and it was not till Easter-day, almost a week after the gentlemen's arrival, that they were honoured by such an attention, and then they were merely asked on leaving church to come there in the evening. For the last week they had seen very little of either Lady Catherine or her daughter. Colonel Fitzwilliam had called at the parsonage more than once during the time, but Mr. Darcy they had only seen at church.

The invitation was accepted of course, and at a proper hour they joined the party in Lady Catherine's drawing room. Her ladyship received them civilly, but it was plain that their company was by no means so acceptable as when she could get nobody else; and she was, in fact, almost engrossed by her nephews, speaking to them, especially to Darcy, much more than to any other person in the room.

Colonel Fitzwilliam seemed really glad to see them; any thing was a welcome relief to him at Rosings; and Mrs. Collins's pretty friend had moreover caught his fancy very much. He now seated himself by her, and talked so agreeably of Kent and Hertfordshire, of travelling and staying at home, of new books and music, that Elizabeth had never been half so well entertained in that room before; and they conversed with so much spirit and flow, as to draw the attention of Lady Catherine herself, as well as of Mr. Darcy. *His* eyes had been soon and repeatedly turned towards them with a look of curiosity; and that her ladyship after a while shared the feeling, was more openly acknowledged, for she did not scruple to call out,

"What is that you are saying, Fitzwilliam? What is it you are talking of? What are you telling Miss Bennet? Let me hear what it is."

"We are speaking of music, Madam," said he, when no longer able to avoid a reply.

"Of music! Then pray speak aloud. It is of all subjects my delight. I must have my share in the conversation, if you are speaking of music. There are few people in England, I suppose, who have more true enjoyment of music than myself, or a better natural taste. If I had ever learnt, I should have been a great proficient.

And so would Anne, if her health had allowed her to apply. I am confident that she would have performed delightfully. How does Georgiana get on, Darcy?"

Mr. Darcy spoke with affectionate praise of his sister's proficiency.

"I am very glad to hear such a good account of her," said Lady Catherine; "and pray tell her from me, that she cannot expect to excel, if she does not practise a great deal."

"I assure you, Madam," he replied, "that she does not need such advice. She practises very constantly."

"So much the better. It cannot be done too much; and when I next write to her, I shall charge her not to neglect it on any account. I often tell young ladies, that no excellence in music is to be acquired, without constant practice. I have told Miss Bennet several times, that she will never play really well, unless she practises more; and though Mrs. Collins has no instrument, she is very welcome, as I have often told her, to come to Rosings every day, and play on the piano forte in Mrs. Jenkinson's room. She would be in nobody's way, you know, in that part of the house."

Mr. Darcy looked a little ashamed of his aunt's ill breeding, and made no answer.

When coffee was over, Colonel Fitzwilliam reminded Elizabeth of having promised to play to him; and she sat down directly to the instrument. He drew a chair near her. Lady Catherine listened to half a song, and then talked, as before, to her other nephew; till the latter walked away from her, and moving with his usual deliberation towards the piano forte, stationed himself so as to command a full view of the fair performer's countenance. Elizabeth saw what he was doing, and at the first convenient pause, turned to him with an arch smile, and said,

"You mean to frighten me, Mr. Darcy, by coming in all this state to hear me? But I will not be alarmed though your sister *does* play so well. There is a stubbornness about me that never can bear to be frightened at the will of others. My courage always rises with every attempt to intimidate me."

"I shall not say that you are mistaken," he replied, "because you could not really believe me to entertain any design of alarming you; and I have had the pleasure of your acquaintance long enough to know, that you find great enjoyment in occasionally professing opinions which in fact are not your own."

Elizabeth laughed heartily at this picture of herself, and said to Colonel Fitzwilliam, "Your cousin will give you a very pretty notion of me, and teach you not to believe a word I say. I am particularly unlucky in meeting with a person so well able to expose my real character, in a part of the world, where I had hoped to pass myself off with some degree of credit. Indeed, Mr. Darcy, it is very ungenerous in you to mention all that you knew to my disadvantage in Hertfordshire—and, give me leave to say, very impolitic too—for it is provoking me to retaliate, and such things may come out, as will shock your relations to hear."

"I am not afraid of you," said he, smilingly.

"Pray let me hear what you have to accuse him of," cried Colonel Fitzwilliam. "I should like to know how he behaves among strangers."

"You shall hear then—but prepare yourself for something very dreadful. The first time of my ever seeing him in Hertfordshire, you must know, was at a ball—and at this ball, what do you think he did? He danced only four dances! I am sorry to pain you—but so it was. He danced only four dances, though gentlemen were scarce; and, to my certain knowledge, more than one young lady was sitting down in want of a partner. Mr. Darcy, you cannot deny the fact."

"I had not at that time the honour of knowing any lady in the assembly beyond my own party."

"True; and nobody can ever be introduced in a ball room. Well, Colonel Fitzwilliam, what do I play next? My fingers wait your orders."

"Perhaps," said Darcy, "I should have judged better, had I sought an introduction, but I am ill qualified to recommend myself to strangers."

"Shall we ask your cousin the reason of this?" said Elizabeth, still addressing Colonel Fitzwilliam. "Shall we ask him why a man of sense and education, and who has lived in the world, is ill qualified to recommend himself to strangers?"

"I can answer your question," said Fitzwilliam, "without applying to him. It is because he will not give himself the trouble."

"I certainly have not the talent which some people possess," said Darcy, "of conversing easily with those I have never seen before. I cannot catch their tone of conversation, or appear interested in their concerns, as I often see done."

"My fingers," said Elizabeth, "do not move over this instrument in the masterly manner which I see so many women's do. They have not the same force or rapidity, and do not produce the same expression. But then I have always supposed it to be my own fault—because I would not take the trouble of practising. It is not that I do not believe *my* fingers as capable as any other woman's of superior execution."

Darcy smiled and said, "You are perfectly right. You have employed your time much better. No one admitted to the privilege of hearing you, can think any thing wanting. We neither of us perform to strangers."

Here they were interrupted by Lady Catherine, who called out to know what they were talking of. Elizabeth immediately began playing again. Lady Catherine approached, and, after listening for a few minutes, said to Darcy,

"Miss Bennet would not play at all amiss, if she practised more, and could have the advantage of a London master. She has a very good notion of fingering, though her taste is not equal to Anne's. Anne would have been a delightful performer, had her health allowed her to learn."

Elizabeth looked at Darcy to see how cordially he assented to his cousin's praise; but neither at the moment nor at any other could she discern any symptom of love; and from the whole of his behaviour to Miss De Bourgh she derived this comfort for Miss Bingley, that he might have been just as likely to marry *her*, had she been his relation.

Lady Catherine continued her remarks on Elizabeth's performance, mixing with them many instructions on execution and taste. Elizabeth received them with all the forbearance of civility; and at the request of the gentlemen remained at the instrument till her Ladyship's carriage was ready to take them all home.

Chapter IX

Elizabeth was sitting by herself the next morning, and writing to Jane, while Mrs. Collins and Maria were gone on business into the village, when she was startled by a ring at the door, the certain signal of a visitor. As she had heard no carriage, she thought it not unlikely to be Lady Catherine, and under that apprehension was putting away her half-finished letter that she might escape all impertinent questions, when the door opened, and to her very great surprise, Mr. Darcy, and Mr. Darcy only, entered the room.

He seemed astonished too on finding her alone, and apologised for his intrusion, by letting her know that he had understood all the ladies to be within.

They then sat down, and when her enquiries after Rosings were made, seemed in danger of sinking into total silence. It was absolutely necessary, therefore, to think of something, and in this emergence recollecting *when* she had seen him last in Hertfordshire, and feeling curious to know what he would say on the subject say on the subject of their hasty departure, she observed,

"How very suddenly you all quitted Netherfield last November, Mr. Darcy! It must have been a most agreeable surprise to Mr.

Bingley to see you all after him so soon; for, if I recollect right, he went but the day before. He and his sisters were well, I hope, when you left London."

"Perfectly so—I thank you."

She found that she was to receive no other answer—and, after a short pause, added,

"I think I have understood that Mr. Bingley has not much idea of ever returning to Netherfield again?"

"I have never heard him say so; but it is probable that he may spend very little of his time there in future. He has many friends, and he is at a time of life when friends and engagements are continually increasing."

"If he means to be but little at Netherfield, it would be better for the neighbourhood that he should give up the place entirely, for then we might possibly get a settled family there. But perhaps Mr. Bingley did not take the house so much for the convenience of the neighbourhood as for his own, and we must expect him to keep or quit it on the same principle."

"I should not be surprised," said Darcy, "if he were to give it up, as soon as any eligible purchase offers."

Elizabeth made no answer. She was afraid of talking longer of his friend; and, having nothing else to say, was now determined to leave the trouble of finding a subject to him.

He took the hint, and soon began with, "This seems a very comfortable house. Lady Catherine, I believe, did a great deal to it when Mr. Collins first came to Hunsford."

"I believe she did—and I am sure she could not have bestowed her kindness on a more grateful object."

"Mr. Collins appears very fortunate in his choice of a wife."

"Yes, indeed; his friends may well rejoice in his having met with one of the very few sensible women who would have accepted him, or have made him happy if they had. My friend has an excellent understanding—though I am not certain that I consider her marrying Mr. Collins as the wisest thing she ever did. She seems perfectly happy, however, and in a prudential light, it is certainly a very good match for her."

"It must be very agreeable to her to be settled within so easy a distance of her own family and friends."

"An easy distance do you call it? It is nearly fifty miles."

"And what is fifty miles of good road? Little more than half a day's journey. Yes, I call it a *very* easy distance."

"I should never have considered the distance as one of the *advantages* of the match," cried Elizabeth. "I should never have said Mrs. Collins was settled *near* her family."

"It is a proof of your own attachment to Hertfordshire. Any

thing beyond the very neighbourhood of Longbourn, I suppose, would appear far."

As he spoke there was a sort of smile, which Elizabeth fancied she understood; he must be supposing her to be thinking of Jane and Netherfield, and she blushed as she answered,

"I do not mean to say that a woman may not be settled too near her family. The far and the near must be relative, and depend on many varying circumstances. Where there is fortune to make the expence of travelling unimportant, distance becomes no evil. But that is not the case *here*. Mr. and Mrs. Collins have a comfortable income, but not such a one as will allow of frequent journeys—and I am persuaded my friend would not call herself *near* her family under less than *half* the present distance."

Mr. Darcy drew his chair a little towards her, and said, "*You* cannot have a right to such very strong local attachment. *You* cannot have been always at Longbourn."

Elizabeth looked surprised. The gentleman experienced some change of feeling; he drew back his chair, took a newspaper from the table, and, glancing over it, said, in a colder voice,

"Are you pleased with Kent?"

A short dialogue on the subject of the country ensued, on either side calm and concise—and soon put an end to by the entrance of Charlotte and her sister, just returned from their walk. The tête a tête surprised them. Mr. Darcy related the mistake which had occasioned his intruding on Miss Bennet, and after sitting a few minutes longer without saying much to any body, went away.

"What can be the meaning of this!" said Charlotte, as soon as he was gone. "My dear Eliza he must be in love with you, or he would never have called on us in this familiar way."

But when Elizabeth told of his silence, it did not seem very likely, even to Charlotte's wishes, to be the case; and after various conjectures, they could at last only suppose his visit to proceed from the difficulty of finding any thing to do, which was the more probable from the time of year. All field sports were over. Within doors there was Lady Catherine, books, and a billiard table, but gentlemen cannot be always within doors; and in the nearness of the Parsonage, or the pleasantness of the walk to it, or of the people who lived in it, the two cousins found a temptation from this period of walking thither almost every day. They called at various times of the morning, sometimes separately, sometimes together, and now and then accompanied by their aunt. It was plain to them all that Colonel Fitzwilliam came because he had pleasure in their society, a persuasion which of course recommended him still more; and Elizabeth was reminded by her own satisfaction in being with him, as well as by his evident admiration of her, of her former favourite George Wickham; and though, in comparing them, she saw there was less captivating softness in Colonel Fitzwilliam's manners, she believed he might have the best informed mind.

But why Mr. Darcy came so often to the Parsonage, it was more difficult to understand. It could not be for society, as he frequently sat there ten minutes together without opening his lips; and when he did speak, it seemed the effect of necessity rather than of choice—a sacrifice to propriety, not a pleasure to himself. He seldom appeared really animated. Mrs. Collins knew not what to make of him. Colonel Fitzwilliam's occasionally laughing at his stupidity, proved that he was generally different, which her own knowledge of him could not have told her; and as she would have liked to believe this change the effect of love, and the object of that love, her friend Eliza, she sat herself seriously to work to find it out.—She watched him whenever they were at Rosings, and whenever he came to Hunsford; but without much success. He certainly looked at her friend a great deal, but the expression of that look was disputable. It was an earnest, steadfast gaze, but she often doubted whether there were much admiration in it, and sometimes it seemed nothing but absence of mind.

She had once or twice suggested to Elizabeth the possibility of his being partial to her, but Elizabeth always laughed at the idea; and Mrs. Collins did not think it right to press the subject, from the danger of raising expectations which might only end in disappointment; for in her opinion it admitted not of a doubt, that all her friend's dislike would vanish, if she could suppose him to be in her power.

In her kind schemes for Elizabeth, she sometimes planned her marrying Colonel Fitzwilliam. He was beyond comparison the pleasantest man; he certainly admired her, and his situation in life was most eligible; but, to counterbalance these advantages, Mr. Darcy had considerable patronage in the church, and his cousin could have none at all.

Chapter X

More than once did Elizabeth in her ramble within the Park, unexpectedly meet Mr. Darcy.—She felt all the perverseness of the mischance that should bring him where no one else was brought; and to prevent its ever happening again, took care to inform him at first, that it was a favourite haunt of hers.—How it could occur a second time therefore was very odd!—Yet it did, and even a third. It seemed like wilful ill-nature, or a voluntary penance, for on these occasions it was not merely a few formal enquiries and an awkward pause and then away, but he actually thought it necessary to turn back and walk with her. He never said a great deal, nor did she give herself the trouble of talking or of listening much; but it struck her in the course of their third rencontre that he was asking some odd unconnected questions—about her pleasure in being at Hunsford, her love of solitary walks, and her opinion of Mr. and Mrs. Collins's happiness; and that in speaking of Rosings and her not perfectly understanding the house, he seemed to expect that whenever she came into Kent again she would be staying *there* too. His words seemed to imply it. Could he have Colonel Fitzwilliam in his thoughts? She supposed, if he meant any thing, he must mean an allusion to what might arise in that quarter. It distressed her a little, and she was quite glad to find herself at the gate in the pales opposite the Parsonage.

She was engaged one day as she walked, in re-perusing Jane's last letter, and dwelling on some passages which proved that Jane had not written in spirits, when, instead of being again surprised by Mr. Darcy, she saw on looking up that Colonel Fitzwilliam was meeting her. Putting away the letter immediately and forcing a smile, she said,

"I did not know before that you ever walked this way."

"I have been making the tour of the Park," he replied, "as I generally do every year, and intend to close it with a call at the Parsonage. Are you going much farther?"

"No, I should have turned in a moment."

And accordingly she did turn, and they walked towards the Parsonage together.

"Do you certainly leave Kent on Saturday?" said she.

"Yes—if Darcy does not put it off again. But I am at his disposal. He arranges the business just as he pleases."

"And if not able to please himself in the arrangement, he has at least great pleasure in the power of choice. I do not know any body who seems more to enjoy the power of doing what he likes than Mr. Darcy."

"He likes to have his own way very well," replied Colonel Fitzwilliam. "But so we all do. It is only that he has better means of having it than many others, because he is rich, and many others are poor. I speak feelingly. A younger son, you know, must be inured to self-denial and dependence."

"In my opinion, the younger son of an Earl can know very little of either. Now, seriously, what have you ever known of self-denial and dependence? When have you been prevented by want of money from going wherever you choose, or procuring any thing you had a fancy for?"

"These are home questions—and perhaps I cannot say that I have experienced many hardships of that nature. But in matters of greater weight, I may suffer from the want of money. Younger sons cannot marry where they like."

"Unless where they like women of fortune, which I think they very often do."

"Our habits of expence make us too dependant, and there are not many in my rank of life who can afford to marry without some attention to money."

"Is this," thought Elizabeth, "meant for me?" and she coloured at the idea; but, recovering herself, said in a lively tone, "And pray, what is the usual price of an Earl's younger son? Unless the elder brother is very sickly, I suppose you would not ask above fifty thousand pounds."

He answered her in the same style, and the subject dropped. To interrupt a silence which might make him fancy her affected with what had passed, she soon afterwards said,

"I imagine your cousin brought you down with him chiefly for the sake of having somebody at his disposal. I wonder he does not marry, to secure a lasting convenience of that kind. But, perhaps his sister does as well for the present, and, as she is under his sole care, he may do what he likes with her."

"No," said Colonel Fitzwilliam, "that is an advantage which he must divide with me. I am joined with him in the guardianship of Miss Darcy."

"Are you, indeed? And pray what sort of guardians do you make? Does your charge give you much trouble? Young ladies of her age, are sometimes a little difficult to manage, and if she has the true Darcy spirit, she may like to have her own way."

As she spoke, she observed him looking at her earnestly, and the manner in which he immediately asked her why she supposed Miss Darcy likely to give them any uneasiness, convinced her that she had somehow or other got pretty near the truth. She directly replied,

"You need not be frightened. I never heard any harm of her; and I dare say she is one of the most tractable creatures in the world. She is a very great favourite with some ladies of my acquaintance. Mrs. Hurst and Miss Bingley. I think I have heard you say that you know them."

"I know them a little. Their brother is a pleasant gentleman-like man—he is a great friend of Darcy's."

"Oh! yes," said Elizabeth drily—"Mr. Darcy is uncommonly kind to Mr. Bingley, and takes a prodigious deal of care of him."

"Care of him!—Yes, I really believe Darcy *does* take care of him in those points where he most wants care. From something that he told me in our journey hither, I have reason to think Bingley very much indebted to him. But I ought to beg his pardon, for I have no right to suppose that Bingley was the person meant. It was all conjecture."

"What is it you mean?"

"It is a circumstance which Darcy of course would not wish to be generally known, because if it were to get round to the lady's family, it would be an unpleasant thing."

"You may depend upon my not mentioning it."

"And remember that I have not much reason for supposing it to be Bingley. What he told me was merely this; that he congratulated himself on having lately saved a friend from the inconveniences of a most imprudent marriage, but without mentioning names or any other particulars, and I only suspected it to be Bingley from believing him the kind of young man to get into a scrape of that sort, and from knowing them to have been together the whole of last summer."

"Did Mr. Darcy give you his reasons for this interference?"

"I understood that there were some very strong objections against the lady."

"And what arts did he use to separate them?"

"He did not talk to me of his own arts," said Fitzwilliam smiling. "He only told me, what I have now told you."

Elizabeth made no answer, and walked on, her heart swelling with indignation. After watching her a little, Fitzwilliam asked her why she was so thoughtful.

"I am thinking of what you have been telling me," said she. "Your cousin's conduct does not suit my feelings. Why was he to be the judge?"

"You are rather disposed to call his interference officious?"

"I do not see what right Mr. Darcy had to decide on the propriety of his friend's inclination, or why, upon his own judgment alone, he was to determine and direct in what manner that friend was to be happy." "But," she continued, recollecting herself, "as we know none of the particulars, it is not fair to condemn him. It is not to be supposed that there was much affection in the case."

"That is not an unatural surmise," said Fitzwilliam, "but it is lessening the honour of my cousin's triumph very sadly."

This was spoken jestingly, but it appeared to her so just a picture of Mr. Darcy, that she would not trust herself with an answer; and, therefore, abruptly changing the conversation, talked on indifferent matters till they reached the parsonage. There, shut into her own room, as soon as their visitor left them, she could think without interruption of all that she had heard. It was not to be supposed that any other people could be meant than those with whom she was connected. There could not exist in the world *two* men, over whom Mr. Darcy could have such boundless influence. That he had been concerned in the measures taken to separate Mr. Bingley and Jane, she had never doubted; but she had always attributed to Miss Bingley the principal design and arrangement of them. If his own vanity, however, did not mislead him, *he* was the cause, his pride and caprice were the cause of all that Jane had suffered, and still continued to suffer. He had ruined for a while every hope of happiness for the most affectionate, generous heart in the world; and no one could say how lasting an evil he might have inflicted.

"There were some very strong objections against the lady," were Colonel Fitzwilliam's words, and these strong objections probably were, her having one uncle who was a country attorney, and another who was in business in London.

"To Jane herself," she exclaimed, "there could be no possibility of objection. All loveliness and goodness as she is! Her understanding excellent, her mind improved, and her manners captivating. Neither could any thing be urged against my father, who, though with some peculiarities, has abilities which Mr. Darcy himself need not disdain, and respectability which he will probably never reach." When she thought of her mother indeed, her confidence gave way a little, but she would not allow that any objections *there* had material weight with Mr. Darcy, whose pride, she was convinced, would receive a deeper wound from the want of importance in his friend's connections, than from their want of sense; and she was quite decided at last, that he had been partly governed by this worst kind of pride, and partly by the wish of retaining Mr. Bingley for his sister.

The agitation and tears which the subject occasioned, brought on a headach; and it grew so much worse towards the evening that, added to her unwillingness to see Mr. Darcy, it determined her not to attend her cousins to Rosings, where they were engaged to drink tea. Mrs. Collins, seeing that she was really unwell, did not press her to go, and as much as possible prevented her husband from pressing her, but Mr. Collins could not conceal his apprehension of Lady Catherine's being rather displeased by her staying at home.

Chapter XI

When they were gone, Elizabeth, as if intending to exasperate herself as much as possible against Mr. Darcy, chose for her employment the examination of all the letters which Jane had written to her since her being in Kent. They contained no actual complaint, nor was there any revival of past occurrences, or any communication of present suffering. But in all, and in almost every line of each, there was a want of that cheerfulness which had been used to characterize her style, and which, proceding from the serenity of a mind at ease with itself, and kindly disposed towards every one, had been scarcely ever clouded. Elizabeth noticed every sentence conveying the idea of uneasiness, with an attention which it had hardly received on the first perusal. Mr. Darcy's shameful boast of what misery he had been able to inflict, gave her a keener sense of her sister's sufferings. It was some consolation to think that his visit to Rosings was to end on the day after the next, and a still greater, that in less than a fortnight she should herself be with Jane again, and enabled to contribute to the recovery of her spirits, by all that affection could do.

She could not think of Darcy's leaving Kent, without remembering that his cousin was to go with him; but Colonel Fitzwilliam had made it clear that he had no intentions at all, and agreeable as he was, she did not mean to be unhappy about him.

While settling this point, she was suddenly roused by the sound of the door bell, and her spirits were a little fluttered by the idea of its being Colonel Fitzwilliam himself, who had once before called late in the evening, and might now come to enquire particularly after her. But this idea was soon banished, and her spirits were very differently affected, when, to her utter amazement, she saw Mr. Darcy walk into the room. In an hurried manner he immediately began an enquiry after her health, imputing his visit to a wish of hearing that she were better. She answered him with cold civility. He sat down for a few moments, and then getting up walked about the room. Elizabeth was surprised, but said not a word. After a silence of several minutes he came towards her in an agitated manner, and thus began,

"In vain have I struggled. It will not do. My feelings will not be repressed. You must allow me to tell you how ardently I admire and love you."

Elizabeth's astonishment was beyond expression. She stared, coloured, doubted, and was silent. This he considered sufficient encouragement, and the avowal of all that he felt and had long felt for her, immediately followed. He spoke well, but there were feelings besides those of the heart to be detailed, and he was not more eloquent on the subject of tenderness than of pride. His sense of her inferiority—of its being a degradation—of the family obstacles which judgment had always opposed to inclination, were dwelt on with a warmth which seemed due to the consequence he was wounding, but was very unlikely to recommend his suit.

In spite of her deeply-rooted dislike, she could not be insensible to the compliment of such a man's affection, and though her intentions did not vary for an instant, she was at first sorry for the pain he was to receive; till, roused to resentment by his subsequent language, she lost all compassion in anger. She tried, however, to compose herself to answer him with patience, when he should have done. He concluded with representing to her the strength of that attachment which, in spite of all his endeavours, he had found impossible to conquer; and with expressing his hope that it would now be rewarded by her acceptance of his hand. As he said this, she could easily see that he had no doubt of a favourable answer. He *spoke* of apprehension and anxiety, but his countenence expressed real security. Such a circumstance could only exasperate farther, and when he ceased, the colour rose into her cheeks, and she said,

"In such cases as this, it is, I believe, the established mode to express a sense of obligation for the sentiments avowed, however unequally they may be returned. It is natural that obligation should be felt, and if I could *feel* gratitude, I would now thank you. But I cannot—I have never desired your good opinion, and you have certainly bestowed it most unwillingly. I am sorry to have occasioned pain to any one. It has been most unconsciously done, however, and I hope will be of short duration. The feelings which, you tell me, have long prevented the acknowledgment of your regard, can have little difficulty in overcoming it after this explanation."

Mr. Darcy, who was leaning against the mantle-piece with his eyes fixed on her face, seemed to catch her words with no less resentment than surprise. His complexion became pale with anger, and the disturbance of his mind was visible in every feature. He was struggling for the appearance of composure, and would not open his lips, till he believed himself to have attained it. The pause was to Elizabeth's feelings dreadful. At length, in a voice of forced calmness, he said,

"And this is all the reply which I am to have the honour of expecting! I might, perhaps, wish to be informed why, with so little *endeavour* at civility, I am thus rejected. But it is of small importance."

"I might as well enquire," replied she, "why with so evident a design of offending and insulting me, you chose to tell me that you liked me against your will, against your reason, and even against your character? Was not this some excuse for incivility, it I *was* uncivil? But I have other provocations. You know I have. Had not my own feelings decided against you, had they been indifferent, or had they even been favourable, do you think that any consideration would tempt me to accept the man, who has been the means of ruining, perhaps for ever, the happiness of a most beloved sister?"

As she pronounced these words, Mr. Darcy changed colour; but the emotion was short, and he listened without attempting to interrupt her while she continued.

"I have every reason in the world to think ill of you. No motive can excuse the unjust and ungenerous part you acted *there*. You dare not, you cannot deny that you have been the principal, if not the only means of dividing them from each other, of exposing one to the censure of the world for caprice and instability, the other to its derision for disappointed hopes, and involving them both in misery of the acutest kind."

She paused, and saw with no slight indignation that he was listening with an air which proved him wholly unmoved by any feeling of remorse. He even looked at her with a smile of affected incredulity.

"Can you deny that you have done it?" she repeated.

With assumed tranquillity he then replied, "I have no wish of denying that I did every thing in my power to separate my friend from your sister, or that I rejoice in my success. Towards *him* I have been kinder than towards myself."

Elizabeth disdained the appearance of noticing this civil reflection, but its meaning did not escape, nor was it likely to conciliate her.

"But it is not merely this affair," she continued, "on which my dislike is founded. Long before it had taken place, my opinion of you was decided. Your character was unfolded in the recital which I received many months ago from Mr. Wickham. On this subject, what can you have to say? In what imaginary act of friendship can you here defend yourself? or under what misrepresentation, can you here impose upon others?"

"You take an eager interest in that gentleman's concerns," said Darcy in a less tranquil tone, and with a heightened colour.

"Who that knows what his misfortunes have been, can help feeling an interest in him?"

"His misfortunes!" repeated Darcy contemptuously; "yes, his

misfortunes have been great indeed."

"And of your infliction," cried Elizabeth with energy. "You have reduced him to his present state of poverty, comparative poverty. You have withheld the advantages, which you must know to have been designed for him. You have deprived the best years of his life, of that independence which was no less his due than his desert. You have done all this! and yet you can treat the mention of his misfortunes with contempt and ridicule."

"And this," cried Darcy, as he walked with quick steps across the room, "is your opinion of me! This is the estimation in which you hold me! I thank you for explaining it so fully. My faults, according to this calculation, are heavy indeed! But perhaps," added he, stopping in his walk, and turning towards her, "these offences might have been overlooked, had not your pride been hurt by my honest confession of the scruples that had long prevented my forming any serious design. These bitter accusations might have been suppressed, had I with greater policy concealed my struggles, and flattered you into the belief of my being impelled by unqualified, unalloyed inclination; by reason, by reflection, by every thing. But disguise of every sort is my abhorrence. Nor am I ashamed of the feelings I related. They were natural and just. Could you expect me to rejoice in the inferiority of your connections? To congratulate myself on the hope of relations, whose condition in life is so decidedly beneath my own?"

Elizabeth felt herself growing more angry every moment; yet she tried to the utmost to speak with composure when she said,

"You are mistaken, Mr. Darcy, if you suppose that the mode of your declaration affected me in any other way, than as it spared me the concern which I might have felt in refusing you, had you behaved in a more gentleman-like manner."

She saw him start at this, but he said nothing, and she continued,

"You could not have made me the offer of your hand in any possible way that would have tempted me to accept it."

Again his astonishment was obvious; and he looked at her with an expression of mingled incredulity and mortification. She went on.

"From the very beginning, from the first moment I may almost say, of my acquaintance with you, your manners impressing me with the fullest belief of your arrogance, your conceit, and your selfish disdain of the feelings of others, were such as to form that ground-work of disapprobation, on which succeeding events have built so immoveable a dislike; and I had not known you a month before I felt that you were the last man in the world whom I could ever be prevailed on to marry."

"You have said quite enough, madam. I perfectly comprehend

your feelings, and have now only to be ashamed of what my own have been. Forgive me for having taken up so much of your time, and accept my best wishes for your health and happiness."

And with these words he hastily left the room, and Elizabeth heard him the next moment open the front door and quit the house.

The tumult of her mind was now painfully great. She knew not how to support herself, and from actual weakness sat down and cried for half an hour. Her astonishment, as she reflected on what had passed, was increased by every review of it. That she should receive an offer of marriage from Mr. Darcy! that he should have been in love with her for so many months! so much in love as to wish to marry her in spite of all the objections which had made him prevent his friend's marrying her sister, and which must appear at least with equal force in his own case, was almost incredible! it was gratifying to have inspired unconsciously so strong an affection. But his pride, his abominable pride, his shameless avowal of what he had done with respect to Jane, his unpardonable assurance in acknowledging, though he could not justify it, and the unfeeling manner in which he had mentioned Mr. Wickham, his cruelty towards whom he had not attempted to deny, soon overcame the pity which the consideration of his attachment had for a moment excited.

She continued in very agitating reflections till the sound of Lady Catherine's carriage made her feel how unequal she was to encounter Charlotte's observation, and hurried her away to her room.

Chapter XII

Elizabeth awoke the next morning to the same thoughts and meditations which had at length closed her eyes. She could not yet recover from the surprise of what had happened; it was impossible to think of any thing else, and totally indisposed for employment, she resolved soon after breakfast to indulge herself in air and exercise. She was proceeding directly to her favourite walk, when the recollection of Mr. Darcy's sometimes coming there stopped her, and instead of entering the park, she turned up the lane, which led her farther from the turnpike road. The park paling was still the boundary on one side, and she soon passed one of the gates into the ground.

After walking two or three times along that part of the lane, she was tempted, by the pleasantness of the morning, to stop at the gates and look into the park. The five weeks which she had now passed in Kent, had made a great difference in the country, and every day was adding to the verdure of the early trees. She was on the point of continuing her walk, when she caught a glimpse of a gentleman within the sort of grove which edged the park; he was moving that way; and fearful of its being Mr. Darcy, she was directly retreating. But the person who advanced, was now near enough to see her, and stepping forward with eagerness, pronounced her name. She had turned away, but on hearing herself called, though in a voice which proved it to be Mr. Darcy, she moved again towards the gate. He had by that time reached it also, and holding out a letter, which she instinctively took, said with a look of haughty composure, "I have been walking in the grove some time in the hope of meeting you. Will you do me the honour of reading that letter?"—And then, with a slight bow, turned again into the plantation,[3] and was soon out of sight.

With no expectation of pleasure, but with the strongest curiosity, Elizabeth opened the letter, and to her still increasing wonder, perceived an envelope containing two sheets of letter paper, written quite through, in a very close hand.—The envelope [4] itself was likewise full.—Pursuing her way along the lane, she then began it. It was dated from Rosings, at eight o'clock in the morning, and was as follows:—

"Be not alarmed, Madam, on receiving this letter, by the apprehension of its containing any repetition of those sentiments, or renewal of those offers, which were last night so disgusting to you. I write without any intention of paining you, or humbling myself, by dwelling on wishes, which, for the happiness of both, cannot be too soon forgotten; and the effort which the formation, and the perusal of this letter must occasion, should have been spared, had not my character required it to be written and read. You must, therefore, pardon the freedom with which I demand your attention; your feelings, I know, will bestow it unwillingly, but I demand it of your justice.

"Two offences of a very different nature, and by no means of equal magnitude, you last night laid to my charge. The first mentioned was, that, regardless of the sentiments of either, I had detached Mr. Bingley from your sister,—and the other, that I had, in defiance of various claims, in defiance of honour and humanity, ruined the immediate prosperity, and blasted the prospects of Mr. Wickham.—Wilfully and wantonly to have thrown off the companion of my youth, the acknowledged favourite of my father, a young man who had scarcely any other dependence than on our patronage, and who had been brought up to expect its exertion, would be a depravity, to which the separation of two

---

3. Wood of planted trees.
4. Sheet of paper used as a cover of the letter. Darcy has written on this sheet too.

young persons, whose affection could be the growth of only a few weeks, could bear no comparison.—But from the severity of that blame which was last night so liberally bestowed, respecting each circumstance, I shall hope to be in future secured, when the following account of my actions and their motives has been read.—If, in the explanation of them which is due to myself, I am under the necessity of relating feelings which may be offensive to your's, I can only say that I am sorry.—The necessity must be obeyed—and farther apology would be absurd.—I had not been long in Hertfordshire, before I saw, in common with others, that Bingley preferred your eldest sister, to any other young woman in the country.—But it was not till the evening of the dance at Netherfield that I had any apprehension of his feeling a serious attachment.—I had often seen him in love before.—At that ball, while I had the honour of dancing with you, I was first made acquainted, by Sir William Lucas's accidental information, that Bingley's attentions to your sister had given rise to a general expectation of their marriage. He spoke of it as a certain event, of which the time alone could be undecided. From that moment I observed my friend's behaviour attentively; and I could then perceive that his partiality for Miss Bennet was beyond what I had ever witnessed in him. Your sister I also watched.—Her look and manners were open, cheerful and engaging as ever, but without any symptom of peculiar regard, and I remained convinced from the evening's scrutiny, that though she received his attentions with pleasure, she did not invite them by any participation of sentiment.—If *you* have not been mistaken here, *I* must have been in an error. Your superior knowledge of your sister must make the latter probable.—If it be so, if I have been misled by such error, to inflict pain on her, your resentment has not been unreasonable. But I shall not scruple to assert, that the serenity of your sister's countenance and air was such, as might have given the most acute observer, a conviction that, however amiable her temper, her heart was not likely to be easily touched.—That I was desirous of believing her indifferent is certain,—but I will venture to say that my investigations and decisions are not usually influenced by my hopes or fears.—I did not believe her to be indifferent because I wished it;—I believed it on impartial conviction, as truly as I wished it in reason.—My objections to the marriage were not merely those, which I last night acknowledged to have required the utmost force of passion to put aside, in my own case; the want of connection could not be so great an evil to my friend as to me.—But there were other causes of repugnance; —causes which, though still existing, and existing to an equal degree in both instances, I had myself endeavoured to forget, because they were not immediately before me.—These causes must be stated, though briefly.—The situation of your mother's family, though objectionable, was nothing in comparison of that total want of propriety so frequently, so almost uniformly betrayed by herself, by your three younger sisters, and occasionally even by your father.—Pardon me.—It pains me to offend you. But amidst your concern for the defects of your nearest relations, and your displeasure at this representation of them, let it give you consolation to consider that, to have conducted yourselves so as to avoid any share of the like censure, is praise no less generally bestowed on you and your eldest sister, than it is honourable to the sense and disposition of both.—I will only say farther, that from what passed that evening, my opinion of all parties was confirmed, and every inducement heightened, which could have led me before, to preserve my friend from what I esteemed a most unhappy connection. —He left Netherfield for London, on the day following, as you, I am certain, remember, with the design of soon returning.—The part which I acted, is now to be explained.—His sisters' uneasiness had been equally excited with my own; our coincidence of feeling was soon discovered; and, alike sensible that no time was to be lost in detaching their brother, we shortly resolved on joining him directly in London.—We accordingly went—and there I readily engaged in the office of pointing out to my friend, the certain evils of such a choice.—I described, and enforced them earnestly.—But, however this remonstrance might have staggered or delayed his determination, I do not suppose that it would ultimately have prevented the marriage, had it not been seconded by the assurance which I hesitated not in giving, of your sister's indifference. He had before believed her to return his affection with sincere, if not with equal regard.—But Bingley has great natural modesty, with a stronger dependence on my judgment than on his own.—To convince him, therefore, that he had deceived himself, was no very difficult point. To persuade him against returning into Hertfordshire, when that conviction had been given, was scarcely the work of a moment.—I cannot blame myself for having done thus much. There is but one part of my conduct in the whole affair, on which I do not reflect with satisfaction; it is that I condescended to adopt the measures of art so far as to conceal from him your sister's being in town. I knew it myself, as it was known to Miss Bingley, but her brother is even yet ignorant of it.—That they might have met without ill consequence, is perhaps probable;—but his regard did not appear to me enough extinguished for him to see her without some danger.—Perhaps this concealment, this disguise, was beneath me.—It is done, however, and it was done for the best.—On this subject I have nothing more to say, no other apology to offer. If I have wounded your sister's feelings, it was unknowingly done; and though the motives which governed me may to you very naturally appear insufficient, I have not yet learnt to condemn them.—With respect to that other, more weighty accusation, of having injured Mr. Wickham, I can only refute it by laying before you the whole of his connection with my family. Of what he has *particularly* accused me I am ignorant; but of the truth of what I shall relate, I can summon more than one witness of undoubted veracity. Mr. Wickham is the son of a very respectable man, who had for many years the management of all the Pemberley estates; and whose good conduct in the discharge of his trust, naturally inclined my father to be of service to him, and on George Wickham, who was his god-son, his kindness was therefore liberally bestowed. My father supported him at school, and afterwards at Cambridge;—most important assistance, as his own father, always poor from the extravagance of his wife, would have been unable to give him a gentleman's education. My father was not only fond of this young man's society, whose manners were always engaging; he had also the highest opinion of him, and hoping the church would be his profession, intended to provide for him in it. As for myself, it is many, many years since I first began to think of him in a very different manner. The vicious propensities —the want of principle which he was careful to guard from the knowledge of his best friend, could not escape the observation of a young man of nearly the same age with himself, and who had opportunities of seeing him in unguarded moments, which Mr. Darcy could not have. Here again I shall give you pain—to what degree you only can tell. But whatever may be the sentiments which Mr. Wickham has created, a suspicion of their nature shall not prevent me from unfolding his real character. It adds even another motive. My excellent father died about five years ago; and his attachment to Mr. Wickham was to the last so steady, that in his will he particularly recommended it to me, to promote his advancement in the best manner that his profession might allow, and if he took orders, desired that a valuable family living might be his as soon as it became vacant. There was also a legacy of one thousand pounds. His own father did not long survive mine, and within half a year from these events, Mr. Wickham wrote to inform me that, having finally resolved against taking orders, he hoped I should not think it unreasonable for him to expect some more immediate pecuniary advantage, in lieu of the preferment, by which he could not be benefited. He had some intention, he added, of studying the law, and I must be aware that the interest of one thousand pounds would be a very insufficient support therein. I rather wished, than believed him to be sincere; but at any rate, was perfectly ready to accede to his proposal. I knew that Mr. Wickham ought not to be a clergyman. The business was therefore soon settled. He resigned all claim to assistance in the church, were it possible that he could ever be in a situation to receive it, and accepted in return three thousand pounds. All connection between us seemed now dissolved. I thought too ill of him, to invite him to Pemberley, or admit his society in town. In town I believe he chiefly lived, but his studying the law was a mere pretence, and being now free from all restraint, his life was a life of idleness and dissipation. For about three years I heard little of him; but on the decease of the incumbent of the living which had been designed for him, he applied to me again by letter for the presentation. His circumstances, he assured me, and I had no difficulty in believing it, were exceedingly bad. He had found the law a most unprofitable study, and was now absolutely resolved on being ordained, if I would present him to the living in question—of which he trusted there could be little doubt, as he was well assured that I had no other person to provide for, and I could not have forgotten my revered father's intentions. You will hardly blame me for refusing to comply with this entreaty, or for resisting every repetition of it. His resentment was in proportion to the distress of his circumstances—and he was doubtless as violent in his abuse of me to others, as in his reproaches to myself. After this period, every appearance of acquaintance was dropt. How he lived I know not. But last summer he was again most painfully obtruded on my notice. I must now mention a circumstance which I would wish to forget myself, and which no obligation less than the present should induce me to unfold to any human being. Having said thus much, I feel no doubt of your secrecy. My sister, who is more than ten years my junior, was left to the guardianship of my mother's nephew, Colonel Fitzwilliam, and myself. About a year ago, she was taken from school, and an establishment formed for her in London; and last summer she went with the lady who presided over it, to Ramsgate; and thither also went Mr. Wickham, undoubtedly by design; for there proved to have been a prior acquaintance between him and Mrs. Younge, in whose character we were most unhappily deceived; and by her connivance and aid, he so far recommended himself to Georgiana, whose affectionate heart retained a strong impression of his kindness to her as a child, that she was persuaded to believe herself in love, and to consent to an elopement. She was then but fifteen, which must be her excuse; and after stating her imprudence, I am happy to add, that I owed the knowledge of it to herself. I joined them unexpectedly a day or two before the intended elopement, and then Georgiana, unable to support the idea of grieving and offending a brother whom she almost looked up to as a father, acknowledged the whole to me. You may imagine what I felt and how I acted. Regard for my sister's credit and feelings prevented any public exposure, but I wrote to Mr. Wickham, who left the place immediately, and Mrs. Younge was of course removed from her charge. Mr. Wickham's chief object was unquestionably my sister's fortune, which is thirty thousand pounds; but I cannot help supposing that the hope of revenging himself on me, was a strong inducement. His revenge would have been complete indeed. This, madam, is a faithful narrative of every event in which we have been concerned together; and if you do not absolutely reject it as false, you will, I hope, acquit me henceforth of cruelty towards Mr. Wickham. I know not in what manner, under what form of falsehood he has imposed on you; but his success is not perhaps to be wondered at. Ignorant as you previously were of every thing concerning either,[5] detection could not be in your power, and suspicion certainly not in your inclination. You may possibly wonder why all this was not told you last night. But I was not then master enough of myself to know what could or ought to be revealed. For the truth of every thing here related, I can appeal more particularly to the testimony of Colonel Fitzwilliam, who from our near relationship and constant intimacy, and still more as one of the executors of my father's will, has been unavoidably acquainted with every particular of these transactions. If your abhorrence of *me* should make *my* assertions valueless, you cannot be prevented by the same cause from confiding in my cousin; and that there may be the possibility of consulting him, I shall endeavour to find some opportunity of putting this letter in your hands in the course of the morning. I will only add, God bless you.

"'FITZWILLIAM DARCY'"

Chapter XIII

If Elizabeth, when Mr. Darcy gave her the letter, did not expect it to contain a renewal of his offers, she had formed no expectation at all of its contents. But such as they were, it may be well supposed how eagerly she went through them, and what a contrariety of emotion they excited. Her feelings as she read were scarcely to be defined. With amazement did she first understand that he believed any apology to be in his power; and stedfastly was she

5. In all editions before Chapman's this passage reads: "* * * to be wondered at, ignorant as you previously were of every thing concerning either. Detection could not * * *." In his text Mr. Chapman accepts an emendation suggested by another close student of Jane Austen's novels, Henry Jackson.

persuaded that he could have no explanation to give, which a just sense of shame would not conceal. With a strong prejudice against every thing he might say, she began his account of what had happened at Netherfield. She read, with an eagerness which hardly left her power of comprehension, and from impatience of knowing what the next sentence might bring, was incapable of attending to the sense of the one before her eyes. His belief of her sister's insensibility, she instantly resolved to be false, and his account of the real, the worst objections to the match, made her too angry to have any wish of doing him justice. He expressed no regret for what he had done which satisfied her; his style was not penitent, but haughty. It was all pride and insolence.

But when this subject was succeeded by his account of Mr. Wickham, when she read with somewhat clearer attention, a relation of events, which, if true, must overthrow every cherished opinion of his worth, and which bore so alarming an affinity to his own history of himself, her feelings were yet more acutely painful and more difficult of definition. Astonishment, apprehension, and even horror, oppressed her. She wished to discredit it entirely, repeatedly exclaiming, "This must be false! This cannot be! This must be the grossest falsehood!"—and when she had gone through the whole letter, though scarcely knowing any thing of the last page or two, put it hastily away, protesting that she would not regard it, that she would never look in it again.

In this perturbed state of mind, with thoughts that could rest on nothing, she walked on; but it would not do; in half a minute the letter was unfolded again, and collecting herself as well as she could, she again began the mortifying perusal of all that related to Wickham, and commanded herself so far as to examine the meaning of every sentence. The account of his connection with the Pemberley family, was exactly what he had related himself; and the kindness of the late Mr. Darcy, though she had not before known its extent, agreed equally well with his own words. So far each recital confirmed the other: but when she came to the will, the difference was great. What Wickham had said of the living was fresh in her memory, and as she recalled his very words, it was impossible not to feel that there was gross duplicity on one side or the other; and, for a few moments, she flattered herself that her wishes did not err. But when she read, and re-read with the closest attention, the particulars immediately following of Wickham's resigning all pretensions to the living, of his receiving in lieu, so considerable a sum as three thousand pounds, again was she forced to hesitate. She put down the letter, weighed every circumstance with what she meant to be impartiality —deliberated on the probability of each statement—but with little success. On both sides it was only assertion. Again she read on. But every line proved more clearly that the affair, which she had believed it impossible that any contrivance could so represent, as to render Mr. Darcy's conduct in it less than infamous, was capable of a turn which must make him entirely blameless throughout the whole.

The extravagance and general profligacy which he scrupled not to lay to Mr. Wickham's charge, exceedingly shocked her; the more so, as she could bring no proof of its injustice. She had never heard of him before his entrance into the ———shire Militia, in which he had engaged at the persuasion of the young man, who, on meeting him accidentally in town, had there renewed a slight acquaintance. Of his former way of life, nothing had been known in Hertfordshire but what he told himself. As to his real character, had information been in her power, she had never felt a wish of enquiring. His countenance, voice, and manner, had established him at once in the possession of every virtue. She tried to recollect some instance of goodness, some distinguished trait of integrity or benevolence, that might rescue him from the attacks of Mr. Darcy; or at least, by the predominance of virtue, atone for those casual errors, under which she would endeavour to class, what Mr. Darcy had described as the idleness and vice of many years continuance. But no such recollection befriended her. She could see him instantly before her, in every charm of air and address; but she could remember no more substantial good than the general approbation of the neighbourhood, and the regard which his social powers had gained him in the mess. After pausing on this point a considerable while, she once more continued to read. But, alas! the story which followed of his designs on Miss Darcy, received some confirmation from what had passed between Colonel Fitzwilliam and herself only the morning before; and at last she was referred for the truth of every particular to Colonel Fitzwilliam himself—from whom she had previously received the information of his near concern in all his cousin's affairs, and whose character she had no reason to question. At one time she had almost resolved on applying to him, but the idea was checked by the awkwardness of the application, and at length wholly banished by the conviction that Mr. Darcy would never have hazarded such a proposal, if he had not been well assured of his cousin's corroboration.

She perfectly remembered every thing that had passed in conversation between Wickham and herself, in their first evening at Mr. Philips's. Many of his expressions were still fresh in her memory. She was *now* struck with the impropriety of such communications to a stranger, and wondered it had escaped her before.

She saw the indelicacy of putting himself forward as he had done, and the inconsistency of his professions with his conduct. She remembered that he had boasted of having no fear of seeing Mr. Darcy—that Mr. Darcy might leave the country, but that *he* should stand his ground; yet he had avoided the Netherfield ball the very next week. She remembered also, that till the Netherfield family had quitted the country, he had told his story to no one but herself; but that after their removal, it had been every where discussed; that he had then no reserves, no scruples in sinking Mr. Darcy's character, though he had assured her that respect for the father, would always prevent his exposing the son.

How differently did every thing now appear in which he was concerned! His attentions to Miss King were now the consequence of views solely and hatefully mercenary; and the mediocrity of her fortune proved no longer the moderation of his wishes, but his eagerness to grasp at any thing. His behaviour to herself could now have had no tolerable motive; he had either been deceived with regard to her fortune, or had been gratifying his vanity by encouraging the preference which she believed she had most incautiously shewn. Every lingering struggle in his favour grew fainter and fainter; and in farther justification of Mr. Darcy, she could not but allow that Mr. Bingley, when questioned by Jane, had long ago asserted his blamelessness in the affair; that proud and repulsive as were his manners, she had never, in the whole course of their acquaintance, an acquaintance which had latterly brought them much together, and given her a sort of intimacy with his ways, seen any thing that betrayed him to be unprincipled or unjust—any thing that spoke him of irreligious or immoral habits. That among his own connections he was esteemed and valued—that even Wickham had allowed him merit as a brother, and that she had often heard him speak so affectionately of his sister as to prove him capable of *some* amiable feeling. That had his actions been what Wickham represented them, so gross a violation of every thing right could hardly have been concealed from the world; and that friendship between a person capable of it, and such an amiable man as Mr. Bingley, was incomprehensible.

She grew absolutely ashamed of herself.—Of neither Darcy nor Wickham could she think, without feeling that she had been blind, partial, prejudiced, absurd.

"How despicably have I acted!" she cried.—"I, who have prided myself on my discernment!—I, who have valued myself on my abilities! who have often disdained the generous candour of my sister, and gratified my vanity, in useless or blameable distrust.—How humiliating is this discovery!—Yet, how just a humiliation!—Had I been in love, I could not have been more wretchedly blind. But vanity, not love, has been my folly.—Pleased with the preference of one, and offended by the neglect of the other, on the very beginning of our acquaintance, I have courted prepossession and ignorance, and driven reason away, where either were concerned. Till this moment, I never knew myself."

From herself to Jane—from Jane to Bingley, her thoughts were in a line which soon brought to her recollection that Mr. Darcy's explanation *there*, had appeared very insufficient; and she read it again. Widely different was the effect of a second perusal.—How could she deny that credit to his assertions, in one instance, which she had been obliged to give in the other?—He declared himself to have been totally unsuspicious of her sister's attachment;—and she could not help remembering what Charlotte's opinion had always been.—Neither could she deny the justice of his description of Jane.—She felt that Jane's feelings, though fervent, were little displayed, and that there was a constant complacency in her air and manner, not often united with great sensibility.

When she came to that part of the letter in which her family were mentioned, in terms of such mortifying, yet merited reproach, her sense of shame was severe. The justice of the charge struck her too forcibly for denial, and the circumstances to which he particularly alluded, as having passed at the Netherfield ball, and as confirming all his first disapprobation, could not have made a stronger impression on his mind than on hers.

The compliment to herself and her sister, was not unfelt. It soothed, but it could not console her for the contempt which had been thus self-attracted by the rest of her family;—and as she considered that Jane's disappointment had in fact been the work of her nearest relations, and reflected how materially the credit of both must be hurt by such impropriety of conduct, she felt depressed beyond any thing she had ever known before.

After wandering along the lane for two hours, giving way to every variety of thought; re-considering events, determining probabilities, and reconciling herself as well as she could, to a change so sudden and so important, fatigue, and a recollection of her long absence, made her at length return home; and she entered the house with the wish of appearing cheerful as usual, and the resolution of repressing such reflections as must make her unfit for conversation.

She was immediately told, that the two gentlemen from Rosings had each called during her absence; Mr. Darcy, only for a few minutes to take leave, but that Colonel Fitzwilliam had been sitting with them at least an hour, hoping for her return, and almost resolving to walk after her till she could be found.—Elizabeth could but just *affect* concern in missing him; she really rejoiced at it. Colonel Fitzwilliam was no longer an object. She could think only of her letter.

Chapter XIV

The two gentlemen left Rosings the next morning; and Mr. Collins having been in waiting near the lodges, to make them his parting obeisance, was able to bring home the pleasing intelligence, of their appearing in very good health, and in as tolerable spirits as could be expected, after the melancholy scene so lately gone through at Rosings. To Rosings he then hastened to console Lady Catherine, and her daughter; and on his return, brought back, with great satisfaction, a message from her Ladyship, importing that she felt herself so dull as to make her very desirous of having them all to dine with her.

Elizabeth could not see Lady Catherine without recollecting, that had she chosen it, she might by this time have been presented to her, as her future niece; nor could she think, without a smile, of what her ladyship's indignation would have been. "What would she have said?—how would she have behaved?" were questions with which she amused herself.

Their first subject was the diminution of the Rosings party.—"I assure you, I feel it execeedingly," said Lady Catherine; "I believe nobody feels the loss of friends so much as I do. But I am particularly attached to these young men; and know them to be so much attached to me!—They were excessively sorry to go! But so they always are. The dear colonel rallied his spirits tolerably till just at last; but Darcy seemed to feel it most acutely, more I think than last year. His attachment to Rosings, certainly increases."

Mr. Collins had a compliment, and an allusion to throw in here, which were kindly smiled on by the mother and daughter.

Lady Catherine observed, after dinner, that Miss Bennet seemed out of spirits, and immediately accounting for it herself, by supposing that she did not like to go home again so soon, she added,

"But if that is the case, you must write to your mother to beg that you may stay a little longer. Mrs. Collins will be very glad of your company, I am sure."

"I am much obliged to your ladyship for your kind invitation," replied Elizabeth, "but it is not in my power to accept it.—I must be in town next Saturday."

"Why, at that rate, you will have been here only six weeks. I expected you to stay two months. I told Mrs. Collins so before you came. There can be no occasion for your going so soon.

Mrs. Bennet could certainly spare you for another fortnight."

"But my father cannot.—He wrote last week to hurry my return."

"Oh! your father of course may spare you, if your mother can.— Daughters are never of so much consequence to a father. And if you will stay another *month* complete, it will be in my power to take one of you as far as London, for I am going there early in June, for a week; and as Dawson does not object to the Barouche box,⁶ there will be very good room for one of you—and indeed, if the weather should happen to be cool, I should not object to taking you both, as you are neither of you large."

"You are all kindness, Madam; but I believe we must abide by our original plan."

Lady Catherine seemed resigned.

"Mrs. Collins, you must send a servant with them. You know I always speak my mind, and I cannot bear the idea of two young women travelling post ⁷ by themselves. It is highly improper. You must contrive to send somebody. I have the greatest dislike in the world to that sort of thing.—Young women should always be properly guarded and attended, according to their situation in life. When my niece Georgiana went to Ramsgate last summer, I made a point of her having two men servants go with her.—Miss Darcy, the daughter of Mr. Darcy, of Pemberley, and Lady Anne, could not have appeared with propriety in a different manner.—I am excessively attentive to all those things. You must send John with the young ladies, Mrs. Collins. I am glad it occured to me to mention it; for it would really be discreditable to *you* to let them go alone."

"My uncle is to send a servant for us."

"Oh!—Your uncle!—He keeps a man-servant, does he?—I am very glad you have somebody who thinks of those things. Where shall you change horses?—Oh! Bromley, of course.—If you mention my name at the Bell, you will be attended to."

Lady Catherine had many other questions to ask respecting their journey, and as she did not answer them all herself, attention was necessary, which Elizabeth believed to be lucky for her; or, with a mind so occupied, she might have forgotten where she was. Reflection must be reserved for solitary hours; whenever she was alone, she gave way to it as the greatest relief; and not a day went by without a solitary walk, in which she might indulge in all the delight of unpleasant recollections.

Mr. Darcy's letter, she was in a fair way of soon knowing by heart. She studied every sentence: and her feelings towards its

6. That is, the servant Dawson does not object to riding on the outside of the carriage.

7. Traveling by carriage and hiring horses at stages of the journey.

writer were at times widely different. When she remembered the style of his address, she was still full of indignation; but when she considered how unjustly she had condemned and upbraided him, her anger was turned against herself; and his disappointed feelings became the object of compassion. His attachment excited gratitude, his general character respect; but she could not approve him; nor could she for a moment repent her refusal, or feel the slightest inclination ever to see him again. In her own past behaviour, there was a constant source of vexation and regret; and in the unhappy defects of her family a subject of yet heavier chagrin. They were hopeless of remedy. Her father, contented with laughing at them, would never exert himself to restrain the wild giddiness of his youngest daughters; and her mother, with manners so far from right herself, was entirely insensible of the evil. Elizabeth had frequently united with Jane in an endeavour to check the imprudence of Catherine and Lydia; but while they were supported by their mother's indulgence, what chance could there be of improvement? Catherine, weak-spirited, irritable, and completely under Lydia's guidance, had been always affronted by their advice; and Lydia, self-willed and careless, would scarcely give them a hearing. They were ignorant, idle, and vain. While there was an officer in Meryton, they would flirt with him; and while Meryton was within a walk of Longbourn, they would be going there for ever.

Anxiety on Jane's behalf, was another prevailing concern, and Mr. Darcy's explanation, by restoring Bingley to all her former good opinion, heightened the sense of what Jane had lost. His affection was proved to have been sincere, and his conduct cleared of all blame, unless any could attach to the implicitness of his confidence in his friend. How grievous then was the thought that, of a situation so desirable in every respect, so replete with advantage, so promising for happiness, Jane had been deprived, by the folly and indecorum of her own family!

When to these recollections was added the developement of Wickham's character, it may be easily believed that the happy spirits which had seldom been depressed before, were now so much affected as to make it almost impossible for her to appear tolerably cheerful.

Their engagements at Rosings were as frequent during the last week of her stay, as they had been at first. The very last evening was spent there; and her Ladyship again enquired minutely into the particulars of their journey, gave them directions as to the best method of packing, and was so urgent on the necessity of placing gowns in the only right way, that Maria thought herself obliged, on her return, to undo all the work of the morning, and pack her trunk afresh.

When they parted, Lady Catherine, with great condescension, wished them a good journey, and invited them to come to Hunsford again next year; and Miss De Bourgh exerted herself so far as to curtsey and hold out her hand to both.

Chapter XV

On Saturday morning Elizabeth and Mr. Collins met for breakfast a few minutes before the others appeared; and he took the opportunity of paying the parting civilities which he deemed indispensably necessary.

"I know not, Miss Elizabeth," said he, "whether Mrs. Collins has yet expressed her sense of your kindness in coming to us, but I am very certain you will not leave the house without receiving her thanks for it. The favour of your company has been much felt, I assure you. We know how little there is to tempt any one to our humble abode. Our plain manner of living, our small rooms, and few domestics, and the little we see of the world, must make Hunsford extremely dull to a young lady like yourself; but I hope you will believe us grateful for the condescension, and that we have done every thing in our power to prevent your spending your time unpleasantly."

Elizabeth was eager with her thanks and assurances of happiness. She had spent six weeks with great enjoyment; and the pleasure of being with Charlotte, and the kind attentions she had received, must make *her* feel the obliged. Mr. Collins was gratified; and with a more smiling solemnity replied,

"It gives me the greatest pleasure to hear that you have passed your time not disagreeably. We have certainly done our best; and most fortunately having it in our power to introduce you to very superior society, and from our connection with Rosings, the frequent means of varying the humble home scene, I think we may flatter ourselves that your Hunsford visit cannot have been entirely irksome. Our situation with regard to Lady Catherine's family is indeed the sort of extraordinary advantage and blessing which few can boast. You see on what a footing we are. You see how continually we are engaged there. In truth I must acknowledge that, with all the disadvantages of this humble parsonage, I should not think any one abiding in it an object of compassion, while they are sharers of our intimacy at Rosings."

Words were insufficient for the elevation of his feelings; and he was obliged to walk about the room, while Elizabeth tried to unite civility and truth in a few short sentences.

"You may, in fact, carry a very favourable report of us into

Hertfordshire, my dear cousin. I flatter myself at least that you will be able to do so. Lady Catherine's great attentions to Mrs. Collins you have been a daily witness of; and altogether I trust it does not appear that your friend has drawn an unfortunate—but on this point it will be as well to be silent. Only let me assure you, my dear Miss Elizabeth, that I can from my heart most cordially wish you equal felicity in marriage. My dear Charlotte and I have but one mind and one way of thinking. There is in every thing a most remarkable resemblance of character and ideas between us. We seem to have been designed for each other."

Elizabeth could safely say that it was a great happiness where that was the case, and with equal sincerity could add that she firmly believed and rejoiced in his domestic comforts. She was not sorry, however, to have the recital of them interrupted by the entrance of the lady from whom they sprung. Poor Charlotte!—it was melancholy to leave her to such society!—But she had chosen it with her eyes open; and though evidently regretting that her visitors were to go, she did not seem to ask for compassion. Her home and her housekeeping, her parish and her poultry, and all their dependent concerns, had not yet lost their charms.

At length the chaise arrived, the trunks were fastened on, the parcels placed within, and it was pronounced to be ready. After an affectionate parting between the friends, Elizabeth was attended to the carriage by Mr. Collins, and as they walked down the garden, he was commissioning her with his best respects to all her family, not forgetting his thanks for the kindness he had received at Longbourn in the winter, and his compliments to Mr. and Mrs. Gardiner, though unknown. He then handed her in, Maria followed, and the door was on the point of being closed, when he suddenly reminded them, with some consternation, that they had hitherto forgotten to leave any message for the ladies of Rosings.

"But," he added, "you will of course wish to have your humble respects delivered to them, with your grateful thanks for their kindness to you while you have been here."

Elizabeth made no objection;—the door was then allowed to be shut, and the carriage drove off.

"Good gracious!" cried Maria, after a few minutes silence, "it seems but a day or two since we first came!—and yet how many things have happened!"

"A great many indeed," said her companion with a sigh.

"We have dined nine times at Rosings, besides drinking tea there twice!—How much I shall have to tell!"

Elizabeth privately added, "And how much I shall have to conceal."

Their journey was performed without much conversation, or any alarm; and within four hours of their leaving Hunsford, they reached Mr. Gardiner's house, where they were to remain a few days.

Jane looked well, and Elizabeth had little opportunity of studying her spirits, amidst the various engagements which the kindness of her aunt had reserved for them. But Jane was to go home with her, and at Longbourn there would be leisure enough for observation.

It was not without an effort meanwhile that she could wait even for Longbourn, before she told her sister of Mr. Darcy's proposals. To know that she had the power of revealing what would so exceedingly astonish Jane, and must, at the same time, so highly gratify whatever of her own vanity she had not yet been able to reason away, was such a temptation to openness as nothing could have conquered, but the state of indecision in which she remained, as to the extent of what she should communicate; and her fear, if she once entered on the subject, of being hurried into repeating something of Bingley, which might only grieve her sister farther.

Chapter XVI

It was the second week in May, in which the three young ladies set out together from Gracechurch-street, for the town of ——— in Hertfordshire; and, as they drew near the appointed inn where Mr. Bennet's carriage was to meet them, they quickly perceived, in token of the coachman's punctuality, both Kitty and Lydia looking out of a dining room up stairs. These two girls had been above an hour in the place, happily employed in visiting an opposite milliner, watching the sentinel on guard, and dressing a sallad and cucumber.

After welcoming their sisters, they triumphantly displayed a table set out with such cold meat as an inn larder usually affords, exclaiming, "Is not this nice? is not this an agreeable surprise?"

"And we mean to treat you all," added Lydia; "but you must lend us the money, for we have just spent ours at the shop out there." Then shewing her purchases: "Look here, I have bought this bonnet. I do not think it is very pretty; but I thought I might as well buy it as not. I shall pull it to pieces as soon as I get home, and see if I can make it up any better."

And when her sisters abused it as ugly, she added, with perfect unconcern, "Oh! but there were two or three much uglier in the shop; and when I have bought some prettier-coloured satin to trim it with fresh, I think it will be very tolerable. Besides, it will not much signify what one wears this summer, after the ———— shire have left Meryton, and they are going in a fortnight."

"Are they indeed?" cried Elizabeth, with the greatest satisfaction.

"They are going to be encamped near Brighton; and I do so want papa to take us all there for the summer! It would be such a delicious scheme, and I dare say would hardly cost any thing at all. Mamma would like to go too of all things! Only think what a miserable summer else we shall have!"

"Yes," thought Elizabeth, "*that* would be a delightful scheme, indeed, and completely do for us at once. Good Heaven! Brighton, and a whole campful of soldiers, to us, who have been overset already by one poor regiment of militia, and the monthly balls of Meryton."

"Now I have got some news for you," said Lydia, as they sat down to table. "What do you think? It is excellent news, capital news, and about a certain person that we all like."

Jane and Elizabeth looked at each other, and the waiter was told that he need not stay. Lydia laughed, and said,

"Aye, that is just like your formality and discretion. You thought the waiter must not hear, as if he cared! I dare say he often hears worse things said than I am going to say. But he is an ugly fellow! I am glad he is gone. I never saw such a long chin in my life. Well, but now for my news: it is about dear Wickham; too good for the waiter, is not it? There is no danger of Wickham's marrying Mary King. There's for you! She is gone down to her uncle at Liverpool; gone to stay. Wickham is safe."

"And Mary King is safe!" added Elizabeth; "safe from a connection imprudent as to fortune."

"She is a great fool for going away, if she liked him."

"But I hope there is no strong attachment on either side," said Jane.

"I am sure there is not on *his*. I will answer for it he never cared three straws about her. Who *could* about such a nasty little freckled thing?"

Elizabeth was shocked to think that, however incapable of such coarseness of *expression* herself, the coarseness of the *sentiment* was little other than her own breast had formerly harboured and fancied liberal!

As soon as all had ate, and the elder ones paid, the carriage was ordered; and after some contrivance, the whole party, with all their boxes, workbags, and parcels, and the unwelcome addition of Kitty's and Lydia's purchases, were seated in it.

"How nicely we are crammed in!" cried Lydia. "I am glad I bought my bonnet, if it is only for the fun of having another bandbox! Well, now let us be quite comfortable and snug, and talk and laugh all the way home. And in the first place, let us hear what has happened to you all, since you went away. Have you seen any pleasant men? Have you had any flirting? I was in great hopes that one of you would have got a husband before you came back. Jane will be quite an old maid soon, I declare. She is almost three and twenty! Lord, how ashamed I should be of not being married before three and twenty! My aunt Philips wants you so to get husbands, you can't think. She says Lizzy had better have taken Mr. Collins; but *I* do not think there would have been any fun in it. Lord! how I should like to be married before any of you; and then I would chaperon you about to all the balls. Dear me! we had such a good piece of fun the other day at Colonel Forster's. Kitty and me were to spend the day there, and Mrs. Forster promised to have a little dance in the evening; (by the bye, Mrs. Forster and me are *such* friends!) and so she asked the two Harringtons to come, but Harriet was ill, and so Pen was forced to come by herself; and then, what do you think we did? We dressed up Chamberlayne in woman's clothes, on purpose to pass for a lady,— only think what fun! Not a soul knew of it, but Col. and Mrs. Forster, and Kitty and me, except my aunt, for we were forced to borrow one of her gowns; and you cannot imagine how well he looked! When Denny, and Wickham, and Pratt, and two or three more of the men came in, they did not know him in the least. Lord! how I laughed! and so did Mrs. Forster. I thought I should have died. And *that* made the men suspect something, and then they soon found out what was the matter."

With such kind of histories of their parties and good jokes, did Lydia, assisted by Kitty's hints and additions, endeavour to amuse her companions all the way to Longbourn. Elizabeth listened as little as she could, but there was no escaping the frequent mention of Wickham's name.

Their reception at home was most kind. Mrs. Bennet rejoiced to see Jane in undiminished beauty; and more than once during dinner did Mr. Bennet say voluntarily to Elizabeth,

"I am glad you are come back, Lizzy."

Their party in the dining-room was large, for almost all the Lucases came to meet Maria and hear the news: and various were the subjects which occupied them; lady Lucas was enquiring of Maria across the table, after the welfare and poultry of her eldest daughter; Mrs. Bennet was doubly engaged, on one hand collecting an account of the present fashions from Jane, who sat some way below her, and on the other, retailing them all to the younger Miss Lucases; and Lydia, in a voice rather louder than any other person's, was enumerating the various pleasures of the morning to any body who would hear her.

"Oh! Mary," said she, "I wish you had gone with us, for we had such fun! as we went along, Kitty and me drew up all the blinds, and pretended there was nobody in the coach; and I should have gone so all the way, if Kitty had not been sick; and when we got to the George, I do think we behaved very handsomely, for we treated the other three with the nicest cold luncheon in the world, and if you would have gone, we would have treated you too. And then when we came away it was such fun! I thought we never should have got into the coach. I was ready to die of laughter. And then we were so merry all the way home! we talked and laughed so loud, that any body might have heard us ten miles off!"

To this, Mary very gravely replied, "Far be it from me, my dear sister, to depreciate such pleasures. They would doubtless be congenial with the generality of female minds. But I confess they would have no charms for *me*. I should infinitely prefer a book."

But of this answer Lydia heard not a word. She seldom listened to any body for more than half a minute, and never attended to Mary at all.

In the afternoon Lydia was urgent with the rest of the girls to walk to Meryton and see how every body went on; but Elizabeth steadily opposed the scheme. It should not be said, that the Miss Bennets could not be at home half a day before they were in pursuit of the officers. There was another reason too for her opposition. She dreaded seeing Wickham again, and was resolved to avoid it as long as possible. The comfort to *her*, of the regiment's approaching removal, was indeed beyond expression. In a fortnight they were to go, and once gone, she hoped there could be nothing more to plague her on his account.

She had not been many hours at home, before she found that the Brighton scheme, of which Lydia had given them a hint at the inn, was under frequent discussion between her parents. Elizabeth saw directly that her father had not the smallest intention of yielding; but his answers were at the same time so vague and equivocal, that her mother, though often disheartened, had never yet despaired of succeeding at last.

Chapter XVII

Elizabeth's impatience to acquaint Jane with what had happened could no longer be overcome; and at length resolving to suppress every particular in which her sister was concerned, and preparing her to be surprised, she related to her the next morning the chief of the scene between Mr. Darcy and herself.

Miss Bennet's astonishment was soon lessened by the strong sisterly partiality which made any admiration of Elizabeth appear perfectly natural; and all surprise was shortly lost in other feelings. She was sorry that Mr. Darcy should have delivered his sentiments in a manner so little suited to recommend them; but still more was she grieved for the unhappiness which her sister's refusal must have given him.

"His being so sure of succeeding, was wrong," said she; "and certainly ought not to have appeared; but consider how much it must increase his disappointment."

"Indeed," replied Elizabeth, "I am heartily sorry for him; but he has other feelings which will probably soon drive away his regard for me. You do not blame me, however, for refusing him?"

"Blame you! Oh, no."

"But you blame me for having spoken so warmly of Wickham."

"No—I do not know that you were wrong in saying what you did."

"But you *will* know it, when I have told you what happened the very next day."

She then spoke of the letter, repeating the whole of its contents as far as they concerned George Wickham. What a stroke was this for poor Jane! who would willingly have gone through the world without believing that so much wickedness existed in the whole race of mankind, as was here collected in one individual. Nor was Darcy's vindication, though grateful to her feelings, capable of consoling her for such discovery. Most earnestly did she labour to prove the probability of error, and seek to clear one, without involving the other.

"This will not do," said Elizabeth. "You never will be able to make both of them good for any thing. Take your choice, but you must be satisfied with only one. There is but such a quantity of merit between them; just enough to make one good sort of man; and of late it has been shifting about pretty much. For my part, I am inclined to believe it all Mr. Darcy's, but you shall do as you chuse."

It was some time, however, before a smile could be extorted from Jane.

"I do not know when I have been more shocked," said she. "Wickham so very bad! It is almost past belief. And poor Mr. Darcy! dear Lizzy, only consider what he must have suffered. Such a disappointment! and with the knowledge of your ill opinion too! and having to relate such a thing of his sister! It is really too distressing. I am sure you must feel it so."

"Oh! no, my regret and compassion are all done away by seeing you so full of both. I know you will do him such ample justice, that I am growing every moment more unconcerned and indifferent. Your profusion makes me saving; and if you lament over him much longer, my heart will be as light as a feather."

"Poor Wickham; there is such an expression of goodness in his countenance! such an openness and gentleness in his manner."

"There certainly was some great mismanagement in the education of those two young men. One has got all the goodness, and the other all the appearance of it."

"I never thought Mr. Darcy so deficient in the *appearance* of it as you used to do."

"And yet I meant to be uncommonly clever in taking so decided a dislike to him, without any reason. It is such a spur to one's genius, such an opening for wit to have a dislike of that kind. One may be continually abusive without saying any thing just; but one cannot be always laughing at a man without now and then stumbling on something witty."

"Lizzy, when you first read that letter, I am sure you could not treat the matter as you do now."

"Indeed I could not. I was uncomfortable enough. I was very uncomfortable, I may say unhappy. And with no one to speak to, of what I felt, no Jane to comfort me and say that I had not been so very weak and vain and nonsensical as I knew I had! Oh! how I wanted you!"

"How unfortunate that you should have used such very strong expressions in speaking of Wickham to Mr. Darcy, for now they *do* appear wholly undeserved."

"Certainly. But the misfortune of speaking with bitterness, is a most natural consequence of the prejudices I had been encouraging. There is one point, on which I want your advice. I want to be told whether I ought, or ought not to make our acquaintance in general understand Wickham's character."

Miss Bennet paused a little and then replied, "Surely there can be no occasion for exposing him so dreadfully. What is your own opinion?"

"That it ought not to be attempted. Mr. Darcy has not authorised me to make his communication public. On the contrary every particular relative to his sister, was meant to be kept as much as possible to myself; and if I endeavour to undeceive people as to the rest of his conduct, who will believe me? The general prejudice against Mr. Darcy is so violent, that it would be the death of half the good people in Meryton, to attempt to place him in an amiable light. I am not equal to it. Wickham will soon be gone; and therefore it will not signify to anybody here, what he really is. Sometime hence it will be all found out, and then we may laugh at their stupidity in not knowing it before. At present

I will say nothing about it."

"You are quite right. To have his errors made public might ruin him for ever. He is now perhaps sorry for what he has done, and anxious to re-establish a character. We must not make him desperate."

The tumult of Elizabeth's mind was allayed by this conversation. She had got rid of two of the secrets which had weighed on her for a fortnight, and was certain of a willing listener in Jane, whenever she might wish to talk again of either. But there was still something lurking behind, of which prudence forbad the disclosure. She dared not relate the other half of Mr. Darcy's letter, nor explain to her sister how sincerely she had been valued by his friend. Here was knowledge in which no one could partake; and she was sensible that nothing less than a perfect understanding between the parties could justify her in throwing off this last incumbrance of mystery. "And then," said she, "if that very improbable event should ever take place, I shall merely be able to tell what Bingley may tell in a much more agreeable manner himself. The liberty of communication cannot be mine till it has lost all its value!"

She was now, on being settled at home, at leisure to observe the real state of her sister's spirits. Jane was not happy. She still cherished a very tender affection for Bingley. Having never even fancied herself in love before, her regard had all the warmth of first attachment, and from her age and disposition, greater steadiness than first attachments often boast; and so fervently did she value his remembrance, and prefer him to every other man, that all her good sense, and all her attention to the feelings of her friends, were requisite to check the indulgence of those regrets, which must have been injurious to her own health and their tranquillity.

"Well, Lizzy," said Mrs. Bennet one day, "what is your opinion *now* of this sad business of Jane's? For my part, I am determined never to speak of it again to anybody. I told my sister Philips so the other day. But I cannot find out that Jane saw any thing of him in London. Well, he is a very undeserving young man—and I do not suppose there is the least chance in the world of her ever getting him now. There is no talk of his coming to Netherfield again in the summer; and I have enquired of every body too, who is likely to know."

"I do not believe that he will ever live at Netherfield any more."

"Oh, well! it is just as he chooses. Nobody wants him to come. Though I shall always say that he used my daughter extremely ill; and if I was her, I would not have put up with it. Well, my comfort is, I am sure Jane will die of a broken heart, and then he will be sorry for what he has done."

But as Elizabeth could not receive comfort from any such expectation, she made no answer.

"Well, Lizzy," continued her mother soon afterwards, "and so the Collinses live very comfortable, do they? Well, well, I only hope it will last. And what sort of table do they keep? Charlotte is an excellent manager, I dare say. If she is half as sharp as her mother, she is saving enough. There is nothing extravagant in *their* housekeeping, I dare say."

"No, nothing at all."

"A great deal of good management, depend upon it. Yes, yes. *They* will take care not to outrun their income. *They* will never be distressed for money. Well, much good may it do them! And so, I suppose, they often talk of having Longbourn when your father is dead. They look upon it quite as their own, I dare say, whenever that happens."

"It was a subject which they could not mention before me."

"No. It would have been strange if they had. But I make no doubt, they often talk of it between themselves. Well, if they can be easy with an estate that is not lawfully their own, so much the better. *I* should be ashamed of having one that was only entailed on me."

Chapter XVIII

The first week of their return was soon gone. The second began. It was the last of the regiment's stay in Meryton, and all the young ladies in the neighbourhood were drooping apace. The dejection was almost universal. The elder Miss Bennets alone were still able to eat, drink, and sleep, and pursue the usual course of their employments. Very frequently were they reproached for this insensibility by Kitty and Lydia, whose own misery was extreme, and who could not comprehend such hardheartedness in any of the family.

"Good Heaven! What is to become of us! What are we to do!" would they often exclaim in the bitterness of woe. "How can you be smiling so, Lizzy?"

Their affectionate mother shared all their grief; she remembered what she had herself endured on a similar occasion, five and twenty years ago.

"I am sure," said she, "I cried for two days together when Colonel Millar's regiment went away. I thought I should have broke my heart."

"I am sure I shall break *mine*," said Lydia.

"If one could but go to Brighton!" observed Mrs. Bennet.

"Oh, yes!—if one could but go to Brighton! But papa is so disagreeable."

"A little sea-bathing would set me up for ever."

"And my aunt Philips is sure it would do *me* a great deal of good," added Kitty.

Such were the kind of lamentations resounding perpetually through Longbourn-house. Elizabeth tried to be diverted by them; but all sense of pleasure was lost in shame. She felt anew the justice of Mr. Darcy's objections; and never had she before been so much disposed to pardon his interference in the views of his friend.

But the gloom of Lydia's prospect was shortly cleared away; for she received an invitation from Mrs. Forster, the wife of the Colonel of the regiment, to accompany her to Brighton. This invaluable friend was a very young woman, and very lately married. A resemblance in good humour and good spirits had recommended her and Lydia to each other, and out of their *three* months' acquaintance they had been intimate *two*.

The rapture of Lydia on this occasion, her adoration of Mrs. Forster, the delight of Mrs. Bennet, and the mortification of Kitty, are scarcely to be described. Wholly inattentive to her sister's feelings, Lydia flew about the house in restless ecstacy, calling for every one's congratulations, and laughing and talking with more violence than ever; whilst the luckless Kitty continued in the parlour repining at her fate in terms as unreasonable as her accent was peevish.

"I cannot see why Mrs. Forster should not ask *me* as well as Lydia," said she, "though I am *not* her particular friend. I have just as much right to be asked as she has, and more too, for I am two years older."

In vain did Elizabeth attempt to make her reasonable, and Jane to make her resigned. As for Elizabeth herself, this invitation was so far from exciting in her the same feelings as in her mother and Lydia, that she considered it as the death-warrant of all possibility of common sense for the latter; and detestable as such a step must make her were it known, she could not help secretly advising her father not to let her go. She represented to him all the improprieties of Lydia's general behaviour, the little advantage she could derive from the friendship of such a woman as Mrs. Forster, and the probability of her being yet more imprudent with such a companion at Brighton, where the temptations must be greater than at home. He heard her attentively, and then said,

"Lydia will never be easy till she has exposed herself in some public place or other, and we can never expect her to do it with so little expense or inconvenience to her family as under the present circumstances."

"If you were aware," said Elizabeth, "of the very great disadvantage to us all, which must arise from the public notice of Lydia's unguarded and imprudent manner; nay, which has already arisen from it, I am sure you would judge differently in the affair."

"Already arisen!" repeated Mr. Bennet. "What, has she frightened away some of your lovers? Poor little Lizzy! But do not be cast down. Such squeamish youths as cannot bear to be connected with a little absurdity, are not worth a regret. Come, let me see the list of the pitiful fellows who have been kept aloof by Lydia's folly."

"Indeed you are mistaken. I have no such injuries to resent. It is not of peculiar, but of general evils, which I am now complaining. Our importance, our respectability in the world, must be affected by the wild volatility, the assurance and disdain of all restraint which mark Lydia's character. Excuse me—for I must speak plainly. If you, my dear father, will not take the trouble of checking her exuberant spirits, and of teaching her that her present pursuits are not to be the business of her life, she will soon be beyond the reach of amendment. Her character will be fixed, and she will, at sixteen, be the most determined flirt that ever made herself and her family ridiculous. A flirt too, in the worst and meanest degree of flirtation; without any attraction beyond youth and a tolerable person; and from the ignorance and emptiness of her mind, wholly unable to ward off any portion of that universal contempt which her rage for admiration will excite. In this danger Kitty is also comprehended. She will follow wherever Lydia leads. Vain, ignorant, idle, and absolutely uncontrouled! Oh! my dear father, can you suppose it possible that they will not be censured and despised wherever they are known, and that their sisters will not be often involved in the disgrace?"

Mr. Bennet saw that her whole heart was in the subject; and affectionately taking her hand, said in reply,

"Do not make yourself uneasy, my love. Wherever you and Jane are known, you must be respected and valued; and you will not appear to less advantage for having a couple of—or I may say, three very silly sisters. We shall have no peace at Longbourn if Lydia does not go to Brighton. Let her go then. Colonel Forster is a sensible man, and will keep her out of any real mischief; and she is luckily too poor to be an object of prey to any body. At Brighton she will be of less importance even as a common flirt than she has been here. The officers will find women better worth their notice. Let us hope, therefore, that her being there may teach her her own insignificance. At any rate, she cannot grow many degrees worse, without authorizing us to lock her up for the rest of her life."

With this answer Elizabeth was forced to be content; but her own opinion continued the same, and she left him disappointed and sorry. It was not in her nature, however, to increase her vexations, by dwelling on them. She was confident of having performed her duty, and to fret over unavoidable evils, or augment them by anxiety, was no part of her disposition.

Had Lydia and her mother known the substance of her conference with her father, their indignation would hardly have found expression in their united volubility. In Lydia's imagination, a visit to Brighton comprised every possibility of earthly happiness. She saw with the creative eye of fancy, the streets of that gay bathing place covered with officers. She saw herself the object of attention, to tens and to scores of them at present unknown. She saw all the glories of the camp; its tents stretched forth in beauteous uniformity of lines, crowded with the young and the gay, and dazzling with scarlet; and to complete the view, she saw herself seated beneath a tent, tenderly flirting with at least six officers at once.

Had she known that her sister sought to tear her from such prospects and such realities as these, what would have been her sensations? They could have been understood only by her mother, who might have felt nearly the same. Lydia's going to Brighton was all that consoled her for the melancholy conviction of her husband's never intending to go there himself.

But they were entirely ignorant of what had passed; and their raptures continued with little intermission to the very day of Lydia's leaving home.

Elizabeth was now to see Mr. Wickham for the last time. Having been frequently in company with him since her return, agitation was pretty well over; the agitations of former partiality entirely so. She had even learnt to detect, in the very gentleness which had first delighted her, an affectation and a sameness to disgust and weary. In his present behaviour to herself, moreover, she had a fresh source of displeasure, for the inclination he soon testified of renewing those attentions which had marked the early part of their acquaintance, could only serve, after what had since passed, to provoke her. She lost all concern for him in finding herself thus selected as the object of such idle and frivolous gallantry; and while she steadily repressed it, could not but feel the reproof contained in his believing, that however long, and for whatever cause, his attentions had been withdrawn, her vanity would be gratified and her preference secured at any time by their renewal.

On the very last day of the regiment's remaining in Meryton, he dined with others of the officers at Longbourn; and so little was Elizabeth disposed to part from him in good humour, that on his making some enquiry as to the manner in which her time had passed at Hunsford, she mentioned Colonel Fitzwilliam's and Mr. Darcy's having both spent three weeks at Rosings, and asked him if he were acquainted with the former.

He looked surprised, displeased, alarmed; but with a moment's recollection and a returning smile, replied, that he had formerly seen him often; and after observing that he was a very gentleman-like man, asked her how she had liked him. Her answer was warmly in his favour. With an air of indifference he soon afterwards added, "How long did you say that he was at Rosings?"

"Nearly three weeks."

"And you saw him frequently?"

"Yes, almost every day."

"His manners are very different from his cousin's."

"Yes, very different. But I think Mr. Darcy improves on acquaintance."

"Indeed!" cried Wickham with a look which did not escape her. "And pray may I ask?" but checking himself, he added in a gayer tone, "Is it in address that he improves? Has he deigned to add ought of civility to his ordinary style? for I dare not hope," he continued in a lower and more serious tone, "that he is improved in essentials."

"Oh, no!" said Elizabeth. "In essentials, I believe, he is very much what he ever was."

While she spoke, Wickham looked as if scarcely knowing whether to rejoice over her words, or to distrust their meaning. There was a something in her countenance which made him listen with an apprehensive and anxious attention, while she added,

"When I said that he improved on acquaintance, I did not mean that either his mind or manners were in a state of improvement, but that from knowing him better, his disposition was better understood."

Wickham's alarm now appeared in a heightened complexion and agitated look; for a few minutes he was silent; till, shaking off his embarrassment, he turned to her again, and said in the gentlest of accents,

"You, who so well know my feelings towards Mr. Darcy, will readily comprehend how sincerely I must rejoice that he is wise enough to assume even the *appearance* of what is right. His pride, in that direction, may be of service, if not to himself, to many others, for it must deter him from such foul misconduct as I have suffered by. I only fear that the sort of cautiousness, to which you, I imagine, have been alluding, is merely adopted on his visits to his aunt, of whose good opinion and judgment he stands much in awe. His fear of her, has always operated, I know, when they were together; and a good deal is to be imputed to his wish of forwarding the match with Miss De Bourgh, which I am certain he has very much at heart."

Elizabeth could not repress a smile at this, but she answered only by a slight inclination of the head. She saw that he wanted to engage her on the old subject of his grievances, and she was in no humour to indulge him. The rest of the evening passed with the *appearance*, on his side, of usual cheerfulness, but with no farther attempt to distinguish Elizabeth; and they parted at last with mutual civility, and possibly a mutual desire of never meeting again.

When the party broke up, Lydia returned with Mrs. Forster to Meryton, from whence they were to set out early the next morning. The separation between her and her family was rather noisy than pathetic. Kitty was the only one who shed tears; but she did weep from vexation and envy. Mrs. Bennet was diffuse in her good wishes for the felicity of her daughter, and impressive in her injunctions that she would not miss the opportunity of enjoying herself as much as possible; advice, which there was every reason to believe would be attended to; and in the clamorous happiness of Lydia herself in bidding farewell, the more gentle adieus of her sisters were uttered without being heard.

Chapter XIX

Had Elizabeth's opinion been all drawn from her own family, she could not have formed a very pleasing picture of conjugal felicity or domestic comfort. Her father captivated by youth and beauty, and that appearance of good humour, which youth and beauty generally give, had married a woman whose weak understanding and illiberal mind, had very early in their marriage put an end to all real affection for her. Respect, esteem, and confidence, had vanished for ever; and all his views of domestic happiness were overthrown. But Mr. Bennet was not of a disposition to seek comfort for the disappointment which his own imprudence had brought on, in any of those pleasures which too often console the unfortunate for their folly or their vice. He was fond of the country and of books; and from these tastes had arisen his principal enjoyments. To his wife he was very little otherwise indebted, than as her ignorance and folly had contributed to his amusement. This is not the sort of happiness which a man would in general wish to owe to his wife; but where other powers of entertainment are wanting, the true philosopher will derive benefit from such as are given.

Elizabeth, however, had never been blind to the impropriety of her father's behaviour as a husband. She had always seen it with pain; but respecting his abilities, and grateful for his affectionate treatment of herself, she endeavoured to forget what she could not overlook, and to banish from her thoughts that continual breach of conjugal obligation and decorum which, in exposing his wife to the contempt of her own children, was so highly reprehensible. But she had never felt so strongly as now, the disadvantages which must attend the children of so unsuitable a marriage, nor ever been so fully aware of the evils arising from so ill-judged a direction of talents; talents which rightly used, might at least have preserved the respectability of his daughters, even if incapable of enlarging the mind of his wife.

When Elizabeth had rejoiced over Wickham's departure, she found little other cause for satisfaction in the loss of the regiment. Their parties abroad were less varied than before; and at home she had a mother and sister whose constant repinings at the dulness of every thing around them, threw a real gloom over their domestic circle; and, though Kitty might in time regain her natural degree of sense, since the disturbers of her brain were removed, her other sister, from whose disposition greater evil might be apprehended, was likley to be hardened in all her folly and assurance, by a situation of such double danger as a watering place and a camp. Upon the whole, therefore, she found, what has been sometimes found before, that an event to which she had looked forward with impatient desire, did not in taking place, bring all the satisfaction she had promised herself. It was consequently necessary to name some other period for the commencement of actual felicity; to have some other point on which her wishes and hopes might be fixed, and by again enjoying the pleasure of anticipation, console herself for the present, and prepare for another disappointment. Her tour to the Lakes was now the object of her happiest thoughts; it was her best consolation for all the uncomfortable hours, which the discontentedness of her mother and Kitty made inevitable; and could she have included Jane in the scheme, every part of it would have been perfect.

"But it is fortunate," thought she, "that I have something to wish for. Were the whole arrangement complete, my disappointment would be certain. But here, by carrying with me one ceaseless source of regret in my sister's absence, I may reasonably hope to have all my expectations of pleasure realized. A scheme of which every part promises delight, can never be successful; and general disappointment is only warded off by the defence of some little peculiar vexation."

When Lydia went away, she promised to write very often and very minutely to her mother and Kitty; but her letters were always long expected, and always very short. Those to her mother, contained little else, than that they were just returned from the library, where such and such officers had attended them, and where she had seen such beautiful ornaments as made her quite wild; that she had a new gown, or a new parasol, which she would have described more fully, but was obliged to leave off in a violent hurry, as Mrs. Forster called her, and they were going to the camp; —and from her correspondence with her sister, there was still less to be learnt—for her letters to Kitty, though rather longer, were much too full of lines under the words to be made public.

After the first fortnight or three weeks of her absence, health, good humour and cheerfulness began to re-appear at Longbourn. Everything wore a happier aspect. The families who had been in town for the winter came back again, and summer finery and summer engagements arose. Mrs. Bennet was restored to her usual querulous serenity, and by the middle of June Kitty was so much recovered as to be able to enter Meryton without tears; an event of such happy promise as to make Elizabeth hope, that by the following Christmas, she might be so tolerably reasonable as not to mention an officer above once a day, unless by some cruel and malicious arrangement at the war-office, another regiment should be quartered in Meryton.

The time fixed for the beginning of their Northern tour was now fast approaching; and a fortnight only was wanting of it, when a letter arrived from Mrs. Gardiner, which at once delayed its commencement and curtailed its extent. Mr. Gardiner would be prevented by business from setting out till a fortnight later in July, and must be in London again within a month; and as that left too short a period for them to go so far, and see so much as they had proposed, or at least to see it with the leisure and comfort they had built on, they were obliged to give up the Lakes, and substitute a more contracted tour; and, according to the present plan, were to go no farther northward than Derbyshire. In that county, there was enough to be seen, to occupy the chief of their three weeks; and to Mrs. Gardiner it had a peculiarly strong attraction. The town where she had formerly passed some years of her life, and where they were now to spend a few days, was probably as great an object of her curiosity, as all the celebrated beauties of Matlock, Chatsworth, Dovedale, or the Peak.

Elizabeth was excessively disappointed; she had set her heart on seeing the Lakes; and still thought there might have been time enough. But it was her business to be satisfied—and certainly her temper to be happy; and all was soon right again.

With the mention of Derbyshire, there were many ideas connected. It was impossible for her to see the word without thinking of Pemberley and its owner. "But surely," said she, "I may enter his county with impunity, and rob it of a few petrified spars [8] without his perceiving me."

The period of expectation was now doubled. Four weeks were to pass away before her uncle and aunt's arrival. But they did pass away, and Mr. and Mrs. Gardiner, with their four children, did at length appear at Longbourn. The children, two girls of six and eight years old, and two younger boys, were to be left under the particular care of their cousin Jane, who was the general favourite, and whose steady sense and sweetness of temper exactly adapted her for attending to them in every way—teaching them, playing with them, and loving them.

The Gardiners staid only one night at Longbourn, and set off the next morning with Elizabeth in pursuit of novelty and amusement. One enjoyment was certain—that of suitableness as companions; a suitableness which comprehended health and temper to bear inconveniences—cheerfulness to enhance every pleasure—and affection and intelligence, which might supply it among themselves if there were disappointments abroad.

It is not the object of this work to give a description of Derbyshire, nor of any of the remarkable places through which their route thither lay; Oxford, Blenheim, Warwick, Kenelworth, Birmingham, &c. are sufficiently known. A small part of Derbyshire is all the present concern. To the little town of Lambton, the scene of Mrs. Gardiner's former residence, and where she had lately learned that some acquaintance still remained, they bent their steps, after having seen all the principal wonders of the country; and within five miles of Lambton, Elizabeth found from her aunt, that Pemberley was situated. It was not in their direct road, nor more than a mile or two out of it. In talking over their route the evening before, Mrs. Gardiner expressed an inclination to see the place again. Mr. Gardiner declared his willingness, and Elizabeth was applied to for her approbation.

"My love, should not you like to see a place of which you have heard so much?" said her aunt. "A place too, with which so many of your acquaintance are connected. Wickham passed all his youth there, you know."

Elizabeth was distressed. She felt that she had no business at Pemberley, and was obliged to assume a disinclination for seeing it. She must own that she was tired of great houses; after

8. Crystallized minerals.

going over so many, she really had no pleasure in fine carpets or satin curtains.

Mrs. Gardiner abused her stupidity. "If it were merely a fine house richly furnished," said she, "I should not care about it myself; but the grounds are delightful. They have some of the finest woods in the country."

Elizabeth said no more—but her mind could not acquiesce. The possibility of meeting Mr. Darcy, while viewing the place, instantly occurred. It would be dreadful! She blushed at the very idea; and thought it would be better to speak openly to her aunt, than to run such a risk. But against this, there were objections; and she finally resolved that it could be the last resource, if her private enquiries as to the absence of the family, were unfavourably answered.

Accordingly, when she retired at night, she asked the chambermaid whether Pemberley were not a very fine place, what was the name of its proprietor, and with no little alarm, whether the family were down for the summer. A most welcome negative followed the last question—and her alarms being now removed, she was at leisure to feel a great deal of curiosity to see the house herself; and when the subject was revived the next morning, and she was again applied to, could readily answer, and with a proper air of indifference, that she had not really any dislike to the scheme.

To Pemberley, therefore, they were to go.

Volume III

Chapter I

Elizabeth, as they drove along, watched for the first appearance of Pemberley Woods with some perturbation; and when at length they turned in at the lodge, her spirits were in a high flutter.

The park was very large, and contained great variety of ground. They entered it in one of its lowest points, and drove for some time through a beautiful wood, stretching over a wide extent.

Elizabeth's mind was too full for conversation, but she saw and admired every remarkable spot and point of view. They gradually ascended for half a mile, and then found themselves at the top of a considerable eminence, where the wood ceased, and

the eye was instantly caught by Pemberley House, situated on
the opposite side of a valley, into which the road with some abruptness wound. It was a large, handsome, stone building, standing
well on rising ground, and backed by a ridge of high woody
hills;—and in front, a stream of some natural importance was
swelled into greater, but without any artificial appearance. Its
banks were neither formal, nor falsely adorned. Elizabeth was
delighted. She had never seen a place for which nature had done
more, or where natural beauty had been so little counteracted
by an awkward taste. They were all of them warm in their admiration; and at that moment she felt, that to be mistress of Pemberley
might be something!

They descended the hill, crossed the bridge, and drove to the
door; and, while examining the nearer aspect of the house, all
her apprehensions of meeting its owner returned. She dreaded
lest the chambermaid had been mistaken. On applying to see
the place, they were admitted into the hall; and Elizabeth, as
they waited for the housekeeper, had leisure to wonder at her
being where she was.

The housekeeper came; a respectable-looking, elderly woman,
much less fine, and more civil, than she had any notion of finding
her. They followed her into the dining-parlour. It was a large,
well-proportioned room, handsomely fitted up. Elizabeth, after
slightly surveying it, went to a window to enjoy its prospect.
The hill, crowned with wood, from which they had descended,
receiving increased abruptness from the distance, was a beautiful
object. Every disposition of the ground was good; and she looked
on the whole scene, the river, the trees scattered on its banks, and
the winding of the valley, as far as she could trace it, with delight.
As they passed into other rooms, these objects were taking different positions; but from every window there were beauties to be
seen. The rooms were lofty and handsome, and their furniture
suitable to the fortune of their proprietor; but Elizabeth saw,
with admiration of his taste, that it was neither gaudy nor uselessly
fine; with less of splendor, and more real elegance, than the furniture of Rosings.

"And of this place," thought she, "I might have been mistress!
With these rooms I might now have been familiarly acquainted!
Instead of viewing them as a stranger, I might have rejoiced in
them as my own, and welcomed to them as visitors my uncle and
aunt.—But no,"—recollecting herself,—"that could never be:
my uncle and aunt would have been lost to me: I should not
have been allowed to invite them."

This was a lucky recollection—it saved her from something
like regret.

She longed to enquire of the housekeeper, whether her master were really absent, but had not courage for it. At length, however, the question was asked by her uncle; and she turned away with alarm, while Mrs. Reynolds replied, that he was, adding, "but we expect him tomorrow, with a large party of friends." How rejoiced was Elizabeth that their own journey had not by any circumstance been delayed a day!

Her aunt now called her to look at a picture. She approached, and saw the likeness of Mr. Wickham suspended, amongst several other miniatures, over the mantlepiece. Her aunt asked her, smilingly, how she liked it. The housekeeper came forward, and told them it was the picture of a young gentleman, the son of her late master's steward, who had been brought up by him at his own expence.—"He is now gone into the army," she added, "but I am afraid he has turned out very wild."

Mrs. Gardiner looked at her niece with a smile, but Elizabeth could not return it.

"And that," said Mrs. Reynolds, pointing to another of the miniatures, "is my master—and very like him. It was drawn at the same time as the other—about eight years ago."

"I have heard much of your master's fine person," said Mrs. Gardiner, looking at the picture; "it is a handsome face. But, Lizzy, you can tell us whether it is like or not."

Mrs. Reynolds's respect for Elizabeth seemed to increase on this intimation of her knowing her master.

"Does that young lady know Mr. Darcy?"

Elizabeth coloured, and said—"A little."

"And do not you think him a very handsome gentleman, Ma'am?"

"Yes, very handsome."

"I am sure *I* know none so handsome; but in the gallery up stairs you will see a finer, larger picture of him than this. This room was my late master's favourite room, and these miniatures are just as they used to be then. He was very fond of them."

This accounted to Elizabeth for Mr. Wickham's being among them.

Mrs. Reynolds then directed their attention to one of Miss Darcy, drawn when she was only eight years old.

"And is Miss Darcy as handsome as her brother?" said Mr. Gardiner.

"Oh! yes—the handsomest young lady that ever was seen; and so accomplished!—She plays and sings all day long. In the next room is a new instrument just come down for her—a present from my master; she comes here to-morrow with him."

Mr. Gardiner, whose manners were easy and pleasant, encouraged her communicativeness by his questions and remarks; Mrs. Reynolds, either from pride or attachment, had evidently great pleasure in talking of her master and his sister.

"Is your master much at Pemberley in the course of the year?"

"Not so much as I could wish, Sir; but I dare say he may spend half his time here; and Miss Darcy is always down for the summer months."

"Except," thought Elizabeth, "when she goes to Ramsgate."

"If your master would marry, you might see more of him."

"Yes, Sir; but I do not know when *that* will be. I do not know who is good enough for him."

Mr. and Mrs. Gardiner smiled. Elizabeth could not help saying, "It is very much to his credit, I am sure, that you should think so."

"I say no more than the truth, and what every body will say that knows him," replied the other. Elizabeth thought this was going pretty far; and she listened with increasing astonishment as the housekeeper added, "I have never had a cross word from him in my life, and I have known him ever since he was four years old."

This was praise, of all others most extraordinary, most opposite to her ideas. That he was not a good-tempered man, had been her firmest opinion. Her keenest attention was awakened; she longed to hear more, and was grateful to her uncle for saying,

"There are very few people of whom so much can be said. You are lucky in having such a master."

"Yes, Sir, I know I am. If I was to go through the world, I could not meet with a better. But I have always observed, that they who are good-natured when children, are good-natured when they grow up; and he was always the sweetest-tempered, most generous-hearted, boy in the world."

Elizabeth almost stared at her.—"Can this be Mr. Darcy!" thought she.

"His father was an excellent man," said Mrs. Gardiner.

"Yes, Ma'am, that he was indeed; and his son will be just like him—just as affable to the poor."

Elizabeth listened, wondered, doubted, and was impatient for more. Mrs. Reynolds could interest her on no other point. She related the subject of the pictures, the dimensions of the rooms, and the price of the furniture, in vain. Mr. Gardiner, highly amused by the kind of family prejudice, to which he attributed her excessive commendation of her master, soon led again to the subject; and she dwelt with energy on his many merits, as they proceeded together up the great staircase.

"He is the best landlord, and the best master," said she, "that ever lived. Not like the wild young men now-a-days, who think of nothing but themselves. There is not one of his tenants or servants but what will give him a good name. Some people call him proud; but I am sure I never saw any thing of it. To my fancy, it is only because he does not rattle away like other young men."

"In what an amiable light does this place him!" thought Elizabeth.

"This fine account of him," whispered her aunt, as they walked, "is not quite consistent with his behaviour to our poor friend."

"Perhaps we might be deceived."

"That is not very likely; our authority was too good."

On reaching the spacious lobby above, they were shewn into a very pretty sitting-room, lately fitted up with greater elegance and lightness than the apartments below; and were informed that it was but just done, to give pleasure to Miss Darcy, who had taken a liking to the room, when last at Pemberley.

"He is certainly a good brother," said Elizabeth, as she walked towards one of the windows.

Mrs. Reynolds anticipated Miss Darcy's delight, when she should enter the room. "And this is always the way with him," she added.—"Whatever can give his sister any pleasure, is sure to be done in a moment. There is nothing he would not do for her."

The picture gallery, and two or three of the principal bed-rooms, were all that remained to be shewn. In the former were many good paintings; but Elizabeth knew nothing of the art; and from such as had been already visible below, she had willingly turned to look at some drawings of Miss Darcy's, in crayons, whose subjects were usually more interesting, and also more intelligible.

In the gallery there were many family portraits, but they could have little to fix the attention of a stranger. Elizabeth walked on in quest of the only face whose features would be known to her. At last it arrested her—and she beheld a striking resemblance of Mr. Darcy, with such a smile over the face, as she remembered to have sometimes seen, when he looked at her. She stood several minutes before the picture in earnest comtemplation, and returned to it again before they quitted the gallery. Mrs. Reynolds informed them, that it had been taken in his father's life time.

There was certainly at this moment, in Elizabeth's mind, a more gentle sensation towards the original, than she had ever felt in the height of their acquaintance. The commendation bestowed on him by Mrs. Reynolds was of no trifling nature. What praise is more valuable than the praise of an intelligent servant? As a brother, a landlord, a master, she considered how many people's happiness were in his guardianship!—How much of pleasure or pain it was in his power to bestow!—How much of good or evil must be done by him! Every idea that had been brought forward by the housekeeper was favourable to his character, and as she stood before the canvas, on which he was represented, and fixed his eyes upon herself, she thought of his regard with a deeper sentiment of gratitude than it had ever raised before; she remembered its warmth, and softened its impropriety of expression.

When all of the house that was open to general inspection had been seen, they returned down stairs, and taking leave of the housekeeper, were consigned over to the gardener, who met them at the hall door.

As they walked across the lawn towards the river, Elizabeth turned back to look again; her uncle and aunt stopped also, and while the former was conjecturing as to the date of the building, the owner of it himself suddenly came forward from the road, which led behind it to the stables.

They were within twenty yards of each other, and so abrupt was his appearance, that it was impossible to avoid his sight. Their eyes instantly met, and the cheeks of each were overspread with the deepest blush. He absolutely started, and for a moment seemed immoveable from surprise; but shortly recovering himself, advanced towards the party, and spoke to Elizabeth, if not in terms of perfect composure, at least of perfect civility.

She had instinctively turned away; but, stopping on his approach, received his compliments with an embarrassment impossible to be overcome. Had his first appearance, or his resemblance to the picture they had just been examining, been insufficient to assure the other two that they now saw Mr. Darcy, the gardener's expression of surprise, on beholding his master, must immediately have told it. They stood a little aloof while he was talking to their niece, who, astonished and confused, scarcely dared lift her eyes to his face, and knew not what answer she returned to his civil enquiries after her family. Amazed at the alteration in his manner since they last parted, every sentence that he uttered was increasing her embarrassment; and every idea of the impropriety of her being found there, recurring to her mind, the few minutes in which they continued together, were some of the most uncomfortable of her life. Nor did he seem much more at ease; when he spoke, his accent had none of its usual sedateness; and he repeated his enquiries as to the time of her having left Longbourn, and of her stay in Derbyshire, so often, and in so hurried a way, as plainly spoke the distraction of his thoughts.

At length, every idea seemed to fail him; and, after standing a few moments without saying a word, he suddenly recollected himself, and took leave.

The others then joined her, and expressed their admiration

of his figure; but Elizabeth heard not a word, and, wholly engrossed by her own feelings, followed them in silence. She was overpowered by shame and vexation. Her coming there was the most unfortunate, the most ill-judged thing in the world! How strange must it appear to him! In what a disgraceful light might it not strike so vain a man! It might seem as if she had purposely thrown herself in his way again! Oh! why did she come? or, why did he thus come a day before he was expected? Had they been only ten minutes sooner, they should have been beyond the reach of his discrimination, for it was plain that he was that moment arrived, that moment alighted from his horse or his carriage. She blushed again and again over the perverseness of the meeting. And his behaviour, so strikingly altered,—what could it mean? That he should even speak to her was amazing!—but to speak with such civility, to enquire after her family! Never in her life had she seen his manners so little dignified, never had he spoken with such gentleness as on this unexpected meeting. What a contrast did it offer to his last address in Rosing's Park, when he put his letter into her hand! She knew not what to think, nor how to account for it.

They had now entered a beautiful walk by the side of the water, and every step was bringing forward a nobler fall of ground, or a finer reach of the woods to which they were approaching; but it was some time before Elizabeth was sensible of any of it; and, though she answered mechanically to the repeated appeals of her uncle and aunt, and seemed to direct her eyes to such objects as they pointed out, she distinguished no part of the scene. Her thoughts were all fixed on that one spot of Pemberley House, whichever it might be, where Mr. Darcy then was. She longed to know what at that moment was passing in his mind; in what manner he thought of her, and whether, in defiance of every thing, she was still dear to him. Perhaps he had been civil, only because he felt himself at ease; yet there had been *that* in his voice, which was not like ease. Whether he had felt more of pain or of pleasure in seeing her, she could not tell, but he certainly had not seen her with composure.

At length, however, the remarks of her companions on her absence of mind roused her, and she felt the necessity of appearing more like herself.

They entered the woods, and bidding adieu to the river for a while, ascended some of the higher grounds; whence, in spots where the opening of the trees gave the eye power to wander, were many charming views of the valley, the opposite hills, with the long range of woods overspreading many, and occasionally part of the stream. Mr. Gardiner expressed a wish of going round the whole Park, but feared it might be beyond a walk. With a triumphant smile, they were told, that it was ten miles round. It settled the matter; and they pursued the accustomed circuit; which brought them again, after some time, in a descent among hanging woods, to the edge of the water, in one of its narrowest parts. They crossed it by a simple bridge, in character with the general air of the scene; it was a spot less adorned than any they had yet visited; and the valley, here contracted into a glen, allowed room only for the stream, and a narrow walk amidst the rough coppice-wood which bordered it. Elizabeth longed to explore its windings; but when they had crossed the bridge, and perceived their distance from the house, Mrs. Gardiner, who was not a great walker, could go no farther, and thought only of returning to the carriage as quickly as possible. Her niece was, therefore, obliged to submit, and they took their way towards the house on the opposite side of the river, in the nearest direction; but their progress was slow, for Mr. Gardiner, though seldom able to indulge the taste, was very fond of fishing, and was so much engaged in watching the occasional appearance of some trout in the water, and talking to the man about them, that he advanced but little. Whilst wandering on in this slow manner, they were again surprised, and Elizabeth's astonishment was quite equal to what it had been at first, by the sight of Mr. Darcy approaching them, and at no great distance. The walk being here less sheltered than on the other side, allowed them to see him before they met. Elizabeth, however astonished, was at least more prepared for an interview than before, and resolved to appear and to speak with calmness, if he really intended to meet them. For a few moments, indeed, she felt that he would probably strike into some other path. This idea lasted while a turning in the walk concealed him from their view; the turning past, he was immediately before them. With a glance she saw, that he had lost none of his recent civility; and, to imitate his politeness, she began, as they met, to admire the beauty of the place; but she had not got beyond the words "delightful," and "charming," when some unlucky recollections obtruded, and she fancied that praise of Pemberley from her, might be mischievously construed. Her colour changed, and she said no more.

Mrs. Gardiner was standing a little behind; and on her pausing, he asked her, if she would do him the honour of introducing him to her friends. This was a stroke of civility for which she was quite unprepared; and she could hardly suppress a smile, at his being now seeking the acquaintance of some of those very people, against whom his pride had revolted, in his offer to herself. "What will be his surprise," thought she, "when he knows who they are!

He takes them now for people of fashion."

The introduction, however, was immediately made; and as she named their relationship to herself, she stole a sly look at him, to see how he bore it; and was not without the expectation of his decamping as fast as he could from such disgraceful companions. That he was *surprised* by the connexion was evident; he sustained it however with fortitude, and so far from going away, turned back with them, and entered into conversation with Mr. Gardiner. Elizabeth could not but be pleased, could not but triumph. It was consoling, that he should know she had some relations for whom there was no need to blush. She listened most attentively to all that passed between them, and gloried in every expression, every sentence of her uncle, which marked his intelligence, his taste, or his good manners.

The conversation soon turned upon fishing, and she heard Mr. Darcy invite him, with the greatest civility, to fish there as often as he chose, while he continued in the neighbourhood, offering at the same time to supply him with fishing tackle, and pointing out those parts of the stream where there was usually most sport. Mrs. Gardiner, who was walking arm in arm with Elizabeth, gave her a look expressive of her wonder. Elizabeth said nothing, but it gratified her exceedingly; the compliment must be all for herself. Her astonishment, however, was extreme; and continually was she repeating, "Why is he so altered? From what can it proceed? It cannot be for *me*, it cannot be for *my* sake that his manners are thus softened. My reproofs at Hunsford could not work such a change as this. It is impossible that he should still love me."

After walking some time in this way, the two ladies in front, the two gentlemen behind, on resuming their places, after descending to the brink of the river for the better inspection of some curious water-plant, there chanced to be a little alteration. It originated in Mrs. Gardiner, who, fatigued by the exercise of the morning, found Elizabeth's arm inadequate to her support, and consequently preferred her husband's. Mr. Darcy took her place by her niece, and they walked on together. After a short silence, the lady first spoke. She wished him to know that she had been assured of his absence before she came to the place, and accordingly began by observing, that his arrival had been very unexpected—"for your housekeeper," she added, "informed us that you would certainly not be here till to-morrow; and indeed, before we left Bakewell, we understood that you were not immediately expected in the country." He acknowledged the truth of it all; and said that business with his steward had occasioned his coming forward a few hours before the rest of the party with whom he had been travelling. "They will join me early to-morrow," he continued, "and among them are some who will claim an acquaintance with you,—Mr. Bingley and his sisters."

Elizabeth answered only by a slight bow. Her thoughts were instantly driven back to the time when Mr. Bingley's name had been last mentioned between them; and if she might judge from his complexion, *his* mind was not very differently engaged.

"There is also one other person in the party," he continued after a pause, "who more particularly wishes to be known to you,—Will you allow me, or do I ask too much, to introduce my sister to your acquaintance during your stay at Lambton?"

The surprise of such an application was great indeed; it was too great for her to know in what manner she acceded to it. She immediately felt that whatever desire Miss Darcy might have of being acquainted with her, must be the work of her brother, and without looking farther, it was satisfactory; it was gratifying to know that his resentment had not made him think really ill of her.

They now walked on in silence; each of them deep in thought. Elizabeth was not comfortable; that was impossible; but she was flattered and pleased. His wish of introducing his sister to her, was a compliment of the highest kind. They soon outstripped the others, and when they had reached the carriage, Mr. and Mrs. Gardiner were half a quarter of a mile behind.

He then asked her to walk into the house—but she declared herself not tired, and they stood together on the lawn. At such a time, much might have been said, and silence was very awkward. She wanted to talk, but there seemed an embargo on every subject. At last she recollected that she had been travelling, and they talked of Matlock and Dove Dale with great perseverance. Yet time and her aunt moved slowly—and her patience and her ideas were nearly worn out before the tete-a-tete was over. On Mr. and Mrs. Gardiner's coming up, they were all pressed to go into the house and take some refreshment; but this was declined, and they parted on each side with the utmost politeness. Mr. Darcy handed the ladies into the carriage, and when it drove off, Elizabeth saw him walking slowly towards the house.

The observations of her uncle and aunt now began; and each of them pronounced him to be infinitely superior to any thing they had expected. "He is perfectly well behaved, polite, and unassuming," said her uncle.

"There *is* something a little stately in him to be sure," replied her aunt, "but it is confined to his air, and is not unbecoming. I can now say with the housekeeper, that though some people may call him proud, *I* have seen nothing of it."

"I was never more surprised than by his behaviour to us. It

was more than civil; it was really attentive; and there was no necessity for such attention. His acquaintance with Elizabeth was very trifling."

"To be sure, Lizzy," said her aunt, "he is not so handsome as Wickham; or rather he has not Wickham's countenance, for his features are perfectly good. But how came you to tell us that he was so disagreeable?"

Elizabeth excused herself as well as she could; said that she had liked him better when they met in Kent than before, and that she had never seen him so pleasant as this morning.

"But perhaps he may be a little whimsical in his civilities," replied her uncle. "Your great men often are; and therefore I shall not take him at his word about fishing, as he might change his mind another day, and warn me off his grounds."

Elizabeth felt that they had entirely mistaken his character, but said nothing.

"From what we have seen of him," continued Mrs. Gardiner, "I really should not have thought that he could have behaved in so cruel a way by any body, as he has done by poor Wickham. He has not an ill-natured look. On the contrary, there is something pleasing about his mouth when he speaks. And there is something of dignity in his countenance, that would not give one an unfavourable idea of his heart. But to be sure, the good lady who shewed us the house, did give him a most flaming character! I could hardly help laughing aloud sometimes. But he is a liberal master, I suppose, and *that* in the eye of a servant comprehends every virtue."

Elizabeth here felt herself called on to say something in vindication of his behaviour to Wickham; and therefore gave them to understand, in as guarded a manner as she could, that by what she had heard from his relations in Kent, his actions were capable of a very different construction; and that his character was by no means so faulty, nor Wickham's so amiable, as they had been considered in Hertfordshire. In confirmation of this, she related the particulars of all the pecuniary transactions in which they had been connected, without actually naming her authority, but stating it to be such as might be relied on.

Mrs. Gardiner was surprised and concerned; but as they were now approaching the scene of her former pleasures, every idea gave way to the charm of recollection; and she was too much engaged in pointing out to her husband all the interesting spots in its environs, to think of any thing else. Fatigued as she had been by the morning's walk, they had no sooner dined than she set off again in quest of her former acquaintance, and the evening was spent in the satisfactions of an intercourse renewed after many years discontinuance.

The occurrences of the day were too full of interest to leave Elizabeth much attention for any of these new friends; and she could do nothing but think, and think with wonder, of Mr. Darcy's civility, and above all, of his wishing her to be acquainted with his sister.

Chapter II

Elizabeth had settled it that Mr. Darcy would bring his sister to visit her, the very day after her reaching Pemberley; and was consequently resolved not to be out of sight of the inn the whole of that morning. But her conclusion was false; for on the very morning after their own arrival at Lambton, these visitors came. They had been walking about the place with some of their new friends, and were just returned to the inn to dress themselves for dining with the same family, when the sound of a carriage drew them to a window, and they saw a gentleman and lady in a curricle,[9] driving up the street. Elizabeth immediately recognising the livery, guessed what it meant, and imparted no small degree of surprise to her relations, by acquainting them with the honour which she expected. Her uncle and aunt were all amazement; and the embarrassment of her manner as she spoke, joined to the circumstance itself, and many of the circumstances of the preceding day, opened to them a new idea on the business. Nothing had ever suggested it before, but they now felt that there was no other way of accounting for such attentions from such a quarter, than by supposing a partiality for their niece. While these newly-born notions were passing in their heads, the perturbation of Elizabeth's feelings was every moment increasing. She was quite amazed at her own discomposure; but amongst other causes of disquiet, she dreaded lest the partiality of the brother should have said too much in her favour; and more than commonly anxious to please, she naturally suspected that every power of pleasing would fail her.

She retreated from the window, fearful of being seen; and as she walked up and down the room, endeavouring to compose herself, saw such looks of enquiring surprise in her uncle and aunt, as made every thing worse.

Miss Darcy and her brother appeared, and this formidable introduction took place. With astonishment did Elizabeth see, that her new acquaintance was at least as much embarrassed

9. A small two-wheeled carriage. According to a contemporary coach-maker quoted in Chapman's appendix "On Carriages and Travel" noted above, a curricle was often chosen as a "genteel kind of carriage" (560).

as herself. Since her being at Lambton, she had heard that Miss Darcy was exceedingly proud; but the observation of a very few minutes convinced her, that she was only exceedingly shy. She found it difficult to obtain even a word from her beyond a monosyllable.

Miss Darcy was tall, and on a larger scale than Elizabeth; and, though little more than sixteen, her figure was formed, and her appearance womanly and graceful. She was less handsome than her brother, but there was sense and good humour in her face, and her manners were perfectly unassuming and gentle. Elizabeth, who had expected to find in her as acute and unembarrassed an observer as ever Mr. Darcy had been, was much relieved by discerning such different feelings.

They had not been long together, before Darcy told her that Bingley was also coming to wait on her; and she had barely time to express her satisfaction, and prepare for such a visitor, when Bingley's quick step was heard on the stairs, and in a moment he entered the room. All Elizabeth's anger against him had been long done away; but, had she still felt any, it could hardly have stood its ground against the unaffected cordiality with which he expressed himself, on seeing her again. He enquired in a friendly, though general way, after her family, and looked and spoke with the same good-humoured ease that he had ever done.

To Mr. and Mrs. Gardiner he was scarcely a less interesting personage than to herself. They had long wished to see him. The whole party before them, indeed, excited a lively attention. The suspicions which had just arisen of Mr. Darcy and their niece, directed their observation towards each with an earnest, though guarded, enquiry; and they soon drew from those enquiries the full conviction that one of them at least knew what it was to love. Of the lady's sensations they remained a little in doubt; but that the gentleman was overflowing with admiration was evident enough.

Elizabeth, on her side, had much to do. She wanted to ascertain the feelings of each of her visitors, she wanted to compose her own, and to make herself agreeable to all; and in the latter object, where she feared most to fail, she was most sure of success, for those to whom she endeavoured to give pleasure were prepossessed in her favour. Bingley was ready, Georgiana was eager, and Darcy determined, to be pleased.

In seeing Bingley, her thoughts naturally flew to her sister; and oh! how ardently did she long to know, whether any of his were directed in a like manner. Sometimes she could fancy, that he talked less than on former occasions, and once or twice pleased herself with the notion that as he looked at her, he was trying to trace a resemblance. But, though this might be imaginary, she could not be deceived as to his behaviour to Miss Darcy, who had been set up as a rival of Jane. No look appeared on either side that spoke particular regard. Nothing occurred between them that could justify the hopes of his sister. On this point she was soon satisfied; and two or three little circumstances occurred ere they parted, which, in her anxious interpretation, denoted a recollection of Jane, not untinctured by tenderness, and a wish of saying more that might lead to the mention of her, had he dared. He observed to her, at a moment when the others were talking together, and in a tone which had something of real regret, that it "was a very long time since he had had the pleasure of seeing her;" and, before she could reply, he added, "It is above eight months. We have not met since the 26th of November, when we were all dancing together at Netherfield."

Elizabeth was pleased to find his memory so exact; and he afterwards took occasion to ask her, when unattended to by any of the rest, whether *all* her sisters were at Longbourn. There was not much in the question, nor in the preceding remark, but there was a look and a manner which gave them meaning.

It was not often that she could turn her eyes on Mr. Darcy himself; but, whenever she did catch a glimpse, she saw an expression of general complaisance, and in all that he said, she heard an accent so far removed from hauteur or disdain of his companions, as convinced her that the improvement of manners which she had yesterday witnessed, however temporary its existence might prove, had at least outlived one day. When she saw him thus seeking the acquaintance, and courting the good opinion of people, with whom any intercourse a few months ago would have been a disgrace; when she saw him thus civil, not only to herself, but to the very relations whom he had openly disdained, and recollected their last lively scene in Hunsford Parsonage, the difference, the change was so great, and struck so forcibly on her mind, that she could hardly restrain her astonishment from being visible. Never, even in the company of his dear friends at Netherfield, or his dignified relations at Rosings, had she seen him so desirous to please, so free from self-consequence, or unbending reserve as now, when no importance could result from the success of his endeavours, and when even the acquaintance of those to whom his attentions were addressed, would draw down the ridicule and censure of the ladies both of Netherfield and Rosings.

Their visitors staid with them above half an hour, and when they arose to depart, Mr. Darcy called on his sister to join him in expressing their wish of seeing Mr. and Mrs. Gardiner, and Miss Bennet, to dinner at Pemberley, before they left the country.

Miss Darcy, though with a diffidence which marked her little in the habit of giving invitations, readily obeyed. Mrs. Gardiner looked at her niece, desirous of knowing how *she*, whom the invitation most concerned, felt disposed as to its acceptance, but Elizabeth had turned away her head. Presuming, however, that this studied avoidance spoke rather a momentary embarrassment, than any dislike of the proposal, and seeing in her husband, who was fond of society, a perfect willingness to accept it, she ventured to engage for her attendance, and the day after the next was fixed on.

Bingley expressed great pleasure in the certainty of seeing Elizabeth again, having still a great deal to say to her, and many enquiries to make after all their Hertfordshire friends. Elizabeth, construing all this into a wish of hearing her speak of her sister, was pleased; and on this account, as well as some others found herself, when their visitors left them, capable of considering the last half hour with some satisfaction, though while it was passing, the enjoyment of it had been little. Eager to be alone, and fearful of enquiries or hints from her uncle and aunt, she staid with them only long enough to hear their favourable opinion of Bingley, and then hurried away to dress.

But she had no reason to fear Mr. and Mrs. Gardiner's curiosity; it was not their wish to force her communication. It was evident that she was much better acquainted with Mr. Darcy than they had before any idea of; it was evident that he was very much in love with her. They saw much to interest, but nothing to justify enquiry.

Of Mr. Darcy it was now a matter of anxiety to think well; and, as far as their acquaintance reached, there was no fault to find. They could not be untouched by his politeness, and had they drawn his character from their own feelings, and his servant's report, without any reference to any other account, the circle in Hertfordshire to which he was known, would not have recognised it for Mr. Darcy. There was now an interest, however, in believing the housekeeper; and they soon became sensible, that the authority of a servant who had known him since he was four years old, and whose own manners indicated respectability, was not to be hastily rejected. Neither had any thing occurred in the intelligence of their Lambton friends, that could materially lessen its weight. They had nothing to accuse him of but pride; pride he probably had, and if not, it would certainly be imputed by the inhabitants of a small market-town, where the family did not visit.[1] It was acknowledged, however, that he was a liberal man, and did much

1. I.e., on whose principal families the residents of Pemberley did not call socially.

good among the poor.

With respect to Wickham, the travellers soon found that he was not held there in much estimation; for though the chief of his concerns, with the son of his patron, were imperfectly understood, it was yet a well known fact that, on his quitting Derbyshire, he had left many debts behind him, which Mr. Darcy afterwards discharged.

As for Elizabeth, her thoughts were at Pemberley this evening more than the last; and the evening, though as it passed it seemed long, was not long enough to determine her feelings towards *one* in that mansion; and she lay awake two whole hours, endeavouring to make them out. She certainly did not hate him. No; hatred had vanished long ago, and she had almost as long been ashamed of ever feeling a dislike against him, that could be so called. The respect created by the conviction of his valuable qualities, though at first unwillingly admitted, had for some time ceased to be repugnant to her feelings; and it was now heightened into somewhat of a friendlier nature, by the testimony so highly in his favour, and bringing forward his disposition in so amiable a light, which yesterday had produced. But above all, above respect and esteem, there was a motive within her of good will which could not be overlooked. It was gratitude.—Gratitude, not merely for having once loved her, but for loving her still well enough, to forgive all the petulance and acrimony of her manner in rejecting him, and all the unjust accusations accompanying her rejection. He who, she had been persuaded, would avoid her as his greatest enemy, seemed, on this accidental meeting, most eager to preserve the acquaintance, and without any indelicate display of regard, or any peculiarity of manner, where their two selves only were concerned, was soliciting the good opinion of her friends, and bent on making her known to his sister. Such a change in a man of so much pride, excited not only astonishment but gratitude—for to love, ardent love, it must be attributed; and as such its impression on her was of a sort to be encouraged, as by no means unpleasing, though it could not be exactly defined. She respected, she esteemed, she was grateful to him, she felt a real interest in his welfare; and she only wanted to know how far she wished that welfare to depend upon herself, and how far it would be for the happiness of both that she should employ the power, which her fancy told her she still possessed, of bringing on the renewal of his addresses.

It had been settled in the evening, between the aunt and niece, that such a striking civility as Miss Darcy's, in coming to them on the very day of her arrival at Pemberley, for she had reached it only to a late breakfast, ought to be imitated, though it could not be equalled, by some exertion of politeness on their side; and, consequently, that it would be highly expedient to wait on her at Pemberley the following morning. They were, therefore, to go.—Elizabeth was pleased, though, when she asked herself the reason, she had very little to say in reply.

Mr. Gardiner left them soon after breakfast. The fishing scheme had been renewed the day before, and a positive engagement made of his meeting some of the gentlemen at Pemberley by noon.

Chapter III

Convinced as Elizabeth now was that Miss Bingley's dislike of her had originated in jealousy, she could not help feeling how very unwelcome her appearance at Pemberley must be to her, and was curious to know with how much civility on that lady's side, the acquaintance would now be renewed.

On reaching the house, they were shewn through the hall into the saloon, whose northern aspect rendered it delightful for summer. Its windows opening to the ground, admitted a most refreshing view of the high woody hills behind the house, and of the beautiful oaks and Spanish chestnuts which were scattered over the intermediate lawn.

In this room they were received by Miss Darcy, who was sitting there with Mrs. Hurst and Miss Bingley, and the lady with whom she lived in London. Georgiana's reception of them was very civil; but attended with all that embarrassment which, though proceeding from shyness and the fear of doing wrong, would easily give to those who felt themselves inferior, the belief of her being proud and reserved. Mrs. Gardiner and her niece, however, did her justice, and pitied her.

By Mrs. Hurst and Miss Bingley, they were noticed only by a curtsey; and on their being seated, a pause, awkward as such pauses must always be, succeeded for a few moments. It was first broken by Mrs. Annesley, a genteel, agreeable-looking woman, whose endeavour to introduce some kind of discourse, proved her to be more truly well bred than either of the others; and between her and Mrs. Gardiner, with occasional help from Elizabeth, the conversation was carried on. Miss Darcy looked as if she wished for courage enough to join in it; and sometimes did venture a short sentence, when there was least danger of its being heard.

Elizabeth soon saw that she was herself closely watched by Miss Bingley, and that she could not speak a word, especially to Miss Darcy, without calling her attention. This observation would not have prevented her from trying to talk to the latter, had they not been seated at an inconvenient distance; but she was not sorry to be spared the necessity of saying much. Her own thoughts were employing her. She expected every moment that some of the gentlemen would enter the room. She wished, she feared that the master of the house might be amongst them; and whether she wished or feared it most, she could scarcely determine. After sitting in this manner a quarter of an hour, without hearing Miss Bingley's voice, Elizabeth was roused by receiving from her a cold enquiry after the health of her family. She answered with equal indifference and brevity, and the other said no more.

The next variation which their visit afforded was produced by the entrance of servants with cold meat, cake, and a variety of all the finest fruits in season; but this did not take place till after many a significant look and smile from Mrs. Annesley to Miss Darcy had been given, to remind her of her post. There was now employment for the whole party; for though they could not all talk, they could all eat; and the beautiful pyramids of grapes, nectarines, and peaches, soon collected them round the table.

While thus engaged, Elizabeth had a fair opportunity of deciding whether she most feared or wished for the appearance of Mr. Darcy, by the feelings which prevailed on his entering the room; and then, though but a moment before she had believed her wishes to predominate, she began to regret that he came.

He had been some time with Mr. Gardiner, who, with two or three other gentlemen from the house, was engaged by the river, and had left him only on learning that the ladies of the family intended a visit to Georgiana that morning. No sooner did he appear, than Elizabeth wisely resolved to be perfectly easy and unembarrassed;—a resolution the more necessary to be made, but perhaps not the more easily kept, because she saw that the suspicions of the whole party were awakened against them, and that there was scarcely an eye which did not watch his behaviour when he first came into the room. In no countenance was attentive curiosity so strongly marked as in Miss Bingley's, in spite of the smiles which overspread her face whenever she spoke to one of its objects; for jealousy had not yet made her desperate, and her attentions to Mr. Darcy were by no means over. Miss Darcy, on her brother's entrance, exerted herself much more to talk; and Elizabeth saw that he was anxious for his sister and herself to get acquainted, and forwarded, as much as possible, every attempt at conversation on either side. Miss Bingley saw all this likewise; and, in the imprudence of anger, took the first opportunity of saying, with sneering civility,

"Pray, Miss Eliza, are not the ————shire militia removed from

Meryton? They must be a great loss to *your* family."

In Darcy's presence she dared not mention Wickham's name; but Elizabeth instantly comprehended that he was uppermost in her thoughts; and the various recollections connected with him gave her a moment's distress; but, exerting herself vigorously to repel the ill-natured attack, she presently answered the question in a tolerably disengaged tone. While she spoke, an involuntary glance shewed her Darcy with an heightened complexion, earnestly looking at her, and his sister overcome with confusion, and unable to lift up her eyes. Had Miss Bingley known what pain she was then giving her beloved friend, she undoubtedly would have refrained from the hint; but she had merely intended to discompose Elizabeth, by bringing forward the idea of a man to whom she believed her partial, to make her betray a sensibility which might injure her in Darcy's opinion, and perhaps to remind the latter of all the follies and absurdities, by which some part of her family were connected with that corps. Not a syllable had ever reached her of Miss Darcy's meditated elopement. To no creature had it been revealed, where secrecy was possible, except to Elizabeth; and from all Bingley's connections her brother was particularly anxious to conceal it, from that very wish which Elizabeth had long ago attributed to him, of their becoming hereafter her own. He had certainly formed such a plan, and without meaning that it should affect his endeavour to separate him from Miss Bennet, it is probable that it might add something to his lively concern for the welfare of his friend.

Elizabeth's collected behaviour, however, soon quieted his emotion; and as Miss Bingley, vexed and disappointed, dared not approach nearer to Wickham, Georgiana also recovered in time, though not enough to be able to speak any more. Her brother, whose eye she feared to meet, scarcely recollected her interest in the affair, and the very circumstance which had been designed to turn his thoughts from Elizabeth, seemed to have fixed them on her more, and more cheerfully.

Their visit did not continue long after the question and answer above-mentioned; and while Mr. Darcy was attending them to their carriage, Miss Bingley was venting her feelings in criticisms on Elizabeth's person, behaviour, and dress. But Georgiana would not join her. Her brother's recommendation was enough to ensure her favour: his judgment could not err, and he had spoken in such terms of Elizabeth, as to leave Georgiana without the power of finding her otherwise than lovely and amiable. When Darcy returned to the saloon, Miss Bingley could not help repeating to him some part of what she had been saying to his sister.

"How very ill Eliza Bennet looks this morning, Mr. Darcy,"

she cried; "I never in my life saw any one so much altered as she is since the winter. She is grown so brown and coarse! Louisa and I were agreeing that we should not have known her again."

However little Mr. Darcy might have liked such an address, he contented himself with coolly replying, that he perceived no other alteration than her being rather tanned,—no miraculous consequence of travelling in the summer.

"For my own part," she rejoined, "I must confess that I never could see any beauty in her. Her face is too thin; her complexion has no brilliancy; and her features are not at all handsome. Her nose wants character; there is nothing marked in its lines. Her teeth are tolerable, but not out of the common way; and as for her eyes, which have sometimes been called so fine, I never could perceive any thing extraordinary in them. They have a sharp, shrewish look, which I do not like at all; and in her air altogether, there is a self-sufficiency without fashion, which is intolerable."

Persuaded as Miss Bingley was that Darcy admired Elizabeth, this was not the best method of recommending herself; but angry people are not always wise; and in seeing him at last look somewhat nettled, she had all the success she expected. He was resolutely silent however; and, from a determination of making him speak, she continued,

"I remember, when we first knew her in Hertfordshire, how amazed we all were to find that she was a reputed beauty; and I particularly recollect your saying one night, after they had been dining at Netherfield, '*She* a beauty!—I should as soon call her mother a wit.' But afterwards she seemed to improve on you, and I believe you thought her rather pretty at one time."

"Yes," replied Darcy, who could contain himself no longer, "but *that* was only when I first knew her, for it is many months since I have considered her as one of the handsomest women of my acquaintance."

He then went away, and Miss Bingley was left to all the satisfaction of having forced him to say what gave no one any pain but herself.

Mrs. Gardiner and Elizabeth talked of all that had occurred, during their visit, as they returned, except what had particularly interested them both. The looks and behaviour of every body they had seen were discussed, except of the person who had mostly engaged their attention. They talked of his sister, his friends, his house, his fruit, of every thing but himself; yet Elizabeth was longing to know what Mrs. Gardiner thought of him, and Mrs. Gardiner would have been highly gratified by her niece's beginning the subject.

Chapter IV

Elizabeth had been a good deal disappointed in not finding a letter from Jane, on their first arrival at Lambton; and this disappointment had been renewed on each of the mornings that had now been spent there; but on the third, her repining was over, and her sister justified by the receipt of two letters from her at once, on one of which was marked that it had been missent elsewhere. Elizabeth was not surprised at it, as Jane had written the direction [2] remarkably ill.

They had just been preparing to walk as the letters came in; and her uncle and aunt, leaving her to enjoy them in quiet, set off by themselves. The one missent must be first attended to; it had been written five days ago. The beginning contained an account of all their little parties and engagements, with such news as the country afforded; but the latter half, which was dated a day later, and written in evident agitation, gave more important intelligence. It was to this effect:

"Since writing the above, dearest Lizzy, something has occurred of a most unexpected and serious nature; but I am afraid of alarming you—be assured that we are all well. What I have to say relates to poor Lydia. An express came at twelve last night, just as we were all gone to bed, from Colonel Forster, to inform us that she was gone off to Scotland with one of his officers; to own the truth, with Wickham!—Imagine our surprise. To Kitty, however, it does not seem so wholly unexpected. I am very, very sorry. So imprudent a match on both sides!—But I am willing to hope the best, and that his character has been misunderstood. Thoughtless and indiscreet I can easily believe him, but this step (and let us rejoice over it) marks nothing bad at heart. His choice is disinterested at least, for he must know my father can give her nothing. Our poor mother is sadly grieved. My father bears it better. How thankful am I, that we never let them know what has been said against him; we must forget it ourselves. They were off Saturday night about twelve, as is conjectured, but were not missed till yesterday morning at eight. The express was sent off directly. My dear Lizzy, they must have passed within ten miles of us. Colonel Forster gives us reason to expect him here soon. Lydia left a few lines for his wife, informing her of their intention. I must conclude, for I cannot be long from my poor mother. I am afraid you will not be able to make it out, but I hardly know what I have written."

Without allowing herself time for consideration, and scarcely

2. Address.

knowing what she felt, Elizabeth on finishing this letter, instantly seized the other, and opening it with the utmost impatience, read as follows: it had been written a day later than the conclusion of the first.

"By this time, my dearest sister, you have received my hurried letter; I wish this may be more intelligible, but though not confined for time, my head is so bewildered that I cannot answer for being coherent. Dearest Lizzy, I hardly know what I would write, but I have bad news for you, and it cannot be delayed. Imprudent as a marriage between Mr. Wickham and our poor Lydia would be, we are now anxious to be assured it has taken place, for there is but too much reason to fear they are not gone to Scotland. Colonel Forster came yesterday, having left Brighton the day before, not many hours after the express. Though Lydia's short letter to Mrs. F. gave them to understand that they were going to Gretna Green,[3] something was dropped by Denny expressing his belief that W. never intended to go there, or to marry Lydia at all, which was repeated to Colonel F. who instantly taking the alarm, set off from B. intending to trace their route. He did trace them easily to Clapham, but no farther; for on entering that place they removed into a hackney-coach and dismissed the chaise that brought them from Epsom. All that is known after this is, that they were seen to continue the London road. I know not what to think. After making every possible enquiry on that side London, Colonel F. came on into Hertfordshire, anxiously renewing them at all the turnpikes, and at the inns in Barnet and Hatfield, but without any success, no such people had been seen to pass through. With the kindest concern he came on to Longbourn, and broke his apprehensions to us in a manner most creditable to his heart. I am sincerely grieved for him and Mrs. F. but no one can throw any blame on them. Our distress, my dear Lizzy, is very great. My father and mother believe the worst, but I cannot think so ill of him. Many circumstances might make it more eligible for them to be married privately in town than to pursue their first plan; and even if *he* could form such a design against a young woman of Lydia's connections, which is not likely, can I suppose her so lost to every thing?—Impossible. I grieve to find, however, that Colonel F. is not disposed to depend upon their marriage; he shook his head when I expressed my hopes, and said he feared W. was not a man to be trusted. My poor mother is really ill and keeps her room. Could she exert herself it would be better, but this is not to be expected; and as to my

3. Scottish law did not require the consent of parents to the marriage of a minor. As the most accessible village on the Scottish side of its border with England, Gretna Green was the customary destination of eloping couples in which one partner was not yet of age.

father, I never in my life saw him so affected. Poor Kitty has anger [4] for having concealed their attachment; but as it was a matter of confidence one cannot wonder. I am truly glad, dearest Lizzy, that you have been spared something of these distressing scenes; but now as the first shock is over, shall I own that I long for your return? I am not so selfish, however, as to press for it, if inconvenient. Adieu. I take up my pen again to do, what I have just told you I would not, but circumstances are such, that I cannot help earnestly begging you all to come here, as soon as possible. I know my dear uncle and aunt so well, that I am not afraid of requesting it, though I have still something more to ask of the former. My father is going to London with Colonel Forster instantly, to try to discover her. What he means to do, I am sure I know not; but his excessive distress will not allow him to pursue any measure in the best and safest way, and Colonel Forster is obliged to be at Brighton again to-morrow evening. In such an exigence my uncle's advice and assistance would be every thing in the world; he will immediately comprehend what I must feel, and I rely upon his goodness."

"Oh! where, where is my uncle?" cried Elizabeth, darting from her seat as she finished the letter, in eagerness to follow him, without losing a moment of the time so precious; but as she reached the door, it was opened by a servant, and Mr. Darcy appeared. Her pale face and impetuous manner made him start, and before he could recover himself enough to speak, she, in whose mind every idea was superseded by Lydia's situation, hastily exclaimed, "I beg your pardon, but I must leave you. I must find Mr. Gardiner this moment, on business that cannot be delayed; I have not an instant to lose."

"Good God! what is the matter?" cried he, with more feeling than politeness; then recollecting himself,

"I will not detain you a minute, but let me, or let the servant, go after Mr. and Mrs. Gardiner. You are not well enough;—you cannot go yourself."

Elizabeth hesitated, but her knees trembled under her, and she felt how little would be gained by her attempting to pursue them. Calling back the servant, therefore, she commissioned him, though in so breathless an accent as made her almost unintelligible, to fetch his master and mistress home, instantly.

On his quitting the room, she sat down, unable to support herself, and looking so miserably ill, that it was impossible for

4. In his notes to the novel Chapman writes of this passage: *"has anger:* the loss of a word has been suspected. But *cf. The Wife and the Mistress,* by Mary Charlton, second edition, 1803, vol. i, p. 263: 'reminded her that she would *get anger* if your lordship should hear of it'; where the italics suggest a colloquialism." Oxford edition, II, 393.

Darcy to leave her, or to refrain from saying, in a tone of gentleness and commiseration, "Let me call your maid. Is there nothing you could take, to give you present relief?—A glass of wine;—shall I get you one?—You are very ill."

"No, I thank you;" she replied, endeavouring to recover herself. "There is nothing the matter with me. I am quite well. I am only distressed by some dreadful news which I have just received from Longbourn."

She burst into tears as she alluded to it, and for a few minutes could not speak another word. Darcy, in wretched suspense, could only say something indistinctly of his concern, and observe her in compassionate silence. At length, she spoke again. "I have just had a letter from Jane, with such dreadful news. It cannot be concealed from any one. My youngest sister has left all her friends —has eloped;—has thrown herself into the power of—of Mr. Wickham. They are gone off together from Brighton. *You* know him too well to doubt the rest. She has no money, no connections, nothing that can tempt him to—she is lost for ever."

Darcy was fixed in astonishment. "When I consider," she added, in a yet more agitated voice, "that *I* might have prevented it!—*I* who knew what he was. Had I but explained some part of it only—some part of what I learnt, to my own family! Had his character been known, this could not have happened. But it is all, all too late now."

"I am grieved, indeed," cried Darcy; "grieved—shocked. But is it certain, absolutely certain?"

"Oh yes!—They left Brighton together on Sunday night, and were traced almost to London, but not beyond; they are certainly not gone to Scotland."

"And what has been done, what has been attempted, to recover her?"

"My father is gone to London, and Jane has written to beg my uncle's immediate assistance, and we shall be off, I hope, in half an hour. But nothing can be done; I know very well that nothing can be done. How is such a man to be worked on? How are they even to be discovered? I have not the smallest hope. It is every way horrible!"

Darcy shook his head in silent acquiescence.

"When *my* eyes were opened to his real character.—Oh! had I known what I ought, what I dared, to do! But I knew not —I was afraid of doing too much. Wretched, wretched, mistake!"

Darcy made no answer. He seemed scarcely to hear her, and was walking up and down the room in earnest meditation; his brow contracted, his air gloomy. Elizabeth soon observed, and instantly understood it. Her power was sinking; every thing *must* sink under such a proof of family weakness, such an assurance of the deepest disgrace. She could neither wonder nor condemn, but the belief of his self-conquest brought nothing consolatory to her bosom, afforded no palliation of her distress. It was, on the contrary, exactly calculated to make her understand her own wishes; and never had she so honestly felt that she could have loved him, as now, when all love must be vain.

But self, though it would intrude, could not engross her. Lydia —the humiliation, the misery, she was bringing on them all, soon swallowed up every private care; and covering her face with her handkerchief, Elizabeth was soon lost to every thing else; and, after a pause of several minutes, was only recalled to a sense of her situation by the voice of her companion, who, in a manner, which though it spoke compassion, spoke likewise restraint, said, "I am afraid you have been long desiring my absence, nor have I any thing to plead in excuse of my stay, but real, though unavailing, concern. Would to heaven that any thing could be either said or done on my part, that might offer consolation to such distress.—But I will not torment you with vain wishes, which may seem purposely to ask for your thanks. This unfortunate affair will, I fear, prevent my sister's having the pleasure of seeing you at Pemberley to day."

"Oh, yes. Be so kind as to apologize for us to Miss Darcy. Say that urgent business calls us home immediately. Conceal the unhappy truth as long as it is possible.—I know it cannot be long."

He readily assured her of his secrecy—again expressed his sorrow for her distress, wished it a happier conclusion than there was at present reason to hope, and leaving his compliments for her relations, with only one serious, parting, look, went away.

As he quitted the room, Elizabeth felt how improbable it was that they should ever see each other again on such terms of cordiality as had marked their several meetings in Derbyshire; and as she threw a retrospective glance over the whole of their acquaintance, so full of contradictions and varieties, sighed at the perverseness of those feelings which would now have promoted its continuance, and would formerly have rejoiced in its termination.

If gratitude and esteem are good foundations of affection, Elizabeth's change of sentiment will be neither improbable nor faulty. But if otherwise, if the regard springing from such sources is unreasonable or unnatural, in comparison of what is so often described as arising on a first interview with its object, and even before two words have been exchanged, nothing can be said in her defence, except that she had given somewhat of a trial to the latter method, in her partiality for Wickham, and that its ill-success might perhaps authorise her to seek the other less interesting mode of attachment. Be that as it may, she saw him go with regret; and in this early example of what Lydia's infamy must produce, found additional anguish as she reflected on that wretched business. Never, since reading Jane's second letter, had she entertained a hope of Wickham's meaning to marry her. No one but Jane, she thought, could flatter herself with such an expectation. Surprise was the least of her feelings on this developement. While the contents of the first letter remained on her mind, she was all surprise—all astonishment that Wickham should marry a girl, whom it was impossible he could marry for money; and how Lydia could ever have attached him, had appeared incomprehensible. But now it was all too natural. For such an attachment as this, she might have sufficient charms; and though she did not suppose Lydia to be deliberately engaging in an elopement, without the intention of marriage, she had no difficulty in believing that neither her virtue nor her understanding would preserve her from falling an easy prey.

She had never perceived, while the regiment was in Hertfordshire, that Lydia had any partiality for him, but she was convinced that Lydia had wanted only encouragement to attach herself to any body. Sometimes one officer, sometimes another had been her favourite, as their attentions raised them in her opinion. Her affections had been continually fluctuating, but never without an object. The mischief of neglect and mistaken indulgence towards such a girl.—Oh! how acutely did she now feel it.

She was wild to be at home—to hear, to see, to be upon the spot, to share with Jane in the cares that must now fall wholly upon her, in a family so deranged; a father absent, a mother incapable of exertion, and requiring constant attendance; and though almost persuaded that nothing could be done for Lydia, her uncle's interference seemed of the utmost importance, and till he entered the room, the misery of her impatience was severe. Mr. and Mrs. Gardiner had hurried back in alarm, supposing, by the servant's account, that their niece was taken suddenly ill;—but satisfying them instantly on that head, she eagerly communicated the cause of their summons, reading the two letters aloud, and dwelling on the postscript of the last, with trembling energy.—Though Lydia had never been a favourite with them, Mr. and Mrs. Gardiner could not but be deeply affected. Not Lydia only, but all were concerned in it; and after the first exclamations of surprise and horror, Mr. Gardiner readily promised every assistance in his power. —Elizabeth, though expecting no less, thanked him with tears of gratitude; and all three being actuated by one spirit, every thing relating to their journey was speedily settled. They were to be off as soon as possible. "But what is to be done about Pemberley?" cried Mrs. Gardiner. "John told us Mr. Darcy was here when you sent for us;—was it so?"

"Yes; and I told him we should not be able to keep our engagement. *That* is all settled."

"That is all settled;" repeated the other, as she ran into her room to prepare. "And are they upon such terms as for her to disclose the real truth! Oh, that I knew how it was!"

But wishes were vain; or at best could serve only to amuse her in the hurry and confusion of the following hour. Had Elizabeth been at leisure to be idle, she would have remained certain that all employment was impossible to one so wretched as herself; but she had her share of business as well as her aunt, and amongst the rest there were notes to be written to all their friends in Lambton, with false excuses for their sudden departure. An hour, however, saw the whole completed; and Mr. Gardiner meanwhile having settled his account at the inn, nothing remained to be done but to go; and Elizabeth, after all the misery of the morning, found herself, in a shorter space of time than she could have supposed, seated in the carriage, and on the road to Longbourn.

Chapter V

"I have been thinking it over again, Elizabeth," said her uncle, as they drove from the town; "and really, upon serious consideration, I am much more inclined than I was to judge as your eldest sister does of the matter. It appears to me so very unlikely, that any young man should form such a design against a girl who is by no means unprotected or friendless, and who was actually staying in his colonel's family, that I am strongly inclined to hope the best. Could he expect that her friends would not step forward? Could he expect to be noticed again by the regiment, after such an affront to Colonel Forster? His temptation is not adequate to the risk."

"Do you really think so?" cried Elizabeth, brightening up for a moment.

"Upon my word," said Mrs. Gardiner, "I begin to be of your uncle's opinion. It is really too great a violation of decency, honour, and interest, for him to be guilty of it. I cannot think so very ill of Wickham. Can you, yourself, Lizzy, so wholly give him up, as to believe him capable of it?"

"Not perhaps of neglecting his own interest. But of every other neglect I can believe him capable. If, indeed, it should be so! But I dare not hope it. Why should they not go on to Scotland, if that had been the case?"

"In the first place," replied Mr. Gardiner, "there is no absolute proof that they are not gone to Scotland."

"Oh! but their removing from the chaise into an hackney coach is such a presumption! And, besides, no traces of them were to be found on the Barnet road."

"Well, then—supposing them to be in London. They may be there, though for the purpose of concealment, for no more exceptionable purpose. It is not likely that money should be very abundant on either side; and it might strike them that they could be more economically, though less expeditiously, married in London, than in Scotland."

"But why all this secrecy? Why any fear of detection? Why must their marriage be private? Oh! no, no, this is not likely. His most particular friend, you see by Jane's account, was persuaded of his never intending to marry her. Wickham will never marry a woman without some money. He cannot afford it. And what claims has Lydia, what attractions has she beyond youth, health, and good humour, that could make him for her sake, forego every chance of benefiting himself by marrying well? As to what restraint the apprehension of disgrace in the corps might throw on a dishonourable elopement with her, I am not able to judge; for I know nothing of the effects that such a step might produce. But as to your other objection, I am afraid it will hardly hold good. Lydia has no brothers to step forward; and he might imagine, from my father's behaviour, from his indolence and the little attention he has ever seemed to give to what was going forward in his family, that *he* would do as little, and think as little about it, as any father could do, in such a matter."

"But can you think that Lydia is so lost to every thing but love of him, as to consent to live with him on any other terms than marriage?"

"It does seem, and it is most shocking indeed," replied Elizabeth, with tears in her eyes, "that a sister's sense of decency and virtue in such a point should admit of doubt. But, really, I know not what to say. Perhaps I am not doing her justice. But she is very young; she has never been taught to think on serious subjects; and for the last half year, nay, for a twelvemonth, she has been given up to nothing but amusement and vanity. She has been allowed to dispose of her time in the most idle and frivolous manner, and to adopt any opinions that came in her way. Since the ———shire were first quartered in Meryton, nothing but love, flirtation, and officers, have been in her head. She has been doing every thing in her power by thinking and talking on the subject, to give greater—what shall I call it? susceptibility to her feelings; which are naturally lively enough. And we all know that Wickham has every charm of person and address that can captivate a woman."

"But you see that Jane," said her aunt, "does not think so ill of Wickham, as to believe him capable of the attempt."

"Of whom does Jane ever think ill? And who is there, whatever might be their former conduct, that she would believe capable of such an attempt, till it were proved against them? But Jane knows, as well as I do, what Wickham really is. We both know that he has been profligate in every sense of the word. That he has neither integrity nor honour. That he is as false and deceitful, as he is insinuating."

"And do you really know all this?" cried Mrs. Gardiner, whose curiosity as to the mode of her intelligence was all alive.

"I do, indeed," replied Elizabeth, colouring. "I told you the other day, of his infamous behaviour to Mr. Darcy; and you, yourself, when last at Longbourn, heard in what manner he spoke of the man, who had behaved with such forbearance and liberality towards him. And there are other circumstances which I am not at liberty—which it is not worth while to relate; but his lies about the whole Pemberley family are endless. From what he said of Miss Darcy, I was thoroughly prepared to see a proud, reserved, disagreeable girl. Yet he knew to the contrary himself. He must know that she was as amiable and unpretending as we have found her."

"But does Lydia know nothing of this? Can she be ignorant of what you and Jane seem so well to understand?"

"Oh, yes!—that, that is the worst of all. Till I was in Kent, and saw so much both of Mr. Darcy and his relation, Colonel Fitz-william, I was ignorant of the truth myself. And when I returned home, the ———shire was to leave Meryton in a week or fort-night's time. As that was the case, neither Jane, to whom I related the whole, nor I, thought it necessary to make our knowl-edge public; for of what use could it apparently be to any one, that the good opinion which all the neighbourhood had of him, should then be overthrown? And even when it was settled that Lydia should go with Mrs. Forster, the necessity of opening her eyes to his character never occurred to me. That *she* could be in any danger from the deception never entered my head. That such a consequence as *this* should ensue, you may easily believe was far enough from my thoughts."

"When they all removed to Brighton, therefore, you had no reason, I suppose, to believe them fond of each other."

"Not the slightest. I can remember no sympton of affection on either side; and had any thing of the kind been perceptible, you must be aware that ours is not a family, on which it could be thrown away. When first he entered the corps, she was ready enough to admire him; but so we all were. Every girl in, or near Meryton, was out of her senses about him for the first two months; but he never distinguished *her* by any particular attention, and, consequently, after a moderate period of extravagant and wild admiration, her fancy for him gave way, and others of the regiment, who treated her with more distinction, again became her favourites."

———

It may be easily believed, that however little of novelty could be added to their fears, hopes, and conjectures, on this interesting subject, by its repeated discussion, no other could detain them from it long, during the whole of the journey. From Elizabeth's thoughts it was never absent. Fixed there by the keenest of all anguish, self reproach, she could find no interval of ease or forgetfulness.

They travelled as expeditiously as possible; and sleeping one night on the road, reached Longbourn by dinner-time the next day. It was a comfort to Elizabeth to consider that Jane could not have been wearied by long expectations.

The little Gardiners, attracted by the sight of a chaise, were standing on the steps of the house, as they entered the paddock; and when the carriage drove up to the door, the joyful surprise that lighted up their faces, and displayed itself over their whole bodies, in a variety of capers and frisks, was the first pleasing earnest of their welcome.

Elizabeth jumped out; and, after giving each of them an hasty kiss, hurried into the vestibule, where Jane, who came running down stairs from her mother's apartment, immediately met her.

Elizabeth, as she affectionately embraced her, whilst tears filled the eyes of both, lost not a moment in asking whether any thing had been heard of the fugitives.

"Not yet," replied Jane. "But now that my dear uncle is come, I hope every thing will be well."

"Is my father in town?"

"Yes, he went on Tuesday as I wrote you word."

"And have you heard from him often?"

"We have heard only once. He wrote me a few lines on Wednesday, to say that he had arrived in safety, and to give me his directions, which I particularly begged him to do. He merely added, that he should not write again, till he had something of importance to mention."

"And my mother—How is she? How are you all?"

"My mother is tolerably well, I trust; though her spirits are greatly shaken. She is up stairs, and will have great satisfaction in seeing you all. She does not yet leave her dressing-room. Mary and Kitty, thank Heaven! are quite well."

"But you—How are you?" cried Elizabeth. "You look pale. How much you must have gone through!"

Her sister, however, assured her, of her being perfectly well; and their conversation, which had been passing while Mr. and Mrs. Gardiner were engaged with their children, was now put an end to, by the approach of the whole party. Jane ran to her uncle and aunt, and welcomed and thanked them both, with alternate smiles and tears.

When they were all in the drawing room, the questions which Elizabeth had already asked, were of course repeated by the others, and they soon found that Jane had no intelligence to give. The sanguine hope of good, however, which the benevolence of her heart suggested, had not yet deserted her; she still expected that it would all end well, and that every morning would bring some letter, either from Lydia or her father, to explain their proceedings, and perhaps announce the marriage.

Mrs. Bennet, to whose apartment they all repaired, after a few minutes conversation together, received them exactly as might be expected; with tears and lamentations of regret, invectives against the villanous conduct of Wickham, and complaints of her own sufferings and ill usage; blaming every body but the person to whose ill judging indulgence the errors of her daughter must be principally owing.

"If I had been able," said she, "to carry my point of going to Brighton, with all my family, *this* would not have happened; but poor dear Lydia had nobody to take care of her. Why did the Forsters ever let her go out of their sight? I am sure there was some great neglect or other on their side, for she is not the kind of girl to do such a thing, if she had been well looked after. I always thought they were very unfit to have the charge of her; but I was over-ruled, as I always am. Poor dear child! And now here's Mr. Bennet gone away, and I know he will fight Wickham, wherever he meets him, and then he will be killed, and what is to become of us all? The Collinses will turn us out, before he is cold in his grave; and if you are not kind to us, brother, I do not know what we shall do."

They all exclaimed against such terrific ideas; and Mr. Gardiner, after general assurances of his affection for her and all her family, told her that he meant to be in London the very next day, and would assist Mr. Bennet in every endeavour for recovering Lydia.

"Do not give way to useless alarm," added he, "though it

is right to be prepared for the worst, there is no occasion to look on it as certain. It is not quite a week since they left Brighton. In a few days more, we may gain some news of them, and till we know that they are not married, and have no design of marrying, do not let us give the matter over as lost. As soon as I get to town, I shall go to my brother, and make him come home with me to Gracechurch Street, and then we may consult together as to what is to be done."

"Oh! my dear brother," replied Mrs. Bennet, "that is exactly what I could most wish for. And now do, when you get to town, find them out, wherever they may be; and if they are not married already, *make* them marry. And as for wedding clothes, do not let them wait for that, but tell Lydia she shall have as much money as she chuses, to buy them, after they are married. And, above all things, keep Mr. Bennet from fighting. Tell him what a dreadful state I am in,—that I am frightened out of my wits; and have such tremblings, such flutterings, all over me, such spasms in my side, and pains in my head, and such beatings at heart, that I can get no rest by night nor by day. And tell my dear Lydia, not to give any directions about her clothes, till she has seen me, for she does not know which are the best warehouses. Oh, brother, how kind you are! I know you will contrive it all."

But Mr. Gardiner, though he assured her again of his earnest endeavours in the cause, could not avoid recommending moderation to her, as well in her hopes as her fears; and, after talking with her in this manner till dinner was on table, they left her to vent all her feelings on the housekeeper, who attended, in the absence of her daughters.

Though her brother and sister were persuaded that there was no real occasion for such a seclusion from the family, they did not attempt to oppose it, for they knew that she had not prudence enough to hold her tongue before the servants, while they waited at table, and judged it better that *one* only of the household, and the one whom they could most trust, should comprehend all her fears and solicitude on the subject.

In the dining-room they were soon joined by Mary and Kitty, who had been too busily engaged in their separate apartments, to make their appearance before. One came from her books, and the other from her toilette. The faces of both, however, were tolerably calm; and no change was visible in either, except that the loss of her favourite sister, or the anger which she had herself incurred in the business, had given something more of fretfulness than usual, to the accents of Kitty. As for Mary, she was mistress enough of herself to whisper to Elizabeth with a countenance of grave reflection, soon after they were seated at table,

"This is a most unfortunate affair; and will probably be much talked of. But we must stem the tide of malice, and pour into the wounded bosoms of each other, the balm of sisterly consolation."

Then, perceiving in Elizabeth no inclination of replying, she added, "Unhappy as the event must be for Lydia, we may draw from it this useful lesson; the loss of virtue in a female is irretrievable—that one false step involves her in endless ruin—that her reputation is no less brittle than it is beautiful,—and that she cannot be too much guarded in her behaviour towards the undeserving of the other sex."

Elizabeth lifted up her eyes in amazement, but was too much oppressed to make any reply. Mary, however, continued to console herself with such kind of moral extractions from the evil before them.

In the afternoon, the two elder Miss Bennets were able to be for half an hour by themselves; and Elizabeth instantly availed herself of the opportunity of making many enquiries, which Jane was equally eager to satisfy. After joining in general lamentations over the dreadful sequel of this event, which Elizabeth considered as all but certain, and Miss Bennet could not assert to be wholly impossible; the former continued the subject, by saying, "But tell me all and every thing about it, which I have not already heard. Give me farther particulars. What did Colonel Forster say? Had they no apprehension of any thing before the elopement took place? They must have seen them together for ever."

"Colonel Forster did own that he had often suspected some partiality, especially on Lydia's side, but nothing to give him any alarm. I am so grieved for him. His behaviour was attentive and kind to the utmost. He *was* coming to us, in order to assure us of his concern, before he had any idea of their not being gone to Scotland: when that apprehension first got abroad, it hastened his journey."

"And was Denny convinced that Wickham would not marry? Did he know of their intending to go off? Had Colonel Forster seen Denny himself?"

"Yes; but when questioned by *him* Denny denied knowing any thing of their plan, and would not give his real opinion about it. He did not repeat his persuasion of their not marrying—and from *that*, I am inclined to hope, he might have been misunderstood before."

"And till Colonel Forster came himself, not one of you entertained a doubt, I suppose, of their being really married?"

"How was it possible that such an idea should enter our brains! I felt a little uneasy—a little fearful of my sister's happiness with him in marriage, because I knew that his conduct had not been always quite right. My father and mother knew nothing of that, they only felt how imprudent a match it must be. Kitty then owned, with a very natural triumph on knowing more than the rest of us, that in Lydia's last letter, she had prepared her for such a step. She had known, it seems, of their being in love with each other, many weeks."

"But not before they went to Brighton?"

"No, I believe not."

"And did Colonel Forster appear to think ill of Wickham himself? Does he know his real character?"

"I must confess that he did not speak so well of Wickham as he formerly did. He believed him to be imprudent and extravagant. And since this sad affair has taken place, it is said, that he left Meryton greatly in debt; but I hope this may be false."

"Oh, Jane, had we been less secret, had we told what we knew of him, this could not have happened!"

"Perhaps it would have been better;" replied her sister. "But to expose the former faults of any person, without knowing what their present feelings were, seemed unjustifiable. We acted with. the best intentions."

"Could Colonel Forster repeat the particulars of Lydia's note to his wife?"

"He brought it with him for us to see."

Jane then took it from her pocket-book, and gave it to Elizabeth. These were the contents:

My dear Harriet,

"You will laugh when you know where I am gone, and I cannot help laughing myself at your surprise tomorrow morning, as soon as I am missed. I am going to Gretna Green, and if you cannot guess with who, I shall think you a simpleton, for there is but one man in the world I love, and he is an angel. I should never be happy without him, so think it no harm to be off. You need not send them word at Longbourn of my going, if you do not like it, for it will make the surprise the greater, when I write to them, and sign my name Lydia Wickham. What a good joke it will be! I can hardly write for laughing. Pray make my excuses to Pratt, for not keeping my engagement, and dancing with him to night. Tell him I hope he will excuse me when he knows all, and tell him I will dance with him at the next ball we meet, with great pleasure. I shall send for my clothes when I get to Longbourn; but

I wish you would tell Sally to mend a great slit in my worked muslin gown, before they are packed up. Good bye. Give my love to Colonel Forster, I hope you will drink to our good journey.

"Your affectionate friend,

"Lydia Bennet."

"Oh! thoughtless, thoughtless Lydia!" cried Elizabeth when she had finished it. "What a letter is this, to be written at such a moment. But at least it shews, that *she* was serious in the object of her journey. Whatever he might afterwards persuade her to, it was not on her side a *scheme* of infamy. My poor father! how he must have felt it!"

"I never saw any one so shocked. He could not speak a word for full ten minutes. My mother was taken ill immediately, and the whole house in such confusion!"

"Oh! Jane," cried Elizabeth, "was there a servant belonging to it, who did not know the whole story before the end of the day?"

"I do not know.—I hope there was.—But to be guarded at such a time, is very difficult. My mother was in hysterics, and though I endeavoured to give her every assistance in my power, I am afraid I did not do so much as I might have done! But the horror of what might possibly happen, almost took from me my faculties."

"Your attendance upon her, has been too much for you. You do not look well. Oh! that I had been with you, you have had every care and anxiety upon yourself alone."

"Mary and Kitty have been very kind, and would have shared in every fatigue, I am sure, but I did not think it right for either of them. Kitty is slight and delicate, and Mary studies so much, that her hours of repose should not be broken in on. My aunt Phillips came to Longbourn on Tuesday, after my father went away; and was so good as to stay till Thursday with me. She was of great use and comfort to us all, and lady Lucas has been very kind; she walked here on Wednesday morning to condole with us, and offered her services, or any of her daughters, if they could be of use to us."

"She had better have stayed at home," cried Elizabeth; "perhaps she *meant* well, but, under such a misfortune as this, one cannot see too little of one's neighbours. Assistance is impossible; condolence, insufferable. Let them triumph over us at a distance, and be satisfied."

She then proceeded to enquire into the measures which her father had intended to pursue, while in town, for the recovery of his daughter.

"He meant, I believe," replied Jane, "to go to Epsom, the

place where they last changed horses, see the postilions, and try if any thing could be made out from them. His principal object must be, to discover the number of the hackney coach which took them from Clapham. It had come with a fare from London; and as he thought the circumstance of a gentleman and lady's removing from one carriage into another, might be remarked, he meant to make enquiries at Clapham. If he could any how discover at what house the coachman had before set down his fare, he determined to make enquiries there, and hoped it might not be impossible to find out the stand and number of the coach. I do not know of any other designs that he had formed: but he was in such a hurry to be gone, and his spirits so greatly discomposed, that I had difficulty in finding out even so much as this."

Chapter VI

The whole party were in hopes of a letter from Mr. Bennet the next morning, but the post came in without bringing a single line from him. His family knew him to be on all common occasions, a most negligent and dilatory correspondent, but at such a time, they had hoped for exertion. They were forced to conclude, that he had no pleasing intelligence to send, but even of *that* they would have been glad to be certain. Mr. Gardiner had waited only for the letters before he set off.

When he was gone, they were certain at least of receiving constant information of what was going on, and their uncle promised, at parting, to prevail on Mr. Bennet to return to Longbourn, as soon as he could, to the great consolation of his sister, who considered it as the only security for her husband's not being killed in a duel.

Mrs. Gardiner and the children were to remain in Hertfordshire a few days longer, as the former thought her presence might be serviceable to her nieces. She shared in their attendance on Mrs. Bennet, and was a great comfort to them, in their hours of freedom. Their other aunt also visited them frequently, and always, as she said, with the design of cheering and heartening them up, though as she never came without reporting some fresh instance of Wickham's extravagance or irregularity, she seldom went away without leaving them more dispirited than she found them.

All Meryton seemed striving to blacken the man, who, but three months before, had been almost an angel of light. He was declared to be in debt to every tradesman in the place, and his intrigues, all honoured with the title of seduction, had been extended into every tradesman's family. Every body declared that he was the wickedest young man in the world; and every body began to find out, that they had always distrusted the appearance of his goodness. Elizabeth, though she did not credit above half of what was said, believed enough to make her former assurance of her sister's ruin still more certain; and even Jane, who believed still less of it, became almost hopeless, more especially as the time was now come, when if they had gone to Scotland, which she had never before entirely despaired of, they must in all probability have gained some news of them.

Mr. Gardiner left Longbourn on Sunday; on Tuesday, his wife received a letter from him; it told them, that on his arrival, he had immediately found out his brother, and persuaded him to come to Gracechurch street. That Mr. Bennet had been to Epsom and Clapham, before his arrival, but without gaining any satisfactory information; and that he was now determined to enquire at all the principal hotels in town, as Mr. Bennet thought it possible they might have gone to one of them, on their first coming to London, before they procured lodgings. Mr. Gardiner himself did not expect any success from this measure, but as his brother was eager in it, he meant to assist him in pursuing it. He added, that Mr. Bennet seemed wholly disinclined at present, to leave London, and promised to write again very soon. There was also a postscript to this effect.

"I have written to Colonel Forster to desire him to find out, if possible, from some of the young man's intimates in the regiment, whether Wickham has any relations or connections, who would be likely to know in what part of the town he has now concealed himself. If there were any one, that one could apply to, with a probability of gaining such a clue as that, it might be of essential consequence. At present we have nothing to guide us. Colonel Forster will, I dare say, do every thing in his power to satisfy us on this head. But, on second thoughts, perhaps Lizzy could tell us, what relations he has now living, better than any other person."

Elizabeth was at no loss to understand from whence this deference for her authority proceeded; but it was not in her power to give any information of so satisfactory a nature, as the compliment deserved.

She had never heard of his having had any relations, except a father and mother, both of whom had been dead many years. It was possible, however, that some of his companions in the ——— shire, might be able to give more information; and, though she was not very sanguine in expecting it, the application was a something to look forward to.

Every day at Longbourn was now a day of anxiety; but the most anxious part of each was when the post was expected. The arrival of letters was the first grand object of every morning's impatience.

Through letters, whatever of good or bad was to be told, would be communicated, and every succeeding day was expected to bring some news of importance.

But before they heard again from Mr. Gardiner, a letter arrived for their father, from a different quarter, from Mr. Collins; which, as Jane had received directions to open all that came for him in his absence, she accordingly read; and Elizabeth, who knew what curiosities his letters always were, looked over her, and read it likewise. It was as follows:

"My dear Sir,

"I feel myself called upon, by our relationship, and my situation in life, to condole with you on the grievous affliction you are now suffering under, of which we were yesterday informed by a letter from Hertfordshire. Be assured, my dear Sir, that Mrs. Collins and myself sincerely sympathise with you, and all your respectable family, in your present distress, which must be of the bitterest kind, because proceeding from a cause which no time can remove. No arguments shall be wanting on my part, that can alleviate so severe a misfortune; or that may comfort you, under a circumstance that must be of all others most afflicting to a parent's mind. The death of your daughter would have been a blessing in comparison of this. And it is the more to be lamented, because there is reason to suppose, as my dear Charlotte informs me, that this licentiousness of behaviour in your daughter, has proceeded from a faulty degree of indulgence, though, at the same time, for the consolation of yourself and Mrs. Bennet, I am inclined to think that her own disposition must be naturally bad, or she could not be guilty of such an enormity, at so early an age. Howsoever that may be, you are grievously to be pitied, in which opinion I am not only joined by Mrs. Collins, but likewise by lady Catherine and her daughter, to whom I have related the affair. They agree with me in apprehending that this false step in one daughter, will be injurious to the fortunes of all the others, for who, as lady Catherine herself condescendingly says, will connect themselves with such a family. And this consideration leads me moreover to reflect with augmented satisfaction on a certain event of last November, for had it been otherwise, I must have been involved in all your sorrow and disgrace. Let me advise you then, my dear Sir, to console yourself as much as possible, to throw off your unworthy child from your affection for ever, and leave her to reap the fruits of her own heinous offence.

"I am, dear Sir, &c. &c."

Mr. Gardiner did not write again, till he had received an answer from Colonel Forster; and then he had nothing of a pleasant

nature to send. It was not known that Wickham had a single relation, with whom he kept up any connection, and it was certain
that he had no near one living. His former acquaintance had
been numerous; but since he had been in the militia, it did not
appear that he was on terms of particular friendship with any
of them. There was no one therefore who could be pointed out,
as likely to give any news of him. And in the wretched state of
his own finances, there was a very powerful motive for secrecy,
in addition to his fear of discovery by Lydia's relations, for it had
just transpired that he had left gaming debts behind him, to a
very considerable amount. Colonel Forster believed that more
than a thousand pounds would be necessary to clear his expences
at Brighton. He owed a good deal in the town, but his debts of
honour were still more formidable. Mr. Gardiner did not attempt
to conceal these particulars from the Longbourn family; Jane heard
them with horror. "A gamester!" she cried. "This is wholly unexpected. I had not an idea of it."

Mr. Gardiner added in his letter, that they might expect to see
their father at home on the following day, which was Saturday.
Rendered spiritless by the ill-success of all their endeavours, he
had yielded to his brother-in-law's intreaty that he would return
to his family, and leave it to him to do, whatever occasion might
suggest to be advisable for continuing their pursuit. When Mrs.
Bennet was told of this, she did not express so much satisfaction
as her children expected, considering what her anxiety for his
life had been before.

"What, is he coming home, and without poor Lydia!" she cried.
"Sure he will not leave London before he has found them. Who
is to fight Wickham, and make him marry her, if he comes away?"

As Mrs. Gardiner began to wish to be at home, it was settled
that she and her children should go to London, at the same time
that Mr. Bennet came from it. The coach, therefore, took them
the first stage of their journey, and brought its master back to
Longbourn.

Mrs. Gardiner went away in all the perplexity about Elizabeth
and her Derbyshire friend, that had attended her from that part
of the world. His name had never been voluntarily mentioned before them by her niece; and the kind of half-expectation which
Mrs. Gardiner had formed, of their being followed by a letter from
him, had ended in nothing. Elizabeth had received none since
her return, that could come from Pemberley.

The present unhappy state of the family, rendered any other
excuse for the lowness of her spirits unnecessary; nothing, therefore, could be fairly conjectured from *that*, though Elizabeth, who

was by this time tolerably well acquainted with her own feelings, was perfectly aware, that, had she known nothing of Darcy, she could have borne the dread of Lydia's infamy somewhat better. It would have spared her, she thought, one sleepless night out of two.

When Mr. Bennet arrived, he had all the appearance of his usual philosophic composure. He said as little as he had ever been in the habit of saying; made no mention of the business that had taken him away, and it was some time before his daughters had courage to speak of it.

It was not till the afternoon, when he joined them at tea, that Elizabeth ventured to introduce the subject; and then, on her briefly expressing her sorrow for what he must have endured, he replied, "Say nothing of that. Who should suffer but myself? It has been my own doing, and I ought to feel it."

"You must not be too severe upon yourself," replied Elizabeth.

"You may well warn me against such an evil. Human nature is so prone to fall into it! No, Lizzy, let me once in my life feel how much I have been to blame. I am not afraid of being over-powered by the impression. It will pass away soon enough."

"Do you suppose them to be in London?"

"Yes; where else can they be so well concealed?"

"And Lydia used to want to go to London," added Kitty.

"She is happy, then," said her father, drily; "and her residence there will probably be of some duration."

Then, after a short silence, he continued, "Lizzy, I bear you no ill-will for being justified in your advice to me last May, which, considering the event, shews some greatness of mind."

They were interrupted by Miss Bennet, who came to fetch her mother's tea.

"This is a parade," cried he, "which does one good; it gives such an elegance to misfortune! Another day I will do the same; I will sit in my library, in my night cap and powdering gown, and give as much trouble as I can,—or, perhaps, I may defer it, till Kitty runs away."

"I am not going to run away, Papa," said Kitty, fretfully; "if I should ever go to Brighton, I would behave better than Lydia."

"*You* go to Brighton!—I would not trust you so near it as East Bourne, for fifty pounds! No, Kitty, I have at last learnt to be cautious, and you will feel the effects of it. No officer is ever to enter my house again, nor even to pass through the village. Balls will be absolutely prohibited, unless you stand up with one of your sisters. And you are never to stir out of doors, till you can prove, that you have spent ten minutes of every day in a rational manner."

Kitty, who took all these threats in a serious light, began to cry.

"Well, well," said he, "do not make yourself unhappy. If you are a good girl for the next ten years, I will take you to a review [5] at the end of them."

Chapter VII

Two days after Mr. Bennet's return, as Jane and Elizabeth were walking together in the shrubbery behind the house, they saw the housekeeper coming towards them, and, concluding that she came to call them to their mother, went forward to meet her; but, instead of the expected summons, when they approached her, she said to Miss Bennet, "I beg your pardon, madam, for interrupting you, but I was in hopes you might have got some good news from town, so I took the liberty of coming to ask."

"What do you mean, Hill? We have heard nothing from town."

"Dear madam," cried Mrs. Hill, in great astonishment, "dont you know there is an express come for master from Mr. Gardiner? He has been here this half hour, and master has had a letter."

Away ran the girls, too eager to get in to have time for speech. They ran through the vestibule into the breakfast room; from thence to the library;—their father was in neither; and they were on the point of seeking him up stairs with their mother, when they were met by the butler, who said,

"If you are looking for my master, ma'am, he is walking towards the little copse."

Upon this information, they instantly passed through the hall once more, and ran across the lawn after their father, who was deliberately pursuing his way towards a small wood on one side of the paddock.

Jane, who was not so light, nor so much in the habit of running as Elizabeth, soon lagged behind, while her sister, panting for breath, came up with him, and eagerly cried out,

"Oh, Papa, what news? what news? have you heard from my uncle?"

"Yes, I have had a letter from him by express."

"Well, and what news does it bring? good or bad?"

"What is there of good to be expected?" said he, taking the letter from his pocket; "but perhaps you would like to read it."

Elizabeth impatiently caught it from his hand. Jane now came up.

5. Review her conduct to see if it warrants a mitigation of the prohibitions he has threatened.

"Read it aloud," said their father, "for I hardly know myself what it is about."

"Gracechurch-street, Monday,
August 2.

"MY DEAR BROTHER,

"At last I am able to send you some tidings of my niece, and such as, upon the whole, I hope will give you satisfaction. Soon after you left me on Saturday, I was fortunate enough to find out in what part of London they were. The particulars, I reserve till we meet. It is enough to know they are discovered, I have seen them both——"

"Then it is, as I always hoped," cried Jane; "they are married!"

Elizabeth read on; "I have seen them both. They are not married, nor can I find there was any intention of being so; but if you are willing to perform the engagements which I have ventured to make on your side, I hope it will not be long before they are. All that is required of you is, to assure to your daughter, by settlement, her equal share of the five thousand pounds, secured among your children after the decease of yourself and my sister; and, moreover, to enter into an engagement of allowing her, during your life, one hundred pounds per annum. These are conditions, which, considering every thing, I had no hesitation in complying with, as far as I thought myself privileged, for you. I shall send this by express, that no time may be lost in bringing me your answer. You will easily comprehend, from these particulars, that Mr. Wickham's circumstances are not so hopeless as they are generally believed to be. The world has been deceived in that respect; and I am happy to say, there will be some little money, even when all his debts are discharged, to settle on my niece, in addition to her own fortune. If, as I conclude will be the case, you send me full powers to act in your name, throughout the whole of this business, I will immediately give directions to Haggerston for preparing a proper settlement. There will not be the smallest occasion for your coming to town again; therefore, stay quietly at Longbourn, and depend on my diligence and care. Send back your answer as soon as you can, and be careful to write explicitly. We have judged it best, that my niece should be married from this house, of which I hope you will approve. She comes to us to-day. I shall write again as soon as any thing more is determined on. Your's, &c.

"EDW. GARDINER."

"Is it possible!" cried Elizabeth, when she had finished. "Can it be possible that he will marry her?"

"Wickham is not so undeserving, then, as we have thought

him;" said her sister. "My dear father, I congratulate you."

"And have you answered the letter?" said Elizabeth.

"No; but it must be done soon."

Most earnestly did she then intreat him to lose no more time before he wrote.

"Oh! my dear father," she cried, "come back, and write immediately. Consider how important every moment is, in such a case."

"Let me write for you," said Jane, "if you dislike the trouble yourself."

"I dislike it very much," he replied; "but it must be done."

And so saying, he turned back with them, and walked towards the house.

"And may I ask?" said Elizabeth, "but the terms, I suppose, must be complied with."

"Complied with! I am only ashamed of his asking so little."

"And they *must* marry! Yet he is *such* a man!"

"Yes, yes, they must marry. There is nothing else to be done. But there are two things that I want very much to know:—one is, how much money your uncle has laid down, to bring it about; and the other, how I am ever to pay him."

"Money! my uncle!" cried Jane, "what do you mean, Sir?"

"I mean, that no man in his senses, would marry Lydia on so slight a temptation as one hundred a-year during my life, and fifty after I am gone."

"That is very true," said Elizabeth; "though it had not occurred to me before. His debts to be discharged, and something still to remain! Oh! it must be my uncle's doings! Generous, good man, I am afraid he has distressed himself. A small sum could not do all this."

"No," said her father, "Wickham's a fool, if he takes her with a farthing less than ten thousand pounds. I should be sorry to think so ill of him, in the very beginning of our relationship."

"Ten thousand pounds! Heaven forbid! How is half such a sum to be repaid?"

Mr. Bennet made no answer, and each of them, deep in thought, continued silent till they reached the house. Their father then went to the library to write, and the girls walked into the breakfast-room.

"And they are really to be married!" cried Elizabeth, as soon as they were by themselves. "How strange this is! And for *this* we are to be thankful. That they should marry, small as is their chance of happiness, and wretched as is his character, we are forced to rejoice! Oh, Lydia!"

"I comfort myself with thinking," replied Jane, "that he certainly would not marry Lydia, if he had not a real regard for her. Though our kind uncle has done something towards clearing him, I cannot believe that ten thousand pounds, or any thing like it, has been advanced. He has children of his own, and may have more. How could he spare half ten thousand pounds?"

"If we are ever able to learn what Wickham's debts have been," said Elizabeth, "and how much is settled on his side on our sister, we shall exactly know what Mr. Gardiner has done for them, because Wickham has not sixpence of his own. The kindness of my uncle and aunt can never be requited. Their taking her home, and affording her their personal protection and countenance, is such a sacrifice to her advantage, as years of gratitude cannot enough acknowledge. By this time she is actually with them! If such goodness does not make her miserable now, she will never deserve to be happy! What a meeting for her, when she first sees my aunt!"

"We must endeavour to forget all that has passed on either side," said Jane: "I hope and trust they will yet be happy. His consenting to marry her is a proof, I will believe, that he is come to a right way of thinking. Their mutual affection will steady them; and I flatter myself they will settle so quietly, and live in so rational a manner, as may in time make their past imprudence forgotten."

"Their conduct has been such," replied Elizabeth, "as neither you, nor I, nor any body, can ever forget. It is useless to talk of it."

It now occurred to the girls that their mother was in all likelihood perfectly ignorant of what had happened. They went to the library, therefore, and asked their father, whether he would not wish them to make it known to her. He was writing, and, without raising his head, coolly replied,

"Just as you please."

"May we take my uncle's letter to read to her?"

"Take whatever you like, and get away."

Elizabeth took the letter from his writing table, and they went up stairs together. Mary and Kitty were both with Mrs. Bennet: one communication would, therefore, do for all. After a slight preparation for good news, the letter was read aloud. Mrs. Bennet could hardly contain herself. As soon as Jane had read Mr. Gardiner's hope of Lydia's being soon married, her joy burst forth, and every following sentence added to its exuberance. She was now in an irritation as violent from delight, as she had ever been fidgetty from alarm and vexation. To know that her daughter would be married was enough. She was disturbed by no fear for her felicity, nor humbled by any remembrance of her misconduct.

"My dear, dear Lydia!" she cried: "This is delightful indeed!—She will be married!—I shall see her again!—She will be married at sixteen!—My good, kind brother!—I knew how it would be—I knew he would manage every thing. How I long to see her! and to see dear Wickham too! But the clothes, the wedding clothes! I will write to my sister Gardiner about them directly. Lizzy, my dear, run down to your father, and ask him how much he will give her. Stay, stay, I will go myself. Ring the bell, Kitty, for Hill. I will put on my things in a moment. My dear, dear Lydia!—How merry we shall be together when we meet!"

Her eldest daughter endeavoured to give some relief to the violence of these transports, by leading her thoughts to the obligations which Mr. Gardiner's behaviour laid them all under.

"For we must attribute this happy conclusion," she added, "in a great measure, to his kindness. We are persuaded that he has pledged himself to assist Mr. Wickham with money."

"Well," cried her mother, "it is all very right; who should do it but her own uncle? If he had not had a family of his own, I and my children must have had all his money you know, and it is the first time we have ever had any thing from him, except a few presents. Well! I am so happy. In a short time, I shall have a daughter married. Mrs. Wickham! How well it sounds. And she was only sixteen last June. My dear Jane, I am in such a flutter, that I am sure I can't write; so I will dictate, and you write for me. We will settle with your father about the money afterwards; but the things should be ordered immediately."

She was then proceeding to all the particulars of calico, muslin, and cambric, and would shortly have dictated some very plentiful orders, had not Jane, though with some difficulty, persuaded her to wait, till her father was at leisure to be consulted. One day's delay she observed, would be of small importance; and her mother was too happy, to be quite so obstinate as usual. Other schemes too came into her head.

"I will go to Meryton," said she, "as soon as I am dressed, and tell the good, good news to my sister Phillips. And as I come back, I can call on Lady Lucas and Mrs. Long. Kitty, run down and order the carriage. An airing would do me a great deal of good, I am sure. Girls, can I do any thing for you in Meryton? Oh! here comes Hill. My dear Hill, have you heard the good news? Miss Lydia is going to be married; and you shall all have a bowl of punch, to make merry at her wedding."

Mrs. Hill began instantly to express her joy. Elizabeth received her congratulations amongst the rest, and then, sick of this folly, took refuge in her own room, that she might think with freedom.

Poor Lydia's situation must, at best, be bad enough; but that it was no worse, she had need to be thankful. She felt it so; and though, in looking forward, neither rational happiness nor worldly prosperity, could be justly expected for her sister; in looking back to what they had feared, only two hours ago, she felt all the advantages of what they had gained.

Chapter VIII

Mr. Bennet had very often wished, before this period of his life, that, instead of spending his whole income, he had laid by an annual sum, for the better provision of his children, and of his wife, if she survived him. He now wished it more than ever. Had he done his duty in that respect, Lydia need not have been indebted to her uncle, for whatever of honour or credit could now be purchased for her. The satisfaction of prevailing on one of the most worthless young men in Great Britain to be her husband, might then have rested in its proper place.

He was seriously concerned, that a cause of so little advantage to any one, should be forwarded at the sole expence of his brother-in-law, and he was determined, if possible, to find out the extent of his assistance, and to discharge the obligation as soon as he could.

When first Mr. Bennet had married, economy was held to be perfectly useless; for, of course, they were to have a son. This son was to join in cutting off the entail, as soon as he should be of age, and the widow and younger children would by that means be provided for. Five daughters successively entered the world, but yet the son was to come; and Mrs. Bennet, for many years after Lydia's birth, had been certain that he would. This event had at last been despaired of, but it was then too late to be saving. Mrs. Bennet had no turn for economy, and her husband's love of independence had alone prevented their exceeding their income.

Five thousand pounds was settled by marriage articles on Mrs. Bennet and the children. But in what proportions it should be divided amongst the latter, depended on the will of the parents. This was one point, with regard to Lydia at least, which was now to be settled, and Mr. Bennet could have no hesitation in acceding to the proposal before him. In terms of grateful acknowledgment for the kindness of his brother, though expressed most concisely, he then delivered on paper his perfect approbation of all that was done, and his willingness to fulfil the engagements that had been made for him. He had never before supposed that, could Wickham be prevailed on to marry his daughter, it would be done with so little inconvenience to himself, as by the present arrangement. He would scarcely be ten pounds a-year the loser, by the hundred that was to be paid them; for, what with her board and pocket allowance, and the continual presents in money, which passed to her, through her mother's hands, Lydia's expences had been very little within that sum.

That it would be done with such trifling exertion on his side, too, was another very welcome surprise; for his chief wish at present, was to have as little trouble in the business as possible. When the first transports of rage which had produced his activity in seeking her were over, he naturally returned to all his former indolence. His letter was soon dispatched; for though dilatory in undertaking business, he was quick in its execution. He begged to know farther particulars of what he was indebted to his brother; but was too angry with Lydia, to send any message to her.

The good news quickly spread through the house; and with proportionate speed through the neighbourhood. It was borne in the latter with decent philosophy. To be sure it would have been more for the advantage of conversation, had Miss Lydia Bennet come upon the town; or, as the happiest alternative, been secluded from the world, in some distant farm house.[6] But there was much to be talked of, in marrying her; and the good-natured wishes for her well-doing, which had proceeded before, from all the spiteful old ladies in Meryton, lost but little of their spirit in this change of circumstances, because with such an husband, her misery was considered certain.

It was a fortnight since Mrs. Bennet had been down stairs, but on this happy day, she again took her seat at the head of her table, and in spirits oppressively high. No sentiment of shame gave a damp to her triumph. The marriage of a daughter, which had been the first object of her wishes, since Jane was sixteen, was now on the point of accomplishment, and her thoughts and her words ran wholly on those attendants of elegant nuptials, fine muslins, new carriages, and servants. She was busily searching through the neighbourhood for a proper situation for her daughter, and, without knowing or considering what their income might be, rejected many as deficient in size and importance.

"Haye-Park might do," said she, "if the Gouldings would quit it, or the great house at Stoke, if the drawing-room were larger; but Ashworth is too far off! I could not bear to have her ten miles from me; and as for Purvis Lodge, the attics are dreadful."

Her husband allowed her to talk on without interruption, while the servants remained. But when they had withdrawn, he said to her, "Mrs. Bennet, before you take any, or all of these houses, for your son and daughter, let us come to a right understanding. Into *one* house in this neighbourhood, they shall never have admittance. I will not encourage the impudence of either, by receiv-

6. Become a prostitute; or be secluded during the term of a pregnancy.

ing them at Longbourn."

A long dispute followed this declaration; but Mr. Bennet was firm: it soon led to another; and Mrs. Bennet found, with amazement and horror, that her husband would not advance a guinea to buy clothes for his daughter. He protested that she should receive from him no mark of affection whatever, on the occasion. Mrs. Bennet could hardly comprehend it. That his anger could be carried to such a point of inconceivable resentment, as to refuse his daughter a privilege, without which her marriage would scarcely seem valid, exceeded all that she could believe possible. She was more alive to the disgrace, which the want of new clothes must reflect on her daughter's nuptials, than to any sense of shame at her eloping and living with Wickham, a fortnight before they took place.

Elizabeth was now most heartily sorry that she had, from the distress of the moment, been led to make Mr. Darcy acquainted with their fears for her sister; for since her marriage would so shortly give the proper termination to the elopement, they might hope to conceal its unfavourable beginning, from all those who were not immediately on the spot.

She had no fear of its spreading farther, through his means. There were few people on whose secrecy she would have more confidently depended; but at the same time, there was no one, whose knowledge of a sister's frailty would have mortified her so much. Not, however, from any fear of disadvantage from it, individually to herself; for at any rate, there seemed a gulf impassable between them. Had Lydia's marriage been concluded on the most honourable terms, it was not to be supposed that Mr. Darcy would connect himself with a family, where to every other objection would now be added, an alliance and relationship of the nearest kind with the man whom he so justly scorned.

From such a connection she could not wonder that he should shrink. The wish of procuring her regard, which she had assured herself of his feeling in Derbyshire, could not in rational expectation survive such a blow as this. She was humbled, she was grieved; she repented, though she hardly knew of what. She became jealous of his esteem, when she could no longer hope to be benefited by it. She wanted to hear of him, when there seemed the least chance of gaining intelligence. She was convinced that she could have been happy with him; when it was no longer likely they should meet.

What a triumph for him, as she often thought, could he know that the proposals which she had proudly spurned only four months ago, would now have been gladly and gratefully received! He was as generous, she doubted not, as the most generous of his sex. But while he was mortal, there must be a triumph.

She began now to comprehend that he was exactly the man, who, in disposition and talents, would most suit her. His understanding and temper, though unlike her own, would have answered all her wishes. It was an union that must have been to the advantage of both; by her ease and liveliness, his mind might have been softened, his manners improved, and from his judgment, information, and knowledge of the world, she must have received benefit of greater importance.

But no such happy marriage could now teach the admiring multitude what connubial felicity really was. An union of a different tendency, and precluding the possibility of the other, was soon to be formed in their family.

How Wickham and Lydia were to be supported in tolerable independence, she could not imagine. But how little of permanent happiness could belong to a couple who were only brought together because their passions were stronger than their virtue, she could easily conjecture.

———

Mr. Gardiner soon wrote again to his brother. To Mr. Bennet's acknowledgments he briefly replied, with assurances of his eagerness to promote the welfare of any of his family; and concluded with intreaties that the subject might never be mentioned to him again. The principal purport of his letter was to inform them, that Mr. Wickham had resolved on quitting the Militia.

"It was greatly my wish that he should do so," he added, "as soon as his marriage was fixed on. And I think you will agree with me, in considering a removal from that corps as highly advisable, both on his account and my niece's. It is Mr. Wickham's intention to go into the regulars; and, among his former friends, there are still some who are able and willing to assist him in the army. He has the promise of an ensigncy in General ———'s regiment, now quartered in the North. It is an advantage to have it is so far from this part of the kingdom. He promises fairly, and I hope among different people, where they may each have a character to preserve, they will both be more prudent. I have written to Colonel Forster, to inform him of our present arrangements, and to request that he will satisfy the various creditors of Mr. Wickham in and near Brighton, with assurances of speedy payment, for which I have pledged myself. And will you give yourself the trouble of carrying similar assurances to his creditors in Meryton, of whom I shall subjoin a list, according to his information. He has given in all his debts; I hope at least he has not deceived us. Haggerston has our directions, and all will be completed in a week. They will then join his regiment, unless they are first invited to Longbourn; and I understand from Mrs. Gardiner, that my niece is very desirous of seeing you all, before she leaves the South. She is well, and begs to be dutifully remembered to you and her mother.—Your's, &c.

"E. GARDINER."

Mr. Bennet and his daughters saw all the advantages of Wickham's removal from the ———shire, as clearly as Mr. Gardiner could do. But Mrs. Bennet, was not so well pleased with it. Lydia's being settled in the North, just when she had expected most pleasure and pride in her company, for she had by no means given up her plan of their residing in Hertfordshire, was a severe disappointment; and besides, it was such a pity that Lydia should be taken from a regiment where she was acquainted with every body, and had so many favourites.

"She is so fond of Mrs. Forster," said she, "it will be quite shocking to send her away! And there are several of the young men, too, that she likes very much. The officers may not be so pleasant in General ———'s regiment."

His daughter's request, for such it might be considered, of being admitted into her family again, before she set off for the North, received at first an absolute negative. But Jane and Elizabeth, who agreed in wishing, for the sake of their sister's feelings and consequence, that she should be noticed on her marriage by her parents, urged him so earnestly, yet so rationally and so mildly, to receive her and her husband at Longbourn, as soon as they were married, that he was prevailed on to think as they thought, and act as they wished. And their mother had the satisfaction of knowing, that she should be able to shew her married daughter in the neighbourhood, before she was banished to the North. When Mr. Bennet wrote again to his brother, therefore, he sent his permission for them to come; and it was settled, that as soon as the ceremony was over, they should proceed to Longbourn. Elizabeth was surprised, however, that Wickham should consent to such a scheme, and, had she consulted only her own inclination, any meeting with him would have been the last object of her wishes.

Chapter IX

Their sister's wedding day arrived; and Jane and Elizabeth felt for her probably more than she felt for herself. The carriage was sent to meet them at ———, and they were to return in it, by dinner-time. Their arrival was dreaded by the elder Miss Bennets; and Jane more especially, who gave Lydia the feelings which would have attended herself, had *she* been the culprit, was wretched in the thought of what her sister must endure.

They came. The family were assembled in the breakfast room, to receive them. Smiles decked the face of Mrs. Bennet, as the carriage drove up to the door; her husband looked impenetrably grave; her daughters, alarmed, anxious, uneasy.

Lydia's voice was heard in the vestibule; the door was thrown open, and she ran into the room. Her mother stepped forwards, embraced her, and welcomed her with rapture; gave her hand with an affectionate smile to Wickham, who followed his lady, and wished them both joy, with an alacrity which shewed no doubt of their happiness.

Their reception from Mr. Bennet, to whom they then turned, was not quite so cordial. His countenance rather gained in austerity; and he scarcely opened his lips. The easy assurance of the young couple, indeed, was enough to provoke him. Elizabeth was disgusted, and even Miss Bennet was shocked. Lydia was Lydia still; untamed, unabashed, wild, noisy, and fearless. She turned from sister to sister, demanding their congratulations, and when at length they all sat down, looked eagerly round the room, took notice of some little alteration in it, and observed, with a laugh, that it was a great while since she had been there.

Wickham was not at all more distressed than herself, but his manners were always so pleasing, that had his character and his marriage been exactly what they ought, his smiles and his easy address, while he claimed their relationship, would have delighted them all. Elizabeth had not before believed him quite equal to such assurance; but she sat down, resolving within herself, to draw no limits in future to the impudence of an impudent man. *She* blushed, and Jane blushed; but the cheeks of the two who caused their confusion, suffered no variation of colour.

There was no want of discourse. The bride and her mother could neither of them talk fast enough; and Wickham, who happened to sit near Elizabeth, began enquiring after his acquaintance in that neighbourhood, with a good humoured ease, which she felt very unable to equal in her replies. They seemed each of them to have the happiest memories in the world. Nothing of the past was recollected with pain; and Lydia led voluntarily to subjects, which her sisters would not have alluded to for the world.

"Only think of its being three months," she cried, "since I went away; it seems but a fortnight I declare; and yet there have been things enough happened in the time. Good gracious! when I went away, I am sure I had no more idea of being married till I came back again! though I thought it would be very good fun if I was."

Her father lifted up his eyes. Jane was distressed. Elizabeth looked expressively at Lydia; but she, who never heard nor saw any thing of which she chose to be insensible, gaily continued, "Oh! mamma, do the people here abouts know I am married to-day? I was afraid they might not; and we overtook William Goulding in his curricle, so I was determined he should know it, and so I let down the side glass next to him, and took off my glove, and let my hand just rest upon the window frame, so that he might see the ring, and then I bowed and smiled like any thing."

Elizabeth could bear it no longer. She got up, and ran out of the room; and returned no more, till she heard them passing through the hall to the dining parlour. She then joined them soon enough to see Lydia, with anxious parade, walk up to her mother's right hand, and hear her say to her eldest sister, "Ah! Jane, I take your place now, and you must go lower, because I am a married woman."

It was not to be supposed that time would give Lydia that embarrassment, from which she had been so wholly free at first. Her ease and good spirits increased. She longed to see Mrs. Phillips, the Lucasses, and all their other neighbours, and to hear herself called "Mrs. Wickham," by each of them; and in the mean time, she went after dinner to shew her ring and boast of being married, to Mrs. Hill and the two housemaids.

"Well, mamma," said she, when they were all returned to the breakfast room, "and what do you think of my husband? Is not he a charming man? I am sure my sisters must all envy me. I only hope they may have half my good luck. They must all go to Brighton. That is the place to get husbands. What a pity it is, mamma, we did not all go."

"Very true; and if I had my will, we should. But my dear Lydia, I don't at all like your going such a way off. Must it be so?"

"Oh, lord! yes;—there is nothing in that. I shall like it of all things. You and papa, and my sisters, must come down and see us. We shall be at Newcastle all the winter, and I dare say there will be some balls, and I will take care to get good partners for them all."

"I should like it beyond any thing!" said her mother.

"And then when you go away, you may leave one or two of my sisters behind you; and I dare say I shall get husbands for them before the winter is over."

"I thank you for my share of the favour," said Elizabeth; "but I do not particularly like your way of getting husbands."

Their visitors were not to remain above ten days with them. Mr. Wickham had received his commission before he left London, and he was to join his regiment at the end of a fortnight.

No one but Mrs. Bennet, regretted that their stay would be

so short; and she made the most of the time, by visiting about with her daughter, and having very frequent parties at home. These parties were acceptable to all; to avoid a family circle was even more desirable to such as did think, than such as did not.

Wickham's affection for Lydia, was just what Elizabeth had expected to find it; not equal to Lydia's for him. She had scarcely needed her present observation to be satisfied, from the reason of things, that their elopement had been brought on by the strength of her love, rather than by his; and she would have wondered why, without violently caring for her, he chose to elope with her at all, had she not felt certain that his flight was rendered necessary by distress of circumstances; and if that were the case, he was not the young man to resist an opportunity of having a companion.

Lydia was exceedingly fond of him. He was her dear Wickham on every occasion; no one was to be put in competition with him. He did every thing best in the world; and she was sure he would kill more birds on the first of September,[7] than any body else in the country.

One morning, soon after their arrival, as she was sitting with her two elder sisters, she said to Elizabeth,

"Lizzy, I never gave *you* an account of my wedding, I believe. You were not by, when I told mamma, and the others, all about it. Are not you curious to hear how it was managed?"

"No really," replied Elizabeth; "I think there cannot be too little said on the subject."

"La! You are so strange! But I must tell you how it went off. We were married, you know, at St. Clement's, because Wickham's lodgings were in that parish. And it was settled that we should all be there by eleven o'clock. My uncle and aunt and I were to go together; and the others were to meet us at the church. Well, Monday morning came, and I was in such a fuss! I was so afraid you know that something would happen to put it off, and then I should have gone quite distracted. And there was my aunt, all the time I was dressing, preaching and talking away just as if she was reading a sermon. However, I did not hear above one word in ten, for I was thinking, you may suppose, of my dear Wickham. I longed to know whether he would be married in his blue coat.

"Well, and so we breakfasted at ten as usual; I thought it would never be over; for, by the bye, you are to understand, that my uncle and aunt were horrid unpleasant all the time I was with them. If you'll believe me, I did not once put my foot out of doors, though I was there a fortnight. Not one party, or scheme, or any thing. To be sure London was rather thin, but however

7. The beginning of the bird-hunting season, which also brings Bingley back to Netherfield.

the little Theatre was open. Well, and so just as the carriage came to the door, my uncle was called away upon business to that horrid man Mr. Stone.[8] And then, you know, when once they get together, there is no end of it. Well, I was so frightened I did not know what to do, for my uncle was to give me away; and if we were beyond the hour, we could not be married all day. But, luckily, he came back again in ten minutes time, and then we all set out. However, I recollected afterwards, that if he *had* been prevented going, the wedding need not be put off, for Mr. Darcy might have done as well."

"Mr. Darcy!" repeated Elizabeth, in utter amazement.

"Oh, yes!—he was to come there with Wickham, you know. But gracious me! I quite forgot! I ought not to have said a word about it. I promised them so faithfully! What will Wickham say? It was to be such a secret!"

"If it was to be secret," said Jane, "say not another word on the subject. You may depend upon my seeking no further."

"Oh! certainly," said Elizabeth, though burning with curiosity; "we will ask you no questions."

"Thank you," said Lydia, "for if you did, I should certainly tell you all, and then Wickham would be angry."

On such encouragement to ask, Elizabeth was forced to put it out of her power, by running away.

But to live in ignorance on such a point was impossible; or at least it was impossible not to try for information. Mr. Darcy had been at her sister's wedding. It was exactly a scene, and exactly among people, where he had apparently least to do, and least temptation to go. Conjectures as to the meaning of it, rapid and wild, hurried into her brain; but she was satisfied with none. Those that best pleased her, as placing his conduct in the noblest light, seemed most improbable. She could not bear such suspense; and hastily seizing a sheet of paper, wrote a short letter to her aunt, to request an explanation of what Lydia had dropt, if it were compatible with the secrecy which had been intended.

"You may readily comprehend," she added, "what my curiosity must be to know how a person unconnected with any of us, and (comparatively speaking) a stranger to our family, should have been amongst you at such a time. Pray write instantly, and let me understand it—unless it is, for very cogent reasons, to remain in the secrecy which Lydia seems to think necessary; and then I must endeavour to be satisfied with ignorance."

"Not that I *shall* though," she added to herself, as she finished the letter; "and my dear aunt, if you do not tell me in an honourable manner, I shall certainly be reduced to tricks and stratagems

8. Haggerstone. See p. 214.

to find it out."

Jane's delicate sense of honour would not allow her to speak to Elizabeth privately of what Lydia had let fall; Elizabeth was glad of it;—till it appeared whether her inquiries would receive any satisfaction, she had rather be without a confidante.

Chapter X

Elizabeth had the satisfaction of receiving an answer to her letter, as soon as she possibly could. She was no sooner in possession of it, than hurrying into the little copse, where she was least likely to be interrupted, she sat down on one of the benches, and prepared to be happy; for the length of the letter convinced her that it did not contain a denial.

"Gracechurch-street, Sept. 6

"MY DEAR NIECE,

"I have just received your letter, and shall devote this whole morning to answering it, as I forsee that a *little* writing will not comprise what I have to tell you. I must confess myself surprised by your application; I did not expect it from *you*. Don't think me angry, however, for I only mean to let you know, that I had not imagined such enquiries to be necessary on *your* side. If you do not choose to understand me, forgive my impertinence. Your uncle is as much surprised as I am—and nothing but the belief of your being a party concerned, would have allowed him to act as he has done. But if you are really innocent and ignorant, I must be more explicit. On the very day of my coming home from Longbourn, your uncle had a most unexpected visitor. Mr. Darcy called, and was shut up with him several hours. It was all over before I arrived; so my curiosity was not so dreadfully racked as *your's* seems to have been. He came to tell Mr. Gardiner that he had found out where your sister and Mr. Wickham were, and that he had seen and talked with them both, Wickham repeatedly, Lydia once. From what I can collect, he left Derbyshire only one day after ourselves, and came to town with the resolution of hunting for them. The motive professed, was his conviction of its being owing to himself that Wickham's worthlessness had not been so well known, as to make it impossible for any young woman of character, to love or confide in him. He generously imputed the whole to his mistaken pride, and confessed that he had before thought it beneath him, to lay his private actions open to the world. His character was to speak for itself. He called it, therefore, his duty to step forward, and endeavour to remedy an evil, which had been brought on by himself. If he *had another* motive, I

am sure it would never disgrace him. He had been some days
in town, before he was able to discover them; but he had something to direct his search, which was more than *we* had; and the
consciousness of this, was another reason for his resolving to follow
us. There is a lady, it seems, a Mrs. Younge, who was some time
ago governess to Miss Darcy, and was dismissed from her charge
on some cause of disapprobation, though he did not say what.
She then took a large house in Edward-street, and has since maintained herself by letting lodgings. This Mrs. Younge was, he knew,
intimately acquainted with Wickham; and he went to her for intelligence of him, as soon as he got to town. But it was two or
three days before he could get from her what he wanted. She
would not betray her trust, I suppose, without bribery and corrup-
tion, for she really did know where her friend was to be found.
Wickham indeed had gone to her, on their first arrival in London,
and had she been able to receive them into her house, they would
have taken up their abode with her. At length, however, our kind
friend procured the wished-for direction. They were in ———
street. He saw Wickham, and afterwards insisted on seeing Lydia.
His first object with her, he acknowledged, had been to persuade
her to quit her present disgraceful situation, and return to her
friends as soon as they could be prevailed on to receive her, offering
his assistance, as far as it would go. But he found Lydia absolutely
resolved on remaining where she was. She cared for none of her
friends, she wanted no help of his, she would not hear of leaving
Wickham. She was sure they should be married some time or
other, and it did not much signify when. Since such were her feelings, it only remained, he thought, to secure and expedite a marriage, which, in his very first conversation with Wickham, he
easily learnt, had never been *his* design. He confessed himself
obliged to leave the regiment, on account of some debts of honour,
which were very pressing; and scrupled not to lay all the ill-
consequences of Lydia's flight, on her own folly alone. He meant
to resign his commission immediately; and as to his future situation,
he could conjecture very little about it. He must go somewhere,
but he did not know where, and he knew he should have nothing
to live on. Mr. Darcy asked him why he had not married your
sister at once. Though Mr. Bennet was not imagined to be very
rich, he would have been able to do something for him, and his
situation must have been benefited by marriage. But he found, in
reply to this question, that Wickham still cherished the hope
of more effectually making his fortune by marriage, in some other
country. Under such circumstances, however, he was not likely
to be proof against the temptation of immediate relief. They met
several times, for there was much to be discussed. Wickham of

course wanted more than he could get; but at length was reduced to be reasonable. Every thing being settled between *them*, Mr. Darcy's next step was to make your uncle acquainted with it, and he first called in Gracechurch-street the evening before I came home. But Mr. Gardiner could not be seen, and Mr. Darcy found, on further enquiry, that your father was still with him, but would quit town the next morning. He did not judge your father to be a person whom he could so properly consult as your uncle, and therefore readily postponed seeing him, till after the departure of the former. He did not leave his name, and till the next day, it was only known that a gentleman had called on business. On Saturday he came again. Your father was gone, your uncle at home, and, as I said before, they had a great deal of talk together. They met again on Sunday, and then *I* saw him too. It was not all settled before Monday: as soon as it was, the express was sent off to Longbourn. But our visitor was very obstinate. I fancy, Lizzy, that obstinacy is the real defect of his character after all. He has been accused of many faults at different times; but *this* is the true one. Nothing was to be done that he did not do himself; though I am sure (and I do not speak it to be thanked, therefore say nothing about it,) your uncle would most readily have settled the whole. They battled it together for a long time, which was more than either the gentleman or lady concerned in it deserved. But at last your uncle was forced to yield, and instead of being allowed to be of use to his niece, was forced to put up with only having the probable credit of it, which went sorely against the grain; and I really believe your letter this morning gave him great pleasure, because it required an explanation that would rob him of his borrowed feathers, and give the praise where it was due. But, Lizzy, this must go no farther than yourself, or Jane at most. You know pretty well, I suppose, what has been done for the young people. His debts are to be paid, amounting, I believe, to considerably more than a thousand pounds, another thousand in addition to her own settled upon *her*, and his commission purchased. The reason why all this was to be done by him alone, was such as I have given above. It was owing to him, to his reserve, and want of proper consideration, that Wickham's character had been so misunderstood, and consequently that he had been received and noticed as he was. Perhaps there was some truth in *this*; though I doubt whether *his* reserve, or *anybody's* reserve, can be answerable for the event. But in spite of all this fine talking, my dear Lizzy, you may rest perfectly assured, that your uncle would never have yielded, if we had not given him credit for *another interest* in the affair. When all this was resolved on, he returned again to his friends, who were still staying at Pem-

berley; but it was agreed that he should be in London once more
when the wedding took place, and all money matters were then
to receive the last finish. I believe I have now told you every thing.
It is a relation which you tell me is to give you great surprise; I
hope at least it will not afford you any displeasure. Lydia came
to us; and Wickham had constant admission to the house. *He*
was exactly what he had been, when I knew him in Hertfordshire;
but I would not tell you how little I was satisfied with *her* behaviour while she staid with us, if I had not perceived, by Jane's
letter last Wednesday, that her conduct on coming home was
exactly of a piece with it, and therefore what I now tell you, can
give you no fresh pain. I talked to her repeatedly in the most serious manner, representing to her all the wickedness of what she
had done, and all the unhappiness she had brought on her family.
If she heard me, it was by good luck, for I am sure she did not
listen. I was sometimes quite provoked, but then I recollected my
dear Elizabeth and Jane, and for their sakes had patience with
her. Mr. Darcy was punctual in his return, and as Lydia informed
you, attended the wedding. He dined with us the next day, and
was to leave town again on Wednesday or Thursday. Will you
be very angry with me, my dear Lizzy, if I take this opportunity
of saying (what I was never bold enough to say before) how much
I like him. His behaviour to us has, in every respect, been as pleasing as when we were in Derbyshire. His understanding and opinions all please me; he wants nothing but a little more liveliness,
and *that*, if he marry *prudently*, his wife may teach him. I thought
him very sly;—he hardly ever mentioned your name. But slyness
seems the fashion. Pray forgive me, if I have been very presuming,
or at least do not punish me so far, as to exclude me from P.
I shall never be quite happy till I have been all round the park.
A low phaeton, with a nice little pair of ponies, would be the
very thing. But I must write no more. The children have been
wanting me this half hour. Your's, very sincerely,

"M. Gardiner."

The contents of this letter threw Elizabeth into a flutter of
spirits, in which it was difficult to determine whether pleasure
or pain bore the greatest share. The vague and unsettled suspicions
which uncertainty had produced of what Mr. Darcy might have
been doing to forward her sister's match, which she had feared
to encourage, as an exertion of goodness too great to be probable,
and at the same time dreaded to be just, from the pain of obligation, were proved beyond their greatest extent to be true! He had
followed them purposely to town, he had taken on himself all
the trouble and mortification attendant on such a research; in
which supplication had been necessary to a woman whom he must

abominate and despise, and where he was reduced to meet, frequently meet, reason with, persuade, and finally bribe, the man whom he always most wished to avoid, and whose very name was punishment to him to pronounce. He had done all this for a girl whom he could neither regard nor esteem. Her heart did whisper, that he had done it for her. But it was a hope shortly checked by other considerations, and she soon felt that even her vanity was insufficient, when required to depend on his affection for her, for a woman who had already refused him, as able to overcome a sentiment so natural as abhorrence against relationship with Wickham. Brother-in-law of Wickham! Every kind of pride must revolt from the connection. He had to be sure done much. She was ashamed to think how much. But he had given a reason for his interference, which asked no extraordinary stretch of belief. It was reasonable that he should feel he had been wrong; he had liberality, and he had the means of exercising it; and though she would not place herself as his principal inducement, she could, perhaps, believe, that remaining partiality for her, might assist his endeavours in a cause where her peace of mind must be materially concerned. It was painful, exceedingly painful, to know that they were under obligations to a person who could never receive a return. They owed the restoration of Lydia, her character, every thing to him. Oh! how heartily did she grieve over every ungracious sensation she had ever encouraged, every saucy speech she had ever directed towards him. For herself she was humbled; but she was proud of him. Proud that in a cause of compassion and honour, he had been able to get the better of himself. She read over her aunt's commendation of him again and again. It was hardly enough; but it pleased her. She was even sensible of some pleasure, though mixed with regret, on finding how steadfastly both she and her uncle had been persuaded that affection and confidence subsisted between Mr. Darcy and herself.

She was roused from her seat, and her reflections, by some one's approach; and before she could strike into another path, she was overtaken by Wickham.

"I am afraid I interrupt your solitary ramble, my dear sister?" said he, as he joined her.

"You certainly do," she replied with a smile; "but it does not follow that the interruption must be unwelcome."

"I should be sorry indeed, if it were. We were always good friends; and now we are better."

"True. Are the others coming out?"

"I do not know. Mrs. Bennet and Lydia are going in the carriage to Meryton. And so, my dear sister, I find from our uncle and aunt, that you have actually seen Pemberley."

She replied in the affirmative.

"I almost envy you the pleasure, and yet I believe it would be too much for me, or else I could take it in my way to Newcastle. And you saw the old housekeeper, I suppose? Poor Reynolds, she was always very fond of me. But of course she did not mention my name to you."

"Yes, she did."

"And what did she say?"

"That you were gone into the army, and she was afraid had— not turned out well. At such a distance as *that*, you know, things are strangely misrepresented."

"Certainly," he replied, biting his lips. Elizabeth hoped she had silenced him; but he soon afterwards said,

"I was surprised to see Darcy in town last month. We passed each other several times. I wonder what he can be doing there."

"Perhaps preparing for his marriage with Miss de Bourgh," said Elizabeth. "It must be something particular, to take him there at this time of year."

"Undoubtedly. Did you see him while you were at Lambton? I thought I understood from the Gardiners that you had."

"Yes; he introduced us to his sister."

"And do you like her?"

"Very much."

"I have heard, indeed, that she is uncommonly improved within this year or two. When I last saw her, she was not very promising. I am very glad you liked her. I hope she will turn out well."

"I dare say she will; she has got over the most trying age."

"Did you go by the village of Kympton?"

"I do not recollect that we did."

"I mention it, because it is the living which I ought to have had. A most delightful place!—Excellent Parsonage House! It would have suited me in every respect."

"How should you have liked making sermons?"

"Exceedingly well. I should have considered it as part of my duty, and the exertion would soon have been nothing. One ought not to repine;—but, to be sure, it would have been such a thing for me! The quiet, the retirement of such a life, would have answered all my ideas of happiness! But it was not to be. Did you ever hear Darcy mention the circumstance, when you were in Kent?"

"I *have* heard from authority, which I thought *as good*, that it was left you conditionally only, and at the will of the present patron."

"You have. Yes, there was something in *that*; I told you so from the first, you may remember."

"I *did* hear, too, that there was a time, when sermon-making was not so palatable to you as it seems to be at present; that you actually declared your resolution of never taking orders, and that the business had been compromised accordingly."

"You did! and it was not wholly without foundation. You may remember what I told you on that point, when first we talked of it."

They were now almost at the door of the house, for she had walked fast to get rid of him; and unwilling for her sister's sake, to provoke him, she only said in reply, with a good-humoured smile,

"Come, Mr. Wickham, we are brother and sister, you know. Do not let us quarrel about the past. In future, I hope we shall be always of one mind."

She held out her hand; he kissed it with affectionate gallantry, though he hardly knew how to look, and they entered the house.

Chapter XI

Mr. Wickham was so perfectly satisfied with this conversation, that he never again distressed himself, or provoked his dear sister Elizabeth, by introducing the subject of it; and she was pleased to find that she had said enough to keep him quiet.

The day of his and Lydia's departure soon came, and Mrs. Bennet was forced to submit to a separation, which, as her husband by no means entered into her scheme of their all going to Newcastle, was likely to continue at least a twelvemonth.

"Oh! my dear Lydia," she cried, "when shall we meet again?"

"Oh, lord! I don't know. Not these two or three years perhaps."

"Write to me very often, my dear."

"As often as I can. But you know married women have never much time for writing. My sisters may write to *me*. They will have nothing else to do."

Mr. Wickham's adieus were much more affectionate than his wife's. He smiled, looked handsome, and said many pretty things.

"He is as fine a fellow," said Mr. Bennet, as soon as they were out of the house, "as ever I saw. He simpers, and smirks, and makes love to us all. I am prodigiously proud of him. I defy even Sir William Lucas himself, to produce a more valuable son-in-law."

The loss of her daughter made Mrs. Bennet very dull for several days.

"I often think," said she, "that there is nothing so bad as parting with one's friends. One seems so forlorn without them."

"This is the consequence you see, Madam, of marrying a daughter," said Elizabeth. "It must make you better satisfied that your other four are single."

"It is no such thing. Lydia does not leave me because she is married; but only because her husband's regiment happens to be so far off. If that had been nearer, she would not have gone so soon."

But the spiritless condition which this event threw her into, was shortly relieved, and her mind opened again to the agitation of hope, by an article of news, which then began to be in circulation. The housekeeper at Netherfield had received orders to prepare for the arrival of her master, who was coming down in a day or two, to shoot there for several weeks. Mrs. Bennet was quite in the fidgets. She looked at Jane, and smiled, and shook her head by turns.

"Well, well, and so Mr. Bingley is coming down, sister," (for Mrs. Phillips first brought her the news.) "Well, so much the better. Not that I care about it, though. He is nothing to us, you know, and I am sure I never want to see him again. But, however, he is very welcome to come to Netherfield, if he likes it. And who knows what *may* happen? But that is nothing to us. You know, sister, we agreed long ago never to mention a word about it. And so, is it quite certain he is coming?"

"You may depend on it," replied the other, "for Mrs. Nicholls was in Meryton last night; I saw her passing by, and went out myself on purpose to know the truth of it; and she told me that it was certain true. He comes down on Thursday at the latest, very likely on Wednesday. She was going to the butcher's, she told me, on purpose to order in some meat on Wednesday, and she has got three couple of ducks, just fit to be killed."

Miss Bennet had not been able to hear of his coming, without changing colour. It was many months since she had mentioned his name to Elizabeth; but now, as soon as they were alone together, she said,

"I saw you look at me to day, Lizzy, when my aunt told us of the present report; and I know I appeared distressed. But don't imagine it was from any silly cause. I was only confused for the moment, because I felt that I *should* be looked at. I do assure you, that the news does not affect me either with pleasure or pain. I am glad of one thing, that he comes alone; because we shall see the less of him. Not that I am afraid of *myself*, but I dread other people's remarks."

Elizabeth did not know what to make of it. Had she not seen him in Derbyshire, she might have supposed him capable of coming there, with no other view than what was acknowledged; but she still thought him partial to Jane, and she wavered as to the greater probability of his coming there *with* his friend's permission, or being bold enough to come without it.

"Yet it is hard," she sometimes thought, "that this poor man cannot come to a house, which he has legally hired, without raising all this speculation! I *will* leave him to himself."

In spite of what her sister declared, and really believed to be her feelings, in the expectation of his arrival, Elizabeth could easily perceive that her spirits were affected by it. They were more disturbed, more unequal, than she had often seen them.

The subject which had been so warmly canvassed between their parents, about a twelvemonth ago, was now brought forward again.

"As soon as ever Mr. Bingley comes, my dear," said Mrs. Bennet, "you will wait on him of course."

"No, no. You forced me into visiting him last year, and promised if I went to see him, he should marry one of my daughters. But it ended in nothing, and I will not be sent on a fool's errand again."

His wife represented to him how absolutely necessary such an attention would be from all the neighbouring gentlemen, on his returning to Netherfield.

" 'Tis an etiquette I despise," said he. "If he wants our society, let him seek it. He knows where we live. I will not spend *my* hours in running after my neighbours every time they go away, and come back again."

"Well, all I know is, that it will be abominably rude if you do not wait on him. But, however, that shan't prevent my asking him to dine here, I am determined. We must have Mrs. Long and the Gouldings soon. That will make thirteen with ourselves, so there will be just room at table for him."

Consoled by this resolution, she was the better able to bear her husband's incivility; though it was very mortifying to know that her neighbours might all see Mr. Bingley in consequence of it, before *they* did. As the day of his arrival drew near,

"I begin to be sorry that he comes at all," said Jane to her sister. "It would be nothing; I could see him with perfect indifference, but I can hardly bear to hear it thus perpetually talked of. My mother means well; but she does not know, no one can know how much I suffer from what she says. Happy shall I be, when his stay at Netherfield is over!"

"I wish I could say any thing to comfort you," replied Elizabeth; "but it is wholly out of my power. You must feel it; and the usual satisfaction of preaching patience to a sufferer is denied me, because you have always so much."

Mr. Bingley arrived. Mrs. Bennet, through the assistance of servants, contrived to have the earliest tidings of it, that the period of anxiety and fretfulness on her side, might be as long as it could. She counted the days that must intervene before their invitation could be sent; hopeless of seeing him before. But on the third morning after his arrival in Hertfordshire, she saw him from her dressing-room window, enter the paddock, and ride towards the house.

Her daughters were eagerly called to partake of her joy. Jane resolutely kept her place at the table; but Elizabeth, to satisfy her mother, went to the window—she looked,—she saw Mr. Darcy with him, and sat down again by her sister.

"There is a gentleman with him, mamma," said Kitty; "who can it be?"

"Some acquaintance or other, my dear, I suppose; I am sure I do not know."

"La!" replied Kitty, "it looks just like that man that used to be with him before. Mr. what's his name. That tall, proud man."

"Good gracious! Mr. Darcy!—and so it does I vow. Well, any friend of Mr. Bingley's will always be welcome here to be sure; but else I must say that I hate the very sight of him."

Jane looked at Elizabeth with surprise and concern. She knew but little of their meeting in Derbyshire, and therefore felt for the awkwardness which must attend her sister, in seeing him almost for the first time after receiving his explanatory letter. Both sisters were uncomfortable enough. Each felt for the other, and of course for themselves; and their mother talked on, of her dislike of Mr. Darcy, and her resolution to be civil to him only as Mr. Bingley's friend, without being heard by either of them. But Elizabeth had sources of uneasiness which could not be suspected by Jane, to whom she had never yet had courage to shew Mrs. Gardiner's letter, or to relate her own change of sentiment towards him. To Jane, he could be only a man whose proposals she had refused, and whose merit she had undervalued; but to her own more extensive information, he was the person, to whom the whole family were indebted for the first of benefits, and whom she regarded herself with an interest, if not quite so tender, at least as reasonable and just, as what Jane felt for Bingley. Her astonishment at his coming—at his coming to Netherfield, to Longbourn, and voluntarily seeking her again, was almost equal to what she had known on first witnessing his altered behaviour in Derbyshire.

The colour which had been driven from her face, returned for half a minute with an additional glow, and a smile of delight added lustre to her eyes, as she thought for that space of time, that his affection and wishes must still be unshaken. But she would not be secure.

"Let me first see how he behaves," said she; "it will then be early enough for expectation."

She sat intently at work, striving to be composed, and without daring to lift up her eyes, till anxious curiosity carried them to the face of her sister, as the servant was approaching the door. Jane looked a little paler than usual, but more sedate than Elizabeth had expected. On the gentlemen's appearing, her colour increased; yet she received them with tolerable ease, and with a propriety of behaviour equally free from any symptom of resentment, or any unnecessary complaisance.

Elizabeth said as little to either as civility would allow, and sat down again to her work, with an eagerness which it did not often command. She had ventured only one glance at Darcy. He looked serious as usual; and she thought, more as he had been used to look in Hertfordshire, than as she had seen him at Pemberley. But, perhaps he could not in her mother's presence be what he was before her uncle and aunt. It was a painful, but not an improbable, conjecture.

Bingley, she had likewise seen for an instant, and in that short period saw him looking both pleased and embarrassed. He was received by Mrs. Bennet with a dergee of civility, which made her two daughters ashamed, especially when contrasted with the cold and ceremonious politeness of her curtsey and address to his friend.

Elizabeth particularly, who knew that her mother owed to the latter the preservation of her favourite daughter from irremediable infamy, was hurt and distressed to a most painful degree by a distinction so ill applied.

Darcy, after enquiring of her how Mr. and Mrs. Gardiner did, a question which she could not answer without confusion, said scarcely any thing. He was not seated by her; perhaps that was the reason of his silence; but it had not been so in Derbyshire. There he had talked to her friends, when he could not to herself. But now several minutes elapsed, without bringing the sound of his voice; and when occasionally, unable to resist the impulse of curiosity, she raised her eyes to his face, she as often found him looking at Jane, as at herself, and frequently on no object but the ground. More thoughtfulness, and less anxiety to please than when they last met, were plainly expressed. She was disappointed, and angry with herself for being so.

"Could I expect it to be otherwise!" said she. "Yet why did he come?"

She was in no humour for conversation with any one but himself; and to him she had hardly courage to speak.

She enquired after his sister, but could do no more.

"It is a long time, Mr. Bingley, since you went away," said

Mrs. Bennet.

He readily agreed to it.

"I began to be afraid you would never come back again. People *did* say, you meant to quit the place entirely at Michaelmas; but, however, I hope it is not true. A great many changes have happened in the neighbourhood, since you went away. Miss Lucas is married and settled. And one of my own daughters. I suppose you have heard of it; indeed, you must have seen it in the papers. It was in the Times and the Courier, I know; though it was not put in as it ought to be. It was only said, 'Lately, George Wickham, Esq. to Miss Lydia Bennet,' without there being a syllable said of her father, or the place where she lived, or any thing. It was my brother Gardiner's drawing up too, and I wonder how he came to make such an awkward business of it. Did you see it?"

Bingley replied that he did, and made his congratulations. Elizabeth dared not lift up her eyes. How Mr. Darcy looked, therefore, she could not tell.

"It is a delightful thing, to be sure, to have a daughter well married," continued her mother, "but at the same time, Mr. Bingley, it is very hard to have her taken such a way from me. They are gone down to Newcastle, a place quite northward, it seems, and there they are to stay, I do not know how long. His regiment is there; for I suppose you have heard of his leaving the——shire, and of his being gone into the regulars. Thank Heaven! he has *some* friends, though perhaps not so many as he deserves."

Elizabeth, who knew this to be levelled at Mr. Darcy, was in such misery of shame, that she could hardly keep her seat. It drew from her, however, the exertion of speaking, which nothing else had so effectually done before; and she asked Bingley, whether he meant to make any stay in the country at present. A few weeks, he believed.

"When you have killed all your own birds, Mr. Bingley," said her mother, "I beg you will come here, and shoot as many as you please, on Mr. Bennet's manor. I am sure he will be vastly happy to oblige you, and will save all the best of the covies for you."

Elizabeth's misery increased, at such unnecessary, such officious attention! Were the same fair prospect to arise at present, as had flattered them a year ago, every thing, she was persuaded, would be hastening to the same vexatious conclusion. At that instant she felt, that years of happiness could not make Jane or herself amends, for moments of such painful confusion.

"The first wish of my heart," said she to herself, "is never more to be in company with either of them. Their society can afford no pleasure, that will atone for such wretchedness as this! Let me never see either one or the other again!"

Yet the misery, for which years of happiness were to offer no compensation, received soon afterwards material relief, from observing how much the beauty of her sister re-kindled the admiration of her former lover. When first he came in, he had spoken to her but little; but every five minutes seemed to be giving her more of his attention. He found her as handsome as she had been last year; as good natured, and as unaffected, though not quite so chatty. Jane was anxious that no difference should be perceived in her at all, and was really persuaded that she talked as much as ever. But her mind was so busily engaged, that she did not always know when she was silent.

When the gentlemen rose to go away, Mrs. Bennet was mindul of her intended civility, and they were invited and engaged to dine at Longbourn in a few days time.

"You are quite a visit in my debt, Mr. Bingley," she added, "for when you went to town last winter, you promised to take a family dinner with us, as soon as you returned. I have not forgot, you see; and I assure you, I was very much disappointed that you did not come back and keep your engagement."

Bingley looked a little silly at this reflection, and said something of his concern, at having been prevented by business. They then went away.

Mrs. Bennet had been strongly inclined to ask them to stay and dine there, that day; but, though she always kept a very good table, she did not think any thing less than two courses, could be good enough for a man, on whom she had such anxious designs, or satisfy the appetite and pride of one who had ten thousand a-year.

Chapter XII

As soon as they were gone, Elizabeth walked out to recover her spirits; or in other words, to dwell without interruption on those subjects that must deaden them more. Mr. Darcy's behaviour astonished and vexed her.

"Why, if he came only to be silent, grave, and indifferent," said she, "did he come at all?"

She could settle it in no way that gave her pleasure.

"He could be still amiable, still pleasing, to my uncle and aunt, when he was in town; and why not to me? If he fears me, why come hither? If he no longer cares for me, why silent? Teazing, teazing, man! I will think no more about him."

Her resolution was for a short time involuntarily kept by the approach of her sister who joined her with a cheerful look, which shewed her better satisfied with their visitors, than Elizabeth.

"Now," said she, "that this first meeting is over, I feel perfectly easy. I know my own strength, and I shall never be embarrassed again by his coming. I am glad he dines here on Tuesday. It will then be publicly seen, that on both sides, we meet only as common and indifferent acquaintance."

"Yes, very indifferent indeed," said Elizabeth, laughingly. "Oh, Jane, take care."

"My dear Lizzy, you cannot think me so weak, as to be in danger now."

"I think you are in very great danger of making him as much in love with you as ever."

They did not see the gentlemen again till Tuesday; and Mrs. Bennet, in the meanwhile, was giving way to all the happy schemes, which the good humour, and common politeness of Bingley, in half an hour's visit, had revived.

On Tuesday there was a large party assembled at Longbourn; and the two, who were most anxiously expected, to the credit of their punctuality as sportsmen, were in very good time. When they repaired to the dining-room, Elizabeth eagerly watched to see whether Bingley would take the place, which, in all their former parties, had belonged to him, by her sister. Her prudent mother, occupied by the same ideas, forbore to invite him to sit by herself. On entering the room, he seemed to hesitate; but Jane happened to look round, and happened to smile: it was decided. He placed himself by her.

Elizabeth, with a triumphant sensation, looked towards his friend. He bore it with noble indifference, and she would have imagined that Bingley had received his sanction to be happy, had she not seen his eyes likewise turned towards Mr. Darcy, with an expression of half-laughing alarm.

His behaviour to her sister was such, during dinner time, as shewed an admiration of her, which, though more guarded than formerly, persuaded Elizabeth, that if left wholly to himself, Jane's happiness, and his own, would be speedily secured. Though she dared not depend upon the consequence, she yet received pleasure from observing his behaviour. It gave her all the animation that her spirits could boast; for she was in no cheerful humour. Mr. Darcy was almost as far from her, as the table could divide them. He was on one side of her mother. She knew how little such a situation would give pleasure to either, or make either appear to advantage. She was not near enough to hear any of their discourse, but she could see how seldom they spoke to each other, and how formal and cold was their manner, whenever they did. Her mother's ungraciousness, made the sense of what they owed him more painful to Elizabeth's mind; and she would, at times, have given any thing to be privileged to tell him, that his kindness was neither unknown nor unfelt by the whole of the family.

She was in hopes that the evening would afford some opportunity of bringing them together; that the whole of the visit would not pass away without enabling them to enter into something more of conversation, than the mere ceremonious salutation attending his entrance. Anxious and uneasy, the period which passed in the drawing-room, before the gentlemen came, was wearisome and dull to a degree, that almost made her uncivil. She looked forward to their entrance, as the point on which all her chance of pleasure for the evening must depend.

"If he does not come to me, *then*," said she, "I shall give him up for ever."

The gentlemen came; and she thought he looked as if he would have answered her hopes; but, alas! the ladies had crowded round the table, where Miss Bennet was making tea, and Elizabeth pouring out the coffee, in so close a confederacy, that there was not a single vacancy near her, which would admit of a chair. And on the gentlemen's approaching, one of the girls moved closer to her than ever, and said, in a whisper,

"The men shan't come and part us, I am determined. We want none of them; do we?"

Darcy had walked away to another part of the room. She followed him with her eyes, envied every one to whom he spoke, had scarcely patience enough to help anybody to coffee; and then was enraged against herself for being so silly!

"A man who has once been refused! How could I ever be foolish enough to expect a renewal of his love? Is there one among the sex, who would not protest against such a weakness as a second proposal to the same woman? There is no indignity so abhorrent to their feelings!"

She was a little revived, however, by his bringing back his coffee cup himself; and she seized the opportunity of saying,

"Is your sister at Pemberley still?"

"Yes, she will remain there till Christmas."

"And quite alone? Have all her friends left her?"

"Mrs. Annesley is with her. The others have been gone on to Scarborough, these three weeks."

She could think of nothing more to say; but if he wished to converse with her, he might have better success. He stood by her, however, for some minutes, in silence; and, at last, on the young lady's whispering to Elizabeth again, he walked away.

When the tea-things were removed, and the card tables placed, the ladies all rose, and Elizabeth was then hoping to be soon joined by him, when all her views were overthrown, by seeing him fall a victim to her mother's rapacity for whist players, and in a few moments after seated with the rest of the party. She now lost every expectation of pleasure. They were confined for the evening at different tables, and she had nothing to hope, but that his eyes were so often turned towards her side of the room, as to make him play as unsuccessfully as herself.

Mrs. Bennet had designed to keep the two Netherfield gentlemen to supper; but their carriage was unluckily ordered before any of the others, and she had no opportunity of detaining them.

"Well girls," said she, as soon as they were left to themselves, "What say you to the day? I think every thing has passed off uncommonly well, I assure you. The dinner was as well dressed as any I ever saw. The venison was roasted to a turn—and everybody said, they never saw so fat a haunch. The soup was fifty times better than what we had at the Lucas's last week; and even Mr. Darcy acknowledged, that the partridges were remarkably well done; and I suppose he has two or three French cooks at least. And, my dear Jane, I never saw you look in greater beauty. Mrs. Long said so too, for I asked her whether you did not. And what do you think she said besides? 'Ah! Mrs. Bennet, we shall have her at Netherfield at last.' She did indeed. I do think Mrs. Long is as good a creature as ever lived—and her nieces are very pretty behaved girls, and not at all handsome: I like them prodigiously."

Mrs. Bennet, in short, was in very great spirits; she had seen enough of Bingley's behaviour to Jane, to be convinced that she would get him at last; and her expectations of advantage to her family, when in a happy humour, were so far beyond reason, that she was quite disappointed at not seeing him there again the next day, to make his proposals.

"It has been a very agreeable day," said Miss Bennet to Elizabeth. "The party seemed so well selected, so suitable one with the other. I hope we may often meet again."

Elizabeth smiled.

"Lizzy, you must not do so. You must not suspect me. It mortifies me. I assure you that I have now learnt to enjoy his conversation as an agreeable and sensible young man, without having a wish beyond it. I am perfectly satisfied from what his manners now are, that he never had any design of engaging my affection. It is only that he is blessed with greater sweetness of address, and a stronger desire of generally pleasing than any other man."

"You are very cruel," said her sister, "you will not let me smile, and are provoking me to it every moment."

"How hard it is in some cases to be believed!"

"And how impossible in others!" [9]

"But why should you wish to persuade me that I feel more than I acknowledge?"

"That is a question which I hardly know how to answer. We all love to instruct, though we can teach only what is not worth knowing. Forgive me; and if you persist in indifference, do not make *me* your confidante."

Chapter XIII

A few days after this visit, Mr. Bingley called again, and alone. His friend had left him that morning for London, but was to return home in ten days time. He sat with them above an hour, and was in remarkably good spirits. Mrs. Bennet invited him to dine with them; but, with many expressions of concern, he confessed himself engaged elsewhere.

"Next time you call," said she, "I hope we shall be more lucky."

He should be particularly happy at any time, &c. &c.; and if she would give him leave, would take an early opportunity of waiting on them.

"Can you come to-morrow?"

Yes, he had no engagement at all for to-morrow; and her invitation was accepted with alacrity.

He came, and in such very good time, that the ladies were none of them dressed. In ran Mrs. Bennet to her daughter's room, in her dressing gown, and with her hair half finished, crying out,

"My dear Jane, make haste and hurry down. He is come—Mr. Bingley is come.—He is, indeed. Make haste, make haste. Here, Sarah, come to Miss Bennet this moment, and help her on with her gown. Never mind Miss Lizzy's hair."

"We will be down as soon as we can," said Jane; "but I dare say Kitty is forwarder than either of us, for she went up stairs half an hour ago."

"Oh! hang Kitty! what has she to do with it? Come be quick, be quick! where is your sash my dear?"

But when her mother was gone, Jane would not be prevailed on to go down without one of her sisters.

9. The three editions which Chapman consulted to make his text all print these two lines as a single speech. Jane Austen recognized the error, and commented on it in one of her letters to her sister Cassandra (4 February 1813). But the error was not corrected in any of the editions printed during Jane Austen's lifetime, a fact which raises questions about how much she had to do with the texts of the second and third editions of the novel.

The same anxiety to get them by themselves, was visible again in the evening. After tea, Mr. Bennet retired to the library, as was his custom, and Mary went up stairs to her instrument. Two obstacles of the five being thus removed, Mrs. Bennet sat looking and winking at Elizabeth and Catherine for a considerable time, without making any impression on them. Elizabeth would not observe her; and when at last Kitty did, she very innocently said, "What is the matter mamma? What do you keep winking at me for? What am I to do?"

"Nothing child, nothing. I did not wink at you." She then sat still five minutes longer; but unable to waste such a precious occasion, she suddenly got up, and saying to Kitty,

"Come here, my love, I want to speak to you," took her out of the room. Jane instantly gave a look at Elizabeth, which spoke her distress at such premeditation, and her intreaty that *she* would not give into it. In a few minutes, Mrs. Bennet half opened the door and called out,

"Lizzy, my dear, I want to speak with you."

Elizabeth was forced to go.

"We may as well leave them by themselves you know;" said her mother as soon as she was in the hall. "Kitty and I are going up stairs to sit in my dressing room."

Elizabeth made no attempt to reason with her mother, but remained quietly in the hall, till she and Kitty were out of sight, then returned into the drawing room.

Mrs. Bennet's schemes for this day were ineffectual. Bingley was every thing that was charming, except the professed lover of her daughter. His ease and cheerfulness rendered him a most agreeable addition to their evening party; and he bore with the ill-judged officiousness of the mother, and heard all her silly remarks with a forbearance and command of countenance, particularly grateful to the daughter.

He scarcely needed an invitation to stay supper; and before he went away, an engagement was formed, chiefly through his own and Mrs. Bennet's means, for his coming next morning to shoot with her husband.

After this day, Jane said no more of her indifference. Not a word passed between the sisters concerning Bingley; but Elizabeth went to bed in the happy belief that all must speedily be concluded, unless Mr. Darcy returned within the stated time. Seriously, however, she felt tolerably persuaded that all this must have taken place with that gentleman's concurrence.

Bingley was punctual to his appointment; and he and Mr. Bennet spent the morning together, as had been agreed on. The latter was much more agreeable than his companion expected.

There was nothing of presumption or folly in Bingley, that could provoke his ridicule, or disgust him into silence; and he was more communicative, and less eccentric than the other had ever seen him. Bingley of course returned with him to dinner; and in the evening Mrs. Bennet's invention was again at work to get every body away from him and her daughter. Elizabeth, who had a letter to write, went into the breakfast room for that purpose soon after tea; for as the others were all going to sit down to cards, she could not be wanted to counteract her mother's schemes.

But on returning to the drawing room, when her letter was finished, she saw, to her infinite surprise, there was reason to fear that her mother had been too ingenious for her. On opening the door, she perceived her sister and Bingley standing together over the hearth, as if engaged in earnest conversation; and had this led to no suspicion, the faces of both as they hastily turned round, and moved away from each other, would have told it all. *Their* situation was awkward enough; but *her's* she thought was still worse. Not a syllable was uttered by either; and Elizabeth was on the point of going away again, when Bingley, who as well as the other had sat down, suddenly rose, and whispering a few words to her sister, ran out of the room.

Jane could have no reserves from Elizabeth, where confidence would give pleasure; and instantly embracing her, acknowledged, with the liveliest emotion, that she was the happiest creature in the world.

" 'Tis too much!" she added, "by far too much. I do not deserve it. Oh! why is not every body as happy?"

Elizabeth's congratulations were given with a sincerity, a warmth, a delight, which words could but poorly express. Every sentence of kindness was a fresh source of happiness to Jane. But she would not allow herself to stay with her sister, or say half that remained to be said, for the present.

"I must go instantly to my mother;" she cried. "I would not on any account trifle with her affectionate solicitude; or allow her to hear it from any one but myself. He is gone to my father already. Oh! Lizzy, to know that what I have to relate will give such pleasure to all my dear family! how shall I bear so much happiness!"

She then hastened away to her mother, who had purposely broken up the card party, and was sitting up stairs with Kitty.

Elizabeth, who was left by herself, now smiled at the rapidity and ease with which an affair was finally settled, that had given them so many previous months of suspense and vexation.

"And this," said she, "is the end of all his friend's anxious circumspection! of all his sister's falsehood and contrivance! the happiest, wisest, most reasonable end!"

In a few minutes she was joined by Bingley, whose conference with her father had been short and to the purpose.

"Where is your sister?" said he hastily, as he opened the door.

"With my mother up stairs. She will be down in a moment I dare say."

He then shut the door, and coming up to her, claimed the good wishes and affection of a sister. Elizabeth honestly and heartily expressed her delight in the prospect of their relationship. They shook hands with great cordiality; and then till her sister came down, she had to listen to all he had to say, of his own happiness, and of Jane's perfections; and in spite of his being a lover, Elizabeth really believed all his expectations of felicity, to be rationally founded, because they had for basis the excellent understanding, and super-excellent disposition of Jane, and a general similarity of feeling and taste between her and himself.

It was an evening of no common delight to them all; the satisfaction of Miss Bennet's mind gave a glow of such sweet animation to her face, as made her look handsomer than ever. Kitty simpered and smiled, and hoped her turn was coming soon. Mrs. Bennet could not give her consent, or speak her approbation in terms warm enough to satisfy her feelings, though she talked to Bingley of nothing else, for half an hour; and when Mr. Bennet joined them at supper, his voice and manner plainly shewed how really happy he was.

Not a word, however, passed his lips in allusion to it, till their visitor took his leave for the night; but as soon as he was gone, he turned to his daughter and said,

"Jane, I congratulate you. You will be a very happy woman."

Jane went to him instantly, kissed him, and thanked him for his goodness.

"You are a good girl;" he replied, "and I have great pleasure in thinking you will be so happily settled. I have not a doubt of your doing very well together. Your tempers are by no means unlike. You are each of you so complying, that nothing will ever be resolved on; so easy, that every servant will cheat you; and so generous, that you will always exceed your income."

"I hope not so. Imprudence or thoughtlessness in money matters, would be unpardonable in *me*."

"Exceed their income! My dear Mr. Bennet," cried his wife, "what are you talking of? Why, he has four or five thousand a-year, and very likely more." Then addressing her daughter, "Oh! my dear, dear Jane, I am so happy! I am sure I sha'nt get a wink of sleep all night. I knew how it would be. I always said it must be so, at last. I was sure you could not be so beautiful for nothing! I remember, as soon as ever I saw him, when he first came into Hertfordshire last year, I thought how likely it was that you should come together. Oh! he is the handsomest young man that ever was seen!"

Wickham, Lydia, were all forgotten. Jane was beyond competition her favourite child. At that moment, she cared for no other. Her younger sisters soon began to make interest with her for objects of happiness which she might in future be able to dispense.

Mary petitioned for the use of the library at Netherfield; and Kitty begged very hard for a few balls there every winter.

Bingley, from this time, was of course a daily visitor at Longbourn; coming frequently before breakfast, and always remaining till after supper; unless when some barbarous neighbour, who could not be enough detested, had given him an invitation to dinner, which he thought himself obliged to accept.

Elizabeth had now but little time for conversation with her sister; for while he was present, Jane had no attention to bestow on any one else; but she found herself considerably useful to both of them, in those hours of separation that must sometimes occur. In the absence of Jane, he always attached himself to Elizabeth, for the pleasure of talking of her; and when Bingley was gone, Jane constantly sought the same means of relief.

"He has made me so happy," said she, one evening, "by telling me, that he was totally ignorant of my being in town last spring! I had not believed it possible."

"I suspected as much," replied Elizabeth. "But how did he account for it?"

"It must have been his sister's doing. They were certainly no friends to his acquaintance with me, which I cannot wonder at, since he might have chosen so much more advantageously in many respects. But when they see, as I trust they will, that their brother is happy with me, they will learn to be contented, and we shall be on good terms again; though we can never be what we once were to each other."

"That is the most unforgiving speech," said Elizabeth, "that I ever heard you utter. Good girl! It would vex me, indeed, to see you again the dupe of Miss Bingley's pretended regard."

"Would you believe it, Lizzy, that when he went to town last November, he really loved me, and nothing but a persuasion of *my* being indifferent, would have prevented his coming down again!"

"He made a little mistake to be sure; but it is to the credit of his modesty."

This naturally introduced a panegyric from Jane on his diffidence, and the little value he put on his own good qualities.

Elizabeth was pleased to find, that he had not betrayed the interference of his friend, for, though Jane had the most generous and forgiving heart in the world, she knew it was a circumstance which must prejudice her against him.

"I am certainly the most fortunate creature that ever existed!" cried Jane. "Oh! Lizzy, why am I thus singled from my family, and blessed above them all! If I could but see *you* as happy! If there *were* but such another man for you!"

"If you were to give me forty such men, I never could be so happy as you. Till I have your disposition, your goodness, I never can have your happiness. No, no, let me shift for myself; and, perhaps, if I have very good luck, I may meet with another Mr. Collins in time."

The situation of affairs in the Longbourn family could not be long a secret. Mrs. Bennet was privileged to whisper it to Mrs. Philips, and *she* ventured, without any permission, to do the same by all her neighbours in Meryton.

The Bennets were speedily pronounced to be the luckiest family in the world, though only a few weeks before, when Lydia had first run away, they had been generally proved to be marked out for misfortune.

Chapter XIV

One morning, about a week after Bingley's engagement with Jane had been formed, as he and the females of the family were sitting together in the dining room,[1] their attention was suddenly drawn to the window, by the sound of a carriage; and they perceived a chaise and four driving up the lawn. It was too early in the morning for visitors, and besides, the equipage did not answer to that of any of their neighbours. The horses were post; and neither the carriage, nor the livery of the servant who preceded it, were familiar to them. As it was certain, however, that somebody was coming, Bingley instantly prevailed on Miss Bennet to avoid the confinement of such an intrusion, and walk away

1. In his notes to the novel Chapman writes of this passage: "*dining room.* On general grounds we should rather expect to find them in the breakfast room at such an hour. There seems to be some confusion; for though it is clear that they waited in the same room for Lady Catherine's appearance, Elizabeth presently 'attended her noble guest *down stairs*'—the dining-room could not be upstairs—and 'as they passed through the hall, Lady Catherine opened the doors into the dining-parlour and drawing-room' and pronounced them 'to be decent looking rooms.' When Elizabeth comes back from the garden she finds Mrs. Bennet 'at the door of the dressing-room' which *was* upstairs; and she often sat there. The simplest solution is probably Mr. Mac-Kinnon's, that *dining room* is a misprint for *dressing room.*" Oxford edition, II, 395–96.

with him into the shrubbery. They both set off, and the conjectures of the remaining three continued, though with little satisfaction, till the door was thrown open, and their visitor entered. It was lady Catherine de Bourgh.

They were of course all intending to be surprised; but their astonishment was beyond their expectation; and on the part of Mrs. Bennet and Kitty, though she was perfectly unknown to them, even inferior to what Elizabeth felt.

She entered the room with an air more than usually ungracious, made no other reply to Elizabeth's salutation, than a slight inclination of the head, and sat down without saying a word. Elizabeth had mentioned her name to her mother, on her ladyship's entrance, though no request of introduction had been made.

Mrs. Bennet all amazement, though flattered by having a guest of such high importance, received her with the utmost politeness. After sitting for a moment in silence, she said very stiffly to Elizabeth,

"I hope you are well, Miss Bennet. That lady I suppose is your mother."

Elizabeth replied very concisely that she was.

"And *that* I suppose is one of your sisters."

"Yes, madam," said Mrs. Bennet, delighted to speak to a lady Catherine. "She is my youngest girl but one. My youngest of all, is lately married, and my eldest is some-where about the grounds, walking with a young man, who I believe will soon become a part of the family."

"You have a very small park here," returned lady Catherine after a short silence.

"It is nothing in comparison of Rosings, my lady, I dare say; but I assure you it is much larger than Sir William Lucas's."

"This must be a most inconvenient sitting room for the evening, in summer; the windows are full west."

Mrs. Bennet assured her that they never sat there after dinner; and then added,

"May I take the liberty of asking your ladyship whether you left Mr. and Mrs. Collins well."

"Yes, very well, I saw them the night before last."

Elizabeth now expected that she would produce a letter for her from Charlotte, as it seemed the only probable motive for her calling. But no letter appeared, and she was completely puzzled.

Mrs. Bennet, with great civility, begged her ladyship to take some refreshment; but Lady Catherine very resolutely, and not very politely, declined eating any thing; and then rising up, said to Elizabeth,

"Miss Bennet, there seemed to be a prettyish kind of a little wilderness on one side of your lawn. I should be glad to take a turn in it, if you will favour me with your company."

"Go, my dear," cried her mother, "and shew her ladyship about the different walks. I think she will be pleased with the hermitage." [2]

Elizabeth obeyed, and running into her own room for her parasol, attended her noble guest down stairs. As they passed through the hall, Lady Catherine opened the doors into the dining-parlour and drawing-room, and pronouncing them, after a short survey, to be decent looking rooms, walked on.

Her carriage remained at the door, and Elizabeth saw that her waiting-woman was in it. They proceeded in silence along the gravel walk that led to the copse; Elizabeth was determined to make no effort for conversation with a woman, who was now more than usually insolent and disagreeable.

"How could I ever think her like her nephew?" said she, as she looked in her face.

As soon as they entered the copse, Lady Catherine began in the following manner:—

"You can be at no loss, Miss Bennet, to understand the reason of my journey hither. Your own heart, your own conscience, must tell you why I come."

Elizabeth looked with unaffected astonishment.

"Indeed, you are mistaken, Madam. I have not been at all able to account for the honour of seeing you here."

"Miss Bennet," replied her ladyship, in an angry tone, "you ought to know, that I am not to be trifled with. But however insincere *you* may choose to be, you shall not find *me* so. My character has ever been celebrated for its sincerity and frankness, and in a cause of such moment as this, I shall certainly not depart from it. A report of a most alarming nature, reached me two days ago. I was told, that not only your sister was on the point of being most advantageously married, but that *you*, that Miss Elizabeth Bennet, would, in all likelihood, be soon afterwards united to my nephew, my own nephew, Mr. Darcy. Though I *know* it must be a scandalous falsehood; though I would not injure him so much as to suppose the truth of it possible, I instantly resolved on setting off for this place, that I might make my sentiments known to you."

"If you believed it impossible to be true," said Elizabeth, colouring with astonishment and disdain, "I wonder you took the trouble of coming so far. What could your ladyship propose by it?"

"At once to insist upon having such a report universally contradicted."

2. A secluded place; here the copse, or bower of small trees, on the grounds.

"Your coming to Longbourn, to see me and my family," said Elizabeth, coolly, "will be rather a confirmation of it; if, indeed, such a report is in existence."

"If! do you then pretend to be ignorant of it? Has it not been industriously circulated by yourselves? Do you not know that such a report is spread abroad?"

"I never heard that it was."

"And can you likewise declare, that there is no *foundation* for it?"

"I do not pretend to possess equal frankness with your ladyship. *You* may ask questions, which *I* shall not choose to answer."

"This is not to be borne. Miss Bennet, I insist on being satisfied. Has he, has my nephew, made you an offer of marriage?"

"Your ladyship has declared it to be impossible."

"It ought to be so; it must be so, while he retains the use of his reason. But *your* arts and allurements may, in a moment of infatuation, have made him forget what he owes to himself and to all his family. You may have drawn him in."

"If I have, I shall be the last person to confess it."

"Miss Bennet, do you know who I am? I have not been accustomed to such language as this. I am almost the nearest relation he has in the world, and am entitled to know all his dearest concerns."

"But you are not entitled to know *mine*; nor will such behaviour as this, ever induce me to be explicit."

"Let me be rightly understood. This match, to which you have the presumption to aspire, can never take place. No, never. Mr. Darcy is engaged to *my daughter*. Now what have you to say?"

"Only this; that if he is so, you can have no reason to suppose he will make an offer to me."

Lady Catherine hesitated for a moment, and then replied,

"The engagement between them is of a peculiar kind. From their infancy, they have been intended for each other. It was the favourite wish of *his* mother, as well as of her's. While in their cradles, we planned the union: and now, at the moment when the wishes of both sisters would be accomplished, in their marriage, to be prevented by a young woman of inferior birth, of no importance in the world, and wholly unallied to the family! Do you pay no regard to the wishes of his friends? To his tacit engagement with Miss De Bourgh? Are you lost to every feeling of propriety and delicacy? Have you not heard me say, that from his earliest hours he was destined for his cousin?"

"Yes, and I had heard it before. But what is that to me? If there is no other objection to my marrying your nephew, I shall certainly not be kept from it, by knowing that his mother and aunt wished him to marry Miss De Bourgh. You both did as much as you could, in planning the marriage. Its completion depended on others. If Mr. Darcy is neither by honour nor inclination confined to his cousin, why is not he to make another choice? And if I am that choice, why may not I accept him?"

"Because honour, decorum, prudence, nay, interest, forbid it. Yes, Miss Bennet, interest; for do not expect to be noticed by his family or friends, if you wilfully act against the inclinations of all. You will be censured, slighted, and despised, by every one connected with him. Your alliance will be a disgrace; your name will never even be mentioned by any of us."

"These are heavy misfortunes," replied Elizabeth. "But the wife of Mr. Darcy must have such extraordinary sources of happiness necessarily attached to her situation, that she could, upon the whole, have no cause to repine."

"Obstinate, headstrong girl! I am ashamed of you! Is this your gratitude for my attentions to you last spring? Is nothing due to me on that score?

"Let us sit down. You are to understand, Miss Bennet, that I came here with the determined resolution of carrying my purpose; nor will I be dissuaded from it. I have not been used to submit to any person's whims. I have not been in the habit of brooking disappointment."

"*That* will make your ladyship's situation at present more pitiable; but it will have no effect on *me*."

"I will not be interrupted. Hear me in silence. My daughter and my nephew are formed for each other. They are descended on the maternal side, from the same noble line; and, on the father's, from respectable, honourable, and ancient, though untitled families. Their fortune on both sides is splendid. They are destined for each other by the voice of every member of their respective houses; and what is to divide them? The upstart pretensions of a young woman without family, connections, or fortune. Is this to be endured! But it must not, shall not be. If you were sensible of your own good, you would not wish to quit the sphere, in which you have been brought up."

"In marrying your nephew, I should not consider myself as quitting that sphere. He is a gentleman; I am a gentleman's daughter; so far we are equal."

"True. You *are* a gentleman's daughter. But who was your mother? Who are your uncles and aunts? Do not imagine me ignorant of their condition."

"Whatever my connections may be," said Elizabeth, "if your nephew does not object to them, they can be nothing to *you*."

"Tell me once for all, are you engaged to him?"

Though Elizabeth would not, for the mere purpose of obliging Lady Catherine, have answered this question; she could not but say, after a moment's deliberation,

"I am not."

Lady Catherine seemed pleased.

"And will you promise me, never to enter into such an engagement?"

"I will make no promise of the kind."

"Miss Bennet I am shocked and astonished. I expected to find a more reasonable young woman. But do not deceive yourself into a belief that I will ever recede. I shall not go away, till you have given me the assurance I require."

"And I certainly *never* shall give it. I am not to be intimidated into anything so wholly unreasonable. Your ladyship wants Mr. Darcy to marry your daughter; but would my giving you the wished-for promise, make *their* marriage at all more probable? Supposing him to be attached to me, would *my* refusing to accept his hand, make him wish to bestow it on his cousin? Allow me to say, Lady Catherine, that the arguments with which you have supported this extraordinary application, have been as frivolous as the application was ill-judged. You have widely mistaken my character, if you think I can be worked on by such persuasions as these. How far your nephew might approve of your interference in *his* affairs, I cannot tell; but you have certainly no right to concern yourself in mine. I must beg, therefore, to be importuned no farther on the subject."

"Not so hasty, if you please. I have by no means done. To all the objections I have already urged, I have still another to add. I am no stranger to the particulars of your youngest sister's infamous elopement. I know it all; that the young man's marrying her, was a patched-up business, at the expence of your father and uncles. And is *such* a girl to be my nephew's sister? Is *her* husband, is the son of his late father's steward, to be his brother? Heaven and earth!—of what are you thinking? Are the shades of Pemberley to be thus polluted?"

"You can *now* have nothing farther to say," she resentfully answered. "You have insulted me, in every possible method. I must beg to return to the house."

And she rose as she spoke. Lady Catherine rose also, and they turned back. Her ladyship was highly incensed.

"You have no regard, then, for the honour and credit of my nephew! Unfeeling, selfish girl! Do you not consider that a connection with you, must disgrace him in the eyes of everybody?"

"Lady Catherine, I have nothing farther to say. You know

my sentiments."

"You are then resolved to have him?"

"I have said no such thing. I am only resolved to act in that manner, which will, in my own opinion, constitute my happiness, without reference to *you*, or to any person so wholly unconnected with me."

"It is well. You refuse, then, to oblige me. You refuse to obey the claims of duty, honour, and gratitude. You are determined to ruin him in the opinion of all his friends, and make him the contempt of the world."

"Neither duty, nor honour, nor gratitude," replied Elizabeth, "have any possible claim on me, in the present instance. No principle of either, would be violated by my marriage with Mr. Darcy. And with regard to the resentment of his family, or the indignation of the world, if the former *were* excited by his marrying me, it would not give me one moment's concern—and the world in general would have too much sense to join in the scorn."

"And this is your real opinion! This is your final resolve! Very well. I shall now know how to act. Do not imagine, Miss Bennet, that your ambition will ever be gratified. I came to try you. I hoped to find you reasonable; but depend upon it I will carry my point."

In this manner Lady Catherine talked on, till they were at the door of the carriage, when turning hastily round, she added,

"I take no leave of you, Miss Bennet. I send no compliments to your mother. You deserve no such attention. I am most seriously displeased."

Elizabeth made no answer; and without attempting to persuade her ladyship to return into the house, walked quietly into it herself. She heard the carriage drive away as she proceeded up stairs. Her mother impatiently met her at the door of the dressing-room, to ask why Lady Catherine would not come in again and rest herself.

"She did not choose it," said her daughter, "she would go."

"She is a very fine-looking woman! and her calling here was prodigiously civil! for she only came, I suppose, to tell us the Collinses were well. She is on her road somewhere, I dare say, and so passing through Meryton, thought she might as well call on you. I suppose she had nothing particular to say to you, Lizzy?"

Elizabeth was forced to give into a little falsehood here; for to acknowledge the substance of their conversation was impossible.

Chapter XV

The discomposure of spirits, which this extraordinary visit threw Elizabeth into, could not be easily overcome; nor could she for many hours, learn to think of it less than incessantly. Lady Catherine it appeared, had actually taken the trouble of this journey from Rosings, for the sole purpose of breaking off her supposed engagement with Mr. Darcy. It was a rational scheme to be sure! but from what the report of their engagement could originate, Elizabeth was at a loss to imagine; till she recollected that *his* being the intimate friend of Bingley, and *her* being the sister of Jane, was enough, at a time when the expectation of one wedding, made every body eager for another, to supply the idea. She had not herself forgotten to feel that the marriage of her sister must bring them more frequently together. And her neighbours at Lucas lodge, therefore, (for through their communication with the Collinses, the report she concluded had reached lady Catherine) had only set *that* down, as almost certain and immediate, which *she* had looked forward to as possible, at some future time.

In revolving lady Catherine's expressions, however, she could not help feeling some uneasiness as to the possible consequence of her persisting in this interference. From what she had said of her resolution to prevent their marriage, it occurred to Elizabeth that she must meditate an application to her nephew; and how *he* might take a similar representation of the evils attached to a connection with her, she dared not pronounce. She knew not the exact degree of his affection for his aunt, or his dependence on her judgment, but it was natural to suppose that he thought much higher of her ladyship than *she* could do; and it was certain, that in enumerating the miseries of a marriage with *one*, whose immediate connections were so unequal to his own, his aunt would address him on his weakest side. With his notions of dignity, he would probably feel that the arguments, which to Elizabeth had appeared weak and ridiculous, contained much good sense and solid reasoning.

If he had been wavering before, as to what he should do, which had often seemed likely, the advice and intreaty of so near a relation might settle every doubt, and determine him at once to be as happy, as dignity unblemished could make him. In that case he would return no more. Lady Catherine might see him in her way through town; and his engagement to Bingley of coming again to Netherfield must give way.

"If, therefore, an excuse for not keeping his promise, should come to his friend within a few days," she added, "I shall know how to understand it. I shall then give over every expectation, every wish of his constancy. If he is satisfied with only regretting me, when he might have obtained my affections and hand, I shall soon cease to regret him at all."

The surprise of the rest of the family, on hearing who their visitor had been, was very great; but they obligingly satisfied it, with the same kind of supposition, which had appeased Mrs. Bennet's curiosity; and Elizabeth was spared from much teazing on the subject.

The next morning, as she was going down stairs, she was met by her father, who came out of his library with a letter in his hand.

"Lizzy," said he, "I was going to look for you; come into my room."

She followed him thither; and her curiosity to know what he had to tell her, was heightened by the supposition of its being in some manner connected with the letter he held. It suddenly struck her that it might be from lady Catherine; and she anticipated with dismay all the consequent explanations.

She followed her father to the fire place, and they both sat down. He then said,

"I have received a letter this morning that has astonished me exceedingly. As it principally concerns yourself, you ought to know its contents. I did not know before, that I had *two* daughters on the brink of matrimony. Let me congratulate you, on a very important conquest."

The colour now rushed into Elizabeth's cheeks in the instantaneous conviction of its being a letter from the nephew, instead of the aunt; and she was undetermined whether most to be pleased that he explained himself at all, or offended that his letter was not rather addressed to herself; when her father continued, "You look conscious. Young ladies have great penetration in such matters as these; but I think I may defy even *your* sagacity, to discover the name of your admirer. This letter is from Mr. Collins."

"From Mr. Collins! and what can *he* have to say?"

"Something very much to the purpose of course. He begins with congratulations on the approaching nuptials of my eldest daughter, of which it seems he has been told, by some of the good-natured, gossiping Lucases. I shall not sport with your impatience, by reading what he says on that point. What relates to yourself, is as follows. "Having thus offered you the sincere congratulations of Mrs. Collins and myself on this happy event, let me now add a short hint on the subject of another; of which we have been advertised by the same authority. Your daughter Elizabeth, it is presumed, will not long bear the name of Bennet, after her elder sister has resigned it, and the chosen partner of her fate, may be reasonably looked up to, as one of the most illustrious personages in this land.""

"Can you possibly guess, Lizzy, who is meant by this?" "This young gentleman is blessed in a peculiar way, with every thing the heart of mortal can most desire,—splendid property, noble kindred, and extensive patronage. Yet in spite of all these temptations, let me warn my cousin Elizabeth, and yourself, of what evils you may incur, by a precipitate closure with this gentleman's proposals, which, of course, you will be inclined to take immediate advantage of."

"Have you any idea, Lizzy, who this gentleman is? But now it comes out."

"My motive for cautioning you, is as follows. We have reason to imagine that his aunt, lady Catherine de Bourgh, does not look on the match with a friendly eye."

"*Mr. Darcy*, you see, is the man! Now, Lizzy, I think I *have* surprised you. Could he, or the Lucases, have pitched on any man, within the circle of our acquaintance, whose name would have given the lie more effectually to what they related? Mr. Darcy, who never looks at any woman but to see a blemish, and who probably never looked at *you* in his life! It is admirable!"

Elizabeth tried to join in her father's pleasantry, but could only force one most reluctant smile. Never had his wit been directed in a manner so little agreeable to her.

"Are you not diverted?"

"Oh! yes. Pray read on."

"After mentioning the likelihood of this marriage to her ladyship last night, she immediately, with her usual condescension, expressed what she felt on the occasion; when it became apparent, that on the score of some family objections on the part of my cousin, she would never give her consent to what she termed so disgraceful a match. I thought it my duty to give the speediest intelligence of this to my cousin, that she and her noble admirer may be aware of what they are about, and not run hastily into a marriage which has not been properly sanctioned." "Mr. Collins moreover adds," "I am truly rejoiced that my cousin Lydia's sad business has been so well hushed up, and am only concerned that their living together before the marriage took place, should be so generally known. I must not, however, neglect the duties of my station, or refrain from declaring my amazement, at hearing that you received the young couple into your house as soon as they were married. It was an encouragement of vice; and had I been the rector of Longbourn, I should very strenuously have opposed it. You ought certainly to forgive them as a christian, but never to admit them in your sight, or allow their names to be mentioned in your hearing." "*That* is his notion of christian forgiveness! The rest of his letter is only about his dear Charlotte's situation, and his expectation of a young olive-branch. But, Lizzy, you look as if you did not enjoy it. You are not going to be *Missish*, I hope, and pretend to be affronted at an idle report. For what do we live, but to make sport for our neighbours, and laugh at them in our turn?"

"Oh!" cried Elizabeth, "I am excessively diverted. But it is so strange!"

"Yes—*that* is what makes it amusing. Had they fixed on any other man it would have been nothing; but *his* perfect indifference, and *your* pointed dislike, make it so delightfully absurd! Much as I abominate writing, I would not give up Mr. Collins's correspondence for any consideration. Nay, when I read a letter of his, I cannot help giving him the preference even over Wickham, much as I value the impudence and hypocrisy of my son-in-law. And pray, Lizzy, what said Lady Catherine about this report? Did she call to refuse her consent?"

To this question his daughter replied only with a laugh; and as it had been asked without the least suspicion, she was not distressed by his repeating it. Elizabeth had never been more at a loss to make her feelings appear what they were not. It was necessary to laugh, when she would rather have cried. Her father had most cruelly mortified her, by what he said of Mr. Darcy's indifference, and she could do nothing but wonder at such a want of penetration, or fear that perhaps, instead of his seeing too *little*, she might have fancied too *much*.

Chapter XVI

Instead of receiving any such letter of excuse from his friend, as Elizabeth half expected Mr. Bingley to do, he was able to bring Darcy with him to Longbourn before many days had passed after Lady Catherine's visit. The gentlemen arrived early; and, before Mrs. Bennet had time to tell him of their having seen his aunt, of which her daughter sat in momentary dread, Bingley, who wanted to be alone with Jane, proposed their all walking out. It was agreed to. Mrs. Bennet was not in the habit of walking, Mary could never spare time, but the remaining five set off together. Bingley and Jane, however, soon allowed the others to outstrip them. They lagged behind, while Elizabeth, Kitty, and Darcy, were to entertain each other. Very little was said by either; Kitty was too much afraid of him to talk; Elizabeth was secretly forming a desperate resolution; and perhaps he might be doing the same.

They walked towards the Lucases, because Kitty wished to call upon Maria; and as Elizabeth saw no occasion for making it a general concern, when Kitty left them, she went boldy on with him alone. Now was the moment for her resolution to be executed, and, while her courage was high, she immediately said,

"Mr. Darcy, I am a very selfish creature; and, for the sake of giving relief to my own feelings, care not how much I may be wounding your's. I can no longer help thanking you for your unexampled kindness to my poor sister. Ever since I have known it, I have been most anxious to acknowledge to you how gratefully I feel it. Were it known to the rest of my family, I should not have merely my own gratitude to express."

"I am sorry, exceedingly sorry," replied Darcy, in a tone of surprise and emotion, "that you have ever been informed of what may, in a mistaken light, have given you uneasiness. I did not think Mrs. Gardiner was so little to be trusted."

"You must not blame my aunt. Lydia's thoughtlessness first betrayed to me that you had been concerned in the matter; and, of course, I could not rest till I knew the particulars. Let me thank you again and again, in the name of all my family, for that generous compassion which induced you to take so much trouble, and bear so many mortifications, for the sake of discovering them."

"If you *will* thank me," he replied, "let it be for yourself alone. That the wish of giving happiness to you, might add force to the other inducements which led me on, I shall not attempt to deny. But your *family* owe me nothing. Much as I respect them, I believe, I thought only of *you*."

Elizabeth was too much embarrassed to say a word. After a short pause, her companion added, "You are too generous to trifle with me. If your feelings are still what they were last April, tell me so at once. My affections and wishes are unchanged, but one word from you will silence me on this subject for ever."

Elizabeth feeling all the more than common awkwardness and anxiety of his situation, now forced herself to speak; and immediately, though not very fluently, gave him to understand, that her sentiments had undergone so material a change, since the period to which he alluded, as to make her receive with gratitude and pleasure, his present assurances. The happiness which this reply produced, was such as he had probably never felt before; and he expressed himself on the occasion as sensibly and as warmly as a man violently in love can be supposed to do. Had Elizabeth been able to encounter his eye, she might have seen how well the expression of heart-felt delight, diffused over his face, became him; but, though she could not look, she could listen, and he told her of feelings, which, in proving of what importance she was to him, made his affection every moment more valuable.

They walked on, without knowing in what direction. There was too much to be thought, and felt, and said, for attention to any other objects. She soon learnt that they were indebted for their present good understanding to the efforts of his aunt, who *did* call on him in her return through London, and there relate her journey to Longbourn, its motive, and the substance of her conversation with Elizabeth; dwelling emphatically on every expression of the latter, which, in her ladyship's apprehension, peculiarly denoted her perverseness and assurance, in the belief that such a relation must assist her endeavours to obtain that promise from her nephew, which *she* had refused to give. But, unluckily for her ladyship, its effect had been exactly contrariwise.

"It taught me to hope," said he, "as I had scarcely ever allowed myself to hope before. I knew enough of your disposition to be certain, that, had you been absolutely, irrevocably decided against me, you would have acknowledged it to Lady Catherine, frankly and openly."

Elizabeth coloured and laughed as she replied, "Yes, you know enough of my *frankness* to believe me capable of *that*. After abusing you so abominably to your face, I could have no scruple in abusing you to all your relations."

"What did you say of me, that I did not deserve? For, though your accusations were ill-founded, formed on mistaken premises, my behaviour to you at the time, had merited the severest reproof. It was unpardonable. I cannot think of it without abhorrence."

"We will not quarrel for the greater share of blame annexed to that evening," said Elizabeth. "The conduct of neither, if strictly examined, will be irreproachable; but since then, we have both, I hope, improved in civility."

"I cannot be so easily reconciled to myself. The recollection of what I then said, of my conduct, my manners, my expressions during the whole of it, is now, and has been many months, inexpressibly painful to me. Your reproof, so well applied, I shall never forget: 'had you behaved in a more gentleman-like manner.' Those were your words. You know not, you can scarcely conceive, how they have tortured me;—though it was some time, I confess, before I was reasonable enough to allow their justice."

"I was certainly very far from expecting them to make so strong an impression. I had not the smallest idea of their being ever felt in such a way."

"I can easily believe it. You thought me then devoid of every proper feeling, I am sure you did. The turn of your countenance I shall never forget, as you said that I could not have addressed you in any possible way, that would induce you to accept me."

"Oh! do not repeat what I then said. These recollections will not do at all. I assure you, that I have long been most heartily ashamed of it."

Darcy mentioned his letter. "Did it," said he, "did it *soon* make you think better of me? Did you, on reading it, give any credit to its contents?"

She explained what its effect on her had been, and how gradually all her former prejudices had been removed.

"I knew," said he, "that what I wrote must give you pain, but it was necessary. I hope you have destroyed the letter. There was one part especially, the opening of it, which I should dread your having the power of reading again. I can remember some expressions which might justly make you hate me."

"The letter shall certainly be burnt, if you believe it essential to the preservation of my regard; but, though we have both reason to think my opinions not entirely unalterable, they are not, I hope, quite so easily changed as that implies."

"When I wrote that letter," replied Darcy, "I believed myself perfectly calm and cool, but I am since convinced that it was written in a dreadful bitterness of spirit."

"The letter, perhaps, began in bitterness, but it did not end so. The adieu is charity itself. But think no more of the letter. The feelings of the person who wrote, and the person who received it, are now so widely different from what they were then, that every unpleasant circumstance attending it, ought to be forgotten. You must learn some of my philosophy. Think only of the past as its remembrance gives you pleasure."

"I cannot give you credit for any philosophy of the kind. *Your* retrospections must be so totally void of reproach, that the contentment arising from them, is not of philosophy, but what is much better, of ignorance. But with *me*, it is not so. Painful recollections will intrude, which cannot, which ought not to be repelled. I have been a selfish being all my life, in practice, though not in principle. As a child I was taught what was *right*, but I was not taught to correct my temper. I was given good principles, but left to follow them in pride and conceit. Unfortunately an only son, (for many years an only *child*) I was spoilt by my parents, who though good themselves, (my father particularly, all that was benevolent and amiable,) allowed, encouraged, almost taught me to be selfish and overbearing, to care for none beyond my own family circle, to think meanly of all the rest of the world, to *wish* at least to think meanly of their sense and worth compared with my own. Such I was, from eight to eight and twenty; and such I might still have been but for you, dearest, loveliest Elizabeth! What do I not owe you! You taught me a lesson, hard indeed at first, but most advantageous. By you, I was properly humbled. I came to you without a doubt of my reception. You shewed me how insufficient were all my pretensions. to please a woman worthy of being pleased."

"Had you then persuaded yourself that I should?"

"Indeed I had. What will you think of my vanity? I believed you to be wishing, expecting my addresses."

"My manners must have been in fault, but not intentionally I assure you. I never meant to deceive you, but my spirits might often lead me wrong. How you must have hated me after *that* evening?"

"Hate you! I was angry perhaps at first, but my anger soon began to take a proper direction."

"I am almost afraid of asking what you thought of me; when we met at Pemberley. You blamed me for coming?"

"No indeed; I felt nothing but surprise."

"Your surprise could not be greater than *mine* in being noticed by you. My conscience told me that I deserved no extraordinary politeness, and I confess that I did not expect to receive *more* than my due.'

"My object *then*," replied Darcy, "was to shew you, by every civility in my power, that I was not so mean as to resent the past; and I hoped to obtain your forgiveness, to lessen your ill opinion, by letting you see that your reproofs had been attended to. How soon any other wishes introduced themselves I can hardly tell, but I believe in about half an hour after I had seen you."

He then told her of Georgiana's delight in her acquaintance, and of her disappointment at its sudden interruption; which naturally leading to the cause of that interruption, she soon learnt that his resolution of following her from Derbyshire in quest of her sister, had been formed before he quitted the inn, and that his gravity and thoughtfulness there, had arisen from no other struggles than what such a purpose must comprehend.

She expressed her gratitude again, but it was too painful a subject to each, to be dwelt on farther.

After walking several miles in a leisurely manner, and too busy to know any thing about it, they found at last, on examining their watches, that it was time to be at home.

"What could become of Mr. Bingley and Jane!" was a wonder which introduced the discussion of *their* affairs. Darcy was delighted with their engagement; his friend had given him the earliest information of it.

"I must ask whether you were surprised?" said Elizabeth.

"Not at all. When I went away, I felt that it would soon happen."

"That is to say, you had given your permission. I guessed as much." And though he exclaimed at the term, she found that it had been pretty much the case.

"On the evening before my going to London," said he "I made a confession to him, which I believe I ought to have made long ago. I told him of all that had occurred to make my former interference in his affairs, absurd and impertinent. His surprise was great. He had never had the slightest suspicion. I told him, moreover, that I believed myself mistaken in supposing, as I had done, that your sister was indifferent to him; and as I could easily perceive that his attachment to her was unabated, I felt no doubt of their happiness together."

Elizabeth could not help smiling at his easy manner of directing his friend.

"Did you speak from your own observation," said she, "when you told him that my sister loved him, or merely from my information last spring?"

"From the former. I had narrowly observed her during the two visits which I had lately made her here; and I was convinced of her affection."

"And your assurance of it, I suppose, carried immediate conviction to him."

"It did. Bingley is most unaffectedly modest. His diffidence had prevented his depending on his own judgment in so anxious a case, but his reliance on mine, made every thing easy. I was obliged to confess one thing, which for a time, and not unjustly, offended him. I could not allow myself to conceal that your sister had been in town three months last winter, that I had known it, and purposely kept it from him. He was angry. But his anger, I am persuaded, lasted no longer than he remained in any doubt of your sister's sentiments. He has heartily forgiven me now."

Elizabeth longed to observe that Mr. Bingley had been a most delightful friend; so easily guided that his worth was invaluable; but she checked herself. She remembered that he had yet to learn to be laught at, and it was rather too early to begin. In anticipating the happiness of Bingley, which of course was to be inferior only to his own, he continued the conversation till they reached the house. In the hall they parted.

Chapter XVII

"My dear Lizzy, where can you have been walking to?" was a question which Elizabeth received from Jane as soon as she entered the room, and from all the others when they sat down to table. She had only to say in reply, that they had wandered about, till she was beyond her own knowledge. She coloured as she spoke; but neither that, nor any thing else, awakened a suspicion of the truth.

The evening passed quietly, unmarked by any thing extraordinary. The acknowledged lovers talked and laughed, the unacknowledged were silent. Darcy was not of a disposition in which happiness overflows in mirth; and Elizabeth, agitated and confused, rather *knew* that she was happy, than *felt* herself to be so; for, besides the immediate embarrassment, there were other evils before her. She anticipated what would be felt in the family when her situation became known; she was aware that no one liked him but Jane; and even feared that with the others it was a *dislike* which not all his fortune and consequence might do away.

At night she opened her heart to Jane. Though suspicion was very far from Miss Bennet's general habits, she was absolutely incredulous here.

"You are joking, Lizzy. This cannot be!—engaged to Mr. Darcy! No, no, you shall not deceive me. I know it to be impossible."

"This is a wretched beginning indeed! My sole dependence was on you; and I am sure nobody else will believe me, if you do not. Yet, indeed, I am in earnest. I speak nothing but the truth. He still loves me, and we are engaged."

Jane looked at her doubtingly. "Oh, Lizzy! it cannot be. I know how much you dislike him."

"You know nothing of the matter. *That* is all to be forgot. Perhaps I did not always love him so well as I do now. But in such cases as these, a good memory is unpardonable. This is the last time I shall ever remember it myself."

Miss Bennet still looked all amazement. Elizabeth again, and more seriously assured her of its truth.

"Good Heaven! can it be really so! Yet now I must believe you," cried Jane. "My dear, dear Lizzy, I would—I do congratulate you —but are you certain? forgive the question—are you quite certain that you can be happy with him?"

"There can be no doubt of that. It is settled between us already, that we are to be the happiest couple in the world. But are you pleased, Jane? Shall you like to have such a brother?"

"Very, very much. Nothing could give either Bingley or myself more delight. But we considered it, we talked of it as impossible. And do you really love him quite well enough? Oh, Lizzy! do any thing rather than marry without affection. Are you quite sure that you feel what you ought to do?"

"Oh, yes! You will only think I feel *more* than I ought to do, when I tell you all."

"What do you mean?"

"Why, I must confess, that I love him better than I do Bingley.

I am afraid you will be angry."

"My dearest sister, now *be* be serious. I want to talk very seriously. Let me know every thing that I am to know, without delay. Will you tell me how long you have loved him?"

"It has been coming on so gradually, that I hardly know when it began. But I believe I must date it from my first seeing his beautiful grounds at Pemberley."

Another intreaty that she would be serious, however, produced the desired effect; and she soon satisfied Jane by her solemn assurances of attachment. When convinced on that article, Miss Bennet had nothing farther to wish.

"Now I am quite happy," said she, "for you will be as happy as myself. I always had a value for him. Were it for nothing but his love of you, I must always have esteemed him; but now, as Bingley's friend and your husband, there can be only Bingley and yourself more dear to me. But Lizzy, you have been very sly, very reserved with me. How little did you tell me of what passed at Pemberley and Lambton! I owe all that I know of it, to another, not to you."

Elizabeth told her the motives of her secrecy. She had been unwilling to mention Bingley; and the unsettled state of her own feelings had made her equally avoid the name of his friend. But now she would no longer conceal from her, his share in Lydia's marriage. All was acknowledged, and half the night spent in conversation.

———

"Good gracious!" cried Mrs. Bennet, as she stood at a window the next morning, "if that disagreeable Mr. Darcy is not coming here again with our dear Bingley! What can he mean by being so tiresome as to be always coming here? I had no notion but he would go a shooting, or something or other, and not disturb us with his company. What shall we do with him? Lizzy, you must walk out with him again, that he may not be in Bingley's way."

Elizabeth could hardly help laughing at so convenient a proposal; yet was really vexed that her mother should be always giving him such an epithet.

As soon as they entered, Bingley looked at her so expressively, and shook hands with such warmth, as left no doubt of his good information; and he soon afterwards said aloud, "Mr. Bennet,[3] have you no more lanes hereabouts in which Lizzy may lose her way again to-day?"

3. In his notes to the novel Chapman writes of this passage: *"Mr. Bennet* should probably be *Mrs. Bennet;* Bingley would be more likely to address her on such a point, and it is she who replies. Mr. Bennet was probably in his library." Oxford edition, II, 397.

"I advise Mr. Darcy, and Lizzy, and Kitty," said Mrs. Bennet, "to walk to Oakham Mount this morning. It is a nice long walk, and Mr. Darcy has never seen the view."

"It may do very well for the others," replied Mr. Bingley; "but I am sure it will be too much for Kitty. Wont it, Kitty?"

Kitty owned that she had rather stay at home. Darcy professed a great curiosity to see the view from the Mount, and Elizabeth silently consented. As she went up stairs to get ready, Mrs. Bennet followed her, saying,

"I am quite sorry, Lizzy, that you should be forced to have that disagreeable man all to yourself. But I hope you will not mind it: it is all for Jane's sake, you know; and there is no occasion for talking to him, except just now and then. So, do not put yourself to inconvenience."

During their walk, it was resolved that Mr. Bennet's consent should be asked in the course of the evening. Elizabeth reserved to herself the application for her mother's. She could not determine how her mother would take it; sometimes doubting whether all his wealth and grandeur would be enough to overcome her abhorrence of the man. But whether she were violently set against the match, or violently delighted with it, it was certain that her manner would be equally ill adapted to do credit to her sense; and she could no more bear that Mr. Darcy should hear the first raptures of her joy, than the first vehemence of her disapprobation.

In the evening, soon after Mr. Bennet withdrew to the library, she saw Mr. Darcy rise also and follow him, and her agitation on seeing it was extreme. She did not fear her father's opposition, but he was going to be made unhappy, and that it should be through her means, that *she*, his favourite child, should be distressing him by her choice, should be filling him with fears and regrets in disposing of her, was a wretched reflection, and she sat in misery till Mr. Darcy appeared again, when, looking at him, she was a little relieved by his smile. In a few minutes he approached the table where she was sitting with Kitty; and, while pretending to admire her work, said in a whisper, "Go to your father, he wants you in the library." She was gone directly.

Her father was walking about the room, looking grave and anxious. "Lizzy," said he, "what are you doing? Are you out of your senses, to be accepting this man? Have not you always hated him?"

How earnestly did she then wish that her former opinions had been more reasonable, her expressions more moderate! It would have spared her from explanations and professions which it was exceedingly awkward to give; but they were now necessary, and she assured him with some confusion, of her attachment to Mr. Darcy.

"Or in other words, you are determined to have him. He is rich, to be sure, and you may have more fine clothes and fine carriages than Jane. But will they make you happy?"

"Have you any other objection," said Elizabeth, "than your belief of my indifference?"

"None at all. We all know him to be a proud, unpleasant sort of man; but this would be nothing if you really liked him."

"I do, I do like him," she replied, with tears in her eyes, "I love him. Indeed he has no improper pride. He is perfectly amiable. You do not know what he really is; then pray do not pain me by speaking of him in such terms."

"Lizzy," said her father, "I have given him my consent. He is the kind of man, indeed, to whom I should never dare refuse any thing, which he condescended to ask. I now give it to *you*, if you are resolved on having him. But let me advise you to think better of it. I know your disposition, Lizzy, I know that you could be neither happy nor respectable, unless you truly esteemed your husband; unless you looked up to him as a superior. Your lively talents would place you in the greatest danger in an unequal marriage. You could scarcely escape discredit and misery. My child, let me not have the grief of seeing *you* unable to respect your partner in life. You know not what you are about."

Elizabeth, still more affected, was earnest and solemn in her reply; and at length, by repeated assurances that Mr. Darcy was really the object of her choice, by explaining the gradual change which her estimation of him had undergone, relating her absolute certainty that his affection was not the work of a day, but had stood the test of many months suspense, and enumerating with energy all his good qualities, she did conquer her father's incredulity, and reconcile him to the match.

"Well, my dear," said he, when she ceased speaking, "I have no more to say. If this be the case, he deserves you. I could not have parted with you, my Lizzy, to any one less worthy."

To complete the favourable impression, she then told him what Mr. Darcy had voluntarily done for Lydia. He heard her with astonishment.

"This is an evening of wonders, indeed! And so, Darcy did every thing; made up the match, gave the money, paid the fellow's debts, and got him his commission! So much the better. It will save me a world of trouble and economy. Had it been your uncle's doing, I must and *would* have paid him; but these violent young lovers carry every thing their own way. I shall offer to pay him to-morrow; he will rant and storm about his love for you, and there will be an end of the matter."

He then recollected her embarrassment a few days before, on his reading Mr. Collins's letter; and after laughing at her some time, allowed her at last to go—saying, as she quitted the room, "If any young men come for Mary or Kitty, send them in, for I am quite at leisure."

Elizabeth's mind was now relieved from a very heavy weight; and, after half an hour's quiet reflection in her own room, she was able to join the others with tolerable composure. Every thing was too recent for gaiety, but the evening passed tranquilly away; there was no longer any thing material to be dreaded, and the comfort of ease and familiarity would come in time.

When her mother went up to her dressing-room at night, she followed her, and made the important communication. Its effect was most extraordinary; for on first hearing it, Mrs. Bennet sat quite still, and unable to utter a syllable. Nor was it under many, many minutes, that she could comprehend what she heard; though not in general backward to credit what was for the advantage of her family, or that came in the shape of a lover to any of them. She began at length to recover, to fidget about in her chair, get up, sit down again, wonder, and bless herself.

"Good gracious! Lord bless me! only think! dear me! Mr. Darcy! Who would have thought it! And is it really true? Oh! my sweetest Lizzy! how rich and how great you will be! What pin-money, what jewels, what carriages you will have! Jane's is nothing to it—nothing at all. I am so pleased—so happy. Such a charming man!—so handsome! so tall!—Oh, my dear Lizzy! pray apologise for my having disliked him so much before. I hope he will overlook it. Dear, dear Lizzy. A house in town! Every thing that is charming! Three daughters married! Ten thousand a year! Oh, Lord! What will become of me. I shall go distracted."

This was enough to prove that her approbation need not be doubted: and Elizabeth, rejoicing that such an effusion was heard only by herself, soon went away, But before she had been three minutes in her own room, her mother followed her.

"My dearest child," she cried, "I can think of nothing else! Ten thousand a year, and very likely more! 'Tis as good as a Lord! And a special licence.[4] You must and shall be married by a special licence. But my dearest love, tell me what dish Mr. Darcy is particularly fond of, that I may have it to-morrow."

This was a sad omen of what her mother's behaviour to the gentleman himself might be; and Elizabeth found, that though in the certain possession of his warmest affection, and secure

4. Permission to marry procured from a bishop or archbishop and used in lieu of the publishing of banns.

of her relations' consent, there was still something to be wished for. But the morrow passed off much better than she expected; for Mrs. Bennet luckily stood in such awe of her intended son-in-law, that she ventured not to speak to him, unless it was in her power to offer him any attention, or mark her deference for his opinion.

Elizabeth had the satisfaction of seeing her father taking pains to get acquainted with him; and Mr. Bennet soon assured her that he was rising every hour in his esteem.

"I admire all my three sons-in-law highly," said he. "Wickham, perhaps, is my favourite; but I think I shall like *your* husband quite as well as Jane's."

Chapter XVIII

Elizabeth's spirits soon rising to playfulness again, she wanted Mr. Darcy to account for his having ever fallen in love with her. "How could you begin?" said she. "I can comprehend your going on charmingly, when you had once made a beginning; but what could set you off in the first place?"

"I cannot fix on the hour, or the spot, or the look, or the words, which laid the foundation. It is too long ago. I was in the middle before I knew that I *had* begun."

"My beauty you had early withstood, and as for my manners—my behaviour to *you* was at least always bordering on the uncivil, and I never spoke to you without rather wishing to give you pain than not. Now be sincere; did you admire me for my impertinence?'

"For the liveliness of your mind, I did."

"You may as well call it impertinence at once. It was very little less. The fact is, that you were sick of civility, of deference, of officious attention. You were disgusted with the women who were always speaking and looking, and thinking for *your* approbation alone. I roused, and interested you, because I was so unlike *them*. Had you not been really amiable you would have hated me for it; but in spite of the pains you took to disguise yourself, your feelings were always noble and just; and in your heart, you thoroughly despised the persons who so assiduously courted you. There—I have saved you the trouble of accounting for it; and really, all things considered, I begin to think it perfectly reasonable. To be sure, you knew no actual good of me—but nobody thinks of *that* when they fall in love."

"Was there no good in your affectionate behaviour to Jane, while she was ill at Netherfield?"

"Dearest Jane! who could have done less for her? But make

a virtue of it by all means. My good qualities are under your protection, and you are to exaggerate them as much as possible; and, in return, it belongs to me to find occasions for teazing and quarrelling with you as often as may be; and I shall begin directly by asking you what made you so unwilling to come to the point at last. What made you so shy of me, when you first called, and afterwards dined here? Why, especially, when you called, did you look as if you did not care about me?"

"Because you were grave and silent, and gave me no encouragement.

"But I was embarrassed."

"And so was I."

"You might have talked to me more when you came to dinner."

"A man who had felt less, might."

"How unlucky that you should have a reasonable answer to give, and that I should be so reasonable as to admit it! But I wonder how long you *would* have gone on, if you had been left to yourself. I wonder when you *would* have spoken, if I had not asked you! My resolution of thanking you for your kindness to Lydia had certainly great effect. *Too much*, I am afraid; for what becomes of the moral, if our comfort springs from a breach of promise, for I ought not to have mentioned the subject? This will never do."

"You need not distress yourself. The moral will be perfectly fair. Lady Catherine's unjustifiable endeavours to separate us, were the means of removing all my doubts. I am not indebted for my present happiness to your eager desire of expressing your gratitude. I was not in a humour to wait for any opening of your's. My aunt's intelligence had given me hope, and I was determined at once to know every thing."

"Lady Catherine has been of infinite use, which ought to make her happy, for she loves to be of use. But tell me, what did you come down to Netherfield for? Was it merely to ride to Longbourn and be embarrassed? or had you intended any more serious consequence?"

"My real purpose was to see *you*, and to judge, if I could, whether I might ever hope to make you love me. My avowed one, or what I avowed to myself, was to see whether your sister were still partial to Bingley, and if she were, to make the confession to him which I have since made."

"Shall you ever have courage to announce to Lady Catherine, what is to befall her?"

"I am more likely to want time than courage, Elizabeth. But it ought to be done, and if you will give me a sheet of paper, it shall be done directly."

"And if I had not a letter to write myself, I might sit by you, and admire the evenness of your writing, as another young lady once did. But I have an aunt, too, who must not be longer neglected."

From an unwillingness to confess how much her intimacy with Mr. Darcy had been over-rated, Elizabeth had never yet answered Mrs. Gardiner's long letter, but now, having *that* to communicate which she knew would be most welcome, she was almost ashamed to find, that her uncle and aunt had already lost three days of happiness, and immediately wrote as follows:

"I would have thanked you before, my dear aunt, as I ought to have done, for your long, kind, satisfactory, detail of particulars; but to say the truth, I was too cross to write. You supposed more than really existed. But *now* suppose as much as you chuse; give a loose to your fancy, indulge your imagination in every possible flight which the subject will afford, and unless you believe me actually married, you cannot greatly err. You must write again very soon, and praise him a great deal more than you did in your last. I thank you, again and again, for not going to the Lakes. How could I be so silly as to wish it! Your idea of the ponies is delightful. We will go round the Park every day. I am the happiest creature in the world. Perhaps other people have said so before, but not one with such justice. I am happier even than Jane; she only smiles, I laugh. Mr. Darcy sends you all the love in the world, that he can spare from me. You are all to come to Pemberley at Christmas. Your's, &c."

Mr. Darcy's letter to Lady Catherine, was in a different style; and still different from either, was what Mr. Bennet sent to Mr. Collins, in reply to his last.

"Dear Sir,

"I must trouble you once more for congratulations. Elizabeth will soon be the wife of Mr. Darcy. Console Lady Catherine as well as you can. But, if I were you, I would stand by the nephew. He has more to give.

"Your's sincerely, &c."

Miss Bingley's congratulations to her brother, on his approaching marriage, were all that was affectionate and insincere. She wrote even to Jane on the occasion, to express her delight, and repeat all her former professions of regard. Jane was not deceived, but she was affected; and though feeling no reliance on her, could not help writing her a much kinder answer than she knew was deserved.

The joy which Miss Darcy expressed on receiving similar information, was as sincere as her brother's in sending it. Four sides of paper were insufficient to contain all her delight, and all her earnest desire of being loved by her sister.

Before any answer could arrive from Mr. Collins, or any congratulations to Elizabeth, from his wife, the Longbourn family heard that the Collinses were come themselves to Lucas lodge. The reason of this sudden removal was soon evident. Lady Catherine had been rendered so exceedingly angry by the contents of her nephew's letter, that Charlotte, really rejoicing in the match, was anxious to get away till the storm was blown over. At such a moment, the arrival of her friend was a sincere pleasure to Elizabeth, though in the course of their meetings she must sometimes think the pleasure dearly bought, when she saw Mr. Darcy exposed to all the parading and obsequious civility of her husband. He bore it however with admirable calmness. He could even listen to Sir William Lucas, when he complimented him on carrying away the brightest jewel of the country, and expressed his hopes of their all meeting frequently at St. James's, with very decent composure. If he did shrug his shoulders, it was not till Sir William was out of sight.

Mrs. Philips's vulgarity was another, and perhaps a greater tax on his forbearance; and though Mrs. Philips, as well as her sister, stood in too much awe of him to speak with the familiarity which Bingley's good humour encouraged, yet, whenever she *did* speak, she must be vulgar. Nor was her respect for him, though it made her more quiet, at all likely to make her more elegant. Elizabeth did all she could, to shield him from the frequent notice of either, and was ever anxious to keep him to herself, and to those of her family with whom he might converse without mortification; and though the uncomfortable feelings arising from all this took from the season of courtship much of its pleasure, it added to the hope of the future; and she looked forward with delight to the time when they should be removed from society so little pleasing to either, to all the comfort and elegance of their family party at Pemberley.

Chapter XIX

Happy for all her maternal feelings was the day on which Mrs. Bennet got rid of her two most deserving daughters. With what delighted pride she afterwards visited Mrs. Bingley and talked of Mrs. Darcy may be guessed. I wish I could say, for the sake of her family, that the accomplishment of her earnest desire in the establishment of so many of her children, produced so happy an effect as to make her a sensible, amiable, well-informed woman for the rest of her life; though perhaps it was lucky for her husband, who might not have relished domestic felicity in so unusual a form, that she still was occasionally nervous and invariably silly.

Mr. Bennet missed his second daughter exceedingly; his affection for her drew him oftener from home than any thing else could do. He delighted in going to Pemberley, especially when he was least expected.

Mr. Bingley and Jane remained at Netherfield only a twelve-month. So near a vicinity to her mother and Meryton relations was not desirable even to *his* easy temper, or *her* affectionate heart. The darling wish of his sisters was then gratified; he bought an estate in a neighbouring county to Derbyshire, and Jane and Elizabeth, in addition to every other source of happiness, were within thirty miles of each other.

Kitty, to her very material advantage, spent the chief of her time with her two elder sisters. In society so superior to what she had generally known, her improvement was great. She was not of so ungovernable a temper as Lydia, and, removed from the influence of Lydia's example, she became, by proper attention and management, less irritable, less ignorant, and less insipid. From the farther disadvantage of Lydia's society she was of course carefully kept, and though Mrs. Wickham frequently invited her to come and stay with her, with the promise of balls and young men, her father would never consent to her going.

Mary was the only daughter who remained at home; and she was necessarily drawn from the pursuit of accomplishments by Mrs. Bennet's being quite unable to sit alone. Mary was obliged to mix more with the world, but she could still moralize over every morning visit; and as she was no longer mortified by comparisons between her sisters' beauty and her own, it was suspected by her father that she submitted to the change without much reluctance.

As for Wickham and Lydia, their characters suffered no revolution from the marriage of her sisters. He bore with philosophy the conviction that Elizabeth must now become acquainted with whatever of his ingratitude and falsehood had before been unknown to her; and in spite of every thing, was not wholly without hope that Darcy might yet be prevailed on to make his fortune. The congratulatory letter which Elizabeth received from Lydia on her marriage, explained to her that, by his wife at least, if not by himself, such a hope was cherished. The letter was to this effect:—

"My Dear Lizzy,

"I wish you joy. If you love Mr. Darcy half as well as I do my dear Wickham, you must be very happy. It is a great comfort to have you so rich, and when you have nothing else to do, I hope you will think of us. I am sure Wickham would like a place at court very much, and I do not think we shall have quite money enough to live upon without some help. Any place would do, of about three or four hundred a year; but, however, do not speak to Mr. Darcy about it, if you had rather not.

"Your's &c."

As it happened that Elizabeth had *much* rather not, she endeavoured in her answer to put an end to every intreaty and expectation of the kind. Such relief, however, as it was in her power to afford, by the practice of what might be called economy in her own private expences, she frequently sent them. It had always been evident to her that such an income as theirs, under the direction of two persons so extravagant in their wants, and heedless of the future, must be very insufficient to their support; and whenever they changed their quarters, either Jane or herself were sure of being applied to, for some little assistance towards discharging their bills. Their manner of living, even when the restoration of peace dismissed them to a home, was unsettled in the extreme. They were always moving from place to place in quest of a cheap situation, and always spending more than they ought. His affection for her soon sunk into indifference; her's lasted a little longer; and in spite of her youth and her manners, she retained all the claims to reputation which her marriage had given her.

Though Darcy could never receive *him* at Pemberley, yet, for Elizabeth's sake, he assisted him farther in his profession. Lydia was occasionally a visitor there, when her husband was gone to enjoy himself in London or Bath; and with the Bingleys they both of them frequently staid so long, that even Bingley's good humour was overcome, and he proceeded so far as to *talk* of giving them a hint to be gone.

Miss Bingley was very deeply mortified by Darcy's marriage; but as she thought it advisable to retain the right of visiting at Pemberley, she dropt all her resentment; was fonder than ever of Georgiana, almost as attentive to Darcy as heretofore, and paid off every arrear of civility to Elizabeth.

Pemberley was now Georgiana's home; and the attachment of the sisters was exactly what Darcy had hoped to see. They were able to love each other, even as well as they intended. Georgiana had the highest opinion in the world of Elizabeth; though at first she often listened with an astonishment bordering on alarm, at her lively, sportive, manner of talking to her brother. He, who had always inspired in herself a respect which almost overcame her affection, she now saw the object of open pleasantry. Her mind received knowledge which had never before fallen in her way. By Elizabeth's instructions she began to comprehend that a woman may take liberties with her husband, which a brother will not always allow in a sister more than ten years younger than himself.

Lady Catherine was extremely indignant on the marriage of her nephew; and as she gave way to all the genuine frankness of her character, in her reply to the letter which announced its arrangement, she sent him language so very abusive, especially of Elizabeth, that for some time all intercourse was at an end. But at length, by Elizabeth's persuasion, he was prevailed on to overlook the offence, and seek a reconciliation; and, after a little farther resistance on the part of his aunt, her resentment gave way, either to her affection for him, or her curiosity to see how his wife conducted herself; and she condescended to wait on them at Pemberley, in spite of that pollution which its woods had received, not merely from the presence of such a mistress, but the visits of her uncle and aunt from the city.

With the Gardiners, they were always on the most intimate terms. Darcy, as well as Elizabeth, really loved them; and they were both ever sensible of the warmest gratitude towards the persons who, by bringing her into Derbyshire, had been the means of uniting them.

FINIS.

Backgrounds

From Jane Austen's Juvenilia

From Jack and Alice†

CHAPTER THE SECOND

***One evening, Alice finding herself some what heated by wine (no very uncommon case) determined to seek a relief for her disordered Head & Love-sick Heart in the Conversation of the intelligent Lady Williams.

She found her Ladyship at home as was in general the Case, for she was not fond of going out, & like the great Sir Charles Grandison scorned to deny herself [1] when at Home, as she looked on that fashionable method of shutting out disagreeable Visitors, as little less than downright Bigamy.

In spite of the wine she had been drinking, poor Alice was uncommonly out of spirits; she could think of nothing but Charles Adams, she could talk of nothing but him, & in short spoke so openly that Lady Williams soon discovered the unreturned affection she bore him, which excited her Pity & Compassion so strongly that she addressed her in the following Manner.

"I perceive but too plainly my dear Miss Johnson, that your Heart has not been able to withstand the fascinating Charms of this young Man & I pity you sincerely. Is it a first Love?"

"It is."

"I am still more grieved [2] to heart *that*; I am myself a sad example of the Miseries, in general attendant on a first Love & I am determined for the future to avoid the like Misfortune. I wish it may not be too late for you to do the same; if it is not endeavour my dear Girl to secure yourself from so great a Danger. A second attachment is seldom attended with any serious consequences; against *that* therefore I have nothing to say. Preserve yourself

† From *Volume the First*, edited by R. W. Chapman (Oxford, 1933), pp. 26–31. Copyright 1933 by the Clarendon Press, Oxford. Reprinted by permission of the publishers. "Jack and Alice" was probably written between 1788 and 1791.

1. Sir Charles Grandison is the hero of a novel published by Samuel Richardson in 1753–54. "Scorned to deny herself": scorned to instruct her servants to tell visitors that she was not at home. 2. The spellings "greived," "freind," "believe," etc., are characteristic (but not consistent) in Jane Austen's manuscripts and have been preserved by her editors.

from a first Love & you need not fear a second."

"You mentioned Madam something of your having yourself been a sufferer by the misfortune you are so good as to wish me to avoid. Will you favour me with your Life & Adventures?"

"Willingly my Love."

CHAPTER THE THIRD

"My Father was a gentleman of considerable Fortune in Berkshire; myself & a few more his only Children. I was but six years old when I had the misfortune of losing my Mother & being at that time young & Tender, my father instead of sending me to School, procured an able handed Governess to superintend my Education at Home. My Brothers were placed at Schools suitable to their Ages & my Sisters being all younger than myself, remained still under the Care of their Nurse.

Miss Dickins was an excellent Governess. She instructed me in the Paths of Virtue; under her tuition I daily became more amiable, & might perhaps by this time have nearly attained perfection, had not my worthy Preceptoress been torn from my arms, e'er I had attained my seventeenth year. I never shall forget her last words. 'My dear Kitty she said Good nightt'ye.' I never saw her afterwards" continued Lady Williams wiping her eyes, "She eloped with the Butler the same night".

"I was invited the following year by a distant relation of my Father's to spend the Winter with her in town. Mrs. Watkins was a Lady of Fashion, Family & fortune; she was in general esteemed a pretty Woman, but I never thought her very handsome, for my part. She had too high a forehead, Her eyes were too small & she had too much colour."

"How can *that* be?" interrupted Miss Johnson reddening with anger; "Do you think that any one can have too much colour?"

"Indeed I do, & I'll tell you why I do my dear Alice; when a person has too great a degree of red in their Complexion, it gives their face in my opinion, too red a look."

"But can a face my Lady have too red a look?"

"Certainly my dear Miss Johnson & I'll tell you why. When a face has too red a look it does not appear to so much advantage as it would were it paler."

"Pray Ma'am proceed in your story."

"Well, as I said before, I was invited by this Lady to spend some weeks with her in town. Many Gentlemen thought her Handsome but in my opinion, Her forehead was too high, her eyes too small & she had too much colour."

"In that Madam as I said before your Ladyship must have been mistaken. Mrs. Watkins could not have too much colour since no one can have too much."

"Excuse me my Love if I do not agree with you in that particular. Let me explain myself clearly; my idea of the case is this. When a Woman has too great a proportion of red in her Cheeks, she must have too much colour."

"But Madam I deny that it is possible for any one to have too great a proportion of red in their Cheeks."

"What my Love not if they have too much colour?"

Miss Johnson was now out of all patience, the more so perhaps as Lady Williams still remained so inflexibly cool. It must be remembered however that her Ladyship had in one respect by far the advantage of Alice; I mean in not being drunk, for heated with wine & raised by Passion, she could have little command of her Temper.

The Dispute at length grew so hot on the part of Alice that "From Words she almost came to Blows" When Mr Johnson luckily entered & with some difficulty forced her away from Lady Williams, Mrs Watkins & her red cheeks.

From A Collection of Letters†

Letter the third

FROM A YOUNG LADY IN DISTRESS'D CIRCUM- STANCES TO HER FREIND.

A few days ago I was at a private Ball given by Mr Ashburnham. As my Mother never goes out she entrusted me to the care of Lady Greville who did me the honour of calling for me in her way & of allowing me to sit forwards, which is a favour about which I am very indifferent especially as I know it is considered as confering a great obligation on me. "So Miss Maria (said her Ladyship as she saw me advancing to the door of the Carriage) you seem very smart tonight—*My* poor Girls will appear quite to disadvantage by *you*. I only hope your Mother may not have distressed herself to set *you* off. Have you got a new Gown on?"

"Yes Ma'am," replied I with as much indifference as I could assume.

† From *Volume the Second*, edited by B. C. Southam (Oxford, 1963), pp. 164–172. Copyright 1963 by the Clarendon Press, Oxford. Reprinted by permission of the publishers. "A Collection of Letters" was probably written before 1792.

"Aye, and a fine one too I think—(feeling it, as by her permission I seated myself by her) I dare say it is all very smart—But I must own, for you know I always speak my mind, that I think it was quite a needless peice of expence—Why could not you have worn your old striped one? It is not my way to find fault with people because they are poor, for I always think that they are more to be despised & pitied than blamed for it, especially if they cannot help it, but at the same time I must say that in my opinion your old striped Gown would have been quite fine enough for its wearer—for to tell you the truth (I always speak my mind) I am very much afraid that one half of the people in the room will not know whether you have a Gown on or not—But I suppose you intend to make your fortune tonight—Well, the sooner the better; & I wish you success."

"Indeed Ma'am I have no such intention.—"

"Who ever heard a Young Lady own that she was a Fortune-hunter?" Miss Greville laughed, but I am sure Ellen felt for me.

"Was your Mother gone to bed before you left her?" said her Ladyship.

"Dear Ma'am" said Ellen, "it is but nine o'clock."

"True Ellen, but Candles cost money, and Mrs Williams is too wise to be extravagant."

"She was just sitting down to supper Ma'am."

"And what had she got for Supper?" "I did not observe". "Bread & Cheese I suppose." "I should never wish for a better supper". said Ellen. "You have never any reason" replied her Mother, "as a better is always provided for you." Miss Greville laughed excessively, as she constantly does at her Mother's wit.

Such is the humiliating Situation in which I am forced to appear while riding in her Ladyship's Coach—I dare not be impertinent, as my Mother is always admonishing me to be humble & patient if I wish to make my way in the world. She insists on my accepting every invitation of Lady Greville, or you may be certain that I would never enter either her House, or her Coach, with the disagreable certainty I always have of being abused for my Poverty while I am in them.— When we arrived at Ashburnham, it was nearly ten o'clock, which was an hour and a half later than we were desired to be there; but Lady Greville is too fashionable (or fancies herself to be so) to be punctual. The Dancing however was not begun as they waited for Miss Greville. I had not been long in the room before I was engaged to dance by Mr. Bernard but just as we were going to stand up, he recollected that his Servant had got his white Gloves, & immediately ran out to fetch them. In the mean time the Dancing began & Lady Greville in passing to another room went exactly before me.— She saw me & instantly stopping, said to me though there were several people close to us;

"Hey day, Miss Maria! What cannot you get a partner? Poor Young Lady! I am afraid your new Gown was put on for nothing. But do not despair; perhaps you may get a hop before the Evening is over." So saying, she passed on without hearing my repeated assurance of being engaged, & leaving me very provoked at being so exposed before every one—Mr Bernard however soon returned & by coming to me the moment he entered the room, and leading me to the Dancers, my Character I hope was cleared from the imputation Lady Greville had thrown on it, in the eyes of all the old Ladies who had heard her speech. I soon forgot all my vexations in the pleasure of dancing and of having the most agreable partner in the room. As he is moreover heir to a very large Estate I could see that Lady Greville did not look very well pleased when she found who had been his Choice.— She was determined to mortify me, and accordingly when we were sitting down between the dances, she came to me with *more* than her usual insulting importance attended by Miss Mason and said loud enough to be heard by half the people in the room, "Pray Miss Maria in what way of business was your Grandfather? for Miss Mason & I cannot agree whether he was a Grocer or a Bookbinder." I saw that she wanted to mortify me and was resolved if I possibly could to prevent her seeing that her scheme succeeded. "Neither Madam; he was a Wine Merchant." "Aye, I knew he was in some such low way—He broke [1] did not he?" "I beleive not Ma'am." "Did not he abscond?" "I never heard that he did" "At least he died insolvent?" "I was never told so before." "Why was not your Father as poor as a Rat?" "I fancy not;" "Was not he in the Kings Bench once?" "I never saw him there." *She* gave me *such* a look, & turned away in a great passion; while I was half delighted with myself for my impertinence, & half afraid of being thought too saucy. As Lady Greville was extremely angry with me, she took no further notice of me all the evening, and indeed had I been in favour I should have been equally neglected, as she was got into a party of great folks & she never speaks to me when she can to any one else. Miss Greville was with her Mother's party at Supper, but Ellen preferred staying with the Bernards & me. We had a very pleasant Dance & as Lady G—slept all the way home, I had a very comfortable ride.

The next day while we were at dinner Lady Greville's Coach stopped at the door, for that is the time of day she generally

---

1. Went bankrupt. The King's Bench to which Lady Greville later refers is a court which hears criminal cases, including bankruptcy cases.

contrives it should. She sent in a message by the Servant to say that "she should not get out but that Miss Maria must come to the Coach-door, as she wanted to speak to her, and that she must make haste & come immediately—" "What an impertinent Message Mama!" said I— "Go Maria—" replied She—Accordingly I went & was obliged to stand there at her Ladyships pleasure though the Wind was extremely high and very cold.

"Why I think Miss Maria you are not quite so smart as you were last night—But I did not come to examine your dress, but to tell you that you may dine with us the day after tomorrow—Not tomorrow, remember, do not come tomorrow, for we expect Lord and Lady Clermont & Sir Thomas Stanley's family—There will be no occasion for your being very fine for I shant send the Carriage—If it rains you may take an umbrella—" I could hardly help laughing at hearing her give me leave to keep myself dry— "and pray remember to be in time, for I shant wait—I hate my Victuals over-done—But you need not come *before* the time—How does your Mother do—? She is at dinner is not she?" "Yes Ma'am we were in the middle of dinner when your Ladyship came." "I am afraid you find it very cold Maria." said Ellen. "Yes, it is an horrible East wind"—said her Mother—"I assure you I can hardly bear the window down—But you are used to be blown about the wind Miss Maria & that is what has made your Complexion so ruddy & coarse. You young Ladies who cannot often ride in a Carriage never mind what weather you trudge in, or how the wind shews your legs. I would not have *my* Girls stand out of doors as you do in such a day as this. But some sort of people have no feelings either of cold or Delicacy—Well, remember that we shall expect you on Thursday at 5 o'clock—You must tell your Maid to come for you at night—There will be no Moon —and you will have an horrid walk home—My Compts [2] to your Mother—I am afraid your dinner will be cold—Drive on—" And away she went, leaving me in a great passion with her as she always does.

Maria Williams

From Catharine[†]

Kitty was by this time perfectly convinced that both in Natural Abilities, & acquired information, Edward Stanley was infinitely superior to his Sister. Her desire of knowing that he was so, had

2. Compliments.
† From *Volume the Third*, edited by R. W. Chapman (Oxford, 1951), pp. 108–115. Copyright 1951 by the Clarendon Press, Oxford. Reprinted by permission of the publishers. "Catharine" was probably written in 1792.

induced her to take every opportunity of turning the Conversation on History and they were very soon engaged in an historical dispute, for which no one was more calculated than Stanley who was so far from being really of any party, that he had scarcely a fixed opinion on the Subject. He could therefore always take either side, & always argue with temper. In his indifference on all such topics he was very unlike his Companion, whose judgement being guided by her feelings which were eager & warm, was easily decided, and though it was not always infallible, she defended it with a Spirit & Enthuisasm which marked her own reliance on it. They had continued therefore for sometime conversing in this manner on the character of Richard the 3^d, which he was warmly defending when he suddenly seized hold of her hand, and exclaiming with great emotion, "Upon my honour you are entirely mistaken," pressed it passionately to his lips, & ran out of the arbour. Astonished at this behaviour, for which she was wholly unable to account, she continued for a few Moments motionless on the seat where he had left her, and was then on the point of following him up the narrow walk through which he had passed, when on looking up the one that lay immediately before the arbour, she saw her Aunt walking towards her with more than her usual quickness. This explained at once the reason of his leaving her, but his leaving her in such Manner was rendered still more inexplicable by it. She felt a considerable degree of confusion at having been seen by her in such a place with Edward, and at having that part of his conduct, for which she could not herself account, witnessed by one to whom all gallantry was odious. She remained therefore confused distressed & irresolute, and suffered her Aunt to approach her, without leaving the Arbour. Mrs Percival's looks were by no means calculated to animate the spirits of her Neice, who in silence awaited her accusation, and in silence meditated her Defence. After a few Moments suspence, for Mrs Peterson [1] was too much fatigued to speak immediately, she began with great Anger and Asperity, the following harangue. "Well; *this* is beyond anything I could have supposed. *Profligate* as I *knew* you to be, I was not prepared for such a sight. This is beyond any thing you ever did *before*; beyond any thing I ever heard of in my Life! Such Impudence, I never witnessed before in such a Girl! And this is the reward for all the cares I have taken in your Education; for all my troubles & Anxieties; and Heaven knows how many they have been! All I wished for, was to breed you up virtuously; I never wanted you to play upon the Harpsichord, or draw better than any one else; but I

1. Mrs. Percival was named Peterson in an earlier version of the story; Jane Austen neglected to revise the manuscript here.

had hoped to see you respectable and good; to see you able &
willing to give an example of Modesty and Virtue to the Young
people here abouts. I bought you Blair's Sermons, and Cœlebs
in Search of a Wife,[2] I gave you the key to my own Library, and
borrowed a great many good books of my Neighbours for you,
all to this purpose. But I might have spared myself the trouble—
Oh! Catherine, you are an abandoned Creature, and I do not
know what will become of you. I am glad however, she continued
softening into some degree of Mildness, to see that you have some
shame for what you have done, and if you are really sorry for it,
and your future life is a life of penitence and reformation perhaps
you may be forgiven. But I plainly see that every thing is going
to sixes & sevens and all order will soon be at an end throughout
the Kingdom."

"Not however Ma'am the sooner, I hope, from any conduct
of mine, said Catherine in a tone of great humility, for upon my
honour I have done nothing this evening that can contribute to
overthrow the establishment of the kingdom."

"You are Mistaken Child, replied she; the welfare of every
Nation depends upon the virtue of it's individuals, and any one
who offends in so gross a manner against decorum & propriety
is certainly hastening it's ruin. You have been giving a bad example
to the World, and the World is but too well disposed to receive
such."

"Pardon me Madam, said her Neice; but I *can* have given an
Example only to *You,* for You alone have seen the offence. Upon
my word however there is no danger to fear from what I have
done; Mr Stanley's behaviour has given me as much surprise,
as it has done to You, and I can only suppose that it was the effect
of his high spirits, authorized in his opinion by our relationship.
But do you consider Madam that it is growing very late? Indeed
You had better return to the house." This speech as she well
knew, would be unanswerable with her Aunt, who instantly
rose, and hurried away under so many apprehensions for her own
health, as banished for the time all anxiety about her Neice, who
walked quietly by her side, revolving within her own Mind the
occurrence that had given her Aunt so much alarm. "I am astonished at my own imprudence, said Mrs Percival; How could I
be so forgetful as to sit down out of doors at such a time of
night. I shall certainly have a return of my rheumatism after
it—I begin to feel very chill already. I must have caught a dreadful
cold by this time—I am sure of being lain-up all the winter

2. *Cœlebs in Search of A Wife* is a
didactic novel by Hannah More published in 1809. Originally the passage
referred to Archbishop Secker's *Lectures on the Catechism of the Church
of England* (1769).

after it—" Then reckoning with her fingers, "Let me see; This is July; the cold weather will soon be coming in—August—September—October—November—December—January—February—March—April—Very likely I may not be tolerable again before May. I must and will have that arbour pulled down—it will be the death of me; who knows *now*, but what I may never recover—Such things *have* happened—My particular freind Miss Sarah Hutchinson's death was occasioned by nothing more—She staid out late one Evening in April, and got wet through for it rained very hard, and never changed her Cloathes when she came home—It is unknown how many people have died in consequence of catching Cold! I do not beleive there is a disorder in the World except the Smallpox which does not spring from it." It was in vain that Kitty endeavoured to convince her that her fears on the occasion were groundless; that it was not yet late enough to catch cold, and that even if it were, she might hope to escape any other complaint, and to recover in less than ten Months. Mrs Percival only replied that she hoped she knew more of Ill health than to be convinced in such a point by a Girl who had always been perfectly well, and hurried up stairs leaving Kitty to make her apologies to M^r & Mrs Stanley for going to bed—.

From Jane Austen's Letters[†]

To Cassandra Austen: [On *Pride and Prejudice*]

Chawton Friday Jan.ʸ 29 [1813]

* * * I want to tell you that I have got my own darling child from London; * * * Miss Benn [1] dined with us on the very day of the books coming & in the evening we set fairly at it, and read half the first vol. to her, prefacing that, having intelligence from Henry that such a work would soon appear, we had desired him to send it whenever it came out, and I believe it passed with her unsuspected. She was amused, poor soul! *That* she could not help, you know, with two such people to lead the way, but she really does seem to admire Elizabeth. I must confess that I think her as delightful a creature as ever appeared in print, and how I shall be able to tolerate those who do not like *her* at least I do not know. There are a few typical errors; and a 'said he,' or a 'said she,' would sometimes make the dialogue more immediately clear; but

I do not write for such dull elves
As have not a great deal of ingenuity themselves.

The second volume is shorter than I could wish, but the difference is not so much in reality as in look, there being a larger proportion of narrative in that part. I have lop't and crop't so successfully, however, that I imagine it must be rather shorter than S. & S. altogether. Now I will try to write of something else, & it shall

† From *Jane Austen's Letters to Her Sister Cassandra and Others*, edited by R. W. Chapman, 2nd edition (London, 1952). Letters 76, 77, 98, 100, 120, 126, 134, 103, 106. Copyright 1952 by Oxford University Press. Reprinted by permission of the publishers.

1. Miss Benn was the daughter of the rector of a village church near Chawton. The attempt to delude Miss Benn by pretending that the "darling child" of *Pride and Prejudice* was simply another novel written by somebody else was part of Jane Austen's reluctance to be identified as the author of her novels. It was not until several months after the publication of *Pride and Prejudice* that she began to be identified outside her family as the author of that novel and of *Sense and Sensibility*. "S. & S." is *Sense and Sensibility;* the "something else" she says she is beginning to write of turned out to be the subjects of *Mansfield Park*.

be a complete change of subject—ordination—I am glad to find
your enquiries have ended so well. If you could discover whether
Northamptonshire is a country of Hedgerows I should be glad
again.

Chawton, Thursday Feby 4 [1813]

My dear Cassandra

Your letter was truly welcome, and I am much obliged to you
all for your praise; it came at a right time, for I had had some
fits of disgust. Our second evening's reading to Miss Benn had
not pleased me so well, but I believe something must be attributed
to my mother's too rapid way of getting on: and though she
perfectly understands the characters herself, she cannot speak
as they ought. Upon the whole, however, I am quite vain enough and
well satisfied enough. The work is rather too light, and bright,
and sparkling; it wants shade; it wants to be stretched out here
and there with a long chapter of sense, if it could be had; if not,
of solemn specious nonsense, about something unconnected with
the story; an essay on writing, a critique on Walter Scott, or
the history of Buonaparté, or anything that would form a contrast,
and bring the reader with increased delight to the playfulness
and epigrammatism of the general style. I doubt your quite agreeing with me here. I know your starched notions.

To Anna Austen: [1] [On the Writing of Fiction]

Chawton Wednesday Aug: 10 [1814]

* * * Wednesday 17.—We have just finished the 1st of the 3
Books I had the pleasure of receiving yesterday; I read it aloud—&
we are all very much amused, & like the work quite as well
as ever.—I depend upon getting through another book before
dinner, but there is really a great deal of respectable reading in
your 48 Pages. I was an hour about it.—I have no doubt that
6 will make a very good sized volume.—You must be quite pleased
to have accomplished so much.—I like Lord P. & his Brother very
much;—I am only afraid that Lord P.—'s good nature will
make most people like him better than he deserves.—The whole
Portman Family are very good—& Lady Anne, who was your great
dread, you have succeeded particularly well with.—Bell Griffin
is just what she should be.—My Corrections have not been more
important than before;—here & there, we have thought the sense

1. Anna Austen was Jane Austen's
niece, the eldest daughter of her
brother James. Anna had sent her aunt
parts of a novel she was writing, and
these two letters are largely given to
Jane Austen's criticism of it. The novel
was never published.

might be expressed in fewer words—and I have scratched out Sir
Tho: from walking with the other Men to the Stables &c the very
day after his breaking his arm—for though I find your Papa *did*
walk out immediately after *his* arm was set, I think it can be
so little usual as to *appear* unnatural in a book—& it does not
seem to be material that Sir Tho: should go with them.—Lyme
will not do. Lyme is towards 40 miles distance from Dawlish &
would not be talked of there.—I have put Starcross indeed. If
you prefer *Exeter*, that must be always safe.—I have also scratched
out the Introduction between Lord P. & his Brother, & Mr. Griffin.
A Country Surgeon (dont tell Mr. C. Lyford) would not be introduced to Men of their rank.—And when Mr. Portman is first
brought in, he w^d not be introduced as *the Honble.—That*
distinction is never mentioned at such times;—at least I beleive
not.—Now, we have finished the 2^d book—or rather the 5th—I
do think you had better omit Lady Helena's postscript;—to those
who are acquainted with P. & P. it will seem an Imitation.—And
your Aunt C. & I both recommend your making a little alteration
in the last scene between Devereux F. and Lady Clanmurray
& her Daughters. We think they press him too much—more than
sensible Women or well-bred Women would do. *Lady C.* at least,
should have discretion enough to be sooner satisfied with his
determination of not going with them.—I am very much pleased
with Egerton as yet.—I did not expect to like him, but I do;
& Susan is a very nice little animated Creature—but St. Julian
is the delight of one's Life. He is quite interesting.—The whole
of his Break-off with Lady H. is very well done.—

Yes—Russel Square is a very proper distance from Berkeley
St.—We are reading the last book.—They must be *two* days
going from Dawlish to Bath; They are nearly 100 miles apart.

Thursday. We finished it last night, after our return from
drinking tea at the G^t House.[2]—The last chapter does not please
us quite so well, we do not thoroughly like the *Play;* perhaps
from having had too much of Plays in that way lately. And
we think you had better not leave England. Let the Portmans
go to Ireland, but as you know nothing of the Manners there,
you had better not go with them. You will be in danger of giving
false representations. Stick to Bath & the Foresters. There you
will be quite at home.—Your Aunt C. does not like desultory
novels, & is rather fearful yours will be too much so, that there
will be too frequent a change from one set of people to another,
& that circumstances will be sometimes introduced of apparent
consequence, which will lead to nothing.—It will not be so great

2. Chawton House, the principal house in the village, then owned by Jane Austen's
brother Edward.

an objection to *me*, if it does. I allow much more Latitude than she does—& think Nature and Spirit cover many sins of a wandering story—and People in general do not care so much about it—for your comfort.

Chawton Sept: 9. [1814]

My dear Anna

We have been very much amused by your 3 books, but I have a good many criticisms to make—more than you will like.—We are not satisfied with Mrs. F.'s settling herself as Tenant & near Neighbour to such a Man as Sir T. H. without having some other inducement to go there; she ought to have some friend living thereabouts to tempt her. A woman, going with two girls just growing up, into a Neighbourhood where she knows nobody but one Man, of not very good character, is an awkwardness which so prudent a woman as Mrs. F. would not be likely to fall into. Remember, she is very prudent;—you must not let her act inconsistently.—Give her a friend, & let that friend be invited to meet her at the Priory, & we shall have no objection to her dining there as she does; but otherwise, a woman in her situation would hardly go there, before she had been visited by other Families. — *** You describe a sweet place, but your descriptions are often more minute than will be liked. You give too many particulars of right hand & left.—Mrs. F. is not careful enough of Susan's health;—Susan ought not to be walking out so soon after Heavy rains, taking long walks in the dirt. An anxious Mother would not suffer it.—I like your Susan very much indeed, she is a sweet creature, her playfulness of fancy is very delightful. I like her as she is *now* exceedingly, but I am not so well satisfied with her behaviour to George R. At first she seemed all over attachment & feeling, & afterwards to have none at all; she is so extremely composed at the Ball, & so well-satisfied apparently with Mr. Morgan. She seems to have changed her Character.—You are now collecting your People delightfully, getting them exactly into such a spot as is the delight of my life;—3 or 4 Families in a Country Village is the very thing to work on—& I hope you will write a great deal more, & make full use of them while they are so very favourably arranged. You are but *now* coming to the heart & beauty of your book; till the heroine grows up, the fun must be imperfect—but I expect a great deal of entertainment from the next 3 or 4 books, & I hope you will not resent these remarks by sending me no more.—

To J. Edward Austen:[1] [On the Character of Her Fiction]

Chawton. Monday Dec: 16 [1816]

* * * Uncle Henry writes very superior Sermons.—You and I must try to get hold of one or two, & put them into our Novels;—it would be a fine help to a volume; & we could make our Heroine read it aloud of a Sunday Evening, just as well as Isabella Wardour in the Antiquary,[2] is made to read the History of the Hartz Demon in the ruins of St. Ruth—though I beleive, upon recollection, Lovell is the Reader.—By the bye, my dear Edward, I am quite concerned for the loss your Mother mentions in her Letter; two Chapters & a half to be missing is monstrous! It is well that *I* have not been at Steventon lately, & therefore cannot be suspected of purloining them;—two strong twigs & a half towards a Nest of my own, would have been something.—I do not think however that any theft of that sort would be really very useful to me. What should I do with your strong, manly, spirited Sketches, full of Variety and Glow?—How could I possibly join them on to the little bit (two Inches wide) of Ivory on which I work with so fine a Brush, as produces little effect after much labour?

To Fanny Knight:[1] [On Love and Courtship]

Chawton Nov: 18. [1814]—Friday

* * * Oh! dear Fanny, your mistake has been one that thousands of women fall into. He was the *first* young Man who attached himself to you. That was the charm, & most powerful it is.— Among the multitudes however that make the same mistake with yourself, there can be few indeed who have so little reason to regret it;—*his* Character and *his* attachment leave you nothing to be ashamed of.—Upon the whole, what is to be done? You certainly *have* encouraged him to such a point as to make him feel almost secure of you—you have no inclination for any other

1. James Edward Austen was Jane Austen's nephew, the son of her eldest brother James. The "Uncle Henry" referred to in this letter is Henry Thomas Austen, another of Jane's brothers. Henry was a banker until he decided to take orders at the age of forty-five.

2. A novel by Scott, published in 1816.
1. Fanny Knight was Jane Austen's niece, the daughter of her brother Edward. Edward took the family name of Knight when Thomas Knight, a distant relative, adopted him as his son and heir.

person—His situation in life, family, friends, & above all his character—his uncommonly amiable mind, strict principles, just notions, good habits—*all* that *you* know so well how to value, *All* that really is of the first importance—everything of this nature pleads his cause most strongly.—You have no doubt of his having superior Abilities—he has proved it at the University—he is I dare say such a scholar as your agreable, idle Brothers would ill bear a comparison with.—Oh! my dear Fanny, the more I write about him, the warmer my feelings become, the more strongly I feel the sterling worth of such a young Man & the desirableness of your growing in love with him again. I recommend this most thoroughly.—There *are* such beings in the World perhaps, one in a Thousand, as the Creature You and I should think perfection, Where Grace & Spirit are united to Worth, where the Manners are equal to the Heart & Understanding, but such a person may not come in your way, or if he does, he may not be the eldest son of a Man of Fortune, the Brother of your particular friend, & belonging to your own County.—Think of all this Fanny. Mr. J. P.—has advantages which do not often meet in one person. His only fault indeed seems Modesty. If he were less modest, he would be more agreable, speak louder & look Impudenter;—and is not it a fine Character of which Modesty is the only defect?—I have no doubt that he will get more lively & more like yourselves as he is more with you;—he will catch your ways if he belongs to you. And as to there being any objection from his *Goodness*, from the danger of his becoming even Evangelical, I cannot admit *that*. I am by no means convinced that we ought not all to be Evangelicals, & am at least persuaded that they who are so from Reason and Feeling, must be happiest & safest.—Do not be frightened from the connection by your Brothers having most wit. Wisdom is better than Wit, & in the long run will certainly have the laugh on her side; & don't be frightened by the idea of his acting more strictly up to the precepts of the New Testament than others.—And now, my dear Fanny, having written so much on one side of the question, I shall turn round & entreat you not to commit yourself farther, & not to think of accepting him unless you really do like him. Anything is to be preferred or endured rather than marrying without Affection; and if his deficiencies of Manner &c &c strike you more than all his good qualities, if you continue to think strongly of them, give him up at once.—Things are now in such a state, that you must resolve upon one or the other, either to allow him to go on as he has done, or whenever you are together behave with a coldness which may convince him that he has been deceiving himself.—I have no doubt of his suffering a good deal for a time, a great deal, when he feels that he must give you up;—but it is no creed of mine, as you must be well aware, that such sort of Disappointments kill anybody.

23 Hans Place, Wednesday Nov: 30 [1814]

* * * Now my dearest Fanny, I will begin a subject which comes in very naturally.—You frighten me out of my wits by your reference. Your affection gives me the highest pleasure, but indeed you must not let anything depend on my opinion. Your own feelings & none but your own, should determine such an important point.—So far however as answering your question, I have no scruple.—I am perfectly convinced that your present feelings supposing you were to marry *now*, would be sufficient for his happiness;—but when I think how very, very far it is from a *Now*, & take everything that *may be*, into consideration, I dare not say, 'Determine to accept him.' The risk is too great for *you*, unless your own Sentiments prompt it.—You will think me perverse perhaps; in my last letter I was urging everything in his favour, & now I am inclining the other way; but I cannot help it; I am at present more impressed with the possible Evil that may arise to *you* from engaging yourself to him—in word or mind—than with anything else.—When I consider how few young Men you have yet seen much of—how capable you are (yes, I do still think you *very* capable) of being really in love—and how full of temptation the next 6 or 7 years of your Life will probably be—(it is the very period of Life for the *strongest* attachments to be formed)—I cannot wish you with your present very cool feelings to devote yourself in honour to him. It is very true that you never may attach another Man, his equal altogether, but if that other Man has the power of attaching you *more*, he will be in your eyes the most perfect.—I shall be glad if you *can* revive past feelings, & from your unbiassed self resolve to go on as you have done, but this I do not expect, and without it I cannot wish you to be fettered. I should not be afraid of your *marrying* him;—with all his worth, you would soon love him enough for the happiness of both; but I should dread the continuance of this sort of tacit engagement, with such an uncertainty as there is, of *when* it may be completed.—Years may pass, before he is Independant.—You like him well enough to marry, but not well enough to wait.—The unpleasantness of appearing fickle is certainly great—but if you think you want Punishment for past Illusions, there it is—and nothing can be compared to the misery of being bound *without* Love, bound to one, & preferring another. *That* is a Punishment which you do *not* deserve.

The Composition of
Pride and Prejudice

R. W. CHAPMAN

Chronology of *Pride and Prejudice*†

The indications of time in *Pride and Prejudice* are frequent and precise; and though only three complete dates are given (that is with the day of the week and month), and one of those is certainly wrong, it is none the less possible to date almost every event with precision and with virtual certainty.

This conclusion has been arrived at by proceeding on the assumption that the dates which are given are mutually consistent. This assumption was justified by Mr. MacKinnon's demonstration that in writing *Mansfield Park* Miss Austen used an almanac. In *Pride and Prejudice* the calculation was for a time upset by the error just mentioned; but in the end we were able to get at the truth from other indications, and finally to correct the error.

There are three main sections in the narrative, in each of which we are able to follow the course of events from day to day. The first is the autumn at Meryton. Here we start from the date of Mr. Collins's visit, *Monday, November 18th*. From that we can reckon the date of the ball at Netherfield as Tuesday, 26 November; it is stated to be *Tuesday*, and the full date is confirmed by Bingley months later, when he says: 'We have not met since the 26th of November.'

The second section, Elizabeth's stay at Hunsford, cannot be precisely dated without inference from what precedes and follows.

In the third section, the events preceding and following the

† From R. W. Chapman, ed., *The Novels of Jane Austen* (Oxford, 1932), 3rd edition, II, 400–407.. Reprinted by permission of the Oxford University Press. I have deleted without indication page references to the Oxford edition, or changed them to accord with the present edition.

elopement, we naturally start from Mr. Gardiner's letter, dated *Monday, August* 2. But this is at once seen to be too early, by about a fortnight, both for what comes before and for what comes after. We must therefore work back from Mrs. Gardiner's letter, which is dated *September* 6.

Now Lydia and Wickham came to Longbourn on their wedding-day, which was a *Monday*, and were to stay 'not above ten days.' 'Soon after their arrival'—say on Wednesday or Thursday—Lydia let out the secret of Darcy's presence at the wedding. Elizabeth at once wrote to her aunt for enlightenment, and the answer, which she received 'as soon as she possibly could', is dated *Sept.* 6. The wedding-day, therefore, should be some six days before 6 September.

Assuming consistency, Mr. MacKinnon argued thus. In a year, following a year in which 18 November is a Monday, 6 September is Saturday in an ordinary year and Sunday in a leap year; the preceding Monday is 1 September in an ordinary year, 31 August in a leap year. But the wedding-day cannot have been 1 September, or Lydia could not, on the evening of that day, be sure that Wickham would 'kill more birds on the first of September, than any body else in the country.' It follows that the wedding was Monday, 31 August, in a leap year. It follows also that the almanacs used by Miss Austen were those of 1811 and 1812. For though 18 November was a Monday in 1799 and again in 1805, 1800 and 1806 were not leap years.

Everything is now clear. The date of Mr. Gardiner's express was not Monday, 2 August, but Monday, 17 August. But an express *was* sent to Longbourn on Sunday, 2 August, from Brighton, to announce the elopement. The most probable explanation of the mistake is that Miss Austen confused these two dates. Otherwise there is no mistake; and it was on Wednesday, 5 August, that Bingley told Elizabeth that 'It is above eight months. We have not met since the 26th of November, when we were all dancing together at Netherfield.'

The Hunsford dates are less precisely indicated; but if we assume consistency as before, the Saturday of Elizabeth's leaving can only have been 18 April; and Easter Day, therefore, can only have been 29 March. Now in 1812 Easter Day *was* 29 March.[1]

The calendar which is appended will make it clear that an almanac was used, and that Miss Austen knew where she was even when she does not tell us. It will be seen that the day on which Mrs. Bennet could get no fish was a Monday.

The dates or parts of dates printed in italics are quoted verbally;

1. Mr. MacKinnon actually arrived at 29 March for Easter Day, while calculating with an ideal calendar, and before consulting that of 1812.

the others, though inferred, are equally certain unless the contrary
is indicated.

1811

Tues. 15 *Oct.*   Mr. Collins's letter.
Tues. 12 Nov.   Jane is invited to dine at Netherfield.
Wed. 13 Nov.   Her illness.
Thurs. 14 Nov.   Mrs. Bennet at Netherfield. Elizabeth remains.
Fri. 15 Nov.   Darcy begins to feel his danger.
Sat. 16 Nov.   Darcy adheres to his book.
Sun. 17 Nov.   The sisters leave Netherfield.
Mon. 18 *Nov.*   Arrival of Mr. Collins. 'There is not a bit of fish
     to be got.'
Tues. 19 Nov.   First appearance of Wickham.
Wed. 20 Nov.   'A little bit of hot supper' with the Philipses.
Thurs. 21 Nov.   The Bingleys visit Longbourn.
Fri., Sat., Sun., Mon., 22–25 Nov.   A succession of rain.
Tues. 26 *Nov.*   The Ball at Netherfield.
Wed. 27 Nov.   Mr. Collins proposes.
     Bingley goes to London.
Thurs. 28 Nov.   The Bingleys leave Netherfield.
Fri. 29 Nov.   Mr. Collins at Lucas Lodge.
Sat. 30 Nov.   Mr. Collins returns to Hunsford.
Tues. 3 Dec.   His promised letter of thanks.
Mon. 16 Dec.   His return to Longbourn.
Sat. 21 Dec.   His departure.
Mon. 23 Dec.   The Gardiners come for Christmas.
Mon. 30 Dec.   They leave, taking Jane.

1812

Early in Jan.   Mr. Collins at Lucas Lodge.
Mon. 6 Jan.   Jane has been a week in town.
Tues. 7 Jan.   She calls in Grosvenor-street.
Wed. 8 Jan.   Charlotte says good-bye.
Thurs. 9 Jan.   The wedding.
Late in Jan.   Four weeks pass away, without Jane's seeing Bingley.
Early in March.   Elizabeth goes to London.
? Thurs. 5 March.   Arrival at Hunsford.
? Fri. 6 March.   Miss de Burgh at the Parsonage.
? Sat. 7 March.   They dine at Rosings.
? Thurs. 12 March.   Sir William leaves.
? Thurs. 19 March.   End of Elizabeth's first fortnight.
Mon. 23 March.   Darcy and Fitzwilliam arrive.
Tues. 24 March.   They call at the Parsonage.
     Jane has been in town these three months
     (30 Dec.–24 March)
Fri. 27 March.   It was doubtless on Good Friday that Darcy was
'seen at church'.

Sun. 29 March, *Easter-day,* 'almost a week after the gentlemen's arrival', the evening is spent at Rosings.
Mon. 30 March. Darcy calls.

Thurs. 9 *April.* Elizabeth's conversation with Colonel Fitzwilliam. Darcy proposes.
Fri. 10 April. Darcy's letter. Elizabeth has spent five weeks in Kent.
Sat. 11 April. Fitzwilliam and Darcy leave Kent, after a stay of 'nearly three weeks'. Dinner at Rosings.
Fri. 17 April. The evening spent at Rosings.
Sat. 18 April. Elizabeth goes to town, after a visit of six weeks (and a few days).

From May to July the dates are approximate only. Jane, Elizabeth, and Maria have left town in the second week in May, and the regiment was then to stay only a fortnight. It seems to have gone about the end of the month, for Lydia, who went with it, had been away three months on 31 August.

Jane and Elizabeth ought not, therefore, to be at Longbourn before Saturday, 9 May, or Monday, 11 May. If so, the statement that Elizabeth or Maria 'were to remain a few days' with the Gardiners is not exact, since they came to them on 18 April.

Again, Elizabeth after her return to Longbourn told Jane the 'secrets which had weighed on her for a fortnight'. She had known the secrets for nearly a month; but the reference seems to be to the period during which she had been with Jane but had not told her.

By the middle of June, Kitty Bennet had begun to recover, and the time fixed for the Northern tour was then a fortnight or more distant—say 1 July. It was then postponed for a fortnight—to say 15 July; and was to last three weeks or a month. The interval from 15 July to 3 August seems about right for the journey through 'Oxford, Blenheim, Warwick, Kenelworth, Birmingham, &c.', and the inspection of 'all the principal wonders' of Derbyshire.

From this point the dates can be determined by reckoning backwards from 6 September.

Sat. 1 Aug. Lydia's elopement (Elizabeth calls it *Sunday* night).
Sun. 2 Aug. Colonel Forster sends an express to Longbourn.
Mon. 3 Aug. Colonel Forster comes to Longbourn.
 The Gardiners and Elizabeth at Bakewell.
Tues. 4 Aug. Mr. Bennet goes to town.
 The Gardiners and Elizabeth visit Pemberley.
Wed. 5 Aug. Colonel Forster is back at Brighton. Mr. Bennet writes to Jane.

Darcy and his sister visit Elizabeth.

Bingley says it is 'above eight months' since 26 Nov.

Thurs. 6 Aug. The Gardiners and Elizabeth at Pemberley.

Fri. 7 Aug. Elizabeth hears from Jane. The dinner at Pemberley is cancelled, and the Gardiners and Elizabeth leave Lambton.

Sat. 8 Aug. They arrive at Longbourn.

Darcy leaves Derbyshire for London.

Sun. 9 Aug. Mr. Gardiner leaves Longbourn.

Tues. 11 Aug. Mrs. Gardiner hears from her husband.

Fri. 14 Aug. Darcy calls in Gracechurch-street.

Sat. 15 Aug. Mr. Bennet returns.

Mr. Gardiner goes back to town.

Darcy calls again, having ascertained that Mr. Bennet is gone.

Sun. 16 Aug. Darcy sees Mr. and Mrs. Gardiner.

Mon. 17 Aug. Mr. Gardiner's express (misdated *August* 2).

Matters 'all settled' between Mr. Gardiner and Darcy.

Lydia goes to Gracechurch-street, where she remains a fortnight.

Mrs. Bennet comes down stairs, for the first time for a fortnight (since 2 Aug.).

Mon. 31 Aug. Wedding of Lydia and Wickham; they come to Longbourn; Lydia is sure Wickham will 'kill more birds on the first of September, than any body else in the country'.

Tues. 1 Sept. Darcy dines with the Gardiners.

Wed. 2 Sept. Jane writes to Mrs. Gardiner.

Wed. 2 Sept., or *Thurs.* 3 Sept. Darcy leaves town.

? Fri. 4 Sept. Elizabeth asks Mrs. Gardiner for an explanation of Lydia's disclosures.

Sun. 6 *Sept.* Mrs. Gardiner replies.

? Thurs. 10 Sept. The Wickhams leave.

Wed. 16 or *Thurs.* 17 Sept. Bingley expected at Netherfield.

It is now 'about a twelvemonth' since Mr. Bennet's waiting upon him had been first canvassed; he was 'to take possession before Michaelmas', 1811.

? Sat. 19 Sept. Bingley and Darcy call.

Tues. 22 Sept. They dine at Longbourn.

? Wed. 23 Sept. Darcy's confession to Bingley.

? Thurs. 24 Sept. Darcy leaves for town, to return in ten days time. Bingley calls alone.

Fri. 25 Sept. He comes to dine, and stays supper.

Sat. 26 Sept. Bingley comes to shoot. He and Jane are engaged.

? Sat. 3 Oct. Lady Catherine's visit, about a week after the engagement, and two days after the 'report of a most alarming nature' had reached her.

Sun. 4 Oct. Mr. Bennet hears from Mr. Collins, who writing no
    doubt on Fri. 2 Oct. says he mentioned the rumour of Eliza-
    beth's engagement to Darcy 'to her ladyship last night'.
? Tues. 6 Oct. Bingley brings Darcy. The proposal.
? Wed. 7 Oct. They walk to Oakham Mount.
? Thurs. 8 Oct. Darcy dines at Longbourn.

Before Christmas. The double wedding. The Gardiners are 'to
    come to Pemberley at Christmas'.

If the conclusions stated are accepted, we must modify the
assumption which is commonly made, though it rests on slender
evidence, that *Pride and Prejudice* as we have it is substantially
the same book as *First Impressions*. But the view we take of the
extent and importance of the revision, performed within a year
or two of publication, does not necessarily affect our view of
the 'dramatic' date. Miss Austen's punctilious observance of the
calendars of 1811 and 1812—if we are right in supposing that
she did so observe them—was for her own satisfaction; she did
not expect her readers to play the detective. We are still free,
therefore, to suppose, if we choose, that she at all times conceived
the events as belonging to the closing decade of the eighteenth
century. One episode, indeed, cannot with strict propriety belong
to any other time. The militia camps at Brighton in 1793, 1794,
and 1795 were important and notorious; and I cannot find that
the militia were there in force in any later year. But the militia
was later again embodied, from 1803 continuously until 1814;
and we are not bound to suppose that Miss Austen conceived
the Brighton episode as 'dating' the story either for herself or
for her readers.

The only other indication of a 'dramatic' date is the reference
in the last chapter to the fortunes of the Wickhams 'when the
restoration of peace dismissed them to a home'. The Peace of
Amiens was concluded in March 1802; and it is permissible to
conjecture that Miss Austen revised her work between this date
and the resumption of hostilities. But it is perhaps equally possible
that in 1812 she looked forward to the peace that was still to
come.

However this may be, I feel a certain difficulty in supposing
that, in publishing *Pride and Prejudice* in 1813, Miss Austen
definitely conceived its action as taking place some ten years (or
more) earlier. It will be remembered that when she in 1816 prepared *Catherine* for publication, she thought it necessary to
apologize for 'those parts of the work which thirteen years have
made comparatively obsolete'; and that in the end she could
not make up her mind to publish. She may, of course, have been
less scrupulous in 1812. But *Pride and Prejudice* has always

seemed to me a book of greater maturity than is credible if we suppose it to have been written, much as we know it, when its author was only one-and-twenty. The disparity between *Pride and Prejudice* and *Sense and Sensibility* is very striking. On the other hand, *Pride and Prejudice* has its immaturities, and it would be difficult to argue, on internal evidence, that it is much later than *Northanger Abbey*.

Q. D. LEAVIS

[Pride and Prejudice and Jane Austen's Early Reading and Writing]†

It is common to speak of Jane Austen's novels as a miracle; the accepted attitude to them is conveniently summarised by Professor Caroline Spurgeon in her address on Jane Austen to the British Academy:

'But Jane Austen is more than a classic; she is also one of the little company whose work is of the nature of a miracle . . . That is to say, there is nothing whatever in the surroundings of these particular writers [Keats, Chatterton, Jane Austen, Emily Brontë], their upbringing, opportunities or training, to account for the quality of their literary work.' [1]

The business of literary criticism is surely not to say 'Inspiration' and fall down and worship, and in the case of Jane Austen it is certainly not entitled to take up such an unprofitable attitude. For in Jane Austen literary criticism has, I believe, a uniquely documented case of the origin and development of artistic expression, and an enquiry into the nature of her genius and the process by which it developed can go very far indeed on sure ground. Thanks to Dr. Chapman's labours we have for some time had at our disposal a properly edited text of nearly all her surviving

† From Q. D. Leavis, "A Critical Theory of Jane Austen's Writings," *Scrutiny*, X (1942), 61–75. Reprinted by permission of the Cambridge University Press and Q. D. Leavis. Mrs. Leavis's long study is continued in *"Lady Susan* into *Mansfield Park," Scrutiny*, X (1942), 114–142 and 272–294. B. C. Southam, in the appendix to *Jane Austen's Literary Manuscripts* (London, 1964), dissents from Mrs. Leavis's "critical theory," especially as it concerns the composition of novels made into their final forms after the composition of *Pride and Prejudice*. See also Marvin Mudrick's book and Robert Liddell's study, both cited in the bibliography, for comments about Mrs. Leavis's claims for the close connections between Jane Austen's early writing and her mature fiction.
1. For the source of Professor Spurgeon's remarks, and of those of Professor Garrod, see the bibliography to this edition. A part of the essay by A. C. Bradley to which Mrs. Leavis refers is reprinted below [*Editor*].

writings, and scholarship, in his person chiefly, has brilliantly made out a number of interesting facts which have not yet however been translated into the language of literary criticism.

Correlated with Professor Spurgeon's attitude to the Austen novels is the classical account of their author as a certain kind of novelist, one who wrote her best at the age of twenty (Professor Oliver Elton), whose work 'shows no development' (Professor Garrod), whose novels 'make exceptionally peaceful reading' (A. C. Bradley); one scholar writes of her primness, another of her 'sunny temper,' with equal infelicity, and all apologize for her inability to dwell on guilt and misery, the French Revolution and the Napoleonic Wars. This account assumes among other things that the novels were written in 'two distinct groups, separated by a considerable interval of time . . . thus, to put it roughly, the first group of three were written between the ages of twenty and twenty-two, and the second group between the ages of thirty-five and forty' and only notices revision where internal dating makes it inevitable—e.g., the mention of Belinda (published 1801) in *Northanger Abbey*, or of Scott as a popular poet in *Sense and Sensibility* (which indicates a revision in 1809). As long ago as 1922 Dr. Chapman pointed out—but cautiously, as becomes a scholar, and with a distinct refusal to commit himself to any positive deductions—that 'the chronology of Miss Austen's novels is unusually obscure' and that for 'the great part of this assumption there is little warrant.' But we can go much farther than this. There are besides the six novels three volumes of early work in manuscript, of which two have been published, and drafts and miscellaneous pieces at various stages, as well as the two volumes of correspondence, which taken together offer the literary detective as well as the literary critic a harvest of clues and evidence; and these writings cover her life from the age of fifteen to her death. Cassandra Austen, besides her notorious work in censoring those of her sister's letters which she did not destroy, left a memorandum of the dates of composition of some of her sister's work; other evidence exists in Jane's *Letters*, and the manuscripts generally tell their own story. Moreover she had a habit of constructing her novels on the current calendar for her own convenience. From these data we can make out the following table of Miss Austen's working life:

Jane Austen, 1775–1817

Between 1789 and 1793 she turned out for the amusement of her family a mass of satiric work (some dramatic and some in epistolary form), some unfinished stories, and many type epistles. From these she selected a number for preservation by copying them at intervals (to judge by the handwriting, over some years) into three volumes. Of these three, *Volume the First* has been edited and published by Dr. Chapman; *Volume the Second* has been published under the title of one of its pieces, *Love and Freindship*; while the third volume has unfortunately never been printed,[1] though a sufficient description of it can be found in the *Life and Letters* published by W. and R. A. Austen-Leigh.

1795 *ca. Elinor and Marianne* was written as a novel in letter-form.

1796–7. *First Impressions* written, as a novel in letter-form.

1797. *Elinor and Marianne* was rewritten as *Sense and Sensibility*; the *Memoir* says 'in its present form' which means only that it was no longer in letters; in some respects at least it could not have been the novel that we know.

1797–8. *Susan*, a novel, probably written up from an unfinished story in *Volume the Third* called 'Catharine, or the Bower.'

1803. *Susan* was rewritten and sent to a publisher.

Before 1805, probably in the interval between the two versions of *Susan*, *Lady Susan*, an epistolary *nouvelle*, was written. It is untitled; its paper is water-marked 1805, but what we have is 'not a draft but a fair copy' and judging by Jane Austen's habits of composition we can assume that this is a rewrite after a period of years.

Between 1806 and 1807 a new novel, *The Watsons*, was started; we have a fair copy corrected, but not finished. Calendar evidence shows it was located in 1807.

1808–9. *Lady Susan*, on my theory, was expanded into *Mansfield Park* (the 1808–9 calendar was used to construct *Mansfield Park*).

1809. *Susan* probably revised again.

1809–10. *Sense and Sensibility* rewritten or revised, for publication in 1811.

1810–12. *Pride and Prejudice* was rewritten for publication in 1813, radically beyond all doubt since it is buit on the punctilious observance of the 1811–1812 calendar.

1811–1813. *Mansfield Park* rewritten as we know it for publication in 1814. Since she spent so long over it, the alterations were probably considerable, and I suspect the 1808–9 version to have been epistolary.

1814–1815. *Emma* written up for publication in 1816 from the earlier story *The Watsons* (as I hope to show).

1815–1816. *The Elliots* written, but not I believe intended for publication as it stands; two of the last chapters towards the final version were completely rewritten, and we have the re-

---

1. Since the appearance of Mrs. Leavis's essay, this volume has been printed as *Volume the Second*, ed. B. C. Southam (Oxford, 1963) [*Editor*].

jected chapter to compare. The prototype, which exists for every other novel, could hardly have not existed for this work, and as the author's hands were full from 1806 onwards, it can possibly be allotted to the pre-1806 gap. Other reasons can be adduced in support of my theory.

1816–17. *Susan* was revised for publication as *Catherine*; it was published posthumously as *Northanger Abbey*, with *The Elliots* as *Persuasion*, by Henry Austen, who gave both these books the names we know them by.

Jan.–March, 1817. *Sanditon*, a new novel of which she was writing the first draft when she died. The MS. remains for us to see what a first draft of hers looked like.

We can see from this table of what Jane Austen chose to preserve of her work and the records, accidentally preserved, of what she preferred to destroy, that our author wrote unceasingly (we should be unjustified in assuming that nothing was being written in the one period, 1798–1803, for which we happen to have no evidence). She had, it appears, some very peculiar habits of composition, which quite destroy the popular notion of her writing by direct inspiration as it were. One habit was to lay down several keels in succession and then do something to each in turn, never having less than three on the stocks but always working at any one over a period of years before launching it, and allowing twelve clear months at least for each final reworking. Another was to start writing her novels much further back in conception than most novelists or perhaps than any other novelist; what is usually a process of rapid and largely unconscious mental selecting, rejecting and reconstituting, was in her case a matter of thoroughly conscious, laborious, separate draftings; in every case except that of *Persuasion* we know, or I hope to show that we know, of early versions which bear little resemblance to the novels as published. Indeed, I propose to argue that her novels are geological structures, the earliest layer going back to her earliest writings, with subsequent accretions from her reading, her personal life and those lives most closely connected with hers, all recast—and this is what gives them their coherence and artistic significance—under the pressure of deep disturbances in her own emotional life at a given time.

This at least is clear, that Miss Austen was not an inspired amateur who had scribbled in childhood and then lightly tossed off masterpieces between callers; she was a steady professional writer who had to put in many years of thought and labour to achieve each novel, and she took her novels very seriously. Her methods were in fact so laborious that it is no wonder that she only produced six novels in twenty-seven years, and the last of those not finally revised, while another (*Northanger Abbey*) was so immature that she despaired of doing anything with it. Another point that emerges is that she was decidedly not precociously mature as an artist. There is no reason whatever to suppose that *Pride and Prejudice, Sense and Sensibility,* and *Northanger Abbey* as we know them agreed in form, tone, content or intention, with those versions which were offered earlier to publishers who (not unnaturally) did not care to publish them. In their original form they were no doubt as thin and flat as *The Watsons,* as sketchy as *Sanditon,* as unsympathetic as *Lady Susan,* and as much dependent for the most part on family jokes as *Northanger Abbey* still is. The novels as we know them are palimpsests through whose surface portions of earlier versions, or of other and earlier compositions quite unrelated, constantly protrude, so that we read from place to place at different levels. Two of the novels, *Emma* and *Mansfield Park,* are the results of an evolutionary process of composition, and bristle with vestigial traits. The novels as a whole then cannot be said to be the work of any given date, but the published versions are certainly to be ascribed to Jane Austen at the final date of revision, since before such final revisions they would probably have been unrecognizable to us now. Thus *Pride and Prejudice* was not the work of a girl of twenty-one but of a woman aged thirty-five to thirty-seven, and we have actually nothing as it was written besides the juvenilia till *Lady Susan,* a slight but accomplished piece of writing in her thirtieth year, and *The Watsons,* a thin sketch for a later novel, written when she was two years older. Since it is not until *Emma,* written when she was nearly forty, that she brings off a mature and artistically perfect novel, in which the various elements are for the first time integrated, we are justified in concluding that she was artistically a late developer as well as a slow and laborious writer. The wit similarly has a pedigree, so have the characters and much of the plots, and even the details of the intrigue. Much more in the novels is dependent on reference to, reaction against, and borrowings from, other novelists than is commonly realized, I believe. *Northanger Abbey* is generally held to be a 'sport,' in its relation to the Gothic novels, but several of her novels were largely, and the others partially, conceived in a similar manner and are as little to be appreciated without at least as much realization of what they are tilting against or referring to. Far from the Austen novels having fallen straight from heaven into the publisher's lap, so to speak, they can be accounted for in even greater detail than other literary compositions, for Jane Austen was not a fertile writer. Her invention except in one limited respect was very meagre; casual jottings of aspects of 'character' and bits of situation and stage business made in her teens turn up at intervals to be worked into the shape required by the story in hand; a great deal of what seems to be creation can be traced through her surviving letters to have originated in life; much of her novels consists of manipulation and differentiation of characters and group-relations made long before in cruder and more general or merely burlesque pieces of writing; rarely is anything abandoned, however slight, Jane Austen's practice being rather thriftily to 'make over.' Her inspiration then turns out to be, as Inspiration so often does, a matter of hard work—radical revision in the light of a maturer taste and a severe self-criticism, and under the pressure of a more and more clearly defined intention over a space of years. Her invention consists chiefly in translating the general into the particular; she proceeds from the crude comprehensive outline and the dashing sketch to something subtle and specialized by splitting up and separating out—in fact her tendency is to overdo this process, so that in the end Mrs. Norris [in *Mansfield Park*] and Elizabeth Elliot and Miss Bingley and Lady Catherine are each too much on one note, rather monotonous and over-attenuated, whereas the original piece of characterization in the void from which they all derive, Lady Greville in the second MS. volume, is more robust in possessing all these facets—she abounds in all these forms of feminine ill-nature instead of exhibiting only the one eternally, and is better comedy because she has no such tendency to get on the reader's nerves. But these later inventions were intended to get on the reader's nerves because they were aspects of social intercourse that had got on Miss Austen's.

I will take one illustration, a particularly neat one, of a process common in her work, from the second MS. volume (which like the first is of the greatest interest to the literary critic). In 'A Collection of Letters' Letter the Third, the only one which is not burlesque, is an account by 'a young lady in reduced circumstances' of a couple of encounters with the local great lady who first takes her to a ball and then calls next day to invite her to dinner. This letter is probably the best-known piece of Austen 'juvenilia' and it has been noticed by one or two critics that Lady Catherine de Bourgh is descended from Lady Greville and that the incident of Charlotte Collins being called out to the carriage in all that wind is also reproduced from this Letter. But anyone who will turn it up in the *Love and Friendship* volume, however sceptically, will have to admit that it indisputably contains all the following:

1. Lady Catherine's general line of impertinence to Elizabeth and some incidents slightly improved in *Pride and Prejudice*.

2. Mrs. Norris's scolding Fanny when she is going out to dine with the Grants—the business about the carriage and walking in spite of the possible rain and the necessity of knowing her place are all there, with just the same tone of voice.

3. The ball itself produces two balls later on, the one in *Pride and Prejudice* where Miss Bingley is rude to Eliza and the one in *Northanger Abbey* where the situation of being engaged to a partner who turns up at the last minute when the heroine is embarrassed at seeming to have no partner, is here first set down. (And this last is borrowed from *Evelina*.)

4. The incident of Miss de Bourgh stopping her carriage, sending for Charlotte to come out in all that wind, 'abominably rude,' etc.

5. The conversation between the Bingley sisters on Eliza's indelicacy in taking a cross-country walk is clearly anticipated in Lady Greville's remarks to the letter-writer in similar phrases.

6. The characters of Lady Catherine and Mrs. Norris are unmistakably delineated in Lady Greville, just as the sensitive and down-trodden Maria Williams who writes the Letter, with the humble mother, is the original of Fanny Price. * * *

The large Austen family, well-born, but not well off, well-educated, singularly united, with tentacles of kinsfolk reaching out into great houses, parsonages rich and poor, Bath and London, the navy and the militia, with its theatricals, dances, flirtations, marriages and invalids was a rich source of raw material for any novelist, but it contributed in two less obvious respects to Jane's equipment. One was that in her capacity of constant visitor to outlying branches she necessarily wrote letters home, addressed it is true to Cassandra, but evidently meant, as Dr. Chapman notes, to be read aloud to a group, keeping them in touch with their friends and relatives; similarly, when at home she wrote to friends, nieces and nephews to transmit family news and give advice. In these letters we can not only find much that later went into the novels, but we can see that material in a preliminary stage, half-way between life and art. The character-sketches, the notes on conduct and social functions, were written for an audience, and written also from a point of view that is the novelist's. There is unfortunately no room here to enlarge on this interesting

relation of the letters to the novels, but I will summarize my argument by saying simply that without the letter-writing one of
the conditions essential to the production of the novels would
not have existed; the letter-writing, like the drafting of story
into novel at different stages of composition, was part of the
process that made possible the unique Austen novels.

The other service this family unit rendered the future novelist
was in providing a literary springboard in its reactions to novels,
which the Austens consumed largely but in no uncritical spirit.
In addition to acting among themselves (these amateur theatricals
have left of course other traces beside the acting in *Mansfield
Park*: a preference after epistolary for dramatic narrative, and a
tendency to characterization too broad for any medium but the
footlights)—in addition to acting plays the Austens by reading
aloud and discussing their reading had evidently acquired by the
time Jane was fifteen a common stock of conversational allusions,
jokes, understandings about the absurdities of their favourite
writers and certain literary criteria. The fruits of this were the
contents of the three manuscript volumes—these items have
mock dedications to members of the family. Some of these remain
private jokes, others are jokes we can understand, while some
though closely related to the rest are positive pieces of original
composition. The trend of this family joke is satiric, but it
implies also a habit of discussing the *theory* of novel composition
and style. Jane was a sound critic of the novel before she began
to be a novelist at all (among other numerous references in the
letters to this subject there is a significant one to Cassandra—'I
know your starched notions' in the matter of digressions in fiction). The family joke and writing for a circle which understood
her allusions gave her the habit of writing with a side-glance at
her audience, which though it has in the earlier novels given us
some cryptic passages is nevertheless the source of that intimate
tone with the reader that has made her so popular. It is the recollection of such a critical audience liable to pounce that accounts
also for her poise—her hold on herself (so disastrously lacking in
George Eliot) which constantly evokes self-ironical touches like
that in *Persuasion* where, after Anne's indulgence in the poetry
of autumn melancholy, she remarks on 'the ploughs at work [that]
spoke the farmer, counteracting the sweets of poetical despond-
ence, and meaning to have spring again.'

The Austen family were hard-headed and demanded not poetry
but uncompromising fidelity to nature in their fiction. There is
hardly anything easier to ridicule in literature than the eighteenth-
century novel by contrasting it with daily life, particularly when
manners, idiom and social conventions changed as rapidly as they

can be seen to have done between *Clarissa* and *Evelina*,[2] and *Evelina* and *Pride and Prejudice*. So the MS. volumes are full of burlesques of the literary conventions, the style and the conversations of Richardson, Goldsmith, Sterne, Fanny Burney, and Henry Mackenzie among others, of the novel of sentiment, the language of sensibility and the language of morality. The value of such a start is obvious when compared with the 'sedulous ape' recipe for training an artist of a century later: dead conventions are not propagated thus, and a study of how other novelists wrote combined with a critical perception of where such writing leads and why and how not to get there, is a tremendous help in finding where one wishes to go oneself. But the burlesque can already be seen in the MS. volumes to have a positive side. Though it is impossible here to enter on a detailed examination of *Volume the First* and *Love and Freindship* a few main strands are worth following.

There is an unconsciously very funny scene in *Evelina* (a novel the Austens seem to have known by heart) where Evelina visits her hitherto unknown father and experiences the correct emotions on the occasion, a hackneyed enough situation in eighteenth-century fiction to be satirized as a type of the false. Make the father a grandfather and multiply the grandchildren, and the burlesque does itself, as can be seen in Letter II of *Love and Freindship*. This device is used again, as we shall see, in *Pride and Prejudice*. Many systematic attempts to prepare booby-traps for the reader and to throw cold water on his expectations are tried out in these pieces for use later in the novels. Many characters in the novels are to be recognized in a certain primitive form and since their origin is an important clue to the way Jane Austen conceived her novels, I will give some illustrations of what I shall call the functional origin of her characters.

The burlesque nature of the early work is visibly the source also of *Northanger Abbey*. Catherine is the anti-heroine of romance, and her family and upbringing and disposition are described entirely in anti-romantic terms. It is essential for the purposes of the joke that the book was meant to be that Catherine should be simple-minded, unsentimental and commonplace, that unsolicited she should fall in love with a young man who snubs and educates her instead of adoring her, and should be launched into the world by an anti-chaperone (for Mrs. Allen, like Catherine, is purely functional—hence her concentration on herself and her inability to advise, instruct or watch over her charge). This is

2. Samuel Richardson's *Clarissa* was published in 1747–48; Fanny Burney's *Evelina* in 1788; and her *Cecilia*, to which Mrs. Leavis refers below, in 1782 [*Editor*].

generally admitted. But *Pride and Prejudice* was originally the same kind of story as *Northanger Abbey* and it is ignorance of this that has led the critics to debate problems such as whether Darcy is, like Mrs. Jennings, an instance of the artist's having changed her mind about the character, whether Elizabeth Bennet is open to the charge of pertness, whether Mr. Collins could possibly have existed. But such problems are non-existent. Besides taking its title from the moral of *Cecilia*, *Pride and Prejudice* takes a great deal beside, part borrowed and part burlesqued. One of the absurdities of Cecilia is her behaviour in defeating, out of the morbid delicacy proper to Burney heroines, the hero Delvile's attempts to come to an explanation with her about his feelings and the obstacles to a union with her (like Darcy he is driven to write her a long letter); it is necessary in her rôle of an anti-Cecilia that Elizabeth should be vigorous-minded, should challenge decorum by her conversation and habits, and eventually invite her lover's proposal; she is 'pert' and of a coming-on disposition, just as necessarily as Catherine is green and dense. Darcy is only Delvile with the minimum of inside necessary to make plausible his conduct (predetermined by the object of the novel). For the original conception of *First Impressions* was undoubtedly to rewrite the story of Cecilia in realistic terms, just as *Susan* or *Catherine* was both to show up *Udolpho* and *The Romance of the Forest* and to contrast the romantic heroine's entry into the world *(Evelina)* with the everyday equivalent. What would be the reactions of a real girl if, like Cecilia, she was appealed to by her lover's family not to marry him because she was an unsuitable match? In *Cecilia* the hero's mother, a 'noble' aristocratic figure, intended to be impressive, attacks Cecilia with all the appeals of which Lady Catherine's arguments to Elizabeth are a close but comic version (and succeeds in her appeal to Cecilia's higher nature!) Now the character of the intolerable great lady was fished out of Letter the Third in the second MS. volume, as I have noted earlier; by putting her into the high-minded Mrs. Delvile's place, changing mother for aunt (the old trick of substituting grandfather for father in burlesque), and suppressing the plausible objections to the marriage which existed in the original (the terms of a will which binds the heiress Cecilia), the *moral* situation is exquisitely burlesqued and the incredibly unrealistic tone of *Cecilia* brought down with a jolt to the level of stage-comedy. Mr. Collins is invented in functional terms for the same purpose; his lengthy proposal is devised to give the author's views on Fanny Burney's preposterous conventions about female behaviour (exhibited by both Evelina and Cecilia)—'the usual practice of elegant females'—and the stilted, grotesquely Johnsonian, diction of Burney lovers (funnier because the professions in Mr. Collins's case are bogus). And the disapproval of Bingley's sisters as a possible bar to his marrying Jane that is put forward by Jane for ridicule by Elizabeth, is also part of the anti-*Cecilia* intention: the Bingley sisters underline the Lady Catherine-Mrs. Delvile skit. The Austens certainly grasped all this, but unless we realize it too, and a whole order of such literary allusions in the novels, we cannot respond to the novels adequately.

A few more of the sources of *Pride and Prejudice* may be noted here. Mary Bennet, who like Mr. Collins has been objected to on the grounds of impossibility, is also a machine for burlesque. She is to be found in isolation in a letter in the second MS. volume called 'The Female Philosopher,' a mock portrait of 'the sensible, the amiable Julia' who 'utters sentiments of Morality worthy of a heart like her own.' A specimen of her utterances:

> 'Mr. Millar observed (and very justly too) that many events had befallen each during that interval of time, which gave occasion to the lovely Julia for making most sensible reflections on the many changes in their situation which so long a period had occasioned, on the advantages of some and the disadvantages of others. From this subject she made a short digression to the instability of human pleasures and the uncertainty of their duration, which led her to observe that all earthly Joys must be imperfect . . .'

On the other hand, there are many positive borrowings from Fanny Burney not in the least in a spirit of satire. The conversation overheard, at the ball where Darcy first appears, by Elizabeth's friend, when Darcy speaks slightingly of Elizabeth, is lifted from *Evelina*, where Evelina's friend overhears the hero speak similarly of Evelina at the ball at which they first meet. Mrs. Bennet in her rôle of embarrassing her superior offspring by her vulgar and insensitive conversation, particularly on the subject of matches, is Mrs. Belfield in *Cecilia*. Elizabeth's twitting of Lady Catherine both at Hunsford and at Longbourn is an echo of the lively impertinence of the Delvile's niece, a Lady Honoria, whose cool wit at the expense of Mr. and Mrs. Delvile's convictions of superiority (his on grounds of family dignity, hers on the score of highmindedness) is quite as amusing and cleverly managed, and rather freer in scope.

But in another function Mrs. Bennet was taken from the first MS. volume. When *Pride and Prejudice* was expanded from an anti-*Cecilia* its theme developed from a contrast between sentimental and intuitive human behaviour in a given situation, to a general examination of a subject to which Jane Austen was certainly giving much thought at this time, the subject of marriage. We can always see where Miss Austen's interests and preoccupations lie in any novel by observing where the stress falls and where the deepest current of feeling flows. The conversations between Jane and Elizabeth about Charlotte's engagements to Mr. Collins, about the disparity between the sexes in courtship and about the sisters' different outlooks on life, and between Elizabeth and Charlotte and Elizabeth and Mrs. Gardiner about marriage and courtship, are noticed by every reader, I suppose, as differing in tone from the rest of the novel. The obverse to the marriage of love in the face of family disapprobation is the marriage of convenience that is approved by worldly wisdom. This idea is used again later in *Mansfield Park* and in *Persuasion*, but it is not new in Jane Austen's writings even in *Pride and Prejudice*. Charlotte Lucas's situation, Mr. Collins's, and his visit with unspecified matrimonial intent to Longbourn, had already been plotted out in an early story in the first MS. volume. This story in letter form is called 'The Three Sisters.'

The situation therein of the mother in the country with £500 a year and three daughters to marry was used later for *Sense and Sensibility*, but the action of the story is that of the Collins-Bennet-Lucas intrigue. Mr. Watts, a desirable *parti* but disagreeable and ridiculous, proposes like Mr. Collins to ally himself with this family, the individual wife being a matter of indifference, and similarly applies first to the eldest daughter, Mary. None of the girls wishes to marry him, but the eldest is anxious to be married and is eventually persuaded by the other two (the second sister is the candid Jane Bennet, the youngest the lively and determined Elizabeth) to accept him for his establishment and from jealous fear that one of her sisters will if she won't. Mary's mamma, like Elizabeth's, engages in battle with her daughters, declaring 'If Mary won't have him Sophy must, and if Sophy won't Georgiana *shall*.' Like Mrs. Bennet's, 'my Mother's resolution I am sorry to say is generally more strictly kept than rationally formed.' [Mrs. Bennet's nerves and silliness, however, were a later inspiration.] More interesting still, there is a half-serious discussion between the younger sisters like that between Jane and Elizabeth where Jane argues that Charlotte has a reasonable prospect of matrimonial happiness, and there is a primitive account of the case for and against a marriage of convenience. But Charlotte Lucas is not Mary Stanhope in disposition (*her* character is used up many years later as Mary Musgrove); though her situation is taken from 'The Three Sisters,' her character comes from another early story, 'Lesley Castle' in the second MS. volume. This original Charlotte (a family joke from *The Sorrows of Werther*) is another functional character, designed solely to set off by excessive in-sensibility the conventional delicacy of feeling of her sister Eloisa the heroine (the contrasted pair provide the Elinor-Marianne relation later). Charlotte Lutterell is wholly taken up with cookery and domestic management (vestigal traits in Charlotte Lucas), the point of this being that when her sister's betrothed dies sud-denly she is distressed by the waste of wedding-victuals but doesn't understand her sister's sufferings. She has for similar reasons exces-sively prosaic (though disinterested) views on marriage that natu-rally acquire an ugly cast when as Charlotte Lucas she puts her views into practice. Colonel Fitzwilliam, who has no necessary part in the plot, was obviously put in to illustrate the theme, and shows signs of having been written down in the final version; his relation to Elizabeth, like that of Wickham and Lydia, Darcy and Elizabeth, Jane and Bingley, Mr. Collins and Charlotte Lucas, and the marriages of convenience desired by their families between Georgiana and Bingley and between Darcy and Miss de Bourgh, are all illustrations of the theme of the book. What we have in *Pride and Prejudice* then is not simply a subject taken over for ridicule, or a realistic instead of a conventional treatment of a plot, nor is it the simple 'borrowing' for a slightly different purpose that is the only recognition its relation to *Cecilia* has received by Dr. Chapman and other scholars. It is the central idea of *Cecilia* given an elaborate orchestration as it were, sometimes guyed (when Lady Catherine and Miss Bingley stand for the digni-fied opposition of Delvile's family to his attachment), more often used as an opportunity for self-exploration on the author's part (Elizabeth's outbreak about Charlotte's marriage and her dis-cussion of 'candour' with her sister are spots where the crust of objective comedy visibly cracks). But what I wish to stress here is the ways in which the author has secured her materials for con-structing a novel which has delighted so many readers, from the severest critics to the least critical. Her writing and reading and living up to the point of the final revision of *Pride and Prejudice* have all tended towards its creation, we might say, and the phases it passed through were necessary to its development into a serious work of art.

Biography

HENRY AUSTEN

Biographical Notice of the Author†

The following pages are the production of a pen which has already contributed in no small degree to the entertainment of the public. And when the public, which has not been insensible to the merits of "Sense and Sensibility," "Pride and Prejudice," "Mansfield Park," and "Emma," shall be informed that the hand which guided that pen is now mouldering in the grave, perhaps a brief account of Jane Austen will be read with a kindlier sentiment than simple curiosity.

Short and easy will be the task of the mere biographer. A life of usefulness, literature, and religion, was not by any means a life of event. To those who lament their irreparable loss, it is consolatory to think that, as she never deserved disapprobation, so, in the circle of her family and friends, she never met reproof; that her wishes were not only reasonable, but gratified; and that to the little disappointments incidental to human life was never added, even for a moment, an abatement of good-will from any who knew her.

Jane Austen was born on the 16th of December, 1775, at Steventon, in the county of Hants. Her father was Rector of that parish upwards of forty years. There he resided, in the conscientious and unassisted discharge of his ministerial duties, until he was turned of seventy years. Then he retired with his wife, our authoress, and her sister, to Bath, for the remainder of his life, a period of about four years. Being not only a profound scholar, but possessing a most exquisite taste in every species of literature, it is not wonderful that his daughter Jane should, at a very early age, have become sensible to the charms of style,

† Henry Austen's biographical sketch of his sister was first published in 1817 as a preface to the posthumous volume containing *Persuasion* and *Northanger Abbey*. It was reprinted in 1833 in the first of the collected editions of Jane Austen's novels. It is here reprinted from R. W. Chapman's edition, *The Novels of Jane Austen* (Oxford, 1933), 3rd edition, V, 3–8, by permission of the Oxford University Press.

and enthusiastic in the cultivation of her own language. On the death of her father she removed, with her mother and sister, for a short time, to Southampton, and finally, in 1809, to the pleasant village of Chawton, in the same county. From this place she sent into the world those novels, which by many have been placed on the same shelf as the works of a D'Arblay [1] and an Edgeworth. Some of these novels had been the gradual perform-ances of her previous life. For though in compositions she was equally rapid and correct, yet an invincible distrust of her own judgement induced her to withhold her works from the public, till time and many perusals had satisfied her that the charm of recent composition was dissolved. The natural constitution, the regular habits, the quiet and happy occupations of our authoress, seemed to promise a long succession of amusement to the public, and a gradual increase of reputation to herself. But the symptoms of a decay, deep and incurable, began to shew themselves in the commencement of 1816. Her decline was at first deceitfully slow; and until the spring of this present year, those who knew their happiness to be involved in her existence could not endure to despair. But in the month of May, 1817, it was found ad-visable that she should be removed to Winchester for the benefit of constant medical aid, which none even then dared to hope would be permanently beneficial. She supported, during two months, all the varying pain, irksomeness, and tedium, attendant on decaying nature, with more than resignation, with a truly elastic cheerfulness. She retained her faculties, her memory, her fancy, her temper, and her affections, warm, clear, and unim-paired, to the last. Neither her love of God, nor of her fellow creatures flagged for a moment. She made a point of receiving the sacrament before excessive bodily weakness might have ren-dered her perception unequal to her wishes. She wrote whilst she could hold a pen, and with a pencil when a pen was become too laborious. The day preceding her death she composed some stanzas replete with fancy and vigour. Her last voluntary speech conveyed thanks to her medical attendant; and to the final ques-tion asked of her, purporting to know her wants, she replied, "I want nothing but death."

She expired shortly after, on Friday the 18th of July, 1817, in the arms of her sister, who, as well as the relator of these events, feels too surely that they shall never look upon her like again.

Jane Austen was buried on the 24th of July, 1817, in the ca-thedral church of Winchester, which, in the whole catalogue of its mighty dead, does not contain the ashes of a brighter genius

1. D'Arblay was the married name of Fanny Burney [*Editor*].

or a sincerer Christian.

Of personal attractions she possessed a considerable share. Her stature was that of true elegance. It could not have been increased without exceeding the middle height. Her carriage and deportment were quiet, yet graceful. Her features were separately good. Their assemblage produced an unrivalled expression of that cheerfulness, sensibility, and benevolence, which were her real characteristics. Her complexion was of the finest texture. It might with truth be said, that her eloquent blood spoke through her modest cheek. Her voice was extremely sweet. She delivered herself with fluency and precision. Indeed she was formed for elegant and rational society, excelling in conversation as much as in composition. In the present age it is hazardous to mention accomplishments. Our authoress would, probably, have been inferior to few in such acquirements, had she not been so superior to most in higher things. She had not only an excellent taste for drawing, but, in her earlier days, evinced great power of hand in the management of the pencil. Her own musical attainments she held very cheap. Twenty years ago they would have been thought more of, and twenty years hence many a parent will expect their daughters to be applauded for meaner performances. She was fond of dancing, and excelled in it. It remains now to add a few observations on that which her friends deemed more important, on those endowments which sweetened every hour of their lives.

If there be an opinion current in the world, that perfect placidity of temper is not reconcileable to the most lively imagination, and the keenest relish for wit, such an opinion will be rejected for ever by those who have had the happiness of knowing the authoress of the following works. Though the frailties, foibles, and follies of others could not escape her immediate detection, yet even on their vices did she never trust herself to comment with unkindness. The affectation of candour is not uncommon; but she had no affectation. Faultless herself, as nearly as human nature can be, she always sought, in the faults of others, something to excuse, to forgive or forget. Where extenuation was impossible, she had a sure refuge in silence. She never uttered either a hasty, a silly, or a severe expression. In short, her temper was as polished as her wit. Nor were her manners inferior to her temper. They were of the happiest kind. No one could be often in her company without feeling a strong desire of obtaining her friendship, and cherishing a hope of having obtained it. She was tranquil without reserve or stiffness; and communicative without intrusion or self-sufficiency. She became an authoress entirely from taste and inclination. Neither the hope of fame nor profit mixed with her early motives. Most of her works, as before observed, were composed many years previous to their publication. It was with extreme difficulty that her friends, whose partiality she suspected whilst she honoured their judgement, could prevail on her to publish her first work. Nay, so persuaded was she that its sale would not repay the expense of publication, that she actually made a reserve from her very moderate income to meet the expected loss. She could scarcely believe what she termed her great good fortune when "Sense and Sensibility" produced a clear profit of about £150. Few so gifted were so truly unpretending. She regarded the above sum as a prodigious recompense for that which had cost her nothing. Her readers, perhaps, will wonder that such a work produced so little at a time when some authors have received more guineas than they have written lines. The works of our authoress, however, may live as long as those which have burst on the world with more éclat. But the public has not been unjust; and our authoress was far from thinking it so. Most gratifying to her was the applause which from time to time reached her ears from those who were competent to discriminate. Still, in spite of such applause, so much did she shrink from notoriety, that no accumulation of fame would have induced her, had she lived, to affix her name to any productions of her pen. In the bosom of her own family she talked of them freely, thankful for praise, open to remark, and submissive to criticism. But in public she turned away from any allusion to the character of an authoress. She read aloud with very great taste and effect. Her own works, probably, were never heard to so much advantage as from her own mouth; for she partook largely in all the best gifts of the comic muse. She was a warm and judicious admirer of landscape, both in nature and on canvass. At a very early age she was enamoured of Gilpin on the Picturesque; and she seldom changed her opinions either on books or men.

Her reading was very extensive in history and belles lettres; and her memory extremely tenacious. Her favourite moral writers were Johnson in prose, and Cowper in verse. It is difficult to say at what age she was not intimately acquainted with the merits and defects of the best essays and novels in the English language. Richardson's power of creating, and preserving the consistency of his characters, as particularly exemplified in "Sir Charles Grandison," gratified the natural discrimination of her mind, whilst her taste secured her from the errors of his prolix style and tedious narrative. She did not rank any work of Fielding quite so high. Without the slightest affectation she recoiled from every thing gross. Neither nature, wit, nor humour, could make her amends for so very low a scale of morals.

Her power of inventing characters seems to have been intuitive, and almost unlimited. She drew from nature; but, whatever may have been surmised to the contrary, never from individuals.

The style of her familiar correspondence was in all respects the same as that of her novels. Every thing came finished from her pen; for on all subjects she had ideas as clear as her expressions were well chosen. It is not hazarding too much to say that she never dispatched a note or letter unworthy of publication.

One trait only remains to be touched on. It makes all others unimportant. She was thoroughly religious and devout; fearful of giving offence to God, and incapable of feeling it towards any fellow creature. On serious subjects she was well-instructed, both by reading and meditation, and her opinions accorded strictly with those of our Established Church.

Reviews and Essays in Criticism

The British Critic †

We had occasion to speak favorably of the former production
of this author or authoress, * * * and we readily do the same of
the present. It is very far superior to almost all the publications
of the kind which have lately come before us. It has a very unex-
ceptionable tendency, the story is well told, the characters remarkably well drawn and supported, and written with great spirit
as well as vigour. The story has no great variety, it is simply this.
The hero is a young man of large fortune and fashionable manners,
whose distinguishing characteristic is personal pride. The heroine,
on the first introduction, conceives a most violent prejudice against
Darcy, which a variety of circumstances well imagined and happily
represented, tend to strengthen and confirm. The under plot
is an attachment between the friend of Darcy and the elder sister
of the principal female character; other personages, of greater or
less interest and importance, complete the dramatis personae,
some of whose characters are exceedingly well drawn. Explanations
of the different perplexities and seeming contrarieties, are gradually
unfolded, and the two principal performers are happily united.

Of the characters, Elizabeth Bennet, the heroine, is supported
with great spirit and consistency throughout; there seems no
defect in the portrait; this is not precisely the case with Darcy
her lover; his early unconcern and fashionable indifference, somewhat abruptly changes [sic] to the ardent lover. The character
of Mr. Collins, the obsequious rector, is excellent. Fancy presents
us with many such, who consider the patron of exalted rank
as the model of all that is excellent on earth, and the patron's
smiles and condescension as the sum of human happiness. Mr.
Bennet, the father of Elizabeth, presents us with some novelty
of character; a reserved, acute, and satirical, but indolent personage,
who sees and laughs at the follies and indiscretions of his depen-
dents, without making any exertions to correct them. The picture
of the younger Miss Bennets, their perpetual visits to the market
town where officers are quartered, and the result, is perhaps exemplified in every provincial town in the kingdom.

It is unnecessary to add, that we have perused these volumes
with much satisfaction and amusement, and entertain very
little doubt that their successful circulation will induce the author
to similar exertions.

† Review of *Pride and Prejudice* in *The British Critic*, XLI (1813), 189–191.

The Critical Review †

Instead of the whole interest of the tale hanging upon one or two characters, as is generally the case in novels, the fair author of the present introduces us, at once, to a whole family, every individual of which excites the interest, and very agreeably divides the attention of the reader.

Mr. Bennet, the father of this family, is represented as a man of abilities, but of a sarcastic humour, and combining a good deal of caprice and reserve in his composition. He possesses an estate of about two thousand a year, and lives at Longbourne, in Hertfordshire, a pleasant walk from the market town of Meryton. This gentleman's estate is made to descend, in default of male issue, to a distant relation. Mr. Bennet, captivated by a handsome face and the appearance of good temper, had married early in life the daughter of a country attorney,

> 'A woman of mean understanding, little information, and uncertain temper. When she was discontented, she fancied herself nervous. The business of her life was to get her daughters married; its solace was visiting and news.'

At a very early period of his marriage, Mr. Bennet finds, that a pretty face is but sorry compensation for the absence of common sense; and that youth and the appearance of good nature, with the want of other good qualities, will not make a rational companion or an estimable wife. The consequence of this discovery of the ill effects of an unequal marriage, is the defalcation of all real affection, confidence, and respect on the side of Mr. Bennet towards his wife. His views of domestic comfort being overthrown, he seeks consolation for a disappointment, which he had brought upon himself, by indulging his fondness for a country life and his love for study. Being, as we said, a man of abilities and sense, though with some peculiarities and eccentricities, he contrives not to be out of temper with the follies which his wife discovers, and is contented to laugh and be amused with her want of decorum and propriety.

> 'This,' as our sensible author remarks, 'is not the sort of happiness which a man would, in general, wish to owe to his wife; but where other powers of entertainment are wanting, the true philosopher will derive benefit from such as are given.'

However this may be, though Mr. Bennet finds amusement in absurdity, it is by no means of advantage to his five daughters,

† Review of *Pride and Prejudice* in *The Critical Review*, III (1813), 318–324.

who, with the help of their silly mother, are looking out for husbands. Jane, the eldest daughter, is very beautiful, and possesses great feeling, good sense, equanimity, cheerfulness, and elegance of manners. Elizabeth, the second, is represented as combining quickness of perception and strength of mind, with a playful vivacity something like that of her father, joined with a handsome person. Mary is a female pedant, affecting great wisdom, though saturated with stupidity. 'She is a lady,' (as Mr. Bennet says), 'of deep reflection, who reads great books and makes extracts.' Kitty is weak-spirited and fretful; but Miss Lydia, the youngest,

> 'is a stout, well-grown girl of fifteen, with a fine complexion and good humoured countenance; a favourite with her mother, whose affection had brought her into public at an early age. She had high animal spirits, and a sort of self-consequence.'

This young lady is mad after the officers who are quartered at Meryton; and from the attentions of these *beaux garçons*, Miss Lydia becomes a most decided flirt.

Although these young ladies claim a great share of the reader's interest and attention, none calls forth our admiration so much as Elizabeth, whose archness and sweetness of manner render her a very attractive object in the familypiece. She is in fact the *Beatrice* of the tale; and falls in love on much the same principles of contrariety.

On the character of Elizabeth, the main interest of the novel depends; and the fair author has shewn considerable ingenuity in the mode of bringing about the final *eclaircissment* between her and Darcy. Elizabeth's sense and conduct are of a superior order to those of the common heroines of novels. From her independence of character, which is kept within the proper line of decorum, and her well-timed sprightliness, she teaches the man of Family-Pride to know himself. * * *

The above is merely the brief outline of this very agreeable novel. An excellent lesson may be learned from the elopement of Lydia:—the work also shows the folly of letting young girls have their own way, and the danger which they incur in associating with the officers, who may be quartered in or near their residence. The character of Wickham is very well pourtrayed;—we fancy, that our authoress had Joseph Surface before her eyes when she sketched it; as well as the lively Beatrice, when she drew the portrait of Elizabeth. Many such silly women as Mrs. Bennet may be found; and numerous parsons like Mr. Collins, who are every thing to every body; and servile in the extreme to their superiors. Mr. Collins is indeed a notable object. * * *

We cannot conclude, without repeating our approbation of

this performance, which rises very superior to any novel we have
lately met with in the delineation of domestic scenes. Nor is
there one character which appears flat, or obtrudes itself upon
the notice of the reader with troublesome impertinence. There
is not one person in the drama with whom we could readily
dispense;—they have all their proper places; and fill their several
stations, with great credit to themselves, and much satisfaction
to the reader.

RICHARD WHATELY

[Technique and Moral Effect in Jane Austen's Fiction] †

The times seem to be past when an apology was requisite from
reviewers for condescending to notice a novel; when they felt
themselves bound in dignity to deprecate the suspicion of paying
much regard to such trifles, and pleaded the necessity of occasionally
stooping to humour the taste of their fair readers. The delights
of fiction, if not more keenly or more generally relished, are
at least more readily acknowledged by men of sense and taste;
and we have lived to hear the merits of the best of this class
of writings earnestly discussed by some of the ablest scholars
and soundest reasoners of the present day.

We are inclined to attribute this change, not so much to
an alternation in the public taste, as in the character of the
productions in question. Novels may not, perhaps, display more
genius now than formerly, but they contain more solid sense;
they may not afford higher gratification, but it is of a nature which
men are less disposed to be ashamed of avowing. We remarked,
in a former Number, in reviewing a work of the author now before
us, that 'a new style of novel has arisen, within the last fifteen
or twenty years, differing from the former in the points upon
which the interest hinges; neither alarming our credulity nor
amusing our imagination by wild variety of incident, or by those
pictures of romantic affection and sensibility, which were formerly
as certain attributes of fictitious characters as they are of rare
occurrence among those who actually live and die. The substitute
for these excitements, which had lost much of their poignancy
by the repeated and injudicious use of them, was the art of copying

† From Richard Whately, "Modern Novels," *Quarterly Review*, XLVII (1821),
352–363.

from nature as she really exists in the common walks of life, and presenting to the reader, instead of the splendid scenes of an imaginary world, a correct and striking representation of that which is daily taking place around him.'[1]

Now, though the origin of this new school of fiction may probably be traced, as we there suggested, to the exhaustion of the mines from which materials for entertainment had been hitherto extracted, and the necessity of gratifying the natural craving of the reader for variety, by striking into an untrodden path; the consequences resulting from this change have been far greater than the mere supply of this demand. When this Flemish painting, as it were, is introduced—this accurate and unexaggerated delineation of events and characters—it necessarily follows, that a novel, which makes good its pretensions of giving a perfectly correct picture of common life, becomes a far more *instructive* work than one of equal or superior merit of the other class; it guides the judgment, and supplies a kind of artificial experience. It is a remark of the great father of criticism, that poetry (i. e. narrative, and dramatic poetry) is of a more philosophical character than history; inasmuch as the latter details what has actually happened, of which many parts may chance to be exceptions to the general rules of probability, and consequently illustrate no general principles; whereas the former shews us what must naturally, or would probably, happen under given circumstances; and thus displays to us a comprehensive view of human nature, and furnishes general rules of practical wisdom. It is evident, that this will apply only to such fictions as are quite *perfect* in respect of the probability of their story; and that he, therefore, who resorts to the fabulist rather than the historian, for instruction in human character and conduct, must throw himself entirely on the judgment and skill of his teacher, and give him credit for talents much more rare than the accuracy and veracity which are the chief requisites in history. We fear, therefore, that the exultation which we can conceive some of our gentle readers to feel, at having Aristotle's warrant for (what probably they had never dreamed of) the *philosophical character* of their studies, must, in practice, be somewhat qualified, by those sundry little violations of probability which are to be met with in most novels; and which so far lower their value, as models of real life, that a person who had no other preparation for the world than is afforded by them, would form, probably, a less accurate idea of things as they are,

1. Whately is quoting here from Sir Walter Scott's review of Jane Austen's *Emma*. Scott's review appeared in the *Quarterly Review*, XIV (1815), 188–201 [*Editor*].

than he would of a lion from studying merely the representations on China tea-pots.

Accordingly, a heavy complaint has long lain against works of fiction, as giving a false picture of what they profess to imitate, and disqualifying their readers for the ordinary scenes and everyday duties of life. And this charge applies, we apprehend, to the generality of what are strictly called novels, with even more justice than to romances. When all the characters and events are very far removed from what we see around us,—when, perhaps, even supernatural agents are introduced, the reader may indulge, indeed, in occasional day-dreams, but will be so little reminded of what he has been reading, by any thing that occurs in actual life, that though he may perhaps feel some disrelish for the tameness of the scene before him, compared with the fairy-land he has been visiting, yet at least his judgment will not be depraved, nor his expectations misled; he will not apprehend a meeting with Algerine banditti on English shores, nor regard the old woman who shews him about an antique country seat, as either an enchantress or the keeper of an imprisoned damsel. But it is otherwise with those fictions which differ from common life in little or nothing but the improbability of the occurrences: the reader is insensibly led to calculate upon some of those lucky incidents and opportune coincidences of which he has been so much accustomed to read, and which, it is undeniable, *may* take place in real life; and to feel a sort of confidence, that however romantic his conduct may be, and in whatever difficulties it may involve him, all will be sure to come right at last, as is invariably the case with the hero of a novel.

On the other hand, so far as these pernicious effects fail to be produced, so far does the example lose its influence, and the exercise of poetical justice is rendered vain. The reward of virtuous conduct being brought about by fortunate accidents, he who abstains (taught, perhaps, by bitter disappointments) from reckoning on such accidents, wants that encouragement to virtue, which alone has been held out to him. 'If I were *a man in a novel*,' we remember to have heard an ingenious friend observe, 'I should certainly act so and so, because I should be sure of being no loser by the most heroic self-devotion, and of ultimately succeeding in the most daring enterprises.' * * *

The change, however, which we have already noticed, as having taken place in the character of several modern novels, has operated in a considerable degree to do away this prejudice; and has elevated this species of composition, in some respects at least, into a much higher class. For most of that instruction which used to be presented to the world in the shape of formal dissertations, or shorter and more desultory moral essays, such as those of the Spectator and Rambler, we may now resort to the pages of the acute and judicious, but not less amusing, novelists who have lately appeared. If their views of men and manners are no less just than those of the essayists who preceded them, are they to be rated lower because they present to us these views, not in the language of general description, but in the form of well-constructed fictitious narrative? If the practical lessons they inculcate are no less sound and useful, it is surely no diminution of their merit that they are conveyed by example instead of precept: nor, if their remarks are neither less wise nor less important, are they the less valuable for being represented as thrown out in the course of conversations suggested by the circumstances of the speakers, and perfectly in character. The praise and blame of the moralist are surely not the less effectual for being bestowed, not in general declamation, on classes of men, but on individuals representing those classes, who are so clearly delineated and brought into action before us, that we seem to be acquainted with them, and feel an interest in their fate. * * *

Among the authors of this school there is no one superior, if equal, to the lady whose last production is now before us, and whom we have much regret in finally taking leave of: her death (in the prime of life, considered as a writer) being announced in this the first publication to which her name is prefixed. We regret the failure not only of a source of innocent amusement, but also of that supply of practical good sense and instructive example, which she would probably have continued to furnish better than any of her contemporaries. * * *

Miss Austin [*sic*] has the merit (in our judgment most essential) of being evidently a Christian writer: a merit which is much enhanced, both on the score of good taste, and of practical utility, by her religion being not at all obtrusive. She might defy the most fastidious critic to call any of her novels, (as Cœlebs was designated, we will not say altogether without reason,) a 'dramatic sermon.' The subject is rather alluded to, and that incidentally, than studiously brought forward and dwelt upon. In fact she is more sparing of it than would be thought desirable by some persons; perhaps even by herself, had she consulted merely her own sentiments; but she probably introduced it as far as she thought would be generally acceptable and profitable: for when the purpose of inculcating a religious principle is made too palpably prominent, many readers, if they do not throw aside the book with disgust, are apt to fortify themselves with that respectful kind of apathy with which they undergo a regular sermon, and prepare themselves as they do to swallow a dose of medicine, endeavouring to *get it down* in large gulps, without tasting it more than is necessary.

The moral lessons also of this lady's novels, though clearly and impressively conveyed, are not offensively put forward, but spring incidentally from the circumstances of the story; they are not forced upon the reader, but he is left to collect them (though without any difficulty) for himself: her's is that unpretending kind of instruction which is furnished by real life; and certainly no author has ever conformed more closely to real life, as well in the incidents, as in the characters and descriptions. Her fables appear to us to be in their own way, nearly faultless; they do not consist (like those of some of the writers who have attempted this kind of common-life novel writing) of a string of unconnected events which have little or no bearing on one main plot, and are introduced evidently for the sole purpose of bringing in characters and conversations; but have all that compactness of plan and unity of action which is generally produced by a sacrifice of probability: yet they have little or nothing that is not probable; the story proceeds without the aid of extraordinary accidents; the events which take place are the necessary or natural consequences of what has preceded; and yet (which is a very rare merit indeed) the final catastrophe is scarcely ever clearly foreseen from the beginning, and very often comes, upon the generality of readers at least, quite unexpected. We know not whether Miss Austin ever had access to the precepts of Aristotle; but there are few, if any, writers of fiction who have illustrated them more successfully. * * *

Miss Austin, though she has in a few places introduced letters with great effect, has on the whole conducted her novels on the ordinary plan, describing, without scruple, private conversations and uncommunicated feelings: but she has not been forgetful of the important maxim, so long ago illustrated by Homer, and afterwards enforced by Aristotle, of saying as little as possible in her own person, and giving a dramatic air to the narrative, by introducing frequent conversations; which she conducts with a regard to character hardly exceeded even by Shakspeare himself. Like him, she shows as admirable a discrimination in the characters of fools as of people of sense; a merit which is far from common. To invent, indeed, a conversation full of wisdom or of wit, requires that the writer should himself possess ability; but the converse does not hold good: it is no fool that can describe fools well; and many who have succeeded pretty well in painting superior characters, have failed in giving individuality to those weaker ones, which it is necessary to introduce in order to give a faithful representation of real life: they exhibit to us mere folly in the abstract, forgetting that to the eye of a skilful naturalist the insects on a leaf present as wide differences as exist between the elephant and the lion. Slender, and Shallow, and Aguecheek, as Shakspeare has painted them, though equally fools, resemble one another no more than Richard, and Macbeth, and Julius Cæsar; and Miss Austin's Mrs. Bennet, Mr. Rushworth [in *Mansfield Park*], and Miss Bates [in *Emma*], are no more alike than her Darcy, Knightley [in *Emma*], and Edmund Bertram [in *Mansfield Park*]. Some have complained, indeed, of finding her fools must (whatever deference they may outwardly pay to received opinions) find the Merry Wives of Windsor and Twelfth Night too much like nature, and consequently tiresome; there is no disputing about tastes; all we can say is, that such critics very tiresome; and that those who look with pleasure at Wilkie's [2] pictures, or those of the Dutch school, must admit that excellence of imitation may confer attraction on that which would be insipid or disagreeable in the reality. * * *

Her minuteness of detail has also been found fault with; but even where it produces, at the time, a degree of tediousness, we know not whether that can justly be reckoned a blemish, which is absolutely essential to a very high excellence. Now, it is absolutely impossible, without this, to produce that thorough acquaintance with the characters, which is necessary to make the reader heartily interested in them. Let any one cut out from the Iliad or from Shakspeare's plays every thing (we are far from saying that either might not lose some parts with advantage, but let him reject every thing) which is absolutely devoid of importance and of interest *in itself*; and he will find that what is left will have lost more than half its charms. We are convinced that some writers have diminished the effect of their works by being scrupulous to admit nothing into them which had not some absolute, intrinsic, and independent merit. They have acted like those who strip off the leaves of a fruit tree, as being of themselves good for nothing, with the view of securing more nourishment to the fruit, which in fact cannot attain its full maturity and flavour without them.

2. David Wilkie (1785–1841) was a Scottish painter famous for his anecdotal paintings of village scenes.

Edinburgh Review: [The Character and Popularity of Jane Austen's Fiction]†

Miss Austen has never been so popular as she deserved to be. Intent on fidelity of delineation, and averse to the commonplace tricks of her art, she has not, in this age of literary quackery, received her reward. Ordinary readers have been apt to judge of her as Partridge, in Fielding's novel, judged of Garrick's acting. He could not see the merit of a man who merely behaved on the stage as any body might be expected to behave under similar circumstances in real life. He infinitely preferred the 'robustious periwig-pated fellow,' who flourished his arms like a windmill, and ranted with the voice of three. It was even so with many of the readers of Miss Austen. She was too natural for them. It seemed to them as if there could be very little merit in making characters act and talk so exactly like the people whom they saw around them every day. They did not consider that the highest triumph of art consists in its concealment; and here the art was so little perceptible, that they believed there was none. Her works, like well-proportioned rooms, are rendered less apparently grand and imposing by the very excellence of their adjustment. It must perhaps be confessed, that she availed herself too little of the ordinary means of attracting attention and exciting interest. Her plots are very simple, formed upon the most rigid view of probabilities, excluding every thing romantic or surprising, or calculated to produce a very powerful emotion, and including only such events as occur in every-day life. Her characters are, for the most part, commonplace people, little distinguished by their mental qualities from the mass of their fellow-creatures, of secondary station, and hardly ever exhibited through that halo of rank and wealth which makes many an ill-drawn sketch pass current with a credulous public 'Materiam superabat opus,' may be said of her works. No novelist perhaps ever employed more unpromising materials, and by none have those materials been more admirably treated. Her forte lay not so much in describing events, as in drawing characters; and in this she stands almost alone. She possessed the rare and difficult art of making her readers intimately acquainted with the characters of all whom she describes. We feel as if we had lived among them; and yet she employs no elaborate description—no metaphysical analysis—no antithetical balance of their good and bad qualities. She scarcely does more

† From "Mrs Gore's *Women as They Are; or, The Manners of the Day*," *Edinburgh Review*, LI (1830), 448–450.

than make them act and talk, and we know them directly. In dialogue she also excelled. Her conversations are never *bookish*—they are just what might have been said; and they are eminently characteristic. We have seen a good deal of spirited dialogue, in which the parts might be transposed and given to other interlocutors, with very little injury to the effect of the whole. This is never the case in the conversations introduced by Miss Austen. Every thing that is said, however short and simple, belongs peculiarly to the person by whom it is uttered, and is indicative of their situation, or turn of mind: And yet they do not seem to talk for effect; they merely say just what it seems most natural they they should have said. In the ridicule of human foibles, she showed great delicacy and address. She never railed in set terms, and seldom launched the shafts of direct satire; but she made us equally sensible of the absurdity or unreasonableness which she wished to expose,—perhaps without even having recourse to one single condemnatory expression. A nicely-regulated vein of humour runs through her writings, never breaking out into broad mirth, but ever ready to communicate a pleasing vivacity to the current of her story. To the above merits may be added those of the purest morality, and most undeviating good sense. Few, if any, fictitious writings have a more decided tendency to improve the hearts of those who read them; and this end is gained without any thing that could be called sermonizing even by the most impatient.

GEORGE HENRY LEWES

The Novels of Jane Austen†

For nearly half a century England has possessed an artist of the highest rank, whose works have been extensively circulated, whose merits have been keenly relished, and whose name is still unfamiliar in men's mouths. One would suppose that great excellence and real success would inevitably produce a loud reputation. Yet in this particular case such a supposition would be singularly mistaken. So far from the name of Miss Austen being constantly cited among the glories of our literature, there are many well-informed persons who will be surprised to hear it mentioned among the best writers. If we look at Hazlitt's account of the

† From *Blackwood's Magazine*, LXXXVI (1859), 99–113.

English novelists, in his *Lectures on the Comic Writers*, we find Mrs Radcliff, Mrs Inchbald, Mrs Opie, Miss Burney, and Miss Edgeworth receiving due honour, and more than is due; but no hint that Miss Austen has written a line. If we cast a glance over the list of English authors republished by Baudry, Galignani, and Tauchnitz, we find there writers of the very smallest pretensions, but not the author of *Emma*, and *Mansfield Park*. Mention the name of Miss Austen to a cultivated reader, and it is probable that the sparkle in his eye will at once flash forth sympathetic admiration, and he will perhaps relate how Scott, Whately, and Macaulay prize this gifted woman, and how the English public has bought her works; but beyond the literary circle we find the name almost entirely unknown; and not simply unknown in the sense of having no acknowledged place among the remarkable writers but unremembered even in connection with the very works which are themselves remembered. We have met with many persons who remembered to have read *Pride and Prejudice*, or *Mansfield Park*, but who had altogether forgotten by whom they were written. "Miss Austen? Oh, yes; she translates from the German, doesn't she?" is a not uncommon question—a vague familiarity with the name of Mrs Austin being uppermost. From time to time also the tiresome twaddle of lady novelists is praised by certain critics, as exhibiting the "quiet truthfulness of Miss Austin."

That Miss Austen is an artist of high rank, in the most rigorous sense of the word, is an opinion which in the present article we shall endeavour to substantiate. That her novels are very extensively read, is not an opinion, but a demonstrated fact; and with this fact we couple the paradoxical fact, of a fine artist, whose works are widely known and enjoyed, being all but unknown to the English public, and quite unknown abroad. The causes which have kept her name in comparative obscurity all the time that her works have been extensively read, and her reputation every year has been settling itself more firmly in the minds of the better critics, may well be worth an inquiry. It is intelligible how the blaze of Scott should have thrown her into the shade, at first: beside his frescoes her works are but miniatures; exquisite miniatures, yet incapable of every filling that space in the public eye which was filled by his massive and masterly pictures. But although it is intelligible why Scott should have eclipsed her, it is not at first so easy to understand why Miss Edgeworth should have done so. Miss Austen, indeed, has taken her revenge with posterity. She will doubtless be read as long as English novels find readers; whereas Miss Edgeworth is already little more than a name, and only finds a public for her children's books. But contemporaries, for the most part, judged otherwise; and in consequence Miss Edgeworth's name has become familiar all over the three kingdoms. Scott, indeed, and Archbishop Whately, at once perceived the superiority of Miss Austen to her more fortunate rival; but the *Quarterly* tells us that "her fame has grown fastest since she died: there was no *éclat* about her first appearance: the public took time to make up its mind; and she, not having staked her hopes of happiness on success or failure, was content to wait for the decision of her claims. Those claims have been long established beyond a question; but the merit of *first* recognising them belongs less to reviewers than to general readers." There is comfort in this for authors who see the applause of reviewers lavished on works of garish effect. Nothing that is really good can fail, at last, in securing its audience; and it is evident that Miss Austen's works must possess elements of indestructible excellence, since, although never "popular," she survives writers who were very popular; and forty years after her death, gains more recognition than she gained when alive. Those who, like ourselves, have read and re-read her works several times, can understand this duration, and this increase of her fame. But the fact that her name is not even now a household word proves that her excellence must be of an unobtrusive kind, shunning the glare of popularity, not appealing to temporary tastes and vulgar sympathies, but demanding culture in its admirers. Johnson wittily says of somebody, "Sir, he managed to make himself public without making himself known." Miss Austen has made herself known without making herself public. There is no portrait of her in the shop windows; indeed, no portrait of her at all. But she is cherished in the memories of those whose memory is fame. * * *

If, as probably few will dispute, the art of the novelist be the representation of human life by means of a story; and if the *truest* representation, effected by the *least expenditure* of means, constitutes the highest claim of art, then we say that Miss Austen has carried the art to a point of excellence surpassing that reached by any of her rivals. Observe we say "the art"; we do not say that she equals many of them in the *interest* excited by the art; that is a separate question. It is probable, nay certain, that the interest excited by the *Antigone* is very inferior to that excited by *Black-eyed Susan*. It is probable that *Uncle Tom* and *Dred* surpassed in interest the *Antiquary* or *Ivanhoe*. It is probable that *Jane Eyre* produced a far greater excitement than the *Vicar of Wakefield*. But the critic justly disregards these fervid elements of immediate success, and fixes his attention mainly on the art which is of eternal substance. Miss Austen has nothing fervid in her works. She is not capable of producing a profound agitation in the mind. In many respects this is a limitation of her powers, a deduction from her claims. But while other writers have had more power over the emotions, more vivid imaginations, deeper sensibilities, deeper insight, and more of what is properly called invention, no novelist has approached her in what we may style the "economy of art," by which is meant the easy adaptation of means to ends, with no aid from extraneous or superfluous elements. Indeed, paradoxical as the juxtaposition of the names may perhaps appear to those who have not reflected much on this subject, we venture to say that the only names we can place above Miss Austen, in respect of this economy of art, are Sophocles and Molière (in *Le Misanthrope*). And if any one will examine the terms of the definition, he will perceive that almost all defects in works of art arise from neglect of this economy. When the *end* is the representation of human nature in its familiar aspects, moving amid every-day scenes, the *means* must likewise be furnished from every-day life: romance and improbabilities must be banished as rigorously as the grotesque exaggeration of peculiar characteristics, or the representation of abstract types. It is easy for the artist to choose a subject from every-day life, but it is *not* easy for him so to represent the characters and their actions that they shall be at once lifelike and interesting; accordingly, whenever ordinary people are introduced, they are either made to speak a language never spoken out of books, and to pursue conduct never observed in life; or else they are intolerably wearisome. But Miss Austen is like Shakespeare; she makes her very noodles inexhaustibly amusing, yet accurately real. We never tire of her characters. They become equal to actual experiences. * * *

But the real secret of Miss Austen's success lies in her having the exquisite and rare gift of dramatic creation of character. Scott says of her, "She had a talent for describing the involvements, and feelings, and characters of ordinary life, which is to me the most wonderful I ever met with. The big bow-wow strain I can do myself like any now going; but the exquisite touch, which renders ordinary commonplace things and characters interesting, from the truth of the description and the sentiment, is denied me. What a pity such a gifted creature died so early!" [1] Generously said; but high as the praise is, it is as much below the real excellence of Miss Austen, as the "big bow-wow strain" is below the incomparable power of the Waverley Novels. Scott felt, but did not define, the excellence of Miss Austen. The

1. Scott's remark was elicited by his reading "for the third time at least Miss Austen's very finely written novel of *Pride and Prejudice*." The entire passage, transcribed more accurately than the version Lewes used, is printed in *The Journal of Sir Walter Scott, 1825–26*, edited by J. G. Tait (Edinburgh and London, 1939), p. 135 [*Editor*].

very word "describing" is altogether misplaced and misleading. She seldom describes anything, and is not felicitous when she attempts it. But instead of *description*, the common and easy resource of novelists, she has the rare and difficult art of *dramatic presentation:* instead of telling us what her characters are, and what they feel, she presents the people, and they reveal themselves. In this she has never perhaps been surpassed not even by Shakespeare himself. If ever living beings can be said to have moved across the page of fiction, as they lived, speaking as they spoke, and feeling as they felt, they do so in *Pride and Prejudice, Emma,* and *Mansfield Park.* What incomparable noodles she exhibits for our astonishment and laughter! What silly, good-natured women! What softly-selfish men! What lively, amiable, honest men and women, whom one would rejoice to have known!

But all her power is dramatic power; she loses her hold on us directly she ceases to speak through the *personœ;* she is then like a great actor *off* the stage. When she is making men and women her mouthpieces, she is exquisitely and inexhaustibly humorous; but when she speaks in her own person, she is apt to be commonplace and even prosing. Her dramatic ventriloquism is such that, amid our tears of laughter and sympathetic exasperation at folly, we feel it almost impossible that she did not hear those very people utter those very words. In many cases this was doubtless the fact. The best invention does not consist in finding *new* language for characters, but in finding the *true* language for them. It is easy to invent a language never spoken by any one out of books; but it is so far from easy to invent—that is, to find out—the language which certain characters would speak and did speak, that in all the thousands of volumes written since Richardson and Fielding, every difficulty is more frequently overcome than *that.* If the reader fails to perceive the extraordinary merit of Miss Austen's representation of character, let him try himself to paint a portrait which shall be at once many-sided and interesting, without employing any but the commonest colours, without calling in the aid of eccentricity, exaggeration, or literary "effects"; or let him carefully compare the writings of Miss Austen with those of any other novelist, from Fielding to Thackeray.

It is probably this same dramatic instinct which makes the construction of her stories so admirable. And by construction, we mean the art which, selecting what is useful and rejecting what is superfluous, renders our interest unflagging, because one chapter evolves the next, one character is necessary to the elucidation of another. In what is commonly called "plot" she does not excel. Her invention is wholly in character and motive, not in situation. Her materials are of the commonest every-day occurence. Neither the emotions of tragedy, nor the exaggerations of farce, seem to have the slightest attraction for her. The reader's pulse never throbs, his curiosity is never intense; but his interest never wanes for a moment. The action begins; the people speak, feel, and act; everything that is said, felt, or done tends towards the entanglement or disentanglement of the plot; and we are almost made actors as well as spectators of the little drama. One of the most difficult things in dramatic writing is so to construct the story that every scene shall advance the denouement by easy evolution, yet at the same time give scope to the full exhibition of the characters. In dramas, as in novels, we almost always see that the action stands still while the characters are being exhibited, and the characters are in abeyance while the action is being unfolded. For perfect specimens of this higher construction demanded by art, we would refer to the jealousy-scenes of *Othello*, and the great scene between Célimène and Arsinoé in *Le Misanthrope*; there is not in these two marvels of art a verse which does not exhibit some *nuance* of character, and thereby, at the same time, tends towards the full development of the action.

So entirely dramatic, and so little descriptive, is the genius of Miss Austen, that she seems to rely upon what her people say and do for the whole effect they are to produce on our imaginations. She no more thinks of describing the physical appearance of her people than the dramatist does who knows that his persons are to be represented by living actors. This is a defect and a mistake in art: a defect, because, although every reader must necessarily conjure up to himself a vivid image of people whose characters are so vividly presented; yet each reader has to do this for himself without aid from the author, thereby missing many of the subtle connections between physical and mental organisation. It is not enough to be told that a young gentleman had a fine countenance and an air of fashion; or that a young gentlewoman was handsome and elegant. As far as any direct information can be derived from the authoress, we might imagine that this was a purblind world, wherein nobody ever saw anybody, except in a dim vagueness which obscured all peculiarities. It is impossible that Mr Collins should not have been endowed by nature with an appearance in some way heralding the delicious folly of the inward man. Yet *all* we hear of this fatuous curate is, that "he was a tall heavy-looking young man of five- and-twenty. His air was grave and stately, and his manners were very formal." Balzac or Dickens would not have been content without making the reader *see* this Mr Collins. Miss Austen is content to make us *know* him, even to the very intricacies of his inward man. It is not stated whether she was shortsighted, but the absence of all sense of the outward world—either scenery or personal appearance—is more remarkable in her than in any writer we remember.

We are touching here on one of her defects which help to an explanation of her limited popularity, especially when coupled with her deficiencies in poetry and passion. She has little or no sympathy with what is picturesque and passionate. This prevents her from painting what the popular eye can see, and the popular heart can feel. The struggles, the ambitions, the errors, and the sins of energetic life are left untouched by her; and these form the subjects most stirring to the general sympathy.

* * *

The absence of breadth, picturesqueness, and passion, will also limit the appreciating audience of Miss Austen to the small circle of cultivated minds; and even these minds are not always capable of greatly relishing her works. We have known very remarkable people who cared little for her pictures of every-day life; and indeed it may be anticipated that those who have little sense of humour, or whose passionate and insurgent activities demand in art a reflection of their own emotions and struggles, will find little pleasure in such homely comedies. Currer Bell may be taken as a type of these. She was utterly without a sense of humour, and was by nature fervid and impetuous. In a letter published in her memoirs she writes,—"Why do you like Miss Austen so very much? I am puzzled on that point. . . . I had not read *Pride and Prejudice* till I read that sentence of yours, and then I got the book. And what did I find? An accurate daguerreotyped portrait of a commonplace face; a carefully-fenced, highly-cultivated garden, with neat borders and delicate flowers; but no glance of a bright, vivid physiognomy, no open country, no fresh air, no blue hill, no bonny beck. I should hardly like to live with her elegant ladies and gentlemen, in their elegant but confined houses." [2] The critical reader will not fail to remark the almost contemptuous indifference to the art of truthful portrait-painting which this passage indicates; and he will understand, perhaps, how the writer of such a passage was herself incapable of drawing more than characteristics, even in her most successful efforts. Jane Eyre, Rochester, and Paul Emmanuel, are very vigorous sketches, but the reader observes them from the *outside*, he does not penetrate their souls, he does not know them. What is said respecting the want of open country, blue hill, and bonny

2. "Currer Bell" was the pen-name of Charlotte Brontë. Her judgment of *Pride and Prejudice* was made in a letter to Lewes written after she had read his remarks on Jane Austen's fiction in *Fraser's Magazine* in 1847 (see bibliography). The letter was printed in Elizabeth Gaskell, *The Life of Charlotte Brontë* (London, 1857), II, 43 [*Editor*].

beck, is perfectly true; but the same point has been more felici-
tously touched by Scott, in his review of *Emma*: "Upon the
whole," he says, "the turn of this author's novels bears the same
relation to that of the sentimental and romantic cast, that cornfields
and cottages and meadows bear to the highly-adorned grounds
of a show mansion, or the rugged sublimities of a mountain landscape. It is neither so captivating as the one, nor so grand as
the other; but it affords those who frequent it a pleasure nearly
allied with the experience of their own social habits." Scott would
also have loudly repudiated the notion of Miss Austen's characters
being "mere daguerreotypes." Having himself drawn both ideal
and real characters, he knew the difficulties of both; and he well
says, "He who paints from *le beau idéal*, if his scenes and sentiments are striking and interesting, is in a great measure exempted
from the difficult task of reconciling them with the ordinary
probabilities of life; but he who paints a scene of common occurrence, places his composition within that extensive range of
criticism which general experience offers to every reader. . . .
Something more than a mere sign-post likeness is also demanded.
The portrait must have spirit and character, as well as resemblance;
and being deprived of all that, according to Bayes, goes 'to
elevate and surprize,' it must make amends by displaying depth
of knowledge and dexterity of execution. We, therefore, bestow
no mean compliment upon the author of *Emma*, when we say
that, keeping close to common incidents, and to such characters
as occupy the ordinary walks of life, she has produced sketches
of such spirit and originality, that we never miss the excitation
which depends upon a narrative of uncommon events, arising
from the consideration of minds, manners, and sentiments, greatly
above our own." [3] * * *

The reader who has yet to make acquaintance with these novels,
is advised to begin with *Pride and Prejudice* or *Mansfield Park*;
and if these do not captivate him, he may fairly leave the others
unread. In *Pride and Prejudice* there is the best story, and the
greatest variety of character: the whole Bennet family is inimitable:
Mr Bennet, caustic, quietly, indolently selfish, but honourable,
and in some respects amiable; his wife, the perfect type of a
gossiping, weak-headed, fussy mother; Jane a sweet creature;
Elizabeth a sprightly and fascinating flesh-and-blood heroine;
Lydia a pretty, but vain and giddy girl; and Mary, plain and
pedantic, studying "thorough bass and human nature." Then
there is Mr Collins, and Sir William Lucas, and the proud foolish
old Lady Catherine de Bourgh, and Darcy, Bingley, and Wickham,

3. Lewes is quoting from Scott's review of *Emma* in the *Quarterly Review*.
Bayes is a foolish, sensation-seeking
playwright in Buckingham's *The Re-
hearsal* (1704) [*Editor*].

all admirable. From the first chapter to the last there is a succession of scenes of high comedy, and the interest is unflagging. * * *

We have endeavoured to express the delight which Miss Austen's works have always given us, and to explain the sources of her success by indicating the qualities which make her a model worthy of the study of all who desire to understand the art of the novelist. But we have also indicated what seem to be the limitations of her genius, and to explain why it is that this genius, moving only amid the quiet scenes of every-day life, with no power over the more stormy and energetic activities which find vent even in every-day life, can never give her a high rank among great artists. Her place is among great artists, but is is not high among them. She sits in the House of Peers, but it is as a simple Baron. The delight derived from her pictures arises from our sympathy with ordinary characters, our relish of humour, and our intellectual pleasure in art for art's sake. But when it is admitted that she never stirs the deeper emotions, that she never fills the soul with a noble aspiration, or brightens it with a fine idea, but, at the utmost, only teaches us charity for the ordinary failings of ordinary people, and sympathy with their goodness, we have admitted an objection which lowers her claims to rank among the great benefactors of the race; and this sufficiently explains why, with all her excellence, her name has not become a household word. Her fame, we think, must endure. Such art as hers can never grow old, never be superseded. But, after all, miniatures are not frescoes, and her works are miniatures. Her place is among the Immortals; but the pedestal is erected in a quiet niche of the great temple.

RICHARD SIMPSON

[Jane Austen as Ironist and Moralist]†

That the critical faculty was in her the ground and support of the artistic faculty there are several reasons for believing. The first reason is her notable deficiency in the poetical faculty. Perhaps there is no author in existence in whom so marvellous a power of exhibiting characters in formation and action is combined with so total a want of the poetical imagination. Heywood has been called a prose Shakespeare; Miss Austen much more really deserves the title. Within her range her characterization is truly Shakes-

† From Richard Simpson, "Jane Austen," *North British Review*, LII (1870), 131–140.

pearian; but she has scarcely a spark of poetry. Her nephew, who has lately written her biography, gives some lines of hers in memory of Mrs. Lefroy, which only show that in serious poetry her model was Johnson, or Cowper in his more prosaic moods, and that the serious imitation of such a model deprived her of all humour, all delicacy of analysis, all subtlety of thought or language, and led her into affectations and commonplaces which in her novels she would have scornfully criticised. She could, however, write pointed epigrams and tolerable charades; in fact she was just so far a poet as a critic might be expected to be. She even seems to have had an ethical dread of the poetic rapture. At least she makes the latest and more carefully drawn of her heroines declare "that she thought it was the misfortune of poetry to be seldom safely enjoyed by those who enjoyed it completely; and that the strong feelings which alone could estimate it truly were the very feelings which ought to taste it but sparingly."

And secondly, the paramount activity of the critical faculty is clearly seen in the didactic purpose and even nomenclature of her novels. *Pride and Prejudice* and *Sense and Sensibility* are both evidently intended to contrast, and by the contrast to teach something about, the qualities or acts named in the titles. In *Persuasion* the risks and advantages of yielding to advice are set forth. *Northanger Abbey* exhibits the unreality of the notions of life which might be picked out of Mrs. Radcliffe's novels; and *Mansfield Park* and *Emma*, though too many-sided and varied to be easily defined by a specific name, are in reality just as didactic as the rest. This didactic intention is even interwoven with the very plots and texture of the novel. The true hero, who at last secures the heroine's hand, is often a man sufficiently her elder to have been her guide and mentor in many of the most difficult crises of her youth. Miss Austen seems to be saturated with the Platonic idea that the giving and receiving of knowledge, the active formation of another's character, or the more passive growth under another's guidance, is the truest and strongest foundation of love. *Pride and Prejudice*, *Emma*, and *Persuasion* all end with the heroes and heroines making comparisons of the intellectual and moral improvement which they have imparted to each other. The author has before her eyes no fear of the old adage, "Wise lovers are the most absurd." Many of her novels are simply expansions of Shakespeare's ballad which tells of the lordling's daughter loving her tutor, then of his being eclipsed by a knight, and then of the lady's perplexities, and her final decision in favour of her first love:

"Then lullaby, the learned man hath got the lady gay."

Her favourite ideal was to exhibit this intelligent love in its germ, to eclipse it for a season by the blaze of a great passion, to quench this glare, and to exhibit the gentle light of the first love reviving and waxing greater till it perfects itself in marriage. So far was she from agreeing with Marlowe's 'mighty saw,'

"He never loved that loved not at first sight,"

that she expressly writes one of her novels, *Sense and Sensibility*, to controvert the view, to show that the sudden passion is not the lasting affection, and to make true love rather an adjunct of the sober common sense than of the impetuous and passionate side of the soul. In *Pride and Prejudice* too she says, "if gratitude and esteem are good foundations of affection," then her heroine is a proper lover; but "if the regard springing from such sources is unreasonable or unnatural in comparison of what is so often described as arising on a first interview, and even before two words have been exchanged," then nothing is to be said for her, except that she had tried the love at first sight, and found it a failure. In this we see clearly enough her habitual exaltation of judgment over passion, of the critical over the poetical and imaginative faculties. And this fact is perhaps even more perceptible in the manifest irony of her whole mass of compositions. As was the bounden duty of a novelist, she concentrated her forces on bringing her heroes and heroines together, and marrying them off happily. But she generally gives us to understand that a sufficient amount of happiness might have been secured for them in other ways. * * * Her plots always presuppose an organized society of families, of fathers and mothers long married, whose existence has been fulfilled in having given birth to the heroes and heroines of the stories. Now, these people are almost always represented as living together in fair comfort; and yet there is scarcely a single pair of them who have not, on the usual novelist's scale of propriety, been wofully mismatched. Sense and stupidity, solidity and frivolity, are represented as in everyday life cosily uniting, and making up the elements of a home with the usual average of happiness and comfort. Miss Austen does not absolutely tell us that the special ends which she takes so much trouble to bring about are anything short of the highest happiness, or that such happiness could possibly be obtained by any other means. On the contrary, she appears as earnest as other novelists for the success of her favourites. But there is enough in her evident opinions, in her bywords, in her arguments, to prove to any sufficiently clear sight that it would be, after all, much the same whether the proper people intermarried, or whether they were mismatched by some malevolent Puck. Dr. Johnson thought it nonsense to say that marriages were made in heaven, and held that any woman and any man might, if they determined upon it, live well enough together, and settle down into the prosaic happiness of a comfortable couple. In similar manner Miss Austen believed in the ultimate possible happiness of every marriage. * * * Thus the great coil Miss Austen makes to bring the right people together is really much ado about nothing. * * * Now, what is this other than taking a humourist's view of that which as a novelist she was treating as the summum bonum of existence? That predestination of love, that preordained fitness, which decreed that one and one only should be the complement and fulfilment of another's being—that except in union with each other each must live miserably, and that no other solace could be found for either than the other's society—she treated as mere moonshine, while she at the same time founded her novels on the assumption of it as a hypothesis. Her biographer and nephew supposes, as a reason of her never marrying, that her notions of love were too exalted for her to find a man who could satisfy her. Those who can only judge upon the evidence derived from her novels must be led to the belief that in her idea love was only an accident of friendship, friendship being the true light of life, while love was often only a troublesome and flickering blaze which interrupted its equable and soothing influence. Friendship, to judge from her novels, was enough for her; she did not want to exaggerate it into passionate love. In it she in fact seems to have found sufficient tenderness and support to satisfy her cravings; she was contented with her home, with her brothers and sister, and did not want a husband. This gave her a great advantage for describing the perturbations of love. She sat apart on her rocky tower, and watched the poor souls struggling in the waves beneath. And her sympathies were not too painfully engaged; for she knew that it was only an Ariel's magic tempest, and that no loss of life was to follow. Hence she could consider the struggles of the mariners with an amused and ironical complacency, and observe minutely all the hairbreadth escapes of their harmless peril. Accordingly her view of the life she described was that of a humourist, but of a very kindly one. She did not precisely think that all she described was vanity and vexation of spirit. But she thought that, in ordinary language, and especially in that of romance-writers, it was screwed up to a higher tension than the facts warranted. She was conscious that, as a novelist, she was speaking somewhat in Cambyses' vein, and that the earnestness of her language was a little outdoing the truth of things. This consciousness gave her a superiority to her subject, which is one element in solving the secret of her wonderful power over it. She is so true because she is consciously exceeding the truth. Others may believe in the stability of raptures, and in the eternity of a momentary fancy; she knows exactly what they are worth; and, though she puts into the mouths of her puppets the language of faith, she knows how to convey to her readers a feeling of her own scepticism. The most she does is to allow that "the cure of unconquerable passions and the transfer of unchanging attachments must vary very much as to time in different people." Hence that disproportion between her language and her judgment, which constitutes the crucial test of her humour. Hers is not humour of the strongest and vividest kind, which awakens the indirect reminiscence of the Infinite through the disproportion of language and imagery to the finite things which they profess to express. It is not the method of Cervantes, magniloquent on trifles, nor of Swift, trifling away magnificence, both of which methods imply a tacit allusion to a common measure, unseen but felt, which equalizes all finite magnitudes by the overwhelming transcendence of its infinity. Her humour is only partial, investing with more importance than they have things of which she owns the importance; but her pervading critical judgment, which never allows her feelings to run away with her, qualifies her humour, and couples her with such writers as Lamb and Thackeray, rather than with the novelists of the type of Scott. * * *

One more instance of the action of her critical faculty must be mentioned. It is well known that Macaulay has given her a place, far indeed below, but nearest to, Shakespeare, for her power of composing characters.[1] She does not give any of them a hobby-horse, like Sterne, nor a ruling passion, like Pope, nor a humour, like Ben Jonson, nor a trick, like Mr. Dickens. They are all natural, all more or less commonplace, but all discriminated from one another beyond the possibility of confusion, by touches so delicate that they defy analysis, and so true that they elude observation, and only produce the effect by their accumulation. She exhibits no ideal characters, no perfect virtue, no perfect vice. She shows strength dashed with feebleness, feebleness braced with some fibres of strength. Even Mrs. Norris, the only one of her characters who is thoroughly and consistently selfish, ends by placing herself in a situation of trouble and sacrifice, in undertaking to be the guardian of her degraded niece. Willoughby [in *Sense and Sensibility*], the nearest to a villain of her developed characters (Mr. Elliott in *Persuasion* is rather described than

---

1. Macaulay compared Jane Austen's ability to individualize character to that of Shakespeare in his essay, "Ma- dame D'Arblay," *Edinburgh Review,* LXXXIX (1843), 561–562 [*Editor*].

seen), gives so plausible an account of himself that he is thoroughly forgiven by those whom he has most injured; and Wickham, the modified villain of *Pride and Prejudice*, has so much charm about him that his sensible and epicurean father-in-law is almost disposed to like him better than his other and more honourable sons. Miss Austen has a most Platonic inclination to explain away knavishness into folly. Wickedness in her characters is neither unmixed with goodness, nor is it merely a defect of will; she prefers to exhibit it as a weakness of intelligence, an inability of the common-sense to rule the passions which it neither comprehends nor commands. It is her philosophy to see not only the soul of goodness in things evil, but also to see on the face of goodness the impress of weakness and caducity. This is one reason which obliges her to compound her characters. Another is even stronger. It is her thorough consciousness that man is a social being, and that apart from society there is not even the individual. She was too great a realist to abstract and isolate the individual, and to give a portrait of him in the manner of Theophrastus or La Bruyère. Even as a unit, man is only known to her in the process of his formation by social influences. She broods over his history, not over his individual soul and its secret workings, nor over the analysis of its faculties and organs. She sees him, not as a solitary being complete in himself, but only as completed in society. Again, she contemplates virtues, not as fixed quantities, or as definable qualities, but as continual struggles and conquests, as progressive states of mind, advancing by repulsing their contraries, or losing ground by being overcome. Hence again the individual mind can only be represented by her as a battle-field, where contending hosts are marshalled, and where victory inclines now to one side, now to another. A character therefore unfolded itself to her, not in statuesque repose, not as a model without motion, but as a dramatic sketch, a living history, a composite force, which could only exhibit what it was by exhibiting what it did. * * *

Thus each of her characters, like Shakespeare's Richard II, "plays in one person many people," contains within him 'a generation of still breeding thoughts," none of which is "self-contained," but all "intermixed," each modified by something else. And neither in the drama of the soul nor in the drams of life did she allow herself to carry her composition of forces too high, or to make the problem too complicated for her analysis. The heroic passions she never touched; all her characters, as Macaulay owns, are commonplace. And heroic combinations of characters are equally beyond her range. Dramatic she is, but it is only within the lines of the domestic drama. She defined her own sphere when she said that three or four families in a country village were the thing for a novelist to work upon. Each of these "little social common wealths" became a distinct personal entity to her imagination, with its own range of ideas, its own subjects of discourse, its own public opinion on all social matters. Indeed there is nothing in her novels to prove that she had any conception of society itself, but only of the coterie of three or four families mixing together, with differences of intellect, wealth, or character, but without any grave social inequalities. Of organized society she manifests no idea. She had no interest for the great political and social problems which were being debated with so much blood in her day. The social combinations which taxed the calculating powers of Adam Smith or Jeremy Bentham were above her powers. She had no knowledge how to keep up the semblance of personality in the representation of a society reckoned by averages, and no method of impersonating the people or any section of the people in the average man. Her clergymen even have very little of their calling about them; there is little attempt to delineate clerical manners as such, except so far as they may be quizzed or caricatured in the solemn inanities of Mr. Collins, and the touchy parochial dignity of Mr. Elton. The other clergymen are a little more serious and learned than the non-clerical characters; but their classification goes no further. They are members of the family, or the coterie of families, with more or less of distinction from their office; but there is no distinctive social force incarnate in them, nor does the official social weight which they carry become interwoven in the web of their characters. In some of her novels she places her coterie of families in Bath, or even in London; and then Bath society comes in as a picturesque background; but it is only pictorial; it has no more to do with the development of her drama or the explication of her characters than the woods and the hills which she is much more fond of describing. There is not the least attempt to bring public opinion to bear on any one. Some of the characters are said to show too much or too little deference to public opinion; but it is only spoken of, not represented. It is an abstract notion, a word not a thing, an idea not a force. Yet if it had been within the sphere of her power she might have made excellent opportunities for using it. She delights in introducing her heroines in their girlhood, shapeless but of good material, like malleable and ductile masses of gold. We have the flower in the germ, the woman's thought dark in the child's brain; the dream of the artist still involved in the marble block which some external force is to chip and carve and mould. She must have known the force of public opinion in doing work of this kind; and she would no doubt have dramatized public opinion, and exhibited its workings, if she had possessed any such knowledge of it as is displayed by George Eliot or by Mrs. Browning. She was perfect in dramatizing the combination of a few simple forces; but it never struck her to try to dramatize the action and reaction of all.

Platonist as she was in her feelings, she could rise to contemplate the soul as a family, but not as a republic. The disturbances in it were not insurrections or revolutions, but only family quarrels; and the scapegrace passion did not necessarily lose the affections of the family ruler. There is no capital punishment, not even transportation or imprisonment for life, in her ethical statute-book. There lives no faculty within us which the soul can spare, says Wordsworth. It was the same in her code: "every qualification is raised at times, by the circumstances of the moment, to more than its real value"; good-breeding is now and then more opportune than good-nature. The same favour which she shows to younger brothers in the plots of her novels she distributes in her philosophy to the qualifications of the mind which usually only play secondary parts in the symphony of life. It may be strange to attribute to the girl who wrote *Pride and Prejudice* and *Sense and Sensibility* a conscious philosophy which had reasoned out and affirmed all these conclusions; but they were just those which her favourite Cowper would lead her into. There is in fact a great similarity in their views; and the estimate of what people should live for, as insinuated in her novels, is adequately expressed in his lines:

> "He that attends to his interior self,
> That has a heart and keeps it; has a mind
> That hungers, and supplies it; and who seeks
> A social, not a dissipated life,
> Has business."

It is true then to say that the perfection, within their limits, of her delicately compounded characters is quite of a piece with her theories, and that artistic instinct need not be postulated to account for what may be a product of judgment; so that even where her originality is most unquestioned and her power most manifest it is a moot point whether she is a born or a made poet.

A. C. BRADLEY

[Jane Austen as Moralist and Humorist]†

To the historian of literary epochs Jane Austen is, or should be, a little inconvenient. She was born a few years later than Wordsworth, Coleridge, and Scott. When she died, Byron was famous, and Shelley and Keats had already published. She belongs therefore to the period commonly entitled that of the Romantic Revival, or the Revival of Imagination. And yet these titles do not suit her in the least. The Waverley Novels are "romantic" in this special sense, but hers are not. They might even be called anti-romantic. Nor are they more imaginative than those of Richardson and Fielding, in the sense implied in the phrase Revival of Imagination. That other favourite title, again, "return to nature," seems to leave her equally untouched. She was, indeed, intensely fond of the country; but scenery plays no great part in her novels, and we find scarcely a trace of the distinctively new modes of feeling towards nature. She resembles Cowper here, not Wordsworth or Shelley. If we take "return to nature" more widely, she still fails to show this return. She does not write of human nature in its most simple, primitive, or unsocial forms. She has no savages or outlaws; the lower orders appear only and casually in a peasant or two, or an hotel waiter; of the few children, most are spoilt; and she is perfectly innocent of the idea that civilization is the fall of man from some paradisal state of nature. The one contemporary poet with whom she has a marked affinity is Crabbe, but it ceases where Crabbe is most imaginative, as in *Sir Eustace Grey*, or *Prisons*, or *Peter Grimes*. She is separated both by her limitations and by her strength from the greater poets of her time. The strangeness of her position is diminished, no doubt, if we remember that those well-worn titles ignore a large part of the prose literature of her day; but that part was, on the whole, second-rate, and the fact remains that she belongs to the first-rate writers, and is an exception among them. We might even say that she got nothing from the Romantic Revival except the opportunity of making fun of Mrs. Radcliffe. Essentially, it appears to me, her novels belong to the age of Johnson and Cowper.

† From A. C. Bradley, "Jane Austen," *A Miscellany*, London, 1929. Pp. 32–72. Copyright 1929 by Macmillan & Company Ltd. Reprinted by permission of the publishers Macmillan & Company Ltd. and The Macmillan Company of Canada.

There are two distinct strains in Jane Austen. She is a moralist and a humorist. These strains are often blended or even completely fused, but still they may be distinguished. It is the first that connects her with Johnson, by whom, I suspect, she was a good deal influenced. With an intellect much less massive, she still observes human nature with the same penetration and the same complete honesty. She is like him in the abstention—no doubt, in her case, much less deliberate—from speculation, and in the orthodoxy and strength of her religion. She is very like him in her contempt for mere sentiment, and for that "cant" of which Boswell was recommended to clear his mind. We remember Johnson in those passages where she refuses to express a deeper concern than she feels for misfortune or grief, and with both there is an occasional touch of brutality in the manner of the refusal. It is a question, however, of manner alone, and when she speaks her mind fully and gravely she speaks for Johnson too; as when she makes Emma say: "I hope it may be allowed that, if compassion has produced exertion and relief to the sufferers, it has done all that is truly important. If we feel for the wretched enough to do all we can for them, the rest is empty sympathy, only distressing to ourselves." Finally, like Johnson, she is, in the strict sense, a moralist. Her morality, that is to say, is not merely embodied in her plots, it is often openly ex-pressed. She followed a fashion of the day in her abstract titles, *Sense and Sensibility*, *Pride and Prejudice*, *Persuasion*; but the fashion coincides with the movement of her mind, and she knew very well the main lesson to be drawn from the other three novels. Her explicit statements and comments are often well worth pondering, though their terminology is sometimes old-fashioned, and though her novels contain infinitely more wisdom than they formulate. * * *

But Jane Austen's favourite attitude, we may even say her instinctive attitude, is, of course, that of the humorist. And this is not all. The foibles, illusions, self-contradictions, of human nature are a joy to her for their own sakes, but also because through action they lead to consequences which may be serious but may also be comic. In that case they produce sometimes matter fit for a comedy, a play in which people's lives fall into an entanglement of errors, misunderstandings, and cross-purposes, from which they are rescued, not by their own wisdom or skill, but by the kindness of Fortune or some Providence with a weak-ness for lovers. This point of view, the point of view not merely of humour but of comedy, is so marked in Jane Austen's novels as to suggest that she was a good deal influenced by the drama.

So at least it seems to me, though I cannot say by what drama; for I have observed no signs of her acquaintance with Restoration Comedy, or even with Goldsmith or Sheridan, and I have little knowledge of the inferior plays current in her time.[1] But we know that the Austen children used to act, that some of Jane's childish compositions were dramatic in form, that she liked going to the theatre, and that the young people in *Mansfield Park* rehearsed a version by Mrs. Inchbald of a play by Kotzebue. There are not a few dialogues in her works which, one imagines, might be transferred with scarcely any change to the stage. Some scenes that are open to criticism as parts of a novel would be quite in place in a drama. For instance, Mr. Collins's proposal to Elizabeth, delightful as it is, suggests farce; and the effect of Willoughby's sudden nocturnal entrance in extreme agitation just at the moment when Elinor, at the crisis of her sister's illness, is awaiting the arrival of their mother, is perhaps a trifle melodramatic. Mary, again, the third of the Bennet sisters, appears always in the same attitude, like a comedy stock-figure. And where no such criticisms can be maintained, it will still be found that many scenes, as well as persons like Mr. Bennet and Sir Walter Elliot, seem almost to be made for the theatre.

But the resemblance to comedy goes further: it extends to the whole story. In all her novels, though in varying degrees, Jane Austen regards the characters, good and bad alike, with ironical amusement, because they never see the situation as it really is and as she sees it. This is the deeper source of our unbroken pleasure in reading her. We constantly share her point of view, and are aware of the amusing difference between the fact and its appearance to the actors. If you fail to perceive and enjoy this, you are not really reading Jane Austen. Some readers do not perceive it, and therefore fail to appreciate her. Others perceive it without enjoying it, and they think her cynical. She is never cynical, and not often merely satirical. A cynic or a mere satirist may be intellectually pleased by human absurdities and illusions, but he does not feel them to be good. But to Jane Austen, so far as they are not seriously harmful, they are altogether pleasant, because they are both ridiculous and right. * * * No doubt there are plenty of things that should not be, but when we so regard them they are not comical. A main point of difference between Jane Austen and Johnson is that to her much more of the world is amusing, and much more of it is right. She is less of a moralist and more of a humorist.

1. Some one in want of a subject for a Degree thesis might turn his attention to this matter. I owe the identification of *Lovers' Vows* to Mr. Mackail.

REGINALD FARRER

[Truth, Reality, and Good Sense in Jane Austen]†

So far we have looked only at the literary aspect of Jane Austen. The secret of her immortality is to be found in that underlying something which is the woman herself; for, of all writers, she it is who pursues truth with most utter and undeviable devotion. The real thing is her only object always. She declines to write of scenes and circumstances that she does not know at first hand; she refuses recognition, and even condonement, to all thought or emotion that conflicts with truth, or burkes it, or fails to prove pure diamond to the solvent of her acid. She is, in fact, the most merciless, though calmest, of iconoclasts; only her calm has obscured from her critics the steely quality, the inexorable rigour of her judgment. Even Butler, her nearest descendant in this generation, never seems really to have recognised his affinity. For Jane Austen has no passion, preaches no gospel, grinds no axe; standing aloof from the world, she sees it, on the whole, as silly. She has no animosity for it; but she has no affection. She does not want to better fools, or to abuse them; she simply sets herself to glean pleasure from their folly. Nothing but the first-rate in life is good enough for her tolerance; remember Anne Elliot's definition [in *Persusion*] of 'good company,' and her cousin's rejoinder, 'That is not good company; that is the best.'

Everything false and feeble, in fact, withers in the demure greyness of her gaze; in 'follies and nonsense, whims and inconsistencies', she finds nothing but diversion, dispassionate but pitiless. For, while no novelist is more sympathetic to real values and sincere emotion, none also is so keen on detecting false currency, or so relentless in exposing it. At times, even, her antagonism to conventionalities and shams betrays her almost to a touch of passion. Yet, if ever she seems cruel, her anger is but just impatience against the slack thought and ready-made pretences that pass current in the world and move her always to her quiet but destructive merriment; as in the famous outburst [in *Persuasion*] about Miss Musgrove's 'large fat sighings over a son whom alive no one had cared for'—*a cri de cœur* for which

† From Reginald Farrer, "Jane Austen," the *Quarterly Review*, CCXXVIII (1917), 11–12, 16–18. Reprinted by permission of the publishers, John Murray (Publishers) Ltd.

the author for once feels immediately bound to come before the curtain, to mitigate it with a quasi-apology quite devoid of either conviction or recantation. Nor will she hear of any reserves in honesty and candour; not only the truth, but the whole truth, must be vital to any character of whom she herself is to approve. * * *

She is consumed with a passion for the real, as apart from the realistic; and the result is that her creations, though obviously observed, are no less obviously generalised into a new identity of their own. She acknowledges no individual portrait, such as those in which alone such essentially unimaginative writers as Charlotte Brontë can deal. And in this intense preoccupation with character, she is frankly bored with events; the accident at Lyme [in *Persuasion*] shows how perfunctorily she can handle a mere occurrence, being concentrated all the time on the emotions that engender it, and the emotions it engenders. Her very style is the mirror of her temperament. Naturally enough, she both writes and makes her people speak an English much more flowing and lucid than is fashionable in ordinary writers and ordinary life; but, allowing for this inevitable blemish, the note of her style is the very note of her nature, in its lovely limpidity, cool and clear and flashing as an alpine stream, without ebulliencies or turbidness of any kind. It is not for nothing that 'rational' is almost her highest word of praise. Good sense, in the widest meaning of the word, is her be-all and end-all; the perfect σωφροσύνη [moderation, self-control] which is also the perfect αὐταρκεῖα [self-sufficiency]. * * *

But now comes the greatest miracle of English Literature. Straight on the heels of 'Lady Susan' and 'Sense and Sensibility' this country parson's daughter of barely twenty-one breaks covert with a book of such effortless mastery, such easy and sustained brilliance, as would seem quite beyond reach of any but the most mature genius. Yet, though 'Pride and Prejudice' has probably given more perfect pleasure than any other novel (Elizabeth, to Jane Austen first, and now to all time, 'is as delightful a creature as ever appeared in print,' literature's most radiant heroine, besides being the most personally redolent of her creator), its very youthful note of joyousness is also the negation of that deeper quality which makes the later work so inexhaustible. Without ingratitude to the inimitable sparkle of this glorious book, even 'Northanger Abbey,' in its different scale, must be recognised as of a more sumptuous vintage. 'Pride and Prejudice' is, in fact, alone among the Immortal Five, a story pure and simple, though unfolded in and by character, indeed, with a dexterity which the author never aimed at repeating. For, as Jane Austen's power and personality unfold, character becomes more and more the very fabric of her works, and the later books are entirely absorbed and dominated by their leading figures; whereas Darcy and Elizabeth are actors among others in their comedy, instead of being the very essence of it, like Anne or Emma. And to the reader, the difference is that, whereas he can never come to an end of the subtle delights that lurk in every sentence of the later books, there does come a point at which he has 'Pride and Prejudice' completely assimilated.

Perhaps Jane Austen never quite recovered this first fine careless rapture; still, the book has other signs of youth. It has a vice-word, 'tolerably,' and its dialogue retains traces of Fanny Burney. Compare the heavy latinised paragraphs of the crucial quarrel between Darcy and Elizabeth (the sentence which proved so indelible a whip-lash to Darcy's pride is hardly capable of delivery in dialogue at all, still less by a young girl in a tottering passion) with the crisp and crashing exchanges in the parallel scene between Elton and Emma. The later book provides another comparison. Throughout, when once its secret is grasped, the reader is left in no doubt that subconsciously Emma was in love with Knightley all the time. In 'Pride and Prejudice' the author has rather fumbled with an analogous psychological situation, and is so far from making clear the real feeling which underlies Elizabeth's deliberately fostered dislike of Darcy, that she has uncharacteristically left herself open to such a monstrous misreading as Sir Walter Scott's, who believed that Elizabeth was subdued to Darcy by the sight of Pemberley. In point of fact, we are expressly told that her inevitable feeling, 'this might have been mine,' is instantly extinguished by the belief that she could not bear it to be hers, at the price of having Darcy too; while her subsequent remark to Jane is emphatically a joke, and is immediately so treated by Jane herself ('another entreaty that she would be serious,' etc.), wiser than some later readers of the scene.

Sir Walter's example should be a warning of how easy it is to trip even amid the looser mesh of Jane Austen's early work. Rapid reading of her is faulty reading. As for Mr. Collins and Lady Catherine, whom some are ungrateful enough to call caricatures, it must definitely be said that they are figures of fun, indeed, but by no means figures of farce. At the same time both are certainly touched with a youthful sheer delight in their absurdity which gives to them an objective ebullience not to be found in more richly comic studies such as Lady Bertram [in *Mansfield Park*] or Mr. Woodhouse [in *Emma*]. Nor does Jane Austen ever again repeat the parallelism between two sisters, that makes the fabric of the two early books. Already, in her incisive treatment of Charlotte Lucas, the later Jane Austen is foreshadowed; and 'Pride and Prejudice' contains the first example of her special invention, the middle-aged married woman whose delightful presence in the middle-distance of the picture reflects an added pleasantness on the different leading figures with which [they] are brought in contact, as foils and confidants.

MARY LASCELLES

[The Narrative Art of *Pride and Prejudice*]†

'I cannot . . . conceive,' Henry James says, 'in any novel worth discussing at all, of a passage of description that is not in its intention narrative, a passage of dialogue that is not in its intention descriptive, a touch of truth of any sort that does not partake of the nature of incident, or an incident that derives its interest from any other source than the general and only source of the success of a work of art—that of being illustrative.' And, having dealt severely with the critics who like compartments and labels, he asseverates: 'I cannot see what is meant by talking as if there were a part of a novel which is the story and part of it which for mystical reasons is not.'

This conviction of the integrity of a good novel—this impression that it must be unprofitable to study 'plot' and 'characters' separately—is strongly borne out by a study of Jane Austen's narrative art, and by particular observation of the course of its development. Whether we approach it in the first place by way of her presentation of character, or of her construction of plot, we shall discover the need—more urgent as we draw towards the later novels—of reaching some central vantage-point, from which the 'old-fashioned distinction between the novel of character and the novel of incident' (as Henry James calls it) is seen to be insignificant. For, 'What' (he demands) 'is character but the determination of incident? What is incident but the illustration of character?'

It is not often that this can be said of those fictitious characters whose internal mechanism is of the simplest kind—characters to which comedy has always been hospitable. They are often curiously intractable—likely, when they are compelled to serve the main interests of the story, to do or suffer injury. If they

† From Mary Lascelles, *Jane Austen and Her Art*, Oxford, 1939. Pp. 146–63. Copyright 1939. Reprinted by permission of the publishers, The Clarendon Press, Oxford.

have been introduced for the sake of suggesting some contrast, they will either give it an unintended turn—throw queer lights on the figure to which they are to act as foil, as Scott's gallant ruffians do on his heroes—or else lose all characteristics but those that serve for this contrast. * * *

Alternatively, one of these simply organized comic characters may be compelled to do a hand's turn in forwarding the action—with disastrous consequences to his own integrity; of which, I suppose, the most obvious example is Mr. Micawber turned detective. And some such misfortune befalls General Tilney [in *Northanger Abbey*]. The burlesque pattern of the story demands a mock villain and Jane Austen creates accordingly one whom Catherine may suspect but must not see through—who, while she is spelling out his most unimpeachable actions in hope of discovering a Montoni, is indeed acting with a petty duplicity which is apparent to all but her. This is very well; but his violent act at the climax of the story sets him nearer to Catherine's image of him than to that which has been presented to us.

On the other hand, these simply organized characters may injure the texture of the story by refusing to serve its ends. The novels of Scott and Dickens are full of comic characters which perform no service at all—which seem to have got into them merely because they presented themselves to the novelist's imagination and asked for employment in such engaging terms that he did not know how to deny them. Scott indeed confesses that he found, when he attempted to follow a plan, that 'personages were rendered important or insignificant, not according to their agency in the original conception . . . , but according to the success, or otherwise, with which I was able to bring them out.' These unexpected developments may play havoc with the story.

Now one would hardly expect usefulness of Mr. Collins, a creature born of his author's youthful fancy in its most hilarious mood. 'Can he be a sensible man, sir?' Elizabeth asks her father, after hearing him read the letter in which their cousin introduces himself; and Mr. Bennet answers: 'No, my dear; I think not. I have great hopes of finding him quite the reverse.' Indeed, he is a being of some exquisitely non-sensible world, of another element than ours, one to which he is 'native and endued.' Whether he bestows his favour upon Elizabeth, pleased to contemplate the notion of her wit 'tempered with silence', or whether he withdraws it—yet gravely explains that she is not excepted from his good wishes for the health of her family—he does not strain probability, as Sir William Lucas strains it by the simplicity of *his* machinery; he transcends it. And so it is not enough to exclaim, 'No one would speak so'; and one is still too moderate if one protests, 'No one would even think so'; for Mr. Collins is the *quintessence* of a character, in Lamb's sense of the word when he defined quintessence as an apple-pie made all of quinces. He does and says not those things which such a man would say and do, nor even those which he would wish to say and do, but those towards which the whole bias of his nature bends him, and from which no thought of consequences, no faintest sense of their possible impact upon other people, deters him. And is such a creature as this to be put into the shafts and draw a plot? Mr. Elton [in *Emma*], his nearest relation, might, and does, perform such a service, for he, with all his comic exuberance, is a being of our familiar element; but can it be exacted of Mr. Collins? It is, and with capital effect. As well as making his own contribution to the story, by the comedy he plays out with Elizabeth and her family and neighbours, he has to draw and hold together Longbourn and Hunsford; to bring Hunsford within range of our imagination awhile before we can be taken there (and incidentally to confirm Elizabeth's ill opinion of every one connected with Darcy), to draw Elizabeth to Hunsford when the time is ripe, and eventually to send Lady Catherine post-haste to Longbourn on her catastrophic visit. It is worth stopping to notice how unobtrusively this last incident is suggested: Lady Catherine, questioned by Mrs. Bennet, mentions that she saw Mr. and Mrs. Collins 'the night before last.' To Elizabeth, she opens her attack by saying: 'A report of a most alarming nature, reached me two days ago'—the report of her engagement to Darcy. We are left to infer a connexion between these two references; and then, after a sufficient interval for the carriage of a letter, comes Mr. Collins's warning to Elizabeth against 'a precipitate closure with the gentleman's proposals': 'We have reason to imagine that his aunt, lady Catherine de Bourgh, does not look on the match with a friendly eye. . . . After mentioning the likelihood of this marriage to her ladyship last night', he has felt it his duty to offer this warning. Such are the care and ingenuity that Jane Austen expends even on the broadly comic characters of her early invention. * * *

The problem which Mrs. Bennet presents is a little different; she is not the sort of character that is likely to embarrass its creator by uncontrollable vitality—as Mrs. Jennings [in *Sense and Sensibility*] had just done, and Mrs. Smith [in *Mansfield Park*] was to do later; Mrs. Bennet was 'a woman of mean understanding, little information, and uncertain temper. When she was discontented she fancied herself nervous. The business of her life was to get her daughters married; its solace was visiting and news.' That, summing up for us the impressions of her that we have gained from her first appearance, seems to dispose of Mrs. Bennet, to set her where she must remain throughout the story. But we are to have a good deal of her company, for her post is at the centre of the action; and she must not become a dead weight. Mr. E. M. Forster, when he divides the characters of fiction into 'round' and 'flat', brings his argument to a head in this sentence: 'The test of a round character is whether it is capable of surprising in a convincing way. If it never surprises, it is flat. If it does not convince, it is a flat pretending to be round.' [1] But it seems to me that this analysis does not allow for such a character as Mrs. Bennet, of whose comic essence it is that she should be incapable of any but her habitual, and therefore inapposite, reaction to life in all its variety. She must indeed surprise us—in order to keep our response to her alive—but may surprise us only by the inexhaustible variety of expression devised for her unvarying reaction to circumstance. And it is in devising this variety of form for what is substantially invariable—for a Mrs. Bennet who is to be left as she was found 'occasionally nervous and invariably silly'—that Jane Austen displays her virtuosity, giving her creature the entail on Longbourn, a theme of specious importance, to play her variations upon. We hear of it first when Mr. Collins offers himself as a visitor, and Mr. Bennet reminds his wife that this cousin 'when I am dead, may turn you all out of this house as soon as he pleases.' ' "Oh my dear," cried his wife, "I cannot bear to hear that metioned. Pray do not talk of that odious man. I do think it is the hardest thing in the world, that your estate should be entailed away from your own children; and I am sure if I had been you, I should have tried long ago to do something or other about it."

'Jane and Elizabeth attempted to explain to her the nature of an entail. They had often attempted it before, but it was a subject on which Mrs. Bennet was beyond the reach of reason . . .' There we are, in the thick of it, knowing what is to be Mrs. Bennet's inevitable response to this subject, ignorant how its mode will be varied—though the close of this very passage promises something:

'. . . She continued to rail bitterly against the cruelty of settling an estate away from a family of five daughters, in favour of a man whom nobody cared anything about.'

Mr. Collins, on arrival, is offered a sufficiently surprising varia-

---

1. *Aspects of the Novel*, p. 106. He admits, however, some flat characters into comedy, provided they give an illusion of intense vitality. Mr. Muir replies to this passage (*The Structure of the Novel,* 1928, ch. vi) with a plea for the flat character as the 'incarnation of habit'—one aspect, that is, of the truth about people; but this does not wholly account for Mrs. Bennet.

tion on this theme: '. . . Such things I know are all chance in this world. There is no knowing how estates will go when once they come to be entailed'—and contributes something to it himself by his proposal of marrying one of his cousins in reparation. And when this falls through—and, worse still, he marries some one else—Mrs. Bennet returns to her favourite subject with fresh energy: 'How any one could have the conscience to entail away an estate from one's own daughters I cannot understand; and all for the sake of Mr. Collins too!—Why should *he* have it more than anybody else?'

And yet she still has something in reserve for us: when Elizabeth returns from visiting Mr. and Mrs. Collins her mother asks her whether they do not 'often talk of having Longbourn when your father is dead. . . . Well, if they can be easy with an estate that is not lawfully their own, so much the better. *I* should be ashamed of having one that was only entailed on me.' And so she leaves us with the assurance that, as she had been talking of this subject before the story began, so she will continue after its close, ever fresh turns of absurdity, happily corresponding with the busy futility of her actions. * * *

Lady Catherine's part in the story of *Pride and Prejudice* is no less precisely planned, but the fun of it is independent of burlesque; for the execution of this plan is so consistent with the comic essence of her character, that not only her appearances but the very anticipation of them (since she is portentously anticipated) compose themselves into a pattern of comedy. The story is shaped by the original misunderstanding and eventual good understanding between Darcy and Elizabeth; and it is Lady Catherine's office to assist at the first, unwittingly, and at the second against her will: her active interference in their affairs—itself finely in character—is the determining circumstance in their coming to understand one another's feelings and their own. Its effect on Elizabeth is direct and obvious; but what a pleasantly ironic invention it is that Darcy, who has alienated Elizabeth by interfering with her sister's affairs, and is by no means ready to repent his interference, should be roused to indignation and action when Lady Catherine tries to interfere with *his*. Her 'unjustifiable endeavours', as he calls them, to separate him from Elizabeth, send him straight to Longbourn; and so, as Elizabeth remarks: 'Lady Catherine has been of infinite use, which ought to make her happy, for she loves to be of use.' And with that most appropriate valedictory the pattern of her part in the story is completed, as though with a flourish. * * *

Pride and Prejudice is no less deliberately shaped [than *Sense and Sensibility*]; its pattern shows an equal delight in the symmetry of correspondence and antithesis; but there is a notable difference in the contrivance. This pattern is formed by diverging and converging lines, by the movement of two people who are impelled apart until they reach a climax of mutual hostility, and thereafter bend their courses towards mutual understanding and amity. It is a pattern very common in fiction, but by no means easy to describe plausibly.

Of the two courses, Jane Austen traces but one by means of a continuous line; that line, however, is firm and fluent. Elizabeth's chief impetus is due to Wickham; but there is hardly a character in the story who contributes no momentum to it, nor any pressure from without to which she does not respond characteristically. Her misunderstanding of Darcy is thus much less simple, much less like the given condition of an invented problem, than Marianne's misunderstanding of Willoughby, or of Elinor [in *Sense and Sensibility*]. Her initial impulse towards this misunderstanding comes, of course, from Darcy himself, in that piece of flamboyant rudeness which I suspect of being a little out of keeping; but from this point on all follows plausibly. Darcy's more characteristic reference to his own implacability prepares her to believe just what she is going to hear of him so soon as Wickham addresses her. And how insinuating that address is! There had been a suspicion of burlesque about Willoughby's mode of entrance into the story—something that recalls the ironic apology for the absence of the hero in the opening of *Northanger Abbey*; chance has disposed it too smoothly to his advantage. Wickham owes no more to chance than that first silent encounter with Darcy that stirs Elizabeth's wakeful curiosity; it is his adroitness that transforms curiosity into sympathetic indignation. What provincial young lady, brought up among the small mysteries and intrigues of Mrs. Bennet's world, would not be flattered into sympathy by his relation of his own story (so nicely corresponding with that of many heroes in popular fiction), or would criticize him for telling or herself for listening to such a private history? Or what young lady of Elizabeth's self-assurance would suspect that she was not to remain its only hearer? Henceforward his adversaries—and even indifferent spectators—play into his hands: Miss Bingley's insolent interference rouses Elizabeth's pride and clouds her judgement; Charlotte Lucas causes her to mistake her own prejudice for generous sentiment; Mr. Collins, by associating Darcy in her mind with the idol of his worship, strengthens every ill impression; Lady Catherine herself, by answering to Wickham's description, confirms part of his story, and by her proprietary praise of Darcy fixes some of its implications; and Colonel Fitzwilliam, by his indiscreet half-confidence, ensures that Elizabeth shall see Darcy's action towards her sister in the harshest light.

Meanwhile, Darcy's ill opinion of the Bennets has been growing, under the influence of these very people and events, until the climax of the ungracious proposal and refusal is reached. And yet, in the centre of this disturbance, forces have begun to stir, and, almost imperceptibly, to allay it. And this entails a change of course which is very difficult to contrive. The initial impulse must not seem to have spent itself—that would leave a fatal impression of lassitude. There must be deflexion; and this, for Jane Austen, means cause and opportunity to reconsider character and action. (Not conduct alone; she has little use for those casual encounters in ambiguous circumstances which are the staple of Fanny Burney's misunderstandings between lovers.) Even while they are drawing yet farther apart, Elizabeth and Darcy have begun to feel unfamiliar doubts; sure as each still is of his and her own critical judgement, both have come to question the standards of their own social worlds. Her mother's behaviour at Netherfield on two uncomfortable occasions disturbs Elizabeth in such a way as to suggest that she had not been embarrassed by it before; and Charlotte Lucas's conduct shocks her. Presently, Colonel Fitzwilliam's manners give her a standard by which to judge Wickham's. In the meantime Darcy has been unwillingly learning to criticize the manners of his world as it is represented by Miss Bingley, and—touching him more smartly—by Lady Catherine.

'"I have told Miss Bennet several times, that she will never play really well, unless she practises more; and though Mrs. Collins has no instrument, she is very welcome, as I have often told her, to come to Rosings every day, and play on the piano forte in Mrs. Jenkinson's room. She would be in nobody's way, you know, in that part of the house." Mr. Darcy looked a little ashamed of his aunt's ill breeding, and made no answer.'

And so, even when the climax of mutual exasperation is reached, Elizabeth's criticism of Darcy meets some response in his consciousness, his statement of his objections to her family means something to her; and the way is open for each to consider anew the actions and character of the other. What Darcy has done is now shown afresh in his letter; this I do not find quite plausible. The manner is right, but not the matter: so much, and such, information would hardly be volunteered by a proud and reserved man—unless under pressure from his author, anxious to get on with the story. And perhaps it may be the same pressure that hastens Elizabeth's complete acceptance of its witness; for there is no time to lose; she must have revised her whole impression of him before her visit to Pemberley—revised it confidently enough to be able to indicate as much clearly to Wickham, for our benefit: 'I think', she says enigmatically in answer to his searching questions, 'Mr. Darcy improves on acquaintance.' This disturbs and provokes him to further inquiry: ' "For I dare not hope," he continued in a lower and more serious tone, "that he is improved in essentials." "Oh, no!" said Elizabeth. "In essentials, I believe, he is very much what he ever was" '—and she develops this proposition to Wickham's discomfort.

The Pemberley visit is to supplement this revised impression of Darcy with evidence as to character: Mrs. Reynolds is a useful piece of machinery—but I do not think that the more exacting Jane Austen of the later novels would have been content with her. It is more to the purpose that here Darcy and Elizabeth see one another for the first time in favourable—even flattering—circumstances: he at his best on his own estate (a piece of nice observation), and she among congenial companions. Lydia's disgrace has still to come—to give him opportunity for proving that he has taken her strictures to heart, to show her how much he values those hopes of a better understanding which it seems bound to frustrate. And Lady Catherine will involuntarily give the last turn to the plot by her interference. But these are needed to bring about rather the marriage than the better understanding. *That* had sprung from the very nature of the misunderstanding, from the interaction of character and circumstance. There had been, for example, something of wilfulness, even of playfulness, in Elizabeth's mood from the first, to promise eventual reaction: 'I dare say you will find him very agreeable', Charlotte Lucas assures her, when she is to dance with Darcy; and she replies: 'Heaven forbid!—*That* would be the greatest misfortune of all!—To find a man agreeable whom one is determined to hate!—Do not wish me such an evil.'

SAMUEL KLIGER

Jane Austen's *Pride and Prejudice* in the Eighteenth-Century Mode†

It is no difficult task to cull from Jane Austen's *Pride and Prejudice* passages reflecting the period's taste in art and employ-

† From the *University of Toronto Quarterly*, XVI (1945–46), 357–371. Reprinted with the permission of the University of Toronto Press.

ing* a critical terminology made widely current throughout the eighteenth century by many formal discussions of aesthetics. Thus, for example, two performances at the piano by Elizabeth Bennet, the heroine, and her sister Mary, are evaluated in terms of the familiar antithesis, drawn in innumerable essays of the period, between "art" and "nature." Elizabeth performs first and the author comments: "Her performance was pleasing, though by no means capital. After a song or two, and before she could reply to the entreaties of several that she would sing again, she was eagerly succeeded at the instrument by her sister Mary, who having, in consequence of being the only plain one in the family, worked hard for knowledge and accomplishments, was always impatient for display." As for the sister, however: "Mary had neither genius nor taste; and though vanity had given her application, it had given her likewise a pedantic air and conceited manner, which would have injured a higher degree of excellence than she had reached. Elizabeth, easy and unaffected, had been listened to with much more pleasure, though not playing half so well."

A century-long discussion, particularly of Shakespeare, is neatly summarized in this passage. Shakespeare, the period agreed, "wanted art"; but, his natural genius offsetting his neglect of art, he was exonerated. Mrs. Griffith, for example, condemned those "mechanists in criticism" who judged Shakespeare "by the cold rules of artful construction." She remarked further: "Would they restrain him within the precincts of art, the height, the depth of whose imagination and creative genius found even the extent of Nature too streightly bounded for it to move in?" [1] Pope, earlier in the century, had also declared for the "grace beyond the reach of art": "A cooler Judgment may commit fewer Faults, and be more approv'd in the Eyes of *One Sort* of Criticks: but that Warmth of Fancy will carry the loudest and more universal Applauses which holds the Heart of a Reader under the strongest Enchantment." [2]

These were critical commonplaces of the period. The contemporary reader of Jane Austen's novel would recognize at once the critical distinctions between "art" and "nature" involved and would concur, perhaps, in extending the palm not to Mary's artful yet unpleasing rendition but to Elizabeth's "natural" singing despite its obvious failures in the "art" of voice cultivation. On the other hand, however, although Jane Austen's partiality

1. Mrs. Elizabeth Griffith, *The Morality of Shakespeare's Drama Illustrated* (London, 1775), 26; cf. R. W. Babcock, *The Genesis of Shakespeare Idolatry* (Chapel Hill, N.C., 1931), 124–5.

2. Pope, Preface to the translation of the *Iliad;* in W. H. Durham, *Critical Essays of the Eighteenth Century* (New Haven, 1915), 341.

for Elizabeth's vivid style is obvious, it would be a serious mistake to conclude that it was possible for either Jane Austen or her period to deprecate "art" altogether. Nothing could be further from the truth of eighteenth-century aesthetic standards, generally speaking. The whole point of the art-nature antithesis was that it was usable as a basis for erecting an apparatus for the critical analysis of painting, literature, and the fine arts, which by manipulation of the two contraries, "art" and "nature," found excellence in a just mixture of these two opposing qualities. In this kind of analysis, faults were identified with excesses in any one extreme or exclusive emphasis on one extreme of style. The rationalistic temper of the period required that excellence be found in a mean between two extremes.[3] Only those readers persuaded by the false classic-romantic dichotomy embalmed in the simpler sort of literary text-books will find in Jane Austen's relative partiality for Elizabeth an absolute condemnation of Mary's "art." As a matter of fact, those who read the novel in this rigid manner will fail to see that by a kind of calculated ambiguity, Jane Austen has purposely set up in the singing scene two alternative possibilities of interpretation: i.e., Elizabeth's "naturalness" is either praiseworthy or to be condemned. Before the novel's end, it will become apparent that, one alternative removed, the remaining alternative fixes the conception of Elizabeth's character and attitudes.[4]

The contrast between Elizabeth's "natural" and Mary's "artful" rendition is soon extended, as anyone can expect who is even moderately well read in eighteenth-century aesthetic discussion, to involve a second set of terms, held in essential opposition: "reason" and "feeling." Thus Mary comments on Elizabeth's decision to walk the three miles to the Bingley home in order to investigate Jane's illness: "I admire the activity of your benevolence, . . . but every impulse of feeling should be guided by reason; and, in my opinion, exertion should always be in proportion to what is required." Art and reason are the terms on one side of the antithesis; nature and benevolence are the terms on the other side. The contextual shift along the line from "art" (a

3. Cf. the brilliant article, from which I have quoted practically verbatim, by R. S. Crane, "English Criticism: Neoclassicism," in *Dictionary of World Literature*, ed. by Joseph T. Shipley (New York, 1943); Crane also quotes appositely from an eighteenth-century source: "The same just moderation must be observed in regard to ornaments; nothing will contribute more to destroy repose than profusion. . . . On the other hand, a work without orna-

ment, instead of simplicity, to which it makes pretensions, has rather the appearance of poverty." (P. 198.)
4. Cf. Reuben A. Brower, "The Controlling Hand: Jane Austen and *Pride and Prejudice*" (*Scrutiny*, XIII, 1945, 99–111); Brower calls attention to this device of calculated ambiguity although he does not deal with the music episode. [A later version of Brower's essay is reprinted below (*Editor*).]

literary norm) to "reason" (an ethical norm) is readily recognizable as a commonplace in the neo-classical idea-complex. From Shaftesbury onwards, taste in art had almost invariably been conceived as a species of virtue. No notion was more characteristic of English neo-classicism than the idea that taste in the fine arts is an ally of morals. The eighteenth century believed that both the feeling for beauty and the prizing of what is decent and proper, perfect the character of the gentleman. As Alexander Gerard expressed it in his *Essay on Taste*: "A man of nice taste will have a stronger abhorrence of vice and a keener relish for virtue, in any given situation, than a person of dull organs can have in the same circumstances." [5] Because of the contextual shift or correlation of art with morals, Elizabeth's emotionalism is to be seen as the correlative of her artless singing. Furthermore, her indecorous behaviour, although clearly motivated by a warm devotion to her sick sister, Jane, also suggests, nevertheless, possibilities of censure, in that the century saw moral excellence as action conforming, as does good art, to a universal criterion of the mean between two extremes. In other words, Elizabeth's emotionalism is not only correlative to her natural style of singing but by calculated ambiguity is purposely presented in the novel in such a way as to suggest possibilities of both praise and censure. By means of this artistic device, the novel's end is practically dictated: that is, the period's rationalistic quest of the mean between two extremes requires that the probabilities for the heroine's behaviour be set up between two alternatives, neither of which is acceptable alone; the rejection of one alternative makes spectacularly clear to the heroine (and the reader) that the solution lies not in the remaining alternative but in a just moderation between the two.

In a third passage, the bi-polar terms "art" and "nature" reveal yet another tension in the neo-classical idea-complex, between "originality" (inspiration, spontaneity, singularity, enthusiasm, excess, the untutored genius—these are all synonymous in current critical usage) and the opposite of originality, the "rules" (regularity, uniformity, propriety, *bon sens*, the appeal to precedent and the example of Greek and Roman antiquity, the disciplined artist—these are all synonyms in the eighteenth-century vocabulary of criticism). The tension is brought to light in Mary's comment on Collins' letter: "In point of composition, . . . , his letter does not seem defective. The idea of the olive branch perhaps is not wholly new, yet I think it is well ex-

5. Quoted by W. G. Howard, "Good Taste and Conscience" (*PMLA*, XXV, 1910, 486–97).

pressed." Mary's measured praise of Collins' epistolary style is in accord with Pope's dictum,

> True wit is Nature to advantage dress'd
> What oft was thought, but ne'er so well express'd,

as only one expression out of many of the period's critical viewpoint towards "originality." Jane Austen's contemporary readers, simply because their values were the same as Jane Austen's, did not need to be reminded, as does the modern reader, either of the critical distinction between the term "originality" and its antithetical correlative "uniformity," or that these concepts were transvaluations of the basic antithesis between "art" and "nature." In the pattern, Mary is the symbol of art, reason, uniformity while Elizabeth is the symbol of nature, benevolence, originality.

The subject of letter-writing, in a fourth passage, causes a shift a second time in the narrative from art and nature, conceived unilaterally in their aesthetic application, to the question of a universal standard of excellence common to art and morals alike. Darcy is composing a letter and Miss Bingley, whose game it is to detract from Elizabeth's charm, monopolizes the conversation. In this sequence, Miss Bingley is twitting Darcy on his slow, laborious writing. In verbal parry and thrust, the information is elicited that Bingley, by contrast, is a rapid writer: "My ideas flow so rapidly that I have not time to express them; by which means my letters sometimes convey no ideas at all to my correspondents." Elizabeth, who is only too eager to humble Darcy's pride—if she can—takes the occasion to praise Bingley's modesty in confessing his epistolary faults. Darcy, however, is not prone to accept her judgment, and he even condemns such modesty as a kind of hypocrisy. As the banter grows, it becomes clear that Darcy reproves "precipitance" (it is his own word) in letter-writing and in social conduct. The tie of friendship between Bingley and himself notwithstanding, there is no point, Darcy is saying, in shrinking from condemning Bingley's epistolary deficiencies. Darcy is offended by Bingley's epistolary improprieties as if they were moral misdemeanors—this, of course, is possible only because the period correlated art with morals. In addition, Darcy is arguing that Elizabeth is compounding the original error in seeking exculpation in friendship. Darcy's overbearing manner may be reprehensible, and before the novel's end he too will approach the mean and allow for the ties of friendship; but because of the century's rationalistic "religion," there is in his reprimand of Elizabeth and Bingley more of a defence of the universe's rational aims and goals than there is a defence of a purely literary standard. Propriety for Darcy is universal and immutable, imbedded in the rational scheme of things, or is, rather, the means of achieving life's rational ends. * * *

These are the passages on art criticism which *Pride and Prejudice* yields to the attentive reader. However, as we have already seen, it is a quite dubious procedure which would attempt to establish a partiality on Jane Austen's part for any one of the critical ideas which the novel expresses. Critical ideas introduced within the context of a novel are not at all the same as critical ideas expressed in a formal treatise on the subject. At any rate, even if we waive the objection, the search for typical eighteenth-century critical ideas in *Pride and Prejudice* would nevertheless tend to miss the whole point, which can be expressed in the following way: in both great and small plots, the novel intends to invoke the same thoughts and attitudes about the antithesis of art and nature. The concentration, in fact, in the small plot on singing, letter-writing, the enjoyment of mountainous sublimity, the appreciation of gardening, carries out Jane Austen's carefully premeditated plan for increasing the availability of the art-nature antithesis for the love plot or basic situation of the novel. In other words, the art-nature antithesis is abstracted into a symbolism adequate to cover the adventures and misadventures which keep Elizabeth and Darcy apart in mutual repulsion at the beginning of the tale and bring them together at the end. Instead, therefore, of selecting passages by an eclectic method in the interest of a systematic exposition of Jane Austen's views on art, the passages ought to be chosen by a formal method, treating the book as an art form with its own laws of development, in the interest of establishing the mutual appropriateness of the art-nature antithesis to the probabilities for action set up in the characters, who are arranged along a scale from one extreme of behaviour suggested by the terms art and reason to the extreme at the opposite end of the scale suggested by the terms nature and emotion.

The purpose of this essay, therefore, is first to establish the art-nature antithesis as the ground of the book's action and its mode of organization and, second, to show that the doctrine of art and reason is extended to morals, to include, in particular, a concept of class relationships. Darcy's pride of class is persistently misunderstood by Elizabeth and what she must learn is that his pride—under proper limitations—is appropriate and a proper human trait. Contrariwise, Darcy must learn that Elizabeth's prejudice for dealing with humans *qua* humans, irrespective of class, is—again under proper limitations—appropriate and an admirable human trait. Thus between the problem posed

in the initial scenes of the novel and its resolution at the book's
end is a dialectic which separates the two leading characters
in the beginning and joins them at the end in a mean between
the two extremes which each respectively represents. Jane Austen
has a host of admirers, but it seems merely idle to praise her
perfection of form without being able to indicate in specific
ways how the perfection is achieved. The governing idea of
Pride and Prejudice is the art-nature antithesis; the perfection
of form is achieved through relating each character and incident
to the basic art-nature dialectic. A concentration on the art-
nature contrast at the book's beginning in the sequence describing
Mary's art and Elizabeth's artlessness prepares the reader to recognize that it is precisely the same dialectic between whose ebb
and flow Elizabeth and Darcy, in their conflicting attitudes
towards class relationships, gyrate. Tracing the art-nature dialectic
will give clearer meaning to *Pride and Prejudice* and will show
how completely dedicated Jane Austen was to the art of fiction.

The ethical expression of the art-nature opposition which
governs the novel appears in an antithesis between primitivism
and society. The reader of Jane Austen's novel should recall
that because of a vogue in the eighteenth century of primitivistic
discussion, the term "nature" had also established itself as one
item of an antithesis on another level between the "arts" (man-
made) and that which is in "nature" (God-made); the antithesis
could be used to indicate whether civilization was progressing
from the primitive state of nature because of man's progress
in the arts, manufactures, organized government, and private
property; or, conversely, whether civilization was retrograding
because the arts, manufactures, government, and private property
represented a perversion of nature. Elizabeth's prejudice toward
Darcy's pride of class, her insistence on dealing with humans
qua humans (naturally, that is) express the ideas at the primitivistic pole of the antithesis; Darcy is the spokesman for civilization, man-made and not in "nature," especially as he speaks in
terms of a theory of class stratification. Elizabeth represents
"man-in-nature," the earlier felicity and joy existing in the class-
less, government-less, property-less conditions surrounding men
in the Garden of Eden before the Fall. Darcy represents the
consequences of the fall of man, the arts of society and government necessary to restrain the wickedness and greed of men resulting from their fall from the bliss of Eden. In Darcy culminates
a centuries-old tradition, carefully nurtured by Christian thinkers
throughout the medieval period and carried down to modern
times without significant change. * * *

We are now at the heart of the Elizabeth-Darcy problem. The issues are clear: (1) A tension is created between the conceptions of man-in-nature and man-in-society; the first deals with humans *qua* humans, the second deals with humans as the "art" of society directs their activities. (2) Pride in class is a proper and justifiable human trait; superiority, so far from being a usurped right, is actually a heavy burden of duties which one assumes; the essential meaning of *noblesse oblige* is this willingness to serve. (3) Since no class exists for itself but is bound by reciprocated rights and duties to classes above and below, social non-compliance is represented either in improper respect for classes above or in delinquency in duty to classes below. (4) The system embodies the universal criterion of the mean between the two extremes; the individual's worth *qua* individual is adjusted to his worth as a member of a social class, whatever his class may be; a dialectic separates the natural man from man as the art of society has created him; nature and art are the juxtaposed terms. Considering the dialectic which separates the two terms, it is instructive to observe how the great Renaissance rationalist, Bishop Hooker, formulated the problem. He pointed out that individuals who are perfectly exemplary are not necessarily the same considered as members of society: "It is both commonly said, and truly, that the best men otherwise are not always the best in regard of society. The reason whereof is, for that the law of men's actions is one, if they be respected only as men; and another, when they are considered as parts of a public body. Many men there are, than whom nothing is more commendable when they are singled; and yet in society with others none less fit to answer the duties which are looked for at their hands." [6]

Since it is Darcy who capitulates first and early in the book, the real concern of the author is evidently Elizabeth's quest of the mean between the two extremes of "art" and "nature." It is Elizabeth who must set her emotional house in order and learn to evaluate all that has happened to her in terms of the mean between the two extremes of the "art" of human relationships and humans in their "natural" associations. In Bishop Hooker's terms, she is an exemplary person as an individual, but she is socially deficient. On the other hand, Darcy is socially exemplary but is deficient in naturalness.

In the letter-writing scene, resentful of Darcy's stiff-necked pride, Elizabeth scores a point for herself, although ostensibly she is defending Bingley's relaxed epistolary style against Darcy's condemnation of such indecorum. She says: "You appear to

<hr />

6. Bishop Hooker, *Of the Laws of Ecclesiastical Politie*, ed. by R. W. Church (Oxford, 1896), I. XVI. 6, pp. 103–4.

me, Mr. Darcy, to allow nothing for the influence of friendship and affection." Elizabeth may be right, but she may be wrong also. Darcy scores a point for reason and the "art" of human relationships when he replies: "Pride—where there is a real superiority of mind—pride will always be under good regulation." Pride, he is saying, is a proper human trait; but Elizabeth is scornful. Her prejudice for dealing with humans *qua* humans, irrespective of class standards, naturally instead of artfully, emotionally instead of rationally, has nearly fatal consequences for her in so far as it almost brings her to a marriage with Wickham.

Wickham precipitates the main action. In the first place, he raises the crucial problem of reciprocated rights and duties. The question is whether the Darcys, father and son, have been true to their class mission of rewarding a faithful servitor. Slyly but shrewdly, Wickham encourages Elizabeth to believe that the younger Darcy has been remiss in his social duties. The entire incident is revealing not only of Wickham's rascality but of Darcy's class idealism and of Elizabeth's failure to consider more sympathetically Darcy's class pride which debars him from expostulating even when he has been seriously libelled.

The fundamental principle of *noblesse oblige* is never to complain, never to explain. No gentleman will either complain or explain when his actions are falsely reported. It is beneath Darcy's pride to explain that Wickham had signed away for cash his right to the Darcy patronage. Darcy by his attitude acknowledges the merit of the phrase *"honi soit qui mal y pense"*—and it is certainly part of Elizabeth's later humiliation that she must recognize her failure to understand Darcy's silence. With perfect consistency, Darcy afterwards serves Elizabeth silently and well in the Lydia-Wickham elopement by removing the financial obstacles in the way of the marriage. On the other hand, Wickham further displays his lack of principles in his loud complaints to Elizabeth.

Elizabeth falls victim to Wickham's strategy only because of her prejudice for dealing with people naturally, irrespective of class. It is characteristic of her that she seeks to measure Darcy for human consistency and she fails for the obvious reason that she is measuring him with the wrong measuring stick. This is brought out in her reply to Wickham that, granting Darcy his pride, his pride alone should have encouraged him to discharge his class obligation to his former steward: "How strange! . . . How abominable! I wonder that the very pride of this Mr. Darcy has not made him just to you! If from no better motive, that he should not have been too proud to be dishonest—for dishonesty I must call it."

In a chastened spirit, Elizabeth learns to respect Darcy's pride of class. Her surrender is expressed explicitly in the words which she intends to remove her father's anxiety about her impending marriage with Darcy: "I love him. Indeed he has no improper pride." A complete surrender of either Darcy or Elizabeth to the other would completely falsify the eighteenth century's ideal of moderation and would obscure the basic art-nature antithesis. As it is, the partial capitulation of each to the other makes clear that each recognizes that every quality has its corresponding defect. With a sudden pleasant surprise, the reader recalls that early in the novel, Jane Austen, with an irony that must have been deliberate, suggests the idea as the premise upon which in the central sequence of the novel the quest proceeds for the mean between extremes when she has Darcy say: "There is, I believe, in every disposition a tendency to some particular evil, a natural defect, which not even the best education can overcome." The exposure of Wickham's perfidy makes Elizabeth, as she reflects backwards on her wilful misunderstanding of Darcy's class idealism, realize her defect of considering people exclusively in their natural relations with corresponding neglect of their opposite qualities arising out of their social relations as the arts of government and society shape them.

It is not intended to suggest that Elizabeth is a doctrinaire revolutionary, aiming to level all classes. There is not a single statement in the novel which can be construed as politically tendentious. On this score alone, the critics are quite right who point out that Jane Austen was totally unaffected by the currents of thought set up by the French Revolution; not even her relative residing in her house, whose husband was beheaded by the guillotine, moved her to interpret the Revolution. Yet *Pride and Prejudice* is not merely a mild satire on manners but, as we have seen, hands down a social verdict. The satire in the novel on social institutions hardly ripples the surface, but the currents underneath are powerful. If the conclusion of the novel makes clear that Elizabeth accepts class relationships as valid, it becomes equally clear that Darcy, through Elizabeth's genius for treating all people with respect for their natural dignity, is reminded that institutions are not an end in themselves but are intended to serve the end of human happiness.

If Elizabeth is not a Leveller, intent on levelling all classes, it is nevertheless interesting to observe how much the spirit of the great seventeenth-century Levellers has entered into her mind. Modern democracy was forged, as we know, in the fiery furnace of the Cromwellian revolution. The noblest words ever spoken for democracy came from the famous Putney Debates in which the question was raised whether property should be a qualification for voting. Rainborough, a Leveller, declared: "For really I think that the poorest he that is in England hath a life to live, as the greatest he." Rainborough was defeated and the property qualification remained. The steady growth, however, of the franchise in England bears witness to the fact that Leveller ideas of respect for natural human dignity have never failed to inspire English political thinking. Perhaps this is merely another way of pointing to the English genius for bringing about the most revolutionary changes in the mildest way possible. The compromise effected between Elizabeth and Darcy represents the same phenomenon, and in this sense Elizabeth is a Leveller and Darcy represents those in the Cromwellian group who argued for the preservation of the property qualification. Elizabeth learns that we must not scorn the accumulated wisdom of past experience which has shaped during centuries the institution of class; Darcy, on the other hand, learns that conservatism need not be impervious to new ideas. And here, perhaps, we have the sufficient answer to those critics of Jane Austen who claim that she was politically and socially obtuse. A livelier appreciation among readers of Jane Austen's novel of the potency of the terms "art" and "nature" in the thinking of such typical eighteenth-century political writers as Burke, Rousseau, Priestley, and Paine, would make it clearer that the art-nature antithesis was an explicit intellectual formulation growing out of the rationalistic spirit of the age. Developed now in aesthetic discussion and now in political discussion, the terms at the bottom were the same since the century sought a universal criterion of a mean between extremes common to art and morals alike.

DOROTHY VAN GHENT

On *Pride and Prejudice*†

It is the frequent response of readers who are making their first acquaintance with Jane Austen that her subject matter is itself so limited—limited to the manners of a small section of English country gentry who apparently never have been worried about death or sex, hunger or war, guilt or God—that it can offer no contiguity with modern interests. This is a very real difficulty in an approach to an Austen novel, and we should not obscure it; for by taking it initially into consideration, we can begin to come

† From Dorothy Van Ghent, *The English Novel*, Form and function. New York, 1953. Pp. 105–23. Copyright 1953. Reprinted by permission of the publishers Holt, Rinehart and Winston, Inc.

closer to the actual toughness and sublety of the Austen quality. The greatest novels have been great in range as well as in technical invention; they have explored human experience a good deal more widely and deeply than Jane Austen was able to explore it. It is wronging an Austen novel to expect of it what it makes no pretense to rival—the spiritual profundity of the very greatest novels. But if we expect artistic mastery of limited materials, we shall not be disappointed.

The exclusions and limitations are deliberate; they do not necessarily represent limitations of Jane Austen's personal experience. Though she led the life of a maiden gentlewoman, it was not actually a sheltered life—not sheltered, that is, from the apparition of a number of the harsher human difficulties. She was a member of a large family whose activities ramified in many directions, in a period when a cousin could be guillotined, when an aunt and uncle could be jailed for a year on a shopkeeper's petty falsification, and when the pregnancies and childbed mortalities of relatives and friends were kept up at a barnyard rate. Her letters show in her the ironical mentality and the eighteenth-century gusto that are the reverse of the puritanism and naïveté that might be associated with the maidenly life. What she excludes from her fictional material does not, then, reflect a personal obliviousness, but, rather, a critically developed knowledge of the character of her gift and a restriction of its exercise to the kind of subject matter which she could shape into most significance. When we begin to look upon these limitations, not as having the negative function of showing how much of human life Jane Austen left out, but as having, rather, the positive function of defining the form and meaning of the book, we begin also to understand that kind of value that can lie in artistic mastery over a restricted range. This "two inches of ivory" (the metaphor which she herself used to describe her work), though it may resemble the handle of a lady's fan when looked on scantly, is in substance an elephant's tusk; it is a savagely probing instrument as well as a masterpiece of refinement.

Time and space are small in *Pride and Prejudice*. Time is a few months completely on the surface of the present, with no abysses of past or future, no room for mystery; there is time only for a sufficiently complicated business of getting wived and husbanded and of adapting oneself to civilization and civilization to oneself. Space can be covered in a few hours of coach ride between London and a country village or estate; but this space is a *physical* setting only in the most generalized sense; it is space as defined by a modern positivistic philosopher—"a place for an argument." The concern is rational and social. What is relevant is the way minds operate in certain social circumstances, and the physical particular has only a derived and subordinate relevance, as it serves to stimulate attitudes between persons. Even the social circumstances are severely restricted: they are the circumstances of marriageable young women coming five to a leisure-class family with reduced funds and prospects. What can be done with this time and space and these circumstances? What Jane Austen does is to dissect—with what one critic has called "regulated hatred" [1] —the monster in the skin of the civilized animal, the irrational acting in the costumes and on the stage of the rational; and to illuminate the difficult and delicate reconciliation of the sensitively developed individual with the terms of his social existence.

"It is a truth universally acknowledged, that a single man in possession of a good fortune must be in want of a wife." This is the first sentence of the book. What we read in it is its opposite— a single woman must be in want of a man with a good fortune— and at once we are inducted into the Austen language, the ironical Austen attack, and the energy, peculiar to an Austen novel, that arises from the compression between a barbaric subsurface marital warfare and a surface of polite manners and civilized conventions. Marriage—that adult initiatory rite that is centrally important in most societies whether barbarous or advanced—is the uppermost concern. As motivated for the story, it is as primitively powerful an urgency as is sex in a novel by D. H. Lawrence. The tale is that of a man hunt, with the female the pursuer and the male a shy and elusive prey. The desperation of the hunt is the desperation of economic survival: girls in a family like that of the Bennets must succeed in running down solvent young men in order to survive. But the marriage motivation is complicated by other needs of a civilized community: the man hunters must observe the most refined behavior and sentiments. The female is a "lady" and the male is a "gentleman"; they must "fall in love." Not only must civilized appearances be preserved before the eyes of the community, but it is even necessary to preserve dignity and fineness of feeling in one's own eyes.

The second sentence outlines the area in which the aforementioned "truth universally acknowledged" is to be investigated —a small settled community, febrile with social and economic rivalry.

> However little known the feelings or views of such a man may be on his first entering a neighborhood, this truth is so well fixed in the minds of the surrounding families, that he is considered as the rightful property of some one or other of their daughters.

Here a high valuation of property is so dominant a culture trait that the word "property" becomes a metaphor for the young man himself; and the phrasing of the sentence, with typical Austen

1. D. W. Harding, "Regulated Hatred: An Aspect of the Work of Jane Aus-   ten," *Scrutiny*, March, 1940.

obliquity, adds a further sly emphasis to this trait when it uses an idiom associated with the possession of wealth—"well fixed" —as a qualifier of the standing of "truth." We are told that the young man may have "feelings or views" of his own (it becomes evident, later, that even daughters are capable of a similar willful subjectivity); and we are warned of the embarrassment such "feelings or views" will cause, whether to the individual or to the community, when we read of those "surrounding families" in whom "truth" is "so well fixed"—portentous pressure! And now we are given a light preliminary draft of the esteemed state of marriage, in the little drama of conflicting perceptions and wills that the first chapter presents between the imbecilic Mrs. Bennet and her indifferent, sarcastic husband. "The experience of three and twenty years had been insufficient to make his wife understand his character." The marriage problem is set broadly before us in this uneasy parental background, where an ill-mated couple must come to terms on the finding of mates for their five daughters. A social call must be made, in any case, on the single gentleman of good fortune who has settled in the neighborhood. With the return of the call, and with the daughters set up for view—some of whom are "handsome," some "good-natured"—no doubt he will buy, that is to say, "fall in love" (with such love, perhaps, as we have seen between Mr. and Mrs. Bennet themselves).

In this first chapter, the fundamental literary unit of the single word—"fortune," "property," "possession," "establishment," "business"—has consistently been setting up the impulsion of economic interest against those nonutilitarian interests implied by the words "feelings" and "love." [2] The implications of the word "marriage" itself are ambivalent; for as these implications are controlled in the book, "marriage" does not mean an act of ungoverned passion (not even in Lydia's and Wickham's rash elopement does it mean this: for Wickham has his eye on a settlement by blackmail, and Lydia's infatuation is rather more with a uniform than with a man); marriage means a complex engagement between the marrying couple and society—that is, it means not only "feelings" but "property" as well. In marrying, the individual marries society as well as his mate, and "property" provides the necessary articles of this other marriage. With marriage so defined, as the given locus of action, the clash and reconciliation of utility interests with interests that are nonutilitarian will provide a subtle drama of manners; for whatever

2. This point of view is developed by Mark Schorer in the essay "Fiction and the 'Analogical Matrix,'" in *Critiques and Essays on Modern Fiction*, edited by John W. Aldridge (New York: The Ronald Press Company, 1952), pp. 83–98. [Schorer's essay was first printed in *Kenyon Review*, XI (1949), 539–560 (*Editor*).]

spiritual creativity may lie in the individual personality, that creativity will be able to operate only within publicly acceptable modes of deportment. These modes of deportment, however public and traditional, must be made to convey the secret life of the individual spirit, much as a lens conveys a vision of otherwise invisible constellations. Language itself is the lens in this case—the linguistic habits of social man.

Below language we do not descend, except by inference, for, in this definitively social world, language is the index of behavior, the special machine which social man has made to register his attitudes and to organize his dealings with others. We have spoken of Jane Austen's exclusion of the physical particular. One might expect that in her treatment of the central problem of marriage she could not avoid some physical particularity—some consciousness of the part played by the flesh and the fleshly passions in marriage. Curiously and quite wonderfully, out of her restricted concern for the rational and social definition of the human performance there does arise a strong implication of the physical. Can one leave this novel without an acute sense of physical characterizations—even of the smells of cosmetic tinctures and obesity in Mrs. Bennet's boudoir, or of the grampus-like erotic wallowings of the monstrous Mr. Collins? Nothing could be stranger to an Austen novel than such representations of the physical. And yet, from her cool, unencumbered understanding of the linguistic exhibitions of the parlor human, she gives us, by the subtlest of implication, the human down to its "naturals," down to where it is human only by grace of the fact that it talks English and has a set of gestures arbitrarily corresponding to rationality.

Among the "daughters" and the "young men of fortune" there are a few sensitive individuals, civilized in spirit as well as in manner. For these few, "feeling" must either succumb to the paralysis of utility or else must develop special delicacy and strength. The final adjustment with society, with "property" and "establishment," must be made in any case, for in this book the individual is unthinkable without the social environment, and in the Austen world that environment has been given once and forever—it is unchangeable and it contains the only possibilities for individual development. For the protagonists, the marriage rite will signify an "ordeal" in that traditional sense of a moral testing which is the serious meaning of initiation in any of the important ceremonies of life. What will be tested will be their integrity of "feeling" under the crudely threatening social pressures. The moral life, then, will be equated with delicacy and integrity of feeling, and its capacity for growth under adverse conditions. In the person of the chief protagonist, Elizabeth, it really will be equated with intelligence. In this conception of the moral life, Jane Austen shows herself the closest kin to Henry James in the tradition of the English novel; for by James, also, the moral life was located in emotional intelligence, and he too limited himself to observation of its workings in the narrow area of a sophisticated civilization.

The final note of the civilized in *Pride and Prejudice* is, as we have said, reconciliation. The protagonists do not "find themselves" by leaving society, divorcing themselves from its predilections and obsessions. In the union of Darcy and Elizabeth, Jane and Bingley, the obsessive social formula of marriage-to-property is found again, but now as the happy reward of initiates who have travailed and passed their "ordeal." The incongruities between savage impulsions and the civilized conventions in which they are buried, between utility and morality, are reconciled in the symoblic act of a marriage which society itself—bent on useful marriages—has paradoxically done everything to prevent. Rightly, the next to the last word in the book is the word "uniting."

We have so far attempted to indicate both the restrictive discipline which Jane Austen accepted from her material and the moral life which she found in it. The significance of a given body of material is a function of the form which the artist gives to the material. Significance is, then, not actually "found" by the artist in his subject matter, as if it were already and obviously present there for anyone to see, but is created by him in the act of giving form to the material (it was in this sense that poets were once called trouvères, or "finders"). The form of the action of *Pride and Prejudice* is a set of "diverging and converging lines" [3] mathematically balanced in their movements, a form whose diagrammatic neatness might be suggested in such a design as that given below, which shows the relationship of correspondence-with-variation between the Darcy-Elizabeth plot and the Jane-Bingley subplot, the complication of the former and the simplicity of the latter, the successive movements toward splitting apart and toward coming together, and the final resolution of movement in "recognition" and reconciliation between conflicting claims, as the total action composes itself in the shape of the lozenge (see the chart on page 368).

But significant form, as we have noted in previous studies, is a far more complex structure of relationships than those merely of plot. An Austen novel offers a particularly luminous illustration of the function of style in determining the major form. Our diagram of the plot movements of *Pride and Prejudice* will serve as visualization of a pattern of antithetical balances found also in the

3. The phrase and the observation are those of Mary Lascelles, in *Jane Austen and Her Art* (New York: Oxford University Press, 1939), p. 160.

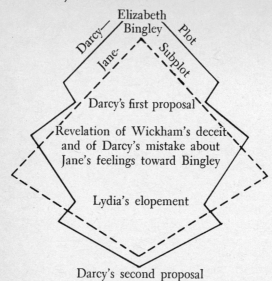

verbal composition of the book. It is here, in style, in the language base itself, that we are able to observe Jane Austen's most deft and subtle exploitation of her material.

The first sentence of the book—"It is a truth universally acknowledged, that a single man in possession of a good fortune must be in want of a wife"—again affords an instance in point. As we have said, the sentence ironically turns itself inside out, thus: a single woman must be in want of a man with a good fortune. In this doubling of the inverse meaning over the surface meaning, a very modest-looking statement sums up the chief conflicting forces in the book: a decorous convention of love (which holds the man to be the pursuer) embraces a savage economic compulsion (the compulsion of the insolvent female to run down male "property"), and in the verbal embrace they appear as a unit. The ironic mode here is a mode of simultaneous opposition and union: civilized convention and economic primitivism unite in the sentence as they do in the action, where "feelings" and "fortune," initially in conflict, are reconciled in the socially creative union of marriage.

This is but one type of verbal manipulation with which the book luxuriates. Another we shall illustrate with a sentence from Mr. Collins' proposal to Elizabeth, where "significant form" lies in elaborate rather than in modest phrasing. Mr. Collins manages to wind himself up almost inextricably in syntax.

"But the fact is, that being as I am, to inherit this estate after the death of your honored father, (who, however, may live many years longer,) I could not satisfy myself without resolving to chuse a wife from among his daughters, that the loss to them might be as little as possible, when the melancholy event takes place—which, however, as I have already said, may not be for several years."

Fancy syntax acts here, not as an expression of moral and intellectual refinement (as Mr. Collins intends it to act), but as an expression of stupidity, the antithesis of that refinement. The elaborate language in which Mr. Collins gets himself fairly *stuck* is a mimesis of an action of the soul, the soul that becomes self dishonest through failure to know itself, and that overrates itself at the expense of the social context, just as it overrates verbalism at the expense of meaning. We have suggested that moral life, in an Austen novel, is identified with emotional intelligence; and it is precisely through failure of intelligence—the wit to know his own limitations—that Mr. Collins appears as a moral monstrosity. Language is the mirror of his degeneracy. Against Mr. Collins' elaborate style of speech we may place the neat and direct phrasing of a sentence such as "It is a truth universally acknowledged . . ." where the balance of overt thesis and buried antithesis acts as a kind of signature of the intelligential life—its syntactical modesty conveying a very deft and energetic mental dance.

Similarly, elaborate epithet ("your honored father," "the melancholy event") is suspect—the sign not of attention but of indifference, of a moldiness of spirit which, far from being innocuous, has the capacity of mold to flourish destructively and to engulf what is clean and sound, as such epithet itself devours sense. Comedy, let us say again, "is a serious matter," and what is serious in this scene of Mr. Collins' proposal is the engulfing capacity of the rapacious Mr. Collins, from whom Elizabeth escapes narrowly. The narrowness of the escape is underlined by the fact that Elizabeth's friend, Charlotte—herself, we assume, intelligent, inasmuch as she is Elizabeth's friend—complacently offers herself as host to this mighty mold. In the civilized community which is our area of observation, emotional intelligence and quickness of moral perception—as we see them, for instance, in Elizabeth—are profoundly threatened by an all-environing imbecility. It is through style that we understand the nature of this threat; for the simplicity and directness of the governing syntax of the book prepares us to find positive values in simplicity and directness, negative values in elaboration and indirection. Even the canny intelligence of Mr. Bennet is not that emotionally informed intelligence—or, shall we say, that intelligence which informs the emotions—that we are led to look upon as desirable; and Mr. Bennet reveals his failure also in "style," a style of speech that shows a little too elaborate consciousness of the pungency of double-talk, of the verbal effect of ironic under-cutting. When Elizabeth suggests that it would be imprudent to send the lightheaded Lydia to Brighton, he says,

> Lydia will never be easy till she has exposed herself in some public place or other, and we can never expect her to do it with so little expense or inconvenience to her family as under the present circumstances.

Being intelligent, Mr. Bennet learns regret for his failure, although (and we delight also in Jane Austen's "realism" here, the tenacity of her psychological grip on her characters) not too much regret —not so much that he ceases to be Mr. Bennet.

From still another point of view, the style of the book is significant of total structure; we refer here to a generalized kind of epithet used in descriptive passages. The park at Pemberley, Darcy's estate, "was very large, and contained great variety of ground"; one drove "through a beautiful wood stretching over a wide extent." What we wish to notice, in diction of this kind, is the merely approximate appropriateness of the qualifier: "large," "great variety," "beautiful wood," "wide extent." This type of diction we might again describe as "modest," or we might speak of it as flatly commonplace; but we shall want to investigate its possibilities of function in the total form of the book. The reader will observe the continued use of the same kind of diction in the passage below, describing the house; what should be noted is the use to which the description is put—its use, not to convey any sense of "naturalistic" particularity, but, rather, to reveal Darcy's taste (of which Elizabeth has been suspicious) and a subtle turn in Elizabeth's feelings about him.

> It was a large, handsome, stone building, standing well on rising ground, and backed by a ridge of high woody hills;—and in front, a stream of some natural importance was swelled into greater, but without any artificial appearance. Its banks were neither formal nor falsely adorned. Elizabeth was delighted. She had never seen a place for which nature had done more, or where natural beauty had been so little counteracted by an awkward taste. They were all of them warm in their admiration; and at that moment she felt that to be mistress of Pemberley might be something!

Wealth applied to the happiest and most dignified creation of environment—that is all we need to know about this setting, a need which the description fulfills by virtue of generalizations— "large," "standing well," "natural importance," "natural beauty," and the series of negations of what is generally understood by "artificial appearance," "falsely adorned," and so forth. More particularity of description would deflect from what is significant in the episode, namely, the effect of the scene upon Elizabeth's attitude toward her lover. Darcy himself has had in her eyes a certain artificiality, unpleasant formality, falseness; he has been lacking in that naturalness which delights her in the present scene, which is his home and which speaks intimately of him; and she has felt that his taste in the handling of human relations was very seriously "awkward." The appearance of Pemberley cannot help putting a slight pressure on her judgment of him, and the description is used with deliberate purpose for this effect. And how shrewd psychologically and warmly human is the remark, "and at that moment she felt that to be mistress of Pemberley might be something!" With all her personal integrity and exacerbated delicacy of feeling about the horrors of acquisitiveness, Elizabeth is smitten with an acquisitive temptation. (No wonder Jane Austen could not find Elizabeth's painted portrait in the galleries, though she was able to find Jane Bennet's there. Elizabeth is quite too human to have a duplicate in paint; only language is able to catch her.) In this final clause, the dramatic concern is solely with the social context—the shifting attitudes of one person toward another, as these attitudes are conditioned by the terms of a narrow, but nevertheless complex, social existence; but as the relationships between persons shift, the individual himself (as Elizabeth, here) is reinterpreted, shows a new aspect of his humanity. In this fashion, the Austen style—here a deliberately generalized and commonplace descriptive style—functions again as determination of significant form, significance in this particular case being the *rational* meaning of a physical setting.

Finally we should remark upon what is perhaps the most formative and conclusive activity of style in the book: the effect of a narrowly mercantile and materialistic vocabulary in setting up meanings. Let us go down a few lists of typical words, categorizing them rather crudely and arbitrarily, but in such a manner as to show their direction of reference. [4] The reader will perhaps be interested in adding to these merely suggestive lists, for in watching the Austen language lies the real excitement of the Austen novel. We shall set up such categories as "trade," "arithmetic," "money," "material possessions," simply in order to indicate the kind of language Jane Austen inherited from her culture and to which she was confined—and in order to suggest what she was able to do with her language, how much of the human drama she was able to get into such confines. We could add such verbal categories as those referring to "patronage," "law," "skill" (a particularly interesting one, covering such words as "design," "cunning,"

4. Mr. Schorer's essay "Fiction and the 'Analogical Matrix,' " cited above, closely examines this aspect of Jane Austen's style.

TRADE	ARITHMETIC	MONEY	MATERIAL POSSESSIONS	SOCIAL INTEGRATION
employed	equally	pounds	estate	town
due form	added	credit	property	society
collect	proportion	capital	owner	civil
receipt	addition	pay	house	neighborhood
buy	enumerate	fortune	manor	county
sell	figure	valuable	tenant	fashion
business	calculated	principal	substantial	breeding
supply	amount	interest	establishment	genteel
terms	amounting	afford	provided	marriage
means	inconsiderable	indebted	foundation	husband
venture	consideration	undervalue	belongs to	connection

"arts," "schemes," and so on; a category obviously converging with the "trade" category, but whose vocabulary, as it appears in this book, is used derogatorily—the stupid people, like Mrs. Bennet, Lady Catherine de Bourgh, Wickham, and Mr. Collins, are the ones who "scheme" and have "designs").

In viewing in the abstract the expressive possibilities open to literary creatorship, we might assume that the whole body of the English language, as it is filed in the dictionary, is perfectly free of access to each author—that each author shares equally and at large in the common stuff of the language. In a sense this is true; the whole body of the language *is* there, virtually, in the dictionary, and anyone can consult it and use it if he wants to. But we have observed fairly frequently, if only by-the-way, in these studies, that each author does not consult the whole body of the language in selecting words for his meanings; that he is driven, as if compulsively, to the selection of a highly particular part of the language; and that the individual character of his work, its connotations and special insights, derive largely from the style he has made his own—that is to say, from the vocabulary and verbal arrangements he has adopted out of the whole gamut of words and rhetorical patterns available in the language. In making these selections, he is acting partly under the compulsions of the culture in which he has been bred and whose unconscious assumptions—as to what is interesting or valuable or necessary or convenient in life—are reflected in the verbal and rhetorical selections common in that culture; and he is acting partly also under compulsions that are individual to his own personal background, but that still maintain subtle links with the common cultural assumptions. The general directions of reference taken by Jane Austen's language, as indicated by such lists as those given above (and the lists, with others like them, could be extended for pages), are clearly materialistic. They reflect a culture whose institutions are solidly defined by materialistic interests—property and banking and trade and the law that keeps order in these matters—institutions which determine, in turn, the character of family relations, the amenities of community life, and the whole complex economy of the emotions. By acknowledgment of the fact that the materialistic assumptions of our own culture are even more pervasive than those reflected in this book, and that their governance over our emotions and our speech habits is even more grim, more sterilizing, and more restrictive, we should be somewhat aided in appreciation of the "contemporaneity" of Jane Austen herself.

But where then, we must ask, does originality lie, if an author's very language is dictated in so large a part by something, as it were, "outside" himself—by the culture into which he is accidentally born? How can there be any free play of individual genius, the free and original play with the language by which we recognize the insight and innovations of genius? The question has to be answered separately for the work of each artist, but as for Jane Austen's work we have been finding answers all along—in her exploitation of antithetical structures to convey ambivalent attitudes, in her ironic use of syntactical elaborations that go against the grain of the language and that convey moral aberrations, and finally in her direct and oblique play with an inherited vocabulary that is materialistic in reference and that she forces—or blandishes or intrigues—into spiritual duties.

The language base of the Austen novel gives us the limiting conditions of the culture. Somehow, using this language of acquisitiveness and calculation and materialism, a language common to the most admirable characters as well as to the basest characters in the book, the spiritually creative persons will have to form their destinies. The project would be so much easier if the intelligent people and the stupid people, the people who are morally alive and the people who are morally dead, had each their different language to distinguish and publicize their differences! But unfortunately for that ease, they have only one language. Fortunately for the drama of the Austen novel, there is this difficulty of the single materialistic language; for drama subsists on difficulty. Within the sterile confines of public assumptions, the Austen protagonists find with difficulty the fertility of honest and intelligent individual feeling. On a basis of communication that is drawn always from the public and savage theology of "property," the delicate lines of spiritual adjustment are explored. The final fought-for recognitions of value are recognitions of the unity of experience—a unity between the common culture and the individual development. No one more knowledgeably than this perceptive and witty woman, ambushed by imbecility, could have conducted such an exploration.

REUBEN A. BROWER

Light and Bright and Sparkling: Irony and Fiction in *Pride and Prejudice*†

The work is rather too light, and bright, and sparkling; it wants shade; it wants to be stretched out here and there with a long chapter of sense, if it could be had; if not, of solemn specious nonsense. . . .

JANE AUSTEN

Many pages of *Pride and Prejudice* can be read as sheer poetry of wit, as Pope without couplets. The antitheses are almost as frequent and almost as varied; the play of ambiguities is certainly as complex; the orchestration of tones is as precise and subtle. As in the best of Pope, the displays of ironic wit are not without imaginative connection; what looks most diverse is really most similar, and ironies are linked by vibrant reference to basic certainties. There are passages too in which the rhythmical pattern of the sentence approaches the formal balance of the heroic couplet:

> Mr. Bennet was so odd a mixture of quick parts, sarcastic humour, reserve, and caprice, that the experience of three and twenty years had been insufficient to make his wife understand his character. *Her* mind *was less difficult* to develope. She was a woman of mean understanding, little information, and uncertain temper. When she was discontented she fancied herself nervous. The business of her life was to get her daughters married; its solace was visiting and news.

The triumph of the novel—whatever its limitations may be—lies in combining such poetry of wit with the dramatic structure of fiction. In historical terms, to combine the traditions of poetic satire with those of the sentimental novel, that was Jane Austen's feat in *Pride and Prejudice*.

For the "bright and sparkling," seemingly centrifugal play of irony is dramatically functional. It makes sense as literary art, the sense with which a writer is most concerned. The repartee, while constantly amusing, delineates characters and their changing relations and points the way to a climactic moment in which the change is most clearly recognized. Strictly speaking, this union

† From Reuben A. Brower, *The Fields of Light*, New York, 1951. Pp. 164–81. Copyright 1951. Reprinted by permission of the publishers, Oxford University Press. An earlier version of this essay was published as "The Controlling Hand: Jane Austen and Pride and Prejudice," in *Scrutiny*, XIII (1945), 99–111.

of wit and drama is achieved with complete success only in the central sequence of *Pride and Prejudice*, in the presentation of Elizabeth's and Darcy's gradual revaluation of each other. Here, if anywhere, Jane Austen met James's demand that the novel should give its readers the maximum of "fun"; at the same time she satisfied the further standard implied in James's remark that the art of the novel is "above all an art of preparations." That she met these demands more continuously in *Emma* does not detract from her achievement in *Pride and Prejudice*.

Her blend of ironic wit and drama may be seen in its simplest form in the first chapter of the novel, in the dialogue between Mr. and Mrs. Bennet on the topic of Mr. Bingley's leasing Netherfield Park. Every remark which each makes, Mrs. Bennet petulantly, and Mr. Bennet perversely, bounces off the magnificent opening sentence:

> It is a truth universally acknowledged, that a single man in possession of a good fortune, must be in want of a wife.

The scene that follows dramatizes the alternatives implied in "universally," Mrs. Bennet reminding us of one; and Mr. Bennet, of the other:

> "My dear Mr. Bennet," said his lady to him one day, "have you heard that Netherfield Park is let at last?"
>
> Mr. Bennet replied that he had not.
>
> "But it is," returned she; "for Mrs. Long has just been here, and she told me all about it."
>
> Mr. Bennet made no answer.
>
> "Do not you want to know who has taken it?" cried his wife impatiently.
>
> "*You* want to tell me, and I have no objection to hearing it."
>
> This was invitation enough.
>
> "Why, my dear, you must know, Mrs. Long says that Netherfield is taken by a young man of large fortune from the north of England; that he came down on Monday in a chaise and four to see the place, and was so much delighted with it that he agreed with Mr. Morris immediately; that he is to take possession before Michaelmas, and some of his servants are to be in the house by the end of next week."
>
> "What is his name?"
>
> "Bingley."
>
> "Is he married or single?"
>
> "Oh! single, my dear, to be sure! A single man of large fortune; four or five thousand a year. What a fine thing for our girls!"
>
> "How so? how can it affect them?"
>
> "My dear Mr. Bennet," replied his wife, "how can you be so tiresome! You must know that I am thinking of his marrying one of them."

"Is that his design in settling here?"

"Design! nonsense, how can you talk so!"

A parallel appears in the opening of Pope's Epistle, "Of the Characters of Women":

> Nothing so true as what you once let fall,
> "Most Women have no Characters at all,"

a pronouncement immediately followed by a series of portraits showing that women have "characters" in one sense if not in another. It is also easy to find counterparts in Pope's satirical mode for Mr. Bennet's extreme politeness of address, his innocent queries, and his epigrammatic turns. The character that emerges from this dialogue is almost that of a professional satirist: Mr. Bennet is a man of quick parts and sarcastic humor, altogether a most unnatural father. Mrs. Bennet speaks another language; *her* talk does not crackle with irony and epigram; *her* sentences run in quite another mold. They either go on too long or break up awkwardly in impulsive exclamations; this is the talk of a person of "mean understanding" and "uncertain temper."

But though the blended art of this scene is admirable, a limitation appears. Mr. and Mrs. Bennet are so perfectly done that little more is left to be expressed. Variety or forward movement in the drama will almost surely be difficult, which obviously proves to be the case. The sequences that depend most closely on the opening scene—those concerned with the business of getting the Bennet daughters married—are all amusingly ironic, but relatively static as drama. As Mrs. Bennet contrives to join Jane and Bingley, to marry one daughter to Mr. Collins, and to further Lydia's exploits with the military, father, mother, and daughters remain in very nearly the same dramatic positions. True enough, the last of these sequences ends in a catastrophe. But the connection between Lydia's downfall and the earlier scenes of ironic comedy in which Mr. and Mrs. Bennet are opposed is not fully expressed. Lydia's behavior "leads to this" in a Richardsonian moral sense, but Lydia is too scantly presented in relation to her parents or to Wickham to prepare us adequately for her bad end. We accept it if at all as literary convention. Incidentally, we might conjecture that the marriage-market sequences belong to the early version of *Pride and Prejudice,* or at least that they are examples of Jane Austen's earlier manner. In the central sequence of *Pride and Prejudice,* especially in its more complex blend of ironic and dramatic design, we can see anticipated the more mature structure of both *Mansfield Park* and *Emma.*

In portraying the gradual change in Elizabeth's estimate of Darcy and in his attitude to her, Jane Austen achieves a perfect harmony between the rich ambiguity of ironic dialogue and the movement toward the climactic scenes in which the new estimate is revealed. I shall limit my discussion to scenes from the Elizabeth-Darcy narrative through the episode in which Elizabeth recognizes her "change in sentiment." Let us first read Jane Austen's dialogue as poetry of wit, disregarding for the time being any forward movement in the drama, and observing the variety of the irony and the unity of effect achieved through recurrent patterns and through assumptions shared by writer and reader. As in our reading of Poe, we may in this way appreciate the extraordinary richness of ironic texture and the imaginative continuity running through the play of wit. In analyzing the ironies and the assumptions, we shall see how intensely dramatic the dialogue is, dramatic in the sense of defining characters through the way they speak and are spoken about.

The aura of implications which surrounds many of the dialogues between Elizabeth and Darcy is complex enough to delight the most pure Empsonian. Take for example the dialogue in which Sir William Lucas attempts to interest Mr. Darcy in dancing:

. . . Elizabeth at that instant moving towards them, he was struck with the notion of doing a very gallant thing, and called out to her,

"My dear Miss Eliza, why are not you dancing?—Mr. Darcy, you must allow me to present this young lady to you as a very desirable partner.—You cannot refuse to dance, I am sure, when so much beauty is before you." And taking her hand, he would have given it to Mr. Darcy, who, though extremely surprised, was not unwilling to receive it, when she instantly drew back, and said with some discomposure to Sir William,

"Indeed, Sir, I have not the least intention of dancing.—I entreat you not to suppose that I moved this way in order to beg for a partner."

Mr. Darcy with grave propriety requested to be allowed the honour of her hand; but in vain. Elizabeth was determined; nor did Sir William at all shake her purpose by his attempt at persuasion.

"You excel so much in the dance, Miss Eliza, that it is cruel to deny me the happiness of seeing you; and though this gentleman dislikes the amusement in general, he can have no objection, I am sure, to oblige us for one half hour."

"Mr. Darcy is all politeness," said Elizabeth, smiling.

"He is indeed—but considering the inducement, my dear Miss Eliza, we cannot wonder at his complaisance; for who would object to such a partner?"

Elizabeth looked archly, and turned away.

"Mr. Darcy is all politeness": the statement, as Elizabeth might say, has a "teazing" variety of meanings. Mr. Darcy is polite in the sense indicated by "grave propriety," that is, he shows the courtesy appropriate to a gentleman—which is the immediate, public meaning of Elizabeth's compliment. But "grave propriety," being a very limited form of politeness, reminds us forcibly of Mr. Darcy's earlier behavior. His "gravity" at the ball had been "forbidding and disagreeable." "Grave propriety" may also mean the bare civility of "the proudest, most disagreeable man in the world." So Elizabeth's compliment has an ironic twist: she smiles and looks "archly." "All politeness" has also quite another meaning. Mr. Darcy "was not unwilling to receive" her hand. He is polite in more than the public proper sense; his gesture shows that he is interested in Elizabeth as a person. Her archness and her smile have for the reader an added ironic value: Elizabeth's interpretation of Darcy's manner may be quite wrong. Finally, there is the embracing broadly comic irony of Sir William's action. "Struck with the notion of doing a very gallant thing," he is pleasantly unconscious of what he is in fact doing and of what Elizabeth's remark may mean to her and to Darcy.

A similar cluster of possibilities appears in another conversation in which Darcy asks Elizabeth to dance with him:

> . . . soon afterwards Mr. Darcy, drawing near Elizabeth, said to her—
>
> "Do not you feel a great inclination, Miss Bennet, to seize such an opportunity of dancing a reel?"
>
> She smiled, but made no answer. He repeated the question, with some surprise at her silence.
>
> "Oh!" said she, "I heard you before; but I could not immediately determine what to say in reply. You wanted me, I know, to say 'Yes,' that you might have the pleasure of despising my taste; but I always delight in overthrowing those kind of schemes, and cheating a person of their premeditated contempt. I have therefore made up my mind to tell you, that I do not want to dance a reel at all—and now despise me if you dare."
>
> "Indeed I do not dare."
>
> Elizabeth, having rather expected to affront him, was amazed at his gallantry; but there was a mixture of sweetness and archness in her manner which made it difficult for her to affront anybody; and Darcy had never been so bewitched by any woman as he was by her. He really believed, that were it not for the inferiority of her connections, he should be in some danger.
>
> Miss Bingley saw, or suspected enough to be jealous; and her great anxiety for the recovery of her dear friend Jane, received some assistance from her desire of getting rid of Elizabeth.
>
> She often tried to provoke Darcy into disliking her guest, by talking of their supposed marriage, and planning his happiness in such an alliance.

Again Mr. Darcy's request may be interpreted more or less pleasantly, depending on whether we connect it with his present or past behavior. Again Elizabeth's attack on Darcy and her archness have an irony beyond the irony intended by the speaker. But the amusement of this dialogue lies especially in the variety of possible tones which we detect in Darcy's speeches. Elizabeth hears his question as expressing "premediated contempt" and scorn of her own taste. But from Mr. Darcy's next remark and the comment which follows, and from his repeating his question and showing "some surprise," we may hear in his request a tone expressive of some interest, perhaps only gallantry, perhaps, as Elizabeth later puts it "somewhat of a friendlier nature." We could take his "Indeed I do not dare" as pure gallantry (Elizabeth's version) or as a sign of conventional "marriage intentions" (Miss Bingley's interpretation), if it were not for the nice reservation, "He really believed, that were it not for the inferiority of her connections, he should be in some danger." We must hear the remark as spoken with this qualification. This simultaneity of tonal layers can be matched only in the satire of Pope, where, as we have seen, the reader feels the impossibility of adjusting his voice to the rapid changes in tone and the difficulty of representing by a single sound the several sounds he hears as equally appropriate and necessary. Analysis such as I have been making shows clearly how arbitrary and how thin any stage rendering of *Pride and Prejudice* must be. No speaking voice could possibly represent the variety of tones conveyed to the reader by such interplay of dialogue and comment.

It would be easy enough to produce more of these dialogues, especially on the subject of music or dancing, each with its range of crisply differentiated meanings. Similar patterns of irony recur many times. Mr. Darcy makes his inquiries (polite or impolite), asking with a smile (scornful or encouraging) questions that may be interpreted as pompous and condescending or gallant and well-disposed. So Mr. Darcy cross-examines Elizabeth in the scene in which their "superior dancing" gives such pleasure to Sir William:

"What think you of books?" said he, smiling.

"Books—Oh! no.—I am sure we never read the same, or not with the same feelings."

"I am sorry you think so; but if that be the case, there can at least be no want of subject.—We may compare our different opinions."

"No—I cannot talk of books in a ball-room; my head is always full of something else."

"The *present* always occupies you in such scenes—does it?" said he, with a look of doubt.

When connected with a hint of Darcy's changing attitude, that "look of doubt," Elizabeth's arch comments take on the added ironic value we have noted in other conversations.

Earlier in this dialogue, Darcy and Elizabeth run through the same sort of question and answer gamut, and with very nearly the same ironic dissonances:

> He smiled, and assured her that whatever she wished him to say should be said.
>
> "Very well.—That reply will do for the present.—Perhaps by and bye I may observe that private balls are much pleasanter than public ones.—But *now* we may be silent."
>
> "Do you talk by rule then, while you are dancing?"
>
> "Sometimes. One must speak a little, you know. It would look odd to be entirely silent for half an hour together, and yet for the advantage of *some*, conversation ought to be so arranged as that they may have the trouble of saying as little as possible."
>
> "Are you consulting your own feelings in the present case, or do you imagine that you are gratifying mine?"
>
> "Both," replied Elizabeth archly; "for I have always seen a great similarity in the turn of our minds.—We are each of an unsocial, taciturn disposition, unwilling to speak, unless we expect to say something that will amaze the whole room, and be handed down to posterity with all the eclat of a proverb."
>
> "This is no very striking resemblance of your own character, I am sure," said he.

When Darcy himself is being quizzed he frequently remarks on his own behavior in a way that may be sublimely smug or simply self-respecting, as for example in his comment on his behavior at the first of the Hertfordshire balls:

> "I certainly have not the talent which some people possess," said Darcy, "of conversing easily with those I have never seen before. I cannot catch their tone of conversation, or appear interested in their concerns, as I often see done."

But these conversations are not simply sets of ironic meanings; they are in more than a trivial sense *jeux d'esprit*, the play of an adult mind. (The sophistication they imply is of a kind which, as John Jay Chapman once remarked, is Greek and French, rather than English.) The fun in Jane Austen's dialogue has a serious point; or rather, the fun *is* the point. The small talk is the focus for her keen sense of the variability of character, for her awareness of the possibility that the same remark or action has very different meanings in different relations. What most satisfies us in reading the dialogue in *Pride and Prejudice* is Jane Austen's awareness that it is difficult to know any complex person, that knowledge of a man like Darcy is an interpretation and a construction, not a

simple absolute. Like the characters of Proust, the chief persons in
Pride and Prejudice are not the same when projected through the
conversation of different people. The *snobisme* of Darcy's talk, like
Swann's, is measured according to the group he is with. Mr. Darcy
is hardly recognizable as the same man when he is described by
Mr. Wickham, by his housekeeper, or Elizabeth, or Mr. Bingley.

But it is only the complex persons, the "intricate characters,"
that require and merit interpretation, as Elizabeth points out in
the pleasant conversation in which she tells Bingley that she "understands him perfectly":

> "You begin to comprehend me, do you?" cried he, turning
> towards her.
> "Oh! yes,—I understand you perfectly."
> "I wish I might take this for a compliment; but to be so
> easily seen through I am afraid is pitiful."
> "That is as it happens. It does not necessarily follow that a
> deep, intricate character is more or less estimable than such a
> one as yours."
> "Lizzy," cried her mother, "remember where you are, and do
> not run on in the wild manner that you are suffered to do at
> home."
> "I did not know before," continued Bingley immediately,
> "that you were a studier of character. It must be an amusing
> study."
> "Yes; but intricate characters are the *most* amusing. They
> have at least that advantage."
> "The country," said Darcy, "can in general supply but few
> subjects for such a study. In a country neighborhood you move
> in a very confined and unvarying society."
> "But people themselves alter so much, that there is something
> new to be observed in them for ever."

Elizabeth's remark with its ironic application to Darcy indicates
the interest that makes the book "go" and shows the type of
awareness we are analyzing. "Intricate characters are the *most*
amusing," because their behavior can be taken in so many ways,
because they are not always the same people. The man we know
today is a different man tomorrow. Naturally, we infer, people will
not be equally puzzling to every judge. Mr. Bingley and Jane
find Mr. Darcy a much less "teazing" man than Elizabeth does. It
is only the Elizabeths, the adult minds, who will observe something new in the "same" people.

Such are the main assumptions behind the irony of *Pride and
Prejudice*, as they are expressed through conversation studies of
Darcy's character. In marked contrast with the opening scene of the
novel, there is in these dialogues no nondramatic statement of
the ironist's position, a further sign that in shaping the Elizabeth-

Darcy sequence Jane Austen was moving away from the modes of satire toward more purely dramatic techniques.

While Jane Austen's irony depends on a sense of variability and intricacy of character, her vision is not one of Proustian relativity. The sense of variability is balanced by a vigorous and positive belief. Elizabeth, in commenting on Charlotte Lucas' choice of Mr. Collins, expresses very emphatically this combination of skepticism and faith:

> "My dear Jane, Mr. Collins is a conceited, pompous, narrow-minded silly man; you know he is, as well as I do; and you must feel, as well as I do, that the woman who marries him, cannot have a proper way of thinking. You shall not defend her, though it is Charlotte Lucas. You shall not, for the sake of one individual, change the meaning of principle and integrity, nor endeavour to persuade yourself or me, that selfishness is prudence, and insensibility of danger, security for happiness."

Though as usual Elizabeth's affirmations have an ironic overtone for the reader, they express a belief that is implied throughout *Pride and Prejudice*. There are persons such as Mr. Collins and Mrs. Bennet and Lady Catherine, about whom there can be no disagreement among people who "have a proper way of thinking." These fixed characters make up a set of certainties against which more intricate exhibitions of pride and prejudice are measured. They are the "fools" which James says are almost indispensable for any piece of fiction. For Jane Austen there can be no doubt about the meaning of "principle and integrity" and similar terms of value. Right-thinking persons know what pride is and when to apply the term. In common with her contemporaries Jane Austen enjoys the belief that some interpretations of behavior are more reasonable than others. The climactic scene of the novel, in which Elizabeth arrives at a new view of Darcy, shows us what is meant by a more reasonable interpretation: it is a reasoned judgment of character reached through long experience and slow weighing of probabilities. The certainty is an achieved certainty.

So the local ironies in Jane Austen, as in Pope, are defined and given larger significance through assumptions shared by the writer and public. The trivial dialogues are constantly being illuminated by a fine sense of the complexity of human nature and by a steady belief in the possibility of making sound judgments. At the same time the playfulness is always serving for "the illustration of character." (The term is Elizabeth's, though in applying it to Darcy, she is as usual unaware of its aptness to her own behavior.) Both she and Darcy are "illustrated" by their ambiguous questions and answers and the alternate interpretations which are so deftly indicated: the poetry of wit in *Pride and Prejudice* is completely dramatic. Certainly nothing could be more dramatic than the assumptions we have been describing: they reflect the practical dramatist's interest in human beings and their behavior, his awareness that character is expressed by what men say and do. The assumption that more reasonable interpretations of conduct are attainable provides for the movement toward a decisive change in relationships at the climax of the novel. It also lays the ground for the resolution of ambiguities and the cancellation of irony at the same moment.

We can now appreciate how beautifully the ironies of the dialogue function in the curve of the main dramatic sequence. The conversations have been skilfully shaped to prepare us for Elizabeth's revised estimate of Darcy, for her recognition that Darcy regards her differently, and for her consequent "change of sentiment" toward him. The preparation for this climax is made mainly through the controlled use of ambiguity that we have been observing. Though we are always being led to make double interpretations, we are never in confusion about what the alternatives are. It is important also that in these ironic dialogues no comment is included that makes us take Darcy's behavior in only an unpleasant sense. When there is comment, it is mainly used to bring out the latent ambiguity without in any way resolving it. So in general the earlier Darcy scenes are left open in preparation for a fresh estimate of his character. The pleasanter interpretation of one of Darcy's or Elizabeth's remarks or of one of the author's comments allows for the later choice and for the consequent recognitions. The pleasanter possibility also gives in passing a hint of Darcy's changing attitude to Elizabeth. For instance, the more favorable meaning of Elizabeth's "Mr. Darcy is all politeness" or of the comment on his "grave propriety" points forward to Darcy's perfect courtesy at Pemberley and to Elizabeth's admission that he was right in objecting to her family's "impropriety of conduct."

This exquisite preparation pays wonderfully at the climactic moment of the novel, when Elizabeth reconsiders the letter in which Darcy justified his conduct toward Bingley and Jane and Wickham. Since more kindly views of Darcy have been introduced through the flow of witty talk, Darcy does not at that point have to be remade, but merely reread. (The tendency to remake a character appears in an obvious form only in the later and lesser scenes of the novel.)

The passages in which Elizabeth reviews the letter present an odd, rather legalistic process. After the more obvious views of Darcy's behavior and the possible alternatives are directly stated, the evidence on both sides is weighed and a reasonable conclusion is reached:

After wandering along the lane for two hours, giving way to every variety of thought; re-considering events, determining probabilities, and reconciling herself as well as she could, to a change so sudden and so important, fatigue, and a recollection of her long absence made her at length return home. . . .

To illustrate her manner of "determining probabilities" we might take one of several examples of Darcy's pride. Immediately after Darcy has proposed to her, she describes his treatment of Jane in rather brutal lanugage:

. . . his pride, his abominable pride, his shameless avowal of what he had done with respect to Jane, his unpardonable assurance in acknowledging, though he could not justify it.

A little later, she rereads the passage in which Darcy explains that Jane had shown no "symptom of peculiar regard" for Bingley. A second perusal reminds Elizabeth that Charlotte Lucas had a similar opinion, and she acknowledges the justice of this account of Jane's outward behavior. In much the same way she reviews other charges, such as Darcy's unfairness to Wickham or his objection to her family's "want of importance," and she is forced by the new evidence to draw "more probable" conclusions.

Jane Austen does not make us suppose that Elizabeth has now discovered the real Darcy or that an intricate person is easily known or known in his entirety, as is very clearly shown by Elizabeth's reply to Wickham's ironic questions about Darcy:

"I dare not hope," he continued in a lower and more serious tone, "that he is improved in essentials."

"Oh, no!" said Elizabeth. "In essentials, I believe, he is very much what he ever was."

While she spoke, Wickham looked as if scarcely knowing whether to rejoice over her words, or to distrust their meaning. There was a something in her countenance which made him listen with an apprehensive and anxious attention, while she added,

"When I said that he improved on acquaintance, I did not mean that either his mind or manners were in a state of improvement, but that from knowing him better, his disposition was better understood."

It is wise not to be dogmatic about "essentials," since in any case they remain "as they were." A sensible person contents himself with "better understanding."

This process of judgment is not merely odd or legalistic, because it is dramatically appropriate. It fits exactly the double presentation of Darcy's character through ironic dialogue and comment, and it fits perfectly the picture of Elizabeth as "a rational creature speaking the truth from her heart," one who adapts her statements to her knowledge. She is quite clear about the meaning of "pride" and "vanity," and she judges herself with complete honesty:

> "Had I been in love, I could not have been more wretchedly blind. But vanity, not love, has been my folly.—Pleased with the preference of one, and offended by the neglect of the other, on the very beginning of our acquaintance, I have courted prepossession and ignorance, and driven reason away, where either were concerned. Till this moment, I never knew myself."

We feel that Elizabeth's judgment of Darcy and of herself is right because the preparation for it has been so complete. The foundations for Elizabeth's choices and her acknowledgment of error were laid in the ambiguous remarks of the earlier scenes of the novel.

The dialogue has been preparing us equally well and with perhaps greater refinement for Elizabeth's realization that she and Darcy now regard one another with very different feelings. The ironic remarks and commentary have included hints that revealed ever so gradually Darcy's developing interest in Elizabeth. Mr. Darcy's "politeness," his "repeated questions," his "gallantry," his "look of doubt," if interpreted favorably, indicate his increasing warmth of feeling. Elizabeth's pert remarks and impertinent questions bear an amusing relation to this change in Darcy's sentiments. Besides being more ambiguous than she supposes, they backfire in another way, by increasing Darcy's admiration. Her accusation of "premeditated contempt" brings out his most gallant reply, and her "mixture of sweetness and archness" leaves him more "bewitched" than ever. In this and other ways the repartee provides local "amusements" while pointing forward to the complete reversal of feeling that follows the meeting at Pemberley.

The judicial process by which Elizabeth earlier "determined probabilities" in judging Darcy's past conduct is matched by the orderly way in which she now "determines her feelings" toward him:

> . . . and the evening, though as it passed it seemed long, was not long enough to determine her feelings towards *one* in that mansion; and she lay awake two whole hours, endeavouring to make them out. She certainly did not hate him. No; hatred had vanished long ago, and she had almost as long been ashamed of ever feeling a dislike against him, that could be so called. The respect created by the conviction of his valuable qualities, though at first unwillingly admitted, had for some time ceased to be repugnant to her feelings; and it was now heightened into

somewhat of a friendlier nature, by the testimony so highly in his favour, and bringing forward his disposition in so amiable a light, which yesterday had produced. But above all, above respect and esteem, there was a motive within her of good will which could not be overlooked. It was gratitude.—Gratitude, not merely for having once loved her, but for loving her still well enough, to forgive all the petulance and acrimony of her manner in rejecting him, and all the unjust accusations accompanying her rejection. He who, she had been persuaded, would avoid her as his greatest enemy, seemed, on this accidental meeting, most eager to preserve the acquaintance, and without any in-delicate display of regard, or any peculiarity of manner, where their two selves only were concerned, was soliciting the good opinion of her friends, and bent on making her known to his sister. Such a change in a man of so much pride, excited not only astonishment but gratitude—for to love, ardent love, it must be attritbuted; and as such its impression on her was of a sort to be encouraged, as by no means unpleasing, though it could not be exactly defined. She respected, she esteemed, she was grateful to him, she felt a real interest in his wel-fare. . . .

In this beautifully graded progress of feeling, from "hatred" or any "dislike" to "respect" to "esteem" to "gratitude" and "a real in-terest" in Darcy's "welfare," each sentiment is defined with an exactness that is perfectly appropriate to Elizabeth's habit of mind as presented earlier in the novel. She defines her sentiments as exactly as her moral judgments.

As all ambiguities are resolved and all irony is dropped, the reader feels the closing in of a structure by its necessary end, the end implied in the crude judgment of Darcy in the first ballroom scene. The harsh exhibit of the way character is decided in this society prepares us to view Mr. Darcy's later actions as open to more than one interpretation:

. . . Mr. Darcy soon drew the attention of the room by his fine, tall person, handsome features, noble mien; and the report which was in general circulation within five minutes after his entrance, of his having ten thousand a year. The gentlemen pronounced him to be a fine figure of a man, the ladies declared he was much handsomer than Mr. Bingley, and he was looked at with great admiration for about half the evening, till his manners gave a disgust which turned the tide of his popularity; for he was discovered to be proud, to be above his company, and above being pleased; and not all his large estate in Derby-shire could then save him from having a most forbidding, dis-agreeable countenance, and being unworthy to be compared with his friend.

. . . His character was decided. He was the proudest, most disagreeable man in the world, and everybody hoped that he would never come there again.

These comments convey above all the aloof vision of the ironist, of Jane Austen herself, who had been described years before as a little girl "who is a judge of character and who remains silent." In the very grammar of the sentences (the passive voice, the *oratio obliqua*), there is an implication of a detached and superior mind that reports both judgments of Darcy, knowing quite well which is the more true, and fully aware that true judgment is considerably more difficult than most people suppose. The display of alternatives in ironic dialogue, the projection by this means of intricate characters, and the movement toward a sounder evaluation of first impressions—all this and more is implicit in the initial view of Darcy and his judges.

Once we have reached the scenes in which the promise of the introduction is fulfilled, the literary design both ironic and dramatic is complete. Thereafter, it must be admitted, *Pride and Prejudice* is not quite the same sort of book. There are fewer passages of equally bright and varied irony and consequently rarer exhibitions of intricacy of character. Mr. Darcy now appears as "humble," not "proud," and even as "perfectly amiable." There are single scenes of a broadly satiric sort, in which Mr. and Mrs. Bennet express characteristic opinions on their daughters' alliances and misalliances. But the close and harmonious relation between ironic wit and dramatic movement is disturbed. A great deal happens, from seductions and mysterious financial transactions to reunions of lovers and weddings. But these events seem to belong to a simpler world where outright judgments of good and bad or of happy and unhappy are in place. The double vision of the ironist is more rarely in evidence.

Occasionally, we feel a recovery of the richer texture of amusement and of the more complex awareness of character revealed in the central sequence. One glancing remark suggests that the final picture of Darcy might have been less simply ideal (Darcy has just been commenting on how well Bingley had taken his confession of having separated Bingley and Jane):

> Elizabeth longed to observe that Mr. Bingley had been a most delightful friend; so easily guided that his worth was invaluable; but she checked herself. She remembered that he had yet to learn to be laught at, and it was rather too early to begin. In anticipating the happiness of Bingley, which of course was to be inferior only to his own, he continued the conversation till they reached the house.

It is perhaps not "rational," as Elizabeth would say, to expect the same complexity when a drama of irony has once arrived at its resolution. But it is probably wise for the novelist to finish up his story as soon as possible after that point has been reached. In *Emma*, the crucial scene of readjustment comes very near the end of the novel. Jane Austen does not run the risk of presenting many scenes in which Emma appears as a wiser and less fanciful young woman. To be sure, the risk is lessened somewhat because the initial and governing vision in Emma is less purely ironic than in *Pride and Prejudice*.

The triumph of *Pride and Prejudice* is a rare one, just because it is so difficult to balance a purely ironic vision with credible presentation of a man and woman undergoing a serious "change of sentiment." Shakespeare achieves an uneasy success in *Much Ado About Nothing*, and Fielding succeeds in *Tom Jones* because he does not expect us to take "love" too seriously. The problem for the writer who essays this difficult blend is one of creating dramatic speech which fulfils his complex intention. In solving this problem of expression, Jane Austen has her special triumph.

MARVIN MUDRICK

Irony as Discrimination: *Pride and Prejudice*†

In *Pride and Prejudice*, for the first time, Jane Austen allows her heroine to share her own characteristic response to the world. Elizabeth Bennet tells Darcy:

> ". . . Follies and nonsense, whims and inconsistencies do divert me, I own, and I laugh at them whenever I can. . . ."

The response is not only characteristic of Elizabeth and her author, but consciously and articulately aimed at by both of them. Both choose diversion; and both, moreover, look for their diversion in the people about them. Elizabeth, despite her youth and the limitations of a rural society, is a busy "studier of character," as Bingley leads her to affirm:

> "You begin to comprehend me, do you?" cried he, turning towards her.
> "Oh! yes—I understand you perfectly."
> "I wish I might take this for a compliment; but to be so easily seen through I am afraid is pitiful."

† From Marvin Mudrick, *Jane Austen: Irony as Defense and Discovery*. Pp. 94–126. Copyright 1952 by Princeton University Press. Reprinted by permission of Marvin Mudrick.

"That is as it happens. It does not necessarily follow that a deep, intricate character is more or less estimable than such a one as yours."

"Lizzy," cried her mother, "remember where you are, and do not run on in the wild manner that you are suffered to do at home."

"I did not know before," continued Bingley immediately, "that you were a studier of character. It must be an amusing study."

"Yes; but intricate characters are the *most* amusing. They have at least that advantage."

"Character" gains a general overtone: with Elizabeth's qualifying adjective, it becomes not only the summation of a single personality, but the summation of a type, the fixing of the individual into a category. So Elizabeth sets herself up as an ironic spectator, able and prepared to judge and classify, already making the first large division of the world into two sorts of people: the simple ones, those who give themselves away out of shallowness (as Bingley fears) or perhaps openness (as Elizabeth implies) or an excess of affectation (as Mr. Collins will demonstrate); and the intricate ones, those who cannot be judged and classified so easily, who are "the most amusing" to the ironic spectator because they offer the most formidable challenge to his powers of detection and analysis. Into one of these preliminary categories, Elizabeth fits everybody she observes.

Elizabeth shares her author's characteristic response of comic irony, defining incongruities without drawing them into a moral context; and, still more specifically, Elizabeth's vision of the world as divided between the simple and the intricate is, in *Pride and Prejudice* at any rate, Jane Austen's vision also. This identification between the author and her heroine establishes, in fact, the whole ground pattern of judgment in the novel. The first decision we must make about anyone, so Elizabeth suggests and the author confirms by her shaping commentary, is not moral but psychological, not whether he is good or bad, but whether he is simple or intricate: whether he may be disposed of as fixed and predictable or must be recognized as variable, perhaps torn between contradictory motives, intellectually or emotionally complex, unsusceptible to a quick judgment.

Once having placed the individual in his category, we must proceed to discriminate him from the others there; and, in the category of simplicity at least, Elizabeth judges as accurately as her author. Jane Austen allows the "simple" characters to have no surprises for Elizabeth, and, consequently, none for us. They perform, they amuse; but we never doubt that we know what they are, and why they act as they do.

We know Mrs. Bennet, for example, at once, in her first conversation with her husband, as she describes the newcomer at Netherfield Park:

> ". . . A single man of large fortune; four or five thousand a year. What a fine thing for our girls."

And the author curtly sums her up at the end of the first chapter:

> She was a woman of mean understanding, little information, and uncertain temper. When she was discontented, she fancied herself nervous. The business of her life was to get her daughters married; its solace was visiting and news.

Two subjects dominate her life and conversation: the injustice of the entail by which Mr. Bennet's estate will descend to his closest male relative rather than to his immediate family, and the problem of getting her daughters married. Out of these fixed ideas, untempered by any altruism, circumspection, wit, or intellect, derive all of her appearances and her total function in the story. The matter of the entail serves mainly to introduce Mr. Collins and to complicate the second and stronger fixed idea; it also provides Mr. Bennet with opportunities to bait his wife:

> "About a month ago I received this letter . . . from my cousin, Mr. Collins, who, when I am dead, may turn you all out of the house as soon as he pleases."
> "Oh; my dear," cried his wife, "I cannot bear to hear that mentioned. Pray do not talk of that odious man. I do think it is the hardest thing in the world, that your estate should be entailed away from your own children; and I am sure if I had been you, I should have tried long ago to do something or other about it."

The problem of getting her daughters married, however, involves her much more directly in the tensions and progress of the narrative. It is her irrepressible vulgarity in discussing Jane's prospective marriage to Bingley which convinces Darcy that any alliance with Mr. Bennet's family—for his friend or for himself— would be imprudent and degrading:

> . . . Mrs. Bennet seemed incapable of fatigue while enumerating the advantages of the match. His being such a charming young man, and so rich, and living but three miles from them, were the first points of self-gratulation. . . . It was, moreover, such a promising thing for her younger daughters as Jane's marrying so greatly must throw them in the way of other rich men. . . .
> In vain did Elizabeth endeavour to check the rapidity of her mother's words, or persuade her to describe her felicity in a less audible whisper; for to her inexpressible vexation, she could perceive that the chief of it was overheard by Mr. Darcy, who

sat opposite to them. Her mother only scolded her for being nonsensical!

"What is Mr. Darcy to me, pray, that I should be afraid of him? I am sure we owe him no such particular civility as to be obliged to say nothing *he* may not like to hear."

Having decided that Darcy is too haughty to pursue any of her daughters, she goes out of her way, in fact, to offend him.

Her feeling toward Mr. Collins swings between extremes of deference and indignation, according as she must consider him a profit or a loss: a suitor, or the holder of the entail. When he is quite unknown to her except as the latter, she detests him. When, in his letter, he barely hints at courting one of the Bennet girls during his coming visit, she thaws almost at once:

"There is some sense in what he says about the girls how-ever; and if he is disposed to make them any amends, I shall not be the person to discourage him."

When, on appearing, he seems quite bent on marriage,

Mrs. Bennet . . . trusted that she might soon have two daughters married; and the man whom she could not bear to speak of the day before, was now high in her good graces.

After Elizabeth, in spite of Mrs. Bennet's strenuous pleading, has turned him down and he marries Charlotte Lucas instead, she can see him only as she saw him at first, gloating—and with a wife now to help him gloat—over the entail:

". . . And so, I suppose, they often talk of having Longbourn when your father is dead. They look upon it as quite their own, I dare say, whenever that happens."

An inadequate mind to begin with, marriage to a man who treats her with contempt only, preoccupation with the insistent material concerns imposed by society upon a woman of her class—they have all combined in Mrs. Bennet's single continuously operating motive: to be herself secure and comfortable, and to fortify her own security by getting her daughters settled in prudent marriage, that condition symbolic of material well-being. For Mrs. Bennet, everything in life reduces itself to the dimensions of this motive; everything except her daughter Lydia.

Lydia is, of course, Mrs. Bennet as she must remember herself at the same age:

Lydia was a stout, well-grown girl of fifteen, with a fine com-plexion and good-humoured countenance; a favourite with her mother, whose affection had brought her into public at an early age. She had high animal spirits, and a sort of natural self-consequence, which the attention of the officers, to whom her uncle's good dinners and her own easy manners recommended her, had increased into assurance.

The coming of a militia regiment to Meryton has determined the course of her life, as far ahead as she cares to look. When the regiment is ordered to Brighton, her world seems ready to collapse, and Mrs. Bennet is scarcely less despairing; but Lydia, at least, is spared by receiving an invitation from her good friend, the colonel's wife, to accompany the regiment to Brighton. Parting from Lydia, Mrs. Bennet

> . . . was diffuse in her good wishes for the felicity of her daughter, and impressive in her injunctions that she would not miss the opportunity of enjoying herself as much as possible; advice, which there was every reason to believe would be attended to. . . .

One of Jane Austen's triumphs in *Pride and Prejudice* is her refusal to sentimentalize Lydia (as well as Mrs. Bennet) once she has fashioned her to a hard and simple consistency. Lydia is a self-assured, highly sexed, wholly amoral and unintellectual girl. When she runs off with Wickham, nothing can lower her spirits or drive her to shame—not all the disapproval of society, not the horror and shame of her family (though her mother, of course, is neither horrified nor ashamed). She has done what she wanted to do; and if her uncle or father or someone else must pay Wickham to persuade him to legalize the union, that is their worry, not hers. She is not defiantly, but simply, impenitent: she recognizes no authority to which penitence or concealment is due. If marriage is valued by some, so much the better; if, for no effect on her part, it gives her a social precedence and dignity, she will take these, though she did not ask for them and could have lived without them. What Elizabeth designates as Lydia's "susceptibility to her feelings," what the author has called her "high animal spirits," is Lydia's only motive, as it must once have been Mrs. Bennet's also; but Lydia has not abandoned it out of prudence or fear, has even seen it assume the unanticipated respectability of marriage:

> "Well, mamma . . . and what do you think of my husband? Is not he a charming man? I am sure my sisters must all envy me. I only hope they may have half my good luck. They must all go to Brighton. That is the place to get husbands. What a pity it is, mamma, we did not all go."
>
> "Very true; and if I had my will, we should. . . ."

And Lydia never repents; neither mother nor daughter even recognizes that there is anything to repent.

Mr. Collins and Lady Catherine, though "simple" also, differ from Lydia and Mrs. Bennet at least to the extent that Elizabeth can observe them more freely, without the sense of shame and responsibility she must feel toward her mother and sister. Mr. Collins is, indeed, so remote from Elizabeth's personal concerns that she and the reader can enjoy him as a pure fool, unweighted by moral import. The fact that he is a clergyman underscores his foolishness and moral nullity:

> ". . . I have been so fortunate as to be distinguished by the patronage of the Right Honorable Lady Catherine de Bourgh, widow of Sir Lewis de Bourgh, whose bounty and beneficence has preferred me to the valuable rectory of this parish, where it shall be my earnest endeavour to demean myself with grateful respect towards her Ladyship, and be ever ready to perform those rites and ceremonies which are instituted by the Church of England."

" '. . . Can he be a sensible man, sir?' " Elizabeth asks; and her father replies:

> "No, my dear; I think not. I have great hopes of finding him quite the reverse. There is a mixture of servility and self-importance in his letter, which promises well. I am impatient to see him."

Mr. Bennet's expectation of amusement is fulfilled many times over. "Mr. Collins was not a sensible man," as the author begins a superfluous descriptive paragraph; and his fatuity, sycophancy, conceit, and resolutely unprejudiced wife-hunting are given ample range. Wherever he goes, whatever he does, he remains unshakably foolish. Elizabeth's declining his proposal, once he can believe that it is not to be ascribed to the "usual practice of elegant females," clouds his jauntiness for a moment; but he recovers soon enough to propose as fervently to Charlotte Lucas three days later, and when he leaves Longbourn he wishes his "fair cousins . . . health and happiness, not excepting my cousin Elizabeth." As he likes to be useful to Lady Catherine, so he is useful to the plot: he provides a place for Elizabeth to visit, where she can observe Lady Catherine and see Darcy again; he draws out his "affable and condescending" patroness for Elizabeth's edification; he serves as a medium through which Lady Catherine's opinions on events in the Bennet family are graciously transmitted to the Bennets. And always he remains firm in the conviction of his importance and dignity, of his place at the center—or a little off the matriarchal center—of the universe.

Like Mr. Collins, Lady Catherine is chiefly amusing because of the incongruity between the importance she assumes to herself and the actual influence she exercises upon the story. At first glance, she is, of course, far more formidable than Mr. Collins; yet, in the story at least, she never does what she thinks she is doing or wishes to do. It is true—as Elizabeth remarks—that "Lady Catherine has been of infinite use, which ought to make her happy, for she loves to be of use." She is useful to the story; but only in ways she is unaware of and would repudiate with outrage if she knew of them. By her insulting condescension toward Elizabeth, she helps Darcy to balance off his distaste of Mrs. Bennet's not dissimilar shortcomings. She provokes Elizabeth into asserting her own independence of spirit, even to the point of impertinence. In her arrogant effort to dissuade Elizabeth from accepting Darcy, she gives Elizabeth the opportunity to set her own proud value upon herself as an individual, and later, having angrily brought the news to Darcy, encourages him to believe that Elizabeth may not refuse him a second time. Lady Catherine is a purely comic figure, not because she is not potentially powerful and dangerous in the authority that rank and wealth confer upon her, but because she is easily known for what she is, and because the lovers are in a position—Darcy by his own rank and wealth, Elizabeth by her spirit and intelligence—to deny her power altogether.

This quality of powerlessness is, indeed, peculiar to Elizabeth's, and the author's, whole category of simplicity: not merely in Mrs. Bennet, Lydia, Mr. Collins, and Lady Catherine, but in the predictably malicious Miss Bingley, in single-postured simpletons like Sir William Lucas and Mary Bennet, down to an unrealized function like Georgiana Darcy. They are powerless, that is, at the center of the story. They cannot decisively divert Elizabeth's or Darcy's mind and purpose because they cannot cope with the adult personality that either of the lovers presents. They are powerless, ultimately, because they are not themselves adult. They convince us of their existence (except, perhaps, Georgiana and Mary), sometimes even brilliantly; but they are not sufficiently complex or self-aware to be taken at the highest level of seriousness. Elizabeth's judgment of them is, then, primarily psychological, not moral: they have not grown to a personal stature significantly measurable by moral law. However Elizabeth may console Bingley that a "deep, intricate character" may be no more "estimable than such a one as yours," the fact is that though she finds simplicity comfortable or amusing, it is only intricacy, complexity of spirit, that she finds fascinating, deserving of pursuit and capture, susceptible to a grave moral judgment.

It may be objected that Jane Bennet belongs in the category of simplicity also, and that Elizabeth, nonetheless, loves and admires her sister above anyone else. Both statements are true; but the latter is true only in a very special sense. There is something maternal, something affectionately envious, something of the nature of a schoolgirl passion in Elizabeth's feeling for Jane.

The difference between her natural, uncomplex, unintuitive, almost unseeing goodness and Elizabeth's conscious, reasoned, perpetual examination into motive—this is a difference not merely between individuals, but between altogether different orders of mind. Elizabeth loves Jane as Jane is a kind and loving sister, she envies Jane her facile solution—to her plain ignorance—of the problems of interpreting personality, she even plays the schoolgirl to her older sister as confidante; but Elizabeth never doubts that Jane's opinions of others have no objective value, and that Jane's response toward people and society is much too simple, even too simple-minded, to be hers. So Elizabeth, as Jane defends Bingley's sisters against her charge of snobbery,

> . . . listened in silence, but was not convinced; their behaviour at the assembly had not been calculated to please in general; and with more quickness of observation and less pliancy of temper than her sister, and with a judgment too unassailed by any attention to herself, she was very little disposed to approve them.

The surest proof of Elizabeth's, and the author's, attitude toward Jane is the lover they are both delighted to supply her with. Bingley is a person of secondary order far more obviously than Jane. He is handsome, very amiable and courteous, lively, properly smitten by Jane almost at first glance. That, and his considerable wealth, make up the extent of his charms. It is significant that Elizabeth never has a twinge of feeling for him, except as he seems a fine catch for her sister. In his conversation with Elizabeth at Netherfield, he fears that he gives himself away out of shallowness; and, despite Elizabeth's graceful denial, he does. There is nothing below the surface. His strong-willed friend, Darcy, leads him about by the nose. Though he is supposed to have fallen seriously in love with Jane, the merest trick of Darcy's and his sister's is enough to send and keep him away from her. As Darcy explains:

> ". . . Bingley is most unaffectedly modest. His diffidence had prevented his depending on his own judgment in so anxious a case, but his reliance on mine, made every thing easy. . . ."

"Modest" is a charitable word here. Darcy has been equally successful, moreover, in turning about and persuading Bingley that Jane *is* in love with him; whereupon

Elizabeth longed to observe that Mr. Bingley had been a most delightful friend; so easily guided that his worth was invaluable. . . .

It is true that Jane pines over Bingley for a long time. She is a sincere and faithful lover; but our admiration of this trait tends to diminish as we think about the object of her love. Jane and Bingley provide us, then, with one of the book's primary ironies: that love is simple, straightforward, and immediate only for very simple people. Jane and Bingley could, of course, have served very well as a pair of story-book lovers, tossed romantically on a sea of circumstances not only beyond their control but beyond their understanding. In the pattern of the novel, however, they have their adult guardians and counterparts—Jane in her sister, Bingley in his friend—to haul them in when the sea gets too rough; and though, like the standard lovers of romance, they will never have to worry about growing up, we are obliged, by the presence of Elizabeth at least, to admit that it *is* possible—perhaps even preferable— for lovers to be complex and mature.

To this point Elizabeth's judgment is as acute and ironic as her author's. Elizabeth, indeed, is far more aware of distinctions in personality than any of the author's previous heroines: Catherine Morland, Elinor or Marianne Dashwood. In *Northanger Abbey*, the author could not allow her heroine to be aware from the outset since her story developed precisely out of Catherine's unawareness of distinctions (a quality suggested, perhaps, by Jane Austen's early tendency to assert an arbitrary omniscience over the objects of her irony). In *Sense and Sensibility*, Jane Austen, yielding for the first time to the moral pressures inevitable upon a woman of her time and class, allowed Elinor only the solemn and easy discriminations of bourgeois morality, and finally smothered the threatening spark of Marianne's much livelier and more observing consciousness. In *Pride and Prejudice*, however, there is no compulsion—personal, thematic, or moral—toward denying the heroine her own powers of judgment. There is, on the contrary, a thematic need for the heroine to display a subtle, accurate, a perceiving mind. In *Pride and Prejudice*, as in the previous novels, Jane Austen deals with the distinction between false moral values and true; but she is also dealing here with a distinction antecedent to the moral judgment—the distinction between the simple personality, unequipped with that self-awareness which alone makes choice seem possible, and the complex personality, whose most crucial complexity is its awareness, of self and others. This distinction, which in her youthful defensive posture Jane Austen has tended to make only between her characters and

herself, she here established internally, between two categories of
personality within the novel. The distinction is, in fact, one that
every character in *Pride and Prejudice* must make if he can; and
the complex characters—Elizabeth and Darcy among them—
justify their complexity by making it, and trying to live by its
implications, through all their lapses of arrogance, prejudice, sensuality, and fear. Elizabeth is aware because, in the novel's climate
of adult decision, she must be so to survive with our respect and
interest.

Yet the distinction must be made in a social setting, by human
beings fallible, if for no other reason, because of their own social
involvement. The province of *Pride and Prejudice*—as always in
Jane Austen's novels—is marriage in an acquisitive society. Elizabeth herself, being young, attractive, and unmarried, is at the
center of it; and it is this position that sets her off from such an
external and imposed commentator as Henry Tilney [in *Northanger Abbey*]. Her position of personal involvement subjects her,
moreover, to a risk of error never run by the detached Mr. Tilney.
She can tag and dismiss the blatantly simple persons very well; it
is when she moves away from these toward ambiguity and self-
concealment, toward persons themselves aware enough to interest
and engage her, that her youth and inexperience and emotional
partiality begin to deceive her.

They deceive her first with Charlotte Lucas. The two girls have
been good friends. Charlotte, according to the author, is a "sensible, intelligent young woman", and she shares Elizabeth's taste
for raillery and social generalization. Even when Charlotte offers
her altogether cynical views on courtship and marriage, Elizabeth
refuses to take her at her word:

> ". . . Happiness in marriage is entirely a matter of chance. If
> the dispositions of the parties are ever so well known to each
> other, or ever so similar before-hand, it does not advance their
> felicity in the least. They always continue to grow sufficiently
> unlike afterwards to have their share of vexation; and it is
> better to know as little as possible of the defects of the person
> with whom you are to pass your life."
>
> "You make me laugh, Charlotte; but it is not sound. You
> know it is not sound, and that you would never act in this way
> yourself."

It is not that Elizabeth misjudges Charlotte's capabilities, but that
she underestimates the strength of the pressures acting upon her.
Charlotte is twenty-seven, unmarried, not pretty, not well-to-do,
living in a society which treats a penniless old maid less as a joke
than as an exasperating burden upon her family. But Elizabeth
is inexperienced enough, at the beginning, to judge in terms of

personality only. She recognizes Mr. Collins' total foolishness and
Charlotte's intelligence, and would never have dreamed that any
pressure could overcome so natural an opposition. Complex and
simple, aware and unaware, do not belong together—except that
in marriages made by economics they often unite, however obvious
the mismatching. Living under a pall of economic anxiety has
withered every desire in Charlotte except the desire for security:

> ". . . I am not romantic. . . . I never was. I ask only a com-
> fortable home; and considering Mr. Collins's character, con-
> nections, and situation in life, I am convinced that my chance
> of happiness with him is as fair, as most people can boast on
> entering the marriage state."

What Charlotte has resolved, finally, is to grow progressively unaware, to reduce herself to simplicity; and, in the meantime, while
that is not yet possible, to close her eyes and ears. Her decision is
clear when Elizabeth visits Hunsford:

> When Mr. Collins said any thing of which his wife might
> reasonably be ashamed, which certainly was not unseldom, she
> involuntarily turned her eye on Charlotte. Once or twice she
> could discern a faint blush; but in general Charlotte wisely did
> not hear.

So the natural antithesis which separates simple from complex,
and which should separate one from the other absolutely in the
closest human relationship, can be upset and annulled by economic
pressure.

Elizabeth's continual mistake is to ignore, or to set aside as un-
influential, the social context. It is a question not merely of
individuals and marriage, but of individuals and marriage in an
acquisitive society. Elizabeth expects nothing except comfort or
amusement from simplicity; but she likes to believe that complexity
means a categorically free will, without social distortion or
qualification.

When complexity and a pleasing manner combine, as they do
in Wickham, Elizabeth is at her least cautious. Wickham is clever
and charming, a smooth social being, and for these qualities
Elizabeth is ready to believe his long, unsolicited tale of being
wronged and even to imagine herself falling in love with him.
What she never allows, until much later, to cast a doubt upon his
testimony is the fact that he is a dispossessed man in an acquisitive
society.

It is with Wickham, nevertheless, that Jane Austen's directing
and organizing irony—which functions doubly, at the same time
through and upon Elizabeth—begins to fail; and the area of failure
is the sexual experience outside marriage.

The first flattening of tone occurs in Darcy's letter, in which Wickham's infamy is revealed. Wickham has attempted to seduce Darcy's sister, Georgiana; and it is this specific attempt, beyond any other evidence of profligacy, that automatically makes him a villain from Darcy's point of view, and from Elizabeth's also as soon as she can accept the truth of the letter. The curious fact is, not that Elizabeth and, here at least, Jane Austen regard seduction as infamous, but that, into an ironic atmosphere elaborated and intensified out of the difficulty of interpreting motive, Jane Austen pushes a standard black-and-white seduction-scene, with all the appurtenances of an ingenuous young girl, a scheming profligate, a wicked governess, and an outraged brother, and with no trace of doubt, shading, or irony. It is hardly enough to say, with Miss Lascelles,[1] that Jane Austen clings to this novelistic convention through almost all her work as to a usable climax, which she met in Richardson and for which she could find no adequate substitute. *Why* she retained this threadbare revelation when, as early as *Pride and Prejudice,* she could demonstrate the most subtle and resourceful skill in representing every other particular of the action, remains a question.

The answer seems to be that, though the nature of her subject makes an approach to the sexual experience inevitable, Jane Austen will not allow herself (as she did in *Love and Freindship* and continues to do in her letters) to assimilate extra-marital sex to her characteristic unifying irony, and that her only other possible response is conventional. She must truncate, flatten, falsify, disapprove, all in the interests of an external morality; and the process in *Pride and Prejudice* is so out of key with its surroundings as to be immediately jarring.

Lydia is the outstanding victim. Not that Lydia is not throughout a wholly consistent and living character. On the solid and simple foundations of her personality she works up to her triumphant end in marriage to Wickham. If she acts from her sensual nature, it is Elizabeth and the author themselves who have proved to us that Lydia, being among the simple spirits who are never really aware and who act only upon their single potentiality, cannot do otherwise. The irony is, or should be, in her unawareness, in her powerlessness to change, in the incongruity between her conviction of vitality and her lack of choice. This irony, though, Jane Austen quite cuts off. She is herself silent, but it is clear that she allows Elizabeth to define the proper attitude toward Lydia. Elizabeth can feel, at first, no sympathy for Lydia at all. Later, however, when the moment of shame is long past, her attitude has not changed except to harden into sarcastic resent-

1. M. Lascelles, *Jane Austen and Her Art* (Oxford, 1939), 72f.

ment: when Lydia offers to give Elizabeth an account of the wedding,

> "No really," replied Elizabeth; "I think there cannot be too little said on the subject."

Elizabeth's ill-tempered efforts to shame Lydia are fruitless, as Elizabeth should have known they would be while Lydia is Lydia still. What they amount to is a kind of floating moral judgment. It seems that both Jane Austen and her heroine feel uneasily that a moral lesson must be taught, though they have already proved that Lydia is incapable of learning it:

> . . . how little of permanent happiness could belong to a couple who were only brought together because their passions were stronger than their virtue, she could easily conjecture.

So Jane Austen suspends her irony, suspends her imagination altogether, while Wickham is engaged in seducing Georgiana or Lydia. Yet, apart from this temporary suspension, Wickham fits admirably into the large pattern of Elizabeth's social education. Not only is he, like Charlotte, an example of the complex personality discarding scruples, discarding candor, making the wrong choice under economic pressure; he is also an evil agent, quite willing to corrupt others as well, to involve them in public disgrace if he can thereby assure his own security. What he uses deliberately is what Mrs. Bennet used, much less deliberately, in her conquest of her husband: sexual attractiveness. It is, then, Wickham who by exploiting sex sets off that other intricate character who passively succumbed to it—Mr. Bennet.

It is, in fact, easy to imagine that when Mr. Bennet calls Wickham his favorite son-in-law he is not merely indulging in habitual paradox, but ironically recognizing the painful contrast between Wickham's awareness, however directed, and his own self-delusion, in the same emotional circumstance. Mr. Bennet made his mistake many years before, and must now stand by it because his class recognizes no respectable way out:

> . . . captivated by youth and beauty, and that appearance of good humour, which youth and beauty generally give, he had married a woman whose weak understanding and illiberal mind, had very early in their marriage put an end to all real affection for her. Respect, esteem, and confidence, had vanished for ever; and all his views of domestic happiness were overthrown. But Mr. Bennet was not of a disposition to seek comfort for the disappointment which his own imprudence had brought on, in any of those pleasures which too often console the unfortunate for their folly or their vice. He was fond of the country and of books; and from these tastes had arisen his principal enjoyments.

To his wife he was very little otherwise indebted, than as her ignorance and folly had contributed to his amusement. This is not the sort of happiness which a man would in general wish to owe to his wife; but where other powers of entertainment are wanting, the true philosopher will derive benefit from such as are given.

Mr. Bennet has become an ironic spectator almost totally self-enclosed, his irony rigidly defensive, a carapace against the plain recognition of his own irrevocable folly. He observes, he stands apart "in silence . . . enjoying the scene," he likes to make blunt comments on the silliness of his daughters, especially of Lydia and Kitty:

> "From all that I can collect by your manner of talking, you must be two of the silliest girls in the country. I have suspected it some time, but I am now convinced."

and, equally, when Charlotte accepts Mr. Collins:

> . . . it gratified him, he said, to discover that Charlotte Lucas, whom he had been used to think tolerably sensible, was as foolish as his wife, and more foolish than his daughter!

He likes to upset, in small ways, the social decorum which has overwhelmed him in its massive and permanent way, he enjoys pointing the contrast between what he ought to think and what he does think. It is a very minor social victory, but the only one now possible for him.

It is true that Lydia's elopement shocks him into exposing himself for as long as it takes him to transact the unpleasant business. When he returns from his futile search in London, in acknowledgment of Elizabeth's

> . . . briefly expressing her sorrow for what he must have endured, he replied, 'Say nothing of that. Who should suffer but myself? It has been my own doing, and I ought to feel it."
> "You must not be too severe upon yourself," replied Elizabeth.
> "You may well warn me against such an evil. Human nature is so prone to fall into it! No, Lizzy, let me once in my life feel how much I have been to blame. I am not afraid of being overpowered by the impression. It will pass away soon enough."

It does soon enough, or at least the impulse to articulate it. With Lydia and Wickham safely married, Mr. Bennet restores himself to what he has been—rather, to what he has seemed. He needs only another letter from Mr. Collins to reaffirm all his amused detachment, to make explicit the only code by which he can tolerate the vacuity, the hopeless failure of sympathy, in his life.

". . . For what do we live, but to make sport for our neighbours, and laugh at them in our turn?"

If Elizabeth cannot answer, it is because she recognizes that there is nothing else left for her father, that his choice was made long ago, that he cannot withdraw or alter it, that he must live by it in the only way endurable for him. Of course his mistake and his despair might be decently masked; things would be better, for his children at least, if he could put up a front of quiet respectability concerning his relations with his wife:

> Elizabeth . . . had never been blind to the impropriety of her father's behaviour as a husband. She had always seen it with pain; but respecting his abilities, and grateful for his affectionate treatment of herself, she endeavoured to forget what she could not overlook, and to banish from her thoughts that continual breach of conjugal obligation and decorum which, in exposing his wife to the contempt of her children, was so highly reprehensible.

But the damage to himself is done and cannot be remedied. Elizabeth knows her father: of the complex characters in the story, he is the only one whom she has known long and well enough to judge accurately from the outset. She has learned from his example that a complex personality may yield to the pressure of sensuality; that marriages made by sex—as well as those made by economics—represent, for the free individual, an abdication of choice, an irremediable self-degradation and defeat.

In his social context, in his status as a gentleman of independent means, Mr. Bennet was lulled into believing that choice was easy, a matter of simple and unexamined inclination; and in the same society Mrs. Bennet could not believe otherwise than that any gentleman of means must make a desirable husband. This much Elizabeth recognizes about the pressures of an acquisitive society, even upon a free individual like her father. The shock of Charlotte's marriage to a fool makes Elizabeth recognize that these pressures act decisively upon other free individuals as well. In spite of examples, however, it takes a long series of vexations and misunderstandings before she can be convinced that the imposed pride of rank and wealth, perhaps the strongest pressure in an acquisitive society, may act, not yet decisively—for the area of decision is marriage—but conditionally upon a free individual like Darcy, to make him behave with an overconfident and unsympathetic obstinacy, to make him seem far different from what he is capable of being behind the façade of pride.

It is the social façade of the complex person that deceives Elizabeth. She can penetrate her father's, out of sympathetic familiarity and concern; but Charlotte's has deceived her. Wickham's takes her in altogether; and by contrast with Wickham's, by the contrast which Wickham himself takes care to emphasize in his own support, Darcy's façade seems disagreeable indeed, or rather a clear window on a disagreeable spirit.

Darcy's function as the character most difficult for the heroine to interpret, and yet most necessary for her to interpret if *she* is to make a proper decision in the only area of choice her society leaves open, his simultaneous role as the heroine's puzzle and her only possible hero, is clearly marked out during the action. From Elizabeth's point of view, in fact, the process of the interpretation of Darcy's personality from disdain through doubt to admiration is represented with an extraordinarily vivid and convincing minuteness.[2] Nevertheless, Darcy himself remains unachieved: we recognize his effects upon Elizabeth, without recognizing that he exists independently of them.

Mrs. Leavis has persuasively documented her belief that *Pride and Prejudice* is an effect to "rewrite the story of *Cecilia* in realistic terms";[3] and she observes, more particularly, that Darcy fails because he does not transcend his derivation: he is a character out of a book, not one whom Jane Austen created or reorganized for her own purpose. But why Darcy alone: why is he, among the major figures in *Pride and Prejudice*, the only one disturbingly derived and wooden?

The reason seems to be the same as that which compelled Jane Austen to falsify her tone and commentary concerning Wickham's seductions and to supply Elinor and Marianne Dashwood with such nonentities for husbands. The socially unmanageable, the personally involving aspects of sex, Jane Austen can no longer treat with irony, nor can she as yet treat them straightforwardly. Darcy is the hero, he is the potential lover of a complex young woman much like the author herself; and as such Jane Austen cannot animate him with emotion, or with her characteristic informing irony. She borrows him from a book; and, though she alters and illuminates everything else, she can do nothing more with him than fit him functionally into the plot.

Even here the author is so uncharacteristically clumsy as to rely on inconsistencies of personality to move her story along. However difficult Elizabeth's task of interpreting Darcy, it is clear from the beginning that, in his consistent functional impact upon the story, he is a proud man with a strong sense of at least external propriety

2. In "The Controlling Hand: Jane Austen and *Pride and Prejudice*," *Scrutiny*, XIII (1945), 99–111, R. A. Brower brilliantly analyzes the process by means of which Elizabeth comes to an understanding of Darcy.

3. Q. D. Leavis, "A Critical Theory of Jane Austen's Writing," *Scrutiny*, X (1941), 71ff.

and dignity, and with no taste whatever for his aunt's vulgar condescension or the kind of sarcasm dispensed by Mr. Bennet. Yet on his first appearance he initiates Elizabeth's prejudice by speaking with a simple vulgarity indistinguishable from his aunt's, and in a voice loud enough to be overheard by the object of his contempt:

> . . . turning round, he looked for a moment at Elizabeth, till catching her eye, he withdrew his own and coldly said, "She is tolerable; but not handsome enough to tempt *me*; and I am in no humour at present to give consequence to young ladies who are slighted by other men. . . ."

In spite of his rigid and principled reserve, in spite of Elizabeth's having just turned down his arrogant proposal, he makes his explanation to Elizabeth in a thoroughly frank and unreserved letter, which—more appropriate to a Richardsonian correspondent than to Darcy as he has been presented—seems an author's gesture of desperation to weight the scales in favor of her predetermined hero.

Out of inconsistency, Darcy emerges into flatness. Only in his sparring with Elizabeth, and then only occasionally, does he establish himself with a degree of solidity, of independent reference, as when Elizabeth tries to tease him into communicativeness while they are dancing:

> ". . . One must speak a little, you know. It would look odd to be entirely silent for half an hour together, and yet for the advantage of *some*, conversation ought to be so arranged as that they may have the trouble of saying as little as possible."
>
> "Are you consulting your own feelings in the present case, or do you imagine that you are gratifying mine?"
>
> "Both," replied Elizabeth archly, "for I have always seen a great similarity in the turn of our minds.—We are each of an unsocial, taciturn disposition, unwilling to speak, unless we expect to say something that will amaze the whole room, and be handed down to posterity with all the éclat of a proverb."
>
> "This is no very striking resemblance of your own character, I am sure," said he. "How near it may be to *mine*, I cannot pretend to say.—*You* think it a faithful portrait undoubtedly."

In dialogue, at least when Elizabeth is an enlivening participant, Jane Austen seems able now and then to overcome her awkwardness in handling Darcy. Otherwise, however, she can only make him serve: he interests us chiefly because he is the center of Elizabeth's interest; and because, in a book in which the individual must choose and in which marriage is the single area of choice, Darcy represents Elizabeth's only plausible, or almost plausible, mate. And when Darcy is ironed out into the conventionally generous and altruistic hero, making devoted efforts to shackle Wickham to Lydia, expending thousands of pounds to restore peace of mind to Elizabeth's family, and all for the love of Elizabeth— when he does all this, with no more of personal depth than Jane Austen allows of moral depth in the whole Lydia-Wickham episode, he comes very close to forfeiting even the functional plausibility that Elizabeth's interest lends him.

The last third of the book, as R. A. Brower has pointed out, does in fact diminish suddenly in density and originality: that is, beginning with Lydia's elopement. We get a conventional chase by an outraged father, a friendly uncle, and a now impeccable hero; we get outbursts of irrelevantly directed moral judgment, and a general simplification of the problems of motive and will down to the level of the Burneyan novel. Jane Austen herself, routed by the sexual question she has raised, is concealed behind a fogbank of bourgeois morality; and the characters, most conspicuously Darcy, must shift for themselves, or, rather, they fall automatically into the grooves prepared for them by hundreds of novels of sentiment and sensibility.

Only Elizabeth does not. She may yield temporarily to a kind of homeless moralizing on Lydia's disgrace, she may be rather obvious and stiff in acquainting herself with Darcy's virtues at last; but the lapses are minor, and they never seriously dim her luminous vigor, her wit, curiosity, discrimination, and independence. If the novel does not collapse in the predictabilities of the denouement, it is because Elizabeth has from the outset been presented in a depth specific and vital enough to resist flattening, because she remains what she has been—a complex person in search of conclusions about people in society, and on the way to her unique and crucial choice.

She observes, and her shield and instrument together is irony. Like Mary Crawford [in *Mansfield Park*] later, Elizabeth is a recognizable and striking aspect of her author; but, unlike Mary's, her sins are all quite venial, her irony unclouded by the author's disapproval and—after a few detours—grandly vindicated in its effect. Jane Austen has not yet made her first unqualified capitulation to the suspicious sobriety of her class, and surrendered her values in exchange for its own. She can, in fact, embody her personal values in her heroine and be delighted with the result; so she writes to her sister about Elizabeth: "I must confess that I think her as delightful a creature as ever appeared in print, and how I shall be able to tolerate those who do not like *her* at least I do not know."

Elizabeth's third dimension is irony; and it is her irony that fills out and sustains the action. Her slightest perception of incongruity reverberates through the scene, and from it out into the atmosphere of the book. When Lydia, having informed Elizabeth that Wickham's wealthy catch has got away, adds:

". . . he never cared three straws about her. Who *could* about such a nasty little freckled thing?"

Elizabeth was shocked to think that, however incapable of such coarseness of *expression* herself, the coarseness of the *sentiment* was little other than her own breast had formerly harboured and fancied liberal!

At Pemberley, she listens as the housekeeper eulogizes Darcy, until her uncle asks:

"Is your master much at Pemberley in the course of the year?"

"Not so much as I could wish, sir; but I dare say he may spend half his time here; and Miss Darcy is always down for the summer months."

"Except," thought Elizabeth, "when she goes to Ramsgate."

recalling by this most astonishing economy of means—like a flashback in intent but with none of its deadening machinery— the whole charged atmosphere of Wickham's earlier attempt at seduction (more successfully than Darcy's letter, our original source of information, had created it at first), recalling the tension of Darcy's insulting and rejected proposal, the excitement of his letter and the depression and change of heart it inevitably brought: and all this richness and clarity of reference out of a single and immediately irrelevant ironic thought.

There is, above all, the perpetual exuberant yet directed irony of her conversation, especially as she uses it to sound Darcy. When Miss Bingley assures her that Darcy cannot be laughed at, Elizabeth exclaims:

"That is an uncommon advantage, and uncommon I hope it will continue, for it would be a great loss to *me* to have many such acquaintance. I dearly love a laugh."

"Miss Bingley," said he, "has given me credit for more than can be. The wisest and the best of men, nay, the wisest and best of their actions, may be rendered ridiculous by a person whose first object in life is a joke."

"Certainly," replied Elizabeth—"there are such people, but I hope I am not one of them. I hope I never ridicule what is wise or good. Follies and nonsense, whims and inconsistencies *do* divert me, I own, and I laugh at them when I can.—But these, I suppose, are precisely what you are without."

Darcy protests that his failings are not of understanding, but of temper:

> ". . . My temper would perhaps be called resentful.—My good opinion once lost is lost for ever."
>
> "*That* is a failing indeed!" cried Elizabeth. "Implacable resentment *is* a shade in a character. You have chosen your fault well.—I really cannot *laugh* at it. You are safe from me."
>
> "There is, I believe, in every disposition a tendency to some particular evil, a natural defect, which not even the best education can overcome."
>
> "And *your* defect is a propensity to hate every body."

Whether Elizabeth is teasing him about his silence at dancing, or, in Lady Catherine's drawing room, explaining her lack of skill at the piano to refute Darcy's claim of having no talent for sociability, she draws him out in the only ways in which he can be drawn out at all, by a challenging indirection just short of impudence, by the appeal of an intelligence as free and aware as that on which he prides himself, by the penetration of a wit which makes its own rules without breaking any significant ones, which even establishes its priority over simple truth:

> "You mean to frighten me, Mr. Darcy, by coming in all this state to hear me? But I will not be alarmed. . . ."
>
> "I shall not say that you are mistaken," he replied, "because you could not really believe me to entertain any design of alarming you; and I have had the pleasure of your acquaintance long enough to know that you find great enjoyment in occasionally professing opinions which in fact are not your own."

If Darcy, finally sounded and known, hardly differs from the stiff-jointed Burneyan aristocratic hero, except as Darcy is provided with a somewhat more explicit personality, the fault is not Elizabeth's, but her author's. Elizabeth has learned what can be learned about him; she has even learned, with Miss Bingley, that Darcy is *not* to be laughed at—not, at least, in the matter of his influence over Bingley:

> Elizabeth longed to observe that Mr. Bingley had been a most delightful friend; so easily guided that his worth was invaluable; but she checked herself. She remembered that he had yet to learn to be laught at, and it was rather too early to begin.

In the process of interpretation, moreover—with its deflections, its spurious evidence, its shocks of awareness and repentance—she has brought to a focus at last all the scattered principles which her overconfidence and lack of experience continually obliged her to underestimate, forget, or abandon.

She never gives up her first principle: to separate the simple personality from the complex, and to concentrate her attention and interest on the latter. Her point of reference is always the complex individual, the individual aware and capable of choice. Her own pride is in her freedom, to observe, to analyze, to choose; her continual mistake is to forget that, even for her, there is only one area of choice—marriage—and that this choice is subject to all the powerful and numbing pressures of an acquisitive society.

The central fact for Elizabeth remains the power of choice. In spite of social pressures, in spite of the misunderstandings and the obstacles to awareness that cut off and confuse the individual, in spite of the individual's repeated failures, the power of choice is all that distinguishes him as a being who acts and who may be judged. There are, certainly, limitations upon his choice, the limitations of an imposed prudence, of living within a social frame in which material comfort is an article of prestige and a sign of moral well-being: since even Elizabeth, though an acute and critical observer, is no rebel, she cannot contemplate the possibility of happiness outside her given social frame. The author is, likewise, pointedly ironic in contrasting Elizabeth's charitable allowances, first for Wickham, and then for Colonel Fitzwilliam, an "Earl's younger son," when her relative poverty obliges them to regard her as ineligible. Yet the irony does not go so far as to invalidate choice or distinctions in choice. Fitzwilliam, no rebel, is prudent in the hope that both prudence and inclination may be satisfied together in the future; but Wickham's "prudence," rather than merely limiting his choice, has deprived him of it entirely. In Elizabeth's feeling, upon touring Darcy's estate, "that to be mistress of Pemberley might be something!" the irony is circumscribed with an equal clarity: Darcy gains by being a rich man with a magnificent estate; but Pemberley is an expression of Darcy's taste as well as of his wealth and rank, and the image of Pemberley cannot divert Elizabeth from her primary concern with Darcy's motives and the meaning of his façade. Pemberley with Mr. Collins, or even with Bingley, would not do at all.

The focus is upon the complex individual; the only quality that distinguishes him from his setting, from the form of courtship and marriage in an acquisitive society, which otherwise standardize and absorb him, is also his unique function—choice. What Elizabeth must choose, within the bounds set by prudence, is an individual equally complex, and undefeated by his social role. The complex individual is, after all, isolated by his freedom, and must be seen so at the end; for even if pressures from without, from the social system and the social class, deflect or overwhelm him, they demonstrate not that he is indistinguishable from his social role, but that he is vulnerable to it. The fact of choice makes him stand, finally, alone, to judge or be judged.

In *Pride and Prejudice,* Jane Austen's irony has developed into an instrument of discrimination between the people who are simple reproductions of their social type and the people with individuality and will, between the unaware and the aware. The defensive —and destructive—weapon of *Northanger Abbey* and *Sense and Sensibility* has here been adapted directly to the theme through the personality of Elizabeth Bennet, who reflects and illustrates her author's vision without ever becoming (except in her malice toward Lydia) merely her author's advocate. The irony is internal, it does not take disturbing tangents toward the author's need for self-vindication: even self-defensive, it is internal and consistent—Mr. Bennet's shying from the consequences of his disastrous mistake, Elizabeth's provocative parrying of Darcy. And if this new control over her irony permits Jane Austen only to be more clever (and not particularly more persuasive) in avoiding a commitment, by Elizabeth in love, for example:

> ". . . Will you tell me how long you have loved him?"
> "It has been coming on so gradually, that I hardly know when it began. But I believe it must date from my first seeing his beautiful grounds at Pemberley."
> Another intreaty that she would be serious, however, produced the desired effect; and she soon satisfied Jane by her solemn assurances of attachment.

the characteristic block of Jane Austen's against direct emotional expression has occasion only very rarely to operate in *Pride and Prejudice*: above all, in the talk and atmosphere of Darcy's proposals, and in his letter—passages which most nearly reproduce the flat or melodramatic textures of *Cecilia,* without any lift of emotion or of irony either. The moment is soon over; and irony is not only back, but back at its proper task of discrimination.

In *Pride and Prejudice,* the flaw of an irrelevant defensiveness has almost vanished; and the flaw of a too obvious personal withdrawal before a moral or emotional issue, as with Lydia and Darcy, is not obtrusive enough, to annul or seriously damage the sustained and organizing power of Jane Austen's irony. Irony here rejects chiefly to discover and illuminate; and, though its setting is the same stratified, materialistic, and severely regulated society, its new text and discovery—its new character, in fact, whom Jane Austen has hitherto allowed only herself to impersonate—is the free individual.

ANDREW H. WRIGHT

[Feeling and Complexity in *Pride and Prejudice*]†

i. *Elizabeth Bennet*

At first glance, perhaps, the two elder Bennet sisters may seem to vie with each other for primacy in *Pride and Prejudice*; but Elizabeth is definitely the heroine: not only does she explicitly represent one of the words of the title of the story; she also quite thoroughly dominates the action—and, by comparison, Jane is a shadowy accessory. The relationship of Miss Bennet to Bingley, which parallels that of Elizabeth and Darcy, is treated much less fully, partly because it is much simpler, but partly because it is intended to be a comment on that of her younger sister and the proud man from Derbyshire. Yet Jane throughout the book has the unqualified approbation of Elizabeth, author, and reader—though we may, with Elizabeth, wish to speak to her with the following affectionate mock-exasperation:

> 'My dear Jane! . . . you are too good. Your sweetness and disinterestedness are really angelic; I do not know what to say to you. I feel as if I had never done you justice, or loved you as you deserve.'

Indeed it is because of—not despite—her perfection that we must reject Jane as the heroine: the author's concern is with the complexity, the interrelationship, of good and bad—the mixture which cannot be unmixed. Jane is a simple character, but ' "intricate characters are the *most* amusing" ', and Jane, like Bingley, is not intricate: she is heroic but minor—she is not a heroine. 'I must confess,' writes Jane Austen of Elizabeth Bennet, 'that I think her as delightful a creature as ever appeared in print, and how I shall be able to tolerate those who do not like *her* at least I do not know.'

To say that Darcy is proud and Elizabeth prejudiced is to tell but half the story. Pride and prejudice are faults; but they are also the necessary defects of desirable merits: self-respect and intelligence. Moreover, the novel makes clear the fact that Darcy's pride leads to prejudice and Elizabeth's prejudice stems from a

† From Andrew H. Wright, *Jane Austen's Novels: A Study in Structure*, London, 1957. Pp. 105–123. Copyright 1957. Reprinted by permission of the publishers, Oxford University Press and Chatto and Windus Ltd.

pride in her own perceptions. So the ironic theme of the book might be said to centre on the dangers of intellectual complexity. Jane Bennet and Bingley are never exposed to these dangers; they are not sufficiently profound. But the hero and the heroine, because of their deep percipience, are, ironically, subject to failures of perception. Elizabeth has good reason to credit herself with the ability to discern people and situations extraordinarily well: she understands her family perfectly, knows William Collins from the first letter he writes, comprehends the merits and deficiencies of the Bingleys almost at once, appreciates Lady Catherine de Bourgh at first meeting. Her failures are with 'intricate' people who moreover stand in a relationship of great intimacy to her: Charlotte Lucas, George Wickham, Fitzwilliam Darcy. And the book is given an added dimension because it shows that intimacy blurs perceptions: intelligence fails if there is insufficient distance between mind and object.

Charlotte Lucas is 'a sensible, intelligent young woman, about twenty-seven . . . Elizabeth's intimate friend'. But we very soon know that in an important respect she differs from Elizabeth—though Elizabeth herself does not know this fact. When, very early in the first volume, they discuss the possibility of an attachment between Jane and Bingley, Charlotte says Jane should make some efforts in this direction; but Elizabeth reminds her friend that Miss Bennet hardly knows him. This, however, does not deter Charlotte:

'I wish Jane success with all my heart; and if she were married to him tomorrow, I should think she had as good a chance of happiness, as if she were to be studying his character for a twelvemonth. Happiness in marriage is entirely a matter of chance. If the dispositions of the parties are ever so well known to each other, or ever so similar before-hand, it does not advance their felicity in the least. They always continue to grow sufficiently unlike afterwards to have their share of vexation; and it is better to know as little as possible of the defects of the person with whom you are to pass your life.'

But Elizabeth does not believe this statement:

'You make me laugh, Charlotte; but it is not sound. You know it is not sound, and that you would never act in this way yourself.'

Why does she refuse to believe Charlotte (who will soon demonstrate quite shockingly that she means every word she says on the subject of marriage)? It is because a natural kindness and affection have blinded Elizabeth to the demerits of her friend; it is because, in the nature of things, involvement (which is so necessary and desirable, in Austenian terms) carries with it the inevitable consequence of obscuring the marvellous clarity and depth of under-standing so necessary to success in personal association.

There is no evidence that Charlotte misunderstands William Collins, but there is much to show that Elizabeth does comprehend him perfectly. ' "Can he be a sensible man, sir?" ' she asks her father rhetorically after hearing the orotund phrases of the clergy-man's letter. Nor is she wrong. At the Netherfield Ball, after dancing with him twice, 'the moment of her release from him was exstacy', but she derives some consolation in discussing his de-merits with Charlotte. The next morning he proposes marriage to Elizabeth (' "And now nothing remains for me but to assure you in the most animated language of the violence of my affection" '), and of course she refuses him summarily. Then she is flabbergasted to learn that Charlotte has accepted Mr. Collins's subsequent pro-posal of marriage to her.

> She had always felt that Charlotte's opinion of matrimony was not exactly like her own, but she could not have supposed it possible that when called into action, she would have sacrificed every better feeling to worldly advantage. Charlotte the wife of Mr. Collins, was a most humiliating picture!

And now, for the first time, she begins to see Charlotte as she really is: and 'felt persuaded that no real confidence could ever subsist between them again'. Elizabeth has learned something from this experience, as is demonstrated in her conversation with Jane not long afterwards:

> 'Do not be afraid of my running into any excess, of my en-croaching on your privilege of universal good will. You need not. There are few people whom I really love, and still fewer of whom I think well. The more I see of the world, the more am I dissatisfied with it; and every day confirms my belief of the inconsistency of all human characters, and of the little dependence that can be placed on the appearance of either merit or sense. I have met with two instances lately; one I will not mention [it is Bingley's 'want of proper resolution']; the other is Charlotte's marriage. It is unaccountable! In every view it is unaccountable.'

Elizabeth does not give Darcy a chance—or rather she does not give herself a chance to know how she really feels about him. The famous first encounter is comically disastrous; it occurs at the assembly where Darcy says to Bingley of Elizabeth, who is sitting down: ' "She is tolerable; but not handsome enough to tempt *me*; and I am in no humour at present to give consequence to young ladies who are slighted by other men" '. And as a natural result, 'Elizabeth remained with no very cordial feelings towards him'.

But at Netherfield, where she has gone to nurse the ailing Jane, Elizabeth makes her extraordinary and attractive personality felt —so strongly that Mrs. Hurst and Miss Bingley take an immediate dislike to her; so strongly that she finds Darcy staring at her.

> She hardly knew how to suppose that she could be an object of admiration to so great a man; and yet that he should look at her because he disliked her, was still more strange. She could only imagine however at last, that she drew his notice because there was a something about her more wrong and reprehensible, according to his ideas of right, than in any other person present. The supposition did not pain her. She liked him too little to care for his approbation.

However, when she refuses to dance with him and says, ' "despise me if you dare" ', he replies in unmistakable accents, ' "Indeed I do not dare" '.

But the insult of the Ball fresh in her mind, she does not like him; she is even willing to overweigh the negative evidence, which now presents itself first from Darcy himself, then from the plausible and attractive Wickham. In the conversation at Netherfield, during which Elizabeth makes her well-known remark, that " 'I hope I never ridicule what is wise and good" ', she finds from Darcy that ' "My good opinion once lost is lost for ever" "—a chilling comment which she acknowledges to be a defect, but not a laughable one.

Then she meets Wickham, and finding him charming, very easily believes his allegations that Darcy has behaved abominably, that the latter has cast the young lieutenant from a promised living in the church, that in fact both Darcy and his sister suffer from very excessive pride. Elizabeth is vexed and even angry when Wickham fails to appear at the Netherfield Ball, again not trying to suppose that there may be something to be said on Darcy's side. Even so, there are signs that she willy-nilly succumbs to his charms—in the pertness of her conversation while they are dancing:

> 'It is *your* turn to say something now, Mr. Darcy.—I talked about the dance, and *you* ought to make some kind of remark on the size of the room, or the number of couples.'
> He smiled, and assured her that whatever she wished him to say should be said.
> 'Very well.—That reply will do for the present.—Perhaps by and bye I may observe that private balls are much pleasanter than public ones.—But *now* we may be silent.'
> 'Do you talk by rule then, while you are dancing?'
> 'Sometimes. One must speak a little, you know. It would look odd to be entirely silent for half an hour together, and yet for the advantage of *some*, conversation ought to be so

arranged as that they may have the trouble of saying as little as possible.'

'Are you consulting your own feelings in the present case, or do you imagine that you are gratifying mine?'

'Both,' replied Elizabeth archly; 'for I have always seen a great similarity in the turn of our minds.—We are each of an unsocial, taciturn disposition, unwilling to speak, unless we expect to say something that will amaze the whole room, and be handeed down to posterity with all the éclat of a proverb.'

However, when she questions him about Wickham, he keeps silent—nor can she understand him, as she readily admits before their dance is finished. It is an artful irony of Jane Austen's that Miss Bingley immediately thereafter tells her that Wickham is entirely in the wrong, and Darcy in the right, in the breach between the two men. Elizabeth disbelieves her for two reasons: first, because she has correctly sized Miss Bingley up as an entirely unreliable source of information; and second, perhaps, because she *wants* to dislike Darcy in order to avoid any entanglement which will cost her her freedom. Nevertheless, she feels mortified when she realizes that Darcy is overhearing Mrs. Bennet boast that Jane and Bingley will soon be engaged.

In the second volume, the relationship of Darcy and Elizabeth is resumed in Kent, at Rosings and at Hunsford, the parsonage to which William Collins has taken his new wife. Everything is unpropitious, so far as Elizabeth herself is concerned: she has agreed to visit Charlotte only because of the memory of their close friendship—'all the comfort of intimacy was over'. Mr. Collins is just as senseless as ever; Miss de Bourgh is ' "sickly and cross.—Yes, she will do for him [Darcy] very well. She will make him a very proper wife" '; and Lady Catherine is quite as insufferable as Wickham has promised. Amongst all these displeasing people comes Darcy, who adds to her annoyance by looking confused when she asks whether he has seen Jane in London (for she suspects that he has warned Bingley off her); and, despite his calls at the parsonage and their 'chance' encounters in Rosings Park, her prejudice against him increases, for she finds apparent corroboration of her suspicions in the conversation with Colonel Fitzwilliam, during which he recounts the fact that Darcy has told him of saving an intimate friend recently from a very imprudent marriage.

And so she is bowled over when Darcy tells her he loves her:

'In vain have I struggled. It will not do. My feelings will not be repressed. You must allow me to tell you how ardently I admire and love you.'

But she is more than astonished: she is gradually angered by the tone and implication of his remarks:

> His sense of her inferiority—of its being a degradation—of the family obstacles which judgment had always opposed to inclination, were dwelt on with a warmth which seemed due to the consequence he was wounding, but was very unlikely to recommend his suit.

So—and not without recrimination for ' "ruining, perhaps for ever, the happiness of a most beloved sister" ' and for his ill-treatment of Wickham—she refuses and dismisses the proud Mr. Fitzwilliam Darcy.

But this is not the end; indeed it is only the beginning of Elizabeth's very gradually successful efforts to know herself thoroughly. The next day she is handed Darcy's justly famous letter, written in proud tones and offering some new light not only on the Jane-Bingley business but upon the supposed unfairness to Wickham's claims. * * *

Elizabeth reads the letter with great astonishment and—at first —with little comprehension. She is, however, even more completely stunned by the account of Wickham, and her first impression is to disbelieve Darcy on that score too. But then, in reflecting on Wickham's behaviour at Meryton (especially with regard to his sudden betrothal to the rich Miss King), she is inclined to think it very probable that Darcy is telling the truth after all.

> She grew absolutely ashamed of herself.—Of neither Darcy nor Wickham could she think, without feeling that she had been blind, partial, prejudiced, absurd.
> 'How despicably have I acted!' she cried.—'I, who have prided myself on my discernment!—I, who have valued myself on my abilities! who have often disdained the generous candour of my sister, and gratified my vanity, in useless or blameable distrust.—How humiliating is this discovery!—Yet, how just a humiliation!—Had I been in love, I could not have been more wretchedly blind.'

In this dramatic moment of self-revelation she has the honesty to see that there may be some justice in what Darcy has said about Jane, for 'she felt that Jane's feelings, though fervent, were little displayed, and that there was a constant complacency in her air and manner, not often united with great sensibility'. She has learned much from the letter, very much indeed; but Jane Austen is too perceptive a reader of character to suppose that all comes clear at once: it is by a marvellous irony that Elizabeth is made to reflect, ' "Had I been in love, I could not have been more wretchedly blind" '. * * *

But why has it been so much easier for her to like George Wickham? It is certainly true that, on their first meeting, he is much more polite than Darcy; his façade is much smoother, and his wit just as sharp. Elizabeth herself says, ' "I have courted pre-possession and ignorance . . ." '. But there is a further reason, that she feels no danger of a permanent attachment to him; and for this second reason, she yields all too willingly to the belief that Darcy is what Wickham says he is.

She deceives herself: Mrs. Gardiner, who is much more per-ceptive in this matter than her niece, warns Elizabeth not to fall in love with the lieutenant. But Elizabeth promises only to go slowly. Nevertheless (and this, it seems to me, proves my second point) she feels not a single pang of regret when Wickham announces his engagement to Miss King, the girl with a dowry of £10,000. As she writes to her aunt,

> 'I am now convinced . . . that I have never been much in love; for had I really experienced that pure and elevating passion, I should at present detest his very name, and wish him all manner of evil. But my feelings are not only cordial towards *him*; they are even impartial towards Miss King. . . . There can be no love in all this.'

And she is right: so she can afford herself the luxury of deciding, before leaving for Kent, that Wickham 'must always be her model of the amiable and pleasing'; she can (or so she thinks) indulge herself in the imperception of denying to Mrs. Gardiner that Wickham's attachment discloses his mercenary motives.

The profundity of her mortification at knowing the truth about him comes then, not merely from the knowledge that her per-ceptions, on which she has prided herself, have been beclouded by prejudice, but from the deeper reason that her relationship to him, because it has not engaged her much, has been able to afford the luxury of quasi-intimacy. Against clarity, in *Pride and Preju-dice*, involvement is set: both are desirable, but each, ironically, works against the other—and the reader cannot believe that the marriage of Darcy and Elizabeth, however happy or beneficial, will ever quite close the breach between these two opposites.

ii. *Fitzwilliam Darcy and George Wickham*

In *Pride and Prejudice*, hero and villain have prominent inter-esting, and convincing parts. Each is present throughout the novel, both attract the heroine, and both receive the marital fates which they deserve. Elizabeth Bennet is a complicated and penetrating heroine; the two men with whom she associates herself roman-tically must also be intricate and intelligent.

If (as we have shown) Elizabeth's prejudices are views in which she takes pride, so ought it be said that Darcy's pride leads to prejudice. But even this is an over-simplification: his austerity of manner, as we learn from his housekeeper at Pemberley, stems partly from an inordinate shyness. It is impossible, however, to explain away his famous remark about Elizabeth (' ". . . tolerable; but not handsome enough to tempt *me* . . ." ' [1]) on the grounds of diffidence alone—nor, indeed, the statement that ' "My good opinion once lost is lost for ever" ', nor the first proposal to Elizabeth; nor his subsequent explanatory letter. He *is* a proud man.

One way in which Jane Austen delineates his character is through his relationship with Bingley. It is partly through this friendship that a certain completeness is given to Darcy's character. Although we are struck, at the very beginning of the book, with Darcy's rudeness and with his pride, we may overlook the solidity of temperament implied in his affection for Bingley.

Despite his early bad impression of Elizabeth, he is soon constrained to like her better: for, ironically, the heroine by behaving disdainfully to him, does just what is necessary to captivate him. Thus at Sir William Lucas's party, her refusal to dance with him only sets him to thinking of her attractiveness; her piquancy at Netherfield leads to the famous conversation in which Elizabeth, while acknowledging that ' "I dearly love a laugh" ', insists that ' "I hope I never ridicule what is wise or good" '.—and from there to Darcy's increased awareness of 'the danger of paying Elizabeth too much attention'.

The next appearance of Darcy comes when Elizabeth is visiting Hunsford, where she has gone to fulfil an unwilling promise of spending some time with Charlotte and William Collins. Besides the unfortunate first impression which the squire of Pemberley has made, there is now the insistent and plausible evidence against his character which Wickham has adduced. Elizabeth cannot understand the why of Darcy's repeated calls at the parsonage, nor can she comprehend the astonishing regularity of their 'unexpected' encounters in the Park. And she is stunned by his declaration of love, and proposal of marriage (critics who censure Jane Austen for an alleged lack of emotion should re-read this chapter).

> Elizabeth's astonishment was beyond expression. She stared, coloured, doubted, and was silent. This he considered sufficient encouragement, and the avowal of all that he felt and had long felt for her, immediately followed. He spoke well, but there

1. This remark, however, does little more than show him to be out of humour. The reader should not make Elizabeth's mistake of judging him too hardly for it.

were feelings besides those of the heart to be detailed, and he was not more eloquent on the subject of tenderness than of pride. His sense of her inferiority—of its being a degradation— of the family obstacles which judgment had always opposed to inclination, were dwelt on with a warmth which seemed due to the consequence he was wounding, but was very unlikely to recommend his suit.

In spite of her deeply-rooted dislike, she could not be insensible to the compliment of such a man's affection, and though her intentions did not vary for an instant, she was at first sorry for the pain he was to receive; till, roused to resentment by his subsequent language, she lost all compassion in anger. She tried, however, to compose herself to answer him with patience, when he should have done. He concluded with representing to her the strength of that attachment which, in spite of all his endeavours, he had found impossible to conquer; and with expressing his hope that it would now be rewarded by her acceptance of his hand. As he said this, she could easily see that he had no doubt of a favourable answer. He *spoke* of apprehension and anxiety, but his countenance expressed real security. Such a circumstance could only exasperate farther. . . .

Elizabeth's angry refusal marks the beginning of the great change in Darcy: he is humbled, though there is but one sentence in the letter which he writes to her, to indicate that he has been mollified: 'I will only add, God bless you'.

Now he disappears from view, until Elizabeth, together with the Gardiners, visits Pemberley. Here Elizabeth's opinion of him softens slightly. And in fact there are a series of circumstances which disclose him to be a much more human person than she has previously thought him.

But this is not all: he behaves heroically, for he hastens to London, seeks out Lydia and Wickham, makes a provison for them, and all but drags them to the altar. These things he does not out of admiration for the eloped couple, but out of love for Elizabeth—which, however, he does not again bring himself to declare, until after Lady Catherine de Bourgh's interview with Elizabeth. This ' "taught me to hope" ', and so he is able to propose again, this time with success.

George Wickham is at once the most plausible and the most villainous of Jane Austen's anti-heroes: he is handsome, persuasive, personable; disingenuous, calculating, and dishonourable. His appearance in the story comes just as Elizabeth, smarting from Darcy's disapprobation, willingly abrogates her critical faculties in favour of a pleasant countenance and manner. She all too readily believes the militia lieutenant's defamation of Darcy's character— though we, the readers, are expected to take note of the warning signals which Elizabeth ignores. In the first place, Jane Bennet declares:

> 'It is impossible. No man of common humanity, no man who had any value for his character, could be capable of it. Can his most intimate friends be so excessively deceived in him? Oh! no.'

In the second place, Miss Bingley plainly warns Elizabeth about Wickham, and indicates his relationship to Darcy:

> 'So, Miss Eliza, I hear you are quite delighted with George Wickham!—Your sister has been talking to me about him, and asking me a thousand questions; and I find that the young man forgot to tell you, among his other communications, that he was the son of old Wickham, the late Mr. Darcy's steward. Let me recommend you, however, as a friend, not to give implicit confidence to all his assertions; for as to Mr. Darcy's using him ill, it is perfectly false; for, on the contrary, he has been always remarkably kind to him, though George Wickham has treated Mr. Darcy in a most infamous manner.'

Jane Austen does not stack the cards, but she is not averse to throwing sand in her readers' eyes: both Jane and Miss Bingley are, as it happens, perfectly correct here; but Elizabeth does not believe either of them, for Jane's unwillingness ever to be unkind does sometimes blind her to people's faults, and Caroline Bingley's careless, insensitive stupidity often leads to complete misapprehension.

So Elizabeth continues to think well of Wickham, and ill of Darcy—even when the former announces his engagement to Miss King, whose dowry is £10,000. This time the heroine ignores the testimony—or rather, the conjecture—of one whose judgment she has always trusted: her aunt, Mrs. Gardiner.

> 'If [says Mrs. Gardiner] you will only tell me what sort of girl Miss King is, I shall know what to think.'
> 'She is a very good kind of girl, I believe. I know no harm of her.'
> 'But he paid her not the smallest attention, till her grandfather's death made her mistress of this fortune.'
> 'No—why should he? If it was not allowable for him to gain *my* affections, because I had no money, what occasion could there be for making love to a girl whom he did not care about, and who was equally poor?'
> 'But there seems indelicacy in directing his attentions towards her, so soon after this event.'
> 'A man in distressed circumstances has not time for all those elegant decorums which other people may observe. If *she* does not object to it, why should *we*?'

'*Her* not objecting, does not justify *him*. It only shews her being deficient in something herself—sense or feeling.'

'Well,' cried Elizabeth, 'have it as you choose. *He* shall be mercenary, and *she* shall be foolish.'

Although she is still unbelieving, however, Elizabeth will remember the doubts which she quashed in her early enthusiasm for Wickham—which, after all, arose partly out of her disdain for Darcy. Her big change dates from her second reading of Darcy's letter; then she excoriates herself for her blindness—though she cannot be expected to have guessed the full measure of Wickham's evil: his complete misrepresentation of Darcy, his planned elopement with Georgiana, his dissipated existence in London.

He gets the fate which he deserves: he marries Lydia, after causing great distress to everyone concerned, except the foolish young girl herself. But, true to his character, he does not lose an ounce of aplomb. On this visit to Longbourn:

> his manners were always so pleasing, that had his character and his marriage been exactly what they ought, his smiles and his easy address, while he claimed their relationship, would have delighted them all. Elizabeth had not before believed him quite equal to such assurance; but she sat down, resolving within herself, to draw no limits in future to the impudence of an impudent man.

Darcy and Wickham are virtually perfect agents of illusionment, and thus of the ironic theme, in *Pride and Prejudice*. Elizabeth is put off by Darcy's rudeness; her vanity is piqued: but she allows herself to over-emphasize his pride, because she comes so dangerously near to involvement with him. She credits Wickham's testimony because it is congenial to her—she misapprehends him because she wants to avoid entanglement with Darcy, while in fact there is nothing to fear from her relationship to Wickham: she is essentially indifferent to him. Thus her clarity of perception, which she genuinely possesses, contains the germs of its own myopia—ironically, when engagement of her affections is threatened.

HOWARD S. BABB

Dialogue with Feeling: A Note on *Pride and Prejudice*†

All the recent studies of Jane Austen have warned us well against taking her work casually. Yet this flood of light on her relation to her culture, her use of irony, and her style [1] has only faintly illuminated the question that haunts one's reading of the novels: how does she dramatize so rich a range of behavior and emotion within so apparently narrow a social tone? I think the answer lies in her management of conversations, which make up the real action in this world that notoriously lacks incident. In them the word becomes an authentic deed.

The dialogues of *Pride and Prejudice*, for example, reveal what deep, what intensive motivations Jane Austen has implanted in Darcy and Elizabeth. In fact the talks between these two are especially important as our only source of truth in this novel, for its point of view is mainly Elizabeth's. And the effect of this is to distort Darcy from his entrance on, to suggest that he is prompted by an ugly pride alone rather than in part by shyness, as he finally explains. But the conversations are more than a technical counterpoint to Elizabeth's prejudiced view; they detail a whole reach of emotional, intellectual, and moral habits. Elizabeth is shown to pride herself on her individuality. She always trusts her immediate perceptions to decide the particular case because she believes that they are grounded in instinctive good sense and unnourished by prejudice. What she resolutely ignores is that these perceptions, along with the generalizations to which she is sometimes driven in support of her judgments, really grow out of her feelings. Darcy is as self-assured in his concern for the merits of the particular case. But he approaches it by way of society's gen-

† This paper was first published in the Spring, 1958, issue of the *Kenyon Review* (XX, 203–216). It subsequently appeared in modified form as part of Chapter V in Mr. Babb's *Jane Austen's Novels: The Fabric of Dialogue*, Columbus, Ohio, 1962. Pp. 113–144. Copyright 1962 by the Ohio State University Press. Used by permission of the author, the *Kenyon Review*, and the Ohio State University Press.

1. I refer respectively to Lionel Trilling's *The Opposing Self* (New York, 1955), pp. 206–230, and Mark Schorer's "Pride Unprejudiced," *The Kenyon Review*, XVIII (1956), 72–91; to Marvin Mudrick's *Jane Austen: Irony as Defense and Discovery* (Princeton, 1952), and Andrew Wright's *Jane Austen's Novels* (London, 1953); and to Mark Schorer's "Fiction and the 'Matrix of Analogy,'" *The Kenyon Review*, XI (1949), 539–560, Dorothy Van Ghent's chapter in *The English Novel: Form and Function* (New York, Toronto, 1953), pp. 99–111, and Reuben Brower's chapter—the most brilliant exposition of Jane Austen's method—in *The Fields of Light* (New York, 1951), pp. 164–181.

eralizations, discarding them only when they are proved lacking. Although he feels that his rank gives authority to his judgments, he is more careful than Elizabeth to root his decisions in reason.

Before we watch the conversations actually generate this life, a final point needs mention. They put in play the word *performance*, whose sense extends from a show, an exhibition, to an act that is expressive of one's entire nature and integrated with it. The term helps to define Elizabeth and Darcy in that each is committed to a different meaning, but it tells us even more. For the word refers to behavior: a person can be known only by the qualities of his performance, and in any performance one mediates between society and oneself. Thus the central issues of the novel, judging from behavior and behaving with judgment, are caught together in *performance*, are realized, that is, in the dialogue, alone with the characters themselves. But it is time for us to test such claims by exploring the conversations directly. We must search out there a more reasonable, more personal Darcy than we usually imagine— and something of Jane Austen's basic method, her speakers' minute variations in tone and suggestive linguistic habits that combine to translate life into language. It is the method of her other novels too, but she exploits it most brilliantly here, especially in the dia- logues before Darcy makes his proposal.

Elizabeth is firmly prejudiced against Darcy even before she speaks with him. This is due in part to society's report that he is "proud . . . and above being pleased," which has been planted in her minds (and ours) when he first appears. More important, Eliza- beth disregards Darcy's intimation that he is shy (and we are likely to do the same) when she overhears him scornfully refuse Bingley's offers to provide a dancing-partner. Their own first talk sets the tone of their relationship, and it introduces the pivotal term of the novel. Elizabeth's interpretation of the word soon allies her with its limited sense, as we shall see, but her immediate behavior does the same thing. For she is led on by Charlotte Lucas and provoked by the mere presence of Darcy to put on an exhibitionistic per- formance for him:

> "Did not you think, Mr. Darcy, that I expressed myself un- commonly well just now, when I was teazing Colonel Forster to give us a ball at Meryton?"
> "With great energy—but it is a subject which always makes a lady energetic."

She proclaims that she is unconventional by "uncommonly well" and that she is feminine by "teazing." Darcy's "great energy" ad- mits that she is an individual, but he then withdraws to a generalization, either to avoid the impropriety of noticing her too personally or to judge sternly all ladies as frivolous. Elizabeth reacts only to the second alternative, accusing him of being unpleasant: "You are severe on us." Although her "us" might seem at first a decorous retreat to the anonymity of a class, it really flaunts the opposition of all her sex to Darcy.

Her antagonism swells when Charlotte, somewhat concerned for Darcy, teases her in turn about the actual performance that is to follow. Elizabeth may pretend to invoke propriety in calling Charlotte "strange," yet she directs attention to her own "vanity" in the act of denying that it has "taken a musical turn":

> "You are a very strange creature by way of a friend!—always wanting me to play and sing before any body and every body!—If my vanity had taken a musical turn, you would have been invaluable, but as it is, I would really rather not sit down before those who must be in the habit of hearing the very best performers. . . . Very well; if it must be so, it must." And gravely glancing at Mr. Darcy, "There is a fine old saying, which every body here is of course familiar with—'Keep your breath to cool your porridge,'—and I shall keep mine to swell my song."

But it is in her closing attack on Darcy that she parades her individuality most openly. Not only does "any body and every body" sneer at him, but she justifies her final impertinence by a generalization that separates him from her circle. Although she mockingly includes herself among the "performers" who delight the idle rich with their skills, it is plain that she thinks of a *performance* as no more than the kind of conscious self-display which she has been enjoying.

Darcy opposes a similarly narrow use of the word by Sir William Lucas on the next pages, then fills out his own sense of it in a scene at Netherfield with Elizabeth and the Bingleys. Caroline equates "performance" with "accomplished"—the second term, with exactly the same range of meaning, is carried through the conversation—in praising Darcy's sister: ". . . so extremely accomplished for her age! Her performance on the pianoforte is exquisite." When Bingley mentions all "young ladies" as "so very accomplished" in his usual warmth of spirit, Caroline flares up at what she considers a devaluation of skills that should belong only to the aristocratic. But Darcy tests Bingley's emotional generalization in the light of his own observation:

> "Your list of the common extent of accomplishments . . . has too much truth. The word is applied to many a woman who deserves it no otherwise than by netting a purse, or cover-

ing a skreen. But I am very far from agreeing with you in your estimation of ladies in general. I cannot boast of knowing more than half a dozen, in the whole range of my acquaintance, that are really accomplished."

Perhaps it would be risky to decide at the moment whether his distinction between "common extent" and "really accomplished" is inspired by a pride like Caroline's in the superficial sense of the word or by a rational grasp of its whole meaning. But he goes further when Caroline generalizes breathlessly to shut out Elizabeth and all except the elegant:

"Oh! certainly," cried his faithful assistant, "no one can be really esteemed accomplished, who does not greatly surpass what is usually met with. A woman must have a thorough knowledge of music, singing, drawing, dancing, and the modern languages, to deserve the word; and besides all this, she must possess a certain something in her air and manner of walking . . . or the word will be but half deserved."

"All this she must possess," added Darcy, "and to all this she must yet add something more substantial, in the improvement of her mind by extensive reading."

His "more substantial" integrates behavior with the reason that comes from "reading." Yet the generalization strikes a more personal note as well, for Caroline has nastily characterized Elizabeth earlier as "a great reader": so this becomes a compliment by including Elizabeth within the select category that Caroline has been jealously hugging to herself.

But Elizabeth's dislike for Darcy, the only voice she can listen to, impels her to make over his sense into an absurd extreme:

"I am no longer surprised at your knowing *only* six accomplished women. I rather wonder now at your knowing *any*."

"Are you so severe upon your own sex, as to doubt the possibility of all this?"

"*I* never saw such a woman. *I* never say such capacity, and taste, and application, and elegance, as you describe, united."

His reply is again utterly rational in bringing out the fullest meaning of "accomplished," and it pays another compliment to the "sex" of which Elizabeth is a member. More than that, it echoes her earlier accusation that he is "severe" on women: isn't he trying to clear himself while hinting gently that she is the biased one? It is hard to tell how much of this Elizabeth takes in; we can only be sure that she rejects both him and his sense of the term to assert the priority of her own experience. Yet Darcy's actual definition and his own responsible performance throughout the scene prove that he comprehends more in the word than Elizabeth does. He recognizes the authority of personal experience and of generalizations based on reason—all without slighting his particular feeling for her.

In fact the dialogues that follow show him taking more and more delighted notice of her. At the Netherfield ball he surprises her into dancing with him, a high compliment when we remember his earlier comments on the pastime, but she,

> suddenly fancying that it would be the greater punishment to her partner to oblige him to talk . . . made some slight observation on the dance. He replied, and was again silent. After a pause of some minutes she addressed him a second time with
> "It is *your* turn to say something now, Mr. Darcy.—I talked about the dance, and *you* ought to make some kind of remark on the size of the room, or the number of couples."

Elizabeth taunts him with another show of willfulness, weighing the silence that she reads as disagreeable pride against her own assumed propriety in conversing. Although she is off on another performance, Darcy yields to her with perfect politeness:

> He smiled, and assured her that whatever she wished him to say should be said.
> "Very well.—That reply will do for the present.—Perhaps by and bye I may observe that private balls are much pleasanter than public ones.—But *now* we may be silent."
> "Do you talk by rule then, while you are dancing?"

And when she parodies decorum to make his stubbornness clear, he tries to cut through her exhibition to her real self, pleading that they overthrow the "rule" of convention and be emotionally direct with each other.

As we would expect, Elizabeth's drive is to put Darcy in his place. Her first generalizations carefully set up the barrier of impersonal propriety again:

> "Sometimes. One must speak a little, you know. It would look odd to be entirely silent for half an hour together, and yet for the advantage of *some*, conversation ought to be so arranged as that they may have the trouble of saying as little as possible."

Her final generalization completes the job of separation by assigning them different standards, and it scarcely masks her disdain for Darcy. Yet he responds with a more personal appeal that digs below her pretense of decorum to get at their private emotions:

> "Are you consulting your own feelings in the present case, or do you imagine that you are gratifying mine?"

"Both," replied Elizabeth archly; "for I have always seen a great similarity in the turn of our minds.—We are each of an unsocial, taciturn disposition, unwilling to speak, unless we expect to say something that will amaze the whole room, and be handed down to posterity with all the eclat of a proverb."

Of course Elizabeth will have none of this. She can spell out his arrogance by condemning herself as well, though she wants her exaggeration in doing so to be plain.

Darcy rejects her typical move to the extreme in order to pursue the truth. But his opening compliment and the warning in his last sentence that she is liable to error make no impression on her:

"This is no very striking resemblance of your own character, I am sure," said he. "How near it may be to *mine*, I cannot pretend to say.—*You* think it a faithful portrait undoubtedly."
"I must not decide on my own performance."

Elizabeth means the word in its thin sense only, carrying on the figure that "portrait" implies to declare her propriety once more. Yet the term's full sense measures her behavior to Darcy with sharp irony, for she is unaware that the role she keeps playing is itself a decision—or that her performance expresses the opposition of her whole nature to Darcy rather than cool reason, as she supposes. And she remains oblivious through the rest of the scene, blithely acting out what she thinks of him while disregarding what he reveals of himself. When she nags him about Wickham, for instance, she never realizes that her advice is better suited to herself: "It is particularly incumbent on those who never change their opinion, to be secure of judging properly at first." Darcy finally resurrects "performance" to hint at her folly:

". . . I could wish, Miss Bennet, that you were not to sketch my character at the present moment, as there is reason to fear that the performance would reflect no credit on either."

Nevertheless he hopes to bring her nearer him by combining their senses of the word. The "performance" he mentions is surely a sketch, but to reproduce reality demands clear insight, which in turn depends on the artist's responsible, unbiased behavior. So, when Elizabeth insists on indulging her skill rather than judging the reality, Darcy shows his anger:

"But if I do not take your likeness now, I may never have another opportunity."
"I would by no means suspend any pleasure of yours," he coldly replied.

The word "pleasure" goes only with a light accomplishment. Since

Elizabeth has blocked every advance toward mutual understanding and a community of feeling, Darcy ends their talk by handing her one-sided interpretation of the word back to her.

So far Jane Austen has used *performance* as something like a gauge for behavior, letting her characters define the range of the concept in their speeches. In the scene at Rosings, she anchors the word in Elizabeth's actual playing of the piano. Now her speakers can keep up the appearance of decorum by pretending to talk of the literal situation. At the same time, though, they manage the situation verbally as a kind of metaphor, revealing intense feelings far beyond their polite social tone. It is the neat trick that Jane Austen repeats periodically in the novels, her way of dramatizing the emotional depth that is so often denied her without fracturing the finished surface.

The conversation opens when Elizabeth accosts Darcy "at the first convenient pause" in her playing; as always, she assumes that he means to be contemptuous:

> "You mean to frighten me, Mr. Darcy, by coming in all this state to hear me? But I will not be alarmed though your sister *does* play so well. There is a stubbornness about me that never can bear to be frightened at the will of others. My courage always rises with every attempt to intimidate me."

The "hear me" and "play so well' maintain decorum, for they seem to speak only of piano-playing. Yet her final, fully emotional generalizations leave no doubt that she is challenging him personally. Although he is conspicuously polite in answering, it is characteristic of Darcy that he also distinguishes between the real and the professed:

> "I shall not say that you are mistaken," he replied, "because you could not really believe me to entertain any design of alarming you; and I have had the pleasure of your acquaintance long enough to know, that you find great enjoyment in occasionally professing opinions which in fact are not your own."

Literally he is accusing Elizabeth of her usual self-willed performance, warning or begging her to recognize the truth about himself.

Elizabeth may appear to joke at this as a false sketch, ironically accepting what Darcy has said while she circumspectly addresses herself to Colonel Fitzwilliam. But she bitterly resents the trust as another proof of Darcy's nastiness:

> Elizabeth laughed heartily at this picture of herself, and said to Colonel Fitzwilliam, "Your cousin will give you a very pretty notion of me, and teach you not to believe a word I say. I am particularly unlucky in meeting with a person so well able to

expose my real character, in a part of the world, where I had hoped to pass myself off with some degree of credit. Indeed, Mr. Darcy, it is very ungenerous in you to mention all that you knew to my disadvantage in Hertfordshire—and, give me leave to say, very impolitic too—for it is provoking me to retaliate, and such things may come out, as will shock your relations to hear."

The phrase "passing myself off" reflects her view of what Darcy tried to do at Netherfield. And she couples "ungenerous" with the threat of laying bare his disagreeable past to attack him more directly. Her "impolitic" is just right, for it implies that she has more sense than Darcy and does so without weakening the emotional power of her assault. Yet he remains utterly polite, and something more: "'I am not afraid of you,' said he, smilingly." Darcy is "not afraid," either because he feels that his own integrity must overcome Elizabeth's willful misinterpretations or because he trusts in the ultimate integrity of her sense and feeling. In either case he puts himself completely in her hands, a real measure of his affection for her.

When Colonel Fitzwilliam invites Elizabeth to go on, she strikes a tone of parody that thinly disguises her indictment of Darcy:

"You shall hear then—but prepare yourself for something very dreadful. The first time of my ever seeing him in Hertfordshire, you must know, was at a ball—and at this ball, what do you think he did? He danced only four dances! I am sorry to pain you—but so it was. He danced only four dances, though gentlemen were scarce; and, to my certain knowledge, more than one young lady was sitting down in want of a partner. Mr. Darcy, you cannot deny the fact."

Such phrases as "to my certain knowledge" and "the fact" allege that Darcy was haughty in refusing to dance with her, though Elizabeth still protects her own feelings by generalizing about "more than one young lady." This deed is the foundation of her prejudice, the reality that she is positive Darcy "cannot deny." But he does. At least he redefines what Elizabeth has always taken to be pride as shyness: "I had not at that time the honour of knowing any lady in the assembly beyond my own party." He is saying in effect: "You have interpreted my performance wrongly as a mere exhibition because you ignore my total character." Elizabeth refuses the explanation he offers to polish him off with a clearly absurd generalization, and then she turns to his friend:

"True; and nobody can ever be introduced in a ball room. Well, Colonel Fitzwilliam, what do I play next? My fingers wait your orders."

"Perhaps," said Darcy, "I should have judged better, had I sought an introduction, but I am ill qualified to recommend myself to strangers."

Yet Darcy insists on his shyness, even admitting that feeling may have swayed his judgment. So, though Elizabeth keeps her tone light by speaking to Colonel Fitzwilliam, she attacks with even more authority. She counts on the impersonal phrasing to provide an air of sense that will decide finally against Darcy:

"Shall we ask your cousin the reason of this?" said Elizabeth, still addressing Colonel Fitzwilliam. "Shall we ask him why a man of sense and education, and who has lived in the world, is ill qualified to recommend himself to strangers?" . . .

"I certainly have not the talent which some people possess," said Darcy, "of conversing easily with those I have never seen before. I cannot catch their tone of conversation, or appear interested in their concerns, as I often see done."

But Elizabeth's hostility is still lurking in the biased rhetorical question. And because Darcy remains unsatisfied that her formula takes account of his real nature, he repeats for the third time, "I cannot put on a skilled performance; I must enact my convictions."

Elizabeth finally resorts to her literal performance on the piano in order to carry the day. She uses it metaphorically so that her thrust may seem decorously oblique, yet she aims her words straight at Darcy's stubbornness:

"My fingers . . . do not move over this instrument in the masterly manner which I see so many women's do. They have not the same force or rapidity, and do not produce the same expression. But then I have always supposed it to be my own fault—because I would not take the trouble of practising. It is not that I do not believe *my* fingers as capable as any other woman's of superior execution."

At the same time this is one of her typical self-displays. But there is another point: since Elizabeth creates the metaphor out of the social situation consciously, using it as a device to illustrate, it is clear that she still thinks of *performance* in its flattest sense.

This allegiance on her part makes Darcy's reply reverberate with meaning:

Darcy smiled and said, "You are perfectly right. You have employed your time much better. No one admitted to the privilege of hearing you, can think any thing wanting. We neither of us perform to strangers."

He expresses his deepest attachment to her in these sentences. The first refuses to dispute her judgment of him; Darcy cheerfully sacrifices the real motives he has been explaining. His second sentence must be sheer feeling, for it destroys the logic of the metaphor that they have all been maintaining so diligently: after all, he has praised his sister at the beginning of the scene because she "practises very constantly," and Elizabeth has just reproached herself for not practicing more often. Darcy can only mean that her behavior towards him, no matter how prejudiced, is more valuable than her piano-playing. In the third sentence he goes back to the metaphor by "hearing you," which really denotes "being with you," but only to keep his extravagant generalization about her charm within bounds of propriety. Yet his last sentence crowns the others. Perhaps he is trying to be gallant by using "perform" in Elizabeth's narrow sense, though the actual situation shows the strain, for she is playing to "strangers." But I think his deeper sense of the word triumphs here in what is really his most fervent plea for intimacy, a plea that quite irrationally disregards the blindness Elizabeth has shown all along: "We reserve our fullest selves, perfectly understood by both of us, for each other." It is his final, almost desperate attempt before the proposal to come to terms with her.

But the proposal soon follows, along with Darcy's revealing letter that brings Elizabeth to a change of mind and heart. So the play with *performance* disappears from *Pride and Prejudice* as Elizabeth and Darcy become more fixed and surer of one another's behavior. By the novel's end they can afford cozy jokes that take their true motives for granted, a far cry from their earlier tense misunderstandings. When he is questioned by Elizabeth, Darcy still defends his behavior, but he can reckon its liabilities:

> "Why, especially, when you called, did you look as if you did not care about me?"
> "Because you were grave and silent, and gave me no encouragement."
> "But I was embarrassed."
> "And so was I."
> "You might have talked to me more when you came to dinner."
> "A man who had felt less, might."
> "How unlucky that you should have a reasonable answer to give, and that I should be so reasonable as to admit it!"

Although Elizabeth puts on something of a show in ironically suggesting that she is disappointed in reason, still her conclusion declares the reasonableness of them both. In spite of its light tone, the talk measures how far they have come in the novel. Darcy has learned that one's total performance may be unacceptable unless it is softened by a gracious display. And Elizabeth has discovered that her exhibitions judging Darcy have been grounded in a prejudice that distorts reason, in an unintegrated performance of her personality. The concept dramatizes the novel's conflict, epitomizes its theme, and is rendered in its dialogue.

E. M. HALLIDAY

Narrative Perspective in *Pride and Prejudice* †

Consider the famous opening sentence of *Pride and Prejudice:* "It is a truth universally acknowledged, that a single man in possession of a good fortune must be in want of a wife." The narrator seems to be standing outside the story, not yet observing the characters but gazing off into the middle distance for some reflections on life in general. But this impression does not last. As Mr. Bennet and "his lady" begin their dialogue, it rapidly becomes clear that the storyteller had them both in view when that opening generalization was made. It is an opinion, we find, that Mrs. Bennet would greet with a clapping of hands and little cries of joy—and one Mr. Bennet would send flying to the paradise of foolish ideas with a shaft of ridicule. The narrator ostensibly takes the responsibility for the opinion; but we see from the beginning that her observations are likely to bear an ironic relation to the views, and points of view, of her characters. This is our introduction to the quality of tough yet gentle irony that will control every page of the novel, making us feel a wonderful balance between sense and sensibility.

This artful control of over-all narrative perspective in the service of Jane Austen's irony is supported by a most subtle manipulation of point of view for the sake of the novel's unity. Even a sleepy reader of this book must be well aware, before he has read very far, that it is Elizabeth Bennet's story. But how does he know this? The title gives no clue, and Elizabeth is not the storyteller. The opening pages make it clear that the matrimonial prospects of the Bennet daughters will direct the action—but there are five daughters. True, three of them look far from promising: Mary is a pedantic bore; Lydia is an empty-headed flirt; Kitty is just empty-headed. But both Jane and Elizabeth are attractive and accomplished, and for several chapters it looks as if Jane's

† From *Nineteenth-Century Fiction*, XV, 65–71. Copyright 1960 by The Regents of the University of California. Re- printed by permission of The Regents and E. M. Halliday.

chances with Bingley will bring the central action into focus, with Elizabeth playing some subsidiary role. How is it, then, that by the time we are quarterway through the novel—say by the time Mr. Collins makes his celebrated proposal to Elizabeth —it has become perfectly clear that Elizabeth is the heroine of *Pride and Prejudice*, and that Jane is only a secondary character?

Partly, this is revealed by the sheer amount of attention the storyteller pays to Elizabeth, which increases rapidly as we move through the first eighteen chapters. This, of course, is itself a function of point of view. The storyteller chooses to gaze upon Elizabeth more and more often, and for longer and longer stretches of time. But the interesting fact is that this deliberate restriction of the narrator's privilege of gazing anywhere and everywhere is most stringently applied when the mechanics of the plot call, quite on the contrary, for attention to Jane. In chapter vii. Jane goes to visit Caroline Bingley at Netherfield. Mrs. Bennet's most sanguine hopes are fulfilled when Jane catches a bad cold on the way, and therefore has to spend several days with the Bingleys. But note that this is reported by letter; for when Jane leaves for Netherfield we do not go with her. The narrative perspective remains focused on the Bennet household, and particularly on Elizabeth; and it is not until Elizabeth decides to put sisterhood above gentility, and walks three miles across muddy fields, that we make our first entry into the Bingley household. Moreover, we see nothing of Jane until Elizabeth goes upstairs to nurse her; and even then we get a scanty glimpse, since Jane evidently is too sick to talk. By this time it begins to be obvious that the narrator is only slightly more interested in Jane than is the feline Miss Bingley, who tolerates her chiefly for the sake of Bingley's interest. Jane's relation to Bingley will be important in the plot, but much less for itself than as a necessary device to help build up Elizabeth's prejudice against Darcy.

Actually, the narrator's audacity in slighting Jane is almost rude. When poor Jane emerges from her sickroom after several days (chap. xi), she is nearly ignored. Everyone greets her politely, of course; but although Bingley "then sat down by her and talked scarcely to anyone else," none of this tête-à-tête between the two nascent lovers is reported. On the other hand, a word-for-word rendering of a most lively conversation including Elizabeth, Bingley, his sister, and Darcy takes up the rest of the chapter; but for all she contributes to the scene, Jane might as well be stretched out asleep on a sofa like the languid Mr. Hurst, who is also present but inaudible.

About this time we also begin to be aware that the narrator's increasing attention to Elizabeth and neglect of Jane is not simply a matter of direction of gaze. We are induced to see much of Elizabeth, and not much of her older sister; but we also begin to see more and more of the action, and of the other characters, from Elizabeth's point of view. In chapter x, for example, just before the one in which Jane becomes so remarkably inconspicuous, we are quite specifically encouraged to identify ourselves with Elizabeth at the beginning of the scene:

> Elizabeth took up some needlework and was sufficiently amused in attending to what passed between Darcy and his companion. The perpetual commendations of the lady either on his handwriting, or on the evenness of his lines, or on the length of his letter, with the perfect unconcern with which her praises were received, formed a curious dialogue, and was exactly in unison with her opinion of each.

We are not told that Elizabeth smiles, or makes any other outward sign of her amusement. The narrative perspective has penetrated to Elizabeth's consciousness; the point of view has become hers not only physically, but psychically.

By means of such skillful technical maneuvering, Jane Austen gradually forces the action of *Pride and Prejudice* to coalesce around Elizabeth, and we are prepared for an essential part of that action to take place in the intimate and subtle chambers of her mind. When we reach the crisis of the novel with Darcy's first proposal to Elizabeth (chap. xxxiv)—which, as a matter of structural nicety, comes exactly halfway through the book—we know that everything that follows must depend on her discovery of his true character. The groundwork is laid very shortly, in chapter xxxvi, which consists entirely of a searching analysis of Elizabeth's inward reactions to Darcy's letter of explanation. And the fact that her discovery is chiefly a psychological process, not an outward action, is stressed by her realization that it involves *self*-discovery. "Had I been in love," she cries (tantalizing the reader with the conditional), "I could not have been more wretchedly blind. . . . I have courted prepossession and ignorance and driven reason away where either were concerned. Till this moment I never knew myself."

Thus the management of narrative perspective plays an essential part in establishing the unity of the action: it is Elizabeth's story, and it is the story of her sense and sensibility rather than her outward behavior. But now an intriguing question occurs. If Elizabeth is to be the center of vision, why is she treated, in in the opening chapters, merely on an equal plane with the other principal characters? Why the delay in establishing her predominance?

There appear to be some very good reasons for this, having to do with the use of point of view to help create suspense. The most violent outward action in *Pride and Prejudice*, perhaps, is Elizabeth's leap over a puddle on her way to Netherfield. Clearly, the suspense in this novel depends not on violent action, or even the threat thereof—despite Mrs. Bennet's nervous fears that Mr. Bennet will fight Wickham. It depends mostly on our waiting for Elizabeth to discover two things: that Darcy is in love with her; and that she is in love with Darcy. The reader must be led to suspect both of these things before Elizabeth does, or the suspense is lost. But if the point of view of the narration had been Elizabeth's from the start, the reader could hardly be aware that Darcy is falling in love; for Elizabeth, blinded by intense prejudice, never dreams of his affection. The storyteller therefore treats us to several direct insights into Darcy's mind in the early stages of the action: he begins by finding her eyes entrancing in chapter vi, and by chapter x is obliged to admit to himself that he "had never been so bewitched by any woman as he was by her." Once it is firmly established that Darcy is slipping, however reluctantly, the narrator can safely project the point of view to that of the prejudiced heroine; and from then on we rarely desert Elizabeth as the center of vision.

As for Elizabeth's falling in love with Darcy, it is something not accomplished until near the end of the book; but we must feel, surely, that it is something *begun* much earlier than Elizabeth herself realizes. To effect this, we must be able to see Darcy apart from Elizabeth's conscious bias: we must see him, almost from the start, as at least potentially worthy of her love. No doubt we begin to take this view of Darcy early, despite his snobbish behavior, partly because we know he is falling in love with Elizabeth. Since we have begun to like her very much ourselves, this stands to his credit in the face of her prejudice; it shows his discrimination. But, as we have seen, our knowledge that Darcy is falling in love would have been impossible if Elizabeth had become the center of vision too soon. Thus our respect for Darcy, which we must feel before believing that so estimable a heroine could fall in love with him, also depends on keeping the point of view away from Elizabeth for a certain length of time.

And what about Elizabeth's specific prejudices against Darcy? If there is to be an interesting degree of suspense, we must not share them wholeheartedly with her: we must believe, long before she does, that the foundations on which they rest are doubtful, so that we may anticipate her change of heart. There are three things Elizabeth seriously holds against Darcy: she thinks he has spoiled Jane's chances with Bingley; that he has done this because he despises the social position of her family; and that he has ruined Wickham's career without due cause. After she has accused Darcy of these faults and hurled his proposal back in his face, he writes her the long, painstaking letter in which he clears himself of the charges. And it deserves attention that most of the grounds upon which he clears himself have been objectively established, early in the story—established, that is, in a way that would have been difficult or impossible in a narration primarily from Elizabeth's point of view. We must be left free to observe these grounds independent of Elizabeth, so that the possibility of romance between her and Darcy can beguile us long before it consciously dawns on her.

Darcy says, first, that Jane never displayed any love for Bingley, so to whisk him away to London could not be thought of as injuring Jane's emotions—and if we look back, we find that the narrator has carefully established this in the early chapters. Jane is so excessively demure that even when her heart is fluttering with romantic passion her manner shows only genteel pleasure and politeness. Even Elizabeth admits this, to Charlotte Lucas, in chapter vi; but it does not occur to her (as it may to the reader) that Bingley won't see through Jane's decorous disguise.

Darcy's explanation of why he wants to prevent marriage between Bingley and Jane is that he could not bear to see his friend marry into a family including such uncommonly ill-bred persons as Mrs. Bennet, Lydia, Kitty, and Mary: and we, the readers, have enjoyed generous exhibitions of their behavior, objectively related, from the opening pages of the novel. Although Darcy's disapproval on this score is damaging to the idea of romance between him and Elizabeth, it is not nearly so much so as her false conviction that he considers her family social station hopelessly beneath him.

Finally, Darcy's explanation of his treatment of Wickham, while it relies mostly on family history, brings to Elizabeth's attention certain improprieties in Wickham's behavior toward her—improprieties that were wide open to the reader's view in chapter xvi, even though at that time they were lost on Elizabeth. This chapter, in fact, is a kind of tour de force of narrative perspective: the point of view seems to be that of Elizabeth; yet in spite of many insights into her mental reaction to Wickham, the reader can maintain a certain detachment of judgment because the bulk of the chapter is fully recorded conversation—and what Wickham says constitutes his impropriety.

Thus the eminent part played by narrative perspective in establishing the artistic unity of *Pride and Prejudice* is achieved only by dint of some very skillful modification for the sake of dramatic suspense. Through a delicate balance between objective and subjective, we are given good reason to anticipate, with delicious anxiety, that Darcy and Elizabeth will wind up in each other's arms; yet Elizabeth, from whose point of view the story as a whole is focused, does not begin to perceive this denouement until near the end.

Two other points about Jane Austen's management of narrative perspective repay study. One has to do with what could be called her "kinaesthetics"—the sense of movement imparted by the author to the story, and the way in which this sense is controlled; the other, closely related, is her selectivity.

Much of *Pride and Prejudice* moves at the pace of life itself: the action is rendered with a degree of detail and fullness of dialogue that gives a highly developed dramatic illusion. But note how fast the storyteller can shift to drastic synopsis when it seems desirable to step up the action and move on to a scene essential to the plot. When Elizabeth is waiting at Longbourn for the Gardiners to come and take her on a tour of the Lake district, she is disappointed by a letter saying that they cannot start until two weeks later than planned, and consequently cannot go so far on their trip. Our shrewd narrator, however, has no intention of making us impatient without a purpose, and disposes of a whole month in two swift sentences: "Four weeks were to pass away before her uncle and aunt's arrival. But they did pass away, and Mr. and Mrs. Gardiner with their four children did at length appear at Longbourn." Geographical setting is dealt with just as jauntily: "It is not the object of this work," we are told a few lines further, "to give a description of Derbyshire, nor of any of the remarkable places through which their route thither lay. Oxford, Blenheim, Warwick, Kenilworth, Birmingham, etc., are sufficiently known." And just two pages later we are treading the plush carpets at Pemberley, ready for the next encounter between Elizabeth and Darcy.

When it comes to selectivity, the filters through which the narrator of *Pride and Prejudice* habitually views the action are much more discriminating than those of any photographer, and they positively cut out much that is the stock in trade of the average novelist. What color is Elizabeth's hair? What did she wear at the Netherfield ball? What in the world do these people eat at all the dinners that are mentioned? What do Mr. and Mrs. Bennet look like? But the answers to these and a hundred similar questions it is the narrator's privilege to withhold: we must take what he (or she) chooses to give us. What Jane Austen chooses to give is pretty well summed up in her observation about Darcy and Elizabeth at the happy moment when Elizabeth finally accepts Darcy's hand: "They walked on, without knowing in what direction. There was too much to be thought and felt and said for attention to any other objects." Thought and feeling, and their verbal expression—this is the world of Jane Austen, so beautifully illuminated for us by her artistic control of narrative perspective.

A. WALTON LITZ

[The Marriage of Antitheses: Structure and Style in *Pride and Prejudice*]†

With *Pride and Prejudice* Jane Austen bid farewell to her early life and to the eighteenth century. We have seen that the recasting of *Sense and Sensibility* in 1809–11 never reached the vital centers of that novel; the original antitheses and conventions protrude through the final structure. But the late revisions of *Pride and Prejudice* (c. 1811–12) were so elaborate, and penetrated so deeply into the novel's language and action, that they amounted to a re-seeing of the entire work. Although it is impossible to reconstruct the details of *First Impressions*, we can say with some assurance that the finished novel was far removed from this early draft. Ten days after the publication of *Pride and Prejudice* Jane Austen wrote to Cassandra: "I am exceedingly pleased that you can say what you do, after having gone thro' the whole work." This remark, as Mary Lascelles has pointed out, suggests a substantial difference between *First Impressions* and the published novel, since Jane Austen would have long been familiar with Cassandra's opinions of the early version.[1] Another indication of the extent of the revisions may be found in the elaborate use of the 1811–12 almanacs; the consistency of the novel's time-scheme could only have resulted from a thorough reworking of the plot. But more important than this historical evidence is the general evidence of the novel's style, which is more uniform and sophisticated than that of *Sense and Sensibility*. In recasting *Sense and Sensibility* Jane Austen was doing the best job she could with a work already moribund in her imagination. But *Pride and Prejudice* remained alive for her, its hero and heroine perpetually interesting.[2] On 24 May 1813, after a visit to "the Exhibition in

† From A. Walton Litz, *Jane Austen: A Study of Her Artistic Development*, New York, 1965. Pp. 97–111. Copyright 1965. Reprinted by permission of the publishers Oxford University Press.
1. Mary Lascelles, *Jane Austen and Her Art* (Oxford, 1939), p. 31.
2. Mary Lascelles remarks [p. 30]

that *Sense and Sensibility* "was never to account for as much, to the author or her family: she would—'if asked'—tell them what became of Miss Steele, but her own imagination did not linger in the world of *Sense and Sensibility* as it was to do in that of *Pride and Prejudice*."

Spring Gardens" held by the Society of Painters in Oil and Water Colours, she wrote to Cassandra:

> It is not thought a good collection, but I was very well pleased —particularly (pray tell Fanny) with a small portrait of Mrs. Bingley, excessively like her. I went in hopes of seeing one of her Sister, but there was no Mrs. Darcy;—perhaps however, I may find her in the Great Exhibition which we shall go to, if we have time . . . Mrs. Bingley's is exactly herself, size, shaped face, features & sweetness; there never was a greater likeness. She is dressed in a white grown, with green ornaments, which convinces me of what I had always supposed, that green was a favourite colour with her. I dare say Mrs. D. will be in Yellow.

And later in the same letter:

> We have been both to the Exhibition & Sir J. Reynolds',—and I am disappointed, for there was nothing like Mrs. D. at either. I can only imagine that Mr. D. prizes any Picture of her too much to like it should be exposed to the public eye.—I can imagine he w^d have that sort of feeling—that mixture of Love, Pride & Delicacy.

It would seem that *Pride and Prejudice* remained fresh and exciting in Jane Austen's imagination for two reasons: first, the charm of the heroine, "as delightful a creature as ever appeared in print;" and second, her pleasure in having successfully reformed the original story to accord with her new ideals in theme and technique. We cannot think of *Pride and Prejudice* as belonging to any one period of Jane Austen's life before 1813; rather it was a summing up of her artistic career, a valedictory to the world of *Sense and Sensibility* and a token of things to come. More than any other of her novels it deserves Henry Austen's description in his Biographical Notice: "Some of these novels had been the gradual performances of her previous life."

One index to the new tones and new attitudes struck in *Pride and Prejudice* is the novel's use of conventions and stock situations drawn from eighteenth-century fiction. Both *Sense and Sensibility* and *Pride and Prejudice* depend upon characters and actions inherited from the Richardson-Fanny Burney tradition: the attractive seducer, the thoughtless young hoyden, ill-mannered relatives, tyrannical aristocrats, elopements and assignations. It is obvious from the *Juvenilia* that Jane Austen recognized the potential absurdity of these conventions; but they were so much a part of her fictional experience, and in some cases so close to the actual world she knew, that she could not exclude them from her art. The superiority of *Pride and Prejudice* to *Sense and Sensibility* lies in the transformation of these stale conventions, which renders them a believable part of the action and a natural vehicle for the novel's themes. This difference may be seen in a comparison of the heroes and villains, Darcy with Colonel Brandon, Wickham with Willoughby. In *Sense and Sensibility* Colonel Brandon has no more life than Lord Orville in Fanny Burney's *Evelina*; we believe in what he represents, but not in him. Yet Darcy, while preserving the virtues of the fictional hero, is entirely believable, since Jane Austen has subjected him to a process of self-evaluation and self-recognition. In him the type has been revivified. Similarly, the story of Willoughby's past behavior (as told by Colonel Brandon) is merely a plot device, a tale of seduction borrowed from fiction in the hope that it will give Willoughby's villainy substance and shape. In fact the tale stamps Willoughby as a two-dimensional figure; it substitutes his prototype in *Evelina* for the man we have glimpsed earlier, and not even the moving final confession can reassert his reality. But in *Pride and Prejudice* Wickham, although a descendant of the eighteenth-century fictional rake, does not suffer from the defects of his originals: his elopement with Lydia is plausible and carefully prepared, not a stale convention dragged in to forward the plot; and Darcy's account of Wickham's past villainies, unlike Colonel Brandon's tale, seems consonant with all we know of the subject's character.

It is important to keep these distinctions between *Sense and Sensibility* and *Pride and Prejudice* in mind when we speak of the latter's origins in late eighteenth-century fiction. Jane Austen's admiration of Fanny Burney is well known, and there can be no doubt that *Pride and Prejudice*—or, more exactly, *First Impressions*—owed a debt to *Cecilia*.[3] Q. D. Leavis exaggerates this debt in her statement that "the original conception of *First Impressions* was undoubtedly to rewrite the story of Cecilia in realistic terms,"[4] but we know that when Jane Austen began work on the story the world of *Evelina* and *Cecilia* held a great reality for her. A niece recollected hearing, as a very young child, Jane Austen "read a part out of *Evelina*, one of the chapters concerning the Branghtons and Mr. Smith, and she thought it sounded like a play."[5] Fanny Burney's fiction is filled with figures who remind us of Colonel Brandon or Willoughby or Lydia or Mrs. Bennet, and although one can argue that these were common types, the

3. For discussion of the relationship between Fanny Burney and Jane Austen, and between *Cecilia* and *Pride and Prejudice*, see C. L. Thompson, *Jane Austen* (London, 1929), pp. 100–106; Elizabeth Jenkins, *Jane Austen* (New York, 1949), pp. 49–57; Q. D. Leavis, "A Critical Theory of Jane Austen's Writings," *Scrutiny*, X (June 1941),

71–2; and R. W. Chapman's Appendix to *Works*, Vol. II. *Evelina* (1778) and *Cecilia* (1782) were well known to Jane Austen before she began *First Impressions* (1796), and *Camilla* was published in that year (with Jane Austen as one of the subscribers).
4. Leavis, *op. cit.*, p. 71.
5. Jenkins, *op. cit.*, p. 51.

details of their treatment in Jane Austen's early work are often reminiscent of Fanny Burney. More significantly, the struggle between personal affection and family pride in *Cecilia* may have suggested the major themes of *Pride and Prejudice*; certainly the title was taken from the conclusion to *Cecilia*, where Dr. Lyster points the story's moral.

> "The whole of this unfortunate business . . . has been the result of PRIDE and PREJUDICE. . . . Yet this, however, remember; if to PRIDE and PREJUDICE you owe your miseries, so wonderfully is good and evil balanced, that to PRIDE and PREJUDICE you will also owe their termination."

But these similarities between *Pride and Prejudice* and Fanny Burney's novels only intensify our sense of Jane Austen's achievement in transforming the conventions of "the land of fiction." Since the limited social world she observed had been the subject of so much previous fiction, she was prevented from seeking originality in new situations and new locales. Instead she had to find her voice within the same range of life explored by many other female writers. Bingley's arrival at Netherfield, the ballroom scene, Wickham's flirtations, Darcy's letter, Lydia's elopement, Lady Catherine's condescending visit—these were standard raw materials, but in *Pride and Prejudice* they were endowed with such a quantity of "felt life," and incorporated so skillfully into the drama, that they took on a new significance. It is this transformation of familiar materials which yields one of the novel's chief pleasures, the sense of subtle variations within a fixed and traditional range of experience. *Pride and Prejudice* bears that hallmark of "classic" art, the discovery of new possibilities within a traditional form.

Although the phrase "Pride and Prejudice" does not suggest as neat an ideological antithesis as "Sense and Sensibility," it would have led a late eighteenth-century reader to expect a schematic drama in which each quality is represented by a separate character or faction. But in *Pride and Prejudice* one cannot equate Darcy with Pride, or Elizabeth with Prejudice; Darcy's pride of place is founded on social prejudice, while Elizabeth's initial prejudice against him is rooted in pride of her own quick perceptions. In this we have a clear indication of the novel's distance from *Cecilia*, for Jane Austen's "internalizing" of the conflicts between proper and improper pride, candor and prejudice, goes far beyond the capabilities of Fanny Burney. Indeed, it was this ability to vest the novel's conflicts in the dynamic development of personality that freed Jane Austen from the world of static values which still dominates in *Sense and Sensibility*. Whereas in *Sense and*

Sensibility the antitheses are resolved by a suppression of one position and an uneasy exaltation of the other, the entire movement of *Pride and Prejudice* tends toward a resolution of conflicts which is a union rather than a compromise, a union in which both parties gain new vigor and freedom of expression. The marriage of Elizabeth and Darcy resolves not only their personal differences but the conflicts they have represented, with the result that the novel provides a final pleasure unique in Jane Austen's fiction, a sense of complete fulfillment analogous to that which marks the end of some musical compositions. It is this sense of a union of opposites—without injury to the identity of either—which prompts the common comparison with Mozart. In *Pride and Prejudice*, for once in her career, Jane Austen allowed the symmetry of her imaginative creation to prevail over the protests of her social self, and the result is a triumph of ideal form. It was a triumph not to be repeated, one that was replaced in the later novels by less comforting views of human nature. Yet it remains valid as the finest expression of one aspect of Jane Austen's personality, her desire to endow human behavior with the order and symmetry of art. *Pride and Prejudice* is a great comedy because it formulates an ideal vision of human possibilities; its ending is "realistic" not because we measure the union of Elizabeth and Darcy against our own experience (that experience which delights in Jane Austen's statement that Mrs. Bennet remained "occasionally nervous and invariably silly"), but because their marriage is a complete fulfillment of the novel's artistic imperatives. Their lives have been the work's structure, and their marriage is a vindication of the artist's power to resolve complexities.

In his penetrating essay on *Mansfield Park* Lionel Trilling defines the special quality that distinguishes *Pride and Prejudice* from Jane Austen's other works.

> The great charm, the charming greatness, of *Pride and Prejudice* is that it permits us to conceive of morality as style. The relation of Elizabeth Bennet to Darcy is real, is intense, but it expresses itself as a conflict and reconciliation of styles: a formal rhetoric, traditional and rigorous, must find a way to accommodate a female vivacity, which in turn must recognize the principled demands of the strict male syntax. The high moral import of the novel lies in the fact that the union of styles is accomplished without injury to either lover.[6]

Pride and Prejudice does more than testify to the artist's capacity for organizing and clarifying the confusions of life; it supports the

6. Lionel Trilling, *The Opposing Self* (New York, 1955), p. 222.

fine illusion that life itself can take on the discrimination and selectivity of art. Throughout the novel aesthetic and moral values are closely related. Darcy and Elizabeth share the common eighteenth-century assumption that a man of real taste is usually a man of sound moral judgment,[7] and when Elizabeth first views Pemberley the tasteful prospect confirms her altered opinion of Darcy's character:

> Elizabeth's mind was too full for conversation, but she saw and admired every remarkable spot and point of view. They gradually ascended for half a mile, and then found themselves at the top of a considerable eminence, where the wood ceased, and the eye was instantly caught by Pemberley House, situated on the opposite side of a valley, into which the road with some abruptness wound. It was a large, handsome, stone building, standing well on rising ground, and backed by a ridge of high woody hills;—and in front, a stream of some natural importance was swelled into greater, but without any artificial appearance. Its banks were neither formal, nor falsely adorned. Elizabeth was delighted. She had never seen a place for which nature had done more, or where natural beauty had been so little counter-acted by an awkward taste. They were all of them warm in their admiration; and at that moment she felt, that to be mistress of Pemberley might be something!

Every evidence of sound aesthetic judgment provided by Pemberley is converted by Elizabeth into evidence of Darcy's natural amiability, and joined with the enthusiastic testimony of the housekeeper, until Pemberley becomes an image of his true nature. Sir Walter Scott was not entirely imperceptive when he made his much-ridiculed remark that Elizabeth "does not perceive that she has done a foolish thing until she accidentally visits a very handsome seat and grounds belonging to her admirer." [8] Pemberley is more than a reminder of lost social and economic possibilities; it is a solid reflection of Elizabeth's new attitude toward Darcy.

This close connection between aesthetic and moral judgments enables Jane Austen to express her moral themes in terms of the novel's movement from complex antitheses to easy resolution. As Darcy and Elizabeth are first presented to us they sum up most of the conflicting forces in Jane Austen's early fiction. Elizabeth possesses the illusion of total freedom; she looks to nature, rather than society or traditional authority, for the basis of her judgments. She is self-reliant and proud of her discernment,

---

7. Shaftesbury gave currency to the notion that the moral sense and the aesthetic sense spring from the same faculties. See William E. Alderman, "Shaftesbury and the Doctrine of Moral Sense in the Eighteenth Century," *PMLA*, XLVI (December 1931), 1087–94.

8. Scott's review of *Emma* in the *Quarterly Review*, XIV (October 1815), 194.

contemptuous of all conventions that constrict the individual's freedom. Darcy, on the other hand, is mindful of his relationship to society, proud of his social place, and aware of the restrictions that inevitably limit the free spirit. Together they dramatize the persistent conflict between social restraint and the individual will, between tradition and self-expression.

Both Darcy and Elizabeth are flanked by figures who parody their basic tendencies: in Mr. Bennet the irony of the detached observer has become sterile, while Lady Catherine de Bourgh represents the worst side of aristocratic self-consciousness. But it is another group that provides the full antidote to pride and prejudice. The Gardiners stand as a rebuke to Darcy's social prejudices and aristocratic pride, an example of natural aristocracy; while Wickham's true nature is a telling blow to Elizabeth's pride of perception, and to her prejudice in favor of "natural" goodness. The marriage of Elizabeth and Darcy is, as Mark Schorer has pointed out, a kind of economic and social merging, an accommodation of traditional values based upon status with the new values personified in the Gardiners.[9] Elizabeth is led to an appreciation of Darcy's "proper" pride—"he has no improper pride," she ultimately protests to Mr. Bennet— while Darcy is disabused of his inherited prejudices based on caste and economic distance. But it would be too much to say, as Schorer does, that Jane Austen embodies her social judgments in Darcy, and her moral judgments in Elizabeth. For it is part of the novel's purpose to demonstrate that Elizabeth's original opinions were not freely arrived at, but conditioned by social prejudice, while Darcy's initial pride had its roots in a feeling of moral superiority. The first two volumes of *Pride and Prejudice* are so complex that no one set of antitheses can define the positions of the hero and heroine, and any attempt to establish rigid patterns leads to absurdity. Under such schematizing Darcy's ambivalent attitude is reduced to the pomposity of Mary's extracts, while Elizabeth's wit becomes as sterile as her father's.

During recent years several intelligent critics have analyzed the stylistic and dramatic techniques used by Jane Austen to mark the subtle changes in the relationship between Darcy and Elizabeth.[10] The most persuasive of these critics, Reuben Brower, has shown that all of the surface wit and irony of the novel is

9. Mark Schorer, "Pride Unprejudiced," *Kenyon Review*, XVIII (Winter 1956), 72–91.
10. See Howard S. Babb, *Jane Austen's Novels: The Fabric of Dialogue* (Columbus, 1962), pp. 113–42; Reuben A. Brower, "Light and Bright and Sparkling: Irony and Fiction in *Pride and Prejudice*," in *The Fields of Light* (New York, 1951), pp. 164–81; R. J. Schoeck, "Jane Austen and the Sense of Exposure: Heuristics in *Pride and Prejudice*," *English Studies*, XXXVI (August 1955), 154–7; and Dorothy Van Ghent, *The English Novel: Form and Function* (New York, 1953), pp. 99–111.

functional, a part of the larger dramatic design. Through a "sheer poetry of wit" Jane Austen conveys multiple views of her major characters, yet never does she lose sight of her fundamental dramatic aims. The greatness of the novel—whatever its limitations may be—lies in her fusion of the poetry of wit with the dramatic structure of fiction. It is this combination of local complexity with a general clarity of design which animates the novel, and redeems a story which could have been as static as that of *Sense and Sensibility*. A perfect example of the organic connection between language and action may be found in the speeches of Elizabeth and Darcy, which change as the differences between them are reconciled. In the novel's early scenes Jane Austen establishes a clear-cut distinction between Elizabeth's lively speech and Darcy's formal language, but this difference in expressive style is gradually modified as each begins to appreciate the other's style of living. When Darcy learns of the changes in Elizabeth's feelings toward him he expresses himself "as sensibly and as warmly as a man violently in love can be supposed to do," while Elizabeth's defense of her engagement to Mr. Bennet is reminiscent of Darcy's earlier remarks on the virtues of proper pride: "Indeed he has no improper pride. He is perfectly amiable." In the conventional final chapter of *Pride and Prejudice*, where the future lives of the characters are confidently charted, Jane Austen can summarize with such easy authority because we have already seen these relationships foreshadowed in the novel's language and action.

The foundation of Jane Austen's success in correlating language and action is her irony, and the nature of this irony is nowhere better displayed than in the permutations of the novel's first sentence: "It is a truth universally acknowledged, that a single man in possession of a good fortune, must be in want of a wife." Out of context this general statement may seem no more significant than its original in *Rambler* No. 115, where Hymenaeus writes:

> "I was known to possess a fortune, and to want a wife; and therefore was frequently attended by those hymeneal solicitors, with whose importunity I was sometimes diverted, and sometimes perplexed; for they contended for me as vultures for a carcase; each employing all his eloquence, and all his artifices, to enforce and promote his own scheme, from the success of which he was to receive no other advantage than the pleasure of defeating others equally eager, and equally industrious."

Yet even in isolation the novel's opening sentence contains a certain irony: the exaggeration of the statement jars against our sense of reality, and prepares us for the discovery in the first chapters of *Pride and Prejudice* that this "truth" is acknowledged only by Mrs. Bennet and her kind. In the context of these chapters the irony is directed at economic motives for marriage, but as the action develops the implications of the opening sentence are modified and extended, until by the end of the novel we are willing to acknowledge that both Bingley and Darcy were "in want of a wife." Thus the sentence is simultaneously a source for irony and a flat statement of the social and personal necessities which dominate the world of *Pride and Prejudice*. The basic truth of the generalization is untouched by its ironic potential, and this suggests an important distinction that must be made in any discussion of Jane Austen's mature art. Her irony is dramatic, not static; complex, not simple; and we can only judge the tenor of the author's comments or the professions of her characters against the total pattern of dramatic action. Take for an example the following dialogue between Darcy and Elizabeth:

"What think you of books?" said he, smiling.

"Books—Oh! no.—I am sure we never read the same, or not with the same feelings."

"I am sorry you think so; but if that be the case, there can at least be no want of subject.—We may compare our different opinions."

"No—I cannot talk of books in a ball-room; my head is always full of something else."

"The *present* always occupies you in such scenes—does it?" said he, with a look of doubt.

"Yes, always," she replied, without knowing what she said, for her thoughts had wandered far from the subject, as soon afterwards appeared by her suddenly exclaiming, "I remember hearing you once say, Mr. Darcy, that you hardly ever forgave, that your resentment once created was unappeasable. You are very cautious, I suppose, as to its *being created*."

"I am," said he, with a firm voice.

"And never allow yourself to be blinded by prejudice?"

"I hope not."

"It is particularly incumbent on those who never change their opinion, to be secure of judging properly at first."

"May I ask to what these questions tend?"

"Merely to the illustration of *your* character," said she, endeavouring to shake off her gravity. "I am trying to make it out."

By the time we have reached this passage in the novel we know enough of Darcy's nature, and Elizabeth's pride of judgment, to realize that the questions tend more to an illustration of *her* character than of his. In this exchange Jane Austen is depending on an immediate grasp of the inherent dramatic irony, and she has carefully prepared her audience by allowing them to see more of the truth of the situation than any one character can perceive. But a first encounter with this passage does not exhaust its ironic implications, and only in retrospect—or upon second reading— do we understand its relation to the total pattern of dramatic action. The point about such complicated irony is that it depends on a full *external* revelation of the characters' inner natures; we rely more upon what they say and do than upon the author's comments. In this passage, as in so many others, we are reminded of the novel's affinities with the best in eighteenth-century drama. The tripartite structure of *Pride and Prejudice*, dictated by the conventional three-decker form of publication, is similar to the structure of a three-act play, and we know from a remark in one of her letters to Cassandra that Jane Austen considered the volumes as separate units:

> The second volume is shorter than I could wish, but the differ- ence is not so much in reality as in look, there being a larger proportion of narrative in that part.

This remark reveals the dramatist's eye for symmetry, but the reference to "a larger proportion of narrative" is scarcely apolo- getic, and we must realize that Jane Austen's method in *Pride and Prejudice* depends heavily on scenic effects but is not limited to them. The first half of the novel could easily be translated into a play; here Darcy and Elizabeth are "on stage," joining with the other characters to dramatize the novel's psychological and social conflicts. Howard S. Babb has shown how Jane Austen plays on the word "performance" in the early dialogues, bringing all the implications of the word together in the great scene at Rosings, where Elizabeth's actual performance at the piano becomes the center of a dramatic confrontation.[11] But after the scene at Rosings, when Darcy's letter begins Elizabeth's movement toward self-recognition, the term "performance" quietly disappears from the novel. The first half of *Pride and Prejudice* has indeed been a dramatic performance, but in the second half a mix- ture of narrative, summary, and scene carries the plot toward its conclusion.

Yet this movement from the predominantly "scenic" construc- tion of the first half of *Pride and Prejudice* into the less dramatic narrative of the second half does not lead to a drop in our interest, nor do we feel that the consistency of the novel's form has been violated. This is because the novel is unified by the indirect presence of Jane Austen's sensibility, and by the direct

11. Babb, *op. cit.*, pp. 132–141.

presence of Elizabeth Bennet as a commanding center of our interest. The shift from the scene at Rosings to Elizabeth's reception of Darcy's letter merely internalizes the drama; and the account of Elizabeth's changing reactions to Darcy's letter reminds us that Jane Austen has not renounced her right to record the inner life of a character with absolute authority. This is not to say that Elizabeth is a Jamesian "center of consciousness"; Jane Austen was too sure of her created world (and of its relation to the actual world) to efface her own personality from the novel, and from first sentence to last we are aware of the artist's command over her fictions. But her early experiments had shown the need for some technique that would counteract the novel's general tendency toward looseness of form by "focusing" action and psychological exposition, and in *The Watsons* she had explored the method of telling a story from the point-of-view of one character while reserving the right to qualify and expand that viewpoint through dramatic irony and direct comment. Such a method is really a compromise: it combines in a limited form the omniscience of traditional third-person narration with the immediacy of first-person narrative, giving the reader a sense of involvement and identification while simultaneously providing the perspective necessary for moral judgment. Of course, this method makes the exacting demand that the novel's central figure be perpetually intelligent and interesting, a demand which Jane Austen could only partially satisfy in *The Watsons*. But in revising *Pride and Prejudice* she created a heroine who could justify the form, and the result was a highly unified work in which the center of our interest is always at the center of the artistic composition.

Selected Bibliography

In the first section of this bibliography I have listed the editions of Jane Austen's works and letters fundamental to a study of her writing, even if these editions have been cited elsewhere in this edition. I have also listed some useful general accounts of her life and work, and three bibliographies which contain references to books and essays I have not listed here. The second section of the bibliography contains the titles of books and essays which either explicitly discuss *Pride and Prejudice* or consider topics in Jane Austen's life, art, and character useful in the study of the novel. I have not cited in this section the titles of any of the books or essays reprinted in whole or in part in the supplementary material to this edition.

JANE AUSTEN: WORKS AND LETTERS

The Novels of Jane Austen, ed. R. W. Chapman, 5 vols., 3rd edition, Oxford, 1933. A sixth volume, containing minor works, was added to this edition in 1954.
Three volumes of Jane Austen's juvenilia have been published:
Volume the First, ed. R. W. Chapman, Oxford, 1933.
Volume the Third, ed. R. W. Chapman, Oxford, 1951.
Volume the Second, ed. B. C. Southam, Oxford, 1963.
Jane Austen's Letters to her Sister Cassandra and Others, ed. R. W. Chapman, 2nd edition, London, 1952.

BIOGRAPHY

Austen-Leigh, J. E. *A Memoir of Jane Austen,* London, 1870. A second edition of this work was published in 1871 which included texts of some early and unpublished fiction.
Austen-Leigh, William and Richard Arthur. *Jane Austen, Her Life and Letters,* London, 1913.
Chapman, R. W. *Jane Austen, Facts and Problems,* Oxford, 1948.
Cornish, Francis Warre. *Jane Austen,* London, 1913. A volume in the English Men of Letters series.
Hubbock, J. H. and Edith C. *Jane Austen's Sailor Brothers,* New York, 1906.
Jenkins, Elizabeth. *Jane Austen,* London, 1938.
Johnson, R. Brimley. *Jane Austen, Her Life, Her Work, Her Family, and Her Critics,* London and New York, 1930.
Pollok, Walter Harries. *Jane Austen, Her Contemporaries, and Herself,* London, 1899.
Smith, Goldwin. *The Life of Jane Austen,* London, 1890.
Villard, Léonie. *Jane Austen,* translated by Veronica Lucas, London, 1924.

BIBLIOGRAPHY

Keynes, Geoffrey. *Jane Austen: A Bibliography,* London, 1929.
Chapman, R. W. *Jane Austen: A Critical Bibliography,* 2nd edition, Oxford, 1955.
Warner, Sylvia Townsend. *Jane Austen, 1775–1817,* revised edition, London, 1961. A volume in the Writers and Their Work series.

JANE AUSTEN: CRITICISM

Alexander, Susan. *The Art of Jane Austen,* London, 1939. First published as an essay in the *Bulletin of the John Rylands Library,* XII (1928), 314–335.
Bowen, Elizabeth. *English Novelists,* London, 1942.
Bradbrook, Frank W. "Style and Judgment in Jane Austen's Novels," *Cambridge Journal,* IV (1950–51), 515–537.
————. "The Letters of Jane Austen," *Cambridge Journal,* VIII (1953–54), 259–276.
Brogan, Howard O. "Science and Narrative Structure in Austen, Hardy, and Woolf," *Nineteenth-Century Fiction,* XI (1956–57), 276–287.

Burchell, Samuel C. "Jane Austen: The Theme of Isolation," *Nineteenth-Century Fiction*, X (1955), 146–150. See also Andrew Wright, "A Reply to Mr. Burchell," *Nineteenth-Century Fiction*, X (1956), 315–319.

Cady, Joseph, and Watt, Ian. "Jane Austen's Critics," *Critical Quarterly*, V (1963), 49–63. A very useful survey of the different virtues and deficiencies different generations of critics have found in her fiction.

Cecil, Lord David. *Jane Austen*, Cambridge, 1935. Reprinted in *Poets and Story-tellers*, New York, 1949, pp. 99–122.

Chapman, R. W. "Jane Austen's Methods," *Times Literary Supplement*, 9 February 1922, pp. 81–82.

Chapman, R. W. "Jane Austen: A Reply to Mr. Garrod," *Essays by Divers Hands . . . Transactions of the Royal Society of Literature*, n. s. X (1931), 17–34. See the essay by Garrod cited below.

"The Charm of Miss Austen," *Spectator*, 22 March 1890, pp. 403–404.

Daiches, David. "Jane Austen, Karl Marx, and the Aristocratic Dance," *American Scholar*, XVII (1948), 289–296.

Drew, Philip. "A Significant Incident in *Pride and Prejudice*," *Nineteenth-Century Fiction*, XIII (1958–59), 356–358.

Elsbree, Langdon. "Jane Austen and the Dance of Fidelity and Complaisance," *Nineteenth-Century Fiction*, XV (1960–61), 113–136. A most ambitious reading of the metaphor of dancing, especially in *Pride and Prejudice*.

Forster, E. M. "Jane Austen," in *Abinger Harvest*, London, 1936, pp. 145–159. Especially acute in discussing Jane Austen's place in her family, and the effect of her family in shaping the character and development of her fiction.

Fox, Robert C. "Elizabeth Bennet: Prejudice or Vanity?", *Nineteenth-Century Fiction*, XVII (1962), 185–187.

Garrod, H. W. "Jane Austen, a Depreciation," *Essays by Divers Hands . . . Transactions of the Royal Society of Literature*, n. s. VIII (1928), 21–40.

Gorer, Geoffrey. "Poor Honey. Some Notes on Jane Austen and Her Mother," *London Magazine*, IV (August, 1957), 35–48.

Greene, D. J. "Jane Austen and the Peerage," *Publications of the Modern Language Association*, LXVIII (1953), 1017–1031. A valuable study of the social status of Jane Austen's own family, and of the knowing accuracy with which she defines the social status of her characters.

Griffin, Cynthia. "The Development of Realism in Jane Austen's Early Novels," *English Literary History*, XXX (1963), 36–52.

Harding, D. W. "Regulated Hatred: An Aspect of the Work of Jane Austen," *Scrutiny*, VIII (1940), 346–362. Considers, as one element in her fiction, her awareness and enactment of the tensions and frustrations which work against easy acceptance of the limits of the society in which she placed her novels.

Hogan, Charles Beecher. "Jane Austen and Her Early Public," *Review of English Studies*, n. s. I (1950), 39–54. Reception of the novels when first published.

Hopkins, Annette B. "Jane Austen, the Critic," *Publications of the Modern Language Association*, XL (1925), 398–425. Her ideas about fiction and other novelists, culled from her letters and writing.

Hutton, Richard Holt. "From Miss Austen to Mr. Trollope," *Spectator*, 16 December 1882, pp. 1609–1611.

Jack, Adolphus Alfred. *Essays on the Novel as Illustrated by Scott and Miss Austen*, London, 1897.

Jack, Ian. "The Epistolary Element in Jane Austen," *English Studies Today*, Second Series, ed. G. A. Bonnard, Berne, 1961, pp. 173–186.

Kaye-Smith, Sheila, and Stern, G. B. *Speaking of Jane Austen*, London and New York, 1944.

———. *More Talk of Jane Austen*, London, 1950.

Kebbel, T. E. "Jane Austen," *Fortnightly Review*, n. s. VII (1870), 187–193.

Kennedy, Margaret. *Jane Austen*, London, 1950.

Leavis, F. R. "The Great Tradition," in *The Great Tradition*, London, 1948, pp. 1–27. Uses her fiction to help define the great tradition of morally engaged novelists, but regrets that he cannot linger to discuss her writing at length.

Lewes, George Henry. "Recent Novels," *Fraser's Magazine*, XXXVI (1847), 687.

———. "The Lady Novelists," *Westminster Review*, LVIII (1852), 129–141.

Lewis, C. S. "A Note on Jane Austen," *Essays in Criticism*, IV (1954), 359–371.

Liddell, Robert. *The Novels of Jane Austen*, London, 1963.

Link, Frederick M. "Jane Austen, Mr. Mudrick, and Critical Monism," *Boston University Studies in English*, III (1957), 60–62.

Litz, Walton. "*The Loiterer*: A Reflection of Jane Austen's Early Environment," *Review of English Studies*, n. s. XII (1961), 251–261. *The Loiterer* was a juvenile magazine prepared and circulated in 1789–90 by Jane Austen's brothers.

Lord, Walter Frewen. "Jane Austen's Novels," *Nineteenth Century*, LII (1902), 665–675.

McCann, Charles J. "Setting and Character in *Pride and Prejudice*," *Nineteenth-Century Fiction*, XIX (1964), 65–75.

Macaulay, Thomas Babington. "Madame D'Arblay," *Edinburgh Review*, LXXXIX (1843), 561–562.

Marcus, Mordecai. "A Major Thematic Pattern in *Pride and Prejudice*," *Nineteenth-Century Fiction*, XVI (1961–62), 274–279.

"Miss Austen and Miss Mitford," *Blackwood's Magazine*, CVII (1870), 290–313.

"Miss Austen's Novels," *Saturday Review*, 23 December 1882, pp. 827–828.

Muir, Edwin. *The Structure of the Novel*, New York, 1929, pp. 42–47.

O'Connor, Frank. "Jane Austen and the Flight from Fancy," *Yale Review*, XLV (1955–56), 31–47.

Parks, Edd Winfield. "Exegesis in Austen's Novels," *South Atlantic Quarterly*, LI (1952), 103–119.

————. "Jane Austen's Art of Rudeness," *University of Toronto Quarterly*, XX (1951), 381–387.

————. "Jane Austen's Lure of the Next Chapter," *Nineteenth-Century Fiction*, VII (1952–53), 56–60.

Pollok, W. F. P. "British Novelists—Richardson, Miss Austen, Scott," *Fraser's Magazine*, LXI (1860), 20–38.

Saintsbury, George. *"Pride and Prejudice,"* in *Prefaces and Essays*, London, 1933, pp. 194–209. First published in 1894.

Schoeck, R. J. "Jane Austen and the Sense of Exposure: Heuristics in *Pride and Prejudice*," *English Studies*, XXXVI (1955), 154–157.

Schorer, Mark. "Pride Unprejudiced," *Kenyon Review*, XVIII (1956), 72–91.

Scott, Sir Walter. "Emma," *Quarterly Review*, XIV (1815), 188–201.

Simon, Irene. "Jane Austen and [Henry James's] *The Art of the Novel*," *English Studies*, XLIII (1962), 225–239.

Southam, B. C. *Jane Austen's Literary Manuscripts*, London, 1964.

Spurgeon, Caroline. "Jane Austen," *Essays by Divers Hands . . . Transactions of the Royal Society of Literature*, n. s. VII (1927), 81–104.

"Thackeray as a Novelist," *North American Review*, LXXVII (1853), 200–219.

Trilling, Lionel. "A Portrait of Western Man," *Listener*, 11 June 1953, pp. 969–971, 974.

Turpin, A. R. "Jane Austen: Limitations or Defects?" *English Review*, LXIV (1937), 53–68.

Ward, Mrs. Humphrey. "Style and Miss Austen," *Macmillan's Magazine*, LI (1884), 84–91.

Wilson, Edmund. "A Long Talk about Jane Austen," in *Classics and Commercials*, New York, 1950, pp. 196–203.

Woolf, Virginia. "Jane Austen," in *The Common Reader*, New York, 1925, pp. 191–206.